o's Ordnance Survey

KT-210-281

STREET ATLAS
Glasgow
and West Central Scotland

Contents

Inside front cover: Strathclyde Passenger
Transport Rail Network map

III Key to map symbols

IV-V Key to map pages

VI-VII Route planning

VIII Administrative and post code boundaries

1 Street maps

240 Extra-large-scale map of Glasgow town centre

242 Index of hospitals, industrial estates, railway
stations, schools, shopping centres, street names
and universities

PHILIP'S

First edition published 1995
First colour edition published 1999 by

Ordnance Survey®   and   George Philip Ltd., a division of
Romsey Road   Octopus Publishing Group Ltd
Maybush   Michelin House
Southampton   81 Fulham Road
SO16 4GU   London SW3 6RB

ISBN 0-540-07651-1 (pocket)

© Crown copyright 1999
© George Philip Ltd 1999

All rights reserved. No part of this publication may be
reproduced, stored in a retrieval system or transmitted, in any
form or by any means, electronic, mechanical, photocopying,
recording or otherwise, without the permission of the Publishers
and the copyright owner.

To the best of the Publishers' knowledge, the information in this
atlas was correct at the time of going to press. No responsibility
can be accepted for any errors or their consequences.

The representation in this atlas of a road, track or path is no
evidence of the existence of a right of way.

**The mapping between pages 1 and 241 (inclusive) in this
atlas is derived from Ordnance Survey® OSCAR® and Land-
Line® data and Landranger® mapping.**

Ordnance Survey, OSCAR, Land-line and Landranger are
registered trade marks of Ordnance Survey, the national
mapping agency of Great Britain.

Printed and bound in Spain by Cayfosa

Digital Data

The exceptionally high-quality
mapping found in this book is
available as digital data in TIFF
format, which is easily convertible
to other bit-mapped (raster) image
formats.

.The index is also available in digital
form as a standard database table.
It contains all the details found in
the printed index together with the
National Grid reference for the map
square in which each entry is
named and feature codes for places
of interest in eight categories such
as education and health.

For further information and to
discuss your requirements, please
contact the Ordnance Survey
Solutions Centre on 01703 792929.

Motorway (with junction number)		Walsall	**Railway station**
Primary route (dual carriageway and single)		**U**	**Glasgow Underground station**
A road (dual carriageway and single)			**Midland Metro**
B road (dual carriageway and single)		**M**	**Metrolink station**
Minor road (dual carriageway and single)			**London Underground station**
Other minor road (dual carriageway and single)		**D**	**Docklands Light Railway station**
Road under construction		**M**	**Tyne and Wear Metro**
Pedestrianised area			**Private railway station**
Postcode boundaries			**Bus, coach station**
County and Unitary Authority boundaries			**Ambulance station**
Railway			**Coastguard station**
Tramway, miniature railway			**Fire station**
Rural track, private road or narrow road in urban area			**Police station**
Gate or obstruction to traffic (restrictions may not apply at all times or to all vehicles)			**Accident and Emergency entrance to hospital**
Path, bridleway, byway open to all traffic, road used as a public path		**H**	**Hospital**
The representation in this atlas of a road, track or path is no evidence of the existence of a right of way		**+**	**Church, place of worship**
		i	**Information Centre** (open all year)
Adjoining page indicators		**P** **P&R**	**Parking, Park and Ride**
		PO	**Post Office**
The map area within the pink band is shown at a larger scale on the page indicated by the red block and arrow		Prim Sch	**Important buildings, schools, colleges, universities and hospitals**

Acad	**Academy**	Meml	**Memorial**
Crem	**Crematorium**	Mon	**Monument**
Cemy	**Cemetery**	Mus	**Museum**
C Ctr	**Civic Centre**	Obsy	**Observatory**
CH	**Club House**	Pal	**Royal Palace**
Coll	**College**	PH	**Public House**
Ent	**Enterprise**	Recn Gd	**Recreation Ground**
Ex H	**Exhibition Hall**	Resr	**Reservoir**
Ind Est	**Industrial Estate**	Ret Pk	**Retail Park**
Inst	**Institute**	Sch	**School**
Ct	**Law Court**	Sh Ctr	**Shopping Centre**
L Ctr	**Leisure Centre**	TH	**Town Hall/House**
LC	**Level Crossing**	Trad Est	**Trading Estate**
Liby	**Library**	Univ	**University**
Mkt	**Market**	YH	**Youth Hostel**

River Medway	**Water name**
	Stream
	River or canal (minor and major)
	Water
	Tidal water
	Woods
	Houses
House	**Non-Roman antiquity**
VILLA	**Roman antiquity**

■ The dark grey border on the inside edge of some pages indicates that the mapping does not continue onto the adjacent page ■ The small numbers around the edges of the maps identify the 1 kilometre National Grid lines

The scale of the maps is 3.92 cm to 1 km (2½ inches to 1 mile)

0	¼		½		¾		1 mile
0	250m	500m	750m	1 kilometre			

The scale of the maps on pages numbered in red is 7.84 cm to 1 km (5 inches to 1 mile)

0	220 yards		440 yards		660 yards	½ mile
0	125m	250m	375m	½ kilometre		

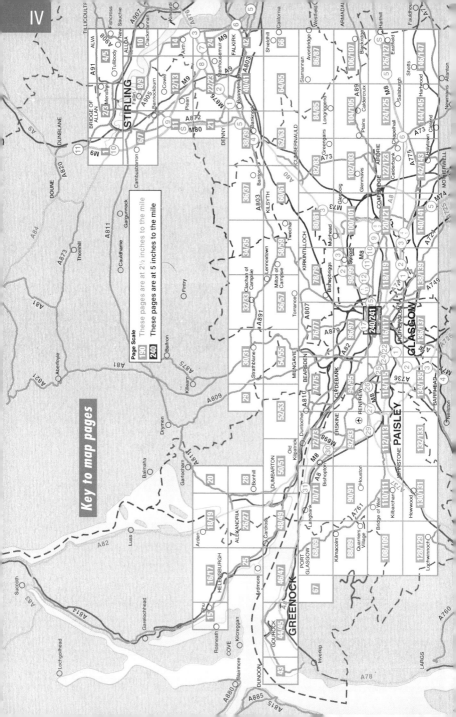

Key to map pages

Page Scale

190 These pages are at 2½ inches to the mile

240 These pages are at 5 inches to the mile

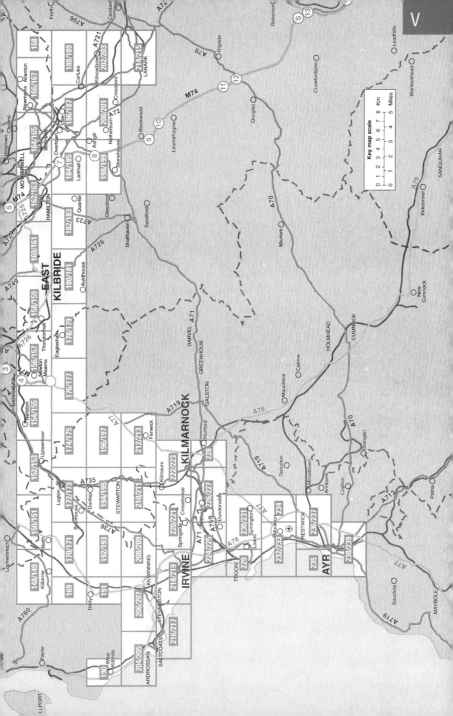

Route planning

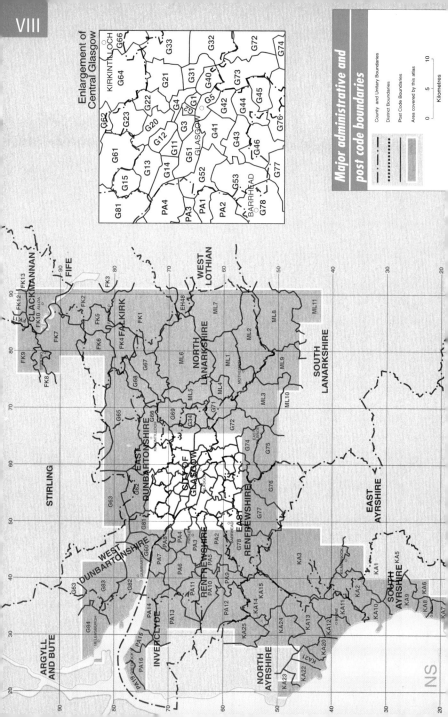

Enlargement of
Central Glasgow

**Major administrative and
post code boundaries**

County and Unitary Boundaries

District Boundaries

Post Code Boundaries

Area covered by this atlas

0   5   10
Kilometres

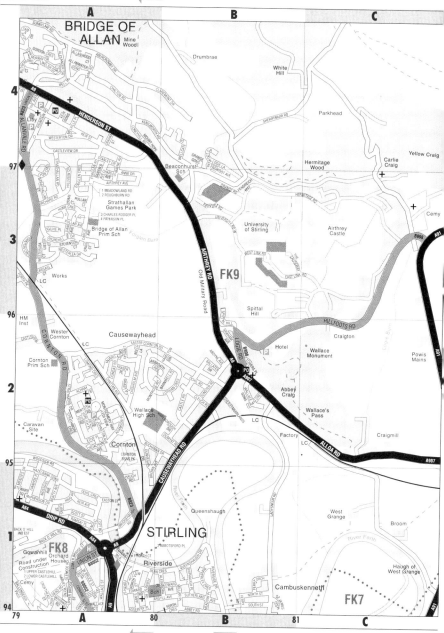

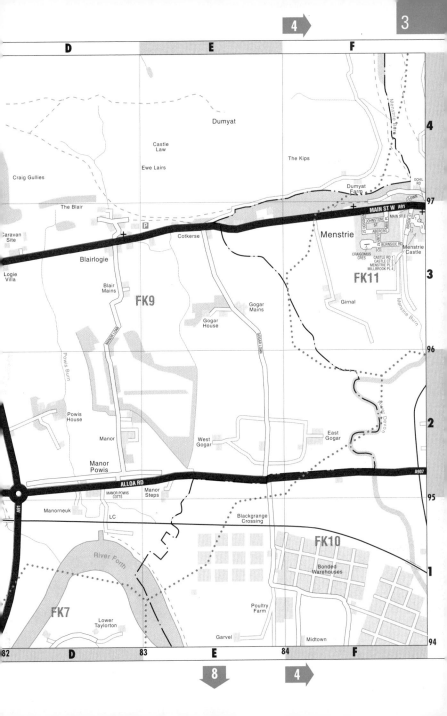

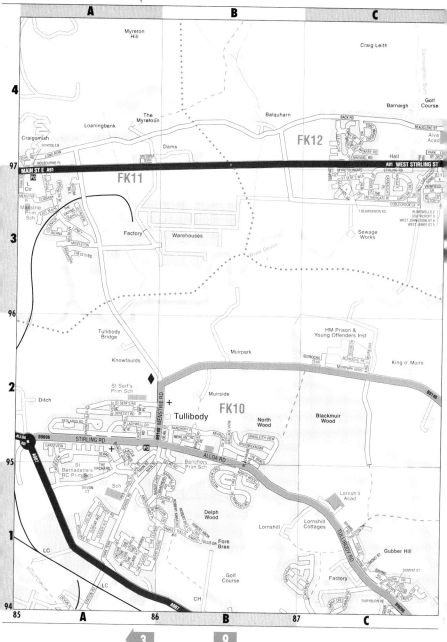

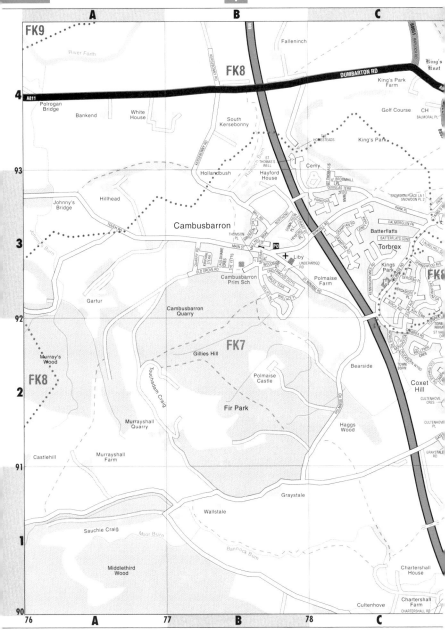

FK9

River Forth

FK8

Falleninch

King's
Knot

DUMBARTON RD

King's Park
Farm

A811

Polrogan
Bridge

Bankend

White
House

South
Kersebonny

Golf Course

CH

BALMORAL PL

THE
HOMESTEADS

King's Park

Hollandbush

Hayford
House

Cemy

ST THOMAS'S
WELL

St Thomas's

Bannock Burn

BROOMHILL
DOUGLAS TERR

SNOWDON PLACE LA 1
SNOWDON PL 2

Johnny's
Bridge

Hillhead

Cambusbarron

THOMSON
PL

MAIN ST

PO

Liby

UNDERWOOD
RD

Batterflatts

BATTERFLATS GDNS

Torbrex

DALMORGLEN PK

Johnny's Burn

TOUCH RD

QUARRY RD

FINTRY
AVE

CALEDONIAN
CRES

THE FEUS

OLD DROVE RD

Cambusbarron
Prim Sch

WOODBURN

UNDERWOOD COTTS

BRUCE TERR

WALLACE PL

BELT RD

ST NINIAN'S RD

Polmaise
Farm

Kings
Park

SYCAMORE P

FERNGROVE RD

DEBRON PL

SPRINGWOOD AVE

LAURELHILL CT

FK8

ST VAL

TOWN
FARM

Gartur

Cambusbarron
Quarry

FK7

Murray's
Wood

Gillies Hill

Bearside

Coxet
Hill

CULTENHOVE
CRES

FK8

Touchadam Craig

Polmaise
Castle

WELLPARK
CRES

TOWN
BURN

CULTENHOVE
PL

Fir Park

Murrayshall
Quarry

Haggs
Wood

GRAYSTALE
RD

Castlehill

Murrayshall
Farm

Graystale

Sauchie Craig

Moor Burn

Wallstale

Bannock Burn

Chartershall
House

Middlethird
Wood

Cultenhove

Chartershall
Farm

CHARTERSHALL RD

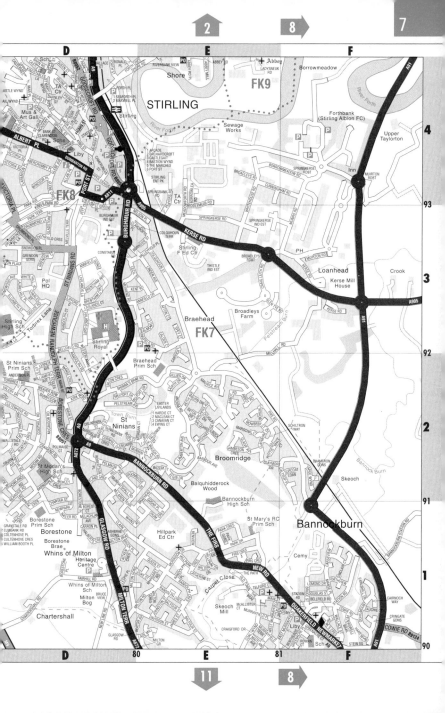

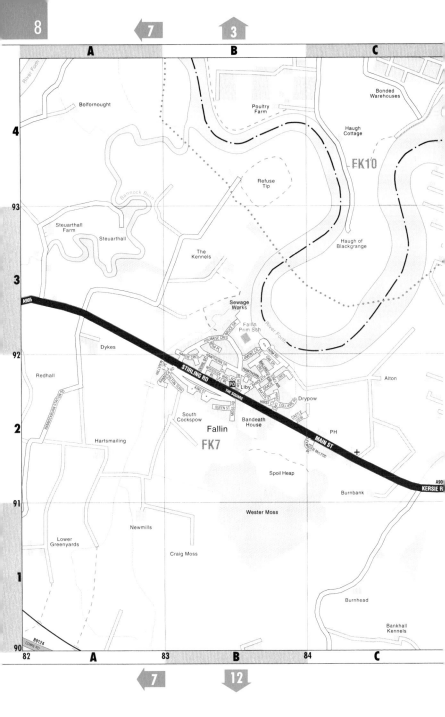

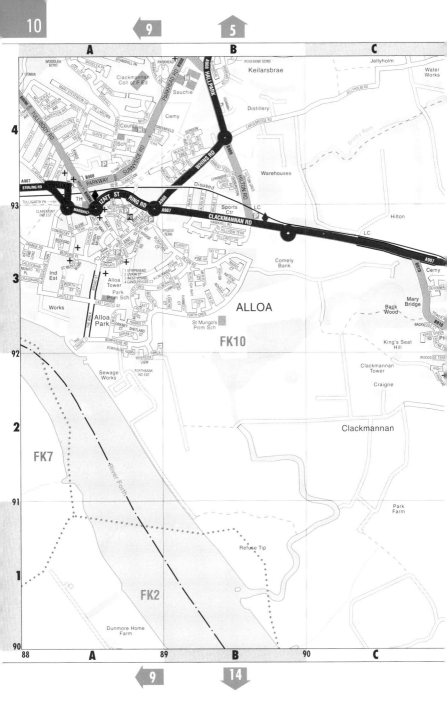

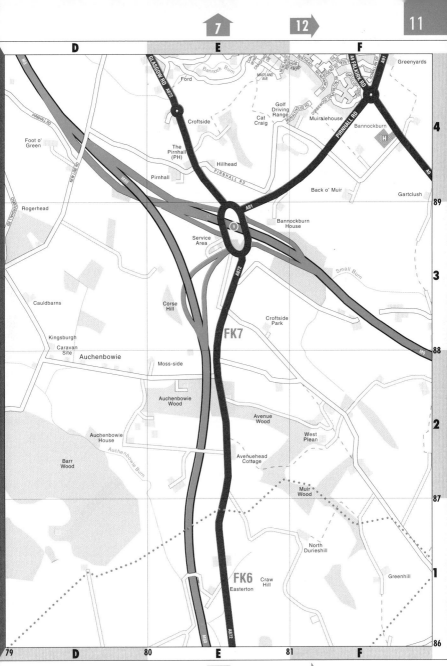

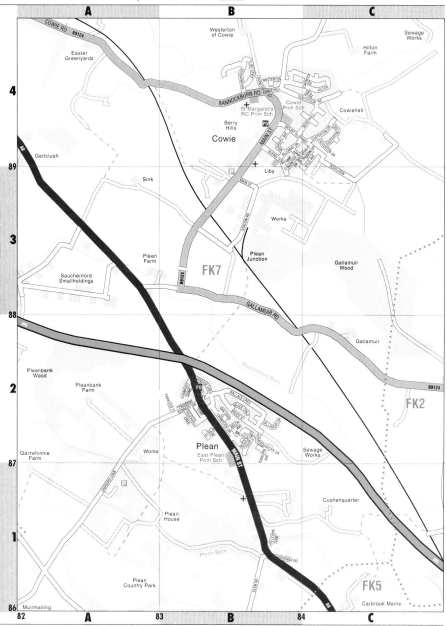

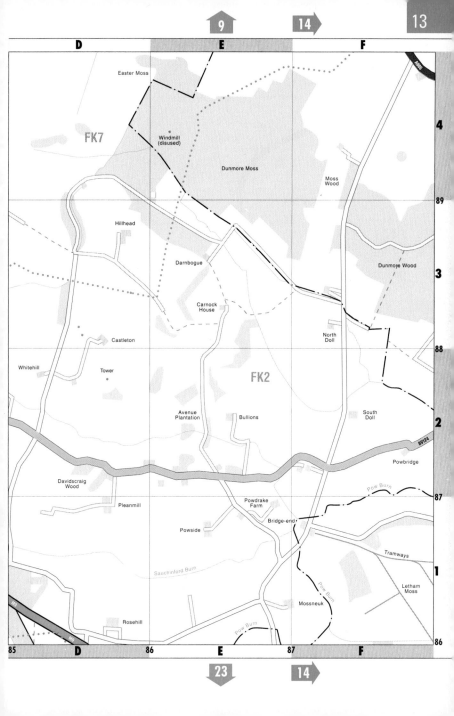

D E F
9 14 13
4
89
3
88
FK2 2
87
1
86
D E F
85 86 87
23 14

Easter Moss

FK7

Windmill
(disused)

Dunmore Moss

Moss
Wood

Hillhead

Darnbogue

Dunmore Wood

Carnock
House

Castleton

North
Doll

Whitehill

Tower

FK2

Avenue
Plantation

Bullions

South
Doll

Powbridge

Davidscraig
Wood

Pow Burn

Pleanmill

Powdrake
Farm

Powside

Bridge-end

Tramways

Sauchinford Burn

Letham
Moss

Pow Burn

Mossneuk

Rosehill

Pow Burn

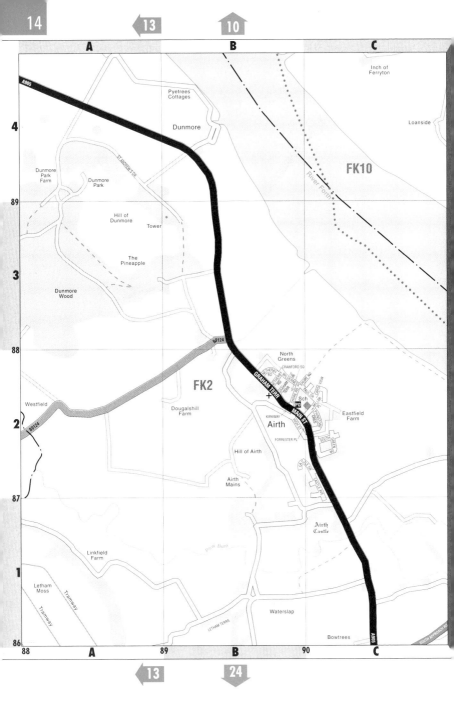

A905

Pyetrees
Cottages

Dunmore

Inch of
Ferryton

Loanside

ST ANDREW'S DR.

Dunmore
Park
Farm

Dunmore
Park

FK10

Hill of
Dunmore

Tower

River Forth

The
Pineapple

Dunmore
Wood

B9124

North
Greens

CRAWFORD SQ

FK2

Dougalshill
Farm

GRAHAM TERR

Sch

Eastfield
Farm

Westfield

B9124

KIRKWAY

Airth

MAIN ST

FORRESTER PL

Hill of Airth

Airth
Mains

Airth
Castle

Linkfield
Farm

Park Burn

Letham
Moss

Tramway

Tramway

Tramway

LETHAM TERRS.

Waterslap

Bowtrees

A905

SOUTH APPROACH RD.

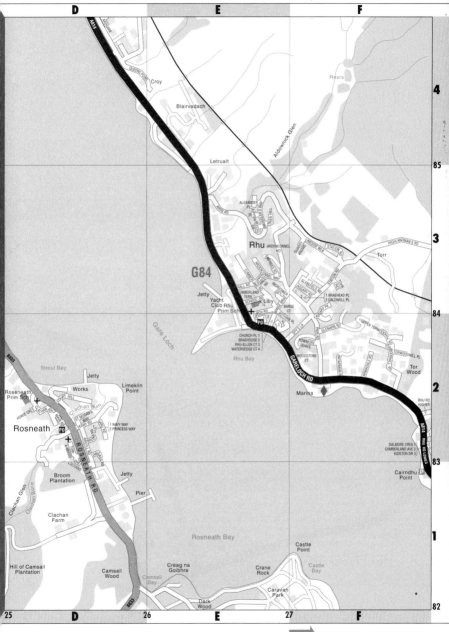

Map labels

D **E** **F**

4 **85** **3** **84** **2** **83** **1** **82**

A814

QUEENS POINT
Croy
Blairvadach
Aldownick Glen
Resrs
Letrualt

ALEXANDER PL
AROS RD
Rhu ARDENCONNEL RD
INVERBECK WK
STATION
HIGHLANDMAN'S RD
Torr
CYPRESS WAY
G84
GLENFIELD RD
1 BRAEHEAD PL
2 CALDWELL PL
Jetty
Yacht
Club Rhu HALL RD
Prim Sch SCHOOL RD
CUMBERLAND
TERR
Liby
BARGE CT
PO
UPPER TORWOODHILL
CT
ROCH RD
CHURCH PL 1
BRAEHOUSE 2
RHU-ELLEN CT 3
WATERSEDGE CT 4
BOWMORE
QUAYS
GLENARN RD
WOODSTONE
CT
TORWOODHILL PL
Gare Loch
Rhu Bay
GARELOCH RD
Tor
Wood
Stroul Bay
Jetty
Works
Limekiln
Point
Marina
RHU RD HIGHER
Roseneath
Prim Sch
COURT HILL
HOWIE CRES
Clachan Burn
Rosneath PO
1 NAVY WAY
2 PRINCESS WAY
ST MODANS WAY
FERRY RD
DALMORE CRES 1
CUMBERLAND AVE 2
KIDSTON DR 3
A814 RHU RD LOWER
Broom
Plantation
ROSNEATH RD
Jetty
Cairndhu
Point
Clachan Glen
Clachan Burn
Pier
Clachan
Farm
Hill of Camsail
Plantation
Camsail
Wood
Rosneath Bay
Castle
Point
Creag na
Goibhre
Crane
Rock
Castle
Bay
Camsail
Bay
Caravan
Park
Dark
Wood
B833

25 **D** **26** **E** **27** **F** **82**

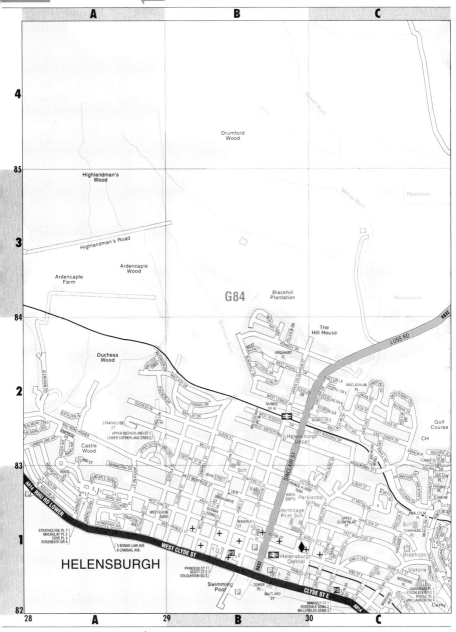

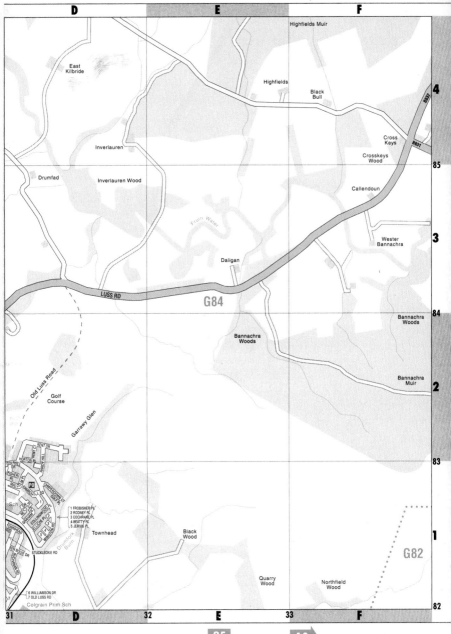

4

Highfields Muir

Highfields
Black
Bull

Cross
Keys

East
Kilbride

Crosskeys
Wood

Inverlauren

85

Drumfad

Inverlauren Wood

Callendoun

Fruin Water

Wester
Bannachra

3

Daligan

LUSS RD

G84

84

Bannachra
Woods

Bannachra
Woods

Old Luss Road

Golf
Course

Bannachra
Muir

2

Garrawy Glen

83

KENT DR

1 FROBISHER PL
2 RODNEY PL
3 COCHRANE PL
4 BEATTY PL
5 JERVIS PL

Black
Wood

Townhead

Drunton Burn

1

G82

STUCKLECKIE RD

6 WILLIAMSON DR
7 OLD LUSS RD

Quarry
Wood

Northfield
Wood

Colgrain Prim Sch

82

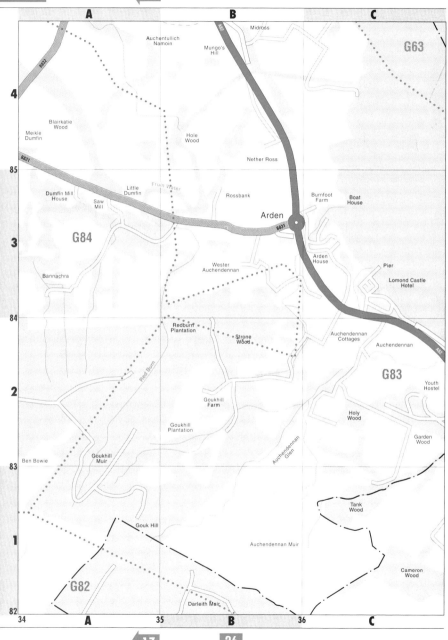

G63

Auchentullich
Namoin

Midross

Mungo's
Hill

Blairkatie
Wood

Meikle
Dumfin

Hole
Wood

Nether Ross

85

Dumfin Mill
House

Little
Dumfin

Fruin Water

Rossbank

Burnfoot
Farm

Boat
House

Saw
Mill

Arden

3

G84

Bannachra

Wester
Auchendennan

Arden
House

Pier

Lomond Castle
Hotel

84

Redburn
Plantation

Strone
Wood

Auchendennan
Cottages

Auchendennan

Red Burn

G83

Youth
Hostel

2

Goukhill
Farm

Goukhill
Plantation

Holy
Wood

Garden
Wood

Ben Bowie

Goukhill
Muir

83

Auchendennan Glen

Tank
Wood

1

Gouk Hill

Auchendennan Muir

Cameron
Wood

G82

Darleith Muir

82

D
E
F

G63

Knockour
Wood

Lorn

4

Knockour
Hill

Black
Roundel

Boat
Houses

85

Boturich
Castle

Loch Lomond

Meikle
Boturich

Whinny Hill

3

84

G83

Ledrishmore
Wood

Burn of Balloch

Over
Balloch

2

Duck
Bay

Cameron Bay

Horsehouse
Wood

Cameron
House

Stable
Wood

Cameron House
Farm

Balloch Castle

83

Cameron
Wildlife Park

Balloch Castle
Country Park

Ledrishbeg

INCHFAD RD

CREINCH
DR

1 McLEAN CRES
2 HARAN RD
3 SHANDON CRES
4 SHANDON RD
5 DUMBAIN RD
6 HALDANE TERR

Balloch
Pier

Moss o' Balloch
Plantations

River Leven

Balloch

1

82

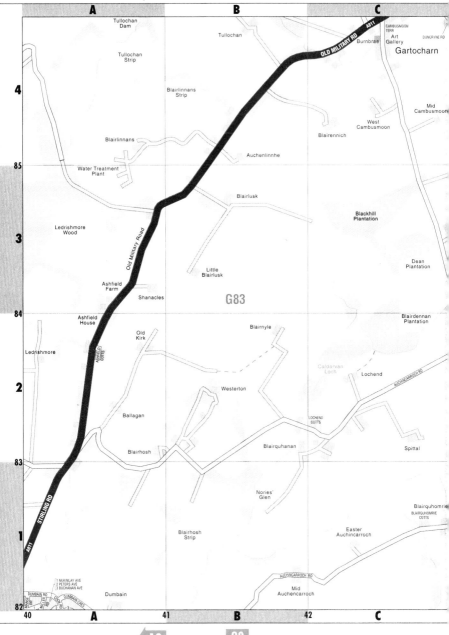

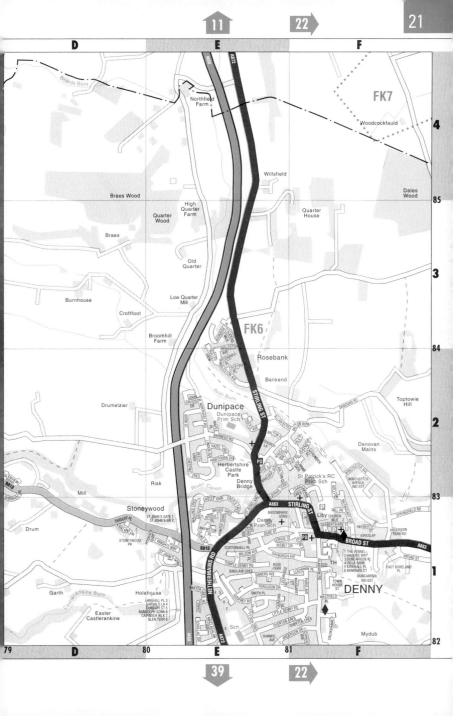

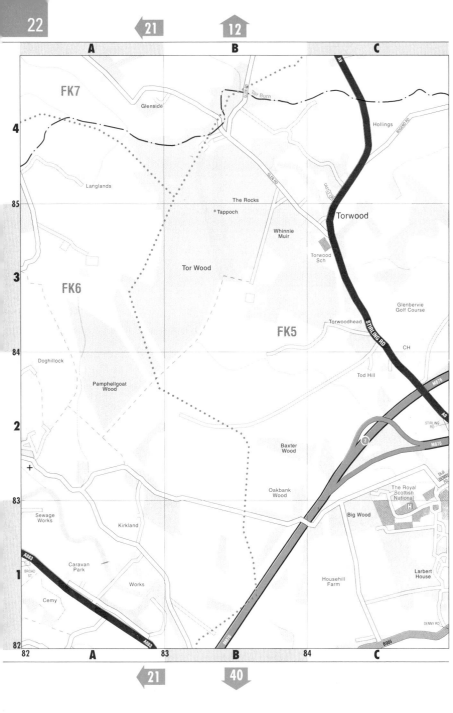

A B C

FK7

Glenside

Tor Burn

Hollings

4

Langlands

The Rocks

85 • Tappoch

Whinnie
Muir

Torwood

Torwood
Sch

3 Tor Wood

FK6

Glenbervie
Golf Course

Torwoodhead

FK5 CH

STIRLING RD

84 Doghillock

Tod Hill

Pamphellgoat
Wood

2

Baxter
Wood

STIRLING
RD

M876

Oakbank
Wood

83 The Royal
Scottish
National

Sewage
Works

Big Wood H

Kirkland

OLD DENNY RD

1

BROAD
ST.

Caravan
Park

Works

Household
Farm

Larbert
House

Cemy

DENNY RD

82 B985

82 A 83 B 84 C

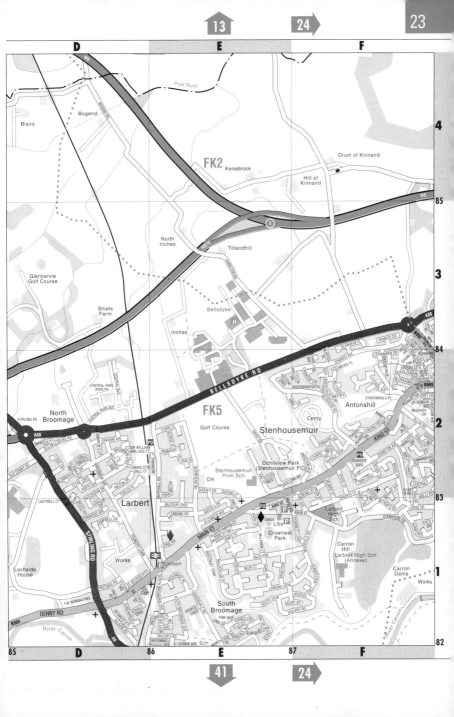

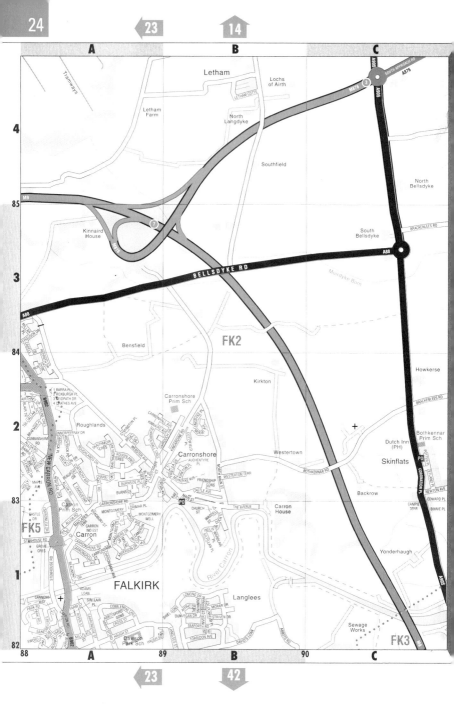

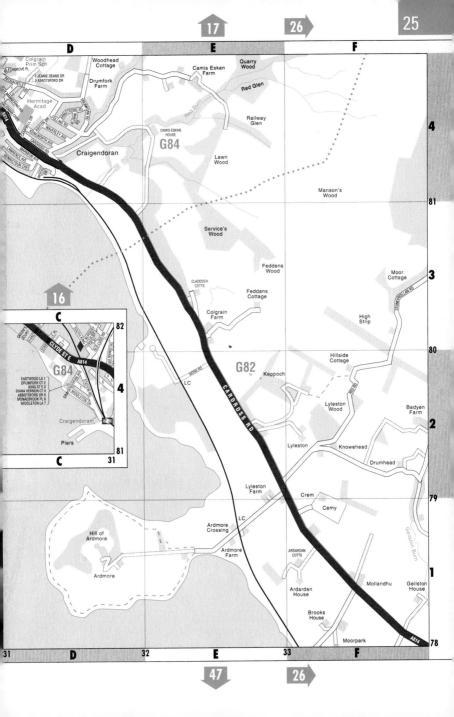

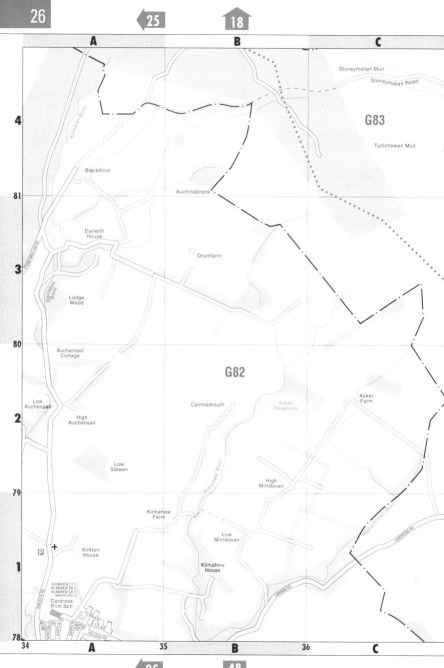

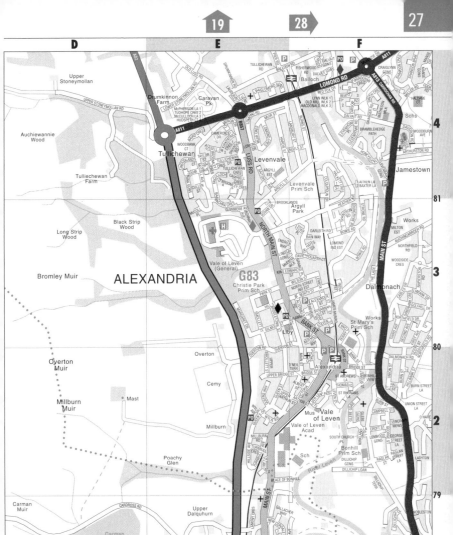

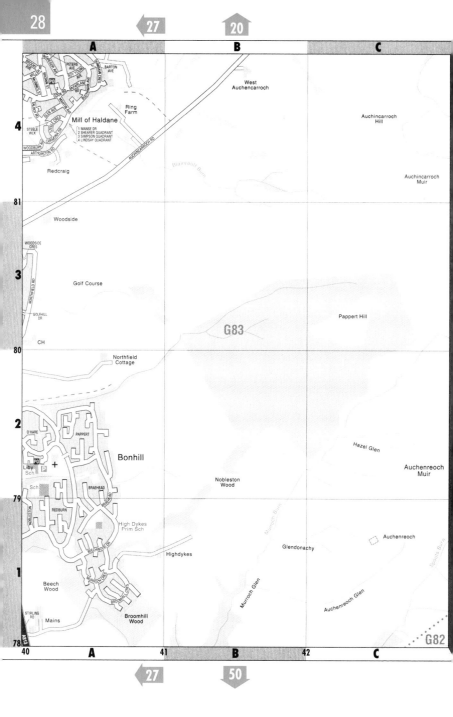

A **B** **C**

West Auchencarroch

Auchincarroch Hill

Auchincarroch Muir

Mill of Haldane

Ring Farm

1 MANSE DR
2 SHEARER QUADRANT
3 SIMPSON QUADRANT
4 LINDSAY QUADRANT

PETERS AVE
BARTON AVE
MILLER ST
BROWN ST
SEA AVE
STEELE WLK

PO

Redcraig

AUCHINCARROCH RD

WOODBURN
ARTHURSTON RD

4

Bunrannoch Burn

81

Woodside

WOODSIDE CRES

NORTHFIELD RD

3

Golf Course

GOLFHILL DR

Pappert Hill

G83

CH

80

Northfield Cottage

O'HARE

PAPPERT

Bonhill

Liby Sch

P

Hazel Glen

Auchenreoch Muir

Sch

BRAEHEAD

2

REDBURN

NOBLESTON DR

BRAEHEAD

Nobleston Wood

79

High Dykes Prim Sch

Highdykes

Auchenreoch

BEECHWOOD DR

Glendonachy

Spouts Burn

Murroch Burn

1

Beech Wood

MURROCH CRES

Broomhill Wood

STIRLING RD

Mains

Murroch Glen

Auchenreoch Glen

G82

78

40 **A** 41 **B** 42 **C**

D   E   F

Quinloch

Quinloch
Wood

Quinloch
Muir

4

Catythirsty
Well

81

Mast

The
Whangie

Queen's
View

3

Auchineden
Hill

Auchengillan

Auchineden

G63

80

Low
Auchengillan

Stables

Works

2

Auchineden
Farm

South
Lodge

79

Auchintroch Burn

Greenan Glen

1

Kilmannan
Resr

78

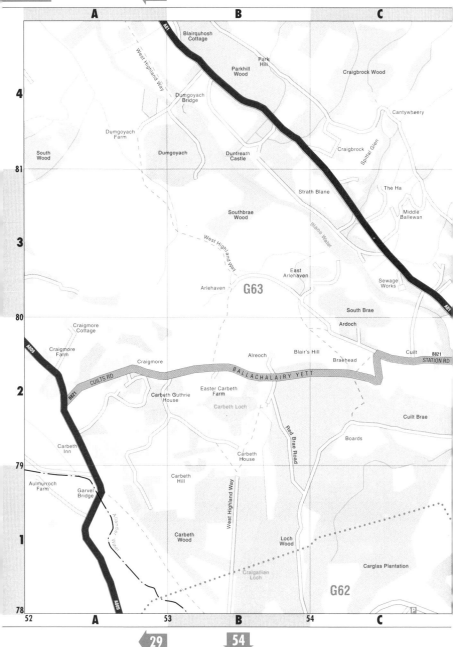

A   B   C

4

Blairquhosh
Cottage

Park
Hill

Parkhill
Wood

Craigbrock Wood

West Highland Way

Dumgoyach
Bridge

Cantywheery

Dumgoyach
Farm

South
Wood

Dumgoyach

Dunfreath
Castle

Craigbrock

Spittal Glen

81

Strath Blane

The Ha

Southbrae
Wood

Middle
Ballewan

Blane Water

3

West Highland Way

East
Arlehaven

Arlehaven

G63

Sewage
Works

80

Craigmore
Cottage

South Brae

Ardoch

Craigmore
Farm

A809

Craigmore

CUILTS RD

BALLACHALAIRY YETT

Alreoch

Blair's Hill

Braehead

Cuilt

B821
STATION RD

2

B821

Carbeth Guthrie
House

Easter Carbeth
Farm

Carbeth Loch

Red Brae Road

Cuilt Brae

Boards

Carbeth
Inn

79

Aulmurroch
Farm

Garvel
Bridge

Carbeth
Hill

Carbeth House

West Highland Way

Allan Dr. Water

1

Carbeth
Wood

Loch
Wood

Carglas Plantation

Craigallian
Loch

G62

A809

78

52   A   53   B   54   C

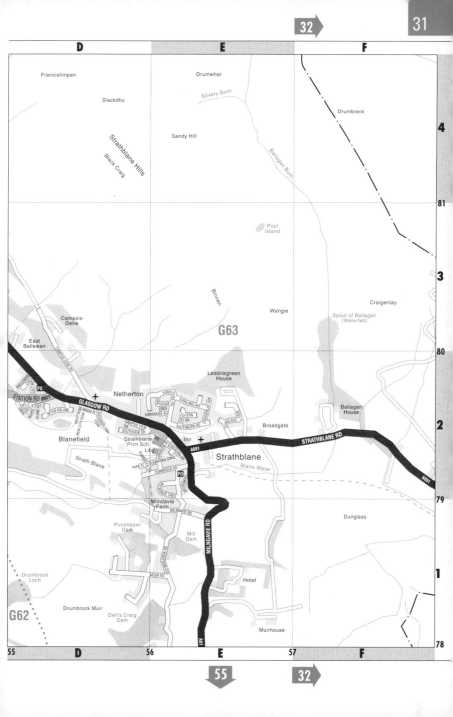

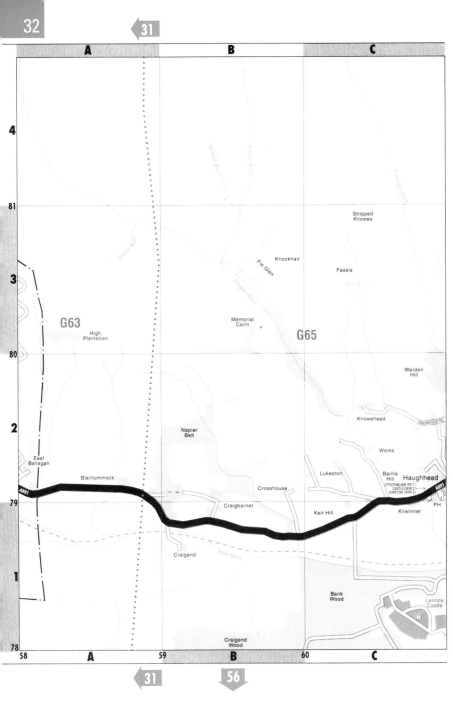

A   B   C

4

81

Stripped
Knowes

3

Fin Glen
Knocknair
Fassis

G63

High
Plantation

Memorial
Cairn

G65

80

Warden
Hill

2

Napier
Belt

Knowehead

KNOWEHEAD RD

Works

East
Ballagan

Lukeston

Baillie
Hill   Haughhead

Blairtummock

Crosshouse

STRATHBLANE RD 1
CASTLEVIEW 2
KIRKTON TERR 3

A891

A891

79

Craigbarnet

Keir Hill

Kilwinnet

PH

Craigend

Pow Burn

1

Bank
Wood

Lennox
Castle

H

78

Craigend
Wood

58   A   59   B   60   C

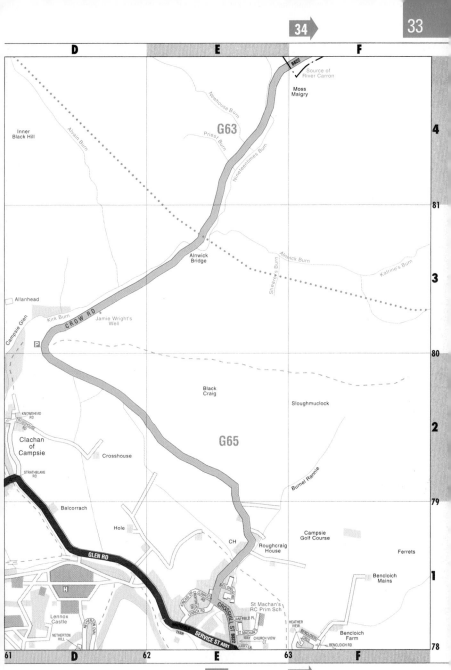

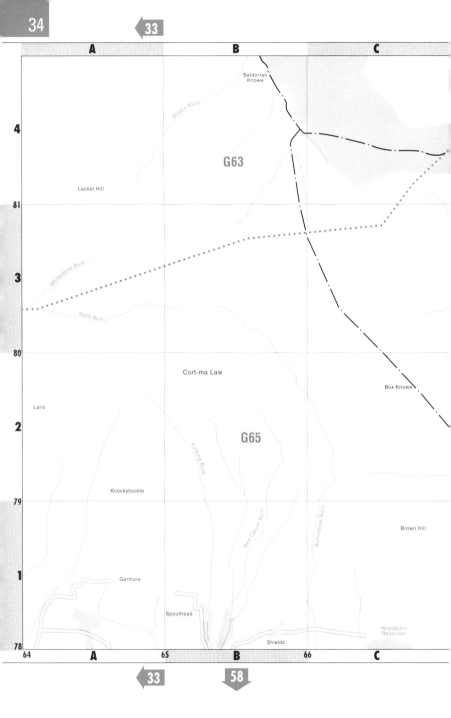

Baldorran
Knowe

4

G63

Lecket Hill

81

Whitestone Burn

3

Back Burn

80

Cort-ma Law

Box Knowe

Lairs

2

G65

Knockybuckle

79

Brown Hill

Folking Burn

Red Cleuch Burn

Burniebrae Burn

1

Garmore

Spouthead

Woodburn
Reservoir

Shields

78

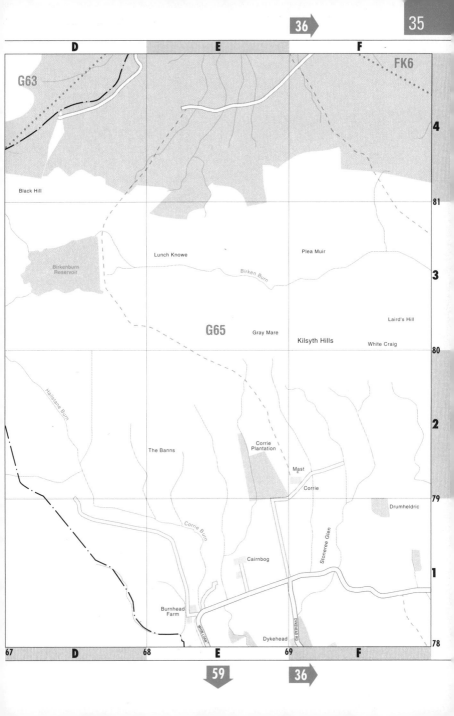

D
E
F

FK6

G63

4

Black Hill

81

Lunch Knowe

Plea Muir

Birkenburn
Reservoir

Birken Burn

3

G65

Gray Mare

Laird's Hill

Kilsyth Hills

White Craig

80

Hellstane Burn

2

The Banns

Corrie
Plantation

Mast

Corrie

79

Corrie Burn

Drumheldric

Stoneree Glen

Cairnbog

1

Burnhead
Farm

DYKEHEAD

Dykehead

78

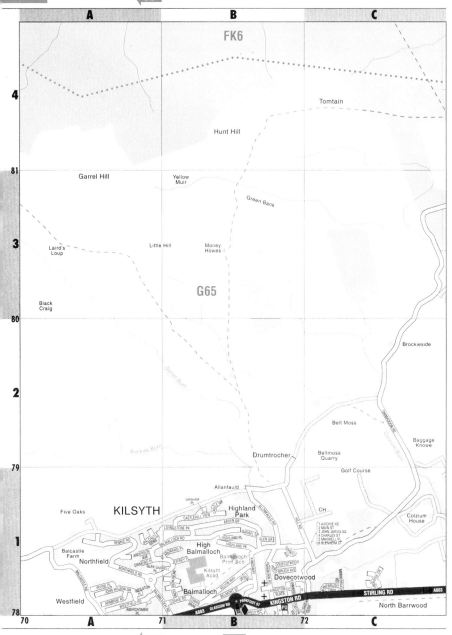

A   B   C

FK6

Tomtain

Hunt Hill

81

Garrel Hill

Yellow
Muir

Green Bank

3

Laird's
Loup

Little Hill

Money
Howes

G65

Black
Craig

80

Brockieside

2

Belt Moss

Baggage
Knowe

Garrel Burn

Bachille Burn

Drumtrocher

Beltmoss
Quarry

Golf Course

79

Allanfauld

CH

Colzium
House

Five Oaks

KILSYTH

GRAHAM

Highland
Park

1 AIRDRIE RD
2 MAIN ST
3 JOHN JARVIS SQ
4 CHARLES ST
5 MAXWELL PL
6 BLENHEIM CT

CASTLEHILL VIEW

LIVINGSTONE PK

ARDEN GR

Highland PK

1

Balcastle
Farm

Northfield

RENNIE RD

ANDERSON
AVE

ALMALLOCH RD

ST ANDREW'S PL

GARREL GR

GLEN GR

High
Balmalloch

HIGHLAND PL

Dovecotwood

DOVECOTWOOD

BRUSH AVE

MONIEBRUGH

WEBRUGH

Balmalloch
Prim Sch

GLEN GARRETT

CRIMOND PL

JEFFREY PL

Kilsyth
Acad

BELMONT ST

KINGSTON
PLACE

Westfield

BALCASTLE RD

IRVINE PL

JOHN WILSON DR

WESLTON

ARMBRAE RD

WESTFIELD RD

ABERCROMBIE

Balmalloch

CORRIE RD

PARKFOOT ST

A803 GLASGOW RD

KINGSTON RD

STIRLING RD **A803**

North Barrwood

78

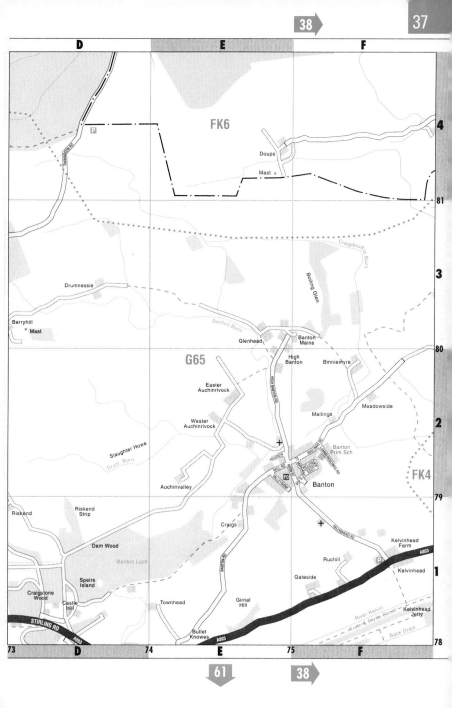

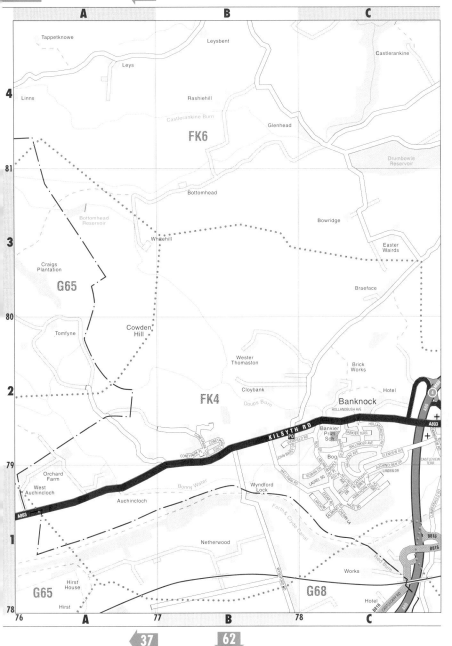

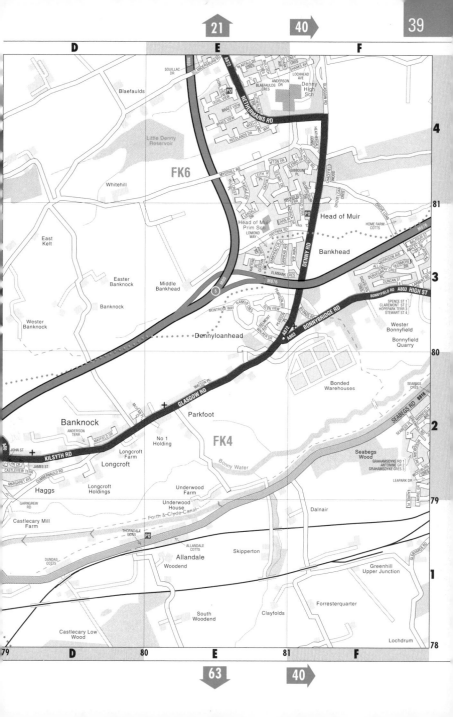

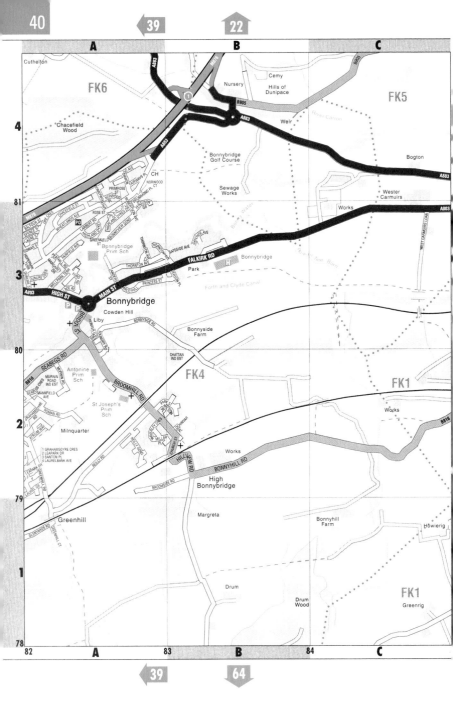

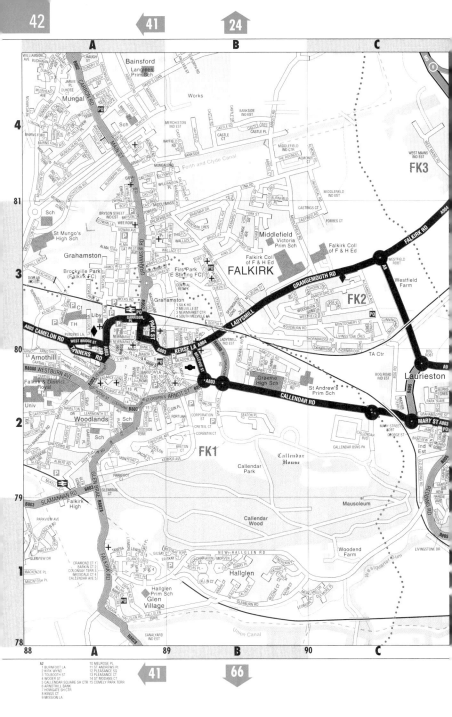

McInroy's Point P
A770

CLOCH RD BALMORAL PL

Hotel   Hotel

EDINBURGH DR STIRLING ST

3

Levan

Cloch Point   TALLOS PARK RD

Works   Levan Burn

Cloch   Levan
Lighthouse   Farm

76

Cloch
Lighthouse   Caravan
Park

Cloch
Plantation

Tannel Hill

Underheugh   PA19   2
Cottage
                                        Burneven Hill

Underheugh

75

Clyde Muirshiel
Regional Park   North Knowe

P   PA16   1

Lunderston Bay

PA16

Curling
Pond

A770   Lunderston

74

43

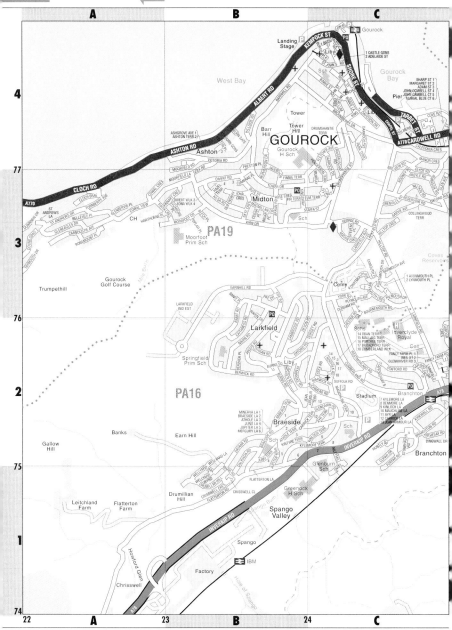

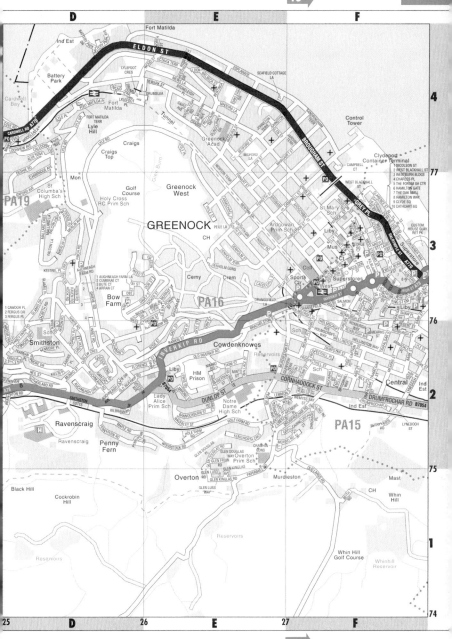

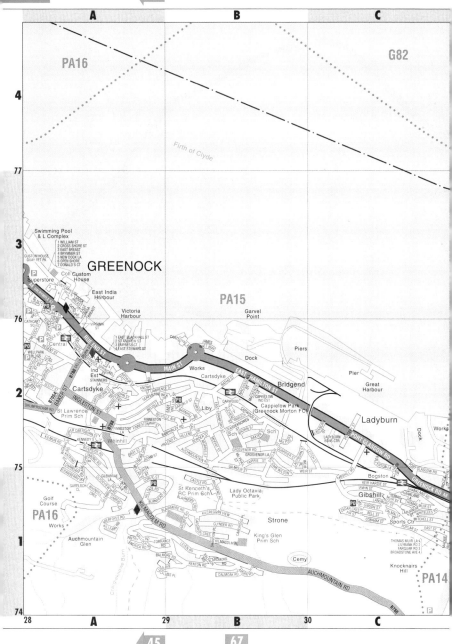

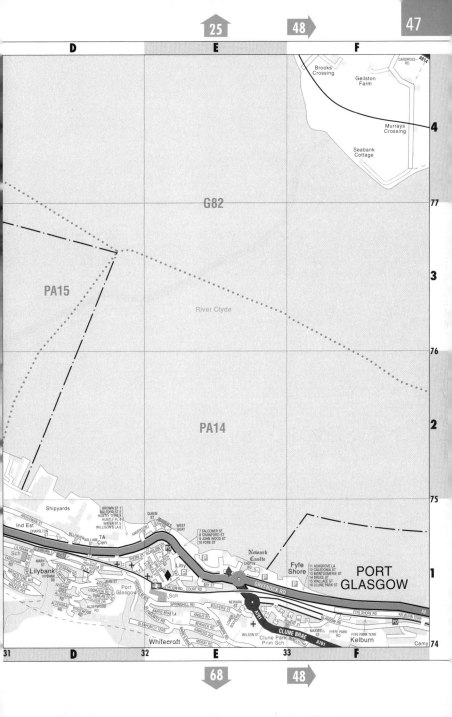

D
E
F

4

77

G82

3

PA15

River Clyde

76

PA14

2

75

Shipyards

BROWN ST 1
BALFOUR ST 2
HUNTLY TERR 3
HUNTLY PL 4
WATER ST 5
WILLISON'S LA 6

QUEEN ST

WEST QUAY

7 FALCONER ST
8 CRAWFORD ST
9 JOHN WOOD ST
10 FORE ST

11 ASHGROVE LA
12 CALEDONIA ST
13 MONTGOMERIE ST
14 BRUCE ST
15 WALLACE ST
16 CLUNE PARK ST

Newark Casite
CASTLE RD

Fyfe Shore

PORT GLASGOW

Ind Est

CHAPELTON ST
ARDGOWAN ST

BELHAVEN
WILLIAM ST

TA Cen

ANDERSON

MURRAY ST

Liby

Lilybank

MARY ST
FAIRD PHAR

Sch
Sch

LOCHVIEW RD
ROBERTSON
HIGHHOLM ST

SHORE ST
SCADLOCK

Port Glasgow
Sch

STATION RD
COURT RD

BAY ST

NEWARK ST

GREENOCK RD

Fyfe Shore

BROADSTONE
MAVIS AVE
MACKIE AVE

IVYBANK
JEAN ST
DUNCAN ST
KINROSS AVE

SPRINGHILL RD

BOUVERIE ST

Clune Park
Prim Sch

GLASGOW RD

FYFE SHORE RD

KELBURN TERR

ALDERBRAE
BOGSTON RD
ALDERWOOD RD

BARRS BRAE LA

ANGUS RD

BERWICK RD

KINROSS AVE

GLENHUNTLY TERR

MORAY RD

WILSON ST

CLUNE BRAE
BENCLUTHA

MAXWELL ST

FYFFE PARK RD

FYFE PARK TERR

Kelburn

Whitecroft

Cemy

74

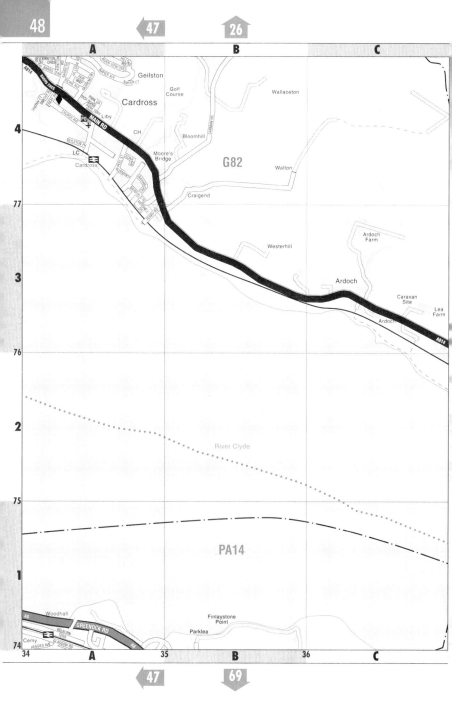

Geilston

Golf Course

Wallaceton

Cardross

Bloomhill

G82

Moore's Bridge

Walton

CH

Craigend

Westerhill

Ardoch Farm

Ardoch

Caravan Site

Lea Farm

Ardoch

River Clyde

PA14

Woodhall

GREENOCK RD

Finlaystone Point

Parklea

Cemy

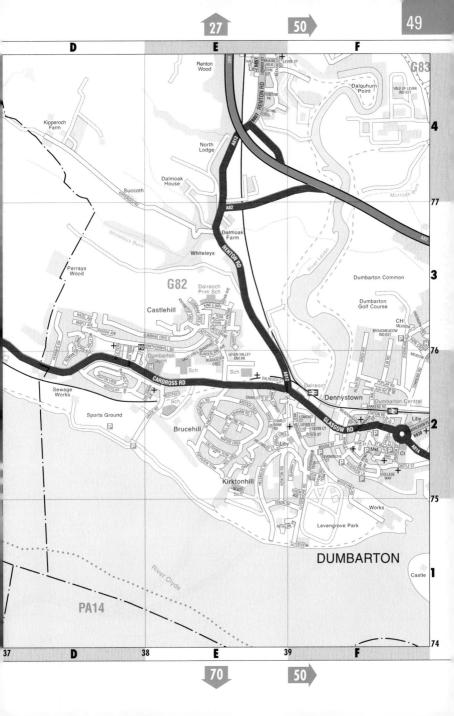

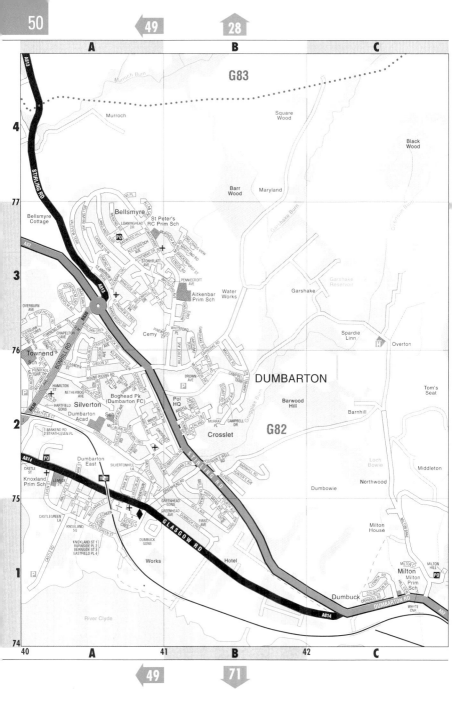

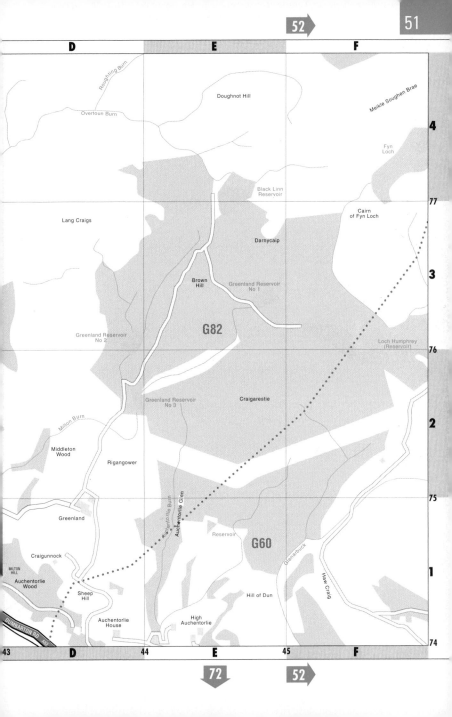

D

E

F

Roughling Burn

Overtoun Burn

Doughnot Hill

Meikle Soughen Brae

4

Fyn
Loch

Black Linn
Reservoir

77

Lang Craigs

Cairn
of Fyn Loch

Darnycaip

3

Brown
Hill

Greenland Reservoir
No 1

Loch Humphrey
(Reservoir)

G82

Greenland Reservoir
No 2

76

Greenland Reservoir
No 3

Craigarestie

2

Milton Burn

Middleton
Wood

Rigangower

75

Greenland

Auchentorlie Burn

Auchentorlie Glen

Reservoir

G60

Glenarbuck

Craigunnock

Haw Craig

MILTON
HILL

1

Auchentorlie
Wood

Sheep
Hill

Hill of Dun

DUMBARTON RD

Auchentorlie
House

High
Auchentorlie

74

43

D

44

E

45

F

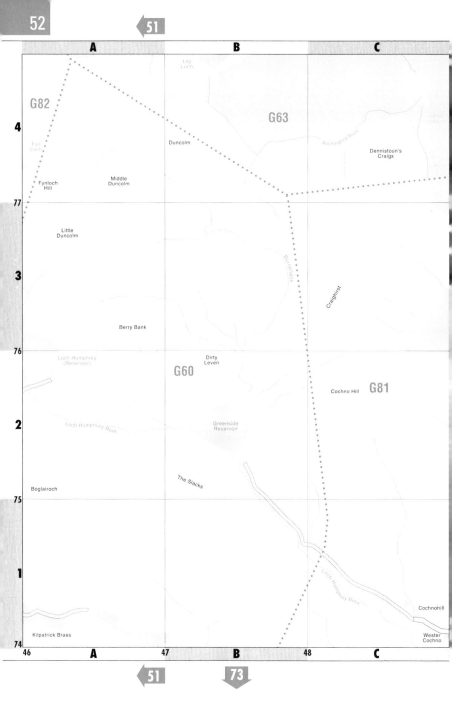

A **B** **C**

D
E
F

Kilmannan
Reservoir

Craigton Burn

Craigenkirn Glen

G63

Tomibeg

Craiganzeoch

Meikle
Longveggan

Windyedge

4

Craigmore

Woodie Craigs

Birny Hills

77

Black
Loch

Dunellan

G62

Craigmore

3

Cochno Loch
(Reservoir)

Cairnhowit

76

Jaw
Reservoir

Long Knowe

G81

2

West
Muirhouses

East
Muirhouses

75

Bog
Wood

Todhill
Wood

Shield Hill
Plantation

Auchenduich
Wood

Jaw Burn

Douglas
Muir

1

Cochno

Lady's
Linn

Cochno Burn

Edinbarnet

G61

COCHNO
RD.

COCHNO
RD.

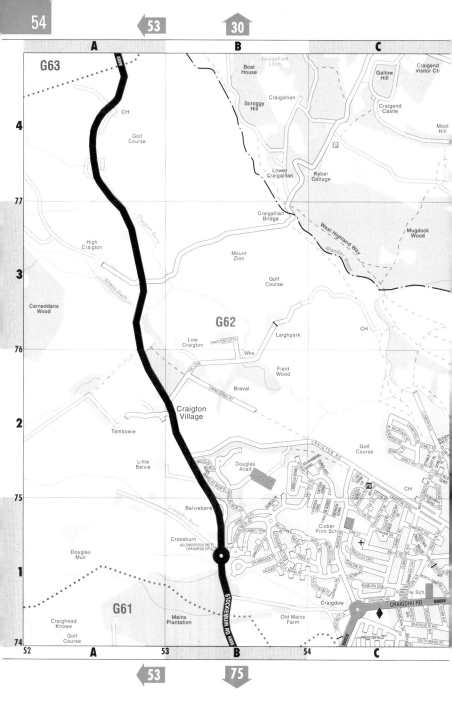

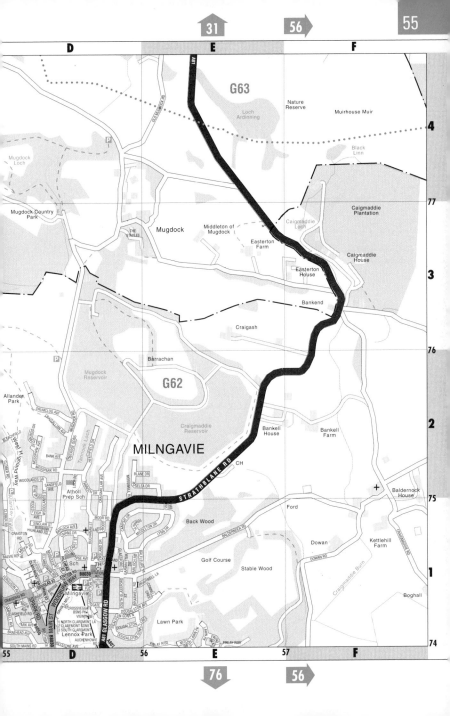

D
E
F

G63

Loch
Ardinning

Nature
Reserve

Muirhouse Muir

4

Black
Linn

77

Mugdock
Loch

Mugdock Country
Park

THE STABLES

Mugdock

Middleton of
Mugdock

Caigmaddie
Loch

Caigmaddie
Plantation

Easterton
Farm

Caigmaddie
House

Easterton
House

3

Bankend

Craigash

76

Barrachan

Mugdock
Reservoir

G62

Craigmaddie
Reservoir

Bankell
House

Bankell
Farm

2

Allander
Park

MILNGAVIE

STRATHBLANE RD

CH

Atholl
Prep Sch

BLANE DR

SELEA DR

Baldernock
House

75

Back Wood

Ford

Dowan

Kettlehill
Farm

Golf Course

Stable Wood

1

Milngavie

Lennox Park

A81 GLASGOW RD

Boghall

Lawn Park

74

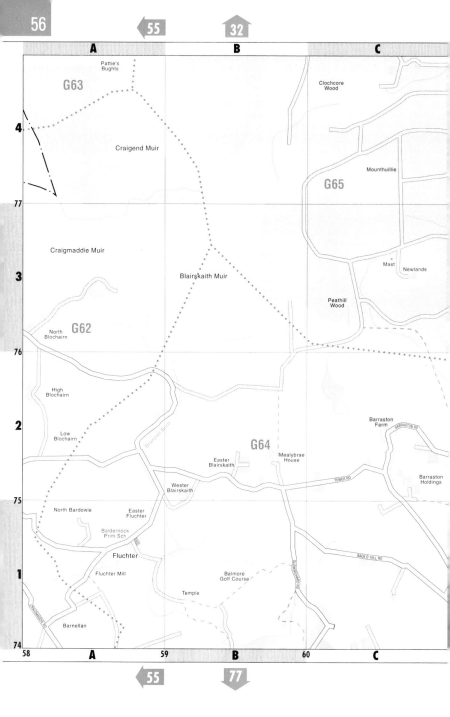

A

B

C

Pattie's
Bughts

G63

Craigend Muir

4

77

Craigmaddie Muir

Blairskaith Muir

Clochcore
Wood

G65

Mounthuillie

Mast

Newlands

Peathill
Wood

3

North
Blochairn

G62

76

High
Blochairn

2

Low
Blochairn

Brannel Burn

G64

Easter
Blairskaith

Mealybrae
House

TOWER RD

Barraston
Farm

BARRASTON RD

Barraston
Holdings

Wester
Blairskaith

75

North Bardowie

Easter
Fluchter

Baldernock
Prim Sch

GLENOACHAR RD

BACK O' HILL RD

Fluchter

1

Fluchter Mill

Balmore
Golf Course

Temple

CRAIGMADDIE RD

Barnellan

74

A

59

B

60

C

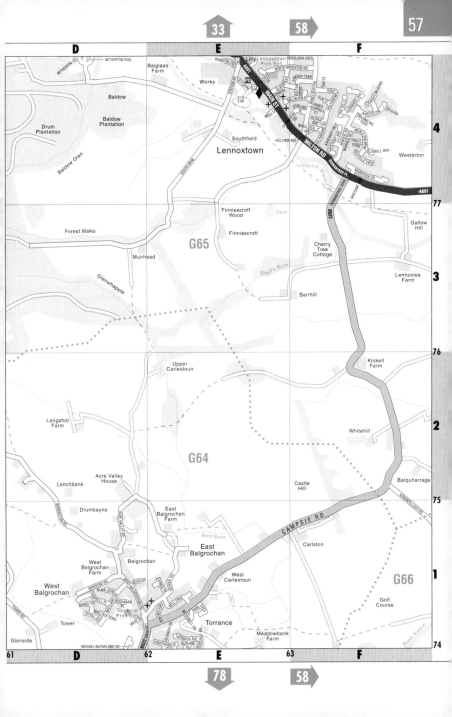

D **E** **F**

NETHERTON HILL
NETHERTON OVAL

Balglass Farm

Works

Baldow

Baldow Plantation

Drum Plantation

Baldow Glen

Southfield

Lennoxtown

4

Liby Lennoxtown Prim Sch
BENCLOICH CRES.
WINSTON CRES.
NORTH BIRBISTON RD
LINDSAY TERR
PINE ST

Westerton

Forest Walks

SOUTH BRAE

Muirhead

Glenwhapple

Finniescroft Wood

Dam

Finniescroft

G65

Glazert Water

77

Cherry Tree Cottage

Boyd's Burn

Barrhill

Gallow Hill

Lennoxlea Farm

3

Upper Carlestoun

76

Kinkell Farm

Langshot Farm

Whitehill

2

G64

Acre Valley House

Leitchbank

Drumbayne

East Balgrochan Farm

Red Burn

Castle Hill

Balquharrage

75

West Balgrochan Farm

Balgrochan

East Balgrochan

West Carlestoun

CAMPSIE RD

Carlston

West Balgrochan

Tower

Torrance Prim Sch

Torrance

Meadowbank Farm

G66

Golf Course

1

Glenside

MICHAEL McPARLAND DR

River Kelvin

74

61 **D** **62** **E** **63** **F**

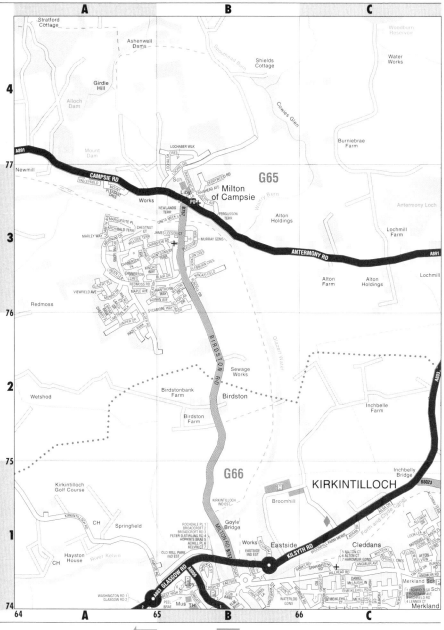

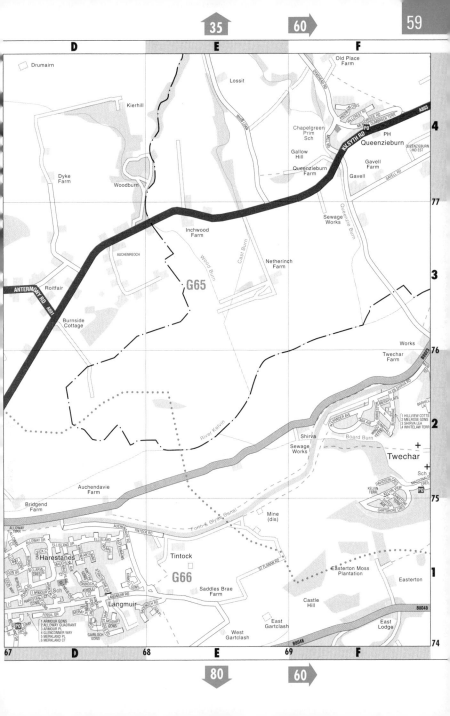

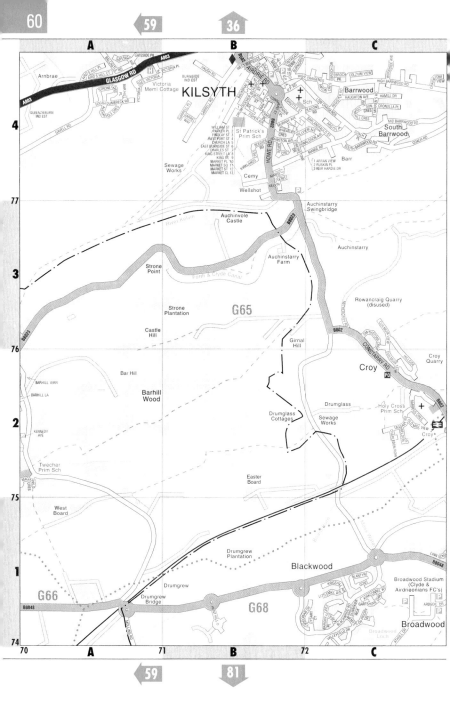

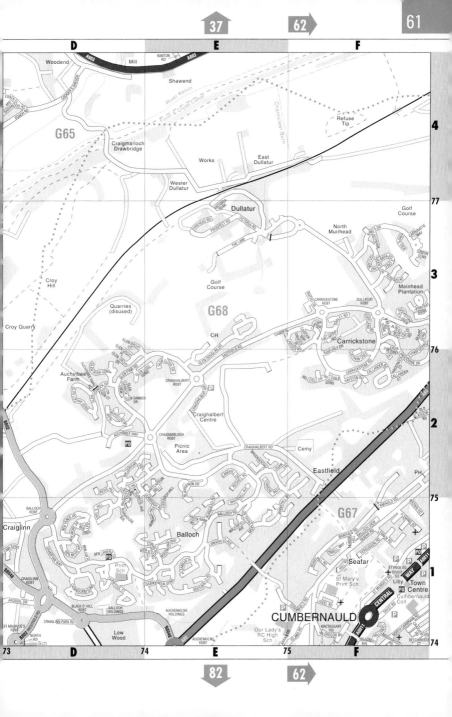

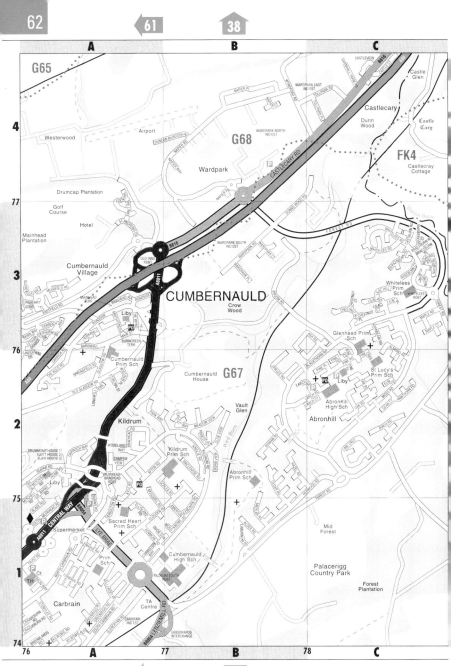

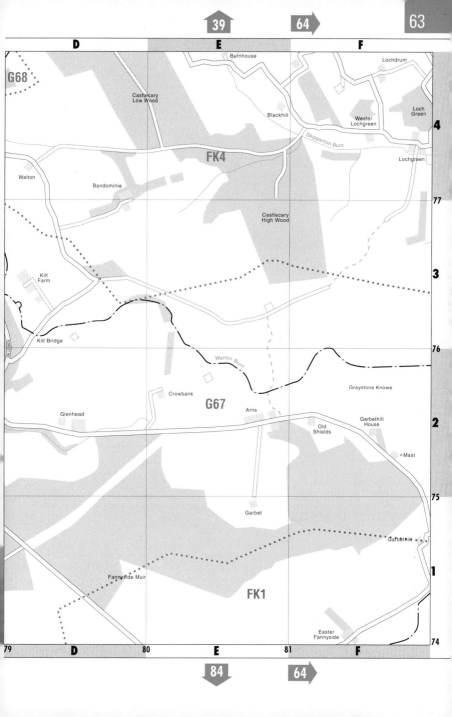

63
40

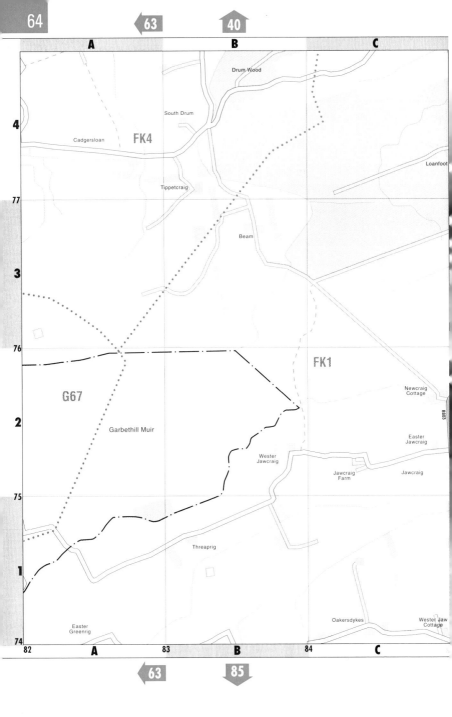

Drum Wood

South Drum

4

Cadgersloan

FK4

Loanfoot

Tippetcraig

77

Beam

3

76

FK1

G67

Newcraig
Cottage

2

Garbethill Muir

Easter
Jawcraig

Wester
Jawcraig

B803

Jawcraig
Farm

Jawcraig

75

Threaprig

1

Oakersdykes

Wester Jaw
Cottage

Easter
Greenrig

74

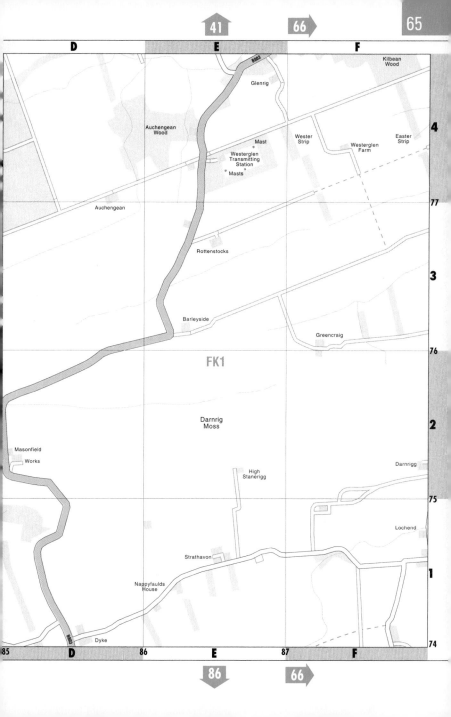

D E F

4

77

3

76

FK1

2

75

1

74

Kilbean Wood

Glenrig

B803

Auchengean Wood

Mast

Westerglen Transmitting Station

Masts

Wester Strip

Westerglen Farm

Easter Strip

Auchengean

Rottenstocks

Barleyside

Greencraig

Darnrig Moss

Masonfield

Works

High Stanerigg

Darnrigg

Lochend

Strathavon

Nappyfaulds House

Dyke

B803

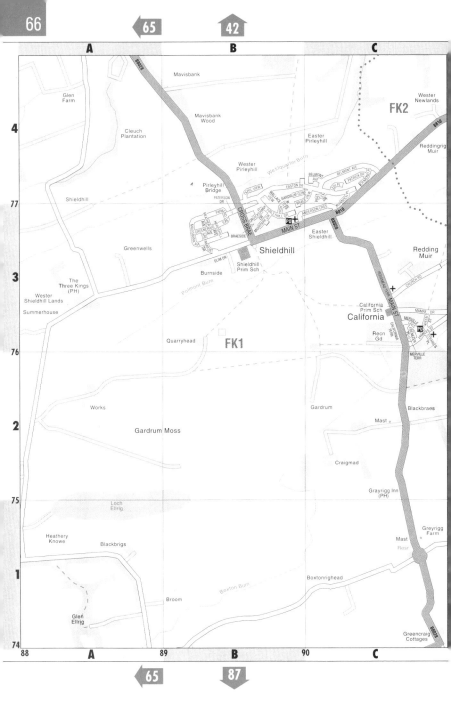

A **B** **C**

4

Glen Farm

Mavisbank

Cleuch Plantation

Mavisbank Wood

Wester Newlands

FK2

BB10

Reddingrig Muir

Easter Pirleyhill

Westquarter Burn

Shieldhill

Wester Pirleyhill

Pirleyhill Bridge

77

PATERSON

BELMONT AVE

BELMONT AVE

PATRICK DR

EASTON DR

GAIL VIEW

WALLACE

GARDRUM GDNS

BRAES DR

ANDERSON CRES

CROSS BRAE

PO

MAIN ST

BB10

Easter Shieldhill

Redding Muir

Greenwells

BRAESIDE

Shieldhill

ELIM DR

Shieldhill Prim Sch

CHURCH RD

California Prim Sch

California

MAIN ST

MANOR

MERVILLE TERR

PO

The Three Kings (PH)

3

Wester Shieldhill Lands

Summerhouse

Burnside

Polmont Burn

Recn Gd

MERVILLE TERR

Quarryhead

FK1

76

Gardrum

Blackbraes

Works

Mast

2

Gardrum Moss

Craigmad

Grayrigg Inn (PH)

75

Loch Ellrig

Greyrigg Farm

Heathery Knowe

Blackbrigs

Mast

Resr

1

Boxton Burn

Boxtonrighead

Broom

Glen Ellrig

Greencraig Cottages

BB28

74

88 **A** 89 **B** 90 **C**

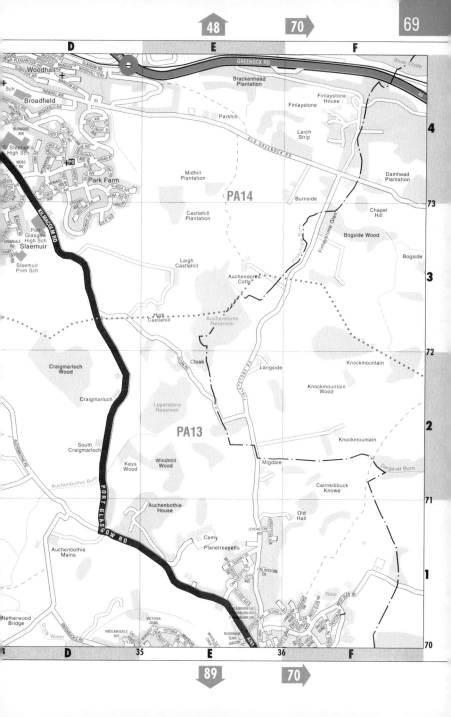

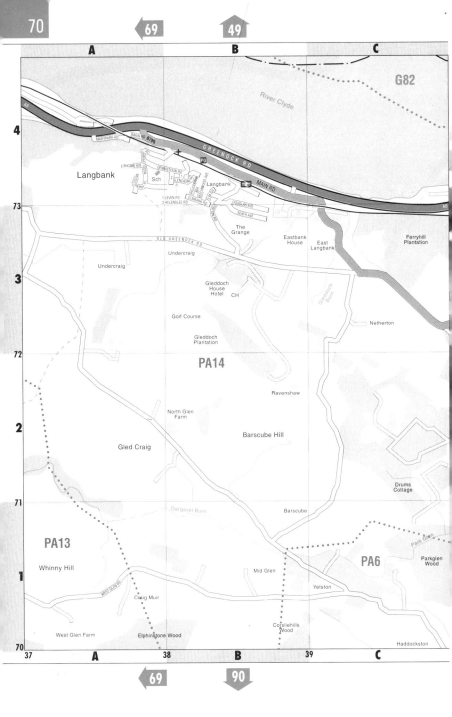

G82

River Clyde

4

MARYPARK RD

MAIN RD B789

GREENOCK RD

Langbank

LITHGOW AVE

DENNISTOUN RD

Sch

GLENCLUNY

MAIN RD

Langbank

73

1 LEVEN RD
2 HELENSLEE RD

DOUGLAS AVE

SEATH AVE

OLD GREENOCK RD

The Grange

Eastbank House

East Langbank

Ferryhill Plantation

Undercraig

Undercraig

3

Gleddoch House Hotel

CH

Gleddoch Burn

Golf Course

Gleddoch Plantation

Netherton

72

PA14

North Glen Farm

Ravenshaw

2

Gled Craig

Barscube Hill

Drums Cottage

71

Dargavel Burn

Barscube

Park Glen

PA13

PA6

Parkglen Wood

1

Whinny Hill

Mid Glen

Yetston

WEST GLENS

Craig Muir

West Glen Farm

Elphinstone Wood

Corsliehills Wood

Haddockston

70

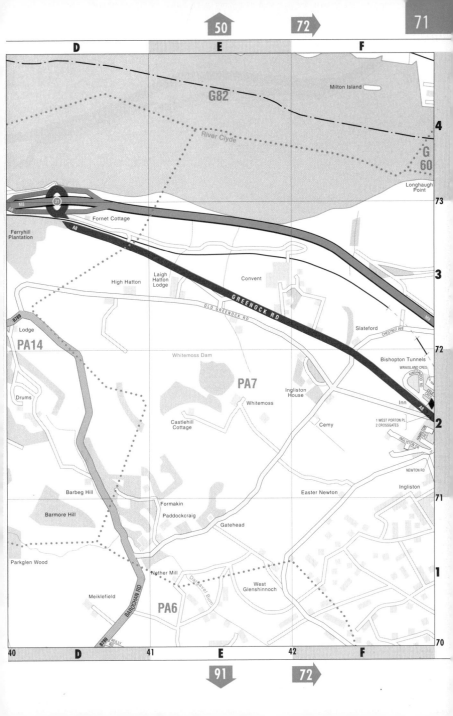

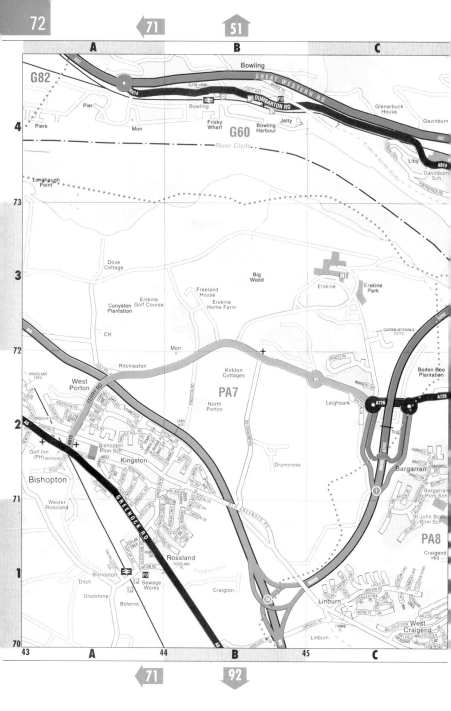

Bowling

G82

GREAT WESTERN RD

A82

CLYDE VIEW

A814

SCOTT RD

RANGE RD

DUMBARTON RD

P

P

PO

Pier

Bowling

Glenarbuck House

Gavinburn

Mon

Frisky Wharf

Jetty

4

Piers

G60

Bowling Harbour

A82

River Clyde

Liby

A814

Gavinburn Sch

Longhaugh Point

FORTPATRICK RD

73

Dove Cottage

Big Wood

A726

3

Erskine

Erskine Park

H

Conyston Plantation

Erskine Golf Course

Freeland House

Erskine Home Farm

GARDEN VETERAN'S COTTS

A8

CH

Mon

PRINCE'S PK

Boden Beo Plantation

72

Ritchieston

BOLT RD

Kirkton Cottages

NURSERY AVE

A726

A726

WRAISLAND CRES

West Porton

HENRY RD

KINGSTON RD

PA7

Laighpark

Toll

A8

Golf Inn (PH)

BRIDGEND

Bishopton Prim Sch

North Porton

LANG AVE

OLD GREENOCK RD

Bargarran

DARROCH DR

Bargarran Prim Sch

CAMERON

2

CROSSGATES

ANDERSON RD

Kingston

Drumcross

MAXWELL DR

GREENOCK RD

Bishopton

Wester Rossland

St John Bosco Prim Sch

71

CARSWELL DR

PA8

Craigend Hill

POPLAR

Rossland

ROSSLAND PL

GAITON RD

Craigton Burn

Linburn

LOCHY RD

LINBURN RD

West Craigend

1

Bishopton

Ditch

Sewage Works

P

PO

P

Craigton

M898

Linburn

MILLFIELD VIEW

MILLFIELD

Gladstone

Bolerno

DARGAVEL RD

LINNHE PL

Linburn

70

A8

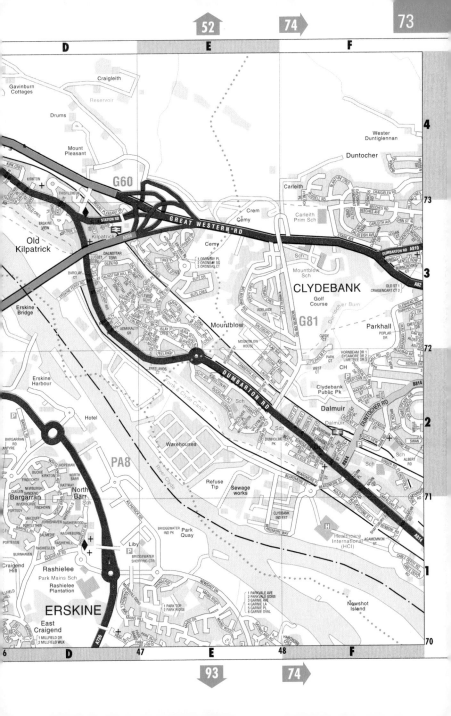

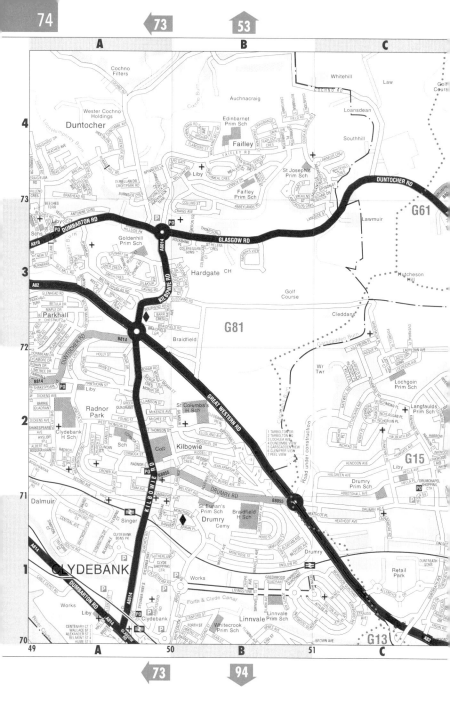

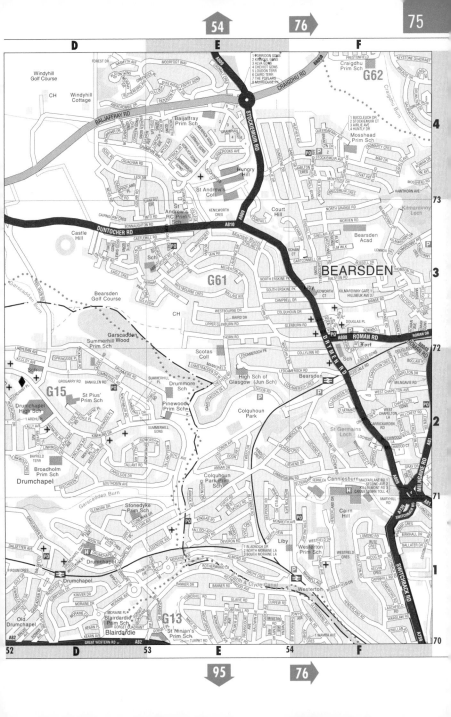

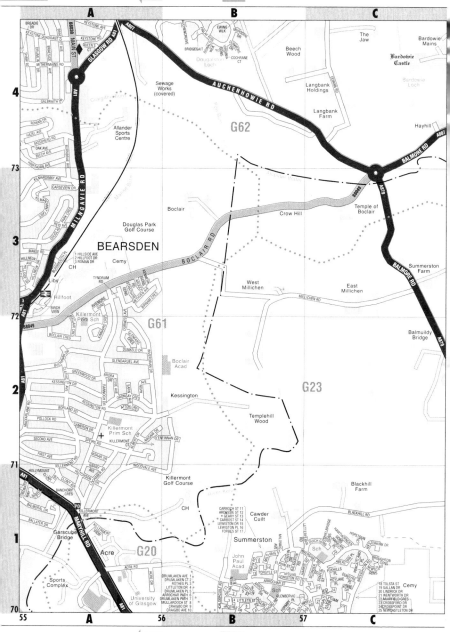

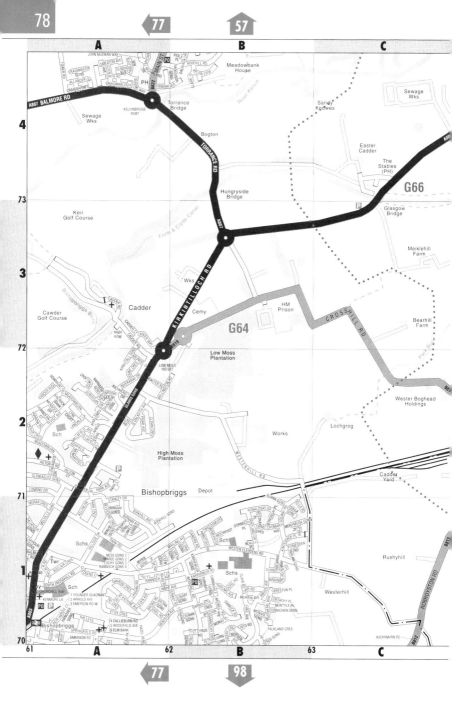

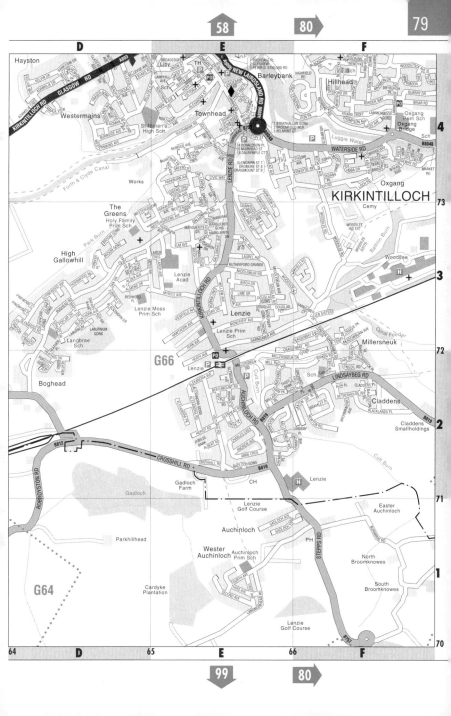

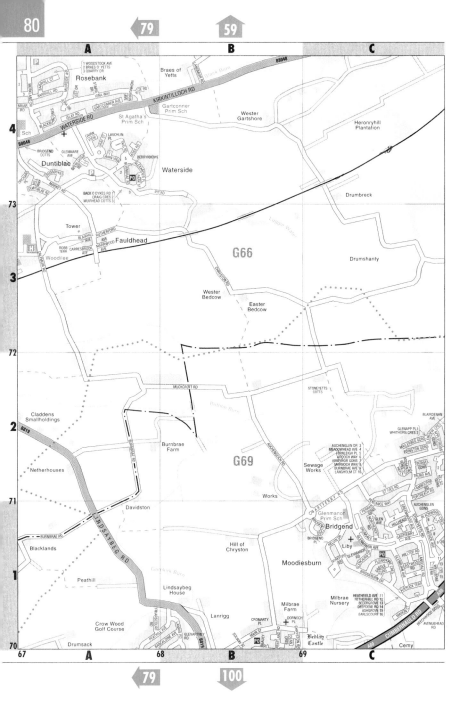

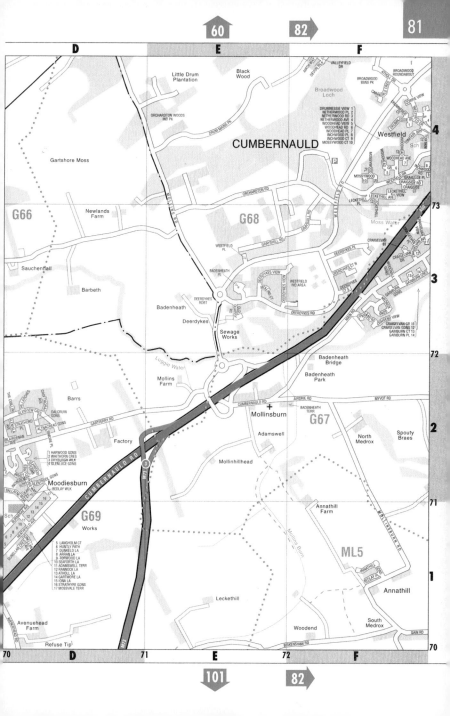

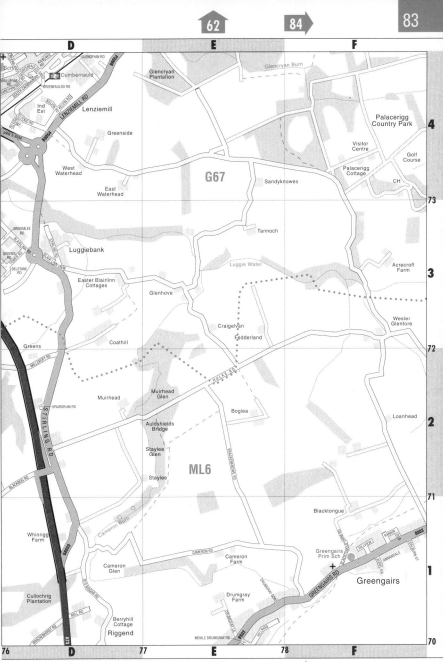

A

B

C

4

Palacerigg Country Park

Golf Course

Fannyside Lochs

Fannyside Mill

Jawhills

Fannyside Lodge

River Avon

Thieves Hill

73

G67

Herd's Hill

West Fannyside

FK1

Scar Hill

Toddle Knowe

Bog Bridge

3

Luggie Water

Avon Water

Black Hill

Blackhill

72

Torbrex

Bogside

Netherton of Glentore

Easter Glentore

B803

2

Langdales

Sheilhill Burn

Easter Glentore

GREENGAIRS RD

ML6

HM Remand Inst

LOCHRIG CRESCENT
SCHOOL RD
BRYAN RD
SLAMADALE RD

Upperton Farm

71

THE CRESCENT

Meadowfield

B803

PH

1

Avalon

Greendykeside

BRIDGE ST

70

79

A

80

B

81

C

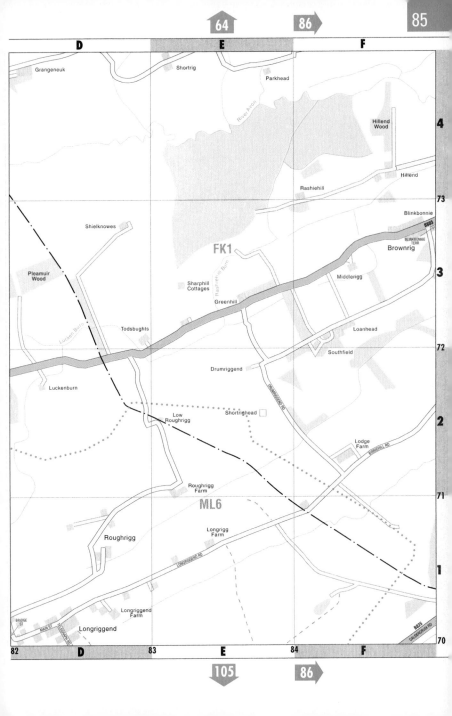

D E F

Grangeneuk

Shortrig

Parkhead

River Avon

Hillend
Wood

4

Hillend

Rashiehill

73

Blinkbonnie

B803

Shielknowes

FK1

BLINKBONNIE
TERR

Brownrig

Pleamuir
Wood

Sharphill
Cottages

Middlerigg

3

Rashiehill Burn

Greenhill

Luckan Burn

Loanhead

Todsbughts

72

Southfield

Drumriggend

Luckenburn

DRUMRIGGEND RD

Low
Roughrigg

Shortrighead

2

Lodge
Farm

BONNHILL RD

Roughrigg
Farm

71

ML6

Roughrigg

Longrigg
Farm

LONGRIGGEND RD

1

BRIDGE
ST

MAIN ST

FLEMINGTON RD

Longriggend
Farm

Longriggend

B825

CALDERCRUIX RD

70

82 D 83 E 84 F

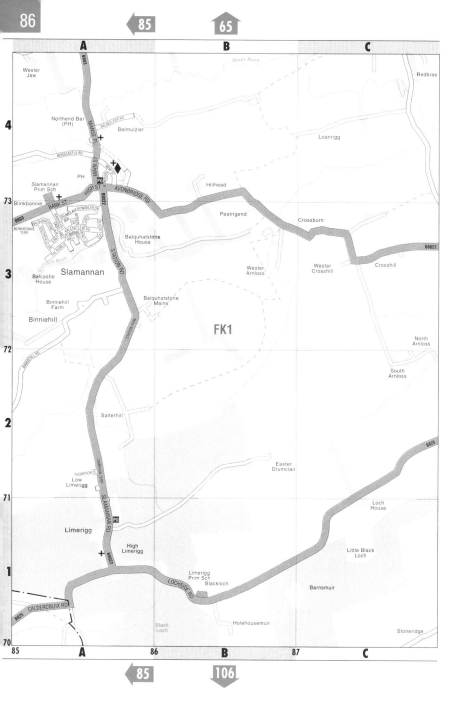

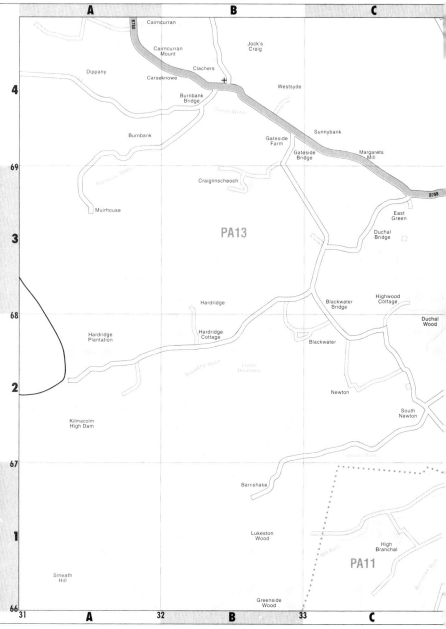

A B C

B7768

Cairncurran

Cairncurran
Mount

Jock's
Craig

Clachers

Dippany

Carseknowe

Westsyde

4

Burnbank
Bridge

Green Water

Burnbank

Gateside
Farm

Sunnybank

Gateside
Bridge

Margarets
Mill

69

Burnbank Water

Craiglinscheoch

B7768

Muirhouse

East
Green

PA13

Duchal
Bridge

3

Hardridge

Blackwater
Bridge

Highwood
Cottage

Duchal
Wood

68

Hardridge
Plantation

Hardridge
Cottage

Blackwater

Blacketty Water

Lower
Reservoir

Newton

2

South
Newton

Kilmacolm
High Dam

67

Barnshake

Mill Burn

1

Lukeston
Wood

High
Branchal

Burnbank Burn

PA11

Smeath
Hill

Greenside
Wood

66

31 A 32 B 33 C

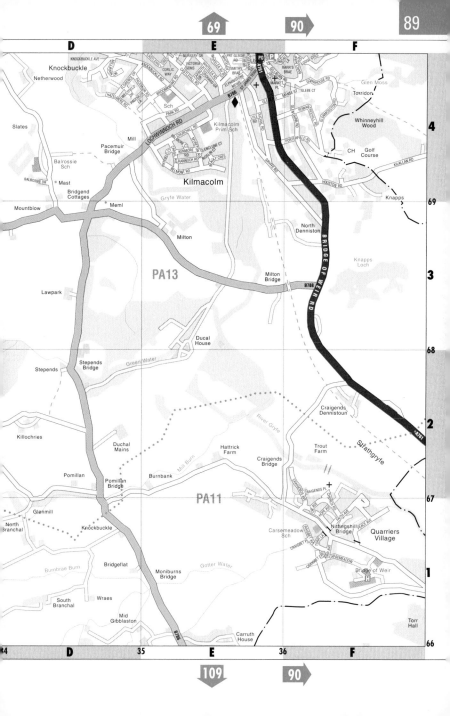

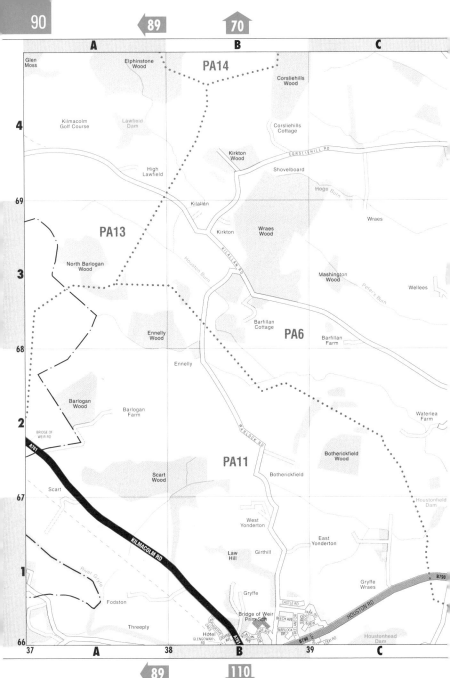

A   **B**   **C**

Glen Moss

Elphinstone Wood

PA14

Corsliehills Wood

Kilmacolm Golf Course

Lawfield Dam

Corsliehills Cottage

4

CORSLIEHILL RD

Kirkton Wood

High Lawfield

Shovelboard

69

Kilalian

Hogs Burn

Wraes

PA13

Kirkton

Wraes Wood

North Barlogan Wood

Houston Burn

KILALIAN RD

Mashington Wood

Peter's Burn

Wellees

3

Barfillan Cottage

PA6

Barfillan Farm

Ennelly Wood

Ennelly

68

Barlogan Wood

Barlogan Farm

Waterlea Farm

WARLOCK RD

2

BRIDGE OF WEIR RD

A761

PA11

Botherickfield

Botherickfield Wood

Scart Wood

Houstonfield Dam

67

Scart

KILMACOLM RD

West Yonderton

East Yonderton

River Gryfe

1

Law Hill

Girthill

Gryffe Wraes

B790

Fodston

Gryffe

CASTLE RD

PARK

BEECH AVE

HOUSTON RD

Threeply

Bridge of Weir Prim Sch

Hotel GLENGOWAN RD

GRYFFE AVE

A761

WARLOCK DR

B790

LOCH RD

Houstonhead Dam

66

37   **A**   **38**   **B**   **39**   **C**

D   E   F

East
Glenshinnoch

PA7

Towncroft Farm

Boghall Cottage

REILLY RD

4

Swinesglen
Plantation

Northbrae
Plantation

Barochan

Reilly
Farm

Corsliehill

Barochancross
Farm

CORSLIEHILL RD

Swines Glen

Barochan Hill

69

Blackleather
Wood

Stabilee

Hops Burn

BAROCHAN RD

Barochan
House

Barochan Moss

3

Swanieston

Chapel
Farm

Low
Wood

Fulwood Wood

TURNINGSHAW RD

Cleaves Farm

PA6

Turningshaw
Farm

68

Barochan Burn

Peter's Burn

CHAPEL RD

KILALLAN RD

Greenhill

2

Houston
Wood

Langdale

Loanhead
Bridge

Loanhead

OLD SCHOOLHOUSE LA 1
CRICKETFIELD LA 2
LYLE'S LAND 3

KD MACOLM RD

Houston
House

North Mains

B790

PH

NORTH ST

Houston
House

+

HOUSTON RD

67

MAIN ST

BRIDGETON ST

SOUTH ST

KINGSLEA
RD

Bogston Hill

SOUTH MAINS COTTS

FLEMING ST

P

CRACK CR

Houston

South
Mains

ST FILLANS DR

HOUSTON RD

Woodend

CROSSFLAT

Ardgryfe
Ford

Nether
Craigends
Farm

HOUSTONFIELD RD

SOUTH MOUND
OLD BRIDGE OF WEIR RD

MANSE CRES

NEUK CRES

RIVERSIDE

+

BRIDGE OF WEIR RD

Gryffe
High Sch

Cemy

NEUK AVE

River Gryfe

1

St Fillan's
RC Prim Sch

DUNNET DR

Weir

Back O' Hill

HOUSTON RD

Houston
Prim Sch

CROSSLEE
CRES

Crosslee Strip

Auchans
Farm

STRAWBERRY FIELD RD 1
BRIERIE AVE 2
BRIERIE-HILL RD 3

BACK O HILL

Crosslee

Craigends

CRAWFORD RD

MAGNUS RD

GRYFEWOOD CR

OSHER AVE

66

40   D   41   E   42   F

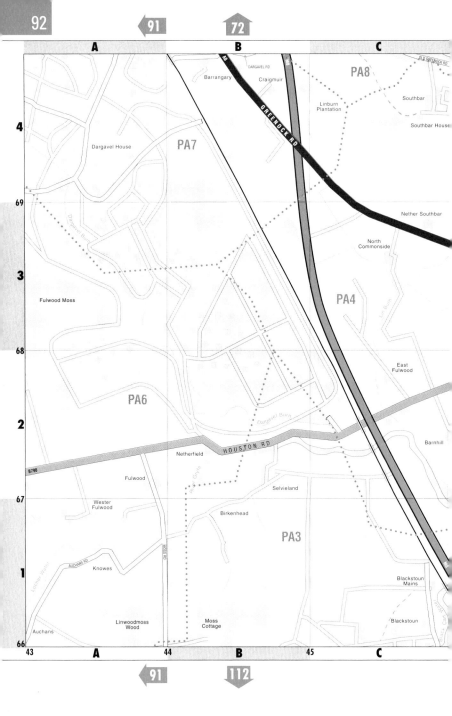

A   B   C

PA8

OLD GREENOCK RD

DARGAVEL RD

Barrangary   Craigmuir

Southbar

Linburn
Plantation

Southbar House

4

Dargavel House

PA7

GREENOCK RD

69

Nether Southbar

North
Commonside

3

Fulwood Moss

PA4

Len Burn

68

East
Fulwood

PA6

Dargavel Burn

2

HOUSTON RD

Netherfield

Barnhill

B790

Fulwood

River Gryfe

Selvieland

67

Wester
Fulwood

Birkenhead

PA3

MOSS RD

1

AUCHANS RD

Knowes

Blackstoun
Mains

Lapwing Water

Linwoodmoss
Wood

Moss
Cottage

Blackstoun

Auchans

66

43   A   44   B   45   C

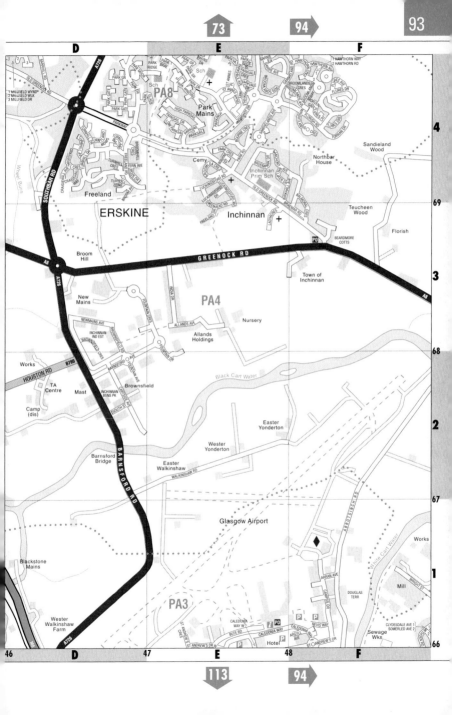

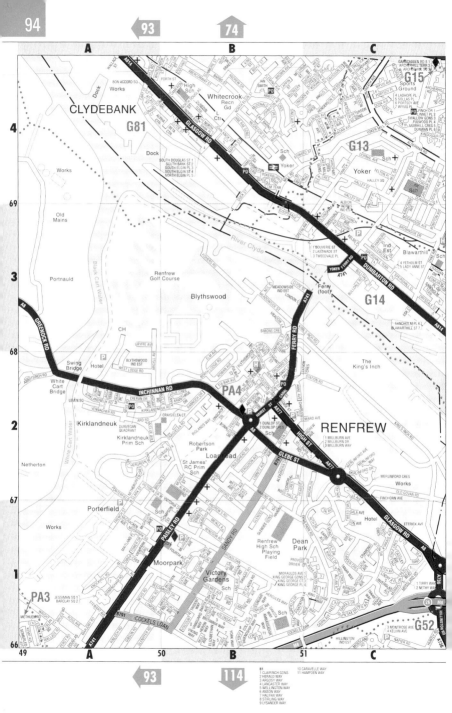

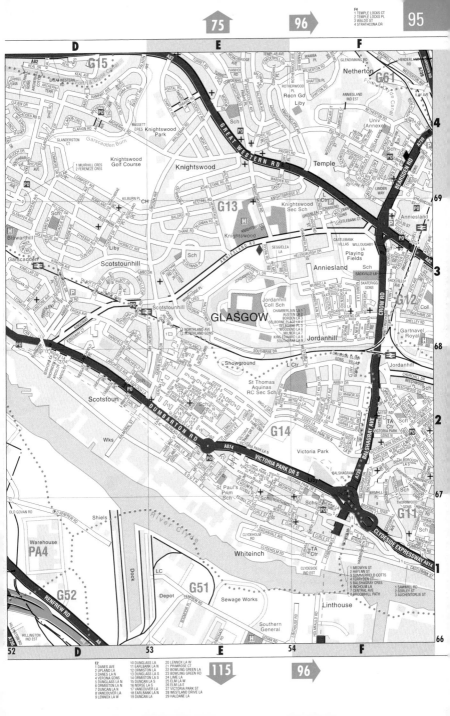

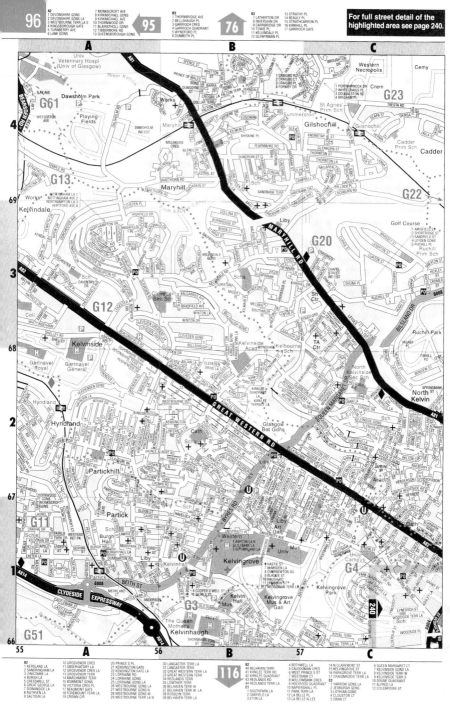

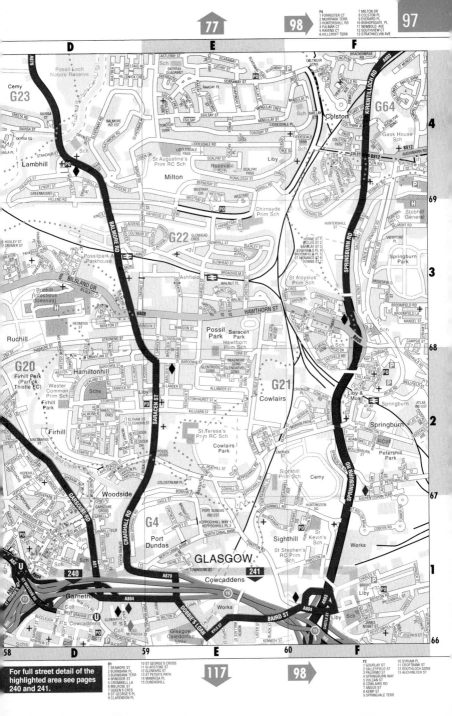

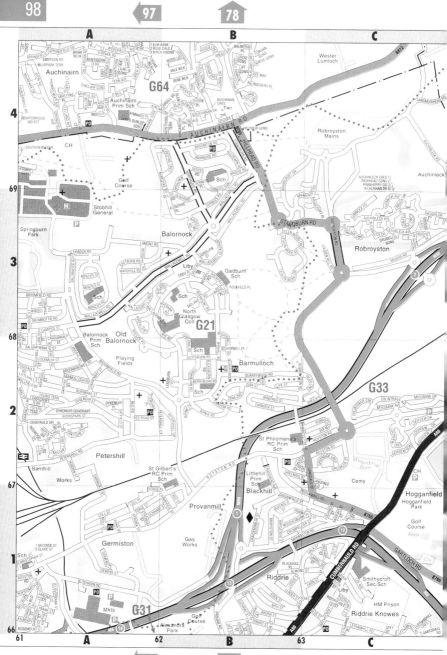

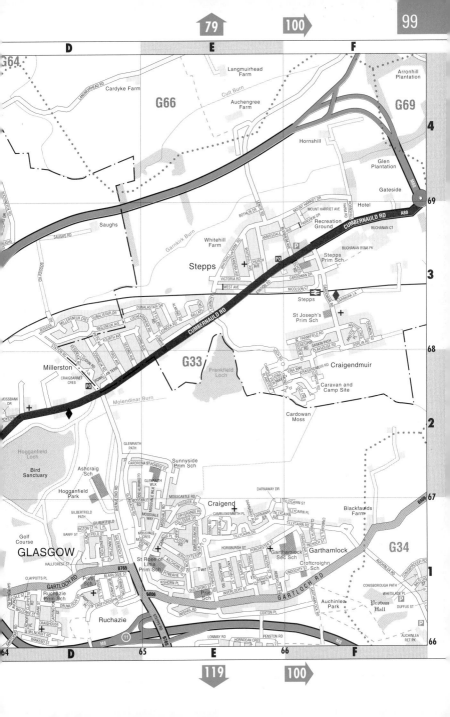

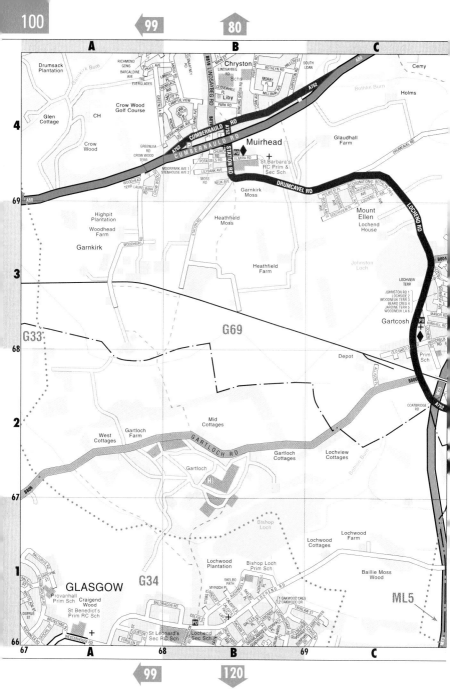

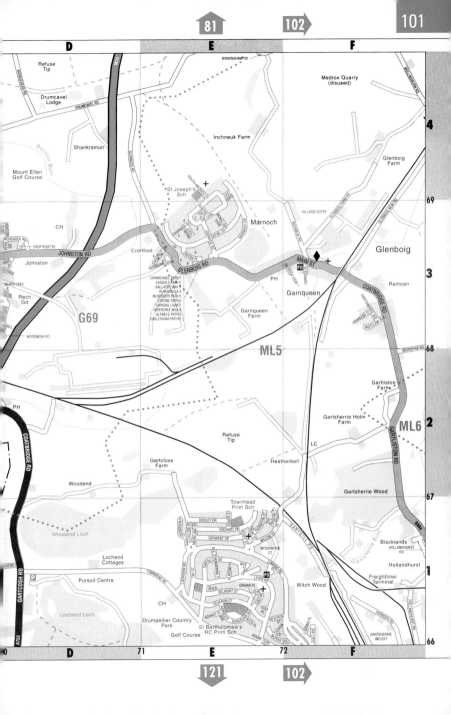

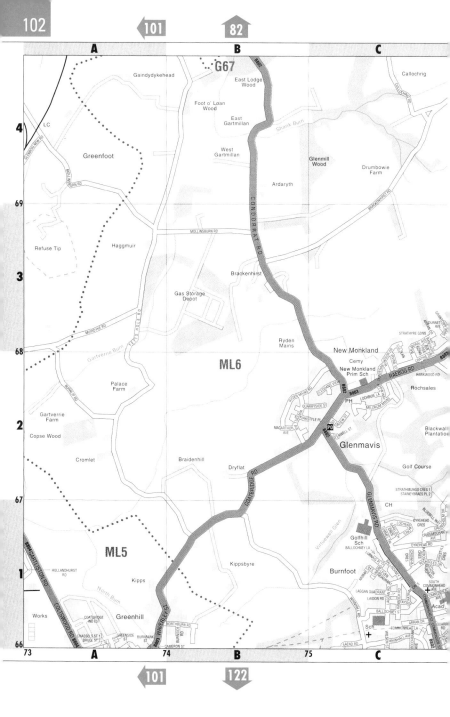

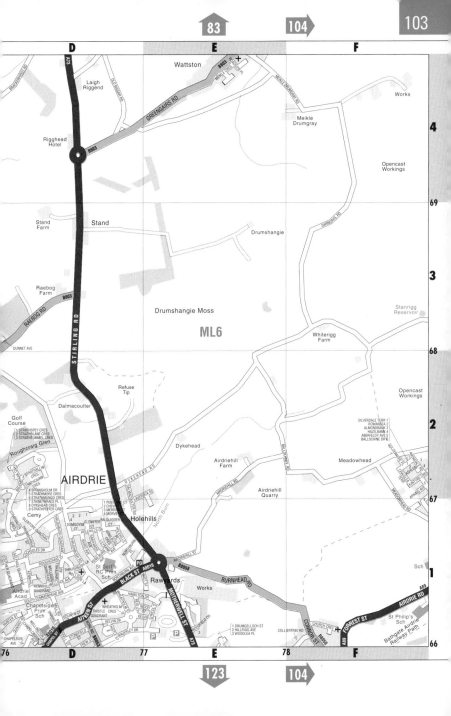

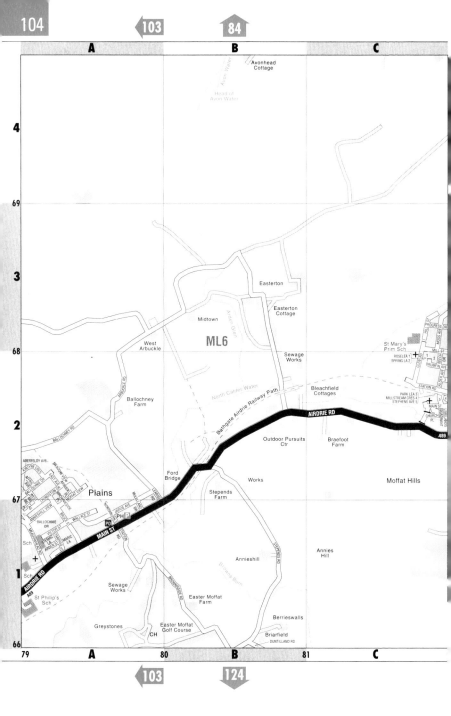

A B C

4

69

3

Avonhead
Cottage

Avon Water

Head of
Avon Water

Easterton

Easterton
Cottage

Midtown

West
Arbuckle

ML6

Artoch Glen

68

St Mary's
Prim Sch

PROGRESS DR

ROSELEA 1
SPRING LA 2

Ballochney
Farm

Sewage
Works

North Calder Water

Bleachfield
Cottages

STATION RD

PARK LEA 3
MILLSTREAM CRES 4
STEPHENS AVE 5

BALLOCHNEY RD

Bathgate Airdrie Railway Path

AIRDRIE RD

CHURCH
PL

A89

2

Outdoor Pursuits
Ctr

Braefoot
Farm

Moffat Hills

Ford
Bridge

ABERFELDY AVE

JOWYNE CRES

MEADOW VIEW

BALLOCHNIE DR

Plains

Works

Stepends
Farm

67

WALLACE ST

PH P

PO

MAIN ST

Sch

MARIG LA

AnniesHill

Annies
Hill

STEPENDS RD

1

AIRDRIE RD

A89

Sch

St Philip's
Sch

Sewage
Works

BROOMSIDE RD

Brooms Burn

Easter Moffat
Farm

Berrieswalls

Briarfield

Greystones

CH

Easter Moffat
Golf Course

DUNTILLAND RD

66

79 A 80 B 81 C

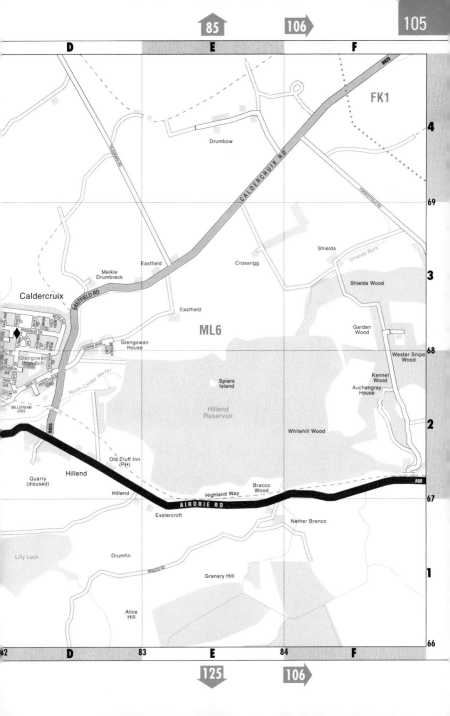

D
E
F

B825

FK1

4

69

CALDERCRUIX RD

Drumbow

FORESTFIELD RD

Shields

Shields Burn

Eastfield

Crossrigg

Shields Wood

3

Meikle
Drumbreck

EASTFIELD RD

Caldercruix

Eastfield

ML6

Garden
Wood

Wester Snipe
Wood

68

GOWAN BRAE

Glengowan
Prim Sch

PROGRESS DR

Glengowan
House

Kennel
Wood

Auchengray
House

North Calder Water

Spiers
Island

MILLSTREAM
CRES

B825

Hillend
Reservoir

Whitehill Wood

2

Old Truff Inn
(PH)

Quarry
(disused)

Hillend

Hillend

Highland Way

Bracco
Wood

A89

67

AIRDRIE RD

Eastercroft

Nether Branco

Lilly Loch

Drumfin

BRACCO RD

Granary Hill

1

Alice
Hill

66

D
83
E
84
F

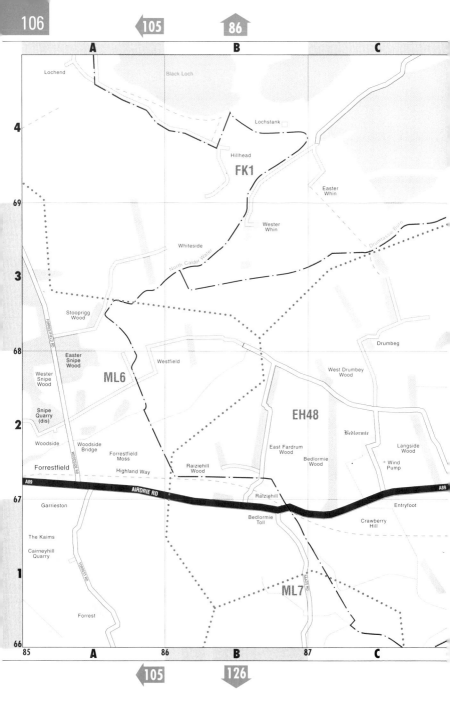

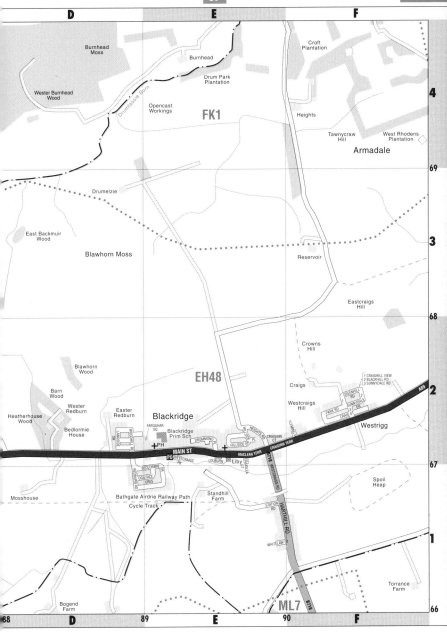

Burnhead
Moss

Croft
Plantation

Burnhead

Drum Park
Plantation

Wester Burnhead
Wood

4

Opencast
Workings

FK1

Heights

Tawnycraw
Hill

West Rhodens
Plantation

Armadale

69

Drumelzie

3

East Backmuir
Wood

Blawhorn Moss

Reservoir

Eastcraigs
Hill

68

Crowns
Hill

Blawhorn
Wood

EH48

Craigs

1 CRAIGHILL VIEW
2 BLACKHILL RD
3 SUNNYDALE RD

Barn
Wood

Westcraigs
Hill

GREENHILL
RD

SUNNYDALE
DR

A89

Heatherhouse
Wood

Wester
Redburn

Easter
Redburn

Blackridge

PARK RD

CRAIG ST

2

Bedlormie
House

FARQUHAR
SQ

WESTCRAIGS

Blackridge
Prim Sch

DRUMMOND

HEIGHTS RD

HILLSIDE PL

CRAIGINN
CT

FLEMING

Westrigg

PH

MAIN ST

PO

MACLEAN TERR

CRAIGINN TERR

67

REDBURN
RD

BEDLORMIE
RD

DUFFTACS
CRES

WOODHILL RD
LANGSIDE

LOUBURN

CRAIGLEA

Liby

WHITBURN RD

HARTHILL RD

Spoil
Heap

Mosshouse

Bathgate Airdrie Railway Path

Standhill
Farm

STATION
RD

Cycle Track

WHITELAW ST

1

Bogend
Farm

ML7

B718

Torrance
Farm

66

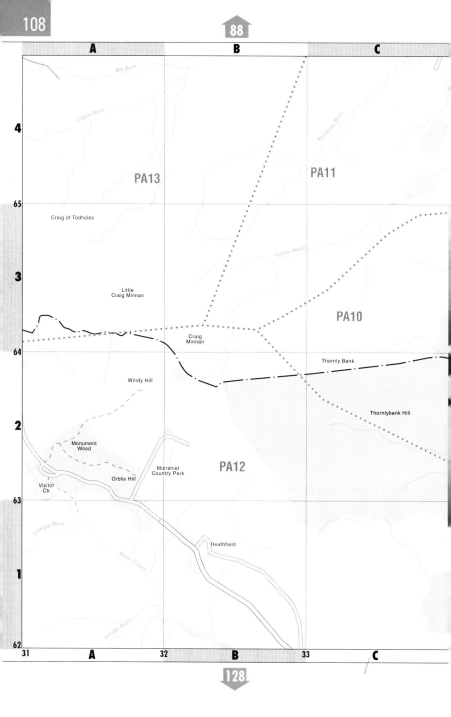

A   B   C

Mill Burn

Copie Burn

4

Bumbrae Burn

PA13   PA11

65

Craig of Todholes

Gotter Water

3

Little
Craig Minnan

PA10

Craig
Minnan

64

Thornly Bank

Windy Hill

Thornlybank Hill

2

Monument
Wood

Muirshiel
Country Park   PA12

Orblis Hill

Visitor
Ctr

63

Cample Burn

River Calder

1

Heathfield

Rough Burn

62
31   A   32   B   33   C

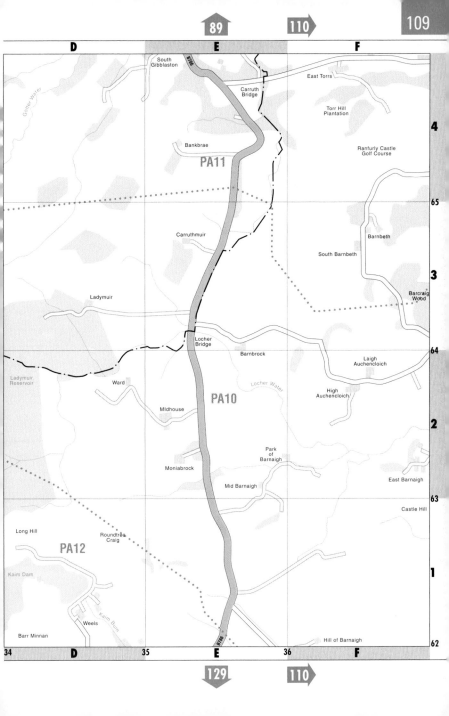

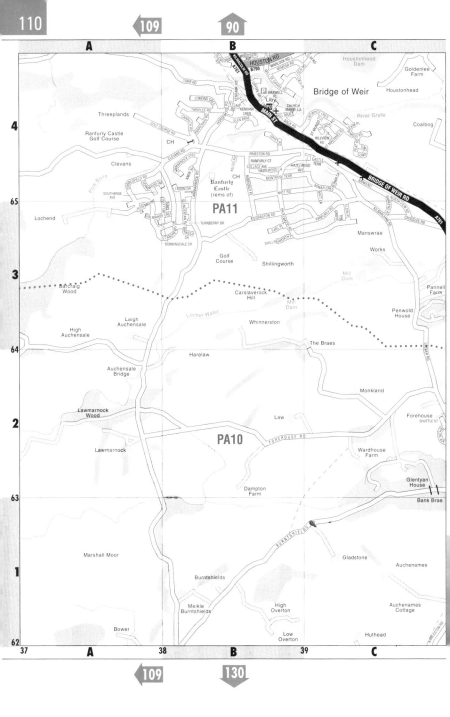

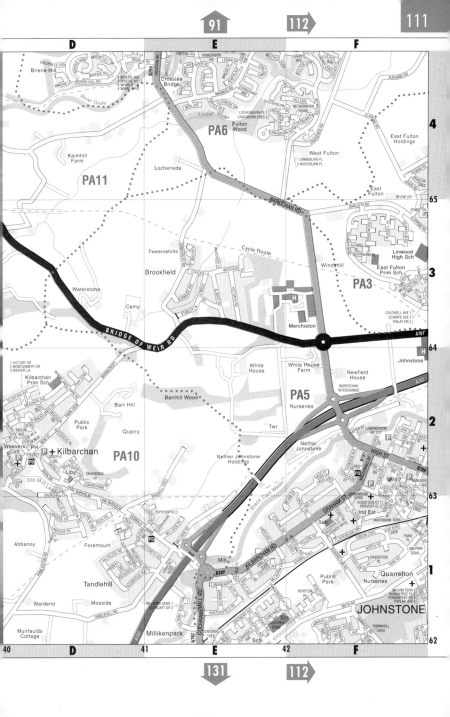

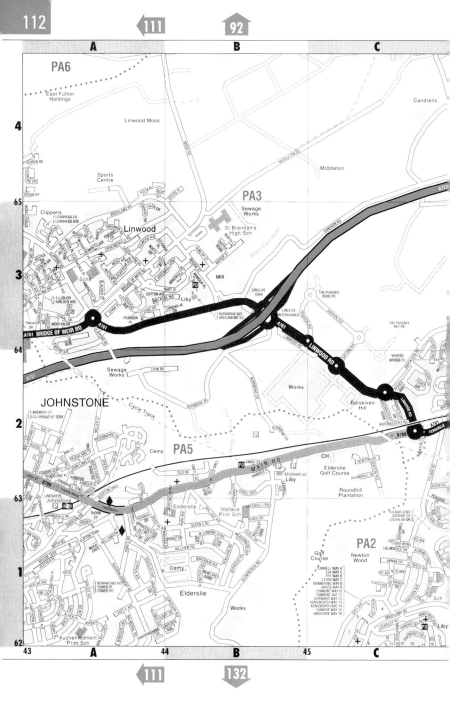

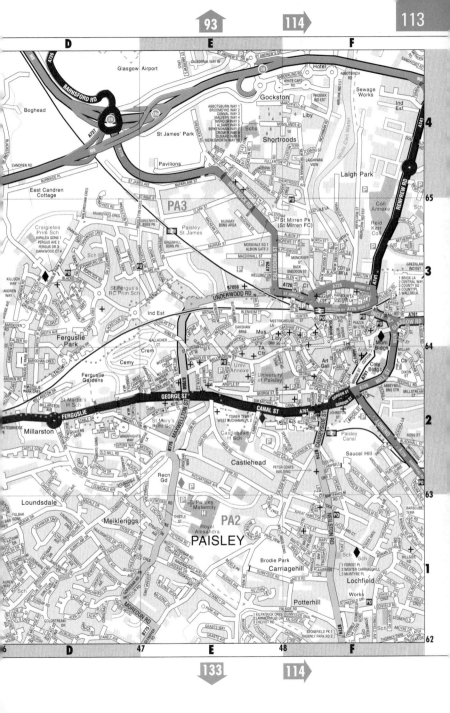

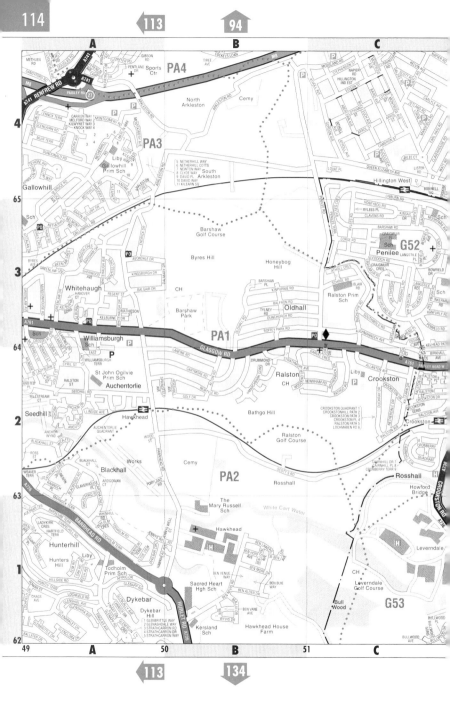

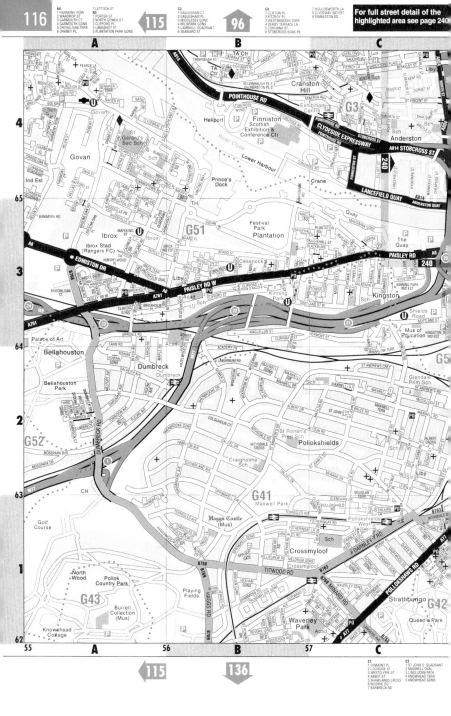

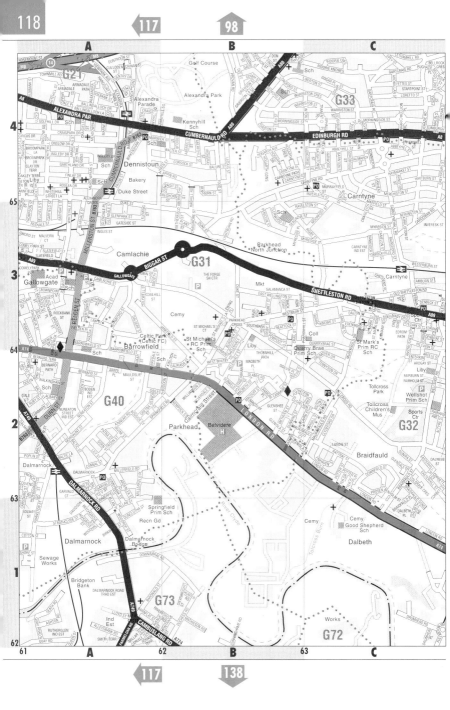

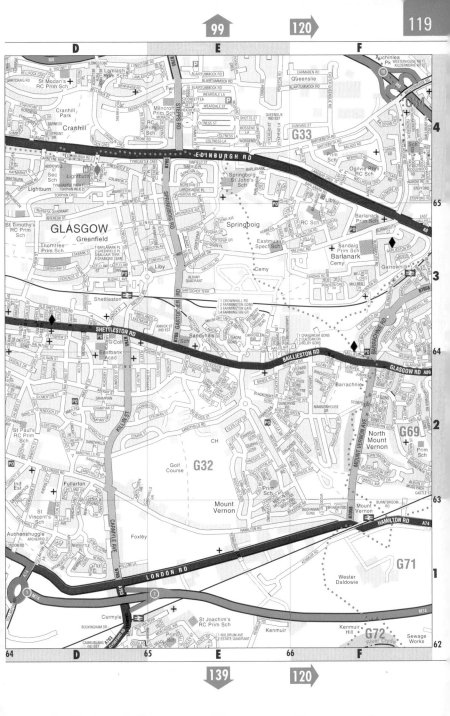

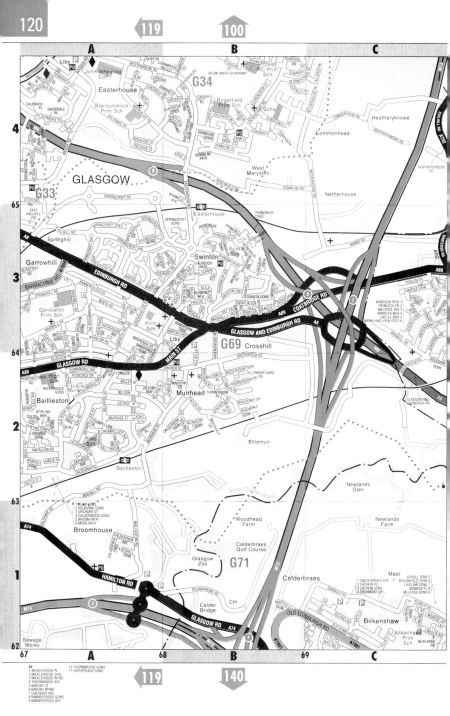

G34

Easterhouse

John Wheatley Coll

Blairtummock Prim Sch

RC Prim Sch

Rogerfield Prim Sch

Heatheryknowe

Commonhead

Netherhouse

GLASGOW

West Maryston

G33

Easterhouse

Springhill

Garrowhill

Barrachnie

EDINBURGH RD

Swinton

Garrowhill Prim Sch

G69 Crosshill

GLASGOW AND EDINBURGH RD

Liby

COATBRIDGE RD

GLASGOW RD

Baillieston

High Sch

Muirhead

Ellismuir

Baillieston

Newlands Glen

Woodhead Farm

Newlands Farm

Broomhouse

1 KELBURNE GDNS
2 KELBURNE GDNS
3 ORCHARD ST
4 CALDERWOOD GDNS
5 BROOM PATH
6 MOSS PATH

Glasgow Zoo

G71

Calderbraes Golf Course

Mast

Calderbraes

HAMILTON RD

Calder Bridge

GLASGOW RD

Birkenshaw

Aitkenhead Prim Sch

Sewage Works

M74

67
68
69
119
140

A3
1 MICKLEHOUSE PL
2 MICKLEHOUSE OVAL
3 MICKLEHOUSE WYND
4 THORNBRIDGE AVE
5 BARONY CT
6 BARONY WYND
7 QUEENSBY AVE
8 BANNERCROSS GDNS
9 BANNERCROSS AVE
10 THORNBRIDGE GDNS
11 HATHERSAGE GDNS

D E F

Drumpellier
Country Park

COLT AVE
LOMOND RD Prim Sch
BLAIRPARK AVE
GARTSHERRIE RD
Summerlee

GILMOUR ST
TER AVE
ST DENIS
WAY
SUMMERLEE
COTTS

MURDYKE RD
Alexander H
HERRIOT ST

Mus

Garnheath
Wood

St Ambrose
Sch
P
Blairhill

NORTH SQ

Gilmourneuk

4

Drumpellier
Home Farm

Coatbridge
Central

Monkland Canal

Golf
Course

Bishop Burn

Drumpellier

CH

COATBRIDGE

Blairhill
BLAIRGROVE MERRYSTONE
CT
MERRYSTON
CT

65

G69

Drumpellier
Golf Course

Langloan
Prim Sch

BANK ST

Prim
Sch

Bargeddie
Prim Sch
CARTCOSH RD

COATBRIDGE RD
Drumpark
1 PRINCESS DR
2 KING PL
3 SUNNYSIDE DR
4 ABERCROMBIE CRES
5 LIBERTY AVE

ML5

GLASGOW RD

Langloan

DUNDYVAN RD

DOUGLAS
ST

MAXWELL
ST

3

Drumpark
Specl Sch

Sewage
Works

Kirkwood

Dundyvan

64

Langmuir RD

Bargeddie
Sch

Mitchell St

ALLAN ST

Kirkwood

Old Monkland
Prim Sch
St Monica's
RC Prim Sch

Liby

Ind Estate
Est

CENTENARY GDNS

Dundyvan

Bargeddie

Crosshill St

HIGHCROSS

Old
Monkland

Old Monkland Rd

St Timothy's
RC Prim Sch
1 BEECH CT
2 PINE CT
3 POPLAR CT
4 MAPLE CT
5 FIR CT
6 SPRUCE CT
7 SYCAMORE CT
8 BIRCH CT

Bargeddie RD

2

Braehead

Woodlands

Cemy

Kirkshaws

Rosehall
High Sch

GLASGOW AND EDINBURGH RD

DOUGLAS
VIEW

63

Aitkenhead

Bankhead

A8

River Burn

G71

North Calder Water

1

Works
1 MONROE DR
2 LINCOLN AVE
3 MONKLAND VIEW
4 BEATSON WYND
5 MACMILLAN GDNS
6 YOUNG PL

TANNOCHSIDE
BSNS PK

Crowflat
Wood

Mill Bank

ML4

Easter
Wood

1 MULBERRY RD
2 REDWOOD CRES
3 WALNUT PL
4 HICKORY CRES

62

70 71 72

D E F

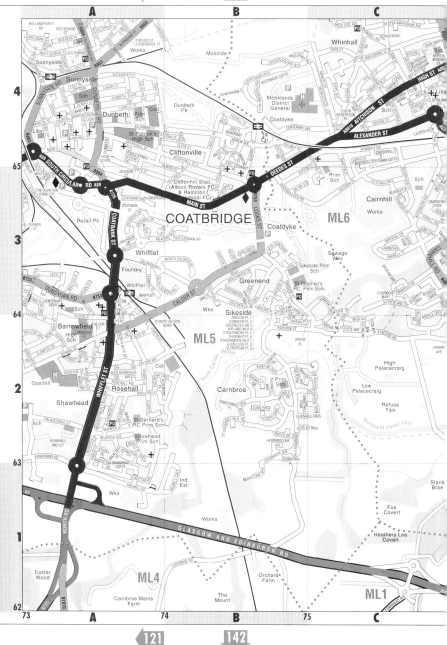

HOLLANDHURST RD
RED BRIDGE

1 BRUCE ST
2 GREENSIDE ST

Works

Mosside

Whinhall

MOSS SIDE AVE
WESTER MAVISBANK AVE

Sunnyside

Sunnyside

4

Dunbeth

Col

Dunbeth Pk

Coatdyke

Monklands
District
General

St Patrick's
High Sch

Cliftonville

TA
Ctr

65

SOUTH CIRCULAR

RD A89

Jackson St

Cliftonhill Stad
(Albion Rovers FC)
& Hamilton
(Academical FC)

MAIN ST

DEEDES ST

Prim
Sch

Sch

Cairnhill

A89

COATBRIDGE

Coatdyke

Works

ML6

Retail Pk

Whifflet

Sewage
Wks

3

Foundry

North Calder Rd

CALDER ST

Greenend

Sikeside Prim
Sch

St Stephen's
RC Prim Sch

Whifflet

Barrowfield
High Sch

Wks

Sikeside
DEESIDE PL 1
DUNAVON PL 2
GREENLEES GR 3
KIPLAND WLK 4
STRATHMORE PL 5
THORNKIP PL 6
STRATHMORE WLK 7
GLEN LUSS PL 8
GLENSPEAN PL 9

High
Palacecraig

64

ML5

Robert Gilson
Gdns

Coathill

H

Rosehall

Carnbroe

Prim
Sch

Low
Palacecraig

Refuse
Tips

2

Shawhead

WHIFFLET ST

Coll

Ind
Est

Monkland Canal (dis)

St Bernard's
RC Prim Sch

Shawhead
Prim Sch

Shawhead
Cotts

63

Rosehall
Ind Est

KIRKSHAWS RD

Wks

A8

Stank
Brae

NORTH RD

Fox
Covert

1

GLASGOW AND EDINBURGH RD

Works

Heathery Lea
Covert

Easter
Wood

ML4

Carnbroe Mains
Farm

The
Mount

Orchard
Farm

ML1

62

73

74

75

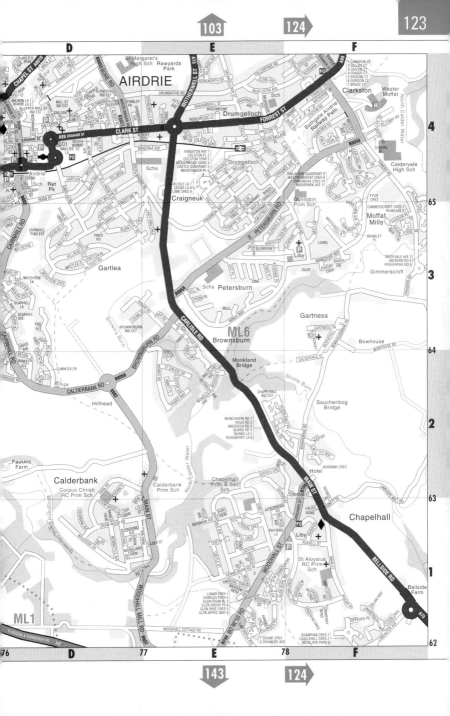

BROWNIESIDE RD

STEPENDS RD

Easter Moffat
Golf Course

Lochhill

DUNTILLAND RD

Brown's Burn

4

Wester
Bracco

Springbank Quarry
(disused)

Lady Bell's
Moss

65

BURNWOOD DR
INVERVALE AVE

Burn
Wood

ROUGHRIGG RD

3

ML6

Roughrigg
Reservoir

BROWNSIDE RD

Clattering Burn

DUNSYSTON RD

Works

64

Easter
Dunsyston

Craigends

2

Gartness
Farm

GARTNESS RD

Craigends
Moss

Turdees

CRAIGENDS RD

Blackrig

Langside

63

Wester
Dunsyston

Bothwellshields

ML1

M

Budshaw

BOTHWELLSHIELDS RD

Longacre

SPRINGFIELD RD

1

Shotts Burn

Peatpots

B7066

GLASGOW AND EDINBURGH RD

ML7

MELLOCH RD
A73

6

B7066

MILL SYKES RD

62

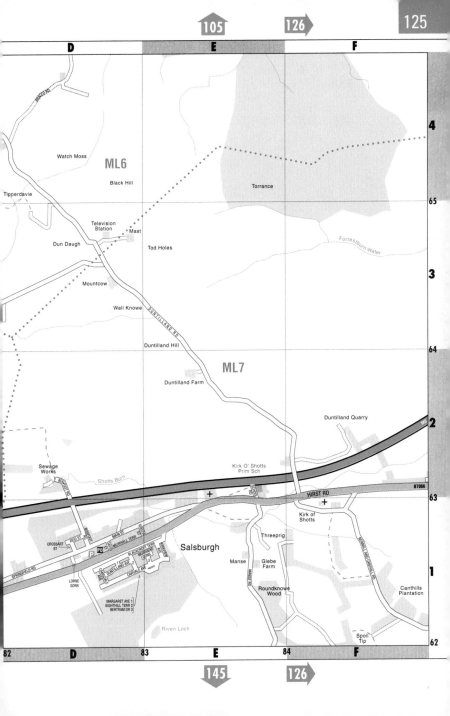

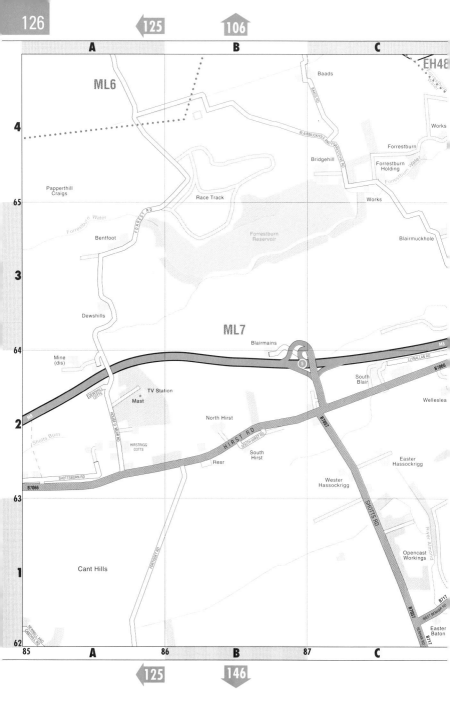

A **B** **C**

EH48

ML6

Baads

BLAIRMUCKHOLE AND FORRESTDYKE RD

BAADS RD

Works

4

Forrestburn

Bridgehill

Forrestburn
Holding

Forrestburn Water

Papperthill
Craigs

65

Race Track

Works

FORREST RD

Forrestburn Water

Forrestburn
Reservoir

Blairmuckhole

Bentfoot

3

Dewshills

ML7

Blairmains

64

M8

Mine
(dis)

LLYNALLAN RD

DEWSHILL COTTS

TV Station

South
Blair

B7066

Mast

Welleslea

HOUSE O MUIR RD

2

North Hirst

HIRST RD

M8

SOUTH HIRST RD

B7057

Shotts Burn

South
Hirst

HIRSTRIGG
COTTS

Easter
Hassockrigg

Resr

SHOTTSBURN RD

Wester
Hassockrigg

SHOTTS RD

B7066

63

River Almond

Opencast
Workings

1

Cant Hills

FORREST RD

West Benhar Rd

B7717

B7057

BENHAR RD

B7717

Easter
Baton

NEWHILL RD
CARLISLE RD

62

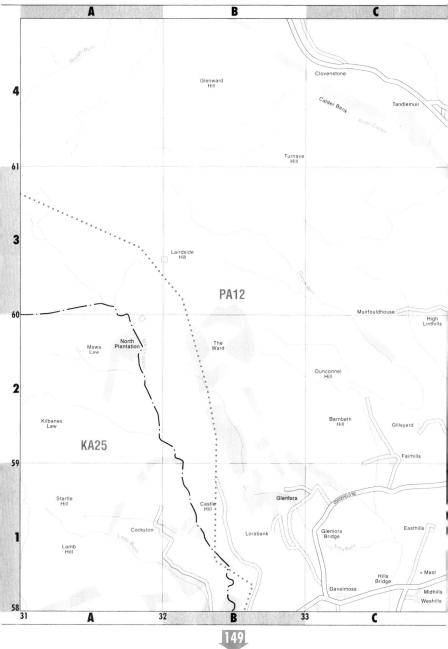

A　　　　　B　　　　　C

4

Rough Burn

Glenward
Hill

Clovenstone

Calder Bank

Tandlemuir

River Calder

Turnave
Hill

61

3

Lairdside
Hill

PA12

Girga Burn

Muirfouldhouse

High
Linthills

60

Maws
Law

North
Plantation

New County

The
Ward

Duncannel
Hill

2

Kilbanes
Law

KA25

Barnbeth
Hill

Gillsyard

Fairhills

59

Startle
Hill

Castle
Hill

Glenlora

CORSEFIELD RD

Glenlora
Bridge

Easthills

1

Lamb
Hill

Cockston

Lady Burn

Lorabank

Lord Burn

Mast

Hills
Bridge

Gavelmoss

Midhills

Weshills

58

31　　　　A　　　　32　　　　B　　　　33　　　　C

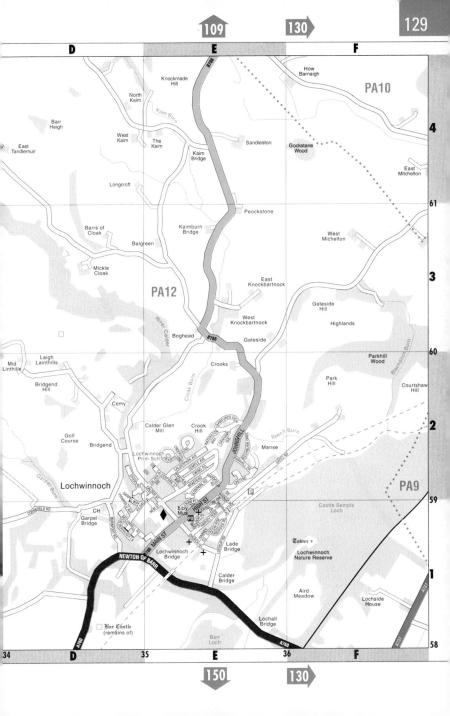

D E F

PA10

How
Barnaigh

Knockmade
Hill

North
Kaim

Barr
Heigh

Kaim Burn

Sandieston

Gockstane
Wood

East
Tandlemuir

West
Kaim

The
Kaim

Kaim
Bridge

East
Mitchelton

4

Longcroft

61

Peockstone

Barrs of
Cloak

Kaimburn
Bridge

West
Michelton

Balgreen

3

Mickle
Cloak

PA12

East
Knockbartnock

Gateside
Hill

Highlands

River Calder

Boghead

West
Knockbartnock

Gateside

Parkhill
Wood

60

Mid
Linthills

Laigh
Lainthills

Crooks

Park
Hill

Courtshaw
Hill

Blackditch Burn

Bridgend
Hill

Cloak Burn

Cemy

Calder Glen
Mill

Crook
Hill

Beech Burn

Manse

2

Golf
Course

Bridgend

Lochwinnoch
Prim Sch

JOHNSHILL

PA9

Garpel Burn

Lochwinnoch

HIGH ST

P

Castle Semple
Loch

59

CROSSFIELD RD

CH

Garpel
Bridge

Liby
Mus

PO

MAIN ST

Lochwinnoch
Bridge

Lade
Bridge

Tower

Lochwinnoch
Nature Reserve

NEWTON OF BARR

Calder
Bridge

1

Aird
Meadow

Lochside
House

Bar Castle
(remains of)

A760

Lochall
Bridge

Barr
Loch

A760

58

34 D A760 35 E 36 F

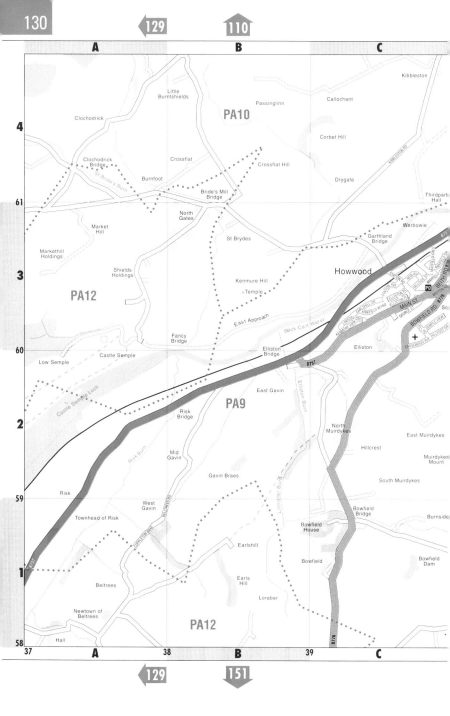

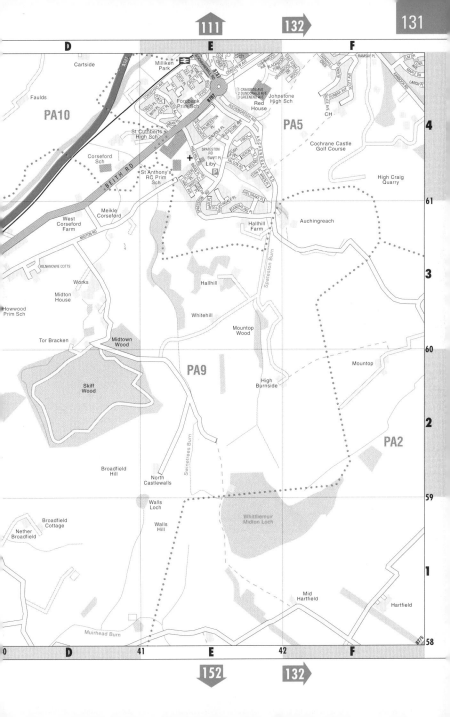

D
E
F

Cartside

Faulds

PA10

Milliken Park

Fordbank Prim Sch

St Cuthbarts High Sch

BEITH RD

Corseford Sch

St Anthony's RC Prim Sch

Meikle Corseford

West Corseford Farm

1 CRAIGBOG AVE
2 DUNDONALD AVE
3 GREENEND AVE

Johnstone High Sch

Red House

PA5

Cochrane Castle Golf Course

High Craig Quarry

4

Spateston Liby

P

MIDTON RD

KILNKNOWIE COTTS

Works

Midton House

Howwood Prim Sch

Tor Bracken

Midtown Wood

Hallhill Farm

Auchingreach

Spateston Burn

Hallhill

Whitehill

Mountop Wood

61

3

PA9

Skiff Wood

Broadfield Hill

North Castlewalls

Swinetrees Burn

High Burnside

Mountop

60

PA2

2

Walls Loch

Broadfield Cottage

Nether Broadfield

Walls Hill

Whittliemuir Midton Loch

59

Mid Hartfield

Hartfield

1

Muirhead Burn

58

0
D
41
E
42
F

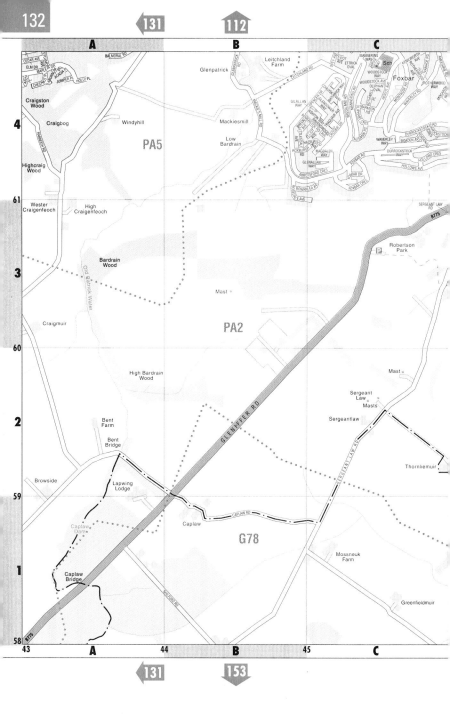

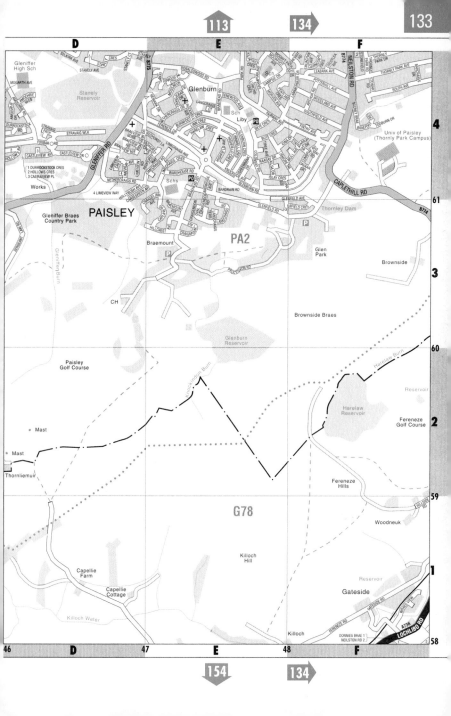

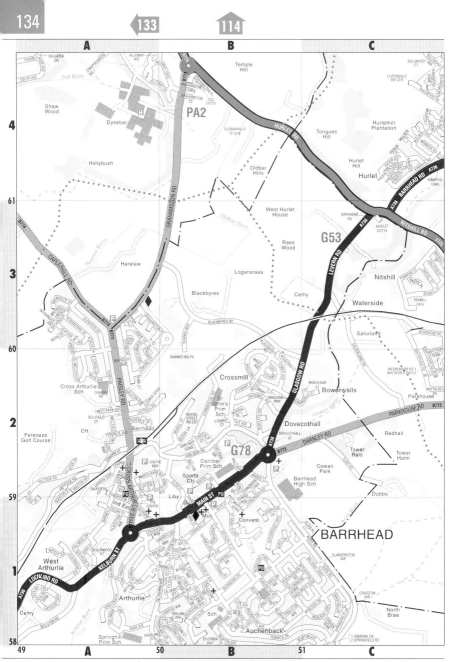

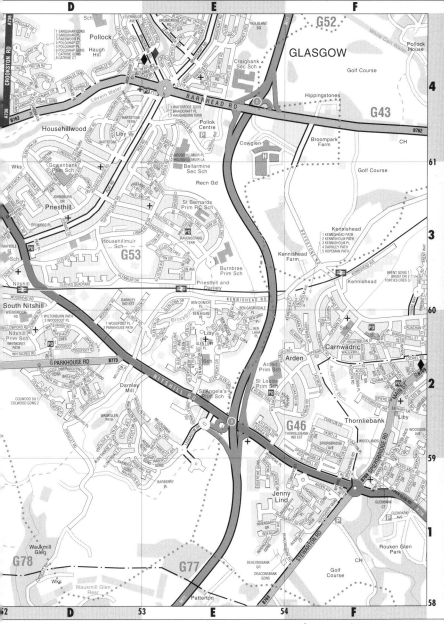

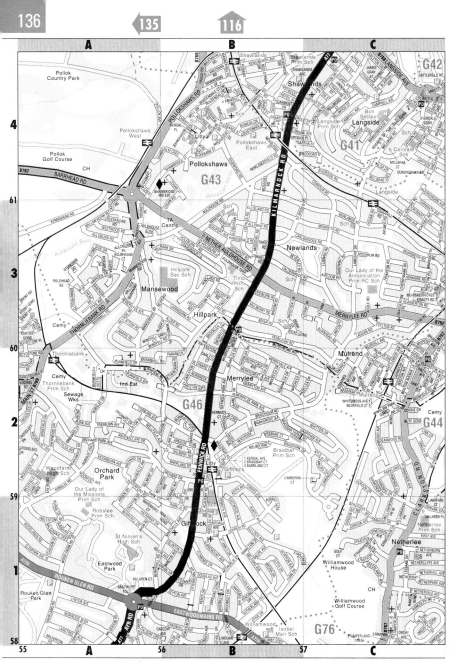

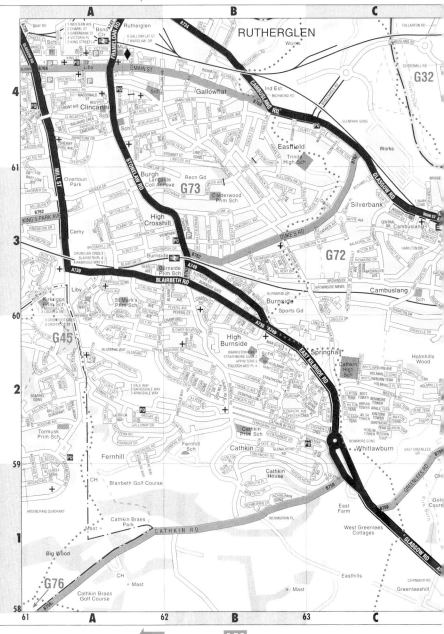

RUTHERGLEN

Works

G32

FULLARTON RD

CLYDESMILL RD

River Clyde

BRIDGE

Gallowflat

Ind Est

Eastfield

Trinity High Sch

Silverbank

Works

CENTRAL BR Cambuslang

Clincarthill

Burgh Langside Coll Annexe

G73

Calderwood Prim Sch

High Crosshill

Cemy

DUKE'S RD

G72

Hamilton Dr

Overtoun Park

Burnside

Burnside Prim Sch

BLAIRBETH RD

Cambuslang

Sch

Kirkriggs Prim Sch

St Mark's Prim Sch

Brownside Mews

G45

High Burnside

Burnside Sports Gd

Springhall

Cathkin High Sch

Holmhills Wood

1 DALE WAY
2 BARRISDALE WAY
3 ARNISDALE WAY

Scarrel Gdns

Tormusk Prim Sch

Fernhill Sch

EAST KILBRIDE RD

Cathkin Prim Sch

Whitlawburn

East Greenlees Gr

Fernhill

Cathkin

Cathkin House

Blairbeth Golf Course

East Farm

West Greenlees Cottages

Big Wood

Cathkin Braes Park

CATHKIN RD

Mast

Mast

Easthills

GLASGOW RD

Greenleeshill

CAIRNMUIR RD

G76

Cathkin Braes Golf Course

CH   Mast   Mast

Gol Cours

Kirk Burn

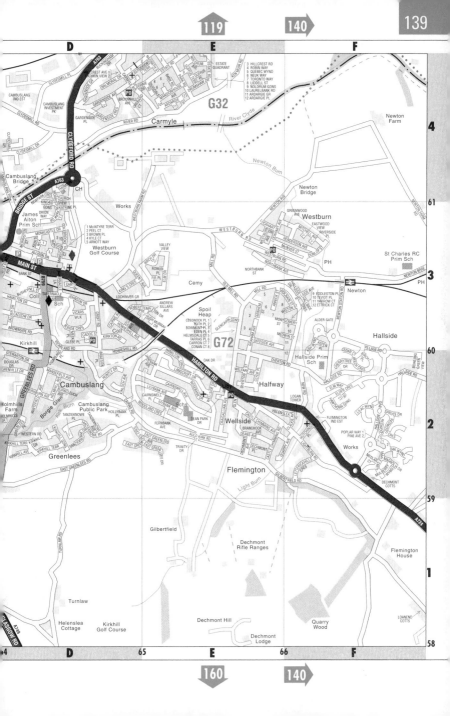

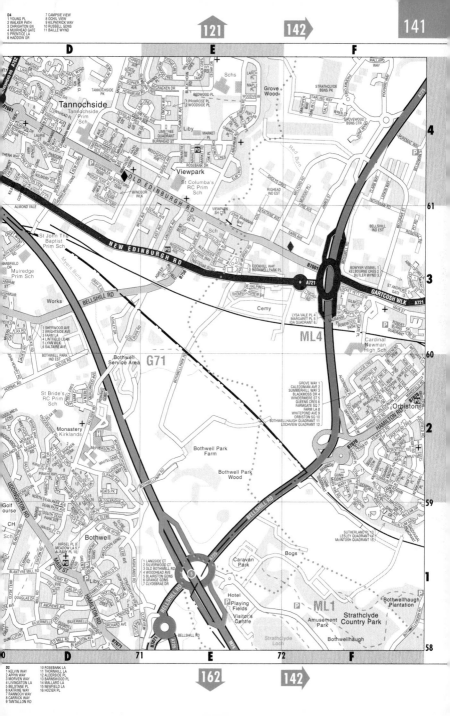

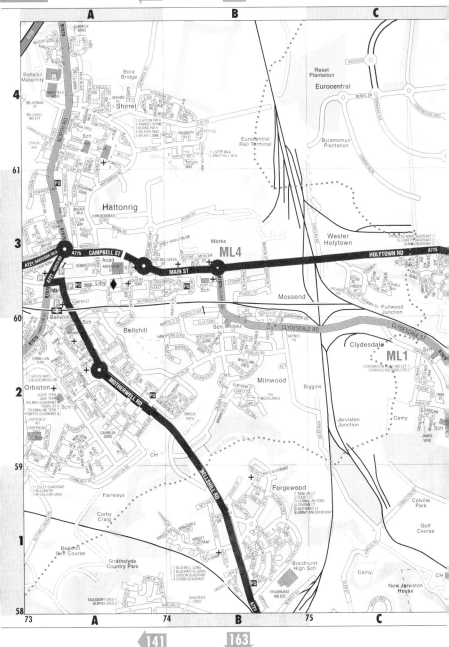

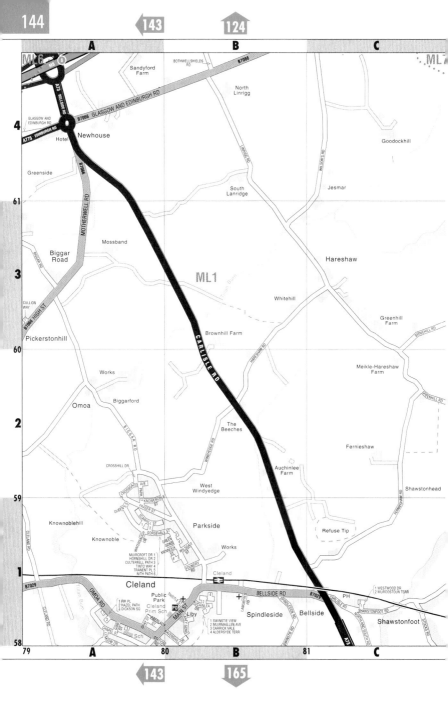

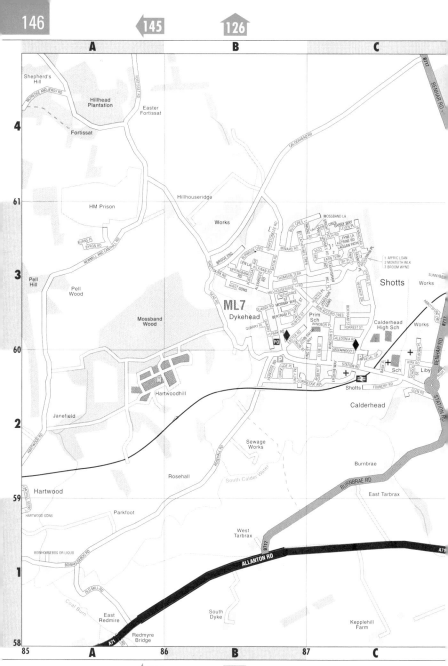

A   **B**   **C**

Shepherd's
Hill

Hillhead
Plantation

Easter
Fortissat

4

Fortissat

MOORHOUSE AND JERSY RD

FORTISSAT RD

CALDERHEAD RD

BENHAR RD

B717

Hillhouseridge

61

HM Prison

Works

BURNS PL
BYRON RD
NEWMILL AND CANTHILL RD

Mossband
La

MOSSBAND CRES
BARRY WAY
FYNE LA
KATRINE RD
LADGAN PATH

3

Pell
Hill

Pell
Wood

Mossband
Wood

BRIDGE END

DEN LA
KILTYNAR RD

DYKEHEAD RD

PEEL PARK RD

HIRST GDNS

SPRINGBANK RD

THOMSON TERR

BENNIE CRES

GRAYSTONE RE RD

MINARD RD

Shotts

Works

SUNNYBANK

ABBOTS DR

1 AFFRIC LOAN
2 MONTEITH WLK
3 BROOM WYND

ML7
Dykehead

HILLHOUSERIDGE

MOTHERDALE
MORNAY WAY

ACCORD CRES

BERTRAM PL

QUARRY PL

QUARRY RD

CALEDONIA ST

BERTRAM ST

WINDSOR ST

Prim
Sch

FORREST ST

HURST RD

Calderhead
High Sch

Works

GREENWOOD ST

60

PO

PARK AVE

CLIVE PL

OLIVE ST

JOE PL

PARKSIDE

CURRIESIDE WK

ROBERT ST

FISKINE AND PL

STATION RD

BANK ST

Sch

KIRK RD

KIRK RD

Liby

Shotts

FOUNDRY RD

GLEN RD

STATION RD

Calderhead

BENHAR RD

B717

Hartwoodhill

H

Janefield

HARTWOOD RD

2

Sewage
Works

Burnbrae

Rosehall

ROSEHALL RD

South Calder Water

BURNBRAE RD

East Tarbrax

59

Hartwood

HARTWOOD GDNS

Parkfoot

West
Tarbrax

B7127

BOWHOUSEBOG OR LIQUO

1

SMITHY CROFT

BOWHO RSEBOG RD

OLD MILL RD

ALLANTON RD

A71

Kepplehill
Farm

Coal Burn

East
Redmire

South
Dyke

A71

58

Redmyre
Bridge

85   **A**   **86**   **B**   **87**   **C**

Fauldhouse

4

61

Golf
Course

CH

Starryshaw
Farm

3

South Calder Water

Spoil
Heap

Stanebent

Cairneyhead

ML7

Stane

STABLE RD

Torbothie

60

Stane
Prim Sch

Torbothie

CEMETERY RD

+

Cemy

1 ETIVE WLK
2 ALLG WAY
3 GAIR WYND
4 BOWMORE WLK
5 TORRIN LOAN
6 SPRINGHILL VIEW
7 DORNIE WYND
8 MORAR WAY
9 CORRIE LOAN
10 SUNA PATH
11 SALEN LOAN

MANSE RD

MAIN ST

NEVIS PL

CHARLOTTE ST

GARTH

LOCHABER
CRES

APPIN TERR

TULLOCH RD

LANSDOWNE CRES

LAGGAN AVE

2

tane

BLINNY CT 1
BRAX PATH 2

B7010

SPRINGHILL RD

Springhill

B7010

59

Works

BELMONT DRIVE

LARCHFIELD LA

NORTHFIELD AVE

TEENWOOD RD

STANE RD

Springhill

Springhill and Leadloch Rd

B715 HEADLESKNOWE RD B715

Works

Knowton
Farm

Lingore Linn

A71

1

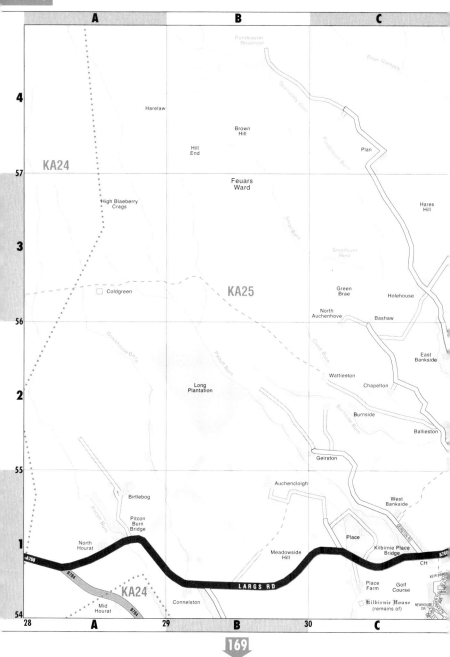

A   B   C

4

Harelaw

Brown
Hill

Hill
End

KA24

Pundeavon
Reservoir

River Garnock

Plan

Hares
Hill

57

Feuars
Ward

3

High Blaeberry
Crags

Smaw Burn

Smallburn
Resr

KA25

Green
Brae

Holehouse

Coldgreen

North
Auchenhove

Bashaw

56

Gateshouse Burn

Pequit Burn

Close Burn

East
Bankside

Wattieston

Chapelton

2

Long
Plantation

Burnside

Burnside Burn

Ballieston

Geirston

55

Auchencloigh

West
Bankside

GEIRSTON RD

Birtlebog

Pitcon Burn

Pitcon
Burn
Bridge

Place

North
Hourat

Meadowside
Hill

Kilbirnie Place
Bridge

A760

1

A760

B784

Place
Farm

Golf
Course

CH

KEIR HARDIE

LARGS RD

KA24

Mid
Hourat

B784

Connelston

Kilbirnie House
(remains of)

NEWHOUSE
DR

54

28   A   29   B   30   C

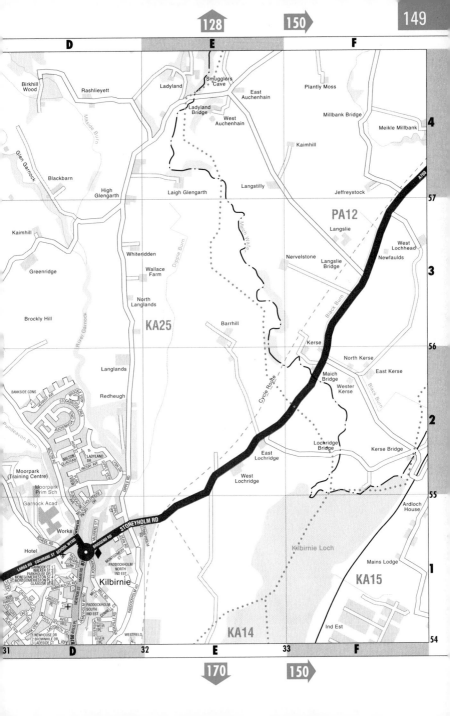

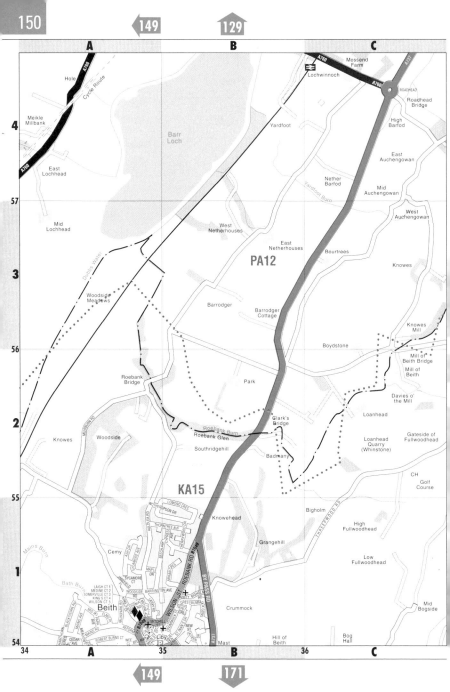

A B C

A760

Hole

Cycle Route

Meikle
Millbank

4

East
Lochhead

A760

Mid
Lochhead

57

Barr
Loch

Yardfoot

Lochwinnoch

Mossend
Farm

A760

ROADHEAD

Roadhead

Roadhead
Bridge

High
Barfod

East
Auchengowan

Mid
Auchengowan

West
Auchengowan

West
Netherhouses

East
Netherhouses

Nether
Barfod

Yardfoot Burn

Bourtrees

Knowes

PA12

3

Dubbs Water

Woodside
Meadows

Barrodger

Barrodger
Cottage

Boydstone

Knowes
Mill

Mill of
Beith Bridge

Mill of
Beith

Davies o'
the Mill

56

Roebank
Bridge

Park

Loanhead

Knowes

Woodside

Roebank Burn

Roebank Glen

Clark's
Bridge

Loanhead
Quarry
(Whinstone)

Gateside of
Fullwoodhead

2

MUIRSIDE RD

Southridgehill

Badmany

CH

Golf
Course

KA15

55

WITHERSPOON DR

LOMOND CRES

THORNTREE AVE

Knowehead

Bigholm

TREETWOOD RD

High
Fullwoodhead

Cemy

SYCAMORE
CT

MAPLE
DR

Grangehill

Low
Fullwoodhead

1

Mains Burn

Bath Burn

LAIGH CT 1
MEDINE CT 2
SOMERVILLE CT 3
KING'S CT 4
WILSON CT 5

WOODSIDE

BARRINGTON AVE

WILSON ST

ROEBANK RD B7049

BY PASS RD

Crummock

Mid
Bogside

Beith

MITCHELL

NEW

Libby

B7049

Mast

Hill of
Beith

Bog
Hall

54

34 A 35 B 36 C

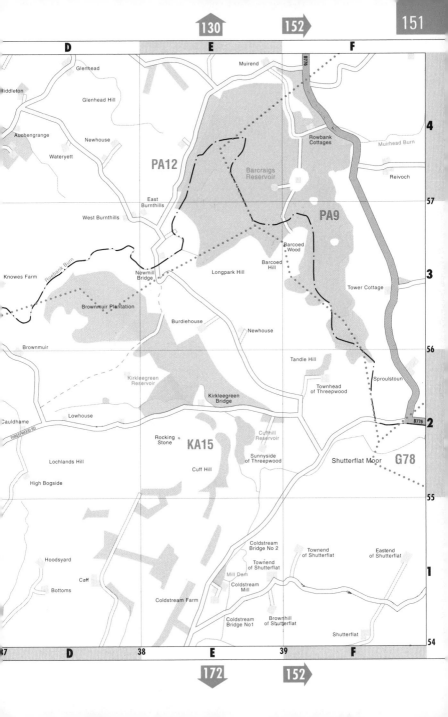

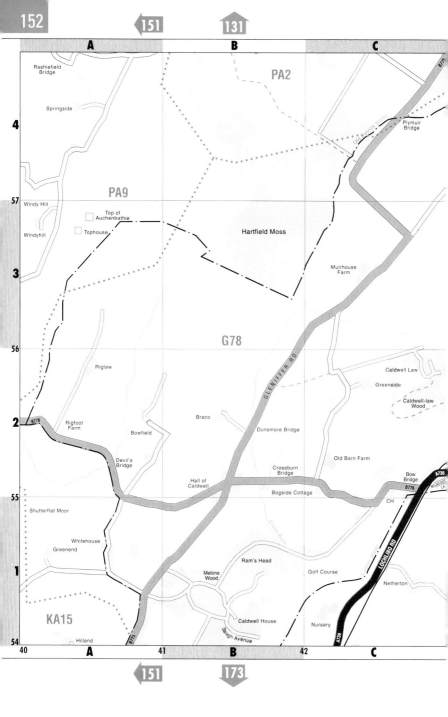

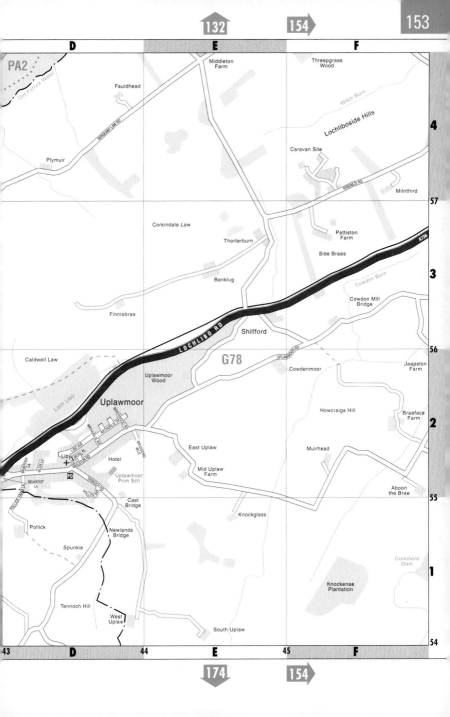

153
133

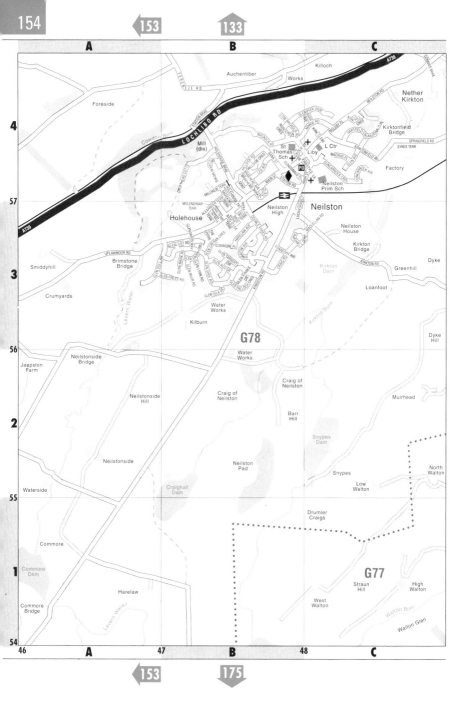

153
175

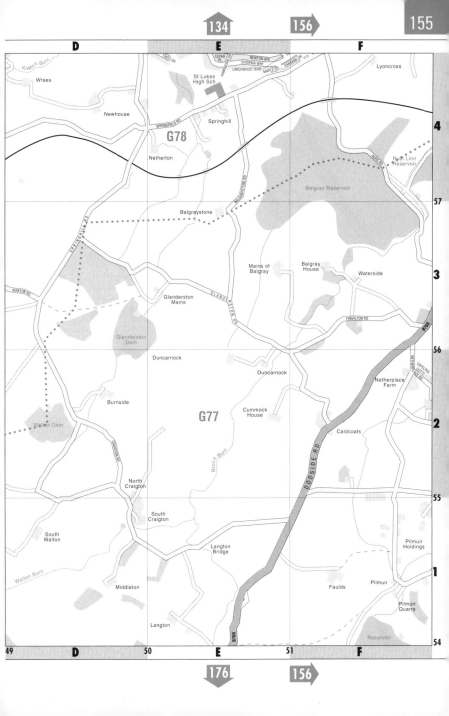

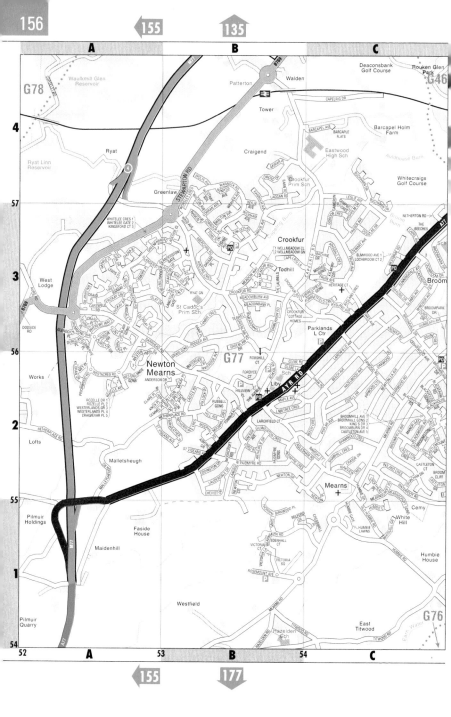

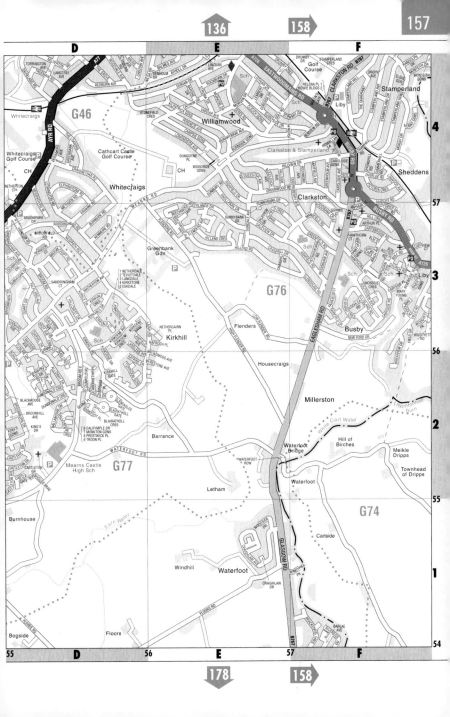

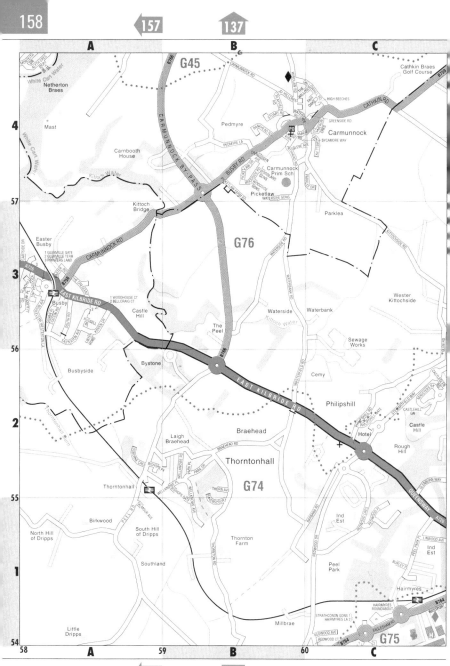

A   B   C

4

White Cart Water

Netherton
Braes

Mast

Carnbooth
House

G45

CARMUNNOCK RD

Cathkin Braes
Golf Course

CATHKIN RD

Pedmyre

Carmunnock

High Beeches

GREENSIDE RD

PO

Carmunnock
Prim Schl

SYCAMORE WAY

57

Kittoch
Bridge

Easter
Busby

1 GLENVILLE GATE
2 GLENVILLE TERR
3 PRINTERS LAND

CARMUNNOCK RD

BUSBY RD

Picketlaw

WATERSIDE GDNS

G76

Parklea

KITTOCHSIDE RD

3

EAST KILBRIDE RD

Busby

1 WOODHOUSE CT
2 BELLCRAIG CT

Castle
Hill

The
Peel

Waterside

Waterbank

Kittoch Water

Wester
Kittochside

56

Busbyside

Bystone

EAST KILBRIDE RD

Sewage
Works

Cemy

2

Laigh
Braehead

BRAEHEAD RD

Braehead

Philipshill

Hotel

CASTLEHILL
GN

Castle
Hill

Rough
Hill

1

North Hill
of Dripps

Birkwood

Thorntonhall

Thorntonhall

South Hill
of Dripps

Southland

THORNTON RD

THORN AVE

G74

Thornton
Farm

Ind
Est

QUEENSWAY

Peel
Park

Ind
Est

Hairmyres

HAIRMYRES
ROUNDABOUT

STRATHCONON GDNS 1
HAIRMYRES LA 2

Millbrae

EAGLESHAM RD

REDWOOD AVE
REDWOOD CT

B764

G75

54

58   A   59   B   60   C

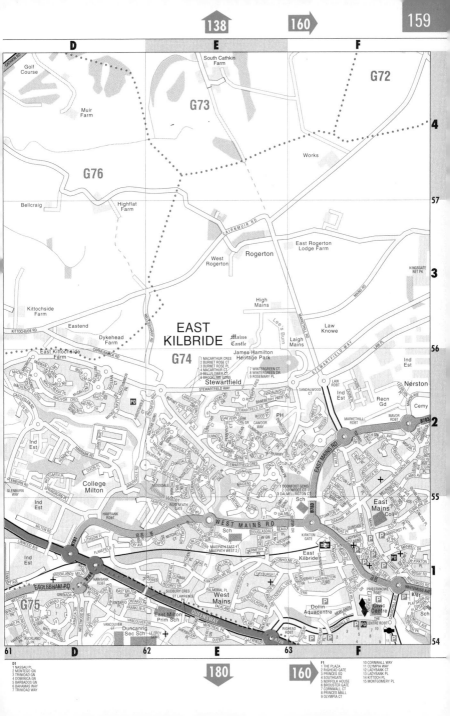

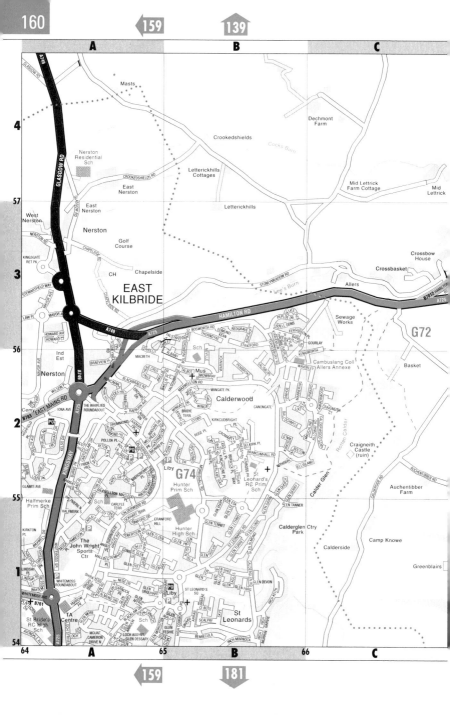

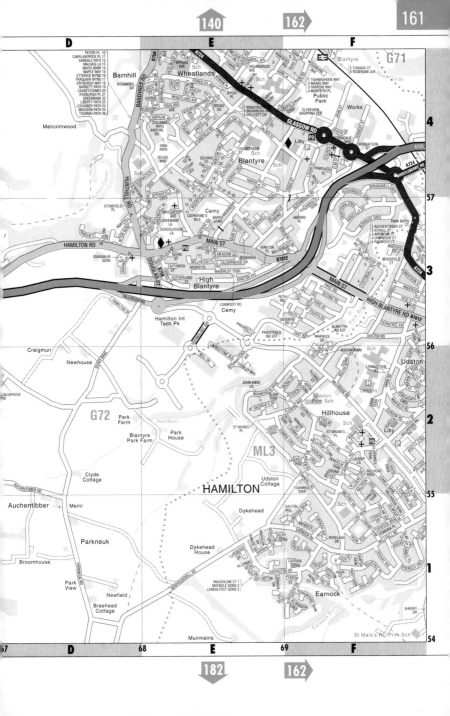

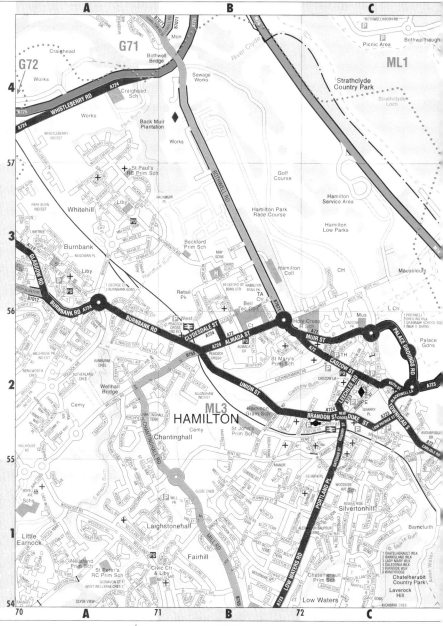

A   B   C

G71

Craighead

G72

Works

ML1

Bothwellhaugh Rd
Picnic Area
Bothwellhaugh

Bothwell Bridge

Sewage Works

Strathclyde Country Park

Strathclyde Loch

4

WHISTLEBERRY RD   A724

Craighead Sch

Works

Back Muir Plantation

Works

Hamilton Service Area

57

St Paul's RC Prim Sch

Whitehill

Liby

Golf Course

Hamilton Park Race Course

Hamilton Low Parks

Mausoleum

3

Burnbank

GLASGOW RD   A724

Sch   Liby

Beckford Prim Sch

Retail Pk

Hamilton Coll

CH

L Ctr

Mote Hill

56

BURNBANK RD   A724

West

CLYDESDALE ST   A72   ALMADA ST

Bell Tec Coll

Holy Cross H Sch

MUIR ST   A72

PALACE GROUNDS RD

Mus

Palace Gdns

Wellhall Bridge

UNION ST

Cadzow Burn

CADZOW ST

FEECHLE RD

TOWNHEAD ST

A723

2

ML3 HAMILTON

Chantinghall

Hamilton Gram Sch

St John's Prim Sch

BRANDON ST   DUKE ST

Central

A723
AVONBRIDGE DR

CAMBIE RD

55

Mill Pk

Laighstonehall

MILL RD

Fairhill

Silvertonhill

Barncluith

1

Little Earnock

Neilsland Prim Sch

St Peter's RC Prim Sch   Civic Ctr & Liby

Chatelherault Prim Sch

LOW WATERS RD   A723

Chatelherault Country Park

Laverock Hill

54

CLYDE VIEW

Low Waters

70   A   71   B   72   C

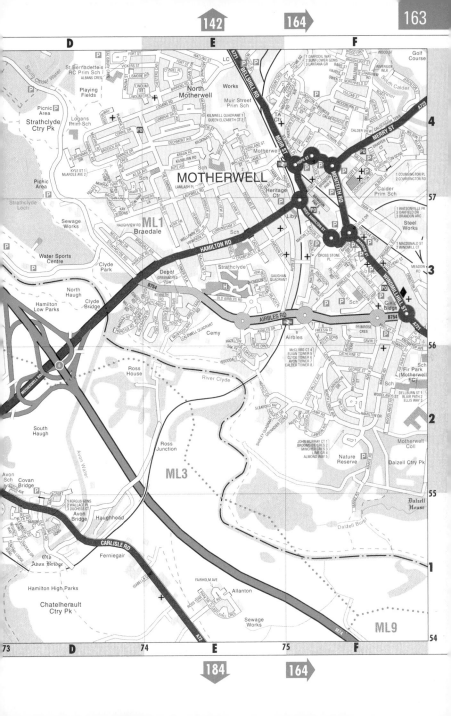

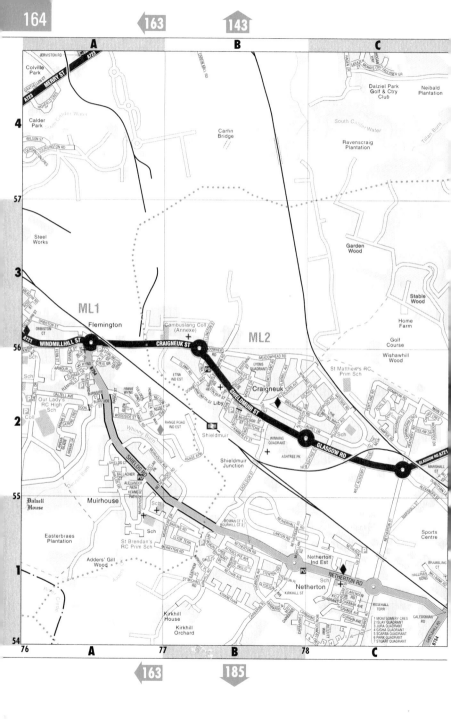

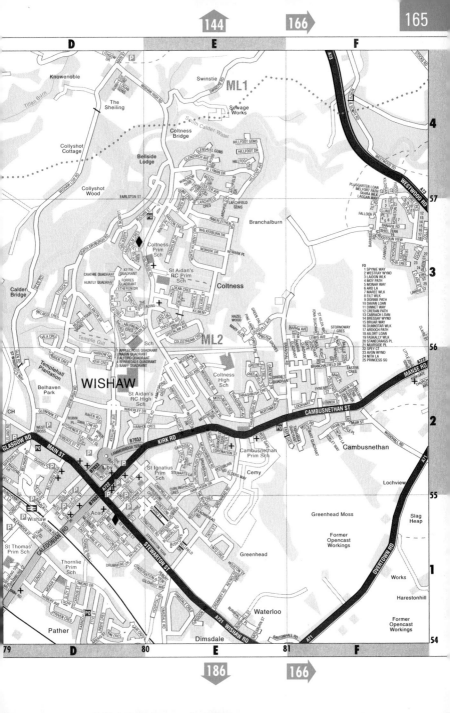

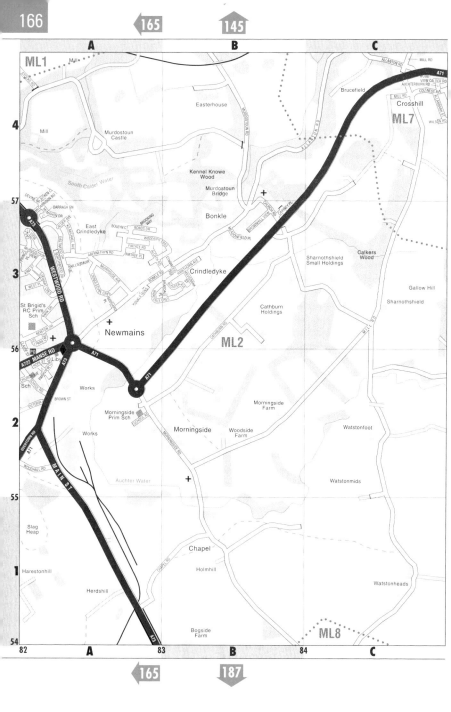

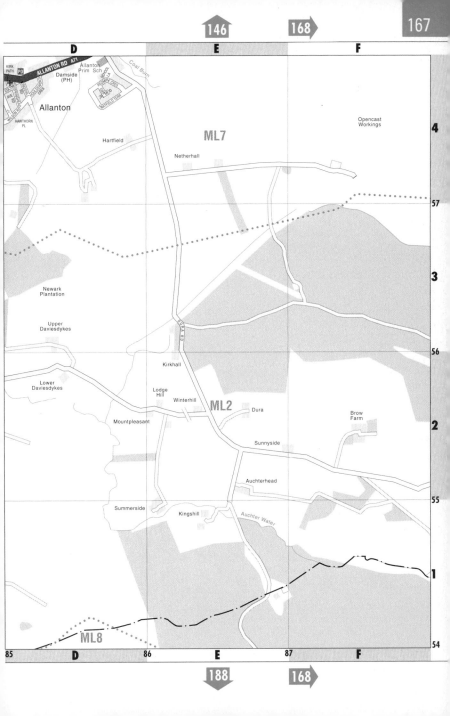

D **E** **F**

KIRK
PATH
PO

ALLANTON RD A71

Allanton
Prim Sch

Damside
(PH)

Allanton

Hartfield

Netherhall

ML7

Opencast
Workings

4

57

Newark
Plantation

3

Upper
Daviesdykes

56

Kirkhall

Lower
Daviesdykes

Lodge
Hill

Winterhill

ML2

Dura

Brow
Farm

2

Mountpleasant

Sunnyside

Auchterhead

55

Summerside

Kingshill

Auchter Water

1

ML8

54

85 **D** **86** **E** **87** **F**

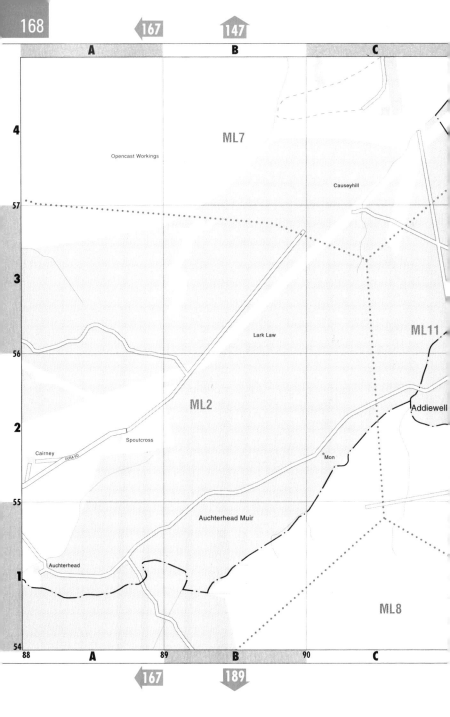

A B C

4

ML7

Opencast Workings

Causeyhill

57

3

Lark Law

ML11

56

ML2

2

Addiewell

Spoutcross

Cairney DURA RD

Mon

55

Auchterhead Muir

1

Auchterhead

ML8

54

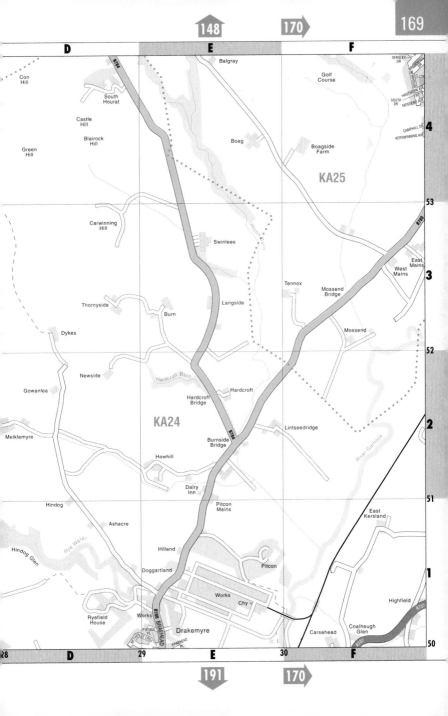

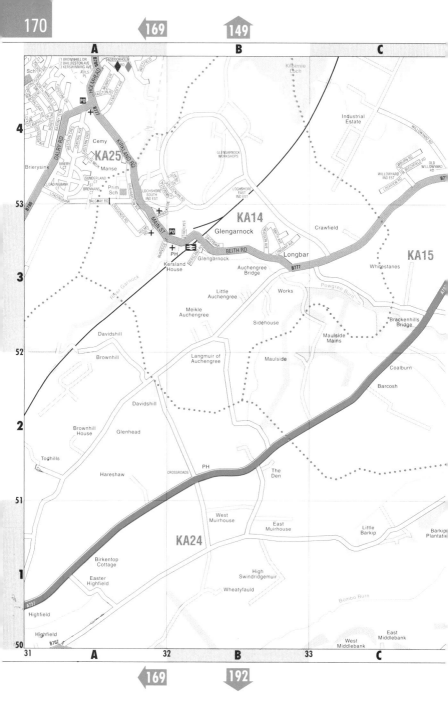

169
149

A **B** **C**

4

Kilbirnie
Loch

Industrial
Estate

KA25

Cemy

Manse

Brierysink

Glengarnock
Workshops

WILLOWYARD IND EST
OLD
WILLOWYARD
RD

53

KA14

Lochshore
South
Ind Est

Glengarnock

Crawfield

Prim
Sch

PH

BEITH RD
Longbar

KA15

Glengarnock

Kersland
House

Auchengree
Bridge

B777

Whitestanes

Powgree Burn

3

River Garnock

Little
Auchengree

Works

Sidehouse

Brackenhills
Bridge

Meikle
Auchengree

Maulside
Mains

Davidshill

52

Brownhill

Langmuir of
Auchengree

Maulside

Coalburn

Barcosh

Davidshill

2

Brownhill
House

Glenhead

Toghills

Hareshaw

CROSSROADS

PH

The
Den

51

West
Muirhouse

East
Muirhouse

Little
Barkip

Barkip
Plantation

KA24

Birkentop
Cottage

High
Swindridgemuir

1

Easter
Highfield

Wheatyfauld

Bombo Burn

Highfield

Highfield
B707

West
Middlebank

East
Middlebank

50

31 **A** **32** **B** **33** **C**

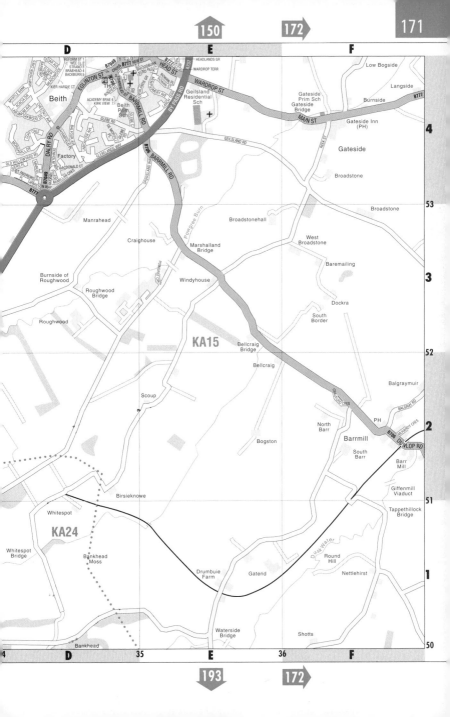

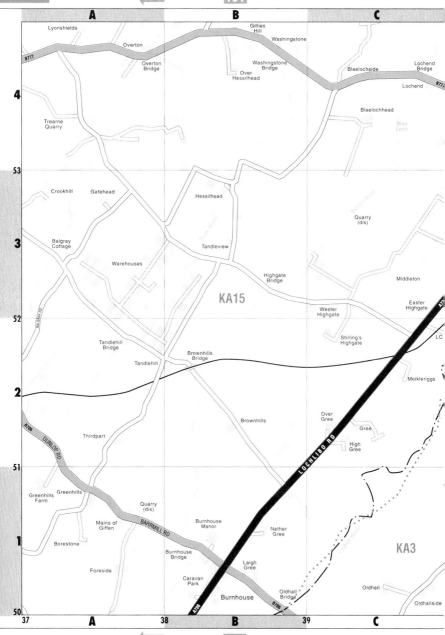

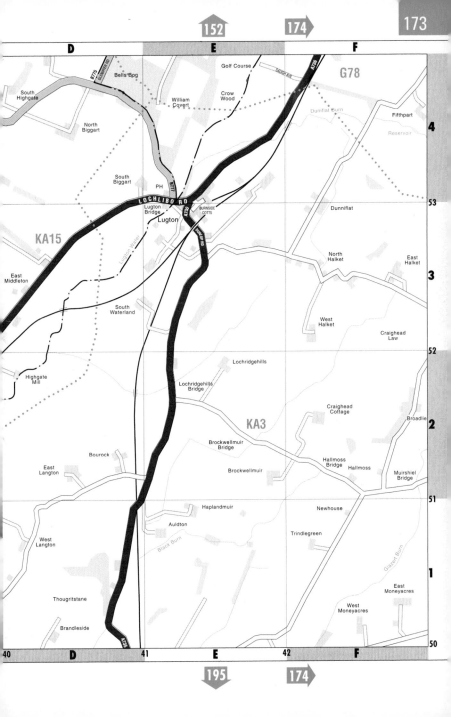

D   E   F

G78

Bells Bog

Golf Course

South Highgate

William Covert

Crow Wood

Dunniflat Burn

Fifthpart

North Biggart

Reservoir

4

South Biggart

PH

KA15

LOCHLIBO RD

Lugton Bridge

Lugton

BURNSIDE COTTS

Dunniflat

53

North Halket

East Halket

East Middleton

South Waterland

West Halket

Craighead Law

3

Lochridgehills

52

Highgate Mill

Lochridgehills Bridge

Craighead Cottage

Broadlie

KA3

Brockwellmuir Bridge

Hallmoss Bridge

Hallmoss

Muirshiel Bridge

2

Bourock

Brockwellmuir

East Langton

Haplandmuir

Newhouse

51

Auldton

Black Burn

Trindlegreen

West Langton

Glazert Burn

1

East Moneyacres

Thougritstane

West Moneyacres

Brandleside

50

40   D   41   E   42   F

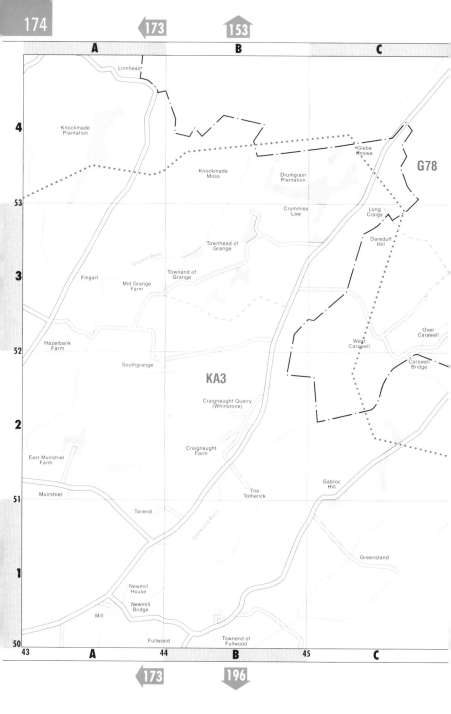

A
B
C

4

Linnhead

Knockmade
Plantation

Knockmade
Moss

Drumgrain
Plantation

Glebe
Knowe

G78

53

Crummies
Law

Long
Craigs

Dareduff
Hill

Townhead of
Grange

Glazert Burn

Townend of
Grange

3

Fingart

Mid Grange
Farm

Over
Carswell

Hazelbank
Farm

52

West
Carswell

Carswell
Bridge

Southgrange

KA3

Craignaught Quarry
(Whinstone)

2

Craignaught
Farm

East Muirshiel
Farm

Gabroc
Hill

51

Muirshiel

The
Totherick

Creikland Burn

Tailend

Greensland

1

Newmill
House

Mill

Newmill
Bridge

50

Fullwood

Townend of
Fullwood

43
A
44
B
45
C

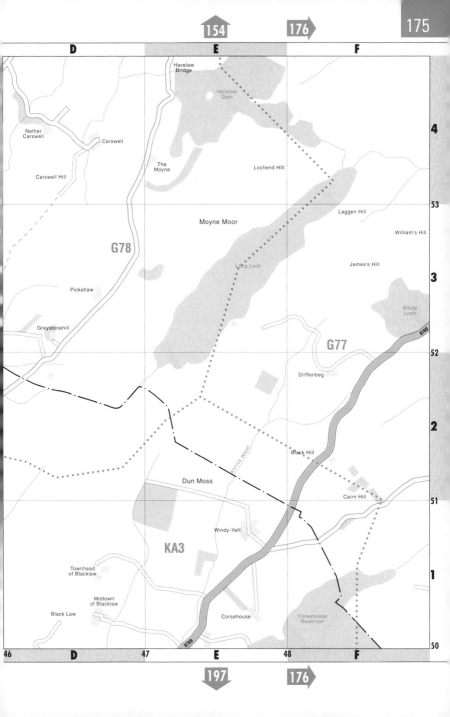

D
E
F

Harelaw Bridge

Harelaw Dam

Nether Carswell

Carswell

The Moyne

Lochend Hill

4

Carswell Hill

53

Moyne Moor

Laggen Hill

William's Hill

G78

James's Hill

Picketlaw

Long Loch

White Loch

3

Greystonehill

G77

52

Driffenbeg

B769

Black Hill

2

Dun Moss

Cairn Hill

51

KA3

Windy-Yett

Townhead of Blacklaw

1

Midtown of Blacklaw

Black Law

Corsehouse

Corsehouse Reservoir

50

46
D
47
E
B709
48
F

A B C

175
175

4

Reservoir
(covered)

B769

DODSIDE RD

Dodside

Dod Hill

Mearns
Law

Golf Course

CH

A77

Reservoir

Barrance Hill

Mearns Muir

53

William's Hill

Bannerbank
Farm

Brother
Loch

Mon

CH

MEARNS RD

3

B769

Byreside
Hill

Hunter Burn

Golf
Course

Loganswell
Farm

Little
Loch

52

G77

Crow Hill

Blacklinch Burn

Brown
Castle

St Martin's

Brownside

Langlee

Nether Cairn

Black Loch

Blackloch
Hill

Fenwick Water

Bennan Burn

Bennan
Farm

2

51

Townhead of
Floak

Floak
Bridge

A77

1

Mid Floak

50

49 A 50 B 51 C

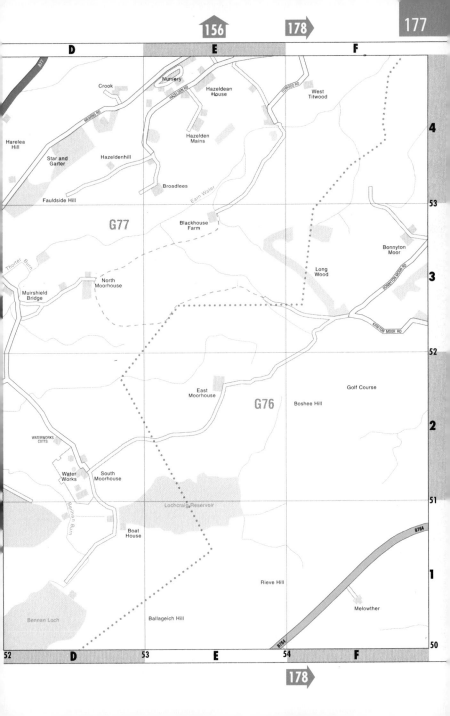

D E F

A77

Crook

Nursery

Hazeldean House

West Titwood

HAZELDEN RD

TITWOOD RD

MEARNS RD

Harelea Hill

4

Star and Garter

Hazeldenhill

Hazelden Mains

Broadlees

Earn Water

Fauldside Hill

53

G77

Blackhouse Farm

Bonnyton Moor

Thortet Burn

Long Wood

3

North Moorhouse

BONNYTON MOOR RD

Muirshield Bridge

KIRKTON MOOR RD

52

East Moorhouse

Golf Course

G76

Boshee Hill

2

WATERWORKS COTTS

Water Works

South Moorhouse

51

Bennan Burn

Lochcraig Reservoir

Boat House

B764

1

Rieve Hill

Melowther

Bennan Loch

Ballageich Hill

B764

50

52 D 53 E 54 F

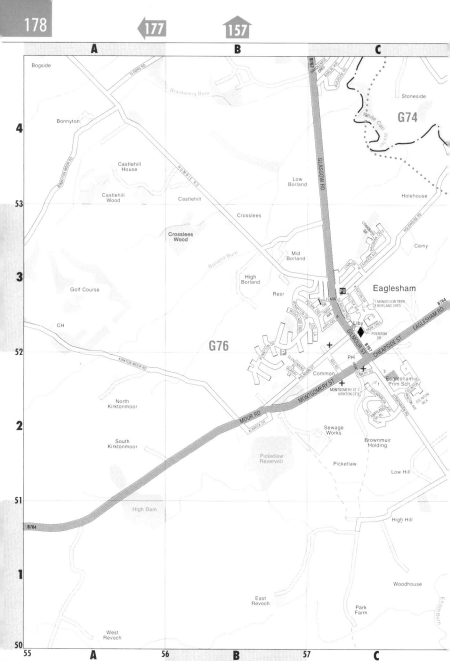

A   B   C

Bogside

Stoneside

B767

G74

White Cart Water

Bonnyton

FLOORS RD

Brackenrig Burn

Low
Borland

GLASGOW RD

Holehouse

Castlehill
House

HUMBIE RD

Castlehill
Wood

Castlehill

Crosslees

53

Crosslees
Wood

Mid
Borland

CRANGAIE
DR

Cemy

Borland Burn

High
Borland

Eaglesham

PO

B764

3

Golf Course

Resr

1 MANSEVIEW TERR
2 BORLAND CRES

CH

Liby

G76

POLNOON
DR

EAGLESHAM RD

CHEAPSIDE ST

GILMOUR ST

B767

52

KIRKTON MOOR RD

Common

PH

Eaglesham
Prim Sch

North
Kirktonmoor

MONTGOMERY ST

MONTGOMERY CT 1
KIRKTON CT 2

2

MOOR RD

South
Kirktonmoor

ALNWICK DR

Sewage
Works

Brownmuir
Holding

Picketlaw
Reservoir

Picketlaw

Low Hill

51

High Dam

High Hill

B764

1

Woodhouse

East
Revoch

Park
Farm

Elvan Burn

West
Revoch

50

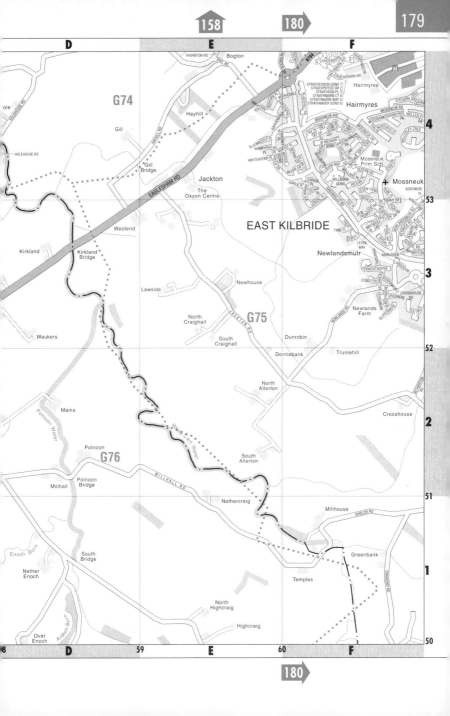

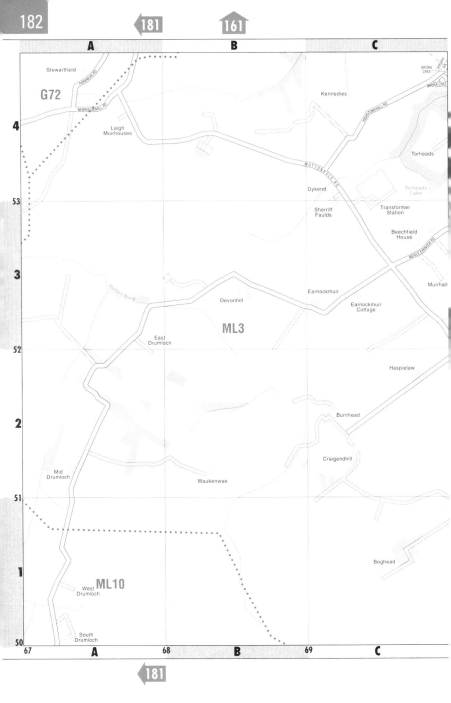

A   B   C

Stewartfield

G72

4

Laigh
Muirhouses

53

3

Rotten Burn

Devonhill

ML3

East
Drumloch

52

2

Mid
Drumloch

Waukenwae

51

1

West
Drumloch   ML10

South
Drumloch

Kennedies

Torheads

Dykend

Sherriff
Faulds

Transformer
Station

Beechfield
House

Earnockmuir

Muirhall

Earnockmuir
Cottage

Haspielaw

Burnhead

Craigendhill

Boghead

Torheads
Lake

MUTTONHOLE RD

HIGH STONEHALL RD

MEIKLE EARNOCK RD

BRORA CRES

BRORA
CRES

CHERRY
DR

PARKHALL RD

NEWHOUSEMILL RD

183 163

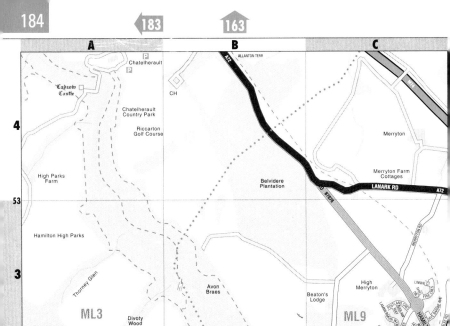

183 198

ML2

ML9

Larkhall

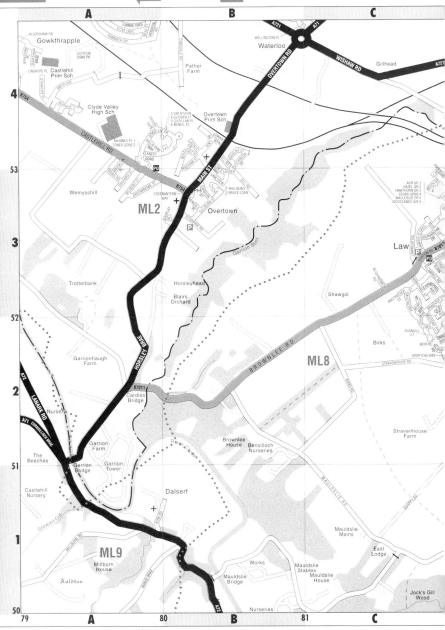

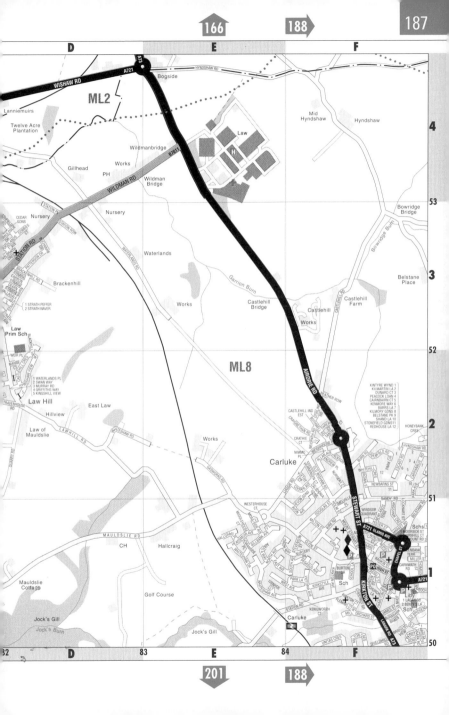

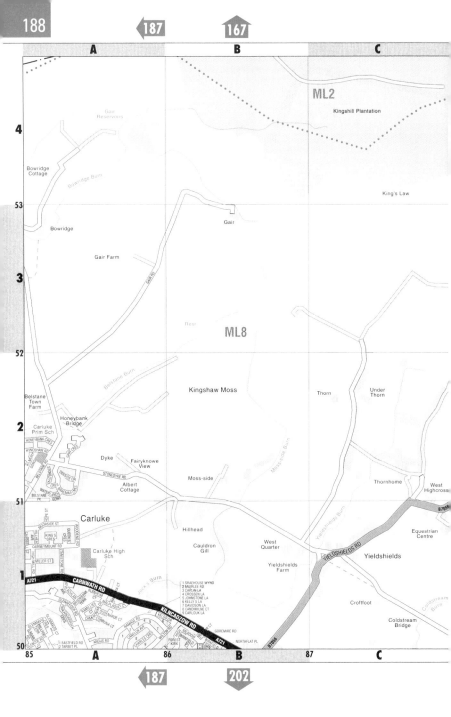

A   B   C

4

ML2

Kingshill Plantation

Gair Reservoirs

Bowridge
Cottage

Bowridge Burn

53

Gair

Bowridge

King's Law

Gair Farm

Gair Rd

3

ML8

Rest

52

Belstane Burn

Kingshaw Moss

Thorn

Under
Thorn

Belstane
Town
Farm

Honeybank
Bridge

Carluke
Prim Sch

Mosssде Burn

HONEYBANK CRES

HYNDSHAW RD

Dyke

Fairyknowe
View

Moss-side

Thornhome

West
Highcross

STONEDYKE RD

Albert
Cottage

51

B7056

Equestrian
Centre

Carluke

Hillhead

Yieldshields Burn

West
Quarter

YIELDSHIELDS RD

Yieldshields

MOSSIDE ST

Carluke High
Sch

Cauldron
Gill

Yieldshields
Farm

KING'S
CRES

CARNEYMOUNT RD

MILLER ST

1

A721

CARNWATH RD

Jock's Burn

1 SRAEHOUSE WYND
2 MUIRLEE RD
3 CARLIN LA
4 CROSSEN LA
5 JOHNSTONE LA
6 KELLY S LA
7 DAVIDSON LA
8 CANDIMILNE CT
9 CARLOUK LA

Croftfoot

Coldstream Burn

KILNCADZOW RD

GOREMIRE RD

A721

NORTHFLAT PL

B7056

Coldstream
Bridge

1 EASTFIELD RD
2 TARBET PL

ANGUS RD

CHARLES CRES

FOREST
KIRK

50

85   A   86   B   87   C

ML2

Black Law

ML8

Thornmuir

Birniehall

Forth

Netherton Burn

Springfield Reservoir

Hill of Westerhouse

Middlehope Farm

Easterseat

Springfield

Knowehead

Middlehouse

YIELDSHIELDS RD

Westerhouse

Damhead

Netherton Burn

East Highcross

Coldstream Burn

Candymill Burn

Mid Coldstream

Craigend

ML11

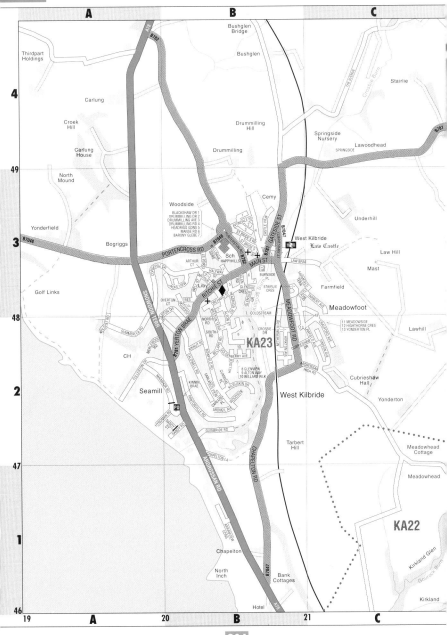

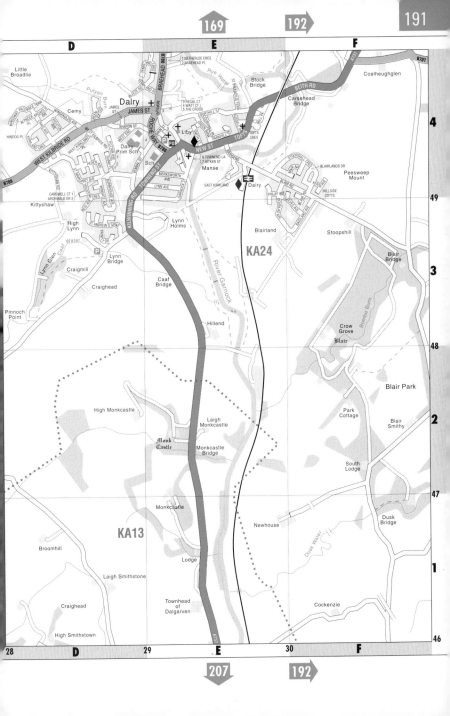

A **B** **C**

B7071

Bellstone

Kerslochmuir

Swindridge Muir

Middlebank Plantation

West Middlebank

East Middlebank

Giffen West Lodge

4

Barjocks Plantation

Bomb's Burn

Glencart

Glencart Plantation

Bowertrapping

Auchenmade Terrace

Knollhead

Whin Hill

49

Lambridden Farm

Pondery Hill

Pencot

Castle Hill

KA24

3

Bathbank Plantation

Templandmuir Farm

Cleeves

Foxcover Plantation

Asseyfauld

South Auchenmade

Dusk Water

Sycamore Hill

48

Cutteith Knowe

Cutteith Wood

Blair Mill

North Lissens

2

Blairmill Bridge

Cleeves Cove

Dusk Glen

South Lissens

47

South Lissens Cottage

Jameston Moss

Lissens Moss

KA13

1

Auchenskeith

Jameston

High Monkredding Plantation

Lylestone Quarry (dis)

Darmule

Jameston Woods

High Gooseloan

Benthead

B778

46

31 **A** 32 **B** 33 **C**

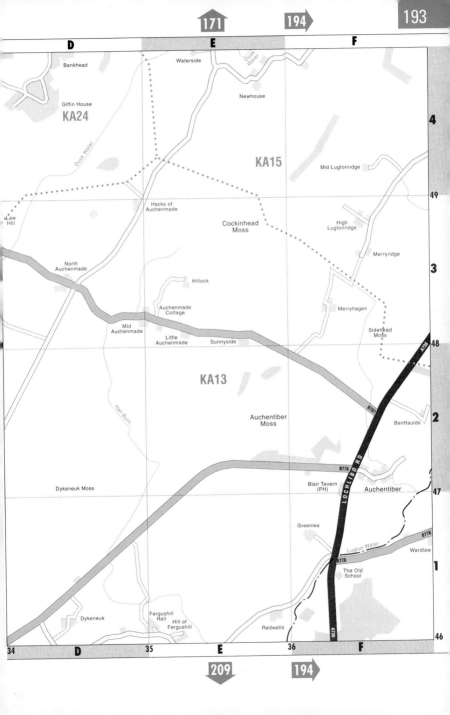

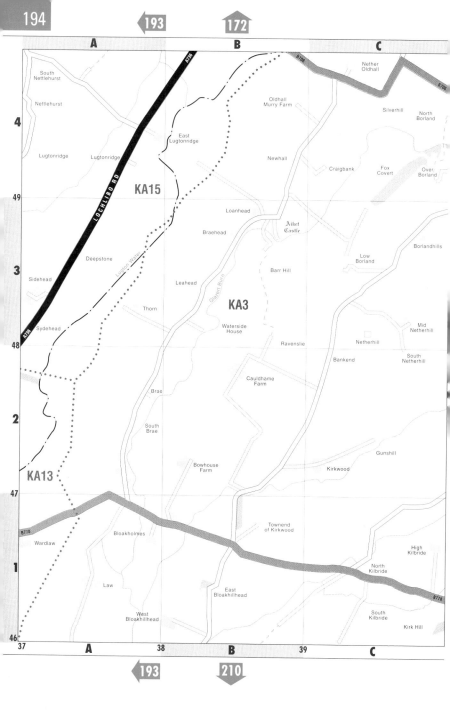

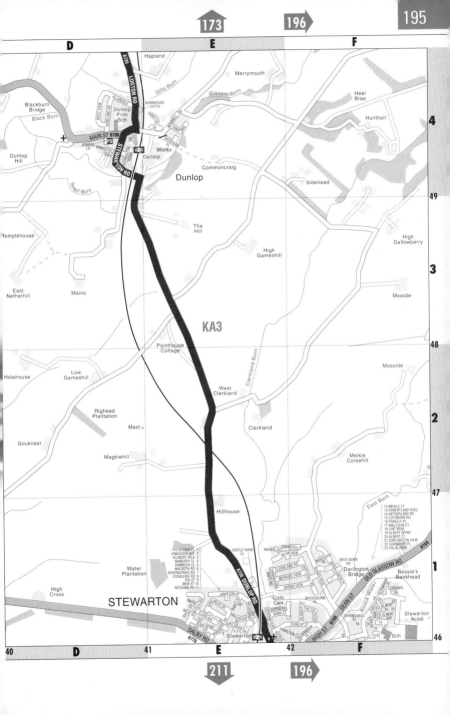

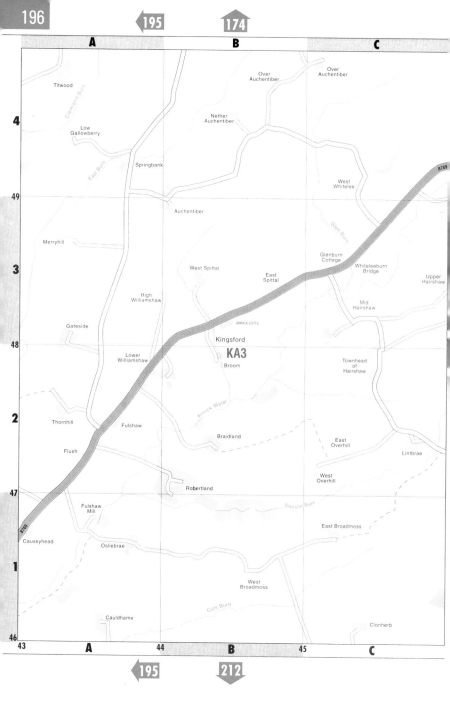

A **B** **C**

Titwood

Cleakland Burn

Over
Auchentiber

Over
Auchentiber

4

Low
Gallowberry

Nether
Auchentiber

East Burn

Springbank

West
Whitelee

49

Auchentiber

Glen Burn

Merryhill

Glenburn
Cottage

Whiteleeburn
Bridge

B769

West Spittal

East
Spittal

Upper
Hairshaw

3

High
Williamshaw

Mid
Hairshaw

Gateside

ANNICK COTTS

Kingsford

Townhead
of
Hairshaw

48

Lower
Williamshaw

KA3

Broom

Annick Water

Thornhill

Fulshaw

Braidland

East
Overhill

2

Flush

West
Overhill

Lintbrae

47

Robertland

Swinzie Burn

B769

Fulshaw
Mill

East Broadmoss

Causeyhead

Osliebrae

1

West
Broadmoss

Cauldhame

Cuts Burn

Clonherb

46

43 **A** **44** **B** **45** **C**

D E F

Blacklawhill

Low
Blacklaw

B769

Corsehouse
Reservoir

G77

4

Blacklaw
Cottage

Blacklaw
Bridge

Glenouther
Rig

Annick Water

East
Whitelee

49

Glenouther
Moor

3

Swinzie Burn

Glenouther

48

KA3

2

Low
Clunch

Clunch
Hill

Blair

High
Clunch

Gree
Law

Harelaw

47

Townhead
of
Gree

A77

Gree
Cottage

Crofthead
of
Gree

Raithill

Kingswell Burn

Tam's
Hill

1

Townend
of
Gree

Damhead
Wood

Drumtee Water

Ladeside

Raithburn

Fenwick Water

Benthouse
Bridge

46

D 47 E 48 F

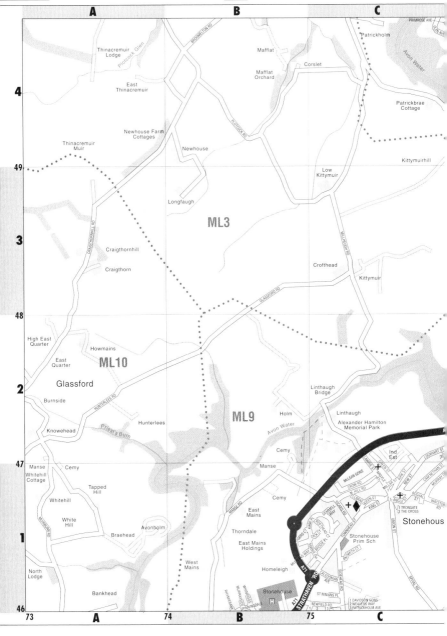

A B C

PRIMROSE AVE

Patrickholm

Avon Water

Thinacremuir
Lodge

Peacock Glen

Mafflat

Corslet

Mafflat
Orchard

East
Thinacremuir

Patrickbrae
Cottage

Newhouse Farm
Cottages

BROOMIELTON RD

PEACOCK RD

Thinacremuir
Muir

Newhouse

Kittymuirhill

49

Low
Kittymuir

Longfaugh

ML3

MILLHEUGH RD

DRAGSTHORNHILL LD

Craigthornhill

Crofthead

Craigthorn

Kittymuir

GLASSFORD RD

48

High East
Quarter

Howmains

East
Quarter

ML10

Linthaugh
Bridge

Glassford

HUNTERLEES RD

Holm

Linthaugh

Burnside

ML9

Alexander Hamilton
Memorial Park

Knowehead

Hunterlees

Priest's Burn

Avon Water

Cemy

47

Manse

Manse

Whitehill
Cottage

Cemy

Ind
Est

MILLBURN RD

Cemy

MANSE RD

Tapped
Hill

East
Mains

Stonehous

Whitehill

White
Hill

Braehead

Avonbolm

Thorndale

East Mains
Holdings

Stonehouse
Prim Sch

1

North
Lodge

West
Mains

Homeleigh

A71

STRATHAVEN RD

ST NINIANS PL

Stonehouse

Bankhead

H

NEWFIELD RD

46

73 A 74 B 75 C

1 DAVIDSON GDNS
2 WEAVERS WAY
3 PATRICKHOLM AVE

Stonehous

1 TRONGATE
2 THE CROSS

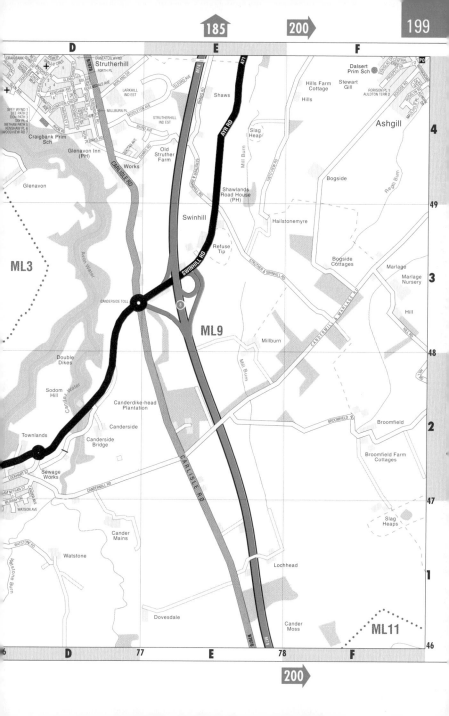

199
186

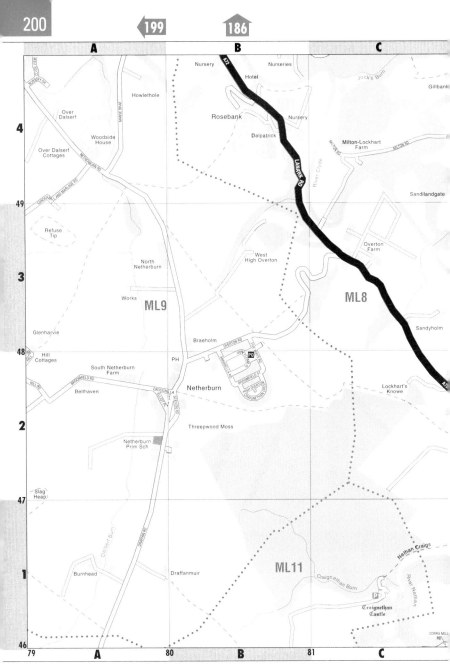

199

A   B   C

4

49

3

ML9

ML8

48

2

47

1

ML11

46

79   A   80   B   81   C

Map labels:

Nursery
Nurseries
Gillbank
Jock's Burn
A72
Howlethole
Hotel
Nursery
Over Dalserf
Rosebank
Nursery
Milton-Lockhart Farm
MILTON RD
Woodside House
Dalpatrick
Over Dalserf Cottages
NETHERBURN RD
MILTON RD
MAYNE RD
CANDER PARK LANE AND DALPATRICK RD
Sandilandgate
LANARK RD
River Clyde
Refuse Tip
North Netherburn
West High Overton
Overton Farm
Works
Sandyholm
Glenharvie
Braeholm
OVERTON RD
Hill Cottages
PH
PO
South Netherburn Farm
Lockhart's Knowe
HILL RD
BROOMFIELD RD
CROSSING LA
FLEMM PL
STATION RD
Netherburn
Bellhaven
BROOMFIELD RD
HIGH OVERTON
CRAIGNETHAN
A72
Threepwood Moss
Netherburn Prim Sch
Slag Heap
DALSERF BURN
DONMAN RD
Nethan Craigs
Burnhead
Draffanmuir
ML11
Craignethan Burn
River Nethan
P
Craignethan Castle
CORRA MILL RD

D E F

Station Rd

Under
Shieldhill

GLENBURN TERR
SHIELDHILL RD
BENTY'S LA
PARK AVE
VIOLET RD
JONQUIL WAY

UNITAS CRES 1
MILTON CRES 2
SPRINGFIELD CRES 3

CARTLAND AVE

Miltonhead
(birthplace of
General Roy)

MILTON RD

South
Hillhead

JURA GDNS

BLUEBELL WAY

Miltonhead
Farm

Wellriggs

Meadowhead

49

Townhead Burn

LANARK RD

A73

Townhead

Oldhill

Tower

Waygateshawhead

Maregill Burn

3

Waygateshaw

Bushelhead

HARESTANES
IND EST

Braidwood

B7056

A73

ML8

Gills

Braidwood
House

Braidwood
Prim Sch

48

HAREMYRES ST
LOCHRANZA ST

BEAMSHIELDS RD

Threepwood

Orchard
Knowe

PO

1 HALL BAR GDNS
2 DONALD GDNS

Poplarglen

BRAIDWOOD RD

Yett
Holm

Woodlands Road

2

Linnside

Woodhall

River Clyde

Swinsy Hill

Halibar
Tower

NUCKERELLA RD

47

Nethanfoot

Orchard
House

WOODHALL RD

Millwood

1 JAMES WILSON PL
2 NETHANFOOT BRIG RD

Lodge

Newpark

Hamper
Hill

LANARK RD

HOLM CRES

Mashock Burn

Derwent
Wood

Hotel

PO

MASHOCK
PATH

Birkhill

BIRKHILL RD

1

BLAIR RD

B7056

Crossford

HARPIN TER

Clyde Valley
Country Estate

Aaronshill
Wood

ML11

Auchenglen

Auchenglen
Hill

NEMPHLAR MOOR RD

Blair
Cottage

A72

Burned Wood

46

2 D 83 E 84 F

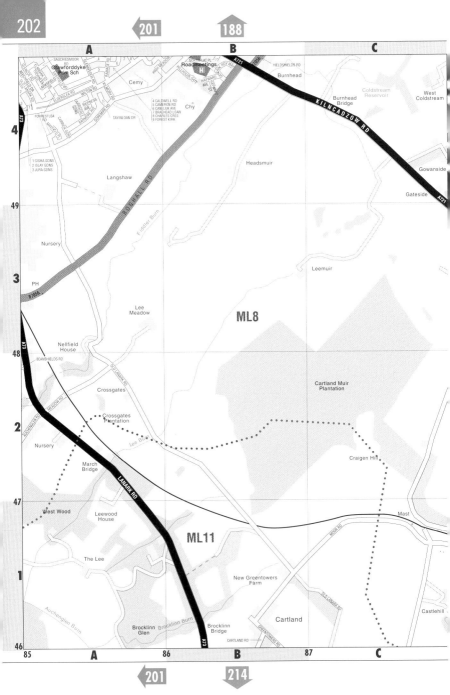

A   **B**   **C**

Sauchiesmoor

Crawforddyke Prim Sch

Cemy

Myrtle Hat Pl
Roadmeetings

Burnhead

Yieldshields Rd

West Coldstream

Coldstream Reservoir

Burnhead Bridge

4 CALDWELL RD
5 CAMERON RD
6 CAMELON AVE
7 BRAEHEAD LOAN
8 CHARLES CRES
9 FOREST KIRK

Chy

KILNCADZOW RD

FORRESTLEA RD

CARNEGIE RD

Tavinloan Dr

4

A73

1 GIGHA GDNS
2 ISLAY GDNS
3 JURA GDNS

Headsmuir

Gowanside

Langshaw

Gateside

A721

Fiddler Burn

B7056 RD

49

Nursery

Leemuir

3

PH

B7056

Lee Meadow

ML8

A73

Nellfield House

BEANSHIELDS RD

48

OLD LANARK RD

Cartland Muir Plantation

Crossgates

2

Crossgates Plantation

Craigen Hill

AUCHENGRAY RD

Nursery

MEADOW RD

Lee Burn

March Bridge

LANARK RD

Mast

47

West Wood

Leewood House

MOOR RD

ML11

The Lee

OLD LANARK RD

New Greentowers Farm

Castlehill

1

GREENTOWERS RD

Cartland

Auchenglen Burn

Brocklinn Glen

Brocklinn Burn

Brocklinn Bridge

A73

CARTLAND RD

46

85   **A**   **86**   **B**   **87**   **C**

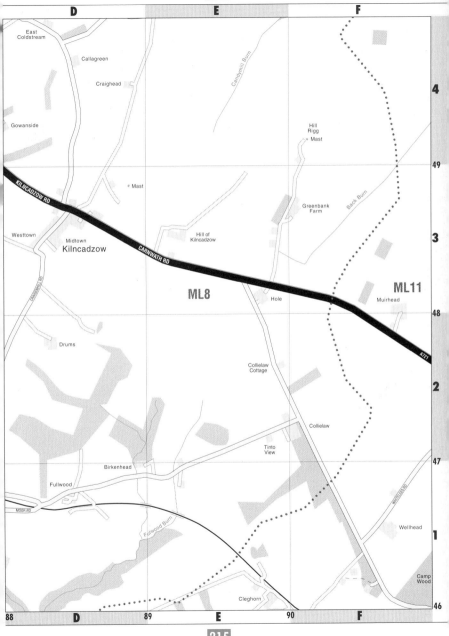

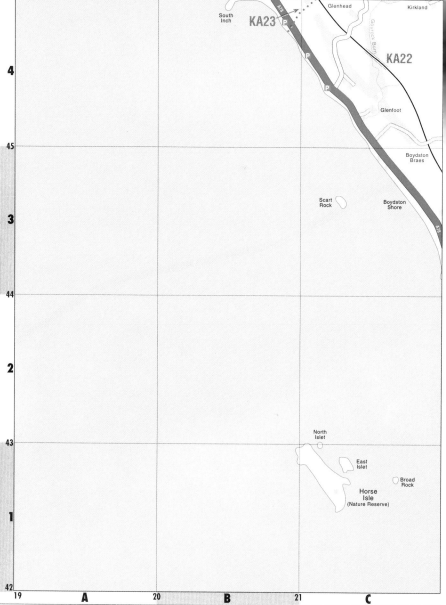

190

A **B** **C**

4

Glenhead Kirkland

South
Inch

KA23

P

P

P

Gourock Burn

KA22

Glenfoot

45

Boydston
Braes

3

Scart
Rock

Boydston
Shore

A78

44

2

43

North
Islet

East
Islet

Broad
Rock

Horse
Isle
(Nature Reserve)

1

42

19 **A** 20 **B** 21 **C**

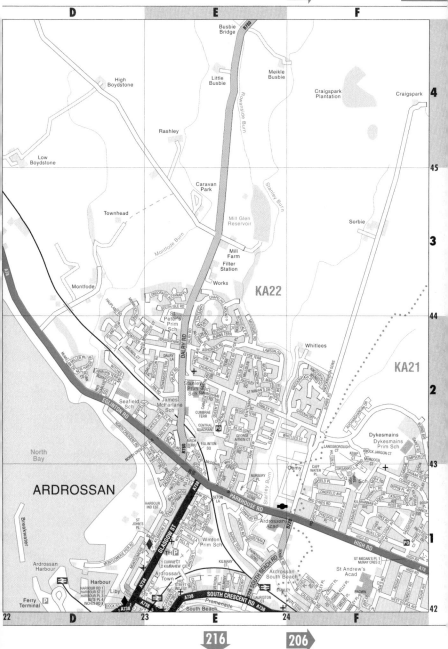

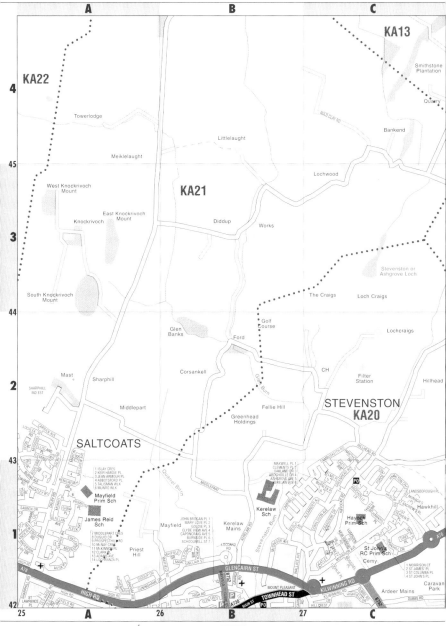

KA13

KA22

Smithstone
Plantation

Quarry

4

Towerlodge

AULD CLAY RD

Littlelaught

Bankend

Meiklelaught

45

Lochwood

West Knockrivoch
Mount

KA21

Knockrivoch

East Knockrivoch
Mount

Diddup

Works

Stevenston or
Ashgrove Loch

3

South Knockrivoch
Mount

The Craigs

Loch Craigs

44

Glen
Banks

Golf
Course

Ford

Lochcraigs

Mast

Sharphill

Corsankell

Glen Burn

CH

Filter
Station

Hillhead

SHARPHILL
IND EST

2

Middlepart

Fellie Hill

STEVENSTON
KA20

Greenhead
Holdings

SALTCOATS

43

MAXWELL PL 1
CLEMENTS PL 2
OAKLAND DR 3
ARDCHOILLE DR 4
ASHGROVE AVE 5
KERELAW AVE 6

Quarrel Burn

1 ISLAY CRES
2 KEIR HARDIE PL
3 JEAN ARMOUR PL
4 ABBOTSFORD PL
5 TALISMAN AVE
6 MUNRO WLK

Mayfield
Prim Sch

Kerelaw
Sch

LANDSBOROUGH PL

PO

James Reid
Sch

MIDDLEPART

Hawkhill

7 MIDDLEPART GDNS
8 DUGUID DR
9 PROSPECTHILL RD
10 McNAY CRES
11 McKINNON PL
12 CLARK PL
13 ADAMS AVE
14 ESPERANZA PL

Mayfield

JOHN BROGAN PL 1
MARY LOVE PL 2
GOUDIE PL 3
CLYDE VIEW AVE 4
CAPONCRAIG AVE 5
BURNSIDE PL 6
SCHOOLWELL ST 7

Kerelaw
Mains

Stevenston Burn

Haysock
Prim Sch

1

Priest
Hill

Luccard

St John's
RC Prim Sch

Cemy

1 MORRISON CT
2 ST JAMES PL
3 ST COLUMBA PL
4 ST JOHN'S PL

GLENCAIRN ST

HIGH RD

A78

TOWNHEAD ST

MOUNT PLEASANT

KILWINNING RD

Caravan
Park

42

ST
LAWRENCE
PL

HIGH RD

GLENCAIRN ST

PO

Ardeer Mains

DUBBS RD

HILLCREST

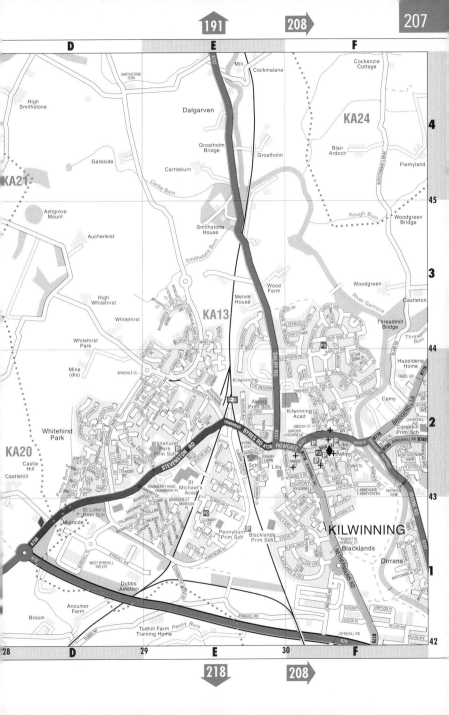

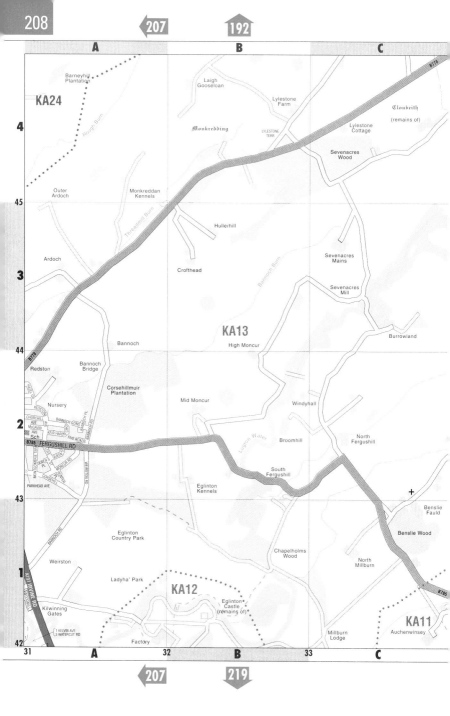

207
192

A

B

C

B778

KA24

Barneyhill
Plantation

Laigh
Gooseloan

Lylestone
Farm

Clonbeith

(remains of)

4

Monkredding

LYLESTONE
TERR

Lylestone
Cottage

Sevenacres
Wood

Rough Burn

Outer
Ardoch

Monkreddan
Kennels

45

Hullerhill

Threadmill Burn

Ardoch

Crofthead

Sevenacres
Mains

Sevenacres
Mill

3

Bannoch Burn

Bannoch

KA13

High Moncur

Burrowland

44

B778

Redston

Bannoch
Bridge

Corsehillmuir
Plantation

Mid Moncur

Windyhall

Nursery

CHURCHILL
AVE

BANNOCH GDNS
LANGHOLM PL

BANNOCH PL

KEIR HARDIE
FIVE ROADS

Lugton Water

Broomhill

North
Fergushill

2

Sch

B785 FERGUSHILL RD

QUEEN

MONCUR RD

WHEATRON RD

South
Fergushill

PARKHEAD AVE

Eglinton
Kennels

43

Benslie
Fauld

BANNOCH RD

Eglinton
Country Park

Benslie Wood

Weirston

Chapelholms
Wood

North
Millburn

1

A737 IRVINE RD

B7080

Ladyha' Park

KA12

Eglinton
Castle
(remains of)

B785

KA11

Kilwinning
Gates

Auchenwinsey

1 KELVIN AVE
2 WATERCUT RD

Factory

Millburn
Lodge

42

31

A

32

B

33

C

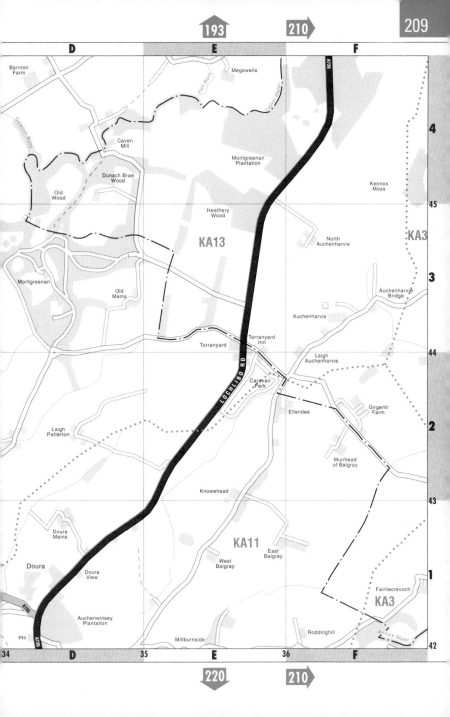

Barnton Farm

Megswells

Caven Mill

Montgreenan Plantation

Dunach Brae Wood

Old Wood

Heathery Wood

Kennox Moss

45

KA13

North Auchenharvie

KA3

Montgreenan

Old Mains

Auchenharvie Bridge

3

Auchenharvie

Torranyard Inn

Torranyard

Laigh Auchenharvie

44

LOCHLIBO RD

Caravan Park

Ellandee

Girgenti Farm

Laigh Patterton

Muirhead of Balgray

2

Knowehead

43

Doura Mains

KA11

Doura

Doura View

West Balgray

East Balgray

1

Fairliecrevoch

KA3

Auchenwinsey Plantation

PH

Millburnside

Roddinghill

Annick Water

42

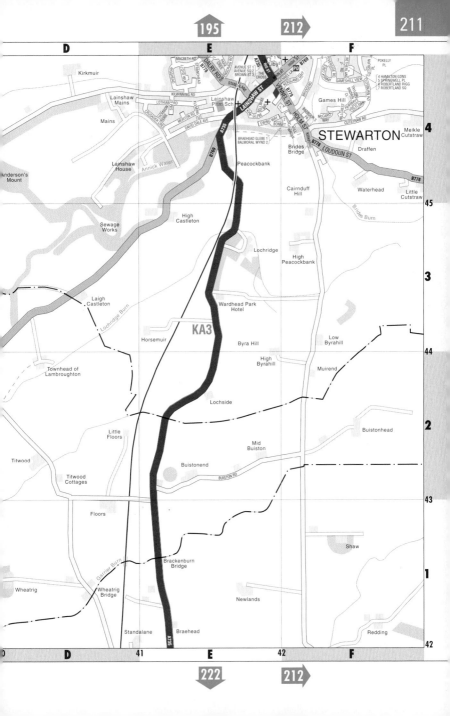

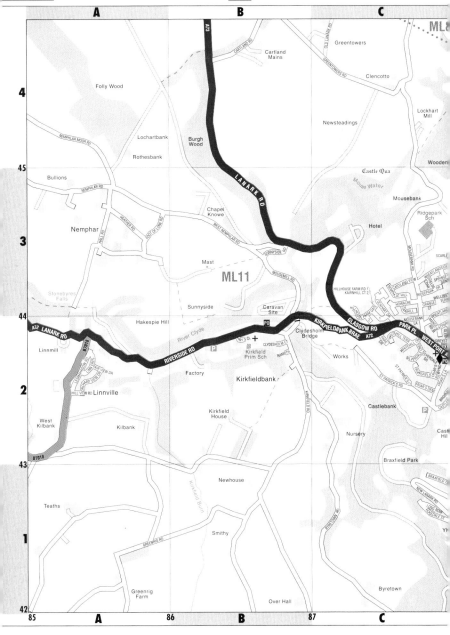

202

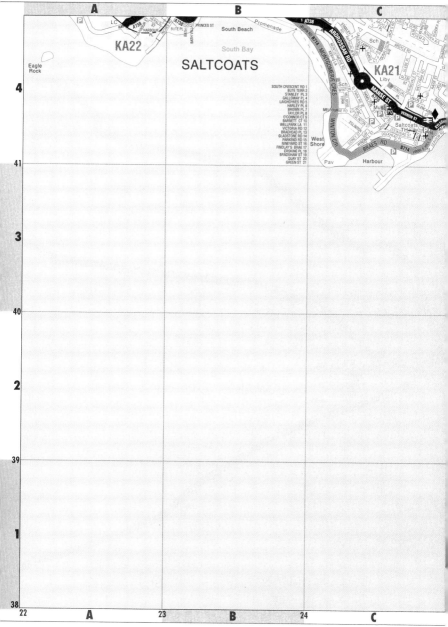

SALTCOATS

South Beach

Promenade

South Bay

KA22

Eagle
Rock

KA21
Liby

Sch

SOUTH CRESCENT RD 1
BUTE TERR 2
STANLEY PL 3
GALLOWAY PL 4
LAUGHDYKES RD 5
HARLEY PL 6
BROWN PL 7
TAYLOR PL 8
O'CONNOR CT 9
BARNETT CT 10
WELLPARK LA 11
VICTORIA RD 12
BRAEHEAD PL 13
GLADSTONE RD 14
PARKEND RD 15
NINEYARD ST 16
FINDLAY'S BRAE 17
ERSKINE PL 18
BRADSHAW ST 19
QUAY ST 20
GREEN ST 21

West
Shore

Saltcoats
TH

Harbour

Pav

BRAES RD

B714

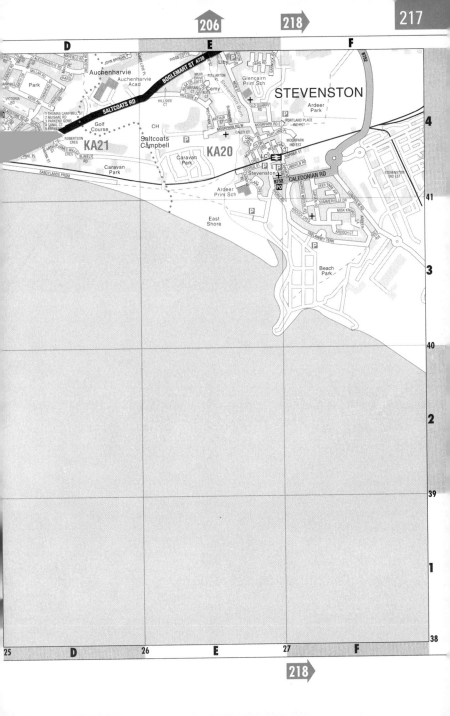

D | E | F

Auchenharvie

JOHN BROGAN P.
MAYFIELD RD
Park
MILLAR RD
MCILWRAITH RD
KERR ST
VICTORIA RD
1 THOMAS CAMPBELL ST
2 McISAAC RD
3 PARKEND GDNS
4 CANAL CT
5 PARKEND
Auchenharvie Acad

BOGLEMART ST A738

SALTCOATS RD

Golf Course

Saltcoats Campbell

KA21

Caravan Park

ROBERTSON CRES
JAMES MILLER CRES
BLAKELY RD
CANAL PL

SANDYLANDS PROM

Liby

RIDGS COTTS
Fullarton
MUIR DRIVE
ARRAN COTTS
BUTE
HILLSIDE CT
WESTPARK ST
ARTHUR ST

CH

Caravan Park

KA20

MOORPARK RD W
BURNS STREET
Stevenston Burn
OLD QUARRY RD
Glencairn Prim Sch
DARG RD
ST JOHNS WAY

STEVENSTON

Ardeer Park

Cemy

PORTLAND PLACE
PORTLAND
MOORPARK RD E
MOORPARK IND EST
MOORPARK ST

Stevenston
CALEY CT
GEORGE ST
GLEBE ST
NEW ST

CALEDONIAN RD
B752
PO

Ardeer Prim Sch

East Shore

LOANHEAD MOOR RD
DEER PARK
SOMMERVILLE DR
TRELAWNEY TERR
ARDOCH CT

MISK KNOWES
GOLF AVE
HAYOCKS RD
LIMEKILN RD
LORNE RD

STEVENSTON IND EST

Beach Park

4

41

3

40

2

39

1

38

217
207

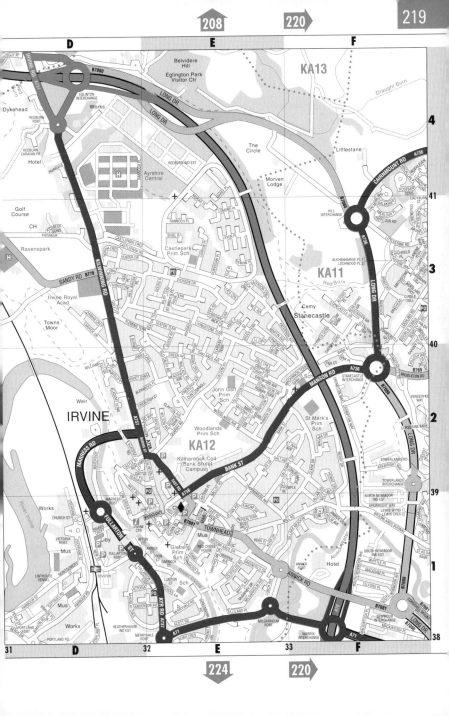

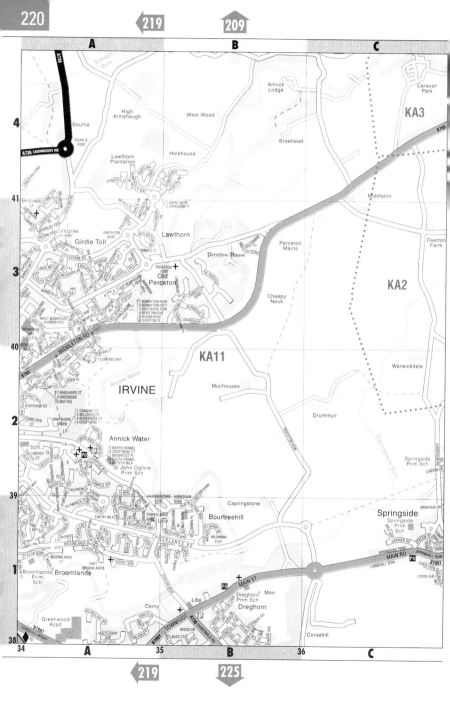

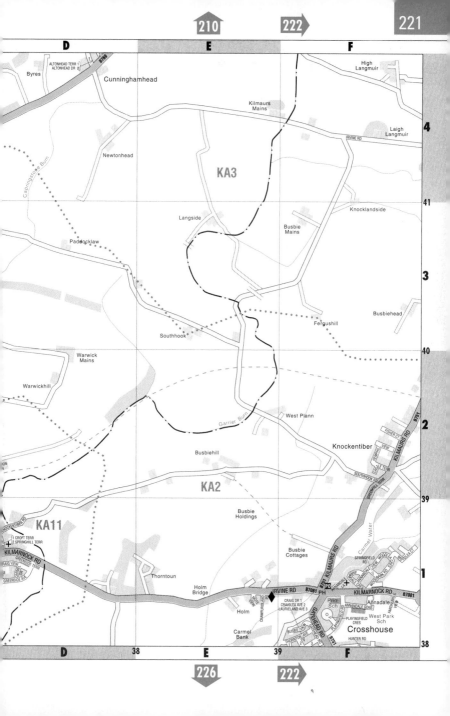

D
E
F

Byres
ALTONHEAD TERR 1
ALTONHEAD DR 2
B769
Cunninghamhead
High Langmuir
Kilmaurs Mains
IRVINE RD
Laigh Langmuir
4
Newtonhead
Capringstone Burn
KA3
41
Langside
Knocklandside
Paddocklaw
Busbie Mains
3
Busbiehead
Southhook
Fergushill
40
Warwick Mains
Warwickhill
West Plann
Garrier Burn
2
Busbiehill
Knockentiber
FISHER CT
VIEW
SOUTHHOOK RD
GREENHILL FARM
KA2
39
KA11
1 CROFT TERR
2 SPRINGHILL TERR
KILMARNOCK RD
GREENSIDE TERR
CRAIG VIEW
GREENSIDE AVE
Busbie Holdings
Carmel Water
Thorntoun
Busbie Cottages
SPRINGFIELD RD
KILMAURS RD
B7081
1
Holm Bridge
IRVINE RD
B7081 PH
CRAIG DR 1
CRAIGLEA AVE 2
LAURIELAND AVE 3
ANNANDALE GDNS
Prim Sch
PLAYINGFIELD CRES
KILMARNOCK RD
B7081
Annadale
West Park Sch
Holm
CRAWFURDLAND
GATEHEAD RD
B751
Carmel Bank
THORNTON AVE
Crosshouse
HUNTER RD
38

D
38
E
39
F

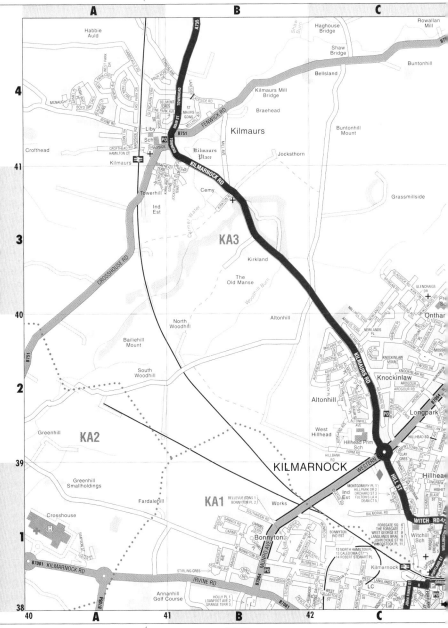

D **E** **F**

Moss Wood

Tannahill

B751

A77

B7038

Dalmusternock

Little Mosside

North Craig Reservoir

Meiklewood

Craufurland Loch

4

Loch Plantation

Northcraig

AUCHENTIBER PL 1
TARBOLTON PL 2
BOYDSTON WAY 3
CROSSHILL WYND 4
DALGARVEN MEWS 5
PORTING CROSS PL 6
LAURISTON WAY 7
LOCHMABEN WYND 8

Wardknowe Plantation

41

DUNURE PL

Fenwick Water

Southcraig Holdings

Borland

Rushybog Plantation

Craufurdland Castle

GLASGOW RD

Borland Bridge

Broombrae

KA3

Greenhead Plantation

3

Hotel

Craufurdland Water

Assloss House

Assloss

Ford

Bringan

CHARESHAW GDNS

REDDING AVE

B7064

WESTERN RD

East Wardlaw

40

Assloss Bridge

Dean Castle Country Park

B7082

GRASSYARDS INTERCHANGE

Hillhouse

2

Dean

Dean Castle

Silverwood Prim Sch

FRASER WLK 1
DUNDAS WLK 2
DONALDSON RD 3

Whinpark

BEANSBURN

Visitor Ctr

DEAN ST

Ford Beansburn

GRASSYARDS RD

39

GILLSBURN GDNS

Kilmarnock Water

Townholm

URQUHART RD

Newhouse

Silverwood

HARRIET RD

WILLIE MAIR'S BRAE

New Farm Loch

St Joseph's Acad

B7082 STRAWBERRYBANK RD

HIGH ST

DEAN LA

Mon

KAY PARK GR

Cemy

MACALISTER PL 1
MACINNES PL 2
MACINTOSH PL 3
MACDOUGALL DR 4
MACMILLAN DR 5
MACMILLAN PL 6
MACEWAN PL 7

PL James Hamilton Acad

1

MORRIS LA
BOULIS ST

Burns Mon & Mus

Park Sch

Ralstonhill

Templetonburn

Coll

KAY PARK TERR

Prim Sch

MILTON RD

A77

8 MACPHERSON WLK
9 MACPHERSON GDNS
10 MACDONALD GDNS
11 MACANDREW PL
12 MACDONALD PL
13 MILTON AVE
14 MACBETH WLK

38

3 **D** **44** **E** **45** **F**

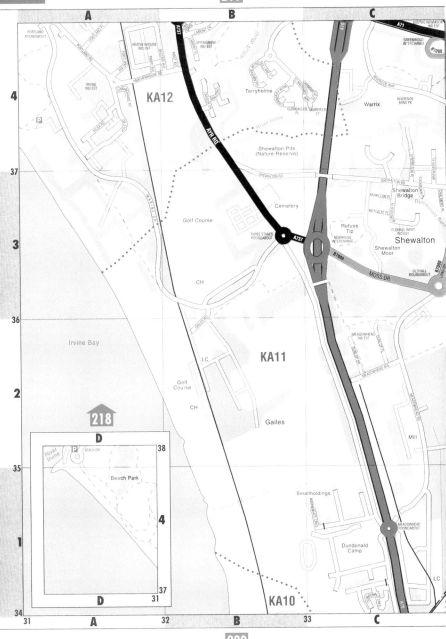

A   B   C

PORTLAND
ROUNDABOUT

HEATHERHOUSE
IND EST

SPRINGBANK
IND EST

GREENWOOD
INTERCHANGE

A71

BOOTHS NEWMOOR
IND EST

IRVINE
IND EST

KA12

Tarryholme

Warrix

RIVERSIDE
BSNS PK

River Irvine

Shewalton Pits
(Nature Reserve)

SHEWALTON RD

SHEWALTON RD

Shewalton
Bridge

Dundonald Burn

Cemetery

Golf Course

THREE STANES
ROUNDABOUT

A737

Refuse
Tip

NEWHOUSE
INTERCHANGE

OLDHALL WEST
IND EST

Shewalton

Shewalton
Moor

OLDHALL
ROUNDABOUT

CH

MOSS DR

Irvine Bay

Golf
Course

GAILES RD

L.C.

KA11

MEADOWHEAD
IND EST

CH

218

Gailes

Mill

Beach Dr

D   38

River
Irvine

Beach Park

4

Smallholdings

MEADOWHEAD
ROUNDABOUT

D   37
31

Dundonald
Camp

LC

KA10

31   A   32   B   33   C

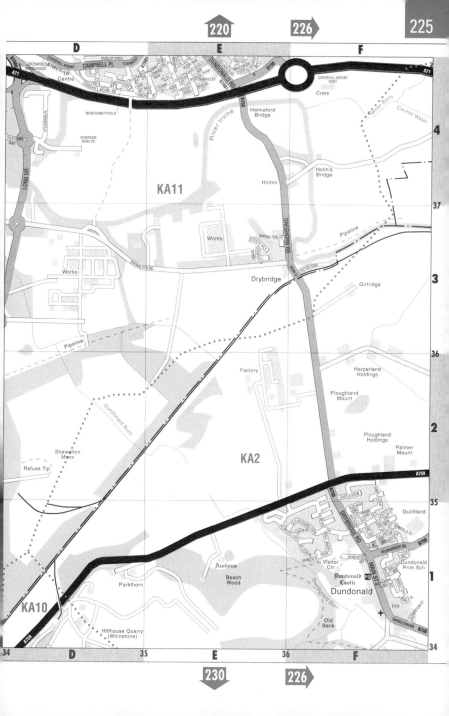

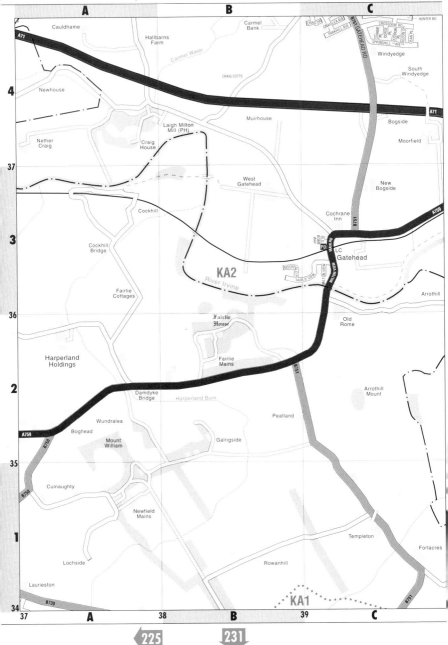

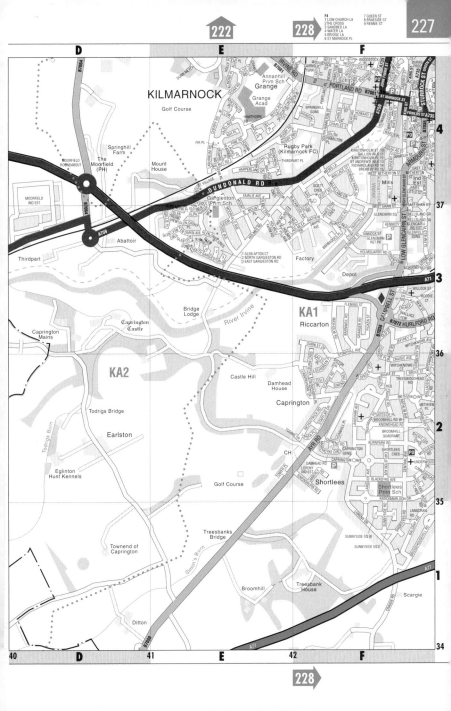

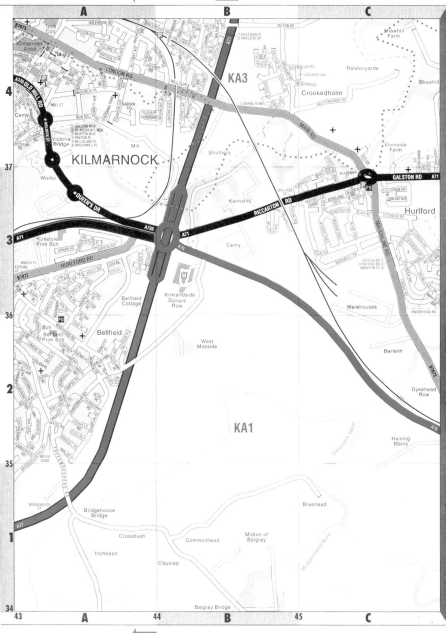

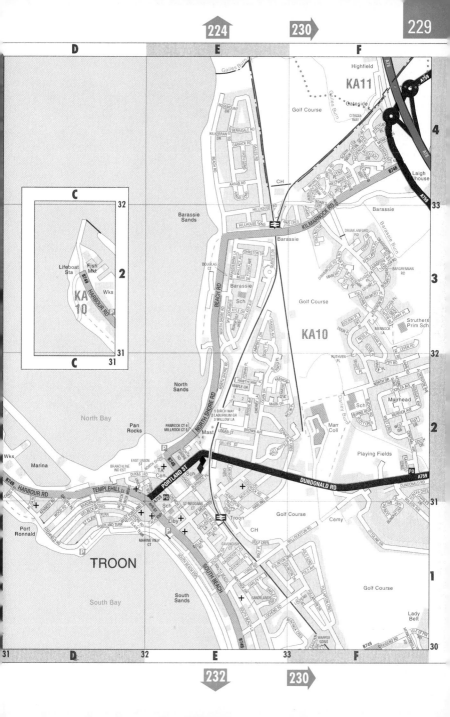

229
225

A **B** **C**

A759

Hillhouse Quarry

Hillhouse

Merkland Loch

Dundonald Burn

Chapel Hill

4

Hallyards Quarry

Highlees

Hallyards

A78

33

Works

Aught Wood

Harpercroft

Highlees Mount

A759

Wardlaw Hill

KA2

Collenan Smallholdings

Mast

Works

3

Clevance

Langholm

WARDLAW CRES 1
CRUMMIEHOLM GDNS 2
CROSSBURN DR 3
CROSSBURN TERR 4
CROSSBURN LA 5

Highgrove House

KA10

32

OLD LOANS RD
SEAVIEW
DORLE WYND

Clevance Cottage

Corraith

MAIN ST
PH

Beattock Burn

Loans

PO

BEECHWOOD PADDOCK

Wester Croft

FULLARTON PL

Craiksland

2

TROON RD
B746

Crossburn

A759 DUNDONALD RD

31

CHARLES DR

B746

Darley Burn

Southside

High Wexford

KA1

OTTOLINE DR

Wexford Cottage

BALCOMIE

1

Southside Cottages

KERSE RD

Darley Plantation

Golf Course

Lady Belt

FULLERTON CLYD

Rumbling Burn

KA9

Crosbie House

ISLE OF PIN RD

Fairlees

Crookside

30

34 **A** **35** **B** **36** **C**

229
233

229

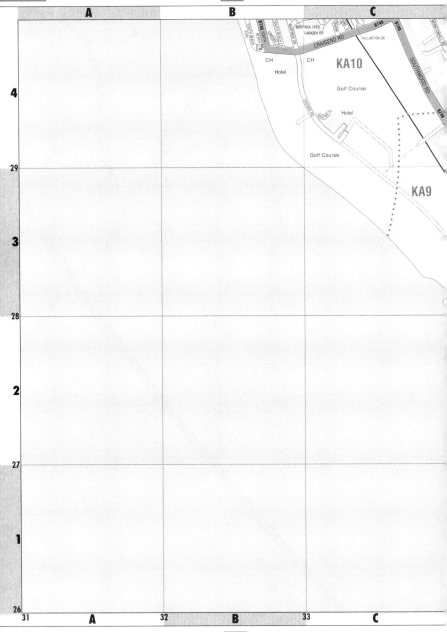

KA10

KA9

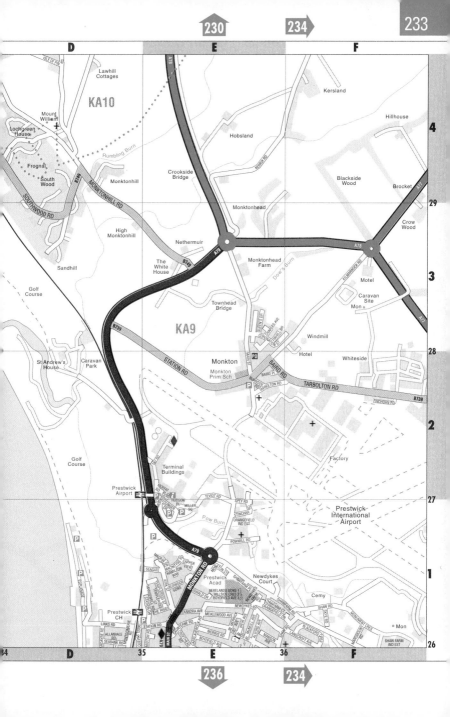

D E F

4

25

3

24

2

23

North
Breakwater

KA8

Dock

South
Pier

BRUCE CRES 1
CATHCART ST 2
ST JOHN ST 3
ACADEMY ST 4
BOAT VENNAL 5
HARBOUR ST 6
SANDGATE 7

AYR
KA7

QUEEN'S TERRACE LA

1

22

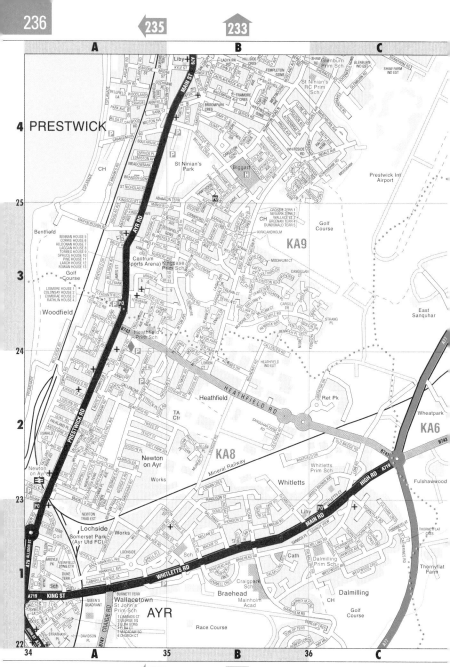

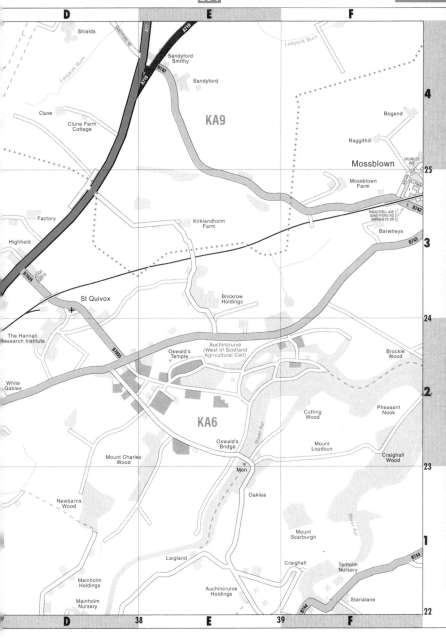

D   E   F

Shields

Ladykirk Burn

Sandyford
Smithy

Sandyford

KA9

Bogend

Clune

Clune Farm
Cottage

Raggithill

4

Mossblown

DRUMLEY
AVE

25

Mossblown
Farm

Factory

Kirklandholm
Farm

B742

Highfield

RAGGITHILL AVE 1
SANDYFORD RD 2
BARWHEYS DR 3

Barwheys

B743

3

St Quivox

Brickrow
Holdings

24

The Hannah
Research Institute

Auchincruive
(West of Scotland
Agricultural Coll)

Brockle
Wood

Oswald's
Temple

White
Gables

KA6

River Ayr

Cutting
Wood

Pheasant
Nook

2

Oswald's
Bridge

Mount
Loudoun

Craighall
Wood

Mount Charles
Wood

Mon

23

Newbarns
Wood

Oaklea

River Ayr

Mount
Scarburgh

1

Laigland

Craighall

Tarholm
Nursery

B744

Mainholm
Holdings

Auchincruive
Holdings

Stanalane

Mainholm
Nursery

B744

22

D   38   E   39   F

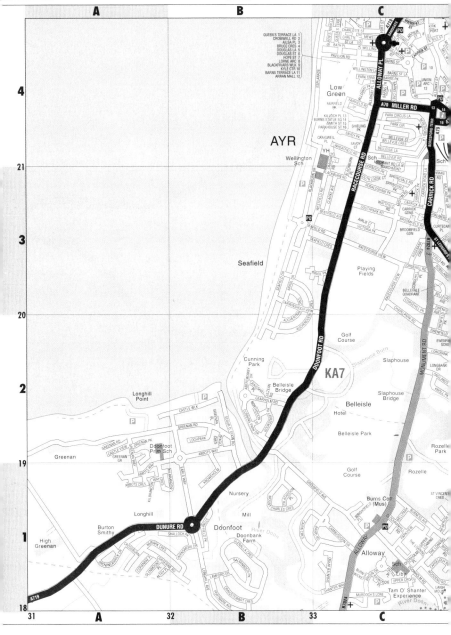

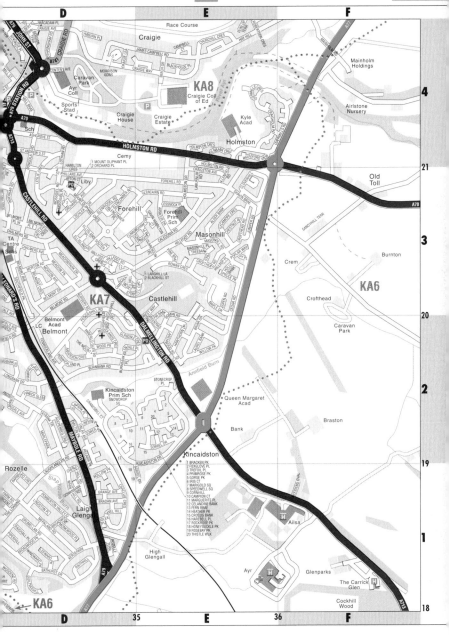

D   E   F

4

JOHN ST
MACADAM PL
CRAIGIE AVE
CRAIGIE RD
TIMBLIN PL
HAYHILL PL
HAY HILL
MAINHOLM CRES
MADER BANK
Craigie
Race Course
JAMES CAMPBELL RD
CAMPBELL
CHURCHILL CRES
A719
CONTENT AVE
MORRISON GDNS
CRAIGIE WAY
BLACKHOUSE PL
Mainholm
Holdings
B744
Caravan
Park
Ayr
Coll
KA8
Craigie Coll
of Ed
Airlstone
Nursery
Sports
Stad
Craigie
House
Craigie
Estate
Kyle
Acad
Sch
ASHGROVE ST
HOLMSTON RD
Holmston
Cemy
OLD
Toll
ST ANDREW'S ST
A713
A70
HAMILTON
CRES
ST PHILLANS AVE
AFTON PL
Liby
1 MOUNT OLIPHANT PL
2 ORCHARD PL
HOLMSTON CRES
HOLMSTON RD
CRAIGSTON AVE
FOREHILL RD
WHITFORD VIEW
21
A70
CASTLEHILL RD
BELMONT
Forehill
GLENCAIRN RD
CESSNOCK PL
Forehill
Prim
Sch
ST LEONARDS RD
SANDYHILL TERR
3
BELMONT
P.W.
TA
Centre
Schs
CHALMERS RD
Masonhill
MASONHILL
TREEBANK
Crem
Burnton
KA6
1 LAIGHHILL LA
2 BLACKHILL ST
ROMAN CRES
Crofthead
KA7
Castlehill
ST EDWARDS RD
Belmont
Acad
Belmont
LC
DALMELLINGTON RD
Caravan
Park
20
MAYBOLE RD
THE MEADOWS
BURNBANK RD
Anfield Burn
STONECROP
Kincaidston
Prim Sch
SNOWDROP
Queen Margaret
Acad
2
Braston
Rozelle
CHALMERS CT
Bank
GRANGE AVE
BRADAN AVE
Kincaidston
1 BRACKEN PK
2 FOXGLOVE PL
3 TREFOIL PL
4 PRIMROSE PK
5 GORSE PK
6 IRIS CT
7 MARIGOLD SQ
8 SPEEDWELL SQ
9 CORNHILL
10 CAMPION CT
11 MARGUERITE PL
12 CELANDINE BANK
13 FERN BRAE
14 HEATHER PK
15 CROCUS BANK
16 HAREBELL PL
17 ROCKROSE PK
18 HONEYSUCKLE PK
19 BUTTERCUP PK
20 THISTLE WLK
19
Laigh
Glengall
Ailsa
A77
High
Glengall
Ayr
Glenparks
The Carrick
Glen
A713
KA6
Cockhill
Wood
18

D   35   E   36   F

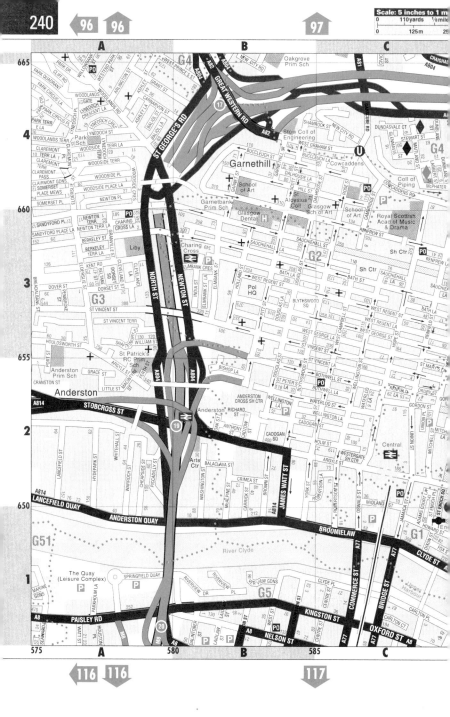

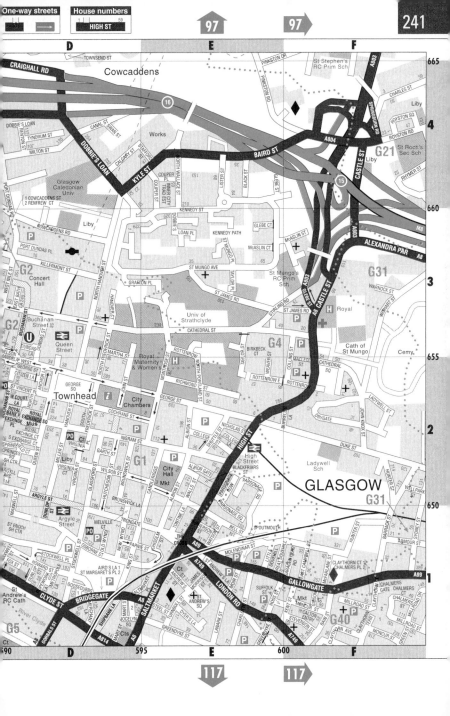

Index

Street names are listed alphabetically and show the locality, the Postcode District, the page number and a reference to the square in which the name falls on the map page

Cumberland Pl **7** Glasgow G5 ..... 117 E2

Full street name
This may have been abbreviated on the map

Location Number
If present, this indicates the street's position on a congested area of the map instead of the name

Town, village or locality in which the street falls.

Postcode District for the street name

Page number of the map on which the street name appears

Grid square in which the centre of the street falls

Schools, hospitals, sports centres, railway stations, shopping centres, industrial estates, public amenities and other places of interest are also listed.

Abbreviations used in the index

App	Approach	Cl	Close	Espl	Esplanade	Mdw	Meadows	S	South
Arc	Arcade	Comm	Common	Est	Estate	N	North	Sq	Square
Ave	Avenue	Cnr	Corner	Gdns	Gardens	Orch	Orchard	Strs	Stairs
Bvd	Boulevard	Cotts	Cottages	Gn	Green	Par	Parade	Stps	Steps
Bldgs	Buildings	Ct	Court	Gr	Grove	Pk	Park	St	Street, Saint
Bsns Pk	Business Park	Ctyd	Courtyard	Hts	Heights	Pas	Passage	Terr	Terrace
Bsns Ctr	Business Centre	Cres	Crescent	Ho	House	Pl	Place	Tk	Track
Bglws	Bungalows	Cswy	Causeway	Ind Est	Industrial Estate	Prec	Precinct	Trad Est	Trading Estate
Cswy	Causeway	Dr	Drive	Intc	Interchange	Prom	Promenade	Wlk	Walk
Ctr	Centre	Dro	Drove	Junc	Junction	Ret Pk	Retail Park	W	West
Circ	Circle	E	East	La	Lane	Rd	Road	Yd	Yard
Cir	Circus	Emb	Embankment	Mans	Mansions	Rdbt	Roundabout		
		Ent	Enterprise						

Town and village index

Airdrie 123 D2	California 66 C3	Fenwick 213 D2	Langbank 70 B4	Renfrew 94 A1
Airth 14 C2	Cambus 9 D4	Fishcross 5 E2	Larbert 23 E1	Renton 27 E1
Alexandria 27 E3	Cambusbarron 6 B3	Fluchter 56 C1	Larkhall 185 D2	Rhu 15 E3
Allandale 39 E1	Cambuslang 139 F3	Forrestfield 106 B1	Laurieston 42 C2	Riggend 83 D1
Alloa 10 B3	Cardross 48 A4	Gartcosh 100 C2	Law 186 C3	Rosneath 15 D2
Alva 5 D4	Carluke 188 A1	Gatehead 226 C3	Lennoxtown 57 F4	Rutherglen 138 B2
Annathill 81 F1	Carmunnock 158 B3	Gateside 171 F4	Letham 24 B4	St Quivox 237 E2
Ardrossan 205 E2	Cartland 202 C1	Glasgow 117 D2	Linwood 112 A3	Salsburgh 125 E1
Ashgill 199 E3	Chapelhall 123 E1	Glenboig 101 E3	Lochwinnoch 129 E2	Saltcoats 216 C4
Avonbridge 87 F3	Chryston 100 B4	Glengarnock 170 A4	Longcroft 39 D2	Seamill 190 B1
Ayr 238 A1	Clachan of Campsie 33 D2	Glenmavis 102 C2	Longriggend 85 E1	Shieldhill 66 C3
Balloch 19 E1	Clackmannan 10 C3	Gourock 44 C4	Lugton 173 E3	Shotts 146 C3
Balmore 77 F4	Clarkston 157 F3	Greengairs 83 F1	Menstrie 3 F3	Skinflats 24 C1
Banknock 38 C1	Cleghorn 215 F4	Greenock 45 E2	Millerston 99 D2	Slamannan 86 A3
Bannockburn 7 F1	Cleland 144 A1	Haggs 39 D2	Milngavie 55 D1	South Alloa 9 F2
Banton 37 F2	Clydebank 74 B3	Hamilton 162 A4	Milton 50 C1	Springside 220 C1
Bardowie 77 D4	Coatbridge 122 A4	Harthill 127 F3	Milton of Campsie 58 A2	Stenhousemuir 23 F1
Bargeddie 121 D2	Cowie 12 B4	Hartwood 146 A1	Monkton 233 E2	Stepps 99 E3
Barrhead 134 A3	Crookedholm 228 B4	Helensburgh 16 C2	Moodiesburn 80 C1	Stevenston 217 D4
Barmill 171 F2	Crossford 201 D1	High Bonnybridge 40 B2	Mossblown 237 F3	Stewarton 211 F4
Bearsden 75 E3	Crosshouse 221 F1	Houston 91 E1	Motherwell 163 F4	Stirling 7 E4
Beith 150 B1	Croy 60 C2	Howwood 130 B1	Mugdock 55 D3	Stonehouse 198 C1
Bellshill 142 A1	Cumbernauld 61 D1	Hurlford 228 C3	Muirhead 100 B4	Strathblane 31 D2
Bishopbriggs 78 B1	Cunninghamhead 221 D4	Inchinnan 93 D2	Neilston 154 A3	Symington 231 E2
Bishopton 72 A1	Dalry 191 E4	Irvine 219 D1	Nemphlar 214 A3	Thorntonhall 158 A1
Blackridge 107 E1	Dalserf 186 A1	Johnstone 112 A1	Netherburn 200 B2	Throsk 9 D3
Blantyre 161 D3	Denny 21 E2	Kilbarchan 111 D1	Newton Mearns 156 B3	Torrance 57 D1
Bonhill 28 A4	Dennyloanhead 39 E3	Kilbirnie 149 D2	Old Kilpatrick 73 D3	Torwood 22 C4
Bonnybridge 40 A3	Drybridge 225 E3	Kilmacolm 89 E4	Overtown 186 A4	Troon 229 E1
Bothwell 141 D1	Dumbarton 49 F2	Kilmarnock 222 B1	Paisley 113 E3	Tullibody 4 A1
Bowling 72 B4	Dundonald 225 F1	Kilmaurs 222 A3	Perceton 220 B2	Twechar 59 F2
Braidwood 201 E1	Dunlop 195 D4	Kilncadzow 203 E3	Plains 104 A2	Uddingston 140 B3
Bridge of Allan 2 A4	Eaglesham 178 C3	Kilsyth 60 B4	Plean 12 B2	Uplawmoor 153 D2
Bridge of Weir 110 B4	East Kilbride 159 D1	Kilwinning 207 D1	Port Glasgow 47 D1	Waterside 213 F2
Brookfield 111 E3	Elderslie 112 B1	Kirkfieldbank 214 B2	Prestwick 236 B3	West Kilbride 190 B2
Burnhouse 172 A1	Erskine 73 D1	Kirkintilloch 79 F4	Quarriers Village 89 F1	Wishaw 165 D1
Calderbank 123 D1	Falkirk 42 B4	Knockentiber 221 F2	Quarter 183 F2	
Caldercruix 105 E1	Fallin 8 C2	Lanark 215 E2	Queenzieburn 59 F4	

Abbey Cl PA1 ... 113 F2
Abbey Craig Rd FK10 ... 5 D1
Abbey Dr G14 ... 95 F2
Abbey Mill FK8 ... 7 E4
Abbey Pl ML6 ... 123 E2
Abbey Prim Sch KA13 ... 207 E2
Abbey Rd Elderslie PA5 ... 112 B1
    Stirling FK8 ... 2 B1
Abbey Rd PI FK6 ... 57 E3
Abbey Wlk ML9 ... 185 D2
Abbeycraig Rd G34 ... 100 C1
Abbeydale Way G73 ... 138 B2
Abbeygate KA13 ... 207 F2
Abbeygreen KA13 ... 207 F2
Abbeygreen St G34 ... 100 C1
Abbeyhill St G32 ... 118 C4
Abbeylands Rd G81 ... 74 B3
Abbeymill Bns Ctr PA1 ... 113 F2
Abbot Ct KA9 ... 236 B3
Abbot Rd FK7 ... 7 E2
Abbot St 4 Glasgow G41 ... 116 C1
    Greenock PA16 ... 45 E2
    Paisley PA3 ... 113 F3
Abbot's Ave KA13 ... 207 F1
Abbot's Pl KA13 ... 207 F2
Abbot's Wlk KA13 ... 207 F2
Abbots Cres KA7 ... 238 A1
Abbots Ct FK2 ... 42 B4
Abbots Moss Dr FK1 ... 41 F1
Abbots Rd FK1 ... 42 B4
Abbots Terr ML6 ... 123 E2
Abbots Way KA7 ... 238 B2
Abbotsburn Way PA3 ... 113 E4
Abbotsford G64 ... 78 B1
Abbotsford Ave
    Cumbernauld G67 ... 162 A4
    Larkhall ML9 ... 185 D1
    Rutherglen G73 ... 138 A4
Abbotsford Brae G74 ... 159 F2
Abbotsford Cres
    Hamilton ML3 ... 162 A3
    Paisley PA2 ... 132 C4
    Shotts ML7 ... 146 C3
    Wishaw ML2 ... 165 E2
Abbotsford Ct G67 ... 82 C4
Abbotsford Dr
    Helensburgh G84 ... 25 C4
    Kirkintilloch G66 ... 79 F4
Abbotsford Gdns FK2 ... 24 A1
Abbotsford La ML4 ... 141 F3
Abbotsford Pl
    Cumbernauld G67 ... 82 C4
    4 Glasgow G5 ... 117 D2
    Glasgow, Laurieston G5 ... 117 D3
    Motherwell ML1 ... 143 D3
    Saltcoats KA21 ... 206 A1
    Stirling FK8 ... 1 B1
Abbotsford Prim Sch G5 ... 117 D2
Abbotsford Rd
    Bearsden G61 ... 75 E3
    Chapelhall ML6 ... 123 F1
    Clydebank G81 ... 74 A1
    Cumbernauld G67 ... 82 C4
    Hamilton ML3 ... 162 A3
    Wishaw ML2 ... 165 E2
Abbotsford St FK2 ... 42 A4
Abbotshall PA13 ... 215 E2
Abbotshall Rd PA13 ... 93 F1
Abbotsinch Rd G14 ... 94 B4
Abbott Cres G81 ... 94 B4
Aberconway St G81 ... 94 B4
Abercorn Ave G52 ... 114 C4
Abercorn Cres ML3 ... 162 C1
Abercorn Ind Est PA3 ... 113 F3
Abercorn Pl G23 ... 76 C1
Abercorn Rd G77 ... 156 B3
Abercorn Sec Sch G77 ... 97 D1
Abercorn St Clydebank G81 ... 74 C4
    Paisley PA3 ... 113 F3
Abercrombie Cres G69 ... 120 C3
Abercrombie Dr G61 ... 75 F4
Abercrombie Pl Kilsyth G65 ... 36 A1
    Menstrie FK11 ... 4 A3
Abercrombie St FK1 ... 41 F3
Abercromby Cres
    East Kilbride G74 ... 160 A2
    Helensburgh G84 ... 16 C2
Abercromby Dr Ayr KA7 ... 238 B2
    Bridge Of A FK9 ... 2 C1
    Glasgow G40 ... 117 F3
Abercromby Pl
    East Kilbride G74 ... 160 A2
    Stirling FK8 ... 7 D4
    Tullibody FK10 ... 4 B1
Abercromby Pl W G84 ... 16 B2
Abercromby Sq 1 G40 ... 117 F3
Abercromby St 7 G40 ... 117 F3
Abercromby St E G84 ... 16 C1
Aberdalgie Rd G34 ... 120 A4
Aberdeen Rd ML6 ... 123 E2
Aberdour St G31 ... 118 B4
Aberfeldy Ave ML6 ... 103 F2
Aberfeldy St G31 ... 118 B4
Aberfeldy Terr KA11 ... 220 A3
Aberfoyle Rd PA15 ... 46 A1
Aberfoyle St G31 ... 118 B4
Aberlady Rd G51 ... 115 F3
Aberlady St ML1 ... 144 A1
Aberlour Pl KA11 ... 219 F3
Aberlour Rd KA13 ... 219 F3
Abernethy Dr PA3 ... 112 A3
Abernethy Pk G74 ... 159 E1
Abernethy Pl G77 ... 157 D2
Abernethy St G31 ... 118 B4
Abernethyn Rd ML2 ... 166 A3
Aberuthven Dr G32 ... 119 D2
Abiagail Pl G72 ... 140 B1

Aboukir St G51 ... 115 F4
Aboyne Ave FK9 ... 2 B2
Aboyne Dr PA2 ... 113 F1
Aboyne St G51 ... 115 F3
Abronhill High Sch G67 ... 62 C2
Abronhill Prim Sch G67 ... 62 B2
Acacia Dr Barrhead G78 ... 134 A3
    Beith KA15 ... 171 D4
    Paisley PA2 ... 113 E1
Acacia Pl PA5 ... 132 A4
Academy Brae KA15 ... 171 D4
Academy Ct Hurlford KA1 ... 228 C3
    Irvine KA12 ... 219 D2
Academy Gdns KA12 ... 219 D2
Academy Pk Ardrossan KA22 ... 205 D1
    Glasgow G51 ... 116 B2
Academy Pl ... 7 F1
Academy Rd Glasgow G46 ... 136 B1
    Irvine KA12 ... 219 D2
    Stirling FK8 ... 7 F1
Academy St Airdrie ML6 ... 123 D4
    Alloa FK10 ... 9 F4
    Ayr KA7 ... 235 F1
    Coatbridge ML5 ... 122 A4
    Glasgow G32 ... 119 D2
    Hurlford KA1 ... 228 C3
    Kilmarnock KA1 ... 227 F3
    Larkhall ML9 ... 185 D2
    Troon KA10 ... 229 E1
Academy Terr ML4 ... 142 A3
Acer Cres PA2 ... 113 D1
Acer Gr ML6 ... 123 F2
Achamore Cres G15 ... 74 C2
Achamore Gr G15 ... 74 C2
Achamore Rd G15 ... 74 C2
Acherhill Gdns G13 ... 95 D4
Achill Pl G60 ... 55 B1
Achnasheen Rd ML6 ... 124 A3
Achray Ave G ... 27 E3
Achray Ct FK10 ... 10 B3
Achray Dr Paisley PA2 ... 113 D1
    Stirling FK9 ... 2 A2
Achray Rd Coatbridge ML5 ... 101 E1
    Milngavie G62 ... 54 B2
Achray Rd G62 ... 82 B3
Acorn Cres G40 ... 117 F2
Acorn Ct G40 ... 117 F2
Acorn St G40 ... 117 F2
Acre Dr G20 ... 76 A1
Acre Rd G20 ... 76 A1
Acre Valley Rd G64 ... 57 D1
Acredyke Cres G21 ... 98 B4
Acredyke Pl G21 ... 98 B3
Acredyke Rd Glasgow G21 ... 98 B4
    Rutherglen G73 ... 137 F4
Acres The ML9 ... 185 E1
Adair Ave KA21 ... 205 F1
Adam Ave ML6 ... 123 D4
Adam Cres FK5 ... 23 F1
Adam St Falkirk FK2 ... 42 B3
    Gourock PA19 ... 44 C4
    Greenock PA15 ... 46 A2
Adam's Gate KA10 ... 229 F3
Adams Ave KA21 ... 205 F1
Adams Court La G1 ... 240 C2
Adams Ct KA13 ... 229 F3
Adams Loan FK2 ... 24 A1
Adams Pl G65 ... 60 B4
Adams Wlk KA12 ... 219 F1
Adamslie Cres G66 ... 79 D4
Adamslie Dr G66 ... 79 D4
Adamson Pl FK9 ... 2 A2
Adamson St ML4 ... 142 B3
Adamswell St G21 ... 97 F2
Adamswell Terr G69 ... 81 D1
Addie St ML1 ... 143 F4
Addiewell Pl ML5 ... 122 A2
Addiewell St G32 ... 119 D4
Addison Gr G46 ... 135 F2
Addison Rd Glasgow G46 ... 135 F2
    Glasgow, Thornliebank G46 ... 135 F2
Adelaide Ct G ... 73 E3
Adelaide Rd G75 ... 180 B4
Adelaide St Gourock PA19 ... 44 C4
    Helensburgh G84 ... 16 C1
Adele St ML1 ... 163 F2
Adelphi St G5 ... 117 E3
Admiral St G41 ... 116 C3
Admiralty Gdns G60 ... 73 D3
Admiralty Gr G60 ... 73 D3
Admiralty Pl G60 ... 73 D3
Advie Pl G42 ... 137 D4
Affric Ave ML6 ... 104 A2
Affric Dr Falkirk FK2 ... 24 B1
    Paisley PA2 ... 114 A1
Affric Loan ML7 ... 146 C3
Afton Ave Kilmarnock KA3 ... 223 D2
    Prestwick KA9 ... 236 B3
Afton Cres G61 ... 76 A2
Afton Ct Ayr KA7 ... 239 D3
    Irvine KA12 ... 219 D1
    Stirling FK7 ... 7 E2
Afton Dr Denny FK6 ... 39 E4
    Renfrew PA4 ... 94 C2
Afton Gdns Blantyre G72 ... 161 D3
    Troon KA10 ... 229 F2
Afton Rd Cumbernauld G67 ... 62 A2
    Stevenston KA20 ... 217 E4
    Stirling, Glasgow G41 ... 116 C1
    Larkhall ML9 ... 185 E1
Afton View KA20 ... 58 C1
Agamemnon St G81 ... 73 F1

Agnew Ave ML6 ... 122 B4
Agnew Gr ML4 ... 141 E3
Agnew La G42 ... 137 D4
Aikenhead House G44 ... 137 E3
Aikenhead Rd G44 ... 137 E4
Aikman Pl G74 ... 160 A2
Aikman Rd ML1 ... 163 D3
Aiknut Rd KA23 ... 190 B2
Ailean Dr G32 ... 119 F2
Ailean Gdns G32 ... 119 F2
Aileymill Gdns PA16 ... 44 C2
Aillort Pl G74 ... 159 F2
Ailort Ave G44 ... 137 D3
Ailort Loan 1 ML2 ... 165 F3
Ailsa Ave Ashgill ML9 ... 199 F4
    Motherwell ML1 ... 163 D4
Ailsa Cres ML1 ... 163 D4
Ailsa Ct Coatbridge ML5 ... 121 F2
    Hamilton ML3 ... 183 E3
Ailsa Dr Bothwell G71 ... 141 D2
    Clydebank G81 ... 74 B3
    Glasgow G42 ... 136 C4
    Kirkintilloch G66 ... 58 C1
    Paisley PA2 ... 133 E4
    Rutherglen G46 ... 157 E4
    Rutherglen, Croftfoot G73 ... 137 F3
    Stevenston KA20 ... 217 E4
Ailsa Gdns KA22 ... 205 E2
Ailsa Hospl KA6 ... 239 F1
Ailsa Pl Ayr KA7 ... 238 A4
    Coatbridge ML5 ... 121 F2
    Kilmarnock KA3 ... 223 D3
Ailsa Rd Bishopbriggs G64 ... 78 A1
    Coatbridge ML5 ... 121 F2
    Gourock PA19 ... 44 B4
    Irvine KA12 ... 224 A4
    Renfrew PA4 ... 94 B1
    Saltcoats KA21 ... 206 A1
    Troon KA10 ... 229 D2
Ailsa St G74 ... 138 C2
Ailsa View KA22 ... 205 F1
Ainsdale Ct KA13 ... 207 D2
Ainslie Ave G52 ... 115 D4
Ainslie Rd Cumbernauld G67 ... 62 B2
    Glasgow G52 ... 115 D4
Airbles Cres ML1 ... 163 E3
Airbles Dr ML1 ... 163 E3
Airbles Farm Rd ML1 ... 163 E3
Airbles Rd ML1 ... 163 E3
Airbles St ML1 ... 163 F3
Aird Ave KA1 ... 227 F4
Aird's La G1 ... 241 D1
Airdale Ave G46 ... 136 B1
Airdrie Acad ML6 ... 123 D3
Airdrie Rd Caldercruix ML6 ... 105 E1
    Carluke ML8 ... 187 F2
    Cumbernauld G67 ... 82 A3
    Cumbernauld, Condorrat G67 ... 82 A4
    Cumbernauld, Mollinsburn
    ... 81 F2
    Kilsyth G65 ... 60 B4
    Plains ML6 ... 103 F1
Airdrie Sta ML6 ... 123 D4
Airdriehill Rd ML6 ... 103 E1
Airdriehill St ML6 ... 103 E1
Airgold Dr G15 ... 74 C2
Airlie Ave G61 ... 75 F4
Airlie Ct KA7 ... 238 C3
Airlie Dr ML4 ... 142 A3
Airlie Gdns G73 ... 138 B2
Airlie La G12 ... 96 A2
Airlie Rd G69 ... 120 A2
Airlie St G12 ... 96 A2
Airlink Ind Est PA3 ... 113 F4
Airlour Rd G43 ... 136 C3
Airth Ct ML1 ... 142 B1
Airth Dr Glasgow G52 ... 115 F2
    Stirling FK7 ... 7 E2
Airth La G52 ... 115 F2
Airth Prim Sch FK2 ... 14 C2
Airth Way G68 ... 81 F4
Airthrey Ave Bridge Of A FK9 ... 2 A3
    Glasgow G14 ... 95 F2
Airthrey Dr FK5 ... 24 A2
Airthrey La G14 ... 95 F2
Airthrey Rd FK9 ... 2 A3
Airylligg Dr G76 ... 178 C3
Aitchison Ct ML6 ... 122 C4
Aitchison Dr FK5 ... 23 D2
Aitchison St ML6 ... 122 C4
Aitken Ct ML2 ... 166 A4
Aitken Cres FK7 ... 7 D1
Aitken Dr Beith KA15 ... 150 B1
    Slamannan FK1 ... 86 A3
Aitken Gdns FK1 ... 41 F1
Aitken La G83 ... 27 F3
Aitken Rd Ardrossan KA22 ... 205 E2
    Lanark ML11 ... 215 D2
Aitken St Airdrie ML6 ... 123 E4
    Dalry KA24 ... 191 E4
    Glasgow G31 ... 118 B4
Aitken Terr FK1 ... 41 E3
Aitkenbar Circ G82 ... 50 A3
Aitkenbar Dr G82 ... 50 A3
Aitkenbar Prim Sch G82 ... 50 A3
Aitkenbrae Dr KA9 ... 236 B4
Aitkenhead Ave ML5 ... 121 D2
Aitkenhead Prim Sch
    G71 ... 120 C1
Aitkenhead Rd
    Chapelhall ML6 ... 123 E1
    Uddingston G71 ... 121 D1
Akarit Rd FK5 ... 23 F1
Alan Wlk FK9 ... 1 C4

Alasdair Ct G78 ... 134 B1
Alba Way ML3 ... 183 E3
Albans Cres ML1 ... 163 D4
Albany C74 ... 160 B2
Albany Ave G32 ... 119 E3
Albany Dr Lanark ML11 ... 215 D2
    Rutherglen G73 ... 138 A3
Albany Pl G71 ... 141 D2
Albany Quadrant G32 ... 119 E3
Albany Rd ML3 ... 183 E4
Albany St Coatbridge ML5 ... 121 F4
    Glasgow G40 ... 118 A2
Albany Terr G72 ... 138 C2
Albany Way ML1 ... 143 D3
Albany Wynd 1 ML9 ... 185 D2
Albert Ave Glasgow G42 ... 117 D1
    Stewarton KA3 ... 195 F1
Albert Cres ML6 ... 123 D4
Albert Cross G41 ... 117 D1
Albert Ct KA3 ... 195 F1
Albert Dr Bearsden G61 ... 76 A2
    Glasgow G41 ... 116 B2
    Helensburgh G84 ... 16 C1
    Larkhall ML9 ... 185 D3
    Rutherglen G73 ... 138 A3
Albert Pl Airdrie ML6 ... 123 D4
    Stewarton KA3 ... 195 F1
    Stirling FK8 ... 7 D4
Albert Prim Sch
    Airdrie ML6 ... 123 D4
    Glasgow G21 ... 97 F3
Albert Quadrant ML1 ... 143 D3
Albert Rd Brookfield PA5 ... 111 E3
    Clydebank G81 ... 74 A2
    Glasgow G42 ... 117 D1
    Gourock PA19 ... 44 B4
    Harthill ML7 ... 127 F3
    Kirkintilloch G66 ... 79 E2
    Renfrew PA4 ... 94 B2
Albert St Alexandria G83 ... 27 F2
    Coatbridge ML5 ... 122 A4
    Hamilton ML3 ... 162 A3
    Helensburgh G84 ... 16 C1
Albert Terr Ayr KA8 ... 239 D4
    Hamilton ML3 ... 162 A3
Albert Wynd KA3 ... 195 F1
Alberta Ave
    Coatbridge ML5 ... 121 F4
    East Kilbride G75 ... 180 B4
Alberta Cres 1 G75 ... 180 B4
Alberta Pk G75 ... 180 B4
Alberta Pl 3 G75 ... 180 B4
Albion Gate Glasgow G1 ... 241 E2
    Paisley PA3 ... 113 E3
Albion St Coatbridge ML5 ... 122 B3
    Glasgow G1 ... 241 E2
    Glasgow, North Mount Vernon
    G69 ... 119 F2
    Motherwell ML1 ... 163 F3
    Paisley PA3 ... 113 F3
Albion Way G75 ... 180 A3
Albion Works Ind Est G13 ... 94 C4
Alcaig Rd G52 ... 115 F1
Alcath Rd ML2 ... 186 B4
Alder Ave Hamilton ML3 ... 162 C1
    Kirkintilloch G66 ... 79 D3
Alder Bank Ayr KA7 ... 239 E3
    Uddingston G71 ... 121 E1
Alder Cres G75 ... 180 B3
Alder Ct G Barrhead G78 ... 134 B2
    East Kilbride G75 ... 180 B3
Alder Gate G72 ... 139 F3
Alder Gn KA11 ... 220 A2
Alder Gr ML5 ... 122 A3
Alder La ML1 ... 143 D2
Alder Pl East Kilbride G75 ... 180 B3
    Glasgow G43 ... 136 B3
    Johnstone PA5 ... 112 A1
    Kilmarnock KA1 ... 227 E4
Alder Rd Clydebank G81 ... 74 A3
    Cumbernauld G67 ... 82 B1
    Dumbarton G82 ... 49 F2
    Glasgow G43 ... 136 B3
    Milton Of C G65 ... 58 A2
Alderbank Rd PA14 ... 47 D1
Alderbrae Rd PA14 ... 47 D1
Alderman Pl G13 ... 95 E3
Alderman Rd G13 ... 95 D3
Alderside Gdns G71 ... 140 C4
Alderside Pl 12 G71 ... 141 D2
Alderstocks G75 ... 180 C3
Alderston Ave KA8 ... 236 A2
Alderston Pk KA8 ... 236 A2
Alderston Pl KA8 ... 236 A2
    Bellshill ML4 ... 141 F2
Alderside Ave Troon KA10 ... 229 D2
    Wishaw ML2 ... 164 B2
Aldersyde Pl G72 ... 140 B1
Aldersyde Terr ML1 ... 144 B1
Alderwood Rd PA14 ... 47 D1
Aldrin Rd G84 ... 25 D4
Alexander Ave
    Eaglesham G76 ... 178 C3
    Falkirk FK2 ... 42 C3
    Stevenston KA20 ... 206 C1
    Twechar G65 ... 59 F2
Alexander Balfour Gdns
    ML3 ... 162 B1
Alexander Dr KA9 ... 233 B1
Alexander Fleming Ave
    KA3 ... 148 C1
Alexander Gdns ML3 ... 163 D1
Alexander Gibson Way
    ML1 ... 163 E3
Alexander Hospl ML5 ... 121 F4

Alexander McLeod Pl FK7 ... 8 C2
Alexander Path ML1 ... 164 A2
Alexander Pl Irvine KA12 ... 219 E2
    Kirkintilloch G66 ... 80 A4
    Rhu G84 ... 15 E4
Alexander Rd ML7 ... 146 B3
Alexander St Airdrie ML6 ... 122 C4
    Clydebank G81 ... 74 A1
    Coatbridge ML5 ... 122 A4
    Dumbarton G82 ... 50 A2
    Renton G82 ... 49 E4
    Wishaw ML2 ... 165 D1
Alexander Terr G78 ... 154 B3
Alexandra Ave
    Kirkintilloch G66 ... 79 E2
    Prestwick KA9 ... 233 E1
    Stepps G33 ... 99 E3
Alexandra Cross G31 ... 118 A4
Alexandra Ct G31 ... 118 A4
Alexandra Dr Alloa FK10 ... 9 F4
    Paisley PA2 ... 113 D2
    Renfrew PA4 ... 94 B2
Alexandra Gdns G66 ... 79 E2
Alexandra Par G31 ... 118 A4
Alexandra Parade Prim Sch
    ... 118 A4
Alexandra Parade Sta
    G31 ... 118 A4
Alexandra Park St G31 ... 118 A4
Alexandra Pk G66 ... 79 E2
Alexandra Pl FK6 ... 2 B1
Alexandra Prim Sch ML6 ... 123 D4
Alexandra Rd G66 ... 79 E2
Alexandra St G66 ... 79 E4
Alexandra Terr Ayr KA6 ... 236 A2
    Kilwinning KA13 ... 207 E2
Alexandra Quadrant ML3 ... 163 D1
Alexandra Sta G31 ... 27 F2
Alford Ave G66 ... 79 D4
Alford Pl Irvine KA11 ... 219 F3
    Linwood PA3 ... 111 F3
Alford Quadrant ML2 ... 165 D3
Alford St G21 ... 97 E2
Alfred La 11 G12 ... 96 C2
Algie St G41 ... 136 C4
Algoma Pl G75 ... 180 A4
Alice Ave ML4 ... 142 A2
Alice St PA2 ... 113 F1
Alice Ct G78 ... 134 A2
Alison Lea G74 ... 160 B2
All Saints RC Sec Sch G21 ... 98 B2
Allan Ave Carluke ML8 ... 187 F2
    Renfrew PA4 ... 94 C1
Allan Barr Ct FK1 ... 42 A1
Allan Cres Alexandria G83 ... 27 F2
    Denny FK6 ... 21 E2
    Dumbarton G82 ... 50 A3
Allan Ct G75 ... 179 F4
Allan Pk FK8 ... 2 A2
Allan Pl Ayr KA8 ... 236 B2
    Dumbarton G82 ... 50 A2
Allan Sq KA12 ... 219 F1
Allan St Coatbridge ML5 ... 121 E3
    Glasgow G40 ... 118 A1
    Motherwell ML1 ... 163 F4
Allan's Prim Sch FK8 ... 7 D4
Allanbank Rd FK7 ... 23 E1
Allanbank St ML7 ... 166 C4
Allandale Ave ML1 ... 143 F3
Allandale Cotts FK4 ... 39 E1
Allander Ave G64 ... 77 D4
Allander Dr G64 ... 78 A4
Allander Gdns G64 ... 77 F2
Allander Rd G62 ... 55 D1
Allands Ave PA4 ... 93 E3
Allanfauld Rd
    Cumbernauld G67 ... 61 F1
    Kilsyth G65 ... 36 B1
Allanshaw Gdns ML3 ... 162 A2
Allanshaw Gr ML3 ... 162 A1
Allanshaw Ind Est ML3 ... 162 A2
Allanshaw St ML3 ... 162 A2
Allanton Ave PA1 ... 114 C2
Allanton Dr G52 ... 115 E3
Allanton Gr ML2 ... 165 D3
Allanton Lea ML3 ... 183 E4
Allanton Pl ML3 ... 162 C1
Allanton Prim Sch ML7 ... 162 F1
Allanton Rd Shotts ML7 ... 146 B1
    Wishaw ML2, ML7 ... 166 C4
Allanton Terr ML3 ... 184 B4
Allanvale KA3 ... 195 D4
Allanvale Rd Bridge Of A FK9 ... 1 C4
    Prestwick KA9 ... 236 A4
Allanwater Gdns FK9 ... 2 A4
Allanwood Ct FK9 ... 2 A4
Allbany Cres ML1 ... 142 C3
Allen Way PA4 ... 94 B1
Allendale G74 ... 159 E2
Allender Rd G61 ... 75 E1
Allenfield Rd KA7 ... 239 E3
Allenshaw Ind Est ML3 ... 162 B2
Allerdyce Dr G15 ... 74 C1
Allershaw Pl ML2 ... 186 B4
Allershaw Rd ML2 ... 186 B4
Allershaw Tower ML2 ... 185 F4
Allerton Gdns G69 ... 119 F2
Alleysbank Rd G73 ... 118 A1
Allison Ave PA8 ... 72 C2
Allison Dr G72 ... 139 D3
Allison Pl Gartcosh G69 ... 100 C2
    3 Glasgow G42 ... 117 D1
    Newton Mearns G77 ... 156 B2

Allison St Ayr KA8 .... 236 A1
Glasgow G42 .... 117 D1
Allnach Pl G34 .... 120 C4
Alloa Acad FK10 .... 9 F4
Alloa Rd Falkirk FK2 .... 24 A2
Fishcross FK10 .... 5 E2
Menstrie FK9 .... 3 D2
Stenhousemuir FK5 .... 23 F2
Tullibody FK10 .... 4 B2
Alloa Tower FK10 .... 10 A3
Alloway KA7 .... 238 C1
Alloway Ave
Kilmarnock KA3 .... 228 A4
Paisley PA2 .... 134 A4
Alloway Cres
Bonnybridge FK4 .... 39 F3
Paisley PA2 .... 134 B4
Rutherglen G73 .... 137 F3
Alloway Ct G66 .... 59 D1
Alloway Dr Clydebank G81 .... 74 B2
Cowie FK7 .... 12 B4
Kirkintilloch G66 .... 59 D1
Newton Mearns G77 .... 157 D2
Paisley PA2 .... 134 A4
Rutherglen G73 .... 137 F3
Alloway Gdns
Hamilton ML3 .... 161 E1
Kirkintilloch G66 .... 59 D1
Alloway Gr G66 .... 58 C1
Alloway Pk KA7 .... 238 C4
Alloway Pl Ardrossan KA22 .... 205 E2
Ayr KA7 .... 238 C4
Alloway Place La KA7 .... 238 C4
Alloway Quadrant G66 .... 59 D1
Alloway Rd Airdrie ML6 .... 123 F4
East Kilbride G74 .... 160 C2
Glasgow G43 .... 136 B3
Alloway St Ayr KA7 .... 238 C4
4 Larkhall ML9 .... 185 E1
Alloway Terr G66 .... 58 C1
Alloway Wynd ML1 .... 143 F2
Alma La FK2 .... 42 A3
Alma St Falkirk FK2 .... 42 A3
Glasgow G40 .... 118 A3
Alma Terr FK2 .... 42 A3
Almada La ML3 .... 162 B2
Almada St ML3 .... 162 B2
Almada St ML3 .... 162 B2
Almond Ave PA4 .... 94 C1
Almond Cres PA2 .... 112 C1
Almond Ct Falkirk FK2 .... 42 C4
Stirling FK7 .... 7 F3
Almond Dr Banknock FK4 .... 38 C1
Bishopton PA7 .... 72 A1
East Kilbride G74 .... 160 A1
Kirkintilloch G66 .... 79 D3
Almond Pl Coatbridge ML5 .... 101 E1
Kilmarnock KA1 .... 227 E4
Motherwell ML1 .... 143 D3
Almond Rd Bearsden G61 .... 75 E1
Cumbernauld G67 .... 62 C2
Falkirk FK2 .... 42 C4
Steeps G33 .... 99 E3
Almond St G33 .... 98 B1
Almond Terr ML7 .... 127 E3
Almond Vale G71 .... 141 D4
Almond Way ML1 .... 163 F2
Almondbank ML6 .... 103 F2
Almswall Rd KA13 .... 207 F2
Alness Cres G52 .... 115 F2
Alness St ML3 .... 162 B1
Alness Terr ML3 .... 162 B1
Alnwick Dr G76 .... 178 B2
Aloa Way **9** ML9 .... 185 E1
Alpha Cr G81 .... 94 B4
Alpine Gr G71 .... 140 C4
Alsatian Ave G81 .... 74 B1
Alsh Terr ML3 .... 162 A1
Alston Ave ML5 .... 122 A4
Alston Gdns G41 .... 75 D4
Altnacreag Gdns G69 .... 81 D2
Altnock Pl KA24 .... 191 D4
Alton Rd PA1 .... 114 B2
Alton St ML3 .... 190 B3
Alton Way KA23 .... 190 B2
Altonhead Dr KA3 .... 210 A1
Altonhead Terr KA3 .... 221 D4
Altonhill Ave KA3 .... 222 C2
Altry Pl KA7 .... 238 A1
Altyre St G32 .... 118 C2
Aluclutha Ave G82 .... 50 A2
Alva Acad FK12 .... 5 D4
Alva Gate G52 .... 115 F2
Alva Gdns Bearsden G61 .... 75 E4
Glasgow G52 .... 115 F2
Alva Glen FK12 .... 5 D4
Alva Ind Est FK12 .... 5 D3
Alva Pl G66 .... 79 F2
Alva Prim Sch FK12 .... 5 D3
Alva Terr PA19 .... 45 D4
Alvord Ave KA9 .... 233 E1
Alwyn Ave PA6 .... 111 E4
Alwyn Ct G74 .... 159 F2
Alwyn Dr G74 .... 159 F2
Alyssum Cres ML1 .... 163 E4
Alyth Cres G76 .... 158 A4
Alyth Gdns Clarkston G76 .... 158 A4
Glasgow G52 .... 115 F2
Ambassador Way PA4 .... 94 B1
Amber Terr ML4 .... 142 A2
Ambleside G75 .... 180 A3
Ambleside Rise ML3 .... 183 E3
Amethyst Ave ML4 .... 142 A4
Amisfield St G20 .... 96 C3
Amlaird Rd KA3 .... 223 D3

Amochrie Dr PA2 .... 133 D4
Amochrie Glen PA2 .... 133 D4
Amulree Pl G32 .... 119 D2
Amulree St G32 .... 119 D2
Ancaster Dr G13 .... 95 F3
Ancaster La G13 .... 95 F3
Anchor Ave PA1 .... 114 A2
Anchor Cres PA1 .... 114 A2
Anchor Dr PA1 .... 114 A2
Anchor La G1 .... 241 D2
Anchor Wynd PA1 .... 114 A2
Ancroft St G20 .... 97 D2
Anderson Ct G75 .... 180 C3
Anderside G75 .... 180 C3
Anderson Ave G65 .... 36 A1
Anderson Cres Ayr KA2 .... 239 D2
Prestwick KA9 .... 236 C4
Queenzieburn G65 .... 59 F4
Sheldhill FK1 .... 66 C3
Anderson Ct ML4 .... 142 A3
Anderson Dr Denny FK6 .... 21 F1
Falkirk FK2 .... 24 A1
Irvine KA12 .... 219 E3
Newton Mearns G77 .... 156 B2
Renfrew PA4 .... 94 B2
Saltcoats KA21 .... 206 A1
Anderson Gdns G72 .... 140 C1
Anderson La ML6 .... 123 D4
Anderson Park Rd FK6 .... 21 F1
Anderson Pl FK7 .... 7 D2
Kilmarnock KA3 .... 223 E1
Stirling FK7 .... 7 D2
Anderson Rd PA7 .... 72 A2
Anderson St Airdrie ML6 .... 123 D3
Bonnybridge FK4 .... 40 A3
Glasgow G11 .... 96 A1
Hamilton ML3 .... 161 F3
Motherwell ML1 .... 163 F3
Port Glasgow PA14 .... 47 E1
Anderson Terr
Ardrossan KA22 .... 205 E1
Longcroft FK4 .... 39 D2
Anderston Cross Sh Ctr
G2 .... 240 B2
Anderston Prim Sch G3 .... 240 A2
Anderston Quay G3 .... 240 A1
Anderston Sta G3 .... 240 B2
Andrew Ave
Kirkintilloch G66 .... 79 E2
Renfrew PA4 .... 94 C2
Andrew Cres FK5 .... 23 E2
Andrew Dr G81 .... 94 B4
Andrew Pl ML8 .... 187 F2
Andrew Sillars Ave G72 .... 139 E3
Andrew St G75 .... 179 F1
Andrews St PA3 .... 113 F3
Anford Pl G72 .... 161 F3
Angela Way G71 .... 140 C3
Angle Gate G14 .... 95 E2
Angle St ML9 .... 198 C1
Angus Ave Airdrie ML6 .... 123 D3
Bishopbriggs G64 .... 78 B1
East Kilbride G74 .... 160 A1
Glasgow G52 .... 115 E2
Hamilton ML3 .... 163 D2
Motherwell ML1 .... 163 E4
Prestwick KA9 .... 236 B4
Angus Gdns G71 .... 140 C4
Angus Oval G52 .... 115 D2
Angus Pl East Kilbride G74 .... 160 A1
Glasgow G52 .... 115 D2
Angus Rd Carluke ML8 .... 188 A1
Greenock PA16 .... 44 B2
Port Glasgow PA14 .... 47 E1
Angus St Alexandria G83 .... 27 F2
Clydebank G81 .... 94 C4
Glasgow G21 .... 97 F2
Angus Wlk G71 .... 141 D4
Ann Ct ML3 .... 162 A3
Ann St Greenock PA15 .... 45 F3
Greenock, Central PA15 .... 45 F2
Hamilton ML3 .... 162 A3
Johnstone PA5 .... 112 A2
Annabella Rd ML9 .... 200 B2
Annan Ave G75 .... 179 F4
Annan Cres ML6 .... 123 E1
Annan Ct FK1 .... 42 A1
Annan Dr Bearsden G61 .... 75 E2
Paisley PA2 .... 112 C1
Rutherglen G73 .... 138 B4
Annan Glade ML1 .... 164 A2
Annan Gr ML1 .... 164 A2
Annan Pl PA5 .... 131 E4
Annan Rd ML1 .... 228 A3
Annan St Glasgow G42 .... 137 D4
Motherwell ML1 .... 164 A2
Annandale ML1 .... 83 F1
Annandale Cres KA2 .... 221 F1
Annandale Gdns KA2 .... 221 F1
Annandale La KA2 .... 221 F1
Annandale View KA2 .... 221 F1
Annandale Way KA11 .... 220 A3
Annanhill Ave KA1 .... 222 B1
Annanhill Pl KA13 .... 207 D2
Annanhill Prim Sch KA1 .... 227 E4
Annathill Gdns ML5 .... 81 F1
Annbank Pl G31 .... 117 F3
Annbank St Glasgow G31 .... 117 F3
Larkhall ML9 .... 184 C2
Anne Ave PA4 .... 94 B2
Anne Cres G66 .... 79 E2
Anne Dr Bridge Of A FK9 .... 2 A3
Stenhousemuir FK5 .... 23 E2
Anne St FK10 .... 9 F4
Annerley Ct ML5 .... 121 F3
Annerley Pl ML5 .... 121 F3
Annes Ct G40 .... 117 F2

Annet Rd FK6 .... 39 E1
Annette St G42 .... 117 D1
Annette Street Prim Sch
G42 .... 117 D1
Annfield Dr FK7 .... 7 E3
Annfield Gdns
Blantyre G72 .... 140 B1
Stirling FK8 .... 7 D3
Annfield Glen Rd KA7 .... 239 D2
Annfield Pl G31 .... 117 F4
Annfield Rd KA9 .... 236 A4
Annfield Terr KA9 .... 236 A4
Annick Cotts KA3 .... 196 B3
Annick Cres KA11 .... 211 F4
Annick Ct KA12 .... 219 E1
Annick Dr Bearsden G61 .... 75 E1
Irvine KA11 .... 220 A1
Annick Pl Kilmarnock KA1 .... 228 A3
Troon KA10 .... 229 F2
Annick Prim Sch KA1 .... 220 A3
Annick Rd
Irvine KA12, KA11 .... 219 F1
Irvine, Broomlands KA11 .... 220 A1
Annick Rdbt KA12 .... 219 F1
Annick St Cambuslang G72 .... 139 E3
Glasgow G32 .... 119 D3
Annick St Ind Est G32 .... 119 E3
Annick View KA12 .... 219 F1
Anniesdale Ave G33 .... 99 E3
Annieshill View ML6 .... 104 A1
Anniesland Coll G12 .... 96 A3
Anniesland Cres G14 .... 95 D3
Anniesland Ind Est G13 .... 95 F4
Anniesland Rd G13 .... 95 E3
Anniesland Sta G13 .... 95 E3
Anniston G65 .... 59 F2
Anniversary Ave G75 .... 180 B4
Annpit Rd KA8 .... 236 A2
Annsfield Rd ML3 .... 183 E4
Ansdell Ave G72 .... 161 F4
Anson Ave FK1 .... 41 F2
Anson St G40 .... 117 F2
Anson Way **6** PA4 .... 94 B1
Anstruther Ct ML8 .... 186 C3
Anstruther St
Glasgow G32 .... 118 C3
Law ML8 .... 186 C3
Antermony Rd G65 .... 58 C3
Anthony St G2 .... 240 B2
Antigua St PA15 .... 46 A2
Antigua Way G75 .... 159 D1
Anton Cres G65 .... 60 C4
Antonine G66 .... 59 D1
Antonine Ave ML1 .... 163 E4
Antonine Gdns
Clydebank G81 .... 74 A3
Falkirk FK1 .... 41 E3
Antonine Gr FK4 .... 39 E2
Antonine Prim Sch FK4 .... 40 A2
Antonine Rd ML1 .... 75 D3
Antonine St FK1 .... 41 E3
Antrim La ML9 .... 185 D2
Anwoth St G32 .... 119 D2
Apollo Path ML1 .... 143 D3
Appin Ct G66 .... 59 D1
Appin Rd G31 .... 118 A4
Appin Terr Hamilton ML3 .... 161 F2
Rutherglen G73 .... 138 B2
Shotts ML7 .... 147 D2
Appin Way
2 Bothwell G71 .... 141 D2
Glenmavis ML6 .... 102 C2
Appleby Ct G75 .... 179 F3
Appleby St G22 .... 97 D2
Applecross Gdns G69 .... 80 C2
Applecross Quadrant
ML1 .... 165 D3
Applecross Rd G66 .... 59 D1
Applecross St G22 .... 97 D2
Appledore Cres G71 .... 141 D2
Appleyard Ct ML4 .... 141 F2
Applin St ML4 .... 141 F2
Apsley La G11 .... 96 A1
Apsley St G11 .... 96 A1
Aqua Ave ML3 .... 161 F1
Aqua Ct ML3 .... 161 F1
Aquila Way ML8 .... 187 E1
Araburn Dr G75 .... 180 C3
Aranthrue Cres PA4 .... 94 B2
Aranthrue Dr PA4 .... 94 B2
Aray St G20 .... 96 B3
Arbroath Ave G52 .... 115 D2
Arbroath Cres FK9 .... 2 A2
Arbroath Gr ML3 .... 162 A2
Arbuckle Pl ML6 .... 104 A2
Arbuckle St KA1 .... 228 A4
Arbuthnot St FK1 .... 41 F3
Arcade FK8 .... 7 D4
Arcadia St Bellshill ML4 .... 142 A4
Glasgow G40 .... 117 F3
Arcan Cres G15 .... 75 D1
Arch Way G65 .... 36 B1
Archerfield Ave G32 .... 119 D1
Archerfield Cres G32 .... 119 D1
Archerfield Dr G32 .... 119 D1
Archerfield Gr G32 .... 119 D1
Archerhill Ave G13 .... 95 D4
Archerhill Cotts G13 .... 95 D4
Archerhill Cres G13 .... 95 D4
Archerhill Gdns G13 .... 95 D4
Archerhill Rd G13 .... 94 C4
Archerhill Sq G13 .... 94 C4
Archerhill Terr G13 .... 95 D4
Archers Ave FK7 .... 7 F2
Archibald Dr KA24 .... 191 D4
Archibald Terr G65 .... 58 B3
Archibald Pl ML4 .... 142 B2
Archray Rd G67 .... 82 A3
Arcon Ave KA4 .... 237 F3
Ard La **6** ML2 .... 165 F3

Ard Loan ML1 .... 143 D3
Ard Rd PA4 .... 94 A2
Ard St G32 .... 119 D2
Ardardan Cotts G82 .... 25 F1
Ardargie Dr G32 .... 139 E4
Ardargie Gr G32 .... 139 E4
Ardargie Pl G32 .... 139 E4
Ardayre Rd KA9 .... 236 A4
Ardbeg Ave
Bishopbriggs G64 .... 78 B1
Kilmarnock KA3 .... 222 C2
Rutherglen G73 .... 138 C2
Ardbeg Ct KA11 .... 219 F3
Ardbeg La G41 .... 117 D1
Ardbeg Rd PA15 .... 46 B1
Ardbeg St G42 .... 117 D1
Ardchoille Dr KA20 .... 206 C1
Ardchoille La KA20 .... 206 C1
Ardchoille St G46 .... 135 F2
Ardeer La KA20 .... 217 F3
Ardeer Prim Sch KA21 .... 217 D4
Arden Ave G46 .... 135 F1
Arden Ct ML3 .... 162 B1
Arden Dr G46 .... 136 A2
Arden Gr G65 .... 36 B1
Arden Hill G44 .... 15 E3
Arden Pl G46 .... 135 F1
Arden Prim Sch G46 .... 135 E2
Arden Rd Greenock PA15 .... 46 B1
Hamilton ML3 .... 162 B2
Arden St ML6 .... 104 A1
Arden Terr ML3 .... 162 B1
Ardencaple Dr G84 .... 16 A1
Ardencaple Quadrant G84 .... 16 A1
Ardenclutha Ave ML3 .... 162 A2
Ardenclutha Dr PA14 .... 47 D1
Ardenconnel Ho G84 .... 15 E3
Ardenconnel Way G84 .... 15 E3
Ardencraig Cres G45 .... 137 E1
Ardencraig Dr G45 .... 138 A1
Ardencraig Pl G45 .... 137 F2
Ardencraig Quadrant G45 .... 137 F1
Ardencraig Rd G45 .... 137 F1
Ardencraig St G45 .... 138 A1
Ardencraig Terr G45 .... 137 F1
Ardenlea G71 .... 140 C4
Ardenlea St G40 .... 118 A2
Ardery St G11 .... 96 A1
Ardessie St G23 .... 76 B1
Ardfern Rd ML6 .... 124 A3
Ardfern St G32 .... 119 D2
Ardfin Ct KA9 .... 236 B3
Ardfin Rd KA9 .... 236 B3
Ardgare G84 .... 15 D4
Ardgay Pl G32 .... 119 D2
Ardgay St G32 .... 119 D2
Ardgay Way G73 .... 138 A2
Ardgour Ct G72 .... 161 F3
Ardgour Dr PA3 .... 112 A3
Ardgour Pl KA3 .... 222 C2
Ardgowan Ave PA2 .... 113 F2
Ardgowan Ct PA2 .... 114 A2
Ardgowan Dr G71 .... 140 C4
Ardgowan Pl ML7 .... 146 C3
Ardgowan Prim Sch PA16 .... 45 E3
Ardgowan St
Greenock PA16 .... 45 F3
Paisley PA2 .... 113 F2
Port Glasgow PA14 .... 47 D1
Ardgowan Terrace La G3 .... 96 B1
Ardgryfe Cres PA6 .... 91 E1
Ardholm St G32 .... 119 D3
Ardhu Pl G15 .... 75 D2
Ardlamont Sq PA3 .... 112 B3
Ardle Ave KA1 .... 228 A3
Ardle Ct G44 .... 136 C3
Ardle Rd G43 .... 136 C2
Ardlui Gdns G62 .... 54 B2
Ardlui St G32 .... 118 C2
Ardmaleish Cres G45 .... 137 F1
Ardmaleish Dr G45 .... 137 F1
Ardmaleish Rd G45 .... 137 F1
Ardmaleish St G45 .... 137 F1
Ardmaleish Terr G45 .... 137 F1
Ardmay Cres G44 .... 137 E4
Ardmillan KA13 .... 207 D1
Ardmillan St G33 .... 118 C4
Ardmore Ct KA11 .... 220 A3
Ardmore Pl PA15 .... 45 F2
Ardmore Rd
Greenock PA15 .... 46 B1
Port Glasgow PA14 .... 68 B4
Ardmory Ave G42 .... 137 E4
Ardmory La G42 .... 137 F4
Ardmory Pl G42 .... 137 E4
Ardnahoe Ave G42 .... 137 F4
Ardnahoe Pl G42 .... 137 E4
Ardneil Ave KA23 .... 190 B2
Ardneil Ct KA22 .... 205 D2
Ardneil Rd G51 .... 115 F4
Ardo Gdns G51 .... 116 A3
Ardoch Cres
Dumbarton G82 .... 49 E2
Stevenston KA20 .... 217 F3
Ardoch Ct G42 .... 137 E4
Ardoch Gdns G72 .... 138 C3
Ardoch Gr G72 .... 138 C3
Ardoch Path **17** ML2 .... 165 F3
Ardoch Rd G60 .... 76 A3
Ardoch St G22 .... 97 E2
Ardoch Way G69 .... 80 C1
Ardochrig G75 .... 180 C3
Ardrossie Pl G20 .... 96 B3
Ardrossan Acad KA22 .... 205 E1

Ardrossan Harbour Sta
KA22 .... 205 D1
Ardrossan High Rd KA13 .... 190 C2
Ardrossan Rd
Saltcoats KA21 .... 216 C4
Seamill KA23 .... 190 B1
Ardrossan South Beach Sta
KA22 .... 205 E1
Ardrossan Town Sta
KA22 .... 205 E1
Ardshiel Rd G51 .... 115 F4
Ardsloy La G14 .... 95 D2
Ardsloy Pl G14 .... 95 D2
Ardtoe Cres G33 .... 99 F3
Ardtoe Pl G33 .... 99 F3
Arduthie Rd G51 .... 115 F4
Ardvreck Pl FK2 .... 24 A2
Ardwell Rd G52 .... 115 F2
Argosy Way **3** PA4 .... 94 B1
Argus Ave ML6 .... 123 E1
Argyle Cres Airdrie ML6 .... 122 C3
Hamilton ML3 .... 161 F2
Argyle Dr ML3 .... 162 A2
Argyle Pk KA8 .... 236 A1
Argyle Pl Kilsyth G65 .... 60 C4
Saltcoats KA21 .... 216 C4
Argyle Pl Bearsden G61 .... 75 F4
Gourock PA19 .... 44 C3
Saltcoats KA21 .... 216 C4
Argyle St Glasgow G2 .... 240 C2
Glasgow, Anderston G3 .... 240 A2
Greenock PA15 .... 45 F3
Paisley PA1 .... 113 E2
Stonehouse ML9 .... 198 C1
Argyle St E G84 .... 16 B1
Argyle St W G84 .... 16 B1
Argyll Arc G1 .... 241 D2
Argyll Ave Dumbarton G82 .... 50 B2
Falkirk FK2 .... 42 B3
Renfrew PA4 .... 93 F1
Stirling FK8 .... 2 B1
Argyll East G83 .... 27 E4
Argyll Gdns ML9 .... 185 D2
Argyll Pl Alloa FK10 .... 10 B4
Bellshill ML4 .... 141 F1
Dumbarton G82 .... 50 B2
East Kilbride G74 .... 160 B2
Rosneath G84 .... 15 D2
Argyll St Alexandria G83 .... 27 E4
Alloa FK10 .... 10 B4
Arisaig Dr Bearsden G61 .... 76 A2
Glasgow G52 .... 115 F2
Arisaig Pl G52 .... 115 F2
Arisdale Cres G77 .... 156 C3
Ark La G31 .... 117 F4
Arkaig Ave ML6 .... 103 F2
Arkaig St ML2 .... 165 D1
Arkle Terr G72 .... 138 C2
Arkleston Cres PA3 .... 114 A4
Arkleston Prim Sch PA4 .... 94 B1
Arkleston Rd PA1 .... 114 A4
Arklet Rd G51 .... 115 F4
Arklet Way ML2 .... 165 F3
Arkwright Way KA11 .... 219 F2
Arkwrights Way PA4 .... 113 D2
Arlington St G3 .... 240 A4
Armadale Ct G31 .... 118 A4
Armadale Path G31 .... 118 A4
Armadale Pl Glasgow G31 .... 118 A4
Greenock PA15 .... 45 F2
Armadale St G31 .... 118 A4
Armine Path ML1 .... 143 E2
Armour Ave Airdrie ML6 .... 122 C4
Cowie FK7 .... 12 B4
Armour Ct Blantyre G72 .... 161 D3
Kirkintilloch G66 .... 59 D1
Armour Dr Ayr KA7 .... 239 E3
Kirkintilloch G66 .... 59 D1
Armour Gdns G66 .... 59 D1
Armour Gr ML1 .... 164 A2
Armour Pl Ardrossan KA22 .... 205 E2
Johnstone PA5 .... 112 B2
Johnstone, Limeroad PA5 .... 112 B3
Kirkintilloch G66 .... 59 D1
Motherwell ML1 .... 143 E2
Stewarton KA3 .... 195 F1
Armour St
Glasgow G4, G31 .... 241 F1
Johnstone PA5 .... 112 A2
Kilmarnock KA1 .... 227 F4
Armstrong Cres G71 .... 141 D4
Armstrong Gr G75 .... 180 B4
Armstrong Rd
Helensburgh G84 .... 25 D4
Kilmarnock KA3 .... 223 E1
Arnbrae Rd G65 .... 36 A1
Arness Terr KA3 .... 222 C2
Arngask Rd G51 .... 115 F4
Arnhall Pl G52 .... 115 F2
Arnhem St G72 .... 139 E3
Arnholm Pl G52 .... 115 F2
Arnisdale Pl G34 .... 120 A4
Arnisdale Rd G34 .... 120 A4
Arnisdale Way G73 .... 138 A2
Arniston St G32 .... 118 C4
Arniston Way PA3 .... 114 A4
Arnol Pl G33 .... 119 F4
Arnold Ave G64 .... 78 A1
Arnold St G20 .... 97 D3
Arnot St FK1 .... 42 B2
Arnothill Bank **6** FK1 .... 42 A2

Arnothill Ct FK1 ... 41 F3
Arnothill Gdns FK1 ... 42 A2
Arnothill La FK1 ... 41 F2
Arnothill Mews FK1 ... 42 A2
Arnott Dr ML5 ... 122 A2
Arnott Quadrant ML1 ... 142 B1
Arnott Way G72 ... 139 D3
Arnprior Pl KA7 ... 238 C1
Arnprior Quadrant G45 ... 137 E2
Arnprior Rd G45 ... 137 E2
Arnprior St G45 ... 137 E2
Arns Gr FK10 ... 9 F4
Arnside Ave G46 ... 136 B2
Arnswell FK10 ... 5 E1
Arnum Gdns ML8 ... 187 F1
Arnum Pl ML8 ... 187 F1
Arnwood Dr G12 ... 96 A3
Aron Terr G72 ... 138 C2
Arondale Rd ML6 ... 103 F2
Aros Dr G52 ... 115 F1
Aros La G52 ... 115 E1
Aros Rd G84 ... 15 E3
Arran G74 ... 160 B1
Arran Ave Coatbridge ML5 ... 122 B2
  Dumbarton G82 ... 49 E3
  Kilmarnock KA3 ... 223 D2
  Port Glasgow PA14 ... 69 D4
  Renfrew PA3 ... 93 F4
Arran Cres KA15 ... 150 B1
Arran Ct Alloa FK10 ... 10 A3
  Greenock PA15 ... 45 D3
  Stevenston KA20 ... 217 E4
Arran Dr Airdrie ML6 ... 99 D2
  Cumbernauld G67 ... 82 B4
  Glasgow G52 ... 115 F2
  Glasgow, Giffnock G46 ... 136 B1
  Glenmavis ML6 ... 102 C3
  Johnstone PA5 ... 111 F1
  Kirkintilloch G66 ... 58 C1
  Paisley PA2 ... 133 F4
Arran Gdns Carluke ML8 ... 201 F4
  Hamilton ML3 ... 162 C1
  Troon KA10 ... 229 E4
Arran La Ardrossan KA22 ... 205 E1
  Moodiesburn G69 ... 81 D1
Arran Mall KA7 ... 238 C4
Arran Pk KA9 ... 236 A3
Arran Pl Ardrossan KA22 ... 205 E1
  Clydebank G81 ... 74 B1
  Coatbridge ML5 ... 122 B2
  Irvine KA12 ... 219 D3
  Linwood PA3 ... 112 A3
  Saltcoats KA21 ... 217 D4
Arran Rd Gourock PA19 ... 44 B3
  Motherwell ML1 ... 163 F4
  Renfrew PA3 ... 94 B1
  Troon KA10 ... 229 E4
Arran Terr Ayr KA7 ... 235 F1
  Falkirk FK1 ... 41 E2
  Rutherglen G73 ... 137 F3
Arran Tower G72 ... 138 C2
Arran View Kilsyth G65 ... 60 B4
  Stewarton KA3 ... 195 F1
Arran Way G72 ... 140 C1
Arranview Ct KA8 ... 236 A2
Arranview Gdns KA23 ... 190 B1
Arranview St ML6 ... 123 F1
Arrochar Ct G23 ... 96 C4
Arrochar Dr G23 ... 76 B1
Arrochar Path G23 ... 76 B1
Arrochar St G23 ... 76 B1
Arrol Cres FK10 ... 10 B4
Arrol Dr KA7 ... 238 B3
Arrol Pk KA7 ... 238 B3
Arrol Pl G40 ... 118 A2
Arrol St G52 ... 114 C4
Arrothill Dr KA1 ... 227 E4
Arrotshole Ct G74 ... 159 D2
Arrotshole Rd G74 ... 159 D2
Arrowsmith Ave G15 ... 95 E4
Artarman Rd G84 ... 15 F2
Arthur Ave Airdrie ML6 ... 123 D3
  Barrhead G78 ... 134 A1
Arthur Ct KA23 ... 190 B3
Arthur Pl G76 ... 157 F3
Arthur Rd PA2 ... 133 F4
Arthur St Alexandria G83 ... 27 F2
  Ayr KA7 ... 238 C4
  Clarkston G76 ... 157 F3
  Glasgow G3 ... 96 B1
  Greenock PA15 ... 46 A2
  Hamilton ML3 ... 162 B3
  Paisley PA1 ... 113 E3
  Saltcoats KA21 ... 217 D4
  Stevenston KA20 ... 217 E4
  West Kilbride KA23 ... 190 B3
Arthur's Dr FK5 ... 23 F1
Arthurlie Ave
  Barrhead G78 ... 134 B1
  Uplawmoor G78 ... 153 D2
Arthurlie Dr Glasgow G46 ... 136 B1
  Newton Mearns G77 ... 156 B2
  Uplawmoor G78 ... 153 D2
Arthurlie Pl KA21 ... 216 C4
Arthurlie St Barrhead G78 ... 134 B1
  Glasgow G51 ... 115 F4
Arthurston Rd G83 ... 28 A4
Arundel Dr
  Bishopbriggs G64 ... 78 A2
  Glasgow G42 ... 137 D4
Ascaig Cres G52 ... 115 F1
Ascog Rd G61 ... 75 F1
Ascog St G42 ... 117 D1
Ascot Ct G12 ... 96 A3
Ascot Ave G12 ... 95 F3

Ash Ave G75 ... 180 B3
Ash Ct G75 ... 180 B3
Ash Dr G75 ... 180 B3
Ash Gr Alloa FK10 ... 10 B3
  Bishopbriggs G64 ... 98 A4
  Kirkintilloch G66 ... 79 D3
  Law ML8 ... 186 C3
  Stenhousemuir FK5 ... 23 F1
  Uddingston G71 ... 141 D4
Ash Pl Banknock FK4 ... 38 C1
  East Kilbride G75 ... 180 B3
  Johnstone PA5 ... 112 A1
  Kilmarnock KA1 ... 227 E4
Ash Rd Clydebank G81 ... 74 A3
  Cumbernauld G67 ... 62 C3
  Dumbarton G82 ... 49 F2
  Glasgow G69 ... 120 A2
Ash Terr FK8 ... 6 C3
Ash Wlk Motherwell ML1 ... 143 D3
  Rutherglen G73 ... 138 B2
Ash Wynd G72 ... 139 F3
Ashbank Cres ML6 ... 123 F2
Ashbrae Gdns FK7 ... 7 D1
Ashburn Gate PA19 ... 44 B4
Ashburn Gdns
  Gourock PA19 ... 44 B4
  Milngavie G62 ... 54 C1
Ashburn Loan ML9 ... 185 D2
Ashburton La G12 ... 96 A3
Ashburton Pk G75 ... 180 A4
Ashburton Rd G12 ... 96 A3
Ashby Cres G13 ... 75 F1
Ashcraig Sch G33 ... 99 D2
Ashcroft G74 ... 160 B3
Ashcroft Ave G65 ... 57 F4
Ashcroft Dr G44 ... 137 F3
Ashcroft Wlk G65 ... 57 F4
Ashdale Ave KA21 ... 205 F1
Ashdale Dr G52 ... 115 F2
Ashdale Rd KA3 ... 222 C2
Ashdene St G22 ... 97 D4
Asher Rd ML6 ... 123 F1
Ashfield G64 ... 78 A1
Ashfield Cotts G83 ... 20 A2
Ashfield Rd Clarkston G76 ... 157 F3
  Law ML8 ... 187 D3
  Milngavie G62 ... 55 D1
Ashfield Sta G22 ... 97 E2
Ashgill Pl G22 ... 97 E3
Ashgill Rd G22 ... 97 E4
Ashgillhead Rd ML9 ... 185 F1
Ashgrove Airdrie ML6 ... 123 E4
  Caldercruix ML6 ... 105 D3
  Coatbridge ML5 ... 122 A2
  Hartwood ML7 ... 145 F2
  Irvine KA12 ... 219 E3
  Moodiesburn G69 ... 80 C1
Ashgrove Ave
  Gourock PA19 ... 44 B4
  Stevenston KA20 ... 206 C1
Ashgrove La PA14 ... 47 E1
Ashgrove Rd
  Ardrossan KA22 ... 205 E2
  Bellshill ML4 ... 142 A4
  Kilwinning KA13 ... 207 E2
Ashgrove St Ayr KA7 ... 239 D4
  Rutherglen G73 ... 118 A1
Ashgrove Workshops
  KA13 ... 207 E2
Ashiestiel Ct G67 ... 82 C4
Ashiestiel Pl G67 ... 82 C4
Ashiestiel Rd G67 ... 82 C4
Ashkirk Dr Ashgill ML9 ... 199 F4
  Glasgow G52 ... 115 E2
Ashland Ave ML3 ... 183 E3
Ashlea Dr G46 ... 136 B2
Ashlea Gdns ML6 ... 103 F2
Ashley Dr G71 ... 141 D3
Ashley La G3 ... 240 A4
Ashley Pk G71 ... 141 E3
Ashley Pl G72 ... 161 E4
Ashley Rise G83 ... 27 F1
Ashley St Bonnybridge FK4 ... 39 F3
  Glasgow G3 ... 240 A4
Ashley Terr FK10 ... 10 A4
Ashmore Rd G43 ... 136 C3
Ashton Dr Helensburgh G84 ... 25 D4
  Hurlford KA1 ... 228 C3
Ashton Gdns G69 ... 101 D3
Ashton Gn G74 ... 159 E1
Ashton La N G12 ... 96 B1
Ashton Pl PA19 ... 44 B4
Ashton Rd Glasgow G12 ... 96 B1
  Gourock PA19 ... 44 B4
  Rutherglen G73 ... 118 A3
Ashton St ML1 ... 142 B1
Ashton Terr PA19 ... 44 B4
Ashton View G82 ... 49 D2
Ashton Way PA2 ... 132 C4
Ashtree Ct G60 ... 73 D3
Ashtree Gr G77 ... 156 B2
Ashtree Pk ML1 ... 164 B2
Ashtree Rd G43 ... 136 B4
Ashvale Cres G21 ... 97 F2
Ashworth Terr ML3 ... 162 A2
Aspen Dr G21 ... 98 A2
Aspen Pl Cambuslang G72 ... 139 F3
  Johnstone PA5 ... 112 A1
Aspen Rd KA7 ... 239 E3
Aspen Way ML3 ... 162 C1
Asquith Pl ML4 ... 142 A3
Aster Dr G45 ... 138 A2
Aster Gdns Glasgow G53 ... 135 E2
  Motherwell ML1 ... 163 F3
Athelstane Dr G67 ... 82 B4

Athelstane Rd G13 ... 95 E4
Athena Way G71 ... 141 D4
Athole Gdns G12 ... 96 B2
Athole La Glasgow G12 ... 96 B2
  Gourock PA16 ... 44 B2
Athole St G84 ... 16 C1
Athole Terr PA16 ... 44 B2
Atholl Ave Paisley G52 ... 114 C4
  Torrance G64 ... 57 D1
Atholl Cres PA1 ... 114 C3
Atholl Ct G66 ... 80 A4
Atholl Dr Cumbernauld G68 ... 81 F4
  Rutherglen G46 ... 157 E4
Atholl Gdns Bearsden G61 ... 75 F4
  Bishopbriggs G64 ... 77 F2
  Kilwinning KA13 ... 207 F2
  Rutherglen G73 ... 138 C2
Atholl La G69 ... 81 D1
Atholl Pl Coatbridge ML5 ... 122 A2
  Linwood PA3 ... 112 A3
  Stirling FK8 ... 1 C1
Atholl Prep Sch G62 ... 55 D2
Atholl Terr G71 ... 121 D1
Atlas Ind Est G21 ... 97 F2
Atlas Pl G21 ... 97 F2
Atlas Rd G21 ... 97 F2
Atlas Sq G21 ... 97 F2
Atlas St G81 ... 94 A4
Atlin Dr ML1 ... 143 D2
Atrium Way H4 ... 40 A2
Attercliffe Ave ML2 ... 164 B1
Attlee Ave G81 ... 74 C1
Attlee Pl G81 ... 74 C1
Attow Rd G43 ... 136 A3
Auburn Dr G78 ... 134 B1
Auchans Ave KA2 ... 225 F1
Auchans Dr KA2 ... 225 F1
Auchans Pl KA3 ... 213 D2
Auchans Rd PA6 ... 92 A1
Auchanshangan Dr KA21 ... 205 F2
Auchenbach Prim Sch
  G78 ... 134 B1
Auchenbeg Cres KA7 ... 239 D2
Auchenbothie Rd PA14 ... 68 C3
Auchencar Rd KA2 ... 222 C2
Auchencrow St G34 ... 120 B4
Auchencruive G62 ... 76 B4
Auchendarroch St PA15 ... 46 B2
Auchendavie Rd G66 ... 59 D1
Auchendoon Cres KA7 ... 238 B2
Auchendores Ave PA14 ... 69 D4
Auchenfoil La PA14 ... 68 B4
Auchenfoil Rd
  Greenock PA14 ... 67 F3
  Port Glasgow, Devol PA14 ... 68 B4
Auchengate KA10 ... 229 F4
Auchengate Cres KA11 ... 224 C1
Auchengeich Rd G69 ... 80 B2
Auchengilloch G75 ... 180 C3
Auchengree Rd G69 ... 80 C1
Auchenglen Gdns G69 ... 80 C1
Auchenglen Rd ML8 ... 201 F2
Auchengreoch Ave PA5 ... 131 E4
Auchengreoch Rd PA5 ... 131 E4
Auchenharvie Acad
  KA21 ... 217 D4
Auchenharvie Pl
  Irvine KA11 ... 219 F3
  Stevenston KA20 ... 206 A1
Auchenharvie Rd KA21 ... 217 D4
Auchenhove Cres KA25 ... 149 D2
Auchenhowie Rd G62 ... 76 B4
Auchenkilns Holdings G68 ... 61 E1
Auchenkilns Rd G67 ... 82 B4
Auchenkilns Rdbt G67 ... 82 A4
Auchenleck La PA14 ... 68 C4
Auchenleck Rd PA14 ... 68 C4
Auchenlodment Prim Sch
  PA5 ... 112 A1
Auchenlodment Rd PA5 ... 112 A2
Auchenreoch Ave G65 ... 59 D3
Auchenreoch Ave G82 ... 50 A3
Auchentibber Pl G72 ... 161 D2
Auchentiber Pl KA3 ... 223 E3
Auchentorlie Quadrant
  PA1 ... 114 A2
Auchentorlie St G11 ... 95 F1
Auchentoshan Ave G81 ... 73 F3
Auchentoshan Prim Sch
  G81 ... 73 F3
Auchentoshan Terr G21 ... 97 F1
Auchentrae Cres KA7 ... 238 B3
Auchentyre Pl FK2 ... 24 B2
Auchinairn Prim Sch G64 ... 98 A4
Auchinairn Rd G64 ... 98 B4
Auchinbaird FK10 ... 5 E2
Auchinbee Farm Rd G68 ... 61 D2
Auchinbee Way G68 ... 61 D2
Auchincampbell Rd ML3 ... 162 B2
Auchincarroch Rd
  Balloch G83 ... 20 C2
  Bonhill G83 ... 28 A4
Auchincloch Dr FK4 ... 38 C1
Auchincruive Ave G46 ... 236 B3
Auchincruive Pl
  (West of Scotland
  Agricultural Coll) KA6 ... 237 E2
Auchineden Ct G61 ... 75 E4
Auchingill Pl G34 ... 100 B1
Auchingill Rd G34 ... 100 B1
Auchingramont Rd ML3 ... 162 B2
Auchinlea Dr ML1 ... 143 E4
Auchinlea Rd G34 ... 99 F1
Auchinlea Ret Pk G34 ... 99 F1
Auchinleck Ave G33 ... 98 C3
Auchinleck Cres G33 ... 98 C3
Auchinleck Dr G33 ... 98 C3

Auchinleck Gdns G33 ... 98 C3
Auchinleck Rd
  Clydebank G81 ... 74 A4
  Glasgow G33 ... 98 C4
Auchinleck Terr G81 ... 74 A4
Auchinloch Prim Sch G66 ... 79 E1
Auchinloch Rd G66 ... 79 E2
Auchinloch St G21 ... 97 F2
Auchinraith Ave ML3 ... 162 B3
Auchinraith Prim Sch
  G72 ... 161 E4
Auchinraith Rd G72 ... 161 F3
Auchinraith Terr G72 ... 161 F3
Auchinvole Cres G65 ... 60 A4
Auchmannoch Ave PA1 ... 114 C3
Auchmead Rd PA16 ... 44 C2
Auchmountain Rd
  Greenock PA15 ... 46 C1
  Greenock, Bridgend PA15 ... 46 B2
  Port Glasgow PA15 ... 67 F4
Auchnacraig Rd G81 ... 74 B4
Auchneagh Ave PA16 ... 45 D2
Auchneagh Cres PA16 ... 45 D2
Auchneagh Farm La PA16 ... 45 D3
Auchneagh Farm Rd PA16 ... 45 D3
Auchneagh Rd PA16 ... 45 D2
Auchter Ave ML2 ... 166 B3
Auchter Rd ML2 ... 165 F2
Auchterburn Rd ML7 ... 166 C4
Auckland Pk G75 ... 159 D1
Auckland Pl G81 ... 73 E2
Auckland St G22 ... 97 D2
Auld Brig Rd FK10 ... 10 A3
Auld Clay Rd KA1 ... 206 C4
Auld Kirk Rd G72 ... 139 E2
Auld Rd The G67 ... 62 A2
Auld St G81 ... 73 F2
Auld's Brae ML6 ... 123 D4
Auldbar Rd G52 ... 115 F1
Auldbar Terr PA2 ... 114 A1
Auldburn Rd G43 ... 136 A3
Auldearn Rd G21 ... 98 B4
Auldgirth Rd G52 ... 115 F2
Auldhame St ML5 ... 121 E4
Auldhouse Ave G43 ... 136 A3
Auldhouse Gdns G43 ... 136 A3
Auldhouse Prim Sch G75 ... 180 B1
Auldhouse Rd
  East Kilbride G75 ... 180 B1
  Glasgow G43 ... 136 B3
Auldhouse Terr G43 ... 136 B3
Auldlea Rd KA15 ... 150 A1
Auldmurroch Dr G62 ... 54 B1
Auldton Terr ML9 ... 185 F1
Aultbea St G22 ... 97 D4
Aultmore Rd G33 ... 119 F4
Aultmore Rdbt G33 ... 119 F4
Aurs Dr G78 ... 134 B1
Aurs Cres G78 ... 134 B1
Aurs Glen G78 ... 134 B1
Aurs Pl G78 ... 134 C1
Aurs Rd G78 ... 134 C1
Aursbridge Cres G78 ... 134 B1
Aursbridge Dr G78 ... 134 B1
Austen La G13 ... 95 F3
Austen Rd G13 ... 95 F3
Austine Dr ML3 ... 183 F4
Aven Dr FK2 ... 42 C2
Avenel Rd G13 ... 75 F1
Avenue End Rd G33 ... 99 D1
Avenue Pk FK9 ... 1 C4
Avenue Sq KA3 ... 211 E4
Avenue St Glasgow G40 ... 118 A3
  Rutherglen G73 ... 118 A1
  Stewarton KA3 ... 195 E1
Avenue The Bridge Of A FK9 ... 2 A4
  Fairlie FK2 ... 24 B1
  Newton Mearns G77 ... 156 B2
  West Kilbride KA23 ... 190 C4
Avenuehead Rd G69 ... 101 D4
Avenuepark St G20 ... 96 C3
Aviemore Gdns G61 ... 76 A3
Aviemore Rd G52 ... 115 F2
Avils Hill KA25 ... 149 D1
Avils Pl KA25 ... 149 D1
Avoch St G34 ... 100 A1
Avon Ave Bearsden G61 ... 76 A2
  Carluke ML8 ... 187 F1
  Longriggend ML6 ... 84 B2
Avon Ct Falkirk FK1 ... 42 B1
  Irvine KA11 ... 220 A2
Avon Dr Bellshill ML4 ... 142 A2
  Linwood PA3 ... 112 A3
Avon Pk FK1 ... 87 F3
Avon Pl Coatbridge ML5 ... 101 E1
  Kilmarnock KA1 ... 228 A3
  Larkhall ML9 ... 185 D1
Avon Rd Bishopbriggs G64 ... 98 A4
  Glasgow G46 ... 136 A1
  Larkhall ML9 ... 199 D4
Avon Sch ML3 ... 163 D2
Avon St Denny FK6 ... 21 F2
  Hamilton ML3 ... 162 C2
  Motherwell ML1 ... 184 C2
  Motherwell ML1 ... 163 F3
Avon Tower ML1 ... 163 F3
Avon Wynd ML1 ... 143 F2
Avonbank Cres ML3 ... 183 F4
Avonbank Rd Larkhall ML9 ... 184 C2
  Rutherglen G73 ... 137 F4
Avonbrae Cres ML3 ... 183 F4
Avonbridge Dr ML3 ... 163 D2
Avonbridge Rd FK1 ... 64 A4
Avondale Ave G74 ... 159 F1
Avondale Dr PA1 ... 114 A3
Avondale Pl G74 ... 181 D4
Avondale Rd KA23 ... 190 B3

Avondale St G33 ... 99 D1
Avonhead G75 ... 180 C3
Avonhead Ave G67 ... 82 B4
Avonhead Gdns G67 ... 82 B4
Avonhead Rd G67 ... 82 B4
Avonmouth Pl H4 ... 44 C3
Avonside Dr FK6 ... 21 E3
Avonside Gr ML3 ... 162 C2
Avonspark St G21 ... 98 A2
Aylmer Rd G43 ... 136 C3
Ayr Ac KA7 ... 235 F1
Ayr Coll KA8 ... 239 D4
Ayr Coll (Newton Annexe)
  KA8 ... 236 A1
Ayr Hospl KA6 ... 236 A3
Ayr Grammar Prim Sch
  KA7 ... 238 C4
Ayr La PA16 ... 44 C2
Ayr Rd Ashgill ML9 ... 185 E1
  Irvine KA11 ... 224 B4
  Kilmarnock KA1 ... 227 F2
  Newton Mearns G77 ... 156 B2
  Prestwick KA9 ... 236 A3
  Rutherglen G46 ... 157 D4
Ayr St Glasgow G21 ... 97 F2
  Troon KA10 ... 229 E3
Ayr Sta KA7 ... 239 D4
Ayr Terr PA16 ... 44 C2
Ayrshire Central Hospl
  KA12 ... 219 D4
Ayton Pk N G74 ... 160 A2
Ayton Pk S G74 ... 160 A2
Aytoun Dr PA8 ... 72 C2
Aytoun Rd G41 ... 116 C2

Baads Rd ML7 ... 106 B1
Baberton Way KA13 ... 207 D2
Babylon Dr ML4 ... 142 A2
Babylon Pl ML4 ... 142 A2
Babylon Rd ML4 ... 142 A2
Back Causeway G31 ... 118 B3
Back Hawkhill Ave KA8 ... 236 A1
Back O Dykes Rd G66 ... 80 A4
Back O Hill Rd ... 91 D1
Back O' Hill Ind Est FK8 ... 2 A1
Back O' Hill Rd
  Fluchter G64 ... 56 C1
  Stirling FK8 ... 2 A1
Back O'Barns ML3 ... 162 C2
Back Peebles St KA8 ... 235 F1
Back Rd Kira FK17 ... 4 C4
Back Sneddon St PA3 ... 113 F3
Back St G82 ... 27 E1
Backbrae St G65 ... 60 B4
Backburn KA15 ... 171 D4
Backmuir Cres ML3 ... 162 A3
Backmuir Pl ML3 ... 162 A3
Backmuir Rd Glasgow G15 ... 75 D2
  Hamilton ML3 ... 162 A3
Backwood Ct FK10 ... 10 C3
Badenheath Pl G68 ... 81 E3
Badenheath Terr G67 ... 81 F2
Badenoch Rd G66 ... 59 E1
Bagnell St G21 ... 97 F3
Bahamas Way G75 ... 159 D1
Baidland Ave KA24 ... 191 F3
Bailie Dr G61 ... 75 E4
Bailie Fyfe Way ML2 ... 186 A4
Baillehill Pl KA1 ... 222 B1
Baillie Gdns ML2 ... 165 F2
Baillie Dr G71 ... 141 D2
Baillie St Bothwell G71 ... 141 D2
  East Kilbride G74 ... 160 B2
Baillie Gdns ML2 ... 165 F2
Baillie Waugh Rd FK7 ... 7 E2
Baillies La ML6 ... 123 D4
Bailliesmuir Pl ML2 ... 166 A3
Baillieston KA4 ... 222 A4
Baillieston Rd
  Glasgow G32 ... 119 F2
  Glasgow, Broomhouse G71 ... 120 A1
Baillieston Station G69 ... 120 A2
Bain Cres G84 ... 16 C2
Bain St G40 ... 241 F1
Bainbridge Dr G83 ... 27 F3
Bainfield Rd G82 ... 48 A4
Baingle Brae FK10 ... 4 A2
Baingle Cres FK10 ... 4 A2
Bainsford Prim Sch FK2 ... 42 A4
Baird Ave Airdrie ML6 ... 103 D1
  Helensburgh G84 ... 16 A1
  Kilwinning KA13 ... 207 F2
  Larkhall ML9 ... 199 E4
  Paisley G52 ... 114 B4
Baird Brae G4 ... 97 D2
Baird Cres Alexandria G83 ... 27 E4
  Cumbernauld G67 ... 82 A4
Baird Ct G81 ... 74 A1
Baird Dr Bearsden G61 ... 75 E3
  Erskine PA8 ... 72 C2
Baird Hill G75 ... 180 C4
Baird Memorial Prim Sch
  G67 ... 82 B4
Baird Pl Bellshill ML4 ... 142 A4
  Kilmarnock KA3 ... 223 D1
  Monkton KA9 ... 233 E2
  Wishaw ML2 ... 165 F2
Baird Rd Ayr KA7 ... 238 C1
  Kilmarnock KA3 ... 223 D1
  Monkton KA9 ... 233 E2

Baird St Coatbridge ML5 .... 122 A4
Falkirk FK1 .... 41 E3
Glasgow G4 .... 241 E4
Baird Terr ML7 .... 127 E3
Bairds Cres ML3 .... 162 B2
Bairdsland View ML4 .... 142 A3
Bairns Ford Ave FK2 .... 42 A4
Bairns Ford Ct FK2 .... 42 A4
Bairns Ford Dr FK2 .... 42 A4
Baker St Glasgow G41 .... 116 C1
Greenock PA15 .... 46 A2
Stirling FK8 .... 7 D4
Bakewell Rd G69 .... 120 A3
Balaclava St G2, G3 .... 240 B2
Balado Rd G33 .... 119 F4
Balbaie Rd ML7 .... 127 F3
Balbeg St G51 .... 115 F3
Balbeggie St G32 .... 119 E2
Balblair Rd G52 .... 115 F1
Balcarres Ave G12 .... 96 B3
Balcastle Gdns G65 .... 36 A1
Balcastle Rd Kilsyth G65 .... 36 A1
Slamannan FK1 .... 86 A3
Balcomie Cres KA10 .... 230 A1
Balcomie St G33 .... 99 D1
Balcomie Terr ML3 .... 183 D4
Balcurvie Rd G34 .... 100 A1
Baldernock Prim Sch
G64 .... 56 A1
Baldernock Rd G62 .... 55 E1
Baldinnie Rd G34 .... 120 A4
Baldoran Cres G68 .... 61 D2
Baldovan Cres G33 .... 119 F4
Baldovie Rd G52 .... 115 E2
Baldragon Rd G34 .... 100 B1
Baldric Rd G13 .... 95 E3
Baldwin Ave G13 .... 95 E4
Balerno Dr G52 .... 115 F2
Balfearn Dr G76 .... 178 C3
Balfleurs St G62 .... 55 D1
Balfluig St G34 .... 99 F1
Balfour Ave KA15 .... 171 D4
Balfour Cres Larbert FK5 .... 23 E1
Plean FK7 .... 12 B2
Balfour Ct KA3 .... 223 E2
Balfour St Alloa FK10 .... 10 B4
Bannockburn FK7 .... 7 E1
Bonnybridge FK4 .... 39 F3
Glasgow G20 .... 96 B3
Port Glasgow PA14 .... 47 D1
Stirling FK8 .... 1 C1
Balfour Terr G75 .... 180 C4
Balfour Wynd ML9 .... 185 E1
Balfron Cres ML3 .... 161 F2
Balfron Rd Glasgow G51 .... 115 F4
Greenock PA15 .... 46 B1
Balgair Dr PA1 .... 114 A3
Balgair St G22 .... 97 D2
Balgair Terr G32 .... 119 D3
Balglass St G22 .... 97 D3
Balgonie Ave PA2 .... 113 D3
Balgonie Dr PA2 .... 113 E1
Balgonie Rd G52 .... 115 F2
Balgonie Woods PA2 .... 113 E1
Balgownie Cres G46 .... 136 A1
Balgray Ave Kilbirnie KA25 .... 170 A4
Kilmarnock KA1 .... 227 F1
Balgray Cres G78 .... 134 C1
Balgray Rd Barrmill KA15 .... 172 A3
Glengarnock KA14 .... 170 A4
Newton Mearns G77 .... 156 A3
Balgray Way KA11 .... 220 A3
Balgraybank St G21 .... 98 A2
Balgrayhill Rd G21 .... 97 F3
Balgraystone Rd
G77, G78 .... 155 E4
Balintore St G32 .... 119 D3
Baliol La G3 .... 240 A4
Baliol St G3 .... 240 A4
Baljaffray Prim Sch G61 .... 75 E4
Baljaffray Rd G61 .... 75 D4
Balkachalarry Tett G63 .... 30 B2
Ballacher Ct ML1 .... 164 A2
Ballagan Pl G62 .... 54 B1
Ballaig Ave G61 .... 75 E3
Ballaig Cres G33 .... 99 E3
Ballantay Quadrant G45 .... 138 A2
Ballantay Rd G45 .... 138 A2
Ballantay Terr G45 .... 138 A2
Ballantine Ave G52 .... 115 D4
Ballantine Dr KA7 .... 238 C3
Ballantrae G74 .... 159 E1
Ballantrae Cres G77 .... 157 D2
Ballantrae Dr G77 .... 157 D2
Ballantrae Rd G72 .... 161 F3
Ballater Cres ML2 .... 165 D3
Ballater Dr Bearsden G61 .... 76 A1
Paisley PA2 .... 93 E4
Renfrew PA4 .... 94 B1
Stirling FK9 .... 2 B2
Ballater Pl G5 .... 117 E2
Ballater St G5 .... 117 E2
Ballayne Dr G69 .... 81 D2
Ballengeich Pass FK8 .... 2 A1
Ballengeich Rd FK8 .... 1 C1
Ballerup Terr G75 .... 181 D4
Balloch High Sch G75 .... 180 A2
Balloch Terr G75 .... 180 C3
Ballevean Cres G60 .... 31 D2
Ballindalloch Dr G31 .... 118 A4
Ballindalloch La G31 .... 118 A4
Ballinkier Ave FK4 .... 38 C2
Balloch Castle G83 .... 19 E1

Balloch Castle Ctry Pk
G83 .... 19 E1
Balloch Gdns G52 .... 115 F2
Balloch Holdings G68 .... 61 D1
Balloch Rd Airdrie ML6 .... 124 A3
Balloch G68 .... 27 E4
Cumbernauld G68 .... 61 E1
Greenock PA15 .... 46 A1
Shotts ML7 .... 146 C3
Balloch Rdbt G68 .... 61 D1
Balloch Sta G83 .... 27 F4
Balloch View G67 .... 61 F1
Ballochmill Rd G73 .... 138 B4
Ballochmyle G74 .... 160 B2
Ballochney La ML6 .... 102 C1
Ballochney Rd ML6 .... 103 F2
Ballochney St ML6 .... 102 C1
Ballochnie Dr ML6 .... 104 A2
Ballogie Rd G44 .... 137 D4
Ballot Rd KA12 .... 219 E2
Balmalloch Prim Sch G65 .... 36 B1
Balmalloch Rd G65 .... 36 B1
Balmartin Rd G23 .... 76 B1
Balmedie PA8 .... 73 D1
Balmeg Ave G46 .... 157 E4
Balmerino Pl G64 .... 98 B4
Balminnoch Pk KA7 .... 238 B1
Balmoral Ave ML6 .... 102 C3
Balmoral Cres
Coatbridge ML5 .... 121 E2
Inchinnan PA4 .... 93 F3
Balmoral Dr Bearsden G61 .... 76 A1
Cambuslang G72 .... 138 C3
Falkirk FK1 .... 41 F2
Glasgow G32 .... 139 D4
Balmoral Gdns
Blantyre G72 .... 140 B1
Uddingston G71 .... 120 C1
Balmoral Path ꞁ ML9 .... 185 E1
Balmoral Pl
East Kilbride G74 .... 159 E1
Gourock PA19 .... 43 F3
Stenhousemuir FK5 .... 23 F2
Stirling FK8 .... 7 D4
Balmoral Rd Elderslie PA5 .... 112 A1
Kilmarnock KA3 .... 222 C1
Balmoral St Falkirk FK1 .... 41 F2
Glasgow G14 .... 95 D2
Balmoral Wynd KA3 .... 211 F4
Balmore Ct PA13 .... 89 E4
Balmore Dr ML3 .... 183 D4
Balmore Ind Est G22 .... 97 D4
Balmore Pl G22 .... 97 D3
Balmore Rd Balmore G64 .... 77 F4
Glasgow G22 .... 97 D3
Greenock PA15 .... 46 B1
Balmore Sq G22 .... 97 D3
Balmuildy Prim Sch G64 .... 77 F2
Balmuildy Rd G64 .... 77 E3
Balmulzier Rd FK1 .... 86 A4
Balornock Prim Sch G21 .... 98 A2
Balornock Rd G21 .... 98 A3
Balquhatstone Cres FK1 .... 86 A3
Balquhidderock FK7 .... 7 E2
Balquidder Ct ML6 .... 103 D1
Balrossie Dr PA13 .... 89 D4
Balrossie Sch PA13 .... 89 D4
Balruddery Pl G64 .... 98 B4
Balshagray Ave G11,G14 .... 95 F2
Balshagray Cres G14 .... 95 F1
Balshagray Dr G11 .... 95 F2
Balshagray La G11 .... 95 F2
Balshagray Pl G11 .... 95 F2
Baltersan Gdns ML3 .... 183 F2
Baltic Ct G40 .... 118 A2
Baltic La G40 .... 118 A2
Baltic Pl G40 .... 118 A2
Baltic St G40 .... 118 A2
Balure Cres FK7 .... 8 B2
Balure St G31 .... 118 B4
Balvaird Cres G73 .... 138 A4
Balvaird Dr G73 .... 138 A4
Balvenie St ML5 .... 122 A2
Balveny St G33 .... 99 E1
Balvicar Dr G42 .... 116 C1
Balvicar St G42 .... 116 C1
Balvie Ave Glasgow G15 .... 75 D1
Glasgow, Giffnock G46 .... 136 B1
Balvie Cres G62 .... 54 C1
Balvie Rd G62 .... 54 C1
Banavie Rd Glasgow G11 .... 96 A2
Wishaw ML2 .... 165 F3
Banchory Ave
Glasgow G43 .... 136 A3
Glenmavis ML6 .... 102 C3
Inchinnan PA4 .... 93 E4
Banchory Cres G61 .... 76 A1
Banchory Pl KA10 .... 4 B2
Banchory Prim Sch FK10 .... 4 B2
Banchory Rd ML2 .... 165 D3
Bandeath Ind Est FK7 .... 9 D3
Bandeath Rd FK7 .... 9 D2
Baneberry Path G74 .... 159 E2
Banff Ave ML6 .... 123 D2
Banff Ct KA3 .... 223 D2
Banff Quadrant ML2 .... 165 D3
Banff Rd PA16 .... 44 B3
Bangorshill St G46 .... 135 F2
Bank Ave G62 .... 55 D2
Bank Ct KA12 .... 219 F2
Bank Pk G75 .... 180 A4
Bank Rd Glasgow G40 .... 118 A1
Kilmarnock KA1 .... 227 F4
Shotts ML7 .... 146 C2
Bank St Glasgow G12 .... 139 E4
Harthill ML7 .... 127 F3

Bank St Airdrie ML6 .... 123 D4
Alexandria G83 .... 27 F3
Alloa FK10 .... 10 A3
Barrhead G78 .... 134 B1
Cambuslang G72 .... 139 D3
Glasgow G12 .... 96 C1
Greenock PA15 .... 45 F2
Irvine KA12 .... 219 E2
Kilbirnie KA25 .... 149 D1
Kilmarnock KA1 .... 227 F4
Kilsyth G65 .... 36 B1
Paisley PA1 .... 113 F3
Prestwick KA9 .... 236 A4
Slamannan FK1 .... 86 A3
Stirling FK8 .... 7 D4
Troon KA10 .... 229 E2
Bank View ML6 .... 123 E1
Bank Way G78 ꞁ ML9 .... 185 D2
Bankbrae Ave G53 .... 135 D3
Bankend PA11 .... 110 C4
Bankend Pl KA3 .... 223 D3
Bankend Rd
Bridge Of W PA11 .... 110 C3
Dumbarton G82 .... 49 F2
Bankend St G33 .... 99 D1
Bankfauld Ave KA25 .... 149 D1
Bankfield Dr ML3 .... 183 E4
Bankfoot Dr G52 .... 115 D2
Bankfoot Pl G77 .... 157 D2
Bankfoot Rd Glasgow G52 .... 115 D2
Paisley PA3 .... 113 D3
Bankglen Rd G15 .... 75 D2
Bankhall St G42 .... 117 D1
Bankhead Ave Airdrie ML6 .... 123 E4
Bellshill ML4 .... 142 A2
Coatbridge ML5 .... 121 E2
Glasgow G13 .... 95 D3
Springvale KA11 .... 221 D1
Bankhead Cres FK4 .... 39 E3
Bankhead Dr G73 .... 138 A4
Bankhead Pl Airdrie ML6 .... 123 E4
Coatbridge ML5 .... 121 E2
Bankhead Prim Sch
Glasgow G13 .... 95 D3
Glasgow, Bankhead G73 .... 137 F4
Bankhead Rd
Kilmacolm PA13 .... 89 E4
Fishcross FK10 .... 5 E2
Kilwinning KA13 .... 207 F2
Kirkintilloch G66 .... 80 A4
Rutherglen G73 .... 137 F4
Bankhead Terr ML1 .... 215 D3
Bankholm Pl G76 .... 157 F3
Bankier Prim Sch FK4 .... 38 C2
Bankier Rd FK4 .... 38 C2
Bankier Terr FK4 .... 38 C2
Banks St G66 .... 58 B1
Bankside Ave PA5 .... 111 F2
Bankside Ct FK6 .... 21 F1
Bankside Gdns KA25 .... 149 D2
Bankside Ind Est FK4 .... 39 F4
Bankside Pl PA5 .... 111 F2
Bankview Dr G66 .... 79 D4
Bannachra Cres G83 .... 27 E3
Bannachra Dr G84 .... 16 A1
Bannatyne Ave G31 .... 118 A4
Bannatyne St ML11 .... 215 D2
Banner Dr G13 .... 75 E1
Banner Rd G13 .... 75 E1
Bannercross Ave G69 .... 120 A3
Bannercross Dr G69 .... 120 A3
Bannercross Gdns ꞁ
G69 .... 120 A3
Bannerman Dr
Bellshill ML4 .... 142 B3
Kilmarnock KA3 .... 223 E1
Bannerman High Sch
G69 .... 120 A2
Bannerman Pl G81 .... 74 A1
Bannock Gdns KA13 .... 208 A2
Bannockburn Ho KA3 .... 223 D1
Bannock Rd KA13 .... 208 A2
Bannock Rd FK7 .... 8 B2
Bannockburn Dr ML9 .... 185 E1
Bannockburn High Sch
FK7 .... 7 E1
Bannockburn Hospl FK7 .... 11 F4
Bannockburn Pl KA3 .... 223 D2
Bannockburn Prim Sch
FK7 .... 7 F1
Bannockburn Rd
Cowie FK7 .... 12 B4
Stirling FK7 .... 7 E2
Bannockburn Sta PA16 .... 45 E3
Bannockburn Station Rd
FK7 .... 8 A2
Bantaskin Prim Sch FK1 .... 41 F2
Bantaskin St G20 .... 96 B4
Bantaskine Dr FK1 .... 41 F2
Bantaskine Gdns FK1 .... 41 F2
Bantaskine St FK1 .... 41 F2
Banton Pl G33 .... 120 A4
Banton Pl Bonnybridge FK4 .... 40 A2
Banton Rd G65 .... 37 F2
Banyan Cres G71 .... 121 E1
Bar Hill Pl G65 .... 60 A4
Barassie G74 .... 159 E2
Barassie Cres G68 .... 61 F3
Barassie Ct G72 .... 140 C1
Barassie Dr PA11 .... 110 B3
Barassie Pl KA3 .... 227 F2

Barassie Prim Sch KA10 .... 229 E3
Barassie St KA10 .... 229 E3
Barassiebank La KA10 .... 229 E3
Barbadoes Rd KA1 .... 227 F3
Barbadoes Rd KA1 .... 227 F3
Barbados Gn ꞁ G75 .... 159 D1
Barbae Pl G71 .... 141 D2
Barbana Rd G74 .... 158 C1
Barbegs Cres G65 .... 60 C2
Barberry Ave G53 .... 135 D1
Barberry Dr KA15 .... 171 D4
Barberry Gdns G53 .... 135 D1
Barberry Pl G53 .... 135 E1
Barbeth Gdns G67 .... 82 A3
Barbeth Pl Cumbernauld G67 .... 82 A3
Irvine KA11 .... 220 A3
Barbeth Rd G67 .... 82 A3
Barbeth Way G67 .... 82 A3
Barbour Ave FK7 .... 7 E2
Barbour's Pk KA3 .... 211 F4
Barbreck Rd ꞁ G42 .... 116 C1
Barcaldine Ave G69 .... 80 A1
Barcapel Ave G77 .... 156 C4
Barcaple Flats G77 .... 156 C4
Barclaven Rd PA13 .... 89 F4
Barclay Ave PA5 .... 112 A1
Barclay Ct G60 .... 73 D3
Barclay Dr Helensburgh G84 .... 16 B2
Kilmarnock KA3 .... 223 E1
Barclay Gdns KA3 .... 220 B3
Barclay Pl KA3 .... 195 E1
Barclay Rd ML1 .... 163 D3
Barclay Sq PA4 .... 94 A1
Barclay St Glasgow G21 .... 97 F3
Old Kilpatrick G60 .... 73 D3
Barcraigs Dr PA2 .... 133 F4
Bard Ave G13 .... 95 D4
Bardowie St G22 .... 97 D2
Bardrain Ave PA5 .... 112 B1
Bardrain Rd PA2 .... 133 E4
Bardrainney Ave PA14 .... 68 C4
Bardrill Dr G64 .... 77 F1
Bardykes Rd G72 .... 161 D4
Barefield St ML9 .... 185 D2
Barfillan Dr G52 .... 115 F3
Bargaran Rd G53 .... 115 D2
Bargarran Prim Sch PA8 .... 72 C1
Bargarran Rd PA8 .... 72 C2
Bargarron Dr PA3 .... 114 A4
Barge Ct G84 .... 15 E3
Bargeddie Prim Sch ML5 .... 121 D3
Bargeddie St G33 .... 98 B1
Bargeny St G53 .... 207 D1
Bargrennan Rd KA10 .... 229 F3
Barhill La G77 .... 156 C4
Barhill Terr G65 .... 60 A2
Barholm Sq G33 .... 99 E1
Barke Rd G67 .... 62 A2
Barkly Terr ꞁ G75 .... 180 B4
Barlae Ave G76 .... 178 C4
Barlanark Ave G32 .... 119 E3
Barlanark Cres G33 .... 119 E4
Barlanark Dr G33 .... 119 E4
Barlanark Pl Glasgow G32 .... 119 F3
Glasgow, Greenfield G32 .... 119 D3
Barlanark Prim Sch G33 .... 119 F3
Barlanark Rd G33 .... 119 E4
Barlandfauld St G65 .... 60 C4
Barleith Ct KA1 .... 228 C3
Barleyhill FK4 .... 40 A3
Barlia Dr G45 .... 137 F2
Barlia St G45 .... 137 F2
Barlia Terr G45 .... 137 F2
Barloan Cres G82 .... 50 A3
Barloan Pl G82 .... 50 A3
Barloch Ave G62 .... 55 D1
Barloch Rd G62 .... 55 D1
Barloch St G22 .... 97 E2
Barlogan Ave G52 .... 115 F3
Barlogan Quadrant G52 .... 115 F3
Barmore Ave KA8 .... 202 A4
Barmouth Ave PA19 .... 44 C3
Barmulloch Prim Sch KA3 .... 98 A2
Barmulloch Rd G21 .... 98 A2
Barn Gn PA10 .... 111 D2
Barn Rd FK8 .... 7 D4
Barnard Gdns G64 .... 78 A2
Barnbeth Rd G53 .... 115 D1
Barncluith Rd ML3 .... 162 C1
Barnego Rd FK6 .... 21 E2
Barnes Rd G64 .... 97 D3
Barnes Rd G78 .... 134 A1
Barnes St G78 .... 134 A1
Barness Pl G33 .... 119 D4
Barnett Cres KA21 .... 216 C4
Barnett Ct KA21 .... 216 C4
Barnett Path ꞁ G72 .... 161 E4
Barnflat St G73 .... 118 A1
Barnford Cres KA7 .... 239 D1
Barnhill Dr Hamilton ML3 .... 161 F3
Tullibody FK10 .... 4 B1
Barnhill Rd G82 .... 50 B2
Barnhill St PA15 .... 46 B2
Barnkirk Ave G15 .... 74 C2
Barns Cres KA7 .... 238 C4
Barns Pk KA7 .... 238 C4
Barns St KA7 .... 238 C4
Barns Terr KA7 .... 238 C4
Barnscroft KA11 .... 111 D2
Barnsdale Ave FK7 .... 7 D2
Barnsford Ave PA4 .... 93 D2

Barnsford Rd PA4 .... 93 D2
Barnsford Pl ꞁ G71 .... 141 D2
Barnton La FK1 .... 42 A2
Barnton St Glasgow G32 .... 118 C4
Stirling FK8 .... 7 D4
Barnweil Rd
Kilmarnock KA3 .... 227 F3
Barnweil Rd KA3 .... 228 C3
Barnwell Rd FK9 .... 2 B2
Barnwell Terr G51 .... 115 F4
Barochan Cres PA3 .... 113 D2
Barochan Rd Bishopton PA6 .... 71 D1
Glasgow G53 .... 115 D2
Houston PA6 .... 91 D3
Baron Ct PA3 .... 163 D1
Baron Rd PA3 .... 114 A3
Baron St PA4 .... 94 B1
Baronald Dr G12 .... 96 A3
Baronald Gate G12 .... 96 A3
Baronald St G73 .... 118 A1
Barone Dr G76 .... 157 E4
Baronhall Dr G72 .... 161 E4
Baronhill G67 .... 62 A2
Barons Gate G71 .... 140 C2
Barons Rd ML1 .... 164 B1
Baronscourt Dr PA3 .... 112 C2
Baronscourt Gdns PA3 .... 112 C2
Baronscourt Rd PA3 .... 112 C2
Barony Ct Ardrossan KA22 .... 205 E1
ꞁ G Glasgow G69 .... 120 A3
Irvine KA11 .... 219 F3
Barony Dr G69 .... 120 A3
Barony Gdns G69 .... 120 A3
Barony Glebe KA23 .... 190 B3
Barony Pl G68 .... 60 C1
Barony Rd KA9 .... 236 B3
Barony Terr KA25 .... 170 A4
Barony Wynd ꞁ G69 .... 120 A3
Barr Ave G78 .... 154 C4
Barr Cres G81 .... 74 A3
Barr Gr G71 .... 141 D4
Barr Pl
Newton Mearns G77 .... 156 B3
Paisley PA1 .... 113 E2
Barr St Ardrossan KA22 .... 205 E1
Glasgow G20 .... 97 D2
Motherwell ML1 .... 163 F4
Barr Terr G74 .... 159 F1
Barr's Brae Kilmacolm PA13 .... 111 D4
Port Glasgow PA14 .... 68 B4
Barr's Brae La PA14 .... 94 B1
Wishaw ML2 .... 165 F3
Barra Cres Irvine KA11 .... 220 B1
Old Kilpatrick G60 .... 73 E3
Barra Dr ML6 .... 123 E3
Barra Gdns G60 .... 73 E3
Barra Pl Irvine KA11 .... 220 B1
Stenhousemuir FK5 .... 24 A2
Barra Rd G60 .... 73 E3
Barra St G20 .... 96 B4
Barrachnie Cres G69 .... 119 F3
Barrachnie Ct G69 .... 119 F3
Barrachnie Rd G69 .... 119 F3
Barrack St Glasgow G4 .... 241 F1
Hamilton ML3 .... 162 B2
Barraston Rd G64 .... 57 D1
Barrcraig Rd PA11 .... 110 B4
Barrhead High Sch G78 .... 134 C2
Barrhead Rd Glasgow G43 .... 135 C4
Newton Mearns G77 .... 156 A3
Paisley PA2 .... 114 A1
Barrhead Sta G78 .... 134 A2
Barrhill Cres PA10 .... 111 E2
Barrhill Rd Beith KA15 .... 171 E4
Burnhouse KA15 .... 172 A1
Barrie Rd East Kilbride G74 .... 160 B3
Glasgow G52 .... 115 D4
Stenhousemuir FK5 .... 23 F2
Barrie Terr KA22 .... 205 E1
Barrie Terr KA22 .... 205 E1
Barriedale Ave ML3 .... 162 A2
Barrington Ave KA15 .... 150 A1
Barrington Dr G4 .... 96 C1
Barrisdale Rd
Glasgow G20 .... 96 B4
Wishaw ML2 .... 165 F3
Barrisdale Way G73 .... 138 A2
Barrland Ct G46 .... 136 B2
Barrland Dr G46 .... 136 B2
Barrland St G41 .... 117 D2
Barrmill Rd Beith KA15 .... 171 E4
Glasgow G43 .... 136 A3
Barrochan Inst PA5 .... 111 F3
Barrochan Rd PA5, PA6 .... 111 F3
Barrowfield Gdns G40 .... 118 A3
Barrowfield St Coatbridge ML5 .... 122 A4
Glasgow G40 .... 118 A3
Barrs Brae La PA14 .... 68 B4
Barrs Cres G82 .... 48 A4
Barrs La G82 .... 26 A1
Barrs Terr G82 .... 48 A4
Barrwood Pl G71 .... 141 D4
Barrwood St G33 .... 98 C2
Barry Gdns G72 .... 161 E3
Barsail Prim Sch PA4 .... 93 E4
Barscube Ave PA14 .... 68 C4
Barscube Terr PA2 .... 114 A3
Barshaw Dr PA1 .... 114 A3
Barshaw Pl PA1 .... 114 C3
Barshaw Rd G52 .... 114 C3
Barskiven Rd PA1 .... 112 C2
Barterholm Rd PA2 .... 113 F1

Bartholomew St G40 .... 118 A2
Bartiebeith Rd G33 .... 119 F4
Bartlands Pl FK6 .... 178 C2
Barton Ave G83 .... 28 A4
Bartonhall Rd ML2 .... 165 E1
Bartonholm Terr KA13 .... 207 F1
Barty's Rd ML4 .... 142 B3
Barwheys Dr KA6 .... 237 F3
Barwood Hill G82 .... 50 A3
Bassett Ave G13 .... 95 D4
Bassett Cres G13 .... 95 D4
Bastion Wynd FK8 .... 7 D4
Bath La G2 .... 240 B3
Bath Pl KA7 .... 238 C4
Bath Sq KA22 .... 216 B4
Bath St Glasgow G2 .... 240 C3
Gourock PA19 .... 44 C4
Kilmarnock KA3 .... 222 C1
Bath Villas KA22 .... 216 B4
Bathgate St G31 .... 118 A3
Bathgow Ave PA1 .... 114 C2
Bathurst Dr KA7 .... 239 D1
Bathville Rd KA25 .... 149 D1
Bathwick Way PA2 .... 132 C4
Baton Rd ML7 .... 146 B3
Baton St G42 .... 117 D1
Batterflats Gdns FK7 .... 6 C3
Battery Park Ave PA16 .... 45 D4
Battery Park Dr PA16 .... 45 D4
Battismains ML11 .... 215 E2
Battle Pl G42 .... 136 C4
Battlefield Ave G42 .... 137 D4
Battlefield Gdns G42 .... 137 D4
Battlefield Prim Sch G42 . 136 C4
Battlefield Rd G42 .... 137 D4
Bavelaw St G33 .... 99 E1
Bawhirley Rd PA15 .... 46 B2
Baxter Cres PA4 .... 43 D2
Baxter La Alexandria G83 .... 27 F4
Lanark ML11 .... 215 D2
Baxter St Fallin FK7 .... 8 B2
Greenock PA15 .... 46 B2
Baxter's Wynd FK1 .... 42 A2
Bay St PA14 .... 47 E1
Bay View Rd PA19 .... 44 C4
Bayfield Ave G15 .... 75 D2
Bayfield Terr G15 .... 75 D2
Bayne St FK8 .... 2 A1
Beach Dr KA12 .... 218 C1
Beach Pk KA10 .... 224 A1
Beach Rd KA10 .... 229 E3
Beaconcrust Sch FK9 .... 2 B3
Beaconsfield Rd G12 .... 96 A3
Beagle Cres KA7 .... 238 B2
Bean Row FK1 .... 42 A2
Beansburn KA3 .... 223 D2
Beanshields Rd ML8 .... 201 F2
Beard Cres G69 .... 100 C3
Beardmore Cotts PA4 .... 93 E3
Beardmore Pl G81 .... 73 F2
Beardmore St G81 .... 73 F2
Beardmore Way PA4 .... 73 E1
Bearford Dr G52 .... 115 D3
Bearhope St PA15 .... 45 F3
Bearsden Acad G61 .... 75 F2
Bearsden Sta G61 .... 75 F2
Bearside Rd FK7 .... 7 D2
Beaton Ave FK7 .... 7 E1
Beaton Rd Balloch G83 .... 27 F4
Glasgow G41 .... 116 C1
Beaton St ML9 .... 184 C3
Beaton Terr KA12 .... 219 E3
Beatrice Dr ML1 .... 142 C3
Beatrice Gdns PA6 .... 111 E4
Beatson Wynd G71 .... 121 D1
Beattock St G31 .... 118 B3
Beattock Wynd ML3 .... 162 A2
Beatty Ave PA4 .... 2 A1
Beatty Pl G84 .... 17 D1
Beatty St G81 .... 73 F2
Beauclerc St FK12 .... 5 D4
Beaufield Gdns KA3 .... 222 A4
Beaufort Ave G43 .... 136 B3
Beaufort Dr Falkirk FK2 .... 24 A2
Kirkintilloch G66 .... 79 D4
Beaufort Gdns G64 .... 77 F1
Beauly Cres Kilmacolm PA13 . 89 E4
Kilmarnock KA1 .... 228 A3
Beauly Ct FK1 .... 42 B1
Beauly Dr PA2 .... 112 C1
Beauly Pl Chryston G69 .... 80 B1
Coatbridge ML5 .... 122 A2
East Kilbride G74 .... 159 E1
Glasgow G20 .... 96 B3
Motherwell ML1 .... 143 D3
Beauly Rd G69 .... 120 A2
Beaumont Dr FK2 .... 24 A1
Beaumont Gate 10 G12 .... 96 B2
Beckford Lodge Maternity
Hosp ML3 .... 162 B3
Beckford Prim Sch ML3 . 162 B3
Beckford St ML3 .... 162 B3
Beda Pl FK7 .... 8 B3
Bedale Rd G69 .... 119 F2
Bedcow View G66 .... 79 F4
Bedford Ave G81 .... 74 B1
Bedford Ct FK10 .... 10 A3
Bedford La 11 Glasgow G5 . 117 D3
Greenock PA16 .... 45 E4
Bedford Pl FK10 .... 10 A3
Bedford St Glasgow G5 .... 117 D3
Greenock PA16 .... 45 E4
Bedlay Ct G69 .... 81 D2
Bedlay Pl ML5 .... 81 F1
Bedlay View G71 .... 141 D4
Bedlay Wlk G69 .... 81 D2

Bedlormie Dr EH48 .... 107 E1
Beech Ave Bearsden G61 .... 76 A4
Beith KA15 .... 150 A1
Bridge Of W PA11 .... 90 B1
Elderslie PA5 .... 112 B1
Glasgow G69 .... 120 A3
Glasgow, Dumbreck G41 .... 116 A2
Irvine KA12 .... 219 E1
Kilmarnock KA1 .... 227 E4
Larkhall ML9 .... 185 A1
Motherwell ML1 .... 143 D2
Newton Mearns G77 .... 156 C2
Paisley PA2 .... 114 A1
Plean FK7 .... 12 B2
Quarter ML3 .... 183 F2
Rutherglen, Cambuslang
G73, G72 .... 138 C3
Rutherglen, High Burnside
G73 .... 138 B2
Beech Cres Cambuslang G72 139 F2
Denny FK6 .... 21 E2
Larbert FK5 .... 41 E4
Motherwell ML1 .... 143 E4
Newton Mearns G77 .... 156 C2
Beech Ct ML5 .... 121 F2
Beech Dr Caldercruix ML6 .. 104 C2
Clydebank G81 .... 74 A3
Beech Gdns G69 .... 120 A3
Beech Gr Ayr KA8 .... 239 E4
East Kilbride G75 .... 180 A3
Gartcosh G69 .... 101 D3
Law ML8 .... 186 C3
Rhu G84 .... 15 E3
Wishaw ML2 .... 165 E4
Beech La FK9 .... 2 A2
Beech Pl Bishopbriggs G64 .. 98 A4
Blantyre G72 .... 161 F4
Gourock PA19 .... 44 B3
Beech Rd Bishopbriggs G64 .. 98 A4
Johnstone PA5 .... 111 E1
Kirkintilloch G66 .... 79 E3
Motherwell ML1 .... 143 E4
Beech Terr ML9 .... 185 D1
Beechbank Ave ML6 .... 102 C1
Beechburn Cres PA12 .... 129 E2
Beeches Ave G81 .... 73 F3
Beeches Rd G81 .... 73 F3
Beeches Terr G81 .... 73 F3
Beeches The Brookfield PA5 111 E3
Houston PA6 .... 91 E1
Lanark ML11 .... 215 D1
Newton Mearns G77 .... 156 C2
Beechfield Dr ML8 .... 202 A4
Beechfield Rd KA15 .... 170 C4
Beechgrove G69 .... 80 C1
Beechgrove Ave G71 .... 141 E4
Beechgrove Pl G84 .... 25 D4
Beechgrove Quadrant
ML1 .... 143 D3
Beechgrove St G40 .... 118 A1
Beechlands Ave G44 .... 136 C1
Beechlands Dr G76 .... 157 E3
Beechmount Ct ML7 .... 147 D1
Beechmount Rd G66 .... 79 F2
Beechtree Terr G65 .... 58 B3
Beechwood Alloa FK10 .... 5 E1
Kilwinning KA13 .... 207 E3
Larkhall ML9 .... 185 D3
Beechwood Ave
Clarkston G76 .... 157 E3
Hamilton ML3 .... 183 D4
Langbank PA14 .... 70 B4
Rutherglen G73 .... 138 B3
Beechwood Cres ML2 .... 165 E1
Beechwood Ct Bearsden G61 75 F2
Cumbernauld G67 .... 61 F1
Beechwood Dr Bonhill G83 .. 28 A1
Coatbridge ML5 .... 122 B3
Glasgow G11 .... 95 F2
Renfrew PA4 .... 94 B1
Beechwood Gdns
Bellshill ML4 .... 142 B2
Moodiesburn G69 .... 80 C1
Beechwood Dr G78 .... 134 B1
Beechwood La G61 .... 75 F2
Beechwood Paddock KA10 230 A2
Beechwood Pl Bellshill ML4 142 B2
Glasgow G11 .... 95 F2
Beechwood Rd G67 .... 82 A4
Beechworth Dr ML1 .... 143 E1
Beecroft Pl G72 .... 140 C1
Begg Ave FK1 .... 41 F2
Beggs Terr KA22 .... 205 E2
Beil Dr G13 .... 94 C4
Beith Dr ML6 .... 123 D2
Beith Prim Sch KA15 .... 171 D4
Beith Rd Dalry KA24 .... 191 F4
Glengarnock KA14 .... 170 B3
Greenock PA16 .... 45 F1
Johnstone PA5 .... 111 F1
Beith St G11 .... 96 A1
Belford Gr G72 .... 156 B1
Belgowan St ML4 .... 141 F4
Belgrave La G12 .... 96 C2
Belgrave St ML4 .... 141 F3
Belhaven Rd Hamilton ML3 .. 162 A1
Wishaw ML2 .... 165 D2
Belhaven St PA14 .... 47 D1
Belhaven Terr
10 Glasgow G12 .... 96 B2
Wishaw ML2 .... 165 D2
Belhaven Terr W 10 G12 ..... 96 B2
Belhaven Terrace La
10 G12 .... 96 B2
Belhaven Terrace West La
10 G12 .... 96 B2
Bell Cres KA12 .... 219 E3
Bell Dr ML3 .... 161 E2

Bell Gn E G75 .... 180 C4
Bell Gn W G75 .... 180 C4
Bell St Airdrie ML6 .... 122 C4
Bellshill ML4 .... 142 A4
Clydebank G81 .... 94 B4
Glasgow G1 .... 241 E1
Greenock PA15 .... 46 C1
Renfrew PA4 .... 94 B2
Wishaw ML2 .... 165 D2
Bell Tec Coll ML3 .... 162 B3
Bell Trees Rd PA9 .... 130 B1
Bell View Ct PA4 .... 94 B2
Bell's Wynd Falkirk FK1 ...... 42 A2
Lanark ML11 .... 215 E3
Bellahouston Acad G41 ...... 116 B3
Bellahouston Acad Annexe
G51 .... 116 B3
Bellahouston Dr G52 .... 115 F2
Bellahouston Prim Sch
G51 .... 116 B3
Bellairs Pl G72 .... 140 B1
Bellard Rd KA23 .... 190 B2
Bellard Wlk KA23 .... 190 B2
Bellarmine Sec Sch G53 .. 135 E3
Bellas Pl ML6 .... 104 A1
Bellcraig Ct G76 .... 158 A3
Belleaire Dr PA16 .... 44 C2
Bellefield Rd ML11 .... 215 D3
Belleisle Ave G71 .... 140 C4
Belleisle Cl KA13 .... 207 E2
Belleisle Cres PA11 .... 110 B3
Belleisle Dr G68 .... 61 F2
Belleisle Gdns G68 .... 61 F2
Belleisle Pk KA7 .... 238 C2
Belleisle Pl Gourock PA19 .... 44 A3
Kilmarnock KA1 .... 227 F3
Belleisle St G42 .... 117 D1
Belleslyhill Ave KA8 .... 236 A2
Belleslyhill Rd KA8 .... 236 A2
Bellevue Quadrant KA7 .. 238 C3
Bellevue Ave G66 .... 79 D3
Bellevue Cres KA7 .... 238 C4
Bellevue Gdns KA1 .... 222 B1
Bellevue La KA7 .... 238 C4
Bellevue Rd Alloa FK10 ...... 9 F3
Ayr KA7 .... 238 C4
Kilmarnock KA1 .... 222 B1
Kirkintilloch G66 .... 79 D4
Prestwick KA9 .... 236 B4
Bellevue St Ayr KA7 .... 238 C4
Falkirk FK1 .... 42 B2
Bellfield Ave KA1 .... 228 B3
Bellfield Cres G78 .... 134 A2
Bellfield Ct Barrhead G78 .. 134 A2
Hurlford KA1 .... 228 B3
Bellfield Dr ML2 .... 165 E1
Bellfield La PA14 .... 47 D1
Bellfield Prim Sch KA1 .... 228 A2
Bellfield Rd Bannockburn FK7 7 F1
Kirkintilloch G66 .... 79 D4
Stirling FK8 .... 7 D3
Bellfield St G31 .... 118 A3
Bellflower Ct G74 .... 159 F2
Bellflower Gdns G53 .... 135 E2
Bellflower Gr G74 .... 159 F2
Bellgrove St G31 .... 117 F3
Bellgrove Sta G31 .... 117 F3
Bellisle Terr ML3 .... 183 D4
Bellrock Ave KA9 .... 236 A3
Bellrock Cres G33 .... 119 D4
Bellrock Ct G33 .... 119 D4
Bellrock Prim Sch G33 .... 119 D4
Bellrock Rd KA9 .... 236 A3
Bellrock St G33 .... 119 D4
Bellscroft Ave G73 .... 137 F4
Bellsdyke Hospl FK5 .... 23 E3
Bellsdyke Rd Airdrie ML6 .. 123 D3
Falkirk FK2 .... 24 B3
Larbert FK5 .... 23 E2
Bellsfield Dr G72 .... 161 F3
Bellshaugh Ct G12 .... 96 B3
Bellshaugh La G12 .... 96 B3
Bellshaugh Pl 2 G12 .... 96 B3
Bellshaugh Rd G12 .... 96 B2
Bellshill Acad ML4 .... 142 A3
Bellshill Ind Est ML4 .... 141 F3
Bellshill Maternity Hospl
ML4 .... 142 A4
Bellshill Rd Bellshill ML4 .... 141 F1
Bothwell G71 .... 141 D3
Motherwell ML1 .... 142 B1
Bellshill Sta ML4 .... 142 A3
Bellside Rd Chapelhall ML6 .. 123 F1
Cleland ML1 .... 144 B1
Motherwell ML1 .... 144 A4
Bellsland Dr KA1 .... 227 F3
Bellsland Gr KA1 .... 227 F3
Bellsland Pl KA1 .... 228 A4
Bellsmeadow Rd FK1 .... 42 B2
Bellsmyre Ave G82 .... 50 A3
Belltree Ave KA3 .... 211 E4
Belltrees Cres PA3 .... 113 D2
Bellvale Ave KA7 .... 239 D3
Bellvue Cres Bellshill ML4 .. 142 A3
Prestwick KA9 .... 236 B4
Bellwood St G41 .... 136 C4
Bellziehill Rd ML4 .... 141 F3
Belman's Ct KA15 .... 150 A1
Belmont Acad KA7 .... 239 D3
Belmont Ave Ayr KA7 .... 239 D3
Dennyloanhead FK4 .... 39 E3
Shieldhill FK1 .... 66 C4
Uddingston G71 .... 140 C4
Belmont Cres Ayr KA7 ...... 239 D3
Glasgow G12 .... 96 C2
Kilmaurs KA3 .... 222 A4
Belmont Ct G66 .... 79 E4

Belmont Dr Ayr KA7 .... 239 D3
Barrhead G78 .... 134 B1
East Kilbride G75 .... 180 A4
Glasgow G46 .... 136 A2
Glasgow G73 .... 138 A4
Shotts ML7 .... 147 D1
Belmont House Sch G77 .. 157 D3
Belmont La G12 .... 96 C2
Belmont Pl E KA7 .... 239 D3
Belmont Pl W KA7 .... 239 D3
Belmont Rd Ayr KA7 .... 239 D3
Cambuslang G72 .... 138 C2
Glasgow G21 .... 97 F3
Kilmacolm PA13 .... 89 E4
Paisley PA3 .... 114 A3
Belmont St Clydebank G81 .. 74 A1
Coatbridge ML5 .... 101 E1
Falkirk FK1 .... 42 B2
Glasgow G12, G20 .... 96 C2
Kilsyth G65 .... 36 B1
Stirling FK8 .... 2 A2
Wishaw ML2 .... 186 A3
Belses Dr G52 .... 115 E3
Belstane Pk ML8 .... 187 F2
Belstane Rd Carluke ML8 .. 188 A2
Cumbernauld G67 .... 82 C3
Belsyde Ave G15 .... 75 D1
Beltane St Glasgow G3 ...... 240 A3
Wishaw ML2 .... 165 D1
Beltrees Ave G53 .... 115 D1
Beltrees Cres G53 .... 115 D1
Beltrees Rd G53 .... 115 D1
Belvidere Cres
Bellshill ML4 .... 142 A2
Bishopbriggs G64 .... 78 A1
Belvidere Hospl G31 .... 118 B2
Belvidere Prim Sch ML4 .. 142 A2
Belvidere Rd ML4 .... 142 A2
Belvidere Terr KA8 .... 236 A1
Belville Ave PA15 .... 46 B2
Belvoir Pl G72 .... 161 E4
Bemersyde G64 .... 78 B1
Bemersyde Ave G43 .... 136 A3
Bemersyde Pl ML9 .... 185 D1
Bemersyde Rd PA2 .... 132 C4
Ben Aigan Dr G53 .... 135 E2
Ben Alder Dr PA2 .... 114 B1
Ben Bouie Dr G84 .... 16 C1
Ben Buie Way PA2 .... 114 B1
Ben Donich Pl G53 .... 135 E2
Ben Edra Pl G53 .... 135 E2
Ben Garrisdale Pl G53 .... 135 E2
Ben Glas Pl G53 .... 135 E2
Ben Hope Ave PA2 .... 114 B1
Ben Laga Pl G53 .... 135 E2
Ben Lawers Dr
Cumbernauld G68 .... 61 D1
Paisley PA2 .... 114 B1
Ben Ledi Ave PA2 .... 114 B1
Ben Ledi Cres G68 .... 61 D1
Ben Lomond View G68 ...... 80 A4
Ben Lui Dr G53 .... 135 E2
Ben Lui Pl
Cumbernauld G68 .... 61 D1
Glasgow G53 .... 135 E2
Ben Macdui Gdns G53 ...... 135 E2
Ben More Dr
Cumbernauld G68 .... 61 D1
Paisley PA2 .... 114 B1
Ben Nevis Rd PA2 .... 114 B1
Ben Nevis Way G68 .... 61 D1
Ben Uird Pl G53 .... 135 E2
Ben Vane Ave PA2 .... 114 B1
Ben Venue Rd G68 .... 61 D1
Ben Venue Way PA2 .... 114 B1
Ben Vorlich Dr G53 .... 135 E2
Ben Wyvis Dr PA2 .... 114 B1
Benalder St G11 .... 96 B1
Benarty Gdns G64 .... 78 A1
Benbain Pl KA11 .... 220 A3
Benbecula G74 .... 160 B1
Benbecula Rd KA3 .... 223 D1
Benbow Rd G81 .... 73 F1
Bencleuch Pl KA11 .... 220 A2
Bencloich Ave G65 .... 57 F4
Bencloich Cres G65 .... 57 F4
Bencloich Rd G65 .... 57 F4
Benculha PA14 .... 48 C4
Bencroft Dr G44 .... 137 F3
Bendigo Pl ML11 .... 215 D2
Benford Ave ML1 .... 143 E2
Benford Knowe ML1 .... 143 F2
Bengairn St G31 .... 118 B4
Bengal Pl G43 .... 136 B4
Bengal St G43 .... 136 B4
Benhar Pl G33 .... 118 C3
Benhar Prim Sch ML7 ...... 127 E3
Benhar Rd Harthill ML7 .... 126 C1
Shotts ML7 .... 127 E3
Benholm St G32 .... 118 C2
Benmore Ka9 .... 236 B3
Benmore La PA16 .... 44 C2
Benmore Tower G72 .... 138 C2
Bennan House KA9 .... 236 A3
Bennan Pl G75 .... 180 B2
Bennan Sq G42 .... 117 E1
Bennoch Pl KA9 .... 236 B3
Benny Lynch Ct G5 .... 117 E3
Benrig Ave KA3 .... 222 A4
Bensley Ave KA1 .... 219 F3
Bensley Rise ML1 .... 219 F3
Benson St ML5 .... 122 A2
Benston Pl PA5 .... 111 F1
Benston Rd PA5 .... 111 F1
Bent Cres G71 .... 141 E3
Bent Rd Chapelhall ML6 .... 123 E2
Hamilton ML3 .... 162 B2

Bar – Bin 247

Bentfield Ave KA7 .... 238 C3
Bentfield Dr KA9 .... 236 A3
Bentfoot Rd ML2 .... 186 B4
Benthall St G5 .... 117 E2
Bentheads FK7 .... 11 F4
Bentinck Cres KA10 .... 229 F1
Bentinck Dr KA10 .... 229 E1
Bentinck St Glasgow G3 ...... 96 C1
Greenock PA16 .... 45 E4
Kilmarnock KA3 .... 227 F4
Bents Rd G69 .... 120 A3
Benty's La ML8 .... 201 F4
Benvie Gdns G64 .... 78 A1
Benview FK7 .... 7 E1
Benview Ave PA4 .... 44 C4
Benview Rd Clarkston G76 .. 157 F4
Port Glasgow PA14 .... 68 C4
Benview St G20 .... 96 C2
Benview Terr Fishcross FK10 .. 5 F2
Paisley PA2 .... 114 A1
Benvue Rd G65 .... 57 F4
Berchem Pl KA21 .... 216 C4
Bereland Ave KA2 .... 226 B4
Berelands Cres G73 .... 137 F4
Berelands Gdns KA4 .... 233 E1
Berelands Pl G73 .... 137 F4
Berelands Rd KA9 .... 233 E1
Beresford Ave G14 .... 95 F2
Beresford Gr KA11 .... 219 F3
Beresford Terr KA7 .... 238 C4
Berkeley St Glasgow G3 .... 240 A3
Stirling FK7 .... 7 D2
Berkeley Terrace La G3 .... 240 A3
Berkley Dr G72 .... 140 B1
Berl Ave PA6 .... 111 E4
Bernadette Ave ML1 .... 143 E1
Bernadette St ML1 .... 143 E2
Bernard Path G40 .... 118 A2
Bernard St G40 .... 118 A2
Bernard Terr G40 .... 118 A2
Bernard's Wynd ML11 ...... 215 D2
Berneray St G22 .... 97 E4
Bernisdale Dr G15 .... 74 C1
Bernisdale Gdns G15 .... 74 C1
Bernisdale Pl G15 .... 74 C1
Berridale G75 .... 179 F4
Berridale Ave G44 .... 137 D3
Berriedale G75 .... 180 C4
Berriedale Ave G69 .... 119 F1
Berriedale Quadrant ML2 .. 165 D3
Berry Dr KA12 .... 219 F2
Berryburn Rd G21 .... 98 B2
Berryhill FK7 .... 12 C4
Berryhill Ave KA11 .... 220 A3
Berryhill Dr G46 .... 136 A1
Berryhill Pl ML7 .... 147 D1
Berryhill Prim Sch ML2 .... 164 C2
Berryhill Rd
Cumbernauld G67 .... 61 F1
Glasgow G46 .... 136 A1
Berryknowe G66 .... 80 A4
Berryknowe Ave G69 .... 100 B4
Berryknowes Ave G52 ...... 115 E3
Berryknowes La G52 .... 115 E3
Berryknowes Rd G52 .... 115 E3
Berryyards Rd PA15 .... 45 F2
Bertram Dr ML7 .... 125 E1
Bertram Pl ML7 .... 146 B3
Bertram St Glasgow G41 .... 116 C1
Hamilton ML3 .... 162 A3
Harthill ML7 .... 127 E3
Larkhall ML9 .... 185 E1
Shotts ML7 .... 147 D1
Bervie St G51 .... 115 F3
Berwick Cres Airdrie ML6 .. 122 C3
Linwood PA3 .... 111 F4
Berwick Dr Glasgow G52 .... 115 D2
Rutherglen G73 .... 138 B3
Berwick Pl Coatbridge ML5 . 122 A2
East Kilbride G74 .... 160 B2
Greenock PA16 .... 44 B2
Berwick Rd Greenock PA16 .. 44 B2
Port Glasgow PA14 .... 47 E1
Berwickshire Rd
Hamilton ML3 .... 162 A3
Bessemer Dr G75 .... 181 D3
Beta Ctr G81 .... 94 B4
Betula Dr G81 .... 74 A3
Bevan Ct KA22 .... 205 D2
Bevan Dr FK12 .... 5 E4
Bevan Gdns KA13 .... 207 F2
Bevan Gr PA5 .... 111 F1
Beveridge Terr ML4 .... 142 B2
Beverley Rd G43 .... 136 B3
Bevin Ave G81 .... 74 B1
Bideford Cres G32 .... 119 E2
Bield The ML3 .... 165 L1
Biggar Rd Chapelhall ML6 .. 123 E1
Chapelhall, Biggar Road
ML1 .... 143 E4
Biggar St G31 .... 118 A3
Biggart Hospl KA9 .... 236 B4
Biggart Rd KA9 .... 236 B4
Bigholm Rd KA15 .... 150 B1
Bigton St G33 .... 99 D1
Bilby Terr KA1 .... 219 E3
Billings Rd ML1 .... 163 D3
Bilsland Ct G20 .... 97 D3
Bilsland Dr G20 .... 97 D3
Bilsland Pl G87 .... 27 E1
Bimson Pl KA12 .... 219 D1
Bimson Row KA12 .... 219 D1
Binend Rd G53 .... 115 E1
Binnie La PA19 .... 44 C4
Binnie Pl Glasgow G40 ...... 117 F3
Skinflats FK2 .... 24 C1
Binnie St PA19 .... 44 C4

Binniehill Rd
Cumbernauld G68 .... 61 E1
Slamannan FK1 .... 85 F2
Binns Rd G33 .... 99 E1
Birch Ave Clarkston G76 ..... 157 F3
Stirling FK8 .... 6 C3
Birch Brae ML3 .... 162 C1
Birch Cotts G84 .... 16 B1
Birch Cres Clarkston G76 ... 157 F3
Johnstone PA5 .... 112 A1
Birch Ct ML5 .... 121 F2
Birch Dr Cambuslang G72 ... 139 E3
Kirkintilloch G66 .... 79 E3
Birch Gr Larkhall ML9 ..... 185 D3
Uddingston G71 .... 141 D4
Birch Knowe G64 .... 98 A4
Birch Pl Blantyre G72 ..... 161 E4
Cambuslang G72 .... 139 F2
Kilmarnock KA1 .... 227 E4
Birch Quadrant ML6 ..... 123 E4
Birch Rd Ayr KA7 .... 239 E2
Clydebank G81 .... 74 A3
Cumbernauld G67 .... 62 C2
Dumbarton G82 .... 49 F2
Birch St Glasgow G5 ..... 117 E2
Motherwell ML1 .... 143 D3
Birch Terr KA22 .... 205 E2
Birch View G61 .... 76 A3
Birch Way KA10 .... 229 F2
Birchfield Dr G14 .... 95 D2
Birchfield Rd ML3 .... 162 A2
Birchgrove PA6 .... 91 E1
Birchlea Dr G46 .... 136 B2
Birchmount Ct ML6 ..... 123 E4
Birchview Dr G76 .... 157 F2
Birchwood FK10 .... 5 E1
Birchwood Ave G32 ..... 119 F2
Birchwood Dr PA2 .... 113 D1
Birchwood Pl G32 .... 119 F2
Birchwood Rd G78 .... 153 D2
Birdsfield Ct G72 .... 161 F3
Birdsfield Dr G72 .... 161 F3
Birdsfield St ML3 .... 161 F3
Birdston Rd Glasgow G21 .. 98 B3
Milton Of C G65 .... 58 B2
Birgidale Ave G45 .... 137 E1
Birgidale Rd G45 .... 137 E1
Birgidale Terr G45 ..... 137 E1
Birkbeck Ct G4 .... 241 E3
Birkdale G74 .... 159 E2
Birkdale Cl KA13 .... 207 E2
Birkdale Ct G72 .... 140 C1
Birken Rd G66 .... 79 F2
Birkenburn Rd G67 ..... 62 C2
Birkenshaw Rd G69, ML5 ... 81 F1
Birkenshaw St G31 ..... 118 A4
Birkenshaw Way PA3 .... 113 F4
Birkfield Loan ML8 ...... 188 B1
Birkfield Pl ML8 .... 188 B1
Birkhall Ave Glasgow G52 .. 115 D2
Inchinnan PA4 .... 93 E4
Birkhall Dr G61 .... 75 F1
Birkhill Ave G64 .... 78 A1
Birkhill Gdns G64 .... 78 A1
Birkhill Rd
Crossford ML11 .... 201 E1
Hamilton ML3 .... 183 E4
Stirling FK7 .... 7 E4
Birkmyre Ave PA14 ..... 47 D1
Birkmyre Rd G51 .... 115 F3
Birks Ct ML8 .... 186 C3
Birks Hill KA11 .... 220 A2
Birks Pl ML11 .... 215 D3
Birks Rd Larkhall ML9 .... 199 D4
Law ML8 .... 186 C2
Birkscairn Pl KA11 ..... 220 B1
Birkscairn Way KA11 .... 220 B1
Birkshaw Brae ML2 ..... 186 A4
Birkshaw Pl ML2 .... 186 A4
Birkshaw Tower ML2 .... 185 F4
Birkwood Pl G77 .... 156 B1
Birkwood St G40 .... 118 A1
Birmingham Rd PA4 ..... 94 A1
Birnam Ave G64 .... 78 A3
Birnam Cres G61 .... 76 A3
Birnam Ct ML3 .... 183 E4
Birnam Gdns G64 .... 78 A1
Birnam Pl Hamilton ML3 ... 161 F2
Newton Mearns G77 .... 156 C2
Birnam Rd G31 .... 118 B2
Birnie Ct G43 .... 136 B4
Birnie Ct G21 .... 98 B2
Birnie Rd G21 .... 98 B2
Birniehill Rd ML1 .... 145 D3
Birniehill Rdbt G71 ..... 181 D4
Birniewell Rd FK1 .... 86 A3
Birnock Ave PA4 .... 94 C1
Birrell Rd G62 .... 54 C2
Birrens Rd ML1 .... 163 A4
Birsay Rd G22 .... 97 D4
Bishop Gdns
Bishopbriggs G64 .... 77 F1
Hamilton ML3 .... 183 F4
Bishop La G2 .... 240 B2
Bishop Loch Prim Sch
G34 .... 100 B1
Bishopbriggs High Sch
G64 .... 77 F4
Bishopbriggs Sta G64 ... 78 A1
Bishopdale G74 .... 159 E2
Bishopmill Pl G21 .... 98 B2
Bishopmill Rd G21 .... 98 B2
Bishops Gate G74 .... 158 B2
Bishops Pk G74 .... 158 A2
Bishopsgate Dr G21 ..... 97 F4

Bishopsgate Gdns G21 .... 97 F4
Bishopsgate Pl [10] G21 .. 97 F4
Bishopsgate Rd G21 ..... 97 F4
Bishopton Prim Sch PA7 .. 72 A2
Bishopton Sta PA7 .... 72 A1
Bishopbriggs Ind Est G21 .. 98 A4
Bissett Cres G81 .... 73 F3
Black O' Hill Rdbt G68 ... 61 D1
Black St Airdrie ML6 ..... 103 D1
Glasgow G4 .... 241 E4
Blackadder Pl G75 .... 179 E4
Blackbog Rd ML6 .... 82 C1
Blackbraes Rd G74 ...... 160 A2
Blackburn Cres
Dumbarton G82 .... 49 E2
Kirkintilloch G66 .... 80 A4
Blackburn Dr KA7 .... 238 C3
Blackburn Pl KA7 .... 238 C3
Blackburn Rd KA7 .... 238 C3
Blackburn Sq G78 .... 134 B1
Blackburn St G51 .... 116 C3
Blackburn St G78 .... 134 B2
Blackbyres Rd G78 ...... 134 B3
Blackcraig Ave G15 ...... 75 D2
Blackcroft Ave ML6 ..... 123 F3
Blackcroft Gdns G32 .... 119 E2
Blackcroft Rd G32 .... 119 E2
Blackcroft Terr ML7 ...... 125 D1
Blackdyke Rd G66 .... 79 F4
Blackfarm Rd G77 .... 156 C2
Blackfauds Dr KA3 ...... 213 D2
Blackfauds Gdns KA3 .... 213 D2
Blackfaulds Rd G73 ...... 137 F4
Blackford Cres KA9 ...... 233 F1
Blackford Rd PA2 .... 114 A2
Blackfriars Prim Sch G5 .. 117 F2
Blackfriars St G1 .... 241 E2
Blackfriars Wlk KA7 ...... 238 C4
Blackhall Ct PA2 .... 114 A2
Blackhall La PA1 .... 113 F2
Blackhall St Paisley PA1 .. 114 A2
Shotts ML7 .... 147 D2
Blackhill Dr G84 .... 16 B2
Blackhill Pl G33 .... 98 B1
Blackhill Rd
Blackridge EH48 .... 107 F2
Glasgow G23 .... 76 C1
Blackhill St KA7 .... 239 D3
Blackhill View ML8 ...... 187 E3
Blackhouse Ave G77 .... 156 C2
Blackhouse Gdns G77 .... 156 C2
Blackhouse Pl KA8 ...... 239 E4
Blackhouse Rd G77 ...... 156 C2
Blackie St G3 .... 96 B1
Blacklands Ave KA13 .... 207 F1
Blacklands Cres KA13 .... 207 F1
Blacklands Pl G66 .... 79 F2
Blacklands Prim Sch
KA13 .... 207 E1
Blacklands Rd G74 ...... 159 E1
Blacklaw Dr G74 .... 181 D4
Blacklaw La PA3 .... 113 F3
Blacklch Cres G74 .... 160 A4
Blacklch Cres PA2 .... 24 A2
Blackmoor Pl ML1 .... 143 D2
Blackmoss Dr ML4 .... 142 A2
Blackmuir Pl FK10 .... 4 B2
Blackness St ML5 .... 122 A2
Blackridge Prim Sch
G48 .... 107 E2
Blackshaw Dr G77 ...... 190 B3
Blackstone Ave G53 .... 135 E4
Blackstone Cres G53 .... 115 E1
Blackstone Rd PA3 ...... 113 D4
Blackstoun Ave PA3 ..... 112 A3
Blackstoun Oval PA3 .... 113 D3
Blackstoun Rd PA3 ...... 113 D3
Blackswell La ML3 ...... 162 C2
Blacksyke Ave KA1 ...... 227 F2
Blackthorn Ave
Beith KA15 .... 150 A1
Kirkintilloch G66 .... 79 D3
Blackthorn Gr G66 ...... 79 D3
Blackthorn Rd
Cumbernauld G67 .... 62 C2
Uddingston G71 .... 141 E4
Blackthorn St G22 ...... 97 F3
Blacktongue Farm Rd
ML6 .... 83 F1
Blackwood G75 .... 180 B3
Blackwood Ave
Kilmarnock KA1 .... 227 F3
Linwood PA3 .... 112 A3
Newton Mearns G77 .... 156 C2
Blackwood Gdns ML1 .... 142 B1
Blackwood Rd
Cumbernauld G68 .... 60 C1
Milngavie G62 .... 54 B1
Blackwood St
Barrhead G78 .... 134 A1
Glasgow G13 .... 95 F4
Blackwood Terr PA5 .... 131 E4
Blackwoods Cres
Bellshill ML4 .... 142 B2
Moodiesburn G69 .... 80 C1
Bladda La PA1 .... 113 F2
Blades Ct G69 .... 101 D3
Bladnoch Dr G15 .... 75 E1
Blaefaulds Cres FK6 ...... 39 E4
Blaeloch Ave G45 .... 137 E1
Blaeloch Dr G45 .... 137 E1
Blaeloch Terr G14 .... 137 E1
Blaeshill Rd G75 .... 179 F4
Blair Athol Dr [20] ML9 .. 185 E1
Blair Ave KA1 .... 228 C3
Blair Cres Glasgow G69 .. 120 A2
Hurlford KA1 .... 228 C3
Blair Dr G65 .... 58 B3

Blair Gdns Gourock PA19 .. 43 F3
Newton Mearns G77 .... 156 A3
Torrance G64 .... 57 D1
Blair House G67 .... 62 A2
Blair Linn View G67 ...... 83 D3
Blair Path ML1 .... 163 F3
Blair Rd Coatbridge ML5 .. 121 F4
Crossford ML8 .... 201 D1
Dalry KA24 .... 191 F4
Hurlford KA1 .... 228 C3
Kilwinning KA13 .... 207 F3
Paisley PA1 .... 114 C3
Blair St Glasgow G32 ..... 118 C3
Kilmarnock KA3 .... 222 C1
Blair Terr FK5 .... 24 A2
Blairafton Wynd KA13 .... 207 E3
Blairatholl Ave G11 ...... 96 A2
Blairatholl Cres G77 .... 157 D2
Blairatholl Gate G77 .... 157 D2
Blairatholl Gdns [11] G11 .. 96 A2
Blairbeth Dr G44 .... 137 D4
Blairbeth Pl G73 .... 138 A3
Blairbeth Rd G73 .... 138 B3
Blairbeth Terr G73 ...... 138 B3
Blairdardie Prim Sch G15 .. 75 D1
Blairdardie Rd G13 ...... 75 E1
Blairdenan Ave G69 ...... 81 D2
Blairdenon Cres FK1 ...... 41 F2
Blairdenon Dr Alloa FK10 .. 5 D1
Cumbernauld G68 .... 61 E2
Blairdenon Rd FK12 ...... 4 C3
Blairdenon Way KA11 .... 220 A1
Blairforkie Dr FK7 .... 1 C4
Blairgowrie Rd G52 ...... 115 E2
Blairgrove Ct ML5 .... 121 F3
Blairhall Ave G41 .... 136 C4
Blairhill Ave G69 .... 80 A3
Blairhill Pl ML5 .... 121 F4
Blairhill St ML5 .... 121 F4
Blairhill Sta ML5 .... 121 F4
Blairholm Dr ML4 .... 142 A2
Blairlinn G64 .... 78 A3
Blairlinn Ind Est G67 .... 82 C3
Blairlinn Rd G67 .... 82 C3
Blairlogie St G33 .... 99 D1
Blairmore Cres PA15 .... 46 B1
Blairmore Rd PA15 ...... 46 B1
Blairmuckhole And
Forrestdyke Rd ML7 .... 126 C4
Blairpark Ave ML5 .... 121 F4
Blairquhomrie Cotts G83 .. 20 C1
Blairston Ave G71 .... 141 D1
Blairston Gdns G71 ...... 141 D1
Blairtum Dr G73 .... 138 A3
Blairtummock Prim Sch
G34 .... 120 A4
Blairtummock Rd
Glasgow G33 .... 119 E4
Glasgow, Queenslie G33 .. 119 F4
Blake Rd G67 .... 62 A1
Blakely Rd KA21 .... 217 D4
Blane Ave G63 .... 31 D2
Blane Cres G63 .... 31 D2
Blane Dr G62 .... 55 D2
Blane Pl G63 .... 31 D2
Blane St ML5 .... 122 A4
Blanefield Ave KA9 ...... 236 B3
Blaneview G33 .... 99 E2
Blantyre Cres G81 .... 73 F4
Blantyre Ct PA8 .... 73 D2
Blantyre Dr PA7 .... 72 A2
Blantyre Farm Rd
G71, G72 .... 140 B3
Blantyre Gdns G68 ...... 60 C1
Blantyre High Sch G72 .. 161 E4
Blantyre Ind Est G72 .... 161 F3
Blantyre Mill Rd G71 .... 141 D1
Blantyre Pl ML5 .... 121 E2
Blantyre Rd G71 .... 141 D1
Blantyre St Coatbridge ML5 .. 121 F2
Glasgow G3 .... 96 B1
Blantyre Sta G72 .... 161 F4
Blaven Ct G69 .... 120 B2
Blawarthill St G14 .... 94 C3
Blawarthill Hospl G14 .... 95 D3
Blawarthill St G14 .... 94 C3
Bleachfield Falkirk FK2 .... 42 A3
Milngavie G62 .... 55 D2
Bleeze Rd KA24 .... 191 D4
Blenheim Ave
East Kilbride G75 .... 180 B4
Glasgow G33 .... 99 F3
Blenheim Ct Carluke ML8 .. 188 A1
Kilsyth G65 .... 36 C1
Blenheim Pl FK5 .... 23 F3
Blindwells FK12 .... 4 C3
Blinkbonnie Terr FK1 .... 86 A3
Blinkbonny Rd FK1 ...... 41 F2
Blinny Ct ML7 .... 147 D2
Blochairn Rd G21 .... 98 A1
Bloomgate ML11 .... 215 D2
Bluebell Gdns
Glasgow G45 .... 138 A1
Motherwell ML1 .... 142 B1
Bluebell Way Airdrie ML6 .. 102 C1
Carluke ML8 .... 201 F4
Lennoxtown G65 .... 57 F4
Bluebell Wlk ML1 .... 143 D2
Blueknowes Rd ML8 ...... 186 C3
Bluevale St G31 .... 118 A3
Blyth Rd G33 .... 119 F3
Blythe Pl G33 .... 119 E3
Blythswood Ave PA4 .... 94 B2
Blythswood Dr PA3 ...... 113 F3
Blythswood Ind Est PA4 .. 94 B2
Blythswood Rd PA4 ...... 94 B2
Blythswood Sq G2 ...... 240 B3

Blythswood St G2 .... 240 B2
Bo'ness Rd Chapelhall ML6 .. 123 E1
Motherwell ML1 .... 143 E4
Boardwalk The G75 ...... 181 D4
Boat Vennel KA7 .... 235 F1
Boblair St G61 .... 76 B2
Boclair Ave G61 .... 75 F2
Boclair Cres Bearsden G61 .. 76 A2
Bishopbriggs G64 .... 78 A1
Boclair Rd Bearsden G61 .. 76 B3
Bishopbriggs G64 .... 78 A1
Boclair St G13 .... 95 F4
Bodden Sq ML1 .... 143 F4
Boden Ind Est G40 ...... 118 A2
Boden Quadrant ML1 .... 142 B1
Boden St G40 .... 118 A2
Bodesbeck Ct KA11 ...... 220 A2
Bodmin Gdns G69 ...... 80 C2
Bog Rd Banknock FK4 .... 38 C2
Launieston FK2 .... 42 C2
Bog Rdbt FK2 .... 42 C2
Bog Road Ind Est FK2 .... 42 C2
Bogany Terr G45 .... 137 F1
Bogbain Rd G34 .... 120 A4
Bogend Rd Bannockburn FK7 .. 11 F4
Bogfield Rd G34 .... 120 A4
Larbert FK2 .... 22 C4
Torwood FK5 .... 22 C4
Bogfoot Rd ML7 .... 125 D1
Bogghknowe G71 .... 140 B4
Boghall Rd Carluke ML8 .. 202 A4
Boghall Rd G69 .... 120 A2
Boghall St Glasgow G33 .. 99 D1
Stonehouse ML9 .... 198 C1
Boghead KA15 .... 171 D4
Boghead Ave G42 ...... 137 D4
Boghead Rd G66 .... 79 E3
Boghead Pk
(Dumbarton FC)
G82 .... 50 A2
Boghead Rd Dumbarton G82 .. 50 A2
Glasgow G21 .... 98 A2
Kirkintilloch G66 .... 79 D3
Bogiewood Rd PA14 ...... 47 D1
Bogle St PA15 .... 46 A2
Boglemart St KA20 ...... 217 E4
Bogleshole Rd G72 ...... 138 C4
Boglestone Ave PA14 .... 68 C4
Boglestone Prim Sch PA14 .. 68 C4
Bogmoor Pl G51 .... 95 E1
Bogmoor Rd G51 .... 115 E4
Bogs View ML4 .... 141 F2
Bogside Rd Ashgill ML9 .. 199 F4
Kilsyth G65 .... 60 B4
Port Glasgow PA14 ...... 68 C4
Bogside St G40 .... 118 A2
Bogston La PA15 .... 46 C1
Bogston Sta PA15 ...... 46 B1
Bogstonhill Rd PA6 ...... 91 D1
Bogton Ave G44 .... 136 C2
Bogton Avenue La G44 .. 136 C2
Bohun Ct FK7 .... 7 E2
Boleyn Ct ML2 .... 166 A3
Boleyn Rd G41 .... 116 C1
Bolingbroke G74 .... 160 B2
Bolivar Terr G42 .... 137 E4
Bolton Dr G42 .... 137 D4
Bolton Terr G65 .... 57 F4
Boman Pl KA3 .... 195 E2
Bon Accord Cres ML7 .... 146 C3
Bon Accord Rd G76 ...... 157 F3
Bon Accord Sq G81 ...... 94 A4
Bon Secours Hospl G41 .. 136 C4
Bonar Cres PA11 .... 110 C4
Bonar La PA11 .... 110 C4
Bonar Law Ave G84 ...... 16 A1
Bonawe St G20 .... 96 C2
Bonds Dr ML2 .... 166 A3
Boness St G40 .... 118 A2
Bonhill Prim Sch G83 .... 27 F2
Bonhill Rd G82 .... 50 A2
Bonhill St G22 .... 97 D2
Bonkle Gdns ML2 .... 166 A3
Bonkle Rd ML2 .... 166 A3
Bonnaughton Rd G61 .... 75 D3
Bonnet Ct KA3 .... 211 F4
Bonnet Rd ML11 .... 215 D2
Bonnhill View G83 ...... 27 F2
Bonnington Ave ML11 .. 215 D2
Bonnybridge Hospl FK4 .. 40 B3
Bonnybridge Prim Sch FK4 .. 40 A3
Bonnybridge Rd FK4 .... 39 F3
Bonnyhill Rd Falkirk FK1 .. 41 D2
High Bonnybridge FK4 .... 40 B2
Bonnyholm Ave G53 .... 115 D2
Bonnyholm Prim Sch G53 .. 115 D2
Bonnyrigg Dr G43 ...... 136 B3
Bonnyside Rd FK4 ...... 40 A3
Bonnyton Dr G76 .... 178 B3
Bonnyton Fonl KA11 .... 220 A3
Bonnyton Ind Est KA11 .. 222 C1
Bonnyton Moor Rd G76 .. 178 A4
Bonnyton Pl Irvine KA11 .. 220 A3
Kilmarnock KA1 .... 222 B1
Bonnyton Row KA11 .... 220 A3
Bonnyview Gdns G69 .... 80 C1
Bonnywood Ave FK4 .... 40 A4
Bontine Ave G82 .... 49 E2
Bonyton Ave G13 .... 94 C3
Bonython Gr G6 .... 75 D1
Booth Pl FK1 .... 42 C2
Boquhanran Pl G81 ...... 74 A2
Boquhanran Rd G81 .... 74 A1
Borden La G13 .... 95 F3
Borden Rd G13 .... 95 F3
Border Ave KA21 .... 216 C4

Border Pl KA21 .... 216 C4
Border St PA15 .... 46 B2
Border Way G66 .... 79 F4
Bore Rd ML6 .... 123 D4
Boreland Dr Glasgow G13 .. 95 D3
Hamilton ML3 .... 161 F1
Boreland Pl G13 .... 95 D3
Borestone Ave KA25 .... 170 A4
Borestone Cres FK7 ...... 7 D2
Borestone Ct FK7 .... 7 D1
Borestone Pl FK7 .... 7 D1
Borestone Prim Sch FK7 .. 7 D1
Borgie Cres G72 .... 139 D3
Borland Cres G76 ...... 178 C3
Borland Dr ML9 .... 199 D4
Borland Rd G61 .... 76 A2
Borron St G4 .... 97 E2
Borrowdale G75 .... 179 F3
Borrowlea Rd FK7 ...... 7 E4
Borrowmeadow Rd FK7 .. 7 F4
Borthwick Dr G75 ...... 179 E4
Borthwick St G33 .... 99 D1
Bosfield Cnr G74 .... 159 F2
Bosfield Pl G74 .... 159 F2
Bosfield Rd G74 .... 159 F2
Boston Dr G84 .... 16 C2
Boswell Ct G42 .... 136 C4
Boswell Dr G72 .... 161 E4
Boswell Pk Ayr KA7 ...... 238 C4
East Kilbride G74 .... 160 B2
Boswell Sq G52 .... 114 C4
Bosworth Rd G74 ...... 160 A3
Botanic Cres G20 ...... 96 B2
Botanic Crescent La G20 .. 96 B2
Bothkennar Prim Sch FK2 .. 24 C2
Bothkennar Rd FK2 ...... 24 C2
Bothlin Dr G33 .... 99 E3
Bothlyn Ave G69 .... 79 F4
Bothlyn Cres G69 ...... 100 C4
Bothlyn Rd G69 .... 100 B4
Bothwell Castle G72 .... 140 B2
Bothwell La Glasgow G2 .. 240 B2
Glasgow, Kelvingrove G12 .. 96 C1
Bothwell Park Ind Est G71 .. 141 D2
Bothwell Park Sch G71 .. 141 E3
Bothwell Pl Coatbridge ML5 .. 121 F4
Paisley PA2 .... 132 C4
Bothwell Prim Sch G71 .. 141 D1
Bothwell Rd Bothwell G71 .. 140 C2
Carluke ML8 .... 187 F2
Hamilton ML3 .... 162 B3
Boturich Dr G83 .... 19 F1
Boundary Rd KA8 ...... 236 B2
Bourhill Ct ML2 .... 164 B1
Bourne Cres PA4 .... 93 E4
Bourne Ct PA4 .... 93 E4
Bourne St ML3 .... 162 C2
Bournemouth Rd PA19 .. 44 C3
Bourock Sq G78 .... 134 C1
Bourtree Pk KA7 .... 239 D4
Bourtree Rd ML3 .... 161 F1
Bouverie St Glasgow G14 .. 94 C3
Port Glasgow PA14 ...... 47 E1
Rutherglen G73 .... 137 F4
Bow St PA16 .... 45 E2
Bow St G14 .... 7 D4
Bowden Dr G52 .... 115 D3
Bowden Pk G75 .... 180 B4
Bower St G12 .... 96 C2
Bowerwalls St G78 ...... 134 C2
Bowes Cres G69 .... 119 F2
Bowes Rigg KA3 .... 195 F1
Bowfield Ave G52 ...... 114 C3
Bowfield Cres G52 ...... 114 C3
Bowfield Pl G52 .... 114 C3
Bowfield Rd Howwood PA9 .. 130 C3
West Kilbride KA23 ...... 190 B2
Bowhouse Gdns FK10 .... 10 A3
Bowhouse Rd Airdrie ML6 .. 123 F3
Alloa FK10 .... 10 A3
Bowhouse Rise KA11 .... 220 A3
Bowhousebog or Liquo
ML7 .... 146 A1
Bowhousebog Rd ML7 .. 146 A1
Bowhousebrae Rd ML6 .. 123 F3
Bowie Rd G83 .... 27 F3
Bowie St G82 .... 49 F2
Bowling Green La [22] G14 .. 95 D2
Bowling Green Rd
Chryston G69 .... 100 B4
Glasgow G44 .... 137 D3
Glasgow G32 .... 119 E2
[22] Glasgow, Whiteinch G14 .. 95 E2
Bowling Green St ML4 .. 142 A3
Bowling Green View G72 .. 139 F2
Bowling St ML5 .... 121 F4
Bowling Sta G60 .... 72 B4
Bowman Rd KA7 .... 238 C3
Bowman St G42 .... 117 D1
Bowmanflat ML9 .... 185 D2
Bowmont Gdns [18] G12 .. 96 B2
Bowmont Hill G64 ...... 78 A2
Bowmont Pl
Cambuslang G72 .... 139 E3
East Kilbride G75 ...... 180 C4
Bowmont Terr G12 ...... 96 B2
Bowmore Ct KA11 ...... 220 A3

Bowmore Gdns
Rutherglen G73 .... 138 C2
Uddingston G71 .... 140 C4
Bowmore Rd G52 .... 115 F3
Bowmore Wlk ML7 .... 147 D2
Bowyer Vennel ML4 .... 141 F3
Boyd Ct KA3 .... 223 D1
Boyd Dr ML1 .... 163 D4
Boyd Orr Cres KA3 .... 222 A4
Boyd Orr Rd KA21 .... 206 A1
Boyd St Falkirk FK2 .... 42 A3
Glasgow G42 .... 117 E1
Kilmarnock KA3 .... 223 D1
Prestwick KA9 .... 236 B4
Boydston Rd KA22 .... 205 E2
Boydston Way KA3 .... 223 C3
Boydstone Pl G46 .... 136 A3
Boydstone Rd G43 .... 135 F3
Boyle St G81 .... 94 B4
Boylestone Rd G78 .... 134 A2
Boyndie St G34 .... 120 A4
Brabloch Cres PA3 .... 113 F3
Bracadale Dr G69 .... 120 B2
Bracadale Gdns G69 .... 120 B2
Bracadale Gr G69 .... 120 B2
Bracadale Rd G69 .... 120 B2
Bracco Rd ML6 .... 105 E1
Brachelston St PA16 .... 45 E2
Bracken Pk KA7 .... 239 E2
Bracken Rd ML1 .... 141 D2
Bracken St Glasgow G22 .... 97 D3
Motherwell ML1 .... 143 D2
Bracken Terr G71 .... 141 D1
Brackenbrae Ave G64 .... 77 F1
Brackenbrae Rd G64 .... 77 F1
Brackendene PA6 .... 91 E1
Brackenhill Ave KA3 .... 223 D3
Brackenhill Dr ML3 .... 183 E4
Brackenhill Rd ML8 .... 187 D3
Brackenhirst Rd ML6 .... 102 C4
Brackenhurst St G82 .... 50 B3
Brackenknowe Rd ML6 .... 83 E2
Brackenlees Rd FK2 .... 24 C2
Brackenrig Cres G76 .... 157 F1
Brackenrig Rd G46 .... 135 F1
Brackla Ave G81 .... 94 C4
Bradan Ave Ayr KA7 .... 239 D1
Clydebank G81 .... 94 C4
Bradan Rd KA10 .... 229 D1
Bradbury St FK2 .... 24 A1
Bradda Ave G73 .... 138 B2
Bradfield Ave G12 .... 96 B3
Bradshaw Cres ML3 .... 161 F2
Bradshaw St KA21 .... 216 C4
Brady Cres G69 .... 81 D2
Brae The Bannockburn FK7 .... 7 E1
Cambusbarron PA7 .... 6 B3
Brae View PA16 .... 45 E3
Braedale Ave Airdrie ML6 .... 123 E4
Motherwell ML1 .... 163 E3
Braedale Cres ML2 .... 166 A3
Braedale Pl ML2 .... 166 B3
Braedale Rd ML11 .... 215 D3
Braeface Rd G67 .... 61 F1
Braefield Dr G46 .... 136 A2
Braefoot KA11 .... 219 F3
Braefoot Ave G62 .... 76 A4
Braefoot Cres Law ML8 .... 186 C3
Paisley PA2 .... 133 F4
Braefoot Ct ML8 .... 186 C3
Braefoot La G79 .... 153 D2
Braehead Alloa FK10 .... 4 B1
Alva FK12 .... 5 D4
Beith KA15 .... 171 D4
Blantyre G72 .... 161 E3
Bonhill G83 .... 28 A2
Langbank PA14 .... 191 E4
Irvine KA11 .... 219 F3
Lochwinnoch PA12 .... 129 E2
Braehead Ave Ayr KA8 .... 236 B1
Clydebank G81 .... 74 A4
Coatbridge ML5 .... 121 E2
Larkhall ML9 .... 184 C1
Lochwinnoch PA12 .... 129 E2
Milngavie G62 .... 54 C1
Neilston G78 .... 154 B4
Tullibody FK10 .... 4 B1
Braehead Cres Ayr KA8 .... 236 B1
Clydebank G81 .... 74 A4
Braehead Ct KA3 .... 223 D1
Braehead Dr ML4 .... 141 F2
Braehead Glebe KA3 .... 211 F4
Braehead Loan ML8 .... 202 A4
Braehead Pl Bellshill ML4 .... 141 F2
Dalry KA24 .... 191 E4
Rhu G84 .... 15 F3
Saltcoats KA21 .... 216 C4
Braehead Prim Sch
Ayr KA8 .... 236 B1
Dumbarton G82 .... 50 A2
Stirling FK7 .... 7 E2
Braehead Quadrant
Motherwell ML1 .... 143 E2
Neilston G78 .... 154 B4
Braehead Rd Ayr KA8 .... 236 B1
Clydebank G81 .... 74 A4
Cumbernauld G67 .... 62 A2
Fenwick KA3 .... 213 D2
Paisley PA2 .... 133 E4
Port Glasgow PA14 .... 68 C4
Stirling FK7 .... 7 E2
Thorntonhall G74 .... 158 B2
Braehead St Glasgow G5 .... 117 E2
Kirkintilloch G66 .... 58 B1
Braehead Terr KA3 .... 222 B3
Braeholm Hospl G84 .... 16 C1
Braehouse G84 .... 15 E2

Braemar Ave G81 .... 73 F2
Braemar Cres Bearsden G61 .... 75 F1
Carluke ML8 .... 188 A2
Falkirk FK2 .... 42 B3
Paisley PA2 .... 113 F1
Braemar Ct G44 .... 136 C2
Braemar Dr Elderslie PA5 .... 112 A1
Falkirk FK2 .... 42 B3
Braemar Gdns FK6 .... 21 E2
Braemar Pl FK5 .... 24 A2
Braemar Rd Inchinnan PA4 .... 93 F3
Rutherglen G73 .... 138 C2
Braemar Sq KA8 .... 236 B1
Braemar St Glasgow G42 .... 136 C4
Hamilton ML3 .... 162 A3
Braemar View G81 .... 73 F3
Braemore Gdns G22 .... 97 E2
Braemore Rd KA3 .... 195 E1
Braemount Ave PA2 .... 133 E3
Braes Ave G81 .... 74 B1
Braes O' Yetts G66 .... 80 A4
Braes Rd KA21 .... 216 C4
Braes The FK10 .... 4 B2
Braes View Denny FK6 .... 39 E4
Shieldhill FK1 .... 66 C4
Braesburn Ct G67 .... 62 C3
Braesburn Pl G67 .... 62 C3
Braesburn Rd G67 .... 62 C3
Braeside Alloa FK10 .... 5 E1
Irvine KA11 .... 219 F3
Kilwinning KA13 .... 207 F3
Shieldhill FK1 .... 66 B3
Braeside Ave Milngavie G62 .... 76 A4
Moodiesburn G69 .... 80 C1
Rutherglen G73 .... 138 B4
Braeside Cres
Barrhead G78 .... 134 C1
Glasgow G69 .... 120 C3
Braeside Dr Barrhead G78 .... 134 C1
Dumbarton G82 .... 50 A3
Braeside Gdns ML3 .... 183 F4
Braeside La Gourock PA16 .... 44 B2
La Larkhall ML9 .... 185 D2
Braeside Pl G72 .... 139 D2
Braeside Rd Ayr KA8 .... 236 B1
Greenock PA16 .... 44 B2
Motherwell ML1 .... 143 E2
Braeside Sch G45 .... 137 F2
Braeside St Glasgow G20 .... 96 C2
Kilmarnock KA1 .... 228 A4
Braeside Way ML9 .... 185 D1
Braeview Laurieston FK2 .... 42 C2
Stenhousemuir FK5 .... 23 E1
Braeview Ave PA2 .... 133 D4
Braeview Dr PA2 .... 133 D4
Braeview Gdns PA2 .... 133 D4
Braeview Pl G74 .... 160 A2
Braeview Rd PA2 .... 133 D4
Braid Ct KA13 .... 207 D2
Braid Sq G4 .... 97 D1
Braid Sq G4 .... 97 D1
Braid's Rd G42 .... 113 F1
Braidbar Ct G46 .... 136 B2
Braidbar Farm Rd G46 .... 136 B2
Braidbar Prim Sch G46 .... 136 B2
Braidbar Rd G46 .... 136 B2
Braidcraft Pl G53 .... 135 E4
Braidcraft Rd G53 .... 115 E1
Braidcraft Terr G53 .... 115 E1
Braidfauld Gdns G32 .... 118 C2
Braidfauld Pl G32 .... 118 C1
Braidfauld Pl G32 .... 118 C1
Braidfield Gr G81 .... 74 A3
Braidfield High Sch G81 .... 74 B1
Braidfield Rd G81 .... 74 A3
Braidholm Ave G46 .... 136 B3
Braidholm Cres G46 .... 136 B3
Braidholm Rd G46 .... 136 B2
Braidhurst High Sch ML1 .... 142 B1
Braidhurst St ML1 .... 163 F4
Braidley Cres G75 .... 180 C3
Braidpark Dr G46 .... 136 B2
Braidwood Pl PA3 .... 111 F3
Braidwood Prim Sch ML8 .... 202 C1
Braidwood Rd
Braidwood ML8 .... 201 C2
Kilwinning KA13 .... 207 F2
Braidwood St ML2 .... 165 E4
Kilmarnock KA9 .... 180 B4
Bramblehedge Path G83 .... 27 F4
Brambling Ct ML2 .... 165 D1
Bramley Pl Airdrie ML6 .... 123 F3
Kirkintilloch G66 .... 79 F3
Brampton G75 .... 179 F3
Branchal Rd ML2 .... 165 E2
Branchalfield Dr ML2 .... 165 F2
Branchalmuir Cres ML2 .... 165 F3
Branchline Ind Est KA10 .... 229 D2
Branchock Ave G72 .... 139 E2
Branchton Rd PA16 .... 44 C2
Branchton Sta PA16 .... 44 C2
Brancumhall Rd G74 .... 160 B2
Brand Pl G51 .... 116 B3
Brand St G51 .... 116 B3
Brandon Arc ML1 .... 163 F3
Brandon Dr G61 .... 75 F4
Brandon Gdns
Cambuslang G72 .... 138 C3
Glasgow G44 .... 136 A4
Brandon Par E ML1 .... 163 F4
Brandon Par S ML1 .... 163 F3
Brandon Pl ML4 .... 141 F2
Brandon St Coatbridge ML5 .... 121 F2
Glasgow G31 .... 117 F3
Hamilton ML3 .... 162 C2
Motherwell ML1 .... 163 F3
Brandon Way ML5 .... 121 E2
Brandyhill FK10 .... 5 F2

Brankholm Brae ML3 .... 161 E2
Brannock Ave ML1 .... 143 E2
Brannock High Sch ML1 .... 143 E2
Brannock Pl ML1 .... 143 E2
Brannock Rd ML1 .... 143 E2
Bransholm Pk FK10 .... 10 A4
Branshill Rd FK10 .... 10 A4
Brassey St G20 .... 96 C3
Braxfield Rd ML11 .... 215 D1
Braxfield Terr ML11 .... 214 C1
Breadalbane Cres ML1 .... 142 B1
Breadalbane Gdns G73 .... 138 B2
Breadalbane St G3 .... 240 A3
Breadie Dr G62 .... 75 F4
Bream Pl PA6 .... 111 E4
Breamish Pl G75 .... 179 F3
Brechin Rd G64 .... 78 B1
Brechin St G3 .... 116 C4
Breck Ave PA2 .... 132 B4
Brediland Prim Sch PA2 .... 113 D1
Brediland Rd
Linwood PA3, PA2 .... 112 A3
Paisley PA2 .... 112 C4
Bredin Way ML1 .... 163 D4
Bredisholm Cres G71 .... 121 E1
Bredisholm Dr G69 .... 120 B2
Bredisholm Rd
Bargeddie G69 .... 121 D2
Coatbridge G69 .... 120 C2
Glasgow G69 .... 120 B2
Bredisholm Terr G69 .... 120 B2
Brenfield Ave G44 .... 136 C2
Brenfield Dr G44 .... 136 C2
Brenfield Rd G44 .... 137 D2
Brent Cres PA6 .... 111 E4
Brent Ct G74 .... 159 F2
Brent Dr G46 .... 135 F3
Brent Gdns G46 .... 135 F3
Brent Rd East Kilbride G74 .... 159 F2
Glasgow G46 .... 135 F3
Brent Way G46 .... 135 F3
Brentwood Ave G53 .... 135 D2
Brentwood Dr G53 .... 135 D2
Brentwood Sq G53 .... 135 D2
Brereton St G42 .... 117 E1
Breslin Terr ML7 .... 127 E3
Bressay G74 .... 159 F2
Bressay Pl KA3 .... 223 D3
Bressay Rd G33 .... 119 F3
Bressay Wynd ML2 .... 165 F3
Bretton PA8 .... 73 E2
Breval Cres G81 .... 74 A4
Brewery Rd KA1 .... 227 F4
Brewery St PA5 .... 111 F2
Brewlands Cres KA1 .... 231 E2
Brewlands Dr KA1 .... 231 E2
Brewlands Rd KA1 .... 231 E2
Brewster Ave PA3 .... 114 A4
Brewster Pl Denny FK6 .... 21 E1
Irvine KA11 .... 224 C3
Brian Bank G65 .... 58 A3
Briar Dr G81 .... 74 A2
Briar Gdns G43 .... 136 B3
Briar Gr Ayr KA7 .... 239 E2
Glasgow G43 .... 136 B3
Briar Neuk G64 .... 98 A4
Briar Pl PA19 .... 44 B3
Briar Rd Glasgow G43 .... 136 B3
Brushbank Way G72 .... 161 E4
Briarcroft Dr G33 .... 98 B4
Briarcroft Pl G33 .... 98 C3
Briarcroft Rd G33 .... 98 B3
Briarcroft St KA9 .... 236 B4
Briarhill Rd KA9 .... 236 B4
Briarhill St KA9 .... 236 B4
Briarlea Dr G46 .... 136 B2
Briars Rd FK10 .... 4 C1
Briarwell La G62 .... 55 D1
Briarwell Rd G62 .... 55 D1
Briarwood Ct G32 .... 119 F1
Briarwood Rd ML2 .... 164 C2
Brick La PA3 .... 113 F3
Bridesburn Pl ML1 .... 195 F1
Bridge Cres FK6 .... 21 E1
Bridge End ML7 .... 146 B3
Bridge La
 Kilmarnock KA1 .... 227 F4
Paisley PA2 .... 113 D2
Bridge of Allan Prim Sch
PA11 .... 89 F1
Bridge of Weir Hospl
PA11 .... 90 B1
Bridge of Weir Prim Sch
PA11 .... 90 B1
Bridge of Weir Rd
Bridge Of W PA11 .... 110 C4
Brookfield PA5, PA3 .... 111 E3
Houston PA6 .... 91 E3
Kilmacolm PA13 .... 89 F3
Linwood PA3 .... 112 A3
Bridge Pl Denny FK6 .... 21 E1
Milngavie G62 .... 55 D1
Shotts ML7 .... 147 D2
Bridge St PA14 .... 68 C4
Bridge St Alexandria G83 .... 27 F2
Bonnybridge FK4 .... 40 A3
Cambuslang G72 .... 139 D3
Clydebank G81 .... 74 B1
Dumbarton G82 .... 49 F2
Glasgow G5 .... 240 C1
Kilbirnie KA25 .... 149 D1
Linwood PA3 .... 112 A3
Longriggend ML6 .... 84 C1

Bridge St continued
Paisley PA1 .... 113 F2
Prestwick KA9 .... 236 A4
Wishaw ML2 .... 164 C2
Bridge Street
 Underground Sta G5 .... 117 D3
Bridge Terr FK10 .... 10 A3
Bridgebar St G78 .... 134 C2
Bridgeburn Dr G69 .... 80 C1
Bridgeford Ave ML4 .... 142 B4
Bridgegait G62 .... 76 B4
Bridgegate Glasgow G1 .... 241 D1
Irvine KA12 .... 219 E1
Bridgehaugh Rd FK9 .... 2 A1
Bridgehouse Ct KA1 .... 228 A1
Bridgehousehill Rd KA1 .... 227 F1
Bridgend Bishopton PA7 .... 72 A2
Dalry KA24 .... 191 E4
Kilwinning KA13 .... 207 F2
Stewarton KA3 .... 211 F4
Bridgend Ave PA14 .... 68 C4
Bridgend Cotts G66 .... 80 A4
Bridgend Cres G69 .... 80 C1
Bridgend La KA13 .... 207 F2
Bridgend Pl G69 .... 80 C1
Bridgend Rd Greenock PA15 . 46 B1
Kilbirnie KA25 .... 149 D1
Bridgend View ML8 .... 187 F1
Bridgend Wlk G78 .... 153 D2
Bridgepark KA22 .... 205 E1
Bridgeton Bsns Ctr
G40 .... 117 F3
Bridgeton Sta G40 .... 117 F2
Bridgewater Ind Pk PA8 .... 73 E1
Bridgewater Shopping Ctr
PA8 .... 73 E1
Bridgeway Ct G66 .... 79 F4
Bridgeway Pl G66 .... 79 F4
Bridgeway Rd G66 .... 79 F4
Bridgeway Terr G66 .... 79 F4
Bridie Terr G74 .... 160 B2
Brierie Ave PA6 .... 91 D1
Brierie Gdns PA6 .... 111 D4
Brierie Hills PA6 .... 91 D1
Brierie La PA6 .... 111 D4
Brierie-Hill Ct PA6 .... 111 D4
Brierie-Hill Gr PA6 .... 111 D4
Brierie-Hill Rd PA6 .... 111 D4
Briery Ct KA25 .... 170 A4
Brierybank Ave ML11 .... 215 D2
Brig O'Lea Terr G78 .... 153 B3
Brig-O-Doon Gr FK7 .... 12 C4
Brigbrae Ave ML4 .... 142 B2
Brigham Pl G23 .... 96 C4
Bright St G21 .... 97 F1
Brighton Pl G51 .... 116 A3
Brighton St G51 .... 116 A3
Brightside Ave
 Port Glasgow PA14 .... 69 D4
Uddingston G71 .... 140 C3
Brigside Gdns ML3 .... 163 D1
Brisbane Ct G46 .... 136 B2
Brisbane Rd PA7 .... 72 A2
Brisbane St Clydebank G81 . 73 E2
Glasgow G42 .... 137 D4
Brisbane Terr G75 .... 180 B4
Britannia Way PA4 .... 94 B1
Briton St KA1 .... 227 E3
Britton Pl KA8 .... 236 A1
Briton St G51 .... 116 A3
Broad Sq G72 .... 161 E4
Broad St Alloa FK10 .... 10 A3
Denny FK6 .... 21 F1
Glasgow G40 .... 118 A3
Stirling FK8 .... 7 D4
Broad Way The ML2 .... 164 C2
Broadcroft G66 .... 58 A1
Broadcroft Rd G66 .... 58 B1
Broadfield Ave PA14 .... 69 D4
Broadford St G4 .... 97 E1
Broadford Terr PA16 .... 44 C2
Broadholm Prim Sch G15 . 75 D2
Broadholm St G22 .... 97 E3
Broadleys Ave G64 .... 77 F1
Broadley's Rd FK7 .... 7 E4
Broadloan PA4 .... 94 B1
Broadmeadow Ind Est G82 . 49 F3
Broadmoss Ave G77 .... 157 E2
Broadwood Dr G44 .... 136 B4
Broadway KA22 .... 205 E1
Broadway Bsns Pk G68 . 81 F4
Broadwood Dr G44 .... 136 B4
Broadwood Prim Sch G15 . 75 D2
Broadwood Stad (Clyde &
 Airdrieonians FC's) G68 . 60 C1
Brock Oval G53 .... 135 E3
Brock Pl G53 .... 135 E4
Brock Rd G53 .... 135 E3
Brock Terr G53 .... 135 E3
Brockburn Cres G53 .... 135 D4
Brockburn Rd G53 .... 135 D4
Brockburn Terr G53 .... 135 E4
Brockburn Pk G75 .... 179 F4
Brockly View KA25 .... 149 D2
Brockville Pk (Falkirk FC)
FK1 .... 42 A3
Brockville St G32 .... 118 C3
Brodick Ave
Kilwinning KA13 .... 207 E2
Motherwell ML1 .... 163 D4

Brodick Cl KA13 .... 207 E2
Brodick Dr
East Kilbride G74 .... 159 E2
Gourock PA19 .... 43 F3
Helensburgh G84 .... 16 C2
Brodick Pl FK1 .... 41 A2
Brodick Rd KA1 .... 222 B1
Brodick St G21 .... 98 A1
Brodie KA10 .... 229 E2
Brodie Park Ave PA2 .... 113 F1
Brodie Park Cres PA2 .... 113 E1
Brodie Park Gdns PA2 .... 113 F1
Brodie Pl East Kilbride G74 . 159 E2
Kilmarnock KA3 .... 223 E1
Stonehouse ML9 .... 198 C1
Brodie Rd G21 .... 98 B4
Brodie St FK2 .... 42 A1
Brogan Cres ML1 .... 163 D4
Broich The FK12 .... 4 C4
Bron Way G67 .... 62 A1
Bronte FK5 .... 24 A2
Bronte St Alva FK12 .... 5 D3
Clydebank G81 .... 73 F2
Glasgow G40 .... 117 F3
Menstrie FK11 .... 3 F3
Brookbank Terr ML8 .... 188 A1
Brooke Ave G83 .... 28 A4
Brookfield Pl PA12 .... 5 D3
Brookfield Rd PA14 .... 68 C4
Brooking Way ML2 .... 166 A3
Brooklands Alexandria G83 . 27 E3
East Kilbride G74 .... 159 D1
Brooklea Dr G46 .... 136 B3
Brooklime Dr G74 .... 159 E2
Brooklime Gdns G74 .... 159 E2
Brooklyn Pl ML2 .... 186 A4
Brookside St G40 .... 118 A3
Broom Ave PA8 .... 93 D4
Broom Cliff G77 .... 156 C2
Broom Cres Barrhead G78 . 134 A3
East Kilbride G75 .... 180 B3
Broom Ct FK7 .... 7 E2
Broom Dr Clydebank G81 . 74 A2
Larkhall ML9 .... 185 D3
Broom Gdns G66 .... 79 D3
Broom Path G69 .... 119 F2
Broom Pk E FK11 .... 4 A3
Broom Pk W FK11 .... 4 A3
Broom Pl
Bridge Of W PA11 .... 110 C4
Coatbridge ML5 .... 121 F2
Kilmarnock KA1 .... 228 A2
Broom Rd Cumbernauld G67 . 62 B3
Glasgow G43 .... 136 B3
Newton Mearns G77 .... 157 D3
Broom Rd E G77 .... 157 D2
Broom Terr PA5 .... 112 A1
Broom Wynd ML7 .... 146 C3
Broomage Ave FK5 .... 23 D2
Broomage Cres FK5 .... 23 D2
Broomage Dr FK5 .... 23 D2
Broomage Pk FK5 .... 23 E1
Broomberry Dr PA19 .... 44 C4
Broomburn Dr G77 .... 157 D2
Broomcroft Rd G77 .... 157 D3
Broomdyke Way PA3 .... 113 E4
Broomelton Rd ML9 .... 184 B1
Broomfauld Gdns KA7 ....
Broomfield Ave
Cambuslang G72 .... 138 B4
Newton Mearns G77 .... 156 C2
Broomfield Gdn KA7 .... 238 C3
Broomfield La G21 .... 97 F3
Broomfield Pl G21 .... 97 F3
Broomfield Rd Ayr KA7 .... 238 C3
Glasgow G21 .... 98 A2
Netherburn ML9 .... 199 D4
Rutherglen G46 .... 157 D3
Broomfield St Airdrie ML6 . 123 D4
Kilwinning KA13 .... 207 E2
Broomfield Terr G71 .... 120 C1
Broomfield Wlk G66 .... 79 E4
Broomgate ML11 .... 215 D2
Broomhill Ave
Glasgow G32 .... 139 D4
Glasgow, Whiteinch G11 . 95 F1
Larbert FK5 .... 23 D1
Newton Mearns G77 .... 156 C2
Broomhill Cres
Bellshill ML4 .... 141 F2
Erskine PA8 .... 93 D4
Broomhill Dr
Kilwinning KA13 .... 207 E3
Larkhall ML9 .... 185 D1
Broomhill Farm Mews
G66 .... 58 C1
Broomhill Gate ML9 .... 185 D1
Broomhill Gdns
Glasgow G11 .... 95 F2
Newton Mearns G77 .... 156 C2
Broomhill La G11 .... 95 F1
Broomhill Path G11 .... 95 F1

Broomhill Pl Denny FK6 .... 21 E2
Broomhill Pl G11 .... 95 F1
Stirling FK7 .... 6 C3
Broomhill Prim Sch G11 .... 95 F2
Broomhill Prim Sch Annexe
G14 .... 95 F2
Broomhill Quadrant KA1 .. 228 A2
Broomhill Rd
Bonnybridge FK4 .... 40 A2
Larkhall ML9 .... 185 D1
Broomhill Rd E KA1 .... 228 A2
Broomhill Rd W KA1 .... 227 F2
Broomhill St
Greenock PA15 .... 45 F2
Harthill ML7 .... 127 E3
Broomhill Terr G11 .... 95 F1
Broomhill View ML9 .... 184 C1
Broomhill Way PA15 .... 45 F2
Broomieknowe FK10 .... 4 B2
Broomieknowe Dr G73 ...... 138 A3
Broomieknowe Rd G73 ...... 138 A3
Broomielaw G1, G2 .... 240 C1
Broomknoll St ML6 .... 123 D4
Broomknowe G68 .... 61 E2
Broomknowe Rd PA13 .... 89 E4
Broomknowes Ave G66 .... 79 F2
Broomknowes Rd G21 .... 98 A2
Broomlands Ave PA8 .... 93 F4
Broomlands Busway
KA11 .... 220 A1
Broomlands Cres PA4 .... 93 F4
Broomlands Ct KA11 .... 220 A1
Broomlands Dr KA12 .... 219 E1
Broomlands Gdns PA8 .... 93 F4
Broomlands Pl KA12 .... 219 E1
Broomlands Prim Sch
KA11 .... 220 A1
Broomlands Rd
Cumbernauld G67 .... 83 D4
Irvine KA11 .... 220 A1
Broomlands St PA1 .... 113 E2
Broomlands Way PA4 .... 93 F4
Broomlea Cres PA4 .... 93 E4
Broomlea Sch G11 .... 95 F1
Broomlee Rd G67 .... 62 A3
Broomley Cres G83 .... 27 E4
Broomley Dr G46 .... 136 B1
Broomley La G46 .... 136 B1
Broomloan Ct G51 .... 116 A3
Broomloan Pl G51 .... 116 A3
Broomloan Rd G51 .... 116 A3
Broompark Ave
Blantyre G72 .... 161 E3
Prestwick KA9 .... 236 B4
Broompark Cir **B** G31 ...... 117 F4
Broompark Cres
Airdrie ML6 .... 103 D2
Prestwick KA9 .... 236 B4
Broompark Dr
Glasgow G31 .... 117 F4
Inchinnan PA4 .... 93 E4
Newton Mearns G77 .... 157 D3
Broompark Gdns FK6 .... 21 F1
Broompark La **7** G31 ...... 117 F4
Broompark Rd
Blantyre G72 .... 161 E4
Wishaw ML2 .... 164 B2
Broompark St **6** G31 ...... 117 F4
Broomridge Rd FK7 .... 7 E2
Broomside Cres ML1 .... 163 F2
Broomside Pl ML5 .... 23 E1
Broomside Rd PA4 .... 40 A2
Broomside St ML1 .... 163 F2
Broomstone Ave G77 .... 156 C2
Broomton Rd G21 .... 98 B4
Broomvale Dr G77 .... 156 C3
Broomward Dr PA5 .... 112 A2
Brora Dr Bearsden G61 .... 76 A2
Glasgow G46 .... 136 B1
Renfrew PA4 .... 94 C2
Brora Gdns G64 .... 78 A1
Brora Rd G64 .... 78 A1
Brora St G33 .... 98 B1
Brosdale Ct FK1 .... 42 A1
Brougham St PA16 .... 45 F4
Broughton G75 .... 180 C3
Broughton Dr G23 .... 96 C3
Broughton Gdns G23 .... 76 C1
Broughton Gn KA11 .... 220 A3
Broughton Pl
Coatbridge ML5 .... 122 A2
Hamilton ML3 .... 162 A2
Broughton Rd G23 .... 76 C1
Broun Dr KA7 .... 238 C1
Brouster Gate **6** G4 ...... 159 F1
Brouster Hill G74 .... 159 F1
Brouster Pl G74 .... 159 F1
Brown Ave Alloa FK10 .... 4 C1
Clydebank G81 .... 94 C4
Dumbarton G82 .... 50 B2
Stirling FK9 .... 2 A1
Troon KA10 .... 229 E2
Brown Pl Cambuslang G72 .. 139 D3
Saltcoats KA21 .... 205 F1
Brown Rd G67 .... 61 F1
Brown St Balloch G83 .... 28 A4
Carluke ML8 .... 187 F2
Coatbridge ML5 .... 122 A3
Falkirk FK1 .... 42 A3
Glasgow G2 .... 240 B2
Greenock PA15 .... 46 B2
Larkhall ML9 .... 185 D2
Motherwell ML1 .... 163 F4
Paisley PA1 .... 113 E3
Port Glasgow PA14 .... 47 D1

Brown St continued
Renfrew PA4 .... 94 A2
Shotts ML7 .... 147 D2
Stewarton KA3 .... 211 E4
Wishaw ML2 .... 166 A2
Brown Wlk KA12 .... 219 E3
Brown's La PA1 .... 113 F2
Browncarrick Dr KA7 .... 238 A1
Brownhill Dr KA25 .... 169 F4
Brownhill Rd G43 .... 136 A2
Brownhill View ML2 .... 166 B3
Brownieside Pl ML6 .... 104 A2
Brownieside Rd ML6 .... 104 B1
Brownlee Rd ML8 .... 186 B2
Brownlie St G42 .... 137 D4
Brownmuir Ave G76 .... 178 C2
Brownsburn Ind Est ML6 .. 123 D3
Brownsburn Rd ML6 .... 123 E3
Brownsdale Rd G73 .... 137 F4
Brownsfield Cres PA4 .... 93 D3
Brownsfield Rd PA4 .... 93 D3
Brownshill Ave ML5 .... 121 F2
Brownside Ave
Barrhead G78 .... 134 A3
Cambuslang G72 .... 138 C3
Brownside Cres G78 .... 134 A3
Brownside Dr
Barrhead G78 .... 134 A3
Glasgow G13 .... 94 C3
Brownside Gr G78 .... 134 A3
Brownside Mews G72 .... 138 C3
Brownside Rd G72 .... 138 C3
Brownside Ave PA2 .... 133 E4
Bruar Way **15** ML2 .... 165 F3
Bruart Ave FK5 .... 23 F2
Bruce Ave
Dundonald KA2 .... 225 F1
Johnstone PA5 .... 131 F4
Motherwell ML1 .... 163 E4
Paisley PA3 .... 114 A4
Prestwick KA9 .... 236 A3
Bruce Cres Ayr KA7 .... 238 C4
Falkirk FK2 .... 24 A2
Kilmarnock KA1 .... 227 F2
Plean FK7 .... 12 B2
Bruce Ct ML6 .... 123 F4
Bruce Dr Falkirk FK7 .... 8 B3
Stenhousemuir FK5 .... 23 F2
Bruce La KA9 .... 236 A3
Bruce Loan ML2 .... 166 B3
Bruce Pl G75 .... 180 C4
Bruce Rd Bishopton PA7 ...... 72 A2
Glasgow G41 .... 116 C2
Motherwell ML1 .... 143 D1
Paisley PA3 .... 114 A4
Renfrew PA4 .... 94 A1
Bruce St Alloa FK10 .... 10 B4
Bannockburn FK7 .... 7 F1
Bellshill ML4 .... 142 A3
Clydebank G81 .... 74 A1
Coatbridge ML5 .... 122 A4
Dumbarton G82 .... 50 A1
Falkirk FK2 .... 42 B3
Greenock PA15 .... 45 F3
Kilmarnock KA1 .... 227 F2
Plains ML6 .... 104 A1
Plean FK7 .... 12 B2
Port Glasgow PA14 .... 47 E1
Stirling FK8 .... 2 A1
Bruce Terr Blantyre G72 .... 140 C1
Cambusbarron FK7 .... 6 B3
East Kilbride G75 .... 180 C4
Irvine KA12 .... 219 E3
Bruce View FK7 .... 7 D1
Bruce's Loan **10** ML9 ...... 185 E1
Brucefield Pl G34 .... 120 B4
Brucehill Rd G82 .... 49 E2
Brunel Way G75 .... 180 C4
Brunstane Rd G34 .... 100 A1
Brunswick La G1 .... 241 D2
Brunswick St G1 .... 241 D2
Brunton St G44 .... 137 D3
Brunton Terr G44 .... 137 D2
Bruntsfield Ave
Glasgow G53 .... 135 D2
Kilwinning KA13 .... 207 D2
Bruntsfield Gdns G53 .... 135 D2
Bryan St ML3 .... 162 A3
Bryce Ave FK2 .... 24 A2
Bryce Gdns ML9 .... 185 D2
Bryce Knox Ct KA11 .... 220 A3
Bryce Pl G75 .... 180 B3
Brydson Pl PA3 .... 112 A3
Brymner St PA15 .... 46 A3
Bryon Ct G71 .... 141 D1
Bryony The FK10 .... 4 A1
Bryson Ct ML3 .... 183 E4
Bryson St Clydebank G81 .... 74 C4
Falkirk FK2 .... 42 A3
Bryson Street Ind Est FK2 .. 42 A3
Buccleuch Ave
Clarkston G76 .... 157 E4
Paisley G52 .... 114 C4
Buccleuch Dr G61 .... 75 F4
Buccleuch La G3 .... 240 B4
Buccleuch St G3 .... 240 B4
Buccleugh St PA15 .... 45 F3
Buchan Gn G74 .... 160 A2
Buchan Rd
Motherwell ML1 .... 143 D1
Stirling FK9 .... 229 F2
Buchan St Hamilton ML3 .. 183 E4
Wishaw ML2 .... 165 D3
Buchan Terr G72 .... 138 C2
Buchanan Ave

Buchanan Cres
Bishopbriggs G64 .... 98 B4
Hamilton ML3 .... 162 A1
Buchanan Ct Falkirk FK2 ...... 42 A4
Stepps G33 .... 99 F3
Buchanan Dr Bearsden G61 .. 76 A2
Bishopbriggs G64 .... 98 B4
Kirkintilloch G66 .... 79 E2
Law ML8 .... 187 D3
Newton Mearns G77 .... 156 C4
Rutherglen G73, G72 .... 138 C3
Rutherglen, Burgh G73, G72 138 B3
Stirling FK9 .... 2 A2
Buchanan Gdns G32 .... 119 F1
Buchanan Gr G69 .... 120 A3
Buchanan Pl
Kilmarnock KA1 .... 228 A3
Torrance G64 .... 57 D1
Buchanan Rd G84 .... 17 D1
Buchanan St Airdrie ML6 .. 123 D4
Coatbridge ML5 .... 121 F3
Dumbarton G82 .... 50 A1
Glasgow G1 .... 240 C2
Glasgow, Baillieston G69 .. 120 A2
Greenock PA16 .... 45 D2
Johnstone PA5 .... 111 F1
Milngavie G62 .... 55 B1
Buchanan Street
Underground Sta G1 ...... 241 D3
Buchandyke Rd G74 .... 160 A2
Buchlyvie Gdns G64 .... 97 F4
Buchlyvie Rd PA1 .... 114 C3
Buchlyvie St G34 .... 120 A4
Buckie PA8 .... 73 D2
Buckie Wlk ML4 .... 142 A3
Buckingham Ct ML3 .... 161 F2
Buckingham Dr
Glasgow G32 .... 139 D4
Rutherglen G73 .... 138 B4
Buckingham St G12 .... 96 B2
Buckingham Terr G12 .... 96 B2
Buckland Cres G52 .... 115 D2
Bucklaw Pl G52 .... 115 E2
Bucklaw Terr G52 .... 115 E2
Buckley St G22 .... 97 E3
Bucksburn Rd G21 .... 98 B2
Buckthorne Pl G53 .... 135 D2
Buddon St G40 .... 118 B2
Budhill Ave G32 .... 119 D3
Budshaw Ave ML6 .... 123 F1
Buiston Rd KA3 .... 211 E2
Bull Rd G76 .... 157 F3
Bull's Cl ML11 .... 215 D2
Bulldale Rd G14 .... 94 C3
Bulldale St G14 .... 94 C3
Bullionslaw Dr G73 .... 138 B3
Bullock Ave G46 .... 136 B1
Bulloch Cres FK6 .... 21 E1
Bullwood Ave G53 .... 134 C4
Bullwood Ct G53 .... 135 D1
Bullwood Dr G53 .... 114 C1
Bullwood Gdns G53 .... 114 C1
Bullwood Pl G53 .... 114 C1
Bunbury Terr **15** G75 .... 180 B4
Bunessan St G52 .... 115 F3
Bungalows The FK5 .... 23 D1
Bunhouse Rd G3 .... 96 B1
Buntine Cres FK7 .... 7 D2
Bunting Pl KA1 .... 228 B4
Burbank G62 .... 55 D1
Burbank Terr PA14 .... 68 B4
Burgh Hall La G11 .... 96 A1
Burgh Hall St G11 .... 96 A1
Burgh La **4** G12 .... 96 B2
Burgh Mews FK10 .... 10 A3
Burgh Prim Sch G73 .... 138 A4
Burgh Rd KA9 .... 236 A4
Burgh Wlk PA10 .... 44 C4
Burghead Dr G51 .... 115 F4
Burghead Pl G51 .... 115 F4
Burgher St G31 .... 118 B3
Burghmuir Ind Est FK8 .... 7 D3
Burghmuir Rd FK7 .... 7 D3
Burleigh Rd G71 .... 141 D2
Burleigh St Coatbridge ML5 122 A2
Glasgow G51 .... 116 A4
Burleigh Way FK10 .... 10 B3
Burley Pl G14 .... 158 C1
Burlington Ave G12 .... 96 A3
Burmola St G22 .... 97 D2
Burn Cres Chapelhall ML6 .. 123 E1
Motherwell ML1 .... 143 D2
Burn Dr FK7 .... 7 E2
Burn La ML1 .... 143 D2
Burn Rd Carluke ML8 .... 187 F2
Saltcoats KA21 .... 216 B4
Burn St G83 .... 27 F2
Burn Street La G83 .... 27 F2
Burn Terr G72 .... 138 C4
Burn View G67 .... 62 B2
Burn's Cres ML5 .... 123 D3
Burn's Pl KA20 .... 206 C1
Burn's Wicket KA7 .... 238 C1
Burnacre Gdns G71 .... 140 C4
Burnbank Braes ML8 .... 187 F1
Burnbank Ctr ML3 .... 162 A3
Burnbank Dr G78 .... 134 B1
Burnbank Gdns ML3 .... 162 A3
Burnbank Pl Ayr KA7 .... 239 D2
2 Glasgow G20 .... 97 D1
Stewarton KA3 .... 195 F1
Burnbank Quadrant ML6 .. 122 C4
Burnbank Rd Ayr KA7 .... 239 D2
Falkirk FK2 .... 42 A4
Hamilton ML3 .... 162 A3
Burnbank St Airdrie ML6 .. 122 C4
Coatbridge ML5 .... 122 A4
Stevenston KA20 .... 217 E4

Burnbrae Terr
3 Glasgow G20 .... 97 D1
Kilsyth G65 .... 36 B1
Burnblea Gdns ML3 .... 162 C1
Burnblea St ML3 .... 162 B1
Burnbrae Alloa FK10 .... 10 B4
Clydebank G81 .... 74 A3
Twechar G65 .... 59 F2
Burnbrae Ave
Bearsden G61 .... 76 A4
Linwood PA3 .... 112 B3
Moodiesburn G69 .... 81 D1
Burnbrae Dr
Elderslie PA3, PA5 .... 112 B2
Perceton KA11 .... 220 A4
Rutherglen G73 .... 138 B3
Burnbrae Gdns Alva FK12 .... 5 D3
Falkirk FK1 .... 42 A3
Burnbrae Pl G74 .... 159 E1
Burnbrae Prim Sch G53 .... 135 E3
Burnbrae Rd Blantyre G72 .. 161 E4
Chryston G69, G66 .... 80 A2
Elderslie PA3 .... 112 B2
Falkirk FK1 .... 42 A3
Harthill ML7 .... 127 F3
Kirkintilloch G69, G66 .... 80 A4
Kirkintilloch, Auchinloch G66 79 F1
Shotts ML7 .... 146 C2
Burnbrae St Clydebank G81 74 B4
Glasgow G21 .... 98 A2
Larkhall ML9 .... 184 C2
Burncleuch Ave G72 .... 139 D2
Burncrooks Ave
Bearsden G61 .... 75 E4
East Kilbride G74 .... 159 E1
Burncrooks Ct G81 .... 73 F3
Burndale La KA13 .... 89 E4
Burndyke Ct G51 .... 116 B4
Burndyke Sq G51 .... 116 B4
Burnee FK10 .... 5 F2
Burness Ave KA7 .... 238 C1
Burnet Rose Ct G74 .... 159 F2
Burnet Rose Gdns G74 ...... 159 E2
Burnet Rose Pl G74 .... 159 E2
Burnett Rd G33 .... 119 F4
Burnfield Ave G46 .... 136 A2
Burnfield Cotts G46 .... 136 A2
Burnfield Dr G43 .... 136 A2
Burnfield Gdns G46 .... 136 A2
Burnfield Pl FK2 .... 42 B4
Burnfield Rd G43 .... 136 A2
Burnfoot G82 .... 48 A4
Burnfoot Ave KA10 .... 229 E3
Burnfoot Cres Paisley PA2 .. 133 F4
Rutherglen G73 .... 138 B3
Burnfoot Dr G52 .... 115 D3
Burnfoot La
Ardrossan KA22 .... 205 D2
1 Falkirk FK1 .... 42 A2
Burnfoot Pl KA3 .... 222 C2
Burnfoot Rd Airdrie ML6 .. 122 C1
Lochwinnoch PA12 .... 129 E1
Burnfoot Way KA10 .... 229 E3
Burngreen G65 .... 60 B4
Burngreen Terr G67 .... 62 A3
Burnhall Pl ML2 .... 165 E1
Burnhall Rd ML2 .... 165 E1
Burnhall St ML2 .... 165 E1
Burnham Rd G14 .... 95 D2
Burnhaven PA8 .... 73 D1
Burnhead La Falkirk FK1 .... 42 B2
Port Glasgow PA14 .... 68 B4
Burnhead Prim Sch G71 .... 141 E4
Burnhead Rd Airdrie ML6 .. 103 E1
Cumbernauld G68 .... 61 E1
Glasgow G43 .... 136 C3
Larbert FK5 .... 23 E2
Larkhall ML9 .... 185 E1
Port Glasgow PA14 .... 68 B4
Burnhead St
Greenock PA15 .... 46 A1
Uddingston G71 .... 141 E4
Burnhill Quadrant G73 .... 137 F4
Burnhill St G73 .... 137 F4
Burnhouse Ave
Cumbernauld G68 .... 61 D1
Dalry KA24 .... 191 D4
Burnhouse Brae G77 .... 157 D2
Burnhouse Cotts KA3 ...... 195 D4
Burnhouse Cres ML3 .... 162 A1
Burnhouse Rd
East Kilbride G75 .... 180 A1
Hamilton ML3 .... 162 A1
Burnhouse St G20 .... 96 B3
Burnieboozle Cres G77 .... 156 C4
Burniebrae Rd ML6 .... 123 F2
Burnlea Cres PA6 .... 91 D2
Burnlea Pl KA20 .... 206 C1
Burnlip Rd G67 .... 82 B2
Burnmouth Ct G33 .... 119 F3
Burnmouth Pl G61 .... 76 A3
Burnmouth Rd G33 .... 119 F3
Burnock Pl G75 .... 179 F4
Burnpark Ave G71 .... 140 B4
Burnpark Rd KA1 .... 227 F2
Burns Ave Bishopton PA7 .... 72 A2
Kilmarnock KA3 .... 223 D2
Saltcoats KA21 .... 205 F2
Burns Cott (Mus) KA7 ...... 238 B1
Burns Cres Harthill ML7 .... 127 F3
Irvine KA11 .... 220 A2
Laurieston FK2 .... 42 C2
Burns Ct G66 .... 79 E2
Burns Dr Johnstone PA5 .... 131 F4
Kirkintilloch G66 .... 79 E2
Burns Gdns G72 .... 140 B1
Burns Gr G46 .... 136 A1

Burns La ML6 .... 123 F2
Burns Loan **11** ML9 .... 185 D2
Burns Path ML4 .... 142 A4
Burns Pk G74 .... 160 A2
Burns Pl Kilwinning KA13 .. 207 F2
Shotts ML7 .... 146 A3
Burns Prec KA1 .... 227 F4
Burns Rd Chapelhall ML6 .. 123 F1
Cumbernauld G67 .... 62 A1
Greenock PA16 .... 44 B2
Kirkintilloch G66 .... 59 D1
Troon KA10 .... 229 F2
Burns Sq Ardrossan KA22 .. 205 E2
Greenock PA16 .... 44 B2
Burns St Alexandria G83 .... 27 F4
Clydebank G81 .... 73 F2
Hamilton ML3 .... 162 B1
Irvine KA12 .... 219 D2
Renton G82 .... 27 E1
Stirling FK8 .... 2 A1
Burns Statue Sq KA7 .... 238 C4
Burns Terr
Ardrossan KA22 .... 205 E2
Cowie FK7 .... 12 B4
Burns Way ML1 .... 143 E2
Burnside G61 .... 75 E4
Burnside Ave
Barrhead G78 .... 134 A2
Bellshill ML4 .... 142 B2
Brookfield PA5 .... 111 E3
Calderbank ML6 .... 123 D1
Kirkintilloch G66 .... 79 D4
Port Glasgow PA14 .... 68 C4
Burnside Cotts KA3 .... 173 E3
Burnside Cres Balloch G83 .. 27 F4
Clydebank G81 .... 74 A4
Hamilton G72 .... 161 F3
Plean FK7 .... 12 B2
Shotts ML7 .... 146 B3
Burnside Ct Bearsden G61 .. 75 E4
Motherwell ML1 .... 164 A2
Rutherglen G73 .... 138 B3
Burnside Gate G73 .... 138 B3
Burnside Gdns
Clarkston G76 .... 157 E4
Johnstone PA10 .... 111 D1
Prestwick KA9 .... 233 E1
Burnside Gr PA5 .... 111 F1
Burnside Ind Est G65 .... 60 B4
Burnside La ML3 .... 162 C1
Burnside Pl Dumbarton G82 .. 50 A1
Irvine KA12 .... 219 D2
Larkhall ML9 .... 185 D2
Paisley PA3 .... 113 D4
Stevenston KA20 .... 206 B1
Troon KA10 .... 229 E2
West Kilbride KA23 .... 190 B3
Burnside Prim Sch G73 .... 138 A3
Burnside Quadrant ML1 .. 143 D3
Burnside Rd Elderslie PA5 .. 112 B1
Glenmavis ML6 .... 102 B1
Gourock PA19 .... 44 C3
Menstrie FK11 .... 3 F3
Monkton KA9 .... 233 E2
Motherwell ML1 .... 143 E2
Prestwick Wlk ML5 .... 121 F3
Rutherglen, High Burnside
G73 .... 138 B2
Burnside St Alloa FK10 .... 5 E1
Dumbarton G82 .... 50 A1
Glengarnock KA14 .... 170 A3
Kilmarnock KA1 .... 227 F3
Motherwell ML1 .... 164 A2
Stirling FK7 .... 7 D2
Burnside Sta G73 .... 138 B3
Burnside Terr KA1 .... 41 F3
Burnside View ML5 .... 121 F3
Burnside Wlk ML5 .... 121 F3
Burntbroom Ct G69 .... 119 F2
Burntbroom Dr G69 .... 119 F1
Burntbroom Gdns G69 ...... 119 F2
Burntbroom Rd G69 .... 119 F1
Burntbroom St G33 .... 119 E4
Burntshields Rd PA10 ...... 130 A1
Burnwood Dr ML6 .... 124 A3
Burra Gdns G64 .... 78 B1
Burrell Collection (Mus)
G43 .... 116 A1
Burrell Ct G41 .... 116 B1
Burrell's La G4 .... 241 F2
Burrelton Rd G43 .... 136 C3
Burstenman's Brae
KA13, KA24 .... 207 F4
Burton La **6** G42 .... 187 F1
Busbie View KA2 .... 221 F1
Busbiehead KA11 .... 220 A3
Busbiehill Pl KA1 .... 222 B1
Busby District Prim Sch
G76 .... 157 F3
Busby Pl KA13 .... 207 F2
Busby Rd Bellshill ML4 ...... 141 F2
Carmunnock G76 .... 158 B4
Clarkston G76 .... 157 F3
Busby Sta G76 .... 157 F4
Bush Cres ML2 .... 165 E1
Bushelhead Rd ML8 .... 201 F3
Bushes Ave PA2 .... 113 E1
Bushes Prim Sch PA2 .... 133 E4
Busheyhill St G72 .... 139 D3
Bute G74 .... 160 B1
Bute Ave Motherwell ML1 .. 163 E4
Port Glasgow PA14 .... 69 D4
Renfrew PA4 .... 94 B1
Bute Cres Bearsden G61 ...... 75 F1
Old Kilpatrick G60 .... 73 D3
Paisley PA2 .... 133 E4
Shotts ML7 .... 146 B3

Bute Ct Greenock PA16 ...... 45 D3
Irvine KA11 ...... 220 B1
Stevenston KA20 ...... 217 E4
Bute Dr Johnstone PA5 ...... 111 E1
Old Kilpatrick G60 ...... 73 E3
Bute Gdns Glasgow G44 ...... 136 C2
Glasgow, Kelvingrove G12 ...... 96 B1
Bute La G12 ...... 96 B1
Bute Pl KA22 ...... 205 E1
Bute Rd Kirkintilloch G66 ...... 80 A4
Renfrew PA3 ...... 93 E1
Bute St Coatbridge ML5 ...... 122 A2
Falkirk FK2 ...... 42 A3
Gourock PA19 ...... 44 B3
Hamilton ML3 ...... 162 A3
Bute Terr Rutherglen G73 ...... 138 A3
Saltcoats KA21 ...... 205 F1
Uddingston G71 ...... 141 D4
Bute Tower G72 ...... 138 C2
Butler Wynd ML4 ...... 141 F3
Bute Ave G84 ...... 16 C2
Butterbiggins Rd G42 ...... 117 D2
Butterdunpark St ML3 ...... 162 B1
Butterfield Pl ⬛ G41 ...... 117 D2
Buttermere G75 ...... 179 F3
By-Pass Rd KA15 ...... 150 B1
By-Pass Rd FK4 ...... 39 F3
Byars Rd G66 ...... 79 D4
Byrebush Rd G53 ...... 115 E1
Byrehill Ave KA13 ...... 207 D1
Byrehill Pl KA13 ...... 207 D1
Byrehill Rd Irvine KA13 ...... 218 C4
Kilwinning KA13 ...... 207 E1
Byres Ave PA3 ...... 114 A3
Byres Cres PA3 ...... 114 A3
Byres Loch KA13 ...... 207 E2
Byres Rd Elderslie PA5 ...... 112 B1
Glasgow G11, G12 ...... 96 B1
Kilwinning KA13 ...... 207 E2
Motherwell ML1 ...... 143 F2
Byresknowe La ML1 ...... 143 D1
Byrestone Ave G77 ...... 157 E2
Byretown Rd ML11 ...... 214 A2
Byron Rd ML7 ...... 146 A3
Byron St Clydebank G81 ...... 74 A2
Glasgow G51 ...... 95 F2
Byshot St G22 ...... 97 E2

Cable Depot Rd G81 ...... 73 F1
Cables Dr G83 ...... 27 F3
Cabrach Loan ⬛ ML2 ...... 165 F3
Cadder Ct G64 ...... 78 A3
Cadder Pl G20 ...... 96 C4
Cadder Prim Sch G64 ...... 78 A3
Cadder Rd Bishopbriggs G64 ...... 78 A3
Glasgow G20 ...... 96 C4
Cadder Way G64 ...... 78 A3
Cadder Way G64 ...... 78 A3
Caddlehill St PA16 ...... 45 E3
Cadell Dr FK2 ...... 24 A3
Cadell Gdns G74 ...... 160 B3
Cadger's Sheuch G65 ...... 61 A2
Cadgers Loan FK7 ...... 12 A1
Cadoc St G72 ...... 139 D3
Cadogan Sq G2 ...... 240 B2
Cadogan St G2 ...... 240 B2
Cadzow Ave G46 ...... 157 D4
Cadzow Cres ML5 ...... 121 F2
Cadzow Dr Bellshill ML4 ...... 142 B2
Cambuslang G72 ...... 139 D3
Cadzow Gn G74 ...... 159 D1
Cadzow Ind Est ML3 ...... 183 E4
Cadzow La ML3 ...... 162 C2
Cadzow Pk ML3 ...... 162 C2
Cadzow Rd ML3 ...... 183 F2
Cadzow St Glasgow G2 ...... 240 B2
Hamilton ML3 ...... 162 C2
Larkhall ML9 ...... 185 D2
Motherwell ML1 ...... 163 E3
Caerlaverock Ave KA9 ...... 236 B4
Caerlaverock Pl G72 ...... 161 E3
Caerlaverock Rd KA9 ...... 236 B4
Caff Water Rd KA21 ...... 205 F1
Caird Ave PA16 ...... 45 E1
Caird Dr 96 A1
Caird Gdns ML3 ...... 162 B3
Caird Pk ML3 ...... 162 B3
Caird St ML3 ...... 162 B3
Caird Terr G61 ...... 75 E4
Cairn Ave PA4 ...... 94 C1
Cairn Cl KA13 ...... 195 E1
Cairn Cres KA7 ...... 238 B1
Cairn Ct G74 ...... 159 F2
Cairn Dr PA3 ...... 112 A3
Cairn Pl G74 ...... 159 F2
Cairn St G21 ...... 97 F3
Cairn View Airdrie ML6 ...... 122 C3
Kirkintilloch G66 ...... 80 A4
Cairnbaan Ct ML8 ...... 187 F2
Cairnban St G51 ...... 115 E3
Cairnbrook Ind Est G34 ...... 120 B4
Cairnbrook Rd G34 ...... 120 B4
Cairncurran Ct PA15 ...... 45 F2
Cairndhu Ave G84 ...... 16 A1
Cairndhu Gdns G84 ...... 16 A1
Cairndow Ave G44 ...... 136 C2
Cairndow Avenue La G44 ...... 136 C2
Cairndow Ct G44 ...... 136 C2
Cairnduff Pl KA3 ...... 195 F1
Cairndyke Cres ML6 ...... 123 D3
Cairney Pl ML2 ...... 166 B3
Cairneymount Rd ML8 ...... 188 A1
Cairnfore Ave KA10 ...... 229 F3
Cairngorm Cres
Barrhead G78 ...... 134 B1
Bearsden G61 ...... 75 D3
Paisley PA2 ...... 133 F4
Wishaw ML2 ...... 164 C2
Cairngorm Ct ML11 ...... 220 A3

Cairngorm Gdns G68 ...... 61 D1
Cairngorm Pl G75 ...... 180 A2
Cairngorm Rd
Glasgow G43 ...... 136 B3
Kilmarnock KA1 ...... 228 A2
Cairnhill Ave ML6 ...... 123 D3
Cairnhill Cir G52 ...... 114 C2
Cairnhill Cres ML5 ...... 122 B2
Cairnhill Ct ML8 ...... 188 A1
Cairnhill Dr G52 ...... 114 C2
Cairnhill Pl G52 ...... 114 C2
Cairnhill Rd Airdrie ML6 ...... 123 D3
Bearsden G61 ...... 75 F1
Cairnhill Trad Est ML6 ...... 123 D3
Cairnhope Ave ML6 ...... 122 C3
Cairnlea Dr G51 ...... 116 A3
Cairnlea Gdns ML4 ...... 142 A2
Cairnlea Rd G62 ...... 54 C1
Cairnmount Rd KA11 ...... 219 F4
Cairnmuir Rd G74 ...... 159 E3
Cairnoch Hill G68 ...... 61 E1
Cairnoch Way FK7 ...... 7 F1
Cairnoch Wlk FK6 ...... 21 E1
Cairnryan G74 ...... 159 E2
Cairns Ave G72 ...... 139 D3
Cairns Dr G62 ...... 55 D1
Cairns Prim Sch The G72 ...... 139 E2
Cairns Rd Bishopton PA7 ...... 72 A2
Cambuslang G72 ...... 139 D2
Cairns St ML1 ...... 163 F3
Cairns Terr KA1 ...... 222 C1
Cairns The FK11 ...... 4 A3
Cairnsgarroch Way KA11 ...... 220 A1
Cairnsmore Dr Ayr KA7 ...... 238 B1
Bearsden G61 ...... 75 D4
Cairnsmore Rd G15 ...... 74 C1
Cairnsmore Way KA11 ...... 220 A1
Cairnswell Ave G72 ...... 139 E2
Cairnswell Pl G72 ...... 139 E2
Cairntoul Ct G68 ...... 61 D1
Cairntoul Dr G14 ...... 95 D3
Cairntoul Pl G14 ...... 95 D3
Cairnview Rd G65 ...... 58 B3
Cairnwood Dr ML6 ...... 122 C3
Caithness Rd
East Kilbride G74 ...... 160 B2
Greenock PA16 ...... 44 B2
Caithness Row ML11 ...... 215 D1
Caithness St Blantyre G72 ...... 161 E3
Glasgow G20 ...... 96 C2
Cala Sona Ct ML2 ...... 185 F4
Calcots Path G34 ...... 100 B1
Calcots Pl G34 ...... 100 B1
Caldarvan St G22 ...... 97 D2
Caldeen Rd ML5 ...... 122 A3
Calder Ave Barrhead G78 ...... 134 B1
Caldercruix ML6 ...... 104 C2
Condorrat G68 ...... 122 A2
Troon KA10 ...... 229 F3
Wishaw ML2 ...... 166 A3
Calder Ct Coatbridge ML5 ...... 122 A2
Stirling FK7 ...... 7 E3
Calder Dr Bellshill ML4 ...... 142 A3
Cambuslang G72 ...... 139 D3
Lochwinnoch PA12 ...... 129 E2
Shotts ML7 ...... 147 D2
Calder Gate G64 ...... 77 F2
Calder Pl Falkirk FK1 ...... 42 B1
Glasgow G69 ...... 120 A2
Kilmarnock KA1 ...... 228 A2
Calder Prim Sch ML1 ...... 163 F4
Calder Rd Bellshill ML4 ...... 142 A3
Cambuslang G72 ...... 139 D3
Paisley PA3 ...... 113 D3
Shotts ML7 ...... 146 C4
Calder St Blantyre G72 ...... 161 E4
Coatbridge ML5 ...... 123 E1
Coatbridge ML5 ...... 122 A2
Glasgow G42 ...... 117 D1
Lochwinnoch PA12 ...... 129 E2
Calder Tower ML1 ...... 163 F3
Calder View Hamilton ML3 ...... 183 D4
Motherwell ML1 ...... 163 F4
Calderbank Prim Sch
...... 123 E2
Calderbank Rd ML6 ...... 123 D2
Calderbank Terr ML1 ...... 163 F3
Calderbank View G69 ...... 120 B2
Calderbraes Ave G71 ...... 140 C4
Caldercuilt Prim Sch G3 ...... 76 C1
Caldercuilt Rd G20 ...... 76 B1
Calderglen Ave G72 ...... 140 B2
Calderglen Ctry Pk G75 ...... 181 E3
Calderglen Rd G74 ...... 160 B1
Caldergrove ML1 ...... 163 F4
Calderhaugh La PA12 ...... 129 E1
Calderhead High Sch
ML7 ...... 146 C3
Calderhead Rd ML7 ...... 146 B4
Calderpark Ave
Glasgow G71 ...... 120 A1
Lochwinnoch PA12 ...... 129 E2
Calderpark Cres G71 ...... 120 A1
Calderpark Pl G71 ...... 129 E2
Calderpark Rd G71 ...... 120 A1
Calderpark St G71 ...... 120 A1
Caldervale Ave G71 ...... 140 C4
Caldervale High Sch ML6 ...... 123 E3
Caldervale St ML6 ...... 123 E3
Calderview Ave ML5 ...... 122 C2
Calderwood G69 ...... 120 A2
Calderwood KA13 ...... 207 F3
Calderwood Ave G69 ...... 120 A2
Calderwood Dr
Blantyre G72 ...... 161 E3
Glasgow G69 ...... 120 A2
Calderwood Gdns
East Kilbride G74 ...... 160 C2
Glasgow G69 ...... 120 A2

Calderwood Jewish Prim
Day Sch G43 ...... 136 B3
Calderwood Prim Sch
G73 ...... 138 B3
Calderwood Rd
East Kilbride G74 ...... 160 A1
Glasgow G43 ...... 136 B3
Rutherglen G73 ...... 138 B4
Calderwood Sq G74 ...... 160 A2
Caldon Rd KA12 ...... 219 E3
Caldwell Ave Glasgow G13 ...... 95 D3
Linwood PA3 ...... 112 A3
Caldwell Gr ML4 ...... 142 A4
Caldwell Pl G84 ...... 15 F3
Caldwell Quadrant ML1 ...... 163 E3
Caldwell Rd Carluke ML8 ...... 202 A4
West Kilbride KA23 ...... 190 B2
Caledon La G12 ...... 96 B1
Caledon St G12 ...... 96 B2
Caledonia Ave Glasgow G5 ...... 117 E2
Rutherglen G73 ...... 138 A4
Caledonia Cres
Ardrossan KA22 ...... 205 E1
Gourock PA19 ...... 45 D4
Caledonia Ct
Ardrossan KA22 ...... 222 C1
Irvine KA11 ...... 220 A2
Caledonia Dr Glasgow G69 ...... 120 A2
Motherwell ML1 ...... 143 F2
Caledonia Gdns ML8 ...... 187 F2
Caledonia Prim Sch
KA21 ...... 216 C4
Caledonia Rd
Ardrossan KA22 ...... 205 E1
Ayr KA7 ...... 239 E3
Beith KA15 ...... 150 A1
Glasgow G69 ...... 120 A2
Glasgow, Gorbals G5 ...... 117 E2
Saltcoats KA21 ...... 216 C4
Shotts ML7 ...... 146 C3
Caledonia St
Clydebank G81 ...... 73 F2
Glasgow G5 ...... 117 E2
Paisley PA3 ...... 113 E3
Port Glasgow PA14 ...... 47 E1
Caledonia Terr Clydebank G81 ...... 49 E2
Greenock PA16 ...... 45 E3
Caledonia Way PA3 ...... 93 E1
Caledonia Way E PA3 ...... 93 F1
Caledonia Way W PA3 ...... 93 F1
Caledonia Wlk ML3 ...... 162 C1
Caledonian Ave
Bellshill ML4 ...... 141 F2
Stenhousemuir FK5 ...... 23 F2
Caledonian Cres ⬛ G12 ...... 96 C1
Caledonian Ct
East Kilbride G74 ...... 180 C4
Falkirk FK2 ...... 42 B4
Caledonian Gdns FK10 ...... 9 F3
Caledonian Pl KA14 ...... 170 A4
Caledonian Prim Sch
G69 ...... 120 A2
Caledonian Rd Alloa FK10 ...... 9 F3
Glengarnock KA14 ...... 170 B4
Larkhall ML9 ...... 185 D2
Stevenston KA20 ...... 217 F4
Wishaw ML2 ...... 165 D1
Caley Brae G71 ...... 140 C3
Caley Ct KA20 ...... 217 E4
Calfhill Rd G53 ...... 115 D1
Calfmuir Rd G66 ...... 80 A3
Calgary Pk G75 ...... 180 B4
Calgary Pl ⬛ G75 ...... 180 B4
Calgary St G4 ...... 241 D4
Callaghan Wynd G72 ...... 140 C1
Callander Ct G68 ...... 61 F2
Callander Dr FK5 ...... 41 E4
Callander Rd
Chapelhall ML6 ...... 123 E1
Cumbernauld G68 ...... 61 F2
Callander St G20 ...... 97 D2
Callendar Ave FK1 ...... 42 A1
Callendar Bsns Pk FK1 ...... 42 C2
Callendar Bvd FK1 ...... 42 C2
Callendar House FK1 ...... 42 B2
Callendar Pl KA8 ...... 236 A2
Callendar Rd FK1 ...... 42 B2
Callendar Riggs FK1 ...... 42 B2
Callendar Square Sch Ctr ⬛
FK1 ...... 42 A2
Callender Rd KA8 ...... 236 B3
Callieburn Rd G64 ...... 98 A4
Callon St ML6 ...... 123 D4
Cally Ave G15 ...... 75 D2
Calside PA2 ...... 113 F2
Calside Ave PA2 ...... 113 F2
Calton Cres FK7 ...... 7 D2
Calton Entry G40 ...... 241 F1
Caltrop Pl FK7 ...... 7 F2
Calvay Cres G33 ...... 119 E4
Calvay Rd G33 ...... 119 E4
Calvinston Rd KA9 ...... 236 B3
Cam'nethan St ML3 ...... 198 C1
Cambourne Rd G69 ...... 80 C1
Cambridge Ave
Clydebank G81 ...... 74 A2
Gourock PA19 ...... 45 D4
Cambridge Rd
Greenock PA16 ...... 44 B2
Renfrew PA4 ...... 94 B1
Cambridge St G2 ...... 240 C3
Camburn St G32 ...... 118 C3
Cambus Pl G33 ...... 99 E1
Cambusbarron Prim Sch
FK7 ...... 6 B3
Cambusdoon Dr KA7 ...... 238 C1
Cambusdoon Pl KA7 ...... 207 E2

Cambusdoon Rd G33 ...... 99 E1
Cambuskeith Rd KA20 ...... 206 C2
Cambuskenneth Gdns
G32 ...... 119 E3
Cambuskenneth Pl G33 ...... 99 E1
Cambuslang Coll Allers
Annexe 160 B2
Cambuslang Coll Annexe
G74 ...... 159 F1
Cambuslang Coll (Annexe)
ML2 ...... 164 B3
Cambuslang Ind Est G72 ...... 139 D4
Cambuslang Investment Pk
G32 ...... 139 D4
Cambuslang Rd
Cambuslang G72 ...... 138 C4
Rutherglen G73, G72 ...... 138 B4
Cambuslang Sta G72 ...... 138 C3
Cambuslea Rd KA8 ...... 236 A2
Cambusmoon Terr G83 ...... 20 C4
Cambusnethan Prim Sch
ML2 ...... 165 E2
Cambusnethan St ML2 ...... 165 F2
Cambustlang Coll G72 ...... 139 D3
Camden St G5 ...... 117 E2
Camelon Cres G72 ...... 161 E4
Camelon Ed Ctr FK1 ...... 41 F3
Camelon Rd FK1 ...... 41 F3
Camelon St G32 ...... 118 C3
Camelon Sta FK1 ...... 41 E3
Cameron Ave PA7 ...... 72 A2
Cameron Cres
Carmunnock G76 ...... 158 C4
Hamilton ML3 ...... 162 B2
Cameron Ct Airdrie ML6 ...... 123 F4
Rutherglen G73 ...... 138 A4
Cameron Dr Alexandria G83 ...... 27 E4
Bearsden G61 ...... 76 A2
Kilmarnock KA3 ...... 223 E1
Newton Mearns G77 ...... 156 C4
Liddingston G71 ...... 141 D4
Cameron Path ML9 ...... 185 E1
Cameron Pl FK2 ...... 24 A1
Cameron Rd Carluke ML8 ...... 202 A4
Greengairs ML6 ...... 83 E1
Cameron Sq G81 ...... 74 B3
Cameron St Clydebank G81 ...... 94 B4
Dumbarton G82 ...... 50 B2
Kilmarnock KA3 ...... 222 C1
Motherwell ML1 ...... 163 E3
Paisley G52 ...... 114 C4
Cameron Terr FK1 ...... 86 A2
Cameronian Ct ML11 ...... 215 E3
Cameronian Dr ML8 ...... 188 A1
Cameronian Pl ML4 ...... 141 F2
Cameronian St FK8 ...... 7 D4
Cameronian Way ⬛ ML9 ...... 185 E1
Cams Eskan House G84 ...... 25 E4
Camlachie St G31 ...... 118 A3
Camp Rd Glasgow G69 ...... 120 A3
Motherwell ML1 ...... 163 F2
Rutherglen G73 ...... 138 A4
Camp St ML1 ...... 163 F3
Campbell Ave
Bishopton PA7 ...... 72 A2
Dumbarton G82 ...... 50 B1
Milngavie G62 ...... 55 D1
Saltcoats KA21 ...... 216 C4
Stevenston KA20 ...... 206 B1
Campbell Cres
Alexandria G83 ...... 27 E4
Bothwell G71 ...... 141 D2
Laurieston FK2 ...... 42 C2
Newton Mearns G77 ...... 156 C3
Campbell Ct Ayr KA8 ...... 239 E4
Greenock PA16 ...... 45 F4
Stirling FK7 ...... 6 C2
Campbell Dr Barrhead G78 ...... 134 B1
Bearsden G61 ...... 75 E3
Dumbarton G82 ...... 50 B2
Helensburgh G84 ...... 25 D4
Larbert FK5 ...... 23 D1
Troon KA10 ...... 229 E3
Campbell La ML3 ...... 162 C2
Campbell Pl
East Kilbride G75 ...... 180 C4
Irvine KA11 ...... 225 D4
Torrance G64 ...... 57 D1
Campbell St Alexandria G83 ...... 27 F2
Ayr KA8 ...... 236 A2
Bellshill ML4 ...... 142 A3
Glasgow G20 ...... 96 C4
Greenock PA16 ...... 45 F3
Hamilton ML3 ...... 162 C2
Helensburgh G84 ...... 16 B2
Johnstone PA5 ...... 111 F1
Kilmarnock KA1 ...... 227 F3
Renfrew PA4 ...... 94 B3
Wishaw ML2 ...... 165 E1
Campbell Terr G82 ...... 50 B2
Campbeltown Dr KA3 ...... 222 C2
Camperdown Ct G84 ...... 17 D1
Campfield St FK2 ...... 42 A3
Camphill PA1 ...... 113 E2
Camphill Ave
Glasgow G41 ...... 136 C4
Kirkintilloch G66 ...... 79 E4
Camphill Ct G77 ...... 170 A4
Camphill Gdns PA7 ...... 72 B2
Camphill Pl ML7 ...... 239 D3
Campie Terr FK2 ...... 24 C1
Campion Ct KA7 ...... 239 D2
Campion Rd ML1 ...... 163 F4
Camps Cres PA4 ...... 94 C1
Campsie Ave Barrhead G78 ...... 134 B1
Irvine KA11 ...... 220 B2
Campsie Cres Airdrie ML6 ...... 122 C4
Kirkintilloch G66 ...... 79 E3
Campsie Ct ML9 ...... 184 C3

Campsie Dene Rd G63 ...... 31 D2
Campsie Dr Bearsden G61 ...... 75 F4
Milngavie G62 ...... 55 D1
Paisley PA2 ...... 133 E4
Renfrew PA4 ...... 114 A4
Renfrew, G'gow Airport PA3 ...... 93 F1
Campsie Gdns G76 ...... 157 E4
Campsie Pl G69 ...... 100 B4
Campsie Rd
East Kilbride G75 ...... 180 A2
Kilmarnock KA1 ...... 228 A2
Kirkintilloch G66 ...... 58 A1
Kirkintilloch, Milton of C G65 ...... 58 A3
Port Glasgow PA14 ...... 69 D3
Torrance G64 ...... 57 F1
Wishaw ML2 ...... 164 C2
Campsie St G21 ...... 98 A3
Campsie View
Chryston G69 ...... 100 B4
Coatbridge G69 ...... 120 C3
Cumbernauld G67 ...... 62 A2
Hamilton ML3 ...... 161 F1
Kirkintilloch G66 ...... 79 D4
Stepps G33 ...... 99 E2
⬛ Uddingston G71 ...... 141 D4
Campsie View KA11 ...... 220 A2
Campsie Way KA11 ...... 220 A2
Campston Pl G33 ...... 99 D1
Camsail Ave G84 ...... 16 A1
Camsail Rd G84 ...... 15 D2
Cambusmore Pl G33 ...... 99 E1
Camsdale Ave ML7 ...... 125 D1
Camstradden Dr E G61 ...... 75 E2
Camstradden Dr W G61 ...... 75 E2
Camus Pl G15 ...... 74 C2
Canal Ave PA5 ...... 112 A2
Canal Cres KA20 ...... 217 E4
Canal Ct KA21 ...... 217 D4
Canal La G66 ...... 58 B1
Canal Pl KA21 ...... 217 D4
Canal Rd PA5 ...... 112 A1
Canal St Elderslie PA5 ...... 112 B2
Falkirk FK2 ...... 42 A4
Falkirk, Camelon FK1 ...... 41 E3
Glasgow G4 ...... 241 D4
Johnstone PA5 ...... 112 A2
Canal Terr PA1 ...... 113 F2
Canalyard Ind Est FK1 ...... 42 A1
Canavan Ct FK7 ...... 7 E2
Canberra Ave G81 ...... 73 E2
Canberra Ct G46 ...... 136 C2
Canberra Dr G75 ...... 180 B4
Canberra Prim Sch G75 ...... 180 A4
Cander Ave ML9 ...... 199 D2
Cander Rigg G64 ...... 78 A2
Cander St ML9 ...... 199 D2
Candermill & Marlage Rd
ML9 ...... 199 F3
Candermill Rd ML9 ...... 199 D3
Candleside Toll ML9 ...... 199 D3
Candimline CE ML8 ...... 188 A1
Candleriggs Alloa FK10 ...... 10 A3
Glasgow G1 ...... 241 E2
Candleriggs Ct FK10 ...... 10 A3
Candren Rd Linwood PA3 ...... 112 C3
Paisley PA3 ...... 113 D2
Canmore Pl ML3 ...... 183 D1
Cangillan Ct KA9 ...... 236 B3
Canmore Cres PA16 ...... 45 D2
Canmore Dr FK5 ...... 23 F2
Canmore Pl Glasgow G31 ...... 118 B2
Stewarton KA3 ...... 195 F1
Canmore St G31 ...... 118 B2
Cannerton Cres G65 ...... 58 A3
Cannerton Pk G65 ...... 58 A3
Cannich Dr PA2 ...... 114 A1
Cannich Pl ML2 ...... 165 F3
Cannisburn Hospl G61 ...... 75 F2
Cannisburn Rd G61 ...... 75 F2
Cannisburn Toll G61 ...... 75 F2
Cannons Way PA2 ...... 24 A1
Canon Ct ML1 ...... 143 E1
Canonbie St G34 ...... 100 B1
Canongate G74 ...... 160 B1
Canonside Ave G71 ...... 120 A1
Canthill Gdns ML7 ...... 146 A2
Cantieslaw Dr G74 ...... 160 B1
Canting Way G51 ...... 116 B4
Canyon Rd ML2 ...... 164 B1
Capel Ave G77 ...... 156 C3
Capel Gr G74 ...... 160 A2
Capel Pl KA11 ...... 220 A1
Capeldrae Cotts G77 ...... 155 F2
Capel Rd
East Kilbride G74 ...... 160 A2
Newton Mearns G77 ...... 156 C4
Capelrig La G77 ...... 156 B3
Capelrig Rd G77 ...... 156 B3
Capelrig St G46 ...... 135 F2
Caplaw Pl ML2 ...... 165 F3
Caplaw Rd Barrhead G78 ...... 132 B1
Paisley PA2 ...... 133 E3
Caplaw Tower ML2 ...... 185 F4
Caplethill Rd
Barrhead G78 ...... 134 A3
Paisley PA2 ...... 133 F4
Caponcraig Ave KA20 ...... 206 B1
Capper View KA9 ...... 233 E1
Cappielow Ind Est PA15 ...... 46 B2

Cappielow Pk (Greenock
Morton FC) PA15 .... 46 B2
Capringstone Foot KA11 .. 220 A3
Caprington Ave KA1 .... 227 F2
Caprington Gdns KA1 ...... 227 F2
Caprington St G33 .... 99 D1
Captain St PA15 .... 45 F2
Cara Dr G51 .... 115 F4
Caravelle Way ⑩ PA4 .... 94 B1
Carbarns ML2 .... 164 C1
Carbarns E ML2 .... 164 B1
Carbarns Rd ML2 .... 164 B1
Carbarns W ML2 .... 164 B1
Carberry Rd G41 .... 116 B1
Carbeth Rd G62 .... 54 C1
Carbeth St G22 .... 97 D2
Carbisdale St G22 .... 97 F3
Carbost St G23 .... 76 B1
Carbrain Ind Est G67 .... 62 A1
Carbrain Prim Sch G67 .... 62 A1
Carbrook Dr FK7 .... 12 B2
Carbrook St Glasgow G21 .... 98 A1
Paisley PA1 .... 113 E2
Carclure Cres KA7 .... 239 D1
Cardarrach St G21 .... 98 A2
Cardean Rd ML4 .... 142 C3
Cardell Ave PA2 .... 113 D2
Cardell Cres ML6 .... 123 E1
Cardell Dr PA2 .... 113 D2
Cardell Rd PA2 .... 113 D2
Cardinal Newman
High Sch ML4 .... 141 F3
Cardon Pl KA11 .... 220 A1
Cardonald Coll G52 .... 115 E2
Cardonald Dr G52 .... 115 D2
Cardonald Gdns G52 .... 115 D2
Cardonald Place Rd G52 .... 115 D2
Cardonald Prim Sch G52 .... 115 D2
Cardonald Sta G52 .... 115 E3
Cardow Cres KA11 .... 220 A3
Cardow Rd G21 .... 98 B2
Cardowan Dr
Cumbernauld G68 .... 60 C1
Stepps G33 .... 99 F3
Cardowan Rd
Glasgow G32 .... 119 D4
Stepps G33 .... 99 F3
Cardrona St G33 .... 99 D2
Cardross Ave PA14 .... 68 C4
Cardross Cres PA15 .... 46 B1
Cardross Ct ⑪ G31 .... 117 F4
Cardross Pl PA15 .... 46 B1
Cardross Prim Sch G82 ...... 26 A1
Cardross Rd
Alexandria G82 .... 26 C1
Dumbarton G82 .... 49 E2
Helensburgh G82 .... 25 E2
Renton G82 .... 27 D1
Cardross St G31 .... 117 F4
Cardross Sta G82 .... 48 A4
Cardrowan Rd FK7 .... 12 B1
Cardwell Rd PA19 .... 44 C4
Cardwell St ⑩ G5 .... 117 D2
Cardyke St G21 .... 98 A2
Carelcroft Rd PA14 .... 68 C4
Careston Pl G64 .... 78 B1
Carey Gdns ML1 .... 144 B1
Carey Rd KA21 .... 205 F2
Carfin Dr ML8 .... 201 E1
Carfin Ind Est ML1 .... 143 D1
Carfin Lourdes Grotto
ML1 .... 143 E1
Carfin Mill Rd ML1 .... 143 E1
Carfin Rd Motherwell ML1 .. 143 E2
Wishaw ML2 .... 164 B2
Carfin St Coatbridge ML5 .... 122 A2
Glasgow G42 .... 117 D1
Motherwell ML1 .... 143 D2
Carfin Sta ML1 .... 143 E1
Carfrae St G3 .... 116 B4
Cargil Ave PA13 .... 89 E4
Cargill Dr KA9 .... 236 B3
Cargill Sq G64 .... 98 B4
Cargill St G31 .... 118 C2
Carham Cres G52 .... 115 E3
Carham Dr G52 .... 115 E3
Caribou Gn G75 .... 180 A4
Carillon Rd G51 .... 116 B3
Carisbrooke Cres G64 .... 78 A2
Carlaverock Rd G43 .... 136 C3
Carleith Ave G81 .... 73 F3
Carleith Prim Sch G81 .... 73 F3
Carleith Quadrant G51 ...... 115 E4
Carleith Terr G81 .... 73 F3
Carleston St G21 .... 97 F2
Carleton Ct G46 .... 136 B2
Carleton Dr G46 .... 136 B2
Carleton Gate G46 .... 136 B2
Carleton Gdns KA9 .... 236 B4
Carlibar Ave G13 .... 94 C4
Carlibar Dr G78 .... 134 B2
Carlibar Gdns G78 .... 134 B2
Carlibar Prim Sch G78 .... 134 B2
Carlibar Rd G78 .... 134 B2
Carlie Ave FK9 .... 2 A3
Carlile Pl PA3 .... 113 F3
Carlin La ML8 .... 188 A1
Carlisle La ML8 .... 123 E4
Carlisle Rd Airdrie ML6 ...... 123 E3
Cleland ML1 .... 144 B3
Hamilton ML3 .... 163 D1
Larkhall ML9 .... 184 C4
Stonehouse ML9 .... 199 E2
Carlisle St G21, G22 .... 97 E2
Carlouk La ML8 .... 188 A1

Carlowrie Ave G72 .... 140 B1
Carlton Ct G5 .... 240 C1
Carlton Pl G5 .... 240 C1
Carluke High Sch ML8 .... 188 A1
Carluke Prim Sch ML8 .... 188 A2
Carluke Sta ML8 .... 187 F2
Carlung Pl KA23 .... 190 B2
Carlyle Ave G52 .... 114 C4
Carlyle Dr G74 .... 160 A1
Carlyle Terr
East Kilbride G74 .... 160 A1
Rutherglen G73 .... 118 A1
Carmaben Rd G33 .... 119 F4
Carman Rd Cardross G82 .... 48 B4
Renton G82 .... 27 E1
Carmel Ave KA1 .... 222 B1
Carmel Dr KA11 .... 221 D1
Carmel Pl Kilmarnock KA1 .. 222 B1
Kilmaurs KA3 .... 222 A4
Carmel Terr KA1 .... 222 B1
Carmen View G82 .... 50 A3
Carment Dr Glasgow G41 .. 136 B4
Stevenston KA20 .... 217 F4
Carmichael Ct ML11 .... 215 E2
Carmichael Path ML5 .... 101 E3
Carmichael Pl G42 .... 136 C4
Carmichael St
Glasgow G51 .... 116 B3
Greenock PA16 .... 45 E3
Law ML8 .... 186 C3
Carmichael Way ML8 .... 186 C3
Carmunnock Dr G83 .... 28 B4
Carmuirs Ave FK1 .... 41 E3
Carmuirs Dr FK1 .... 41 E3
Carmuirs Prim Sch FK1 ...... 41 E3
Carmuirs St FK1 .... 41 E3
Carmunnock By-Pass
G76 .... 158 B4
Carmunnock Prim Sch
G76 .... 158 B4
Carmunnock Rd
Clarkston G76 .... 158 A3
Glasgow G44 .... 137 E3
Carmyle Ave G32 .... 139 D4
Carmyle Pl KA20 .... 217 E4
Carmyle Prim Sch G32 ...... 119 E1
Carmyle Station G32 .... 119 D1
Carna Dr G44 .... 137 E3
Carnarvon St G3 .... 240 A4
Carnaughton Pl FK12 .... 4 C3
Carnbooth Ct G45 .... 137 F1
Carnbroe Prim Sch ML5 .... 122 B2
Carnbroe Rd ML5 .... 122 B2
Carneddans Rd G62 .... 54 B2
Carnegie Dr FK1 .... 41 E3
Carnegie Hill G75 .... 180 B4
Carnegie Pl G75 .... 180 B4
Carnegie Rd G52 .... 115 D3
Carnell Cres KA9 .... 236 B4
Carnell Terr KA9 .... 236 B4
Carnoch St G23 .... 76 B1
Carnock Cres G78 .... 134 A1
Carnock Gdns G62 .... 54 C1
Carnock Rd G53 .... 135 E4
Carnock St Cowie FK7 .... 12 C4
Greenock PA15 .... 46 A2
Carnoustie Ave PA19 .... 44 A3
Carnoustie Cres
Bishopbriggs G64 .... 78 B1
East Kilbride G75 .... 180 A3
Carnoustie Ct
Bothwell G72 .... 140 C1
Kilwinning KA13 .... 207 D2
Carnoustie Pl
Bellshill ML4 .... 142 A4
Glasgow G5 .... 116 C3
Irvine KA12 .... 224 C4
Carnoustie St G5 .... 116 C3
Carnoustie Way G60 .... 61 F3
Carntyne Ind Est G32 .... 118 C3
Carntyne Path G32 .... 118 B4
Carntyne Pl G32 .... 118 B4
Carntyne Prim Sch G33 .... 118 B4
Carntyne Rd G32 .... 118 C4
Carntyne Sta G32 .... 118 C3
Carntynehall Rd G32 .... 118 C3
Carnwadric Prim Sch
G46 .... 135 F2
Carnwadric Rd G46 .... 135 F2
Carnwath Ave G43 .... 136 C3
Carnwath Rd Carluke ML8 .. 188 A1
Kilncadzow ML8 .... 203 E3
Caroline Cres FK12 .... 4 C3
Caroline St G31 .... 118 C3
Carolside Ave G76 .... 157 F4
Carolside Dr G15 .... 75 D2
Carolside Gdns G76 .... 157 F4
Carolside Prim Sch G76 .... 157 F3
Carousel Cres ML2 .... 165 E2
Carradale Ave FK1 .... 41 E2
Carradale Cres G68 .... 81 F4
Carradale Dr KA9 .... 236 B3
Carradale Gdns
Bishopbriggs G64 .... 78 B1
Carluke ML8 .... 202 A4
Carradale Pl PA3 .... 112 A3
Carradale St ML5 .... 121 F4
Carranbuie Rd ML8 .... 187 F2
Carrbridge Dr ⑨ G20 .... 96 B3
Carresbrook Ave G66 .... 80 A3
Carriagehill Ave PA2 .... 113 F1
Carriagehill Dr PA2 .... 113 F1
Carrick Ave Ayr KA7 .... 238 C3
Saltcoats KA21 .... 206 A2
Carrick Cres Glasgow G46 .. 136 B1
Wishaw ML2 .... 165 D2
Carrick Ct Kirkintilloch G66 .. 59 D1
Stirling FK7 .... 7 E3

Carrick Dr Coatbridge ML5 .. 121 E4
Glasgow G32 .... 119 F2
Irvine KA12 .... 219 D3
Rutherglen G73 .... 138 A3
Carrick Gdns Ayr KA7 .... 238 C3
Bellshill ML4 .... 142 A4
Blantyre G72 .... 161 E3
Carluke ML8 .... 202 A4
Hamilton ML3 .... 161 F1
Carrick Glen Hospl The
KA6 .... 239 F1
Carrick Gr G32 .... 119 F2
Carrick La PA16 .... 44 C2
Carrick Pk KA7 .... 238 C3
Carrick Pl Ardrossan KA22 .. 205 E2
Bellshill ML4 .... 121 E4
Coatbridge ML5 .... 122 A4
Falkirk FK2 .... 24 A2
Falkirk, Tamfourhill FK1 .... 41 E2
Glenboig ML5 .... 101 F3
Larkhall ML9 .... 185 D2
Prestwick KA9 .... 236 A4
Carrick Rd Ayr KA7 .... 238 C3
Bishopbriggs G64 .... 78 B1
Bishopton PA7 .... 72 B1
Cumbernauld G67 .... 62 A2
East Kilbride G74 .... 159 F2
Rutherglen G73 .... 137 F3
Troon KA10 .... 229 E4
Carrick Road La KA7 .... 238 C3
Carrick St Ayr KA7 .... 238 C4
Glasgow G2 .... 240 B2
Larkhall ML9 .... 185 E1
Carrick Terr
Dumbarton G82 .... 49 D2
Greenock PA16 .... 44 C2
Carrick Vale Ave ML1 .... 144 B1
Carrick View ML5 .... 101 F3
Carrick Way ⑧ G71 .... 141 D2
Carrickarden Rd G61 .... 75 F2
Carrickstone Rd G68 .... 61 F2
Carrickstone Rdbt G68 ...... 61 F3
Carrickstone View G68 ...... 61 F3
Carrington St G4 .... 96 C1
Carrochan Cres G83 .... 27 F4
Carrochan Rd G83 .... 27 F4
Carroglen Gdns G32 .... 119 E3
Carroglen Gr G32 .... 119 E3
Carroll Cres ML1 .... 143 E1
Carron Ave KA1 .... 228 A3
Carron Cres Bearsden G61 .. 75 E2
Bishopbriggs G64 .... 78 A1
Glasgow G22 .... 97 F2
Kirkintilloch G66 .... 79 F2
Carron Ct Cambuslang G72 .. 139 E3
Hamilton ML3 .... 162 A1
Carron Dr PA7 .... 72 B1
Carron Ind Est FK2 .... 24 A4
Carron Pl Coatbridge ML5 .. 101 E1
East Kilbride G75 .... 180 C3
Glasgow G22 .... 97 F3
Irvine KA12 .... 219 E3
Stirling FK7 .... 7 D1
Carron Prim Sch FK2 .... 24 A1
Carron Rd FK2 .... 24 A4
Carron St Glasgow G22 ...... 97 F3
Wishaw ML2 .... 165 D1
Carron Way
Motherwell ML1 .... 143 E2
Paisley PA3 .... 114 A4
Carronbank Ave FK2 .... 24 A1
Carronbank Cres FK6 .... 21 F2
Carronbank Ct FK2 .... 24 A1
Carrongrove Ave FK2 .... 24 A1
Carrongrove Rd FK2 .... 24 A2
Carronhall Ave FK2 .... 24 B2
Carronlea Dr FK2 .... 24 A1
Carronshore Prim Sch
FK2 .... 24 B2
Carronshore Rd FK2 .... 24 A1
Carronside Pl FK6 .... 21 F2
Carronside St FK2 .... 42 A4
Carronvale Ave FK5 .... 23 E1
Carronvale Rd FK5 .... 23 E1
Carronview FK5 .... 23 E1
Carrour Gdns G64 .... 77 F1
Carruth Dr PA13 .... 89 E4
Carruth Rd PA11 .... 110 B4
Carsaig Ct FK9 .... 2 A3
Carsaig Dr G52 .... 115 F3
Carsaig Loan ML5 .... 101 E3
Carscallan Rd ML3 .... 183 F3
Carse Terr FK10 .... 9 F4
Carse View FK2 .... 14 C2
Carsebridge Rd FK10 .... 10 B4
Carsegreen Ave PA2 .... 133 D4
Carseloch Rd KA7 .... 238 C1
Carsemeadow PA11 .... 89 F1
Carsemeadow Sch PA11 .... 89 F1
Carseview Bannockburn FK7 .. 7 F1
Tullibody FK10 .... 4 A1
Carseview Dr G61 .... 76 A3
Carsewood Ave PA9 .... 130 C3
Carson Dr KA12 .... 224 B4
Carson Rd G83 .... 27 F4
Carstairs St G40 .... 118 A1
Carswell Ct KA24 .... 191 D4
Carswell Gdns G41 .... 116 C1
Carswell Rd G77 .... 156 A3
Cart La PA3 .... 113 F3
Cartbank Gr G44 .... 137 D2
Cartbank Rd G44 .... 137 D2
Cartcraigs Rd G43 .... 136 A3
Carters Pl KA12 .... 219 E1
Cartha Cres PA2 .... 114 A2
Cartha St G42 .... 136 C4
Cartland Ave ML8 .... 201 F4
Cartland Rd ML11 .... 214 B4
Cartland View ML11 .... 214 C3

Cartsbridge Rd G76 .... 157 F3
Cartsburn St PA15 .... 46 A2
Cartsdyke Ave PA15 .... 46 B2
Cartsdyke Sta PA15 .... 46 B2
Cartside Ave Inchinnan PA4 .. 93 D2
Johnstone PA5 .... 111 E1
Cartside Dr G76 .... 158 A3
Cartside Pl G76 .... 158 A3
Cartside Quadrant G42 .... 137 D4
Cartside Rd G76 .... 157 F3
Cartside St G42 .... 136 C4
Cartvale La PA3 .... 113 F3
Cartvale Rd G42 .... 137 D4
Cartvale Sch G42 .... 136 C4
Cartview Ct G76 .... 157 F3
Carvale Ave ML7 .... 125 D1
Carwinshoch View KA7 .... 238 B3
Carwood Ct PA15 .... 46 B2
Carwood St PA15 .... 46 B2
Caskie Dr G72 .... 140 C1
Cassels Gr ML1 .... 142 B1
Cassels St Carluke ML8 .... 187 F1
Motherwell ML1 .... 163 F4
Cassillis St KA7 .... 238 C4
Cassiltoun Gdns G45 .... 137 E1
Cassley Ave PA4 .... 94 C1
Casthurn Rd G67 .... 62 C3
Castings Ave FK2 .... 42 A4
Castings Ct Falkirk FK2 .... 42 A4
Falkirk, Middlefield FK2 .... 42 A3
Castings Dr FK2 .... 42 A3
Castings Rd FK2 .... 42 C3
Castle Ave Airth FK2 .... 14 C2
Balloch G83 .... 19 F1
Bothwell G72 .... 140 C2
Elderslie PA5 .... 112 A1
Falkirk FK2 .... 24 B2
Helensburgh G84 .... 16 A1
Motherwell ML1 .... 143 D3
Stevenston KA20 .... 206 C1
Castle Bsns Pk The FK8 ...... 1 C1
Castle Chimmins Ave G72 .. 139 E2
Castle Chimmins Rd G72 .. 139 E2
Castle Cres Bishopton PA7 .. 72 A1
Denny FK6 .... 21 E1
Falkirk FK2 .... 42 B4
Torwood FK5 .... 22 C4
Castle Ct Cumbernauld G68 .. 62 A1
Falkirk FK2 .... 42 B4
Kirkintilloch G66 .... 79 E4
Menstrie FK11 .... 3 F3
Stirling FK8 .... 7 D4
Castle Dr Airth FK2 .... 14 C2
Dundonald KA2 .... 225 F1
Falkirk FK2 .... 42 B4
Kilbirnie KA25 .... 149 D1
Kilmarnock KA3 .... 223 D2
Motherwell ML1 .... 143 D3
Stenhousemuir FK5 .... 23 F1
West Kilbride KA23 .... 190 B3
Castle Farm Ct KA3 .... 195 E1
Castle Gait PA1 .... 113 F2
Castle Gate Bothwell G71 .. 140 C3
Newton Mearns G77 .... 157 D2
Castle Gdns Chryston G69 .. 80 C1
Gourock PA19 .... 44 C4
Paisley PA2 .... 113 D2
Castle Gr Kilbirnie KA25 .... 149 D1
Kilsyth G65 .... 36 B3
Castle Mains Rd G62 .... 54 B1
Castle Pl Falkirk FK2 .... 42 B4
Irvine KA12 .... 219 D2
Uddingston G71 .... 140 C3
Castle Quadrant ML6 .... 123 E4
Castle Rd Airdrie ML6 ...... 123 E4
Ardrossan KA22 .... 205 E2
Bridge Of W PA11 .... 90 B1
Dumbarton G82 .... 50 A1
Elderslie PA5 .... 112 B2
Falkirk FK2 .... 42 B4
Greenock PA15 .... 46 B1
Menstrie FK11 .... 3 F3
Newton Mearns G77 .... 156 B2
Port Glasgow PA14 .... 47 E1
Stirling FK9 .... 2 B2
Castle Sq G81 .... 73 F2
Castle St Alloa FK10 .... 10 A3
Chapelhall ML6 .... 123 E1
Clydebank G81 .... 73 F2
Dumbarton G82 .... 49 F3
Glasgow G4 .... 241 F3
Glasgow, Baillieston G69 .. 120 A2
Glasgow, Kelvinhaugh G11 .. 96 B1
Hamilton ML3 .... 162 C2
Irvine KA12 .... 219 D2
Paisley PA1 .... 113 E2
Rutherglen G73 .... 138 A4
Castle Terr
Bridge Of W PA11 .... 110 C4
Denny FK6 .... 21 E1
Knockentiber KA2 .... 222 A1
Castle View Ayr KA7 .... 238 A2
Fallin FK7 .... 8 B2
West Kilbride KA23 .... 190 B3
Wishaw ML2 .... 166 A3
Castle Way
Coatbridge G69 .... 120 C3
Cumbernauld G67 .... 62 B2
Castle Wlk KA7 .... 238 B2
Castle Wynd Bothwell G71 .. 141 D1
Quarter ML3 .... 183 F2
Castlebank Cres G11 .... 96 A1
Castlebank Ct G13 .... 95 F3
Castlebank Gdns G13 .... 95 F3
Castlebank St G11 .... 96 A1
Castlebank Villas G13 .... 95 F3
Castlebay Dr G22 .... 77 E1

Castlebay Pl G22 .... 97 E4
Castlebay St G22 .... 97 E4
Castlebrae G82 .... 49 E3
Castlecary Rd G68 .... 62 B4
Castlecroft Gdns G71 .... 140 C3
Castlefern Rd G73 .... 138 A2
Castlefield Gdns G75 .... 180 A2
Castlefield Prim Sch G75 .. 180 A3
Castlegait FK3 .... 7 D4
Castlegate ML11 .... 215 D2
Castleglen Rd G74 .... 159 D2
Castlegreen Cres G82 .... 50 A1
Castlegreen La G82 .... 50 A1
Castlegreen St G82 .... 50 A1
Castlehead High Sch PA1 .. 113 E2
Castlehill
Port Glasgow PA14 .... 69 D4
Stamannan FK1 .... 86 A3
Castlehill Cres Ayr KA7 .... 239 D3
Banknock FK4 .... 38 C1
Chapelhall ML6 .... 123 F1
Hamilton ML3 .... 162 C2
Hamilton, Allanton ML3 .. 163 E1
Kilmacolm PA13 .... 89 E4
Law ML8 .... 187 D2
Renfrew PA4 .... 94 B2
Castlehill Dr G77 .... 156 C2
Castlehill Gdns ML3 .... 162 C1
Castlehill Gn G74 .... 158 C2
Castlehill Ind Est ML8 ...... 187 F2
Castlehill Prim Sch
Bearsden G61 .... 75 E3
Wishaw ML2 .... 186 A4
Castlehill Quadrant G82 .... 49 E3
Castlehill Rd Ayr KA7 .... 239 D3
Bearsden G61 .... 75 E3
Dullatur G68 .... 187 F3
Kilmacolm PA13 .... 89 E4
Overtown ML2 .... 186 A4
Stewarton KA3 .... 195 F1
Castlehill View G65 .... 36 B1
Castlelaurie St FK2 .... 42 B4
Castlelaw Gdns G32 .... 119 D3
Castlelaw St G32 .... 119 D3
Castlelaw Gdns G32 .... 119 D3
Castlemilk Arc G45 .... 137 E2
Castlemilk Cres G44 .... 137 F3
Castlemilk Dr G45 .... 137 F2
Castlemilk High Sch G45 .. 137 F1
Castlemilk Rd G44 .... 137 E3
Castlemount Ave G77 ...... 156 C2
Castlepark Cres KA21 ...... 219 D3
Castlepark Prim Sch
KA12 .... 219 E3
Castleton Ave
Bishopbriggs G64 .... 97 F4
Newton Mearns G77 .... 157 D2
Castleton Cres G77 .... 156 C2
Castleton Ct Glasgow G45 .. 137 F1
Newton Mearns G77 .... 156 C2
Castleton Dr G77 .... 156 C2
Castleton Gr G77 .... 156 C2
Castleview Clachan of C G65 .. 62 C4
Cumbernauld G68 .... 62 C4
Dundonald KA2 .... 225 F2
Stirling FK9 .... 2 A2
Castleview Ave PA2 .... 133 D4
Castleview Dr Bridge Of A FK9 .. 2 A4
Paisley PA2 .... 133 D4
Castleview Pl PA2 .... 133 D4
Castleview Terr FK4 .... 39 D2
Catacol Ave KA21 .... 205 F1
Cath of St Mungo G4 ...... 241 F3
Cathay St G22 .... 97 E4
Cathburn Rd ML2 .... 166 B3
Cathcart Cres PA2 .... 114 A2
Cathcart Pl G73 .... 137 F4
Cathcart Rd Glasgow G42 .. 117 D1
Rutherglen G73 .... 137 F4
Cathcart Sq PA15 .... 45 F3
Cathcart St Ayr KA7 .... 235 F1
Greenock PA15 .... 46 A3
Cathcart Sta G44 .... 137 D3
Cathedral Sq G4 .... 241 F2
Cathedral St G1, G4 .... 241 E3
Catherine Pl KA3 .... 222 B3
Catherine St
Bannockburn FK7 .... 7 F1
Kirkintilloch G66 .... 79 E4
Motherwell ML1 .... 163 F2
Catherine Way ML1 .... 142 C2
Catherine's Wlk G72 ...... 161 E3
Cathkin Ave
Rutherglen G73, G72 .... 138 C3
Rutherglen, Gallowflat
G73, G72 .... 138 B4
Cathkin By-Pass G73 .... 138 B2
Cathkin Cres G68 .... 61 F2
Cathkin Ct G45 .... 137 F1
Cathkin Dr G76 .... 157 E4
Cathkin Gdns G71 .... 120 C1
Cathkin High Sch G73 ...... 138 C2
Cathkin Pl
Cambuslang G72 .... 138 C3
Kilwinning KA13 .... 207 D2
Cathkin Prim Sch G73 ...... 138 B2
Cathkin Rd Glasgow G42 .. 136 C4
Rutherglen G73 .... 138 B1
Uddingston G71 .... 120 B1
Cathkin View G32 .... 139 D4
Cathkinview Pl G42 .... 137 D4
Cathkinview Rd G42 .... 137 D4
Catrine G74 .... 159 E1
Catrine Cres ML1 .... 164 A2
Catrine Ct G53 .... 135 D4
Catrine Gdns G53 .... 135 D4

Catrine St 11 ML9 ... 185 E1
Catriona Way ML1 ... 143 D2
Catter Gdns G62 ... 54 C2
Cauldhame Cres PK7 ... 6 83
Cauldstream The FK9 ... 2 83
Causewayhead Rd FK9 ... 2 82
Causewayside Cres G32 ... 119 D2
Causewayside St G32 ... 119 D1
Causeyfoot Dr KA25 ... 149 D1
Causeyside St PA1 ... 113 F2
Causeystanes G72 ... 161 E4
Cavendish Ct
5 Glasgow G5 ... 117 D2
Troon KA10 ... 229 E1
Cavendish Dr G77 ... 156 C3
Cavendish La KA10 ... 229 E1
Cavendish Pl Glasgow G5 ... 117 D2
Troon KA10 ... 229 E1
Cavendish St G5 ... 117 D2
Cavin Dr G45 ... 137 F2
Cavin Rd G45 ... 137 F2
Cawder Ct G68 ... 61 E3
Cawder Gdns FK9 ... 1 C4
Cawder Pl G68 ... 61 E3
Cawder Rd Bridge Of A FK9 ... 1 C4
Cumbernauld G68 ... 61 E3
Cawder View G68 ... 61 F3
Cawder Way G68 ... 61 F3
Cawdor Cres Bishopton PA7 ... 72 A1
Greenock PA16 ... 45 D2
Cawdor Pl PA16 ... 45 D2
Cawdor Way G14 ... 159 E2
Cayton Gdns G69 ... 119 F2
Cecil St Clarkston G76 ... 157 F4
Coatbridge ML5 ... 122 A3
Glasgow G12 ... 96 B2
Stirling FK7 ... 7 D3
Cedar Ave Beith KA15 ... 171 D4
Clydebank G81 ... 73 E2
Johnstone PA5 ... 132 A4
Stirling FK9 ... 6 C3
Uddingston G71 ... 141 D4
Cedar Cres Greenock PA16 ... 46 C1
Hamilton ML3 ... 162 C1
Cedar Ct Cambuslang G72 ... 139 F2
East Kilbride G75 ... 180 B3
Glasgow G20 ... 97 D1
Kilbarchan PA10 ... 111 D2
Cedar Dr East Kilbride G75 ... 180 B3
Kirkintilloch G66 ... 79 E3
Milton Of C G65 ... 58 B3
Uddingston G71 ... 141 E4
Cedar Gdns Law ML8 ... 186 C3
Motherwell ML1 ... 143 E2
Rutherglen G73 ... 138 B2
Cedar Gr Cardross G82 ... 48 A4
Stenhousemuir FK5 ... 23 E1
Cedar La Airdrie ML6 ... 123 E4
Motherwell ML1 ... 143 D2
Cedar Pl Barrhead G78 ... 155 E4
Blantyre G72 ... 140 B1
East Kilbride G75 ... 180 B3
Gourock PA19 ... 44 B3
Cedar Rd Ayr KA7 ... 239 E3
Banknock FK4 ... 38 C1
Bishopbriggs G64 ... 98 A4
Cumbernauld G67 ... 62 B2
Irvine KA12 ... 219 E2
Kilmarnock KA1 ... 227 E4
Cedar St G20 ... 97 D1
Cedar Wlk G64 ... 98 A4
Cedars The FK10 ... 4 A1
Cedarwood Ave G60 ... 73 D4
Cedarwood Rd G77 ... 156 C2
Cedric Pl G13 ... 95 E4
Cedric Rd G13 ... 95 E4
Celandine Bank ML4 ... 239 E2
Celtic Pk (Celtic FC) G40 ... 118 A3
Celtic St G20 ... 96 B4
Cemetery Rd Blantyre G72 ... 161 E3
Glasgow G52 ... 115 F2
Shotts ML7 ... 147 D2
Centenary Ave ML4 ... 122 B4
Centenary Ct G81 ... 74 A1
Centenary Gdns
Coatbridge ML5 ... 122 A3
Hamilton ML3 ... 162 C1
Centenary Pl KA22 ... 205 E2
Centenary Quadrant ML1 ... 143 D3
Central Ave
Ardrossan KA22 ... 205 E2
Cambuslang G72 ... 138 C3
Clydebank G81 ... 74 A3
Glasgow G11 ... 95 F1
Glasgow, North Mount Vernon G32 ... 119 F2
Hamilton G72 ... 161 F3
Kilbirnie KA25 ... 170 A4
Kilmarnock KA1 ... 227 F2
Motherwell ML1 ... 143 D1
Motherwell, Holytown ML1 ... 142 C3
Troon KA10 ... 229 F2
Uddingston G71 ... 141 E3
Central Bvd FK5 ... 23 D2
Central Cres ML9 ... 199 F4
Central Dr FK5 ... 23 F2
Central Gr
Cambuslang G72 ... 138 C3
Glasgow G32 ... 119 D2
Central Park Ave FK5 ... 23 D2
Central Park Bsns Pk FK5 ... 23 D2
Central Path G32 ... 119 F2
Central Quadrant KA22 ... 205 E2
Central Rd PA1 ... 113 F3
Central Ret Pk FK1 ... 42 B3
Central Sta Glasgow G2 ... 240 C2
Hamilton ML3 ... 162 C2

Central Way
Cumbernauld G67 ... 61 F1
Paisley PA1 ... 113 F3
Centre Rdbt The G74 ... 159 F1
Centre St Chapelhall ML6 ... 123 E1
Glasgow G5 ... 117 D3
Glenboig ML5 ... 101 E3
Centre The G78 ... 134 A1
Centre Way G78 ... 134 A2
Centrum (Sports Arena)
KA9 ... 236 A3
Ceres Gdns G64 ... 78 B1
Cessnock Ave KA1 ... 228 C3
Cessnock Dr KA1 ... 228 C3
Cessnock Pl Ayr KA7 ... 239 E3
Cambuslang G72 ... 139 E3
Cessnock Rd Hurlford KA1 ... 228 C3
Millerston G33 ... 99 D2
Troon KA10 ... 229 E2
Cessnock St G51 ... 116 A3
Cessnock Underground Sta
G51 ... 116 B3
Cessock Pl KA1 ... 228 A3
Chacefield St FK4 ... 40 A3
Chacefield Wood FK6 ... 39 F4
Chalmers Ave KA7 ... 239 D3
Chalmers Cres G75 ... 180 C4
Chalmers Ct G40 ... 241 F1
Chalmers Dr G75 ... 180 C4
Chalmers Gate G40 ... 241 F1
Chalmers Pl Glasgow G40 ... 241 F1
Irvine KA11 ... 224 C2
Chalmers Rd KA7 ... 239 D3
Chalmers St Clydebank G81 ... 74 A1
Glasgow G40 ... 241 F1
Gourock PA19 ... 44 C4
Chalmerston Rd FK9 ... 1 A2
Chalton Rd FK9 ... 2 A4
Chamberlain La G13 ... 95 F3
Chamberlain Rd G13 ... 95 F3
Chambers Dr FK2 ... 24 A1
Chamfron Gdns FK7 ... 7 F2
Chancellor St G11 ... 96 B1
Chantinghall Rd ML3 ... 162 A2
Chantinghall Terr ML3 ... 162 A2
Chapel Cres ML3 ... 24 A2
Chapel Ct G73 ... 137 F4
Chapel Dr FK3 ... 23 F2
Chapel La Falkirk FK1 ... 42 A3
Irvine KA12 ... 219 E1
Chapel Rd Clydebank G81 ... 74 A3
Houston PA6 ... 91 D2
Wishaw ML2 ... 166 B1
Chapel St Airdrie ML6 ... 123 D4
Carluke ML8 ... 187 F1
Cleland ML1 ... 144 A1
Glasgow G20 ... 96 C3
Gourock PA19 ... 44 C4
Greenock PA15 ... 46 A2
Lennoxtown G65 ... 57 E4
Rutherglen G73 ... 137 F4
Chapel Street Ind Est G20 ... 96 C3
Chapelacre Gr G84 ... 16 C1
Chapelcross Ave ML6 ... 103 D1
Chapelgill Pl KA11 ... 220 A2
Chapelgreen Prim Sch G65 ... 59 F4
Chapelhall Ind Est ML6 ... 123 E2
Chapelhall Prim & Sec Sch
ML6 ... 123 E1
Chapelhill Mount KA22 ... 205 E3
Chapelhill Rd PA2 ... 114 A1
Chapelknowe Rd ML1 ... 143 F1
Chapelpark Rd KA7 ... 238 C2
Chapelside Ave ML6 ... 123 D4
Chapelside Prim Sch ML6 ... 103 D3
Chapelside Rd G74 ... 160 A3
Chapelton Ave
Bearsden G61 ... 75 F2
Dumbarton G82 ... 50 A3
Chapelton Gdns
Bearsden G61 ... 75 F2
Dumbarton G82 ... 50 A3
Chapelton La KA23 ... 190 B2
Chapelton Rd
Cumbernauld G67 ... 82 B3
West Kilbride KA23 ... 190 B1
Chapelton St Glasgow G22 ... 97 D3
Port Glasgow PA14 ... 47 D1
Chapeltoun Terr KA3 ... 216 C2
Chapelwell St KA21 ... 216 D4
Chapland Rd ML10 ... 215 D3
Chaplet Ave G13 ... 95 E4
Chapman Ave ML5 ... 101 E3
Chapman St 4 G42 ... 117 D1
Chapmans Terr KA1 ... 228 A4
Chappell St G78 ... 134 A2
Charing Cross ML9 ... 185 D2
Charing Cross La G3 ... 240 A3
Charing Cross Sta G2 ... 240 A3
Charles Ave Bridge Of A FK9 ... 2 A4
Monkton KA9 ... 233 D3
Renfrew PA4 ... 94 B2
Charles Cres Carluke ML8 ... 188 A1
Kirkintilloch G66 ... 79 E2
Charles Dr Larbert FK5 ... 41 E4
Irvine KA10 ... 229 F1
Charles Path ML6 ... 123 E1
Charles Pl Greenock PA15 ... 45 F3
Kilmarnock KA1 ... 227 F4
Charles Quadrant ML1 ... 143 D3
Charles Rodger Pl FK9 ... 2 A3
Charles St Alloa FK10 ... 9 F4
Glasgow G21 ... 97 F1
Kilmarnock KA1 ... 227 F4
Kilsyth G65 ... 36 B1
Shotts ML7 ... 147 D2
Stirling FK8 ... 7 D3
Wishaw ML2 ... 164 B2

Charleson Row G65 ... 60 C2
Charlotte Ave G64 ... 78 A4
Charlotte Hill Ct FK5 ... 23 D2
Charlotte Path ML9 ... 185 D1
Charlotte Pl PA2 ... 113 F1
Charlotte St Ayr KA7 ... 238 C4
Dumbarton G82 ... 49 E2
Glasgow G1 ... 241 E1
Helensburgh G84 ... 16 C1
Shotts ML7 ... 147 D2
Charlotte Street La KA7 ... 238 C4
Charnwood Ave PA5 ... 131 E4
Charter St FK7 ... 7 D1
Chartershall Rd KA7 ... 72 A2
Chartwell Rd PA7 ... 72 A2
Chassels St ML5 ... 122 A4
Chateau Gr ML3 ... 163 D1
Chatelherault Ave G72 ... 138 C3
Chatelherault Cres ML3 ... 162 C1
Chatelherault Prim Sch ML3 ... 162 C1
Chatelherault Wlk ML3 ... 162 C1
Chatham G75 ... 180 B4
Chattan Ave FK9 ... 2 A2
Chattan Ind Est FK4 ... 40 B2
Chatton St G23 ... 76 B1
Cheapside St
Eaglesham G76 ... 178 C3
Glasgow G3 ... 240 A2
Chelmsford Dr G12 ... 96 A3
Cherry Bank G66 ... 79 D3
Cherry Cres G81 ... 74 A2
Cherry Gdns KA11 ... 219 F3
Cherry Hill Rd KA7 ... 239 D1
Cherry La Banknock FK4 ... 38 C1
Troon KA10 ... 229 E2
Cherry Pl Bishopbriggs G64 ... 98 A4
Johnstone PA5 ... 112 A1
Milton Of C G65 ... 58 A2
Motherwell ML1 ... 143 D3
Uddingston G71 ... 141 F4
Cherry Rd KA1 ... 227 E4
Cherrybank Rd G43 ... 136 C3
Cherrybank Wlk ML6 ... 122 B4
Cherryhill View ML1 ... 184 C2
Cherrytree Cres ML9 ... 185 D3
Cherrytree Dr G72 ... 139 F2
Cherrywood Dr KA15 ... 150 B1
Cherrywood Rd PA5 ... 112 B1
Chester Rd PA16 ... 44 C2
Chester St G32 ... 119 D3
Chesterfield Ave G12 ... 96 A3
Chesters Cres ML1 ... 163 E4
Chesters Pl G73 ... 138 A4
Chesters Rd G61 ... 75 E2
Chestnut Ave Beith KA15 ... 171 D4
Bishopton PA7 ... 71 F3
Cumbernauld G67 ... 62 C3
Chestnut Cres Denny FK6 ... 21 E2
East Kilbride G75 ... 180 B3
Hamilton ML3 ... 162 C1
Uddingston G71 ... 141 E4
Chestnut Ct
Cumbernauld G67 ... 62 C3
Milton Of C G65 ... 58 A3
Chestnut Dr Clydebank G81 ... 74 A3
Kirkintilloch G66 ... 79 D3
Chestnut Gr Blantyre G72 ... 161 E4
Carluke ML8 ... 187 F1
Glenboig ML5 ... 101 E3
Larkhall ML9 ... 185 D3
Motherwell ML1 ... 163 E2
Stenhousemuir FK5 ... 23 F2
Chestnut Pl
Cumbernauld G67 ... 62 C3
Johnstone PA5 ... 131 E4
Kilwinning KA13 ... 208 A2
Chestnut St G22 ... 97 E3
Cheviot Ave G78 ... 134 B1
Cheviot Cres
East Kilbride G75 ... 180 A2
Wishaw ML2 ... 164 C2
Cheviot Ct Airdrie ML6 ... 103 E1
Irvine KA11 ... 220 A2
Cheviot Dr G77 ... 156 B2
Cheviot Gdns G61 ... 75 E4
Cheviot Head KA11 ... 219 F2
Cheviot Rd Glasgow G43 ... 136 B3
Hamilton ML3 ... 162 A1
Larkhall ML9 ... 185 E1
Paisley PA2 ... 113 F1
Cheviot St G72 ... 161 E3
Cheviot Way KA11 ... 220 A2
Chillin Pl ML9 ... 185 E1
Chirmorie Pl G53 ... 115 D1
Chirnside Ct G77 ... 161 F3
Chirnside Pl G52 ... 115 D3
Chirnside Rd G52 ... 115 D3
Chirnyside Prim Sch G22 ... 97 E3
Chisholm Ave
Bishopton PA7 ... 72 B2
Stirling FK9 ... 2 A2
Chisholm Dr G77 ... 156 C3
Chisholm St ML5 ... 122 A4
Chisolm St G1 ... 241 E1
Chrighton Gn 3 G71 ... 141 D4
Chriss Ave ML3 ... 183 E4
Christ the King Prim Sch
ML1 ... 143 E3
Christchurch Pl G75 ... 180 A4
Christian St G43 ... 136 B4
Christie Gdns KA21 ... 216 C4
Christie La PA3 ... 113 F3
Christie Park Prim Sch G83 ... 27 E3
Christie Pl G72 ... 139 D3

Christie St Bellshill ML4 ... 142 B3
Paisley PA1 ... 113 F3
Christie Terr FK5 ... 23 F2
Christopher St G21 ... 98 A1
Chromars Pl PA15 ... 45 F2
Chryston Prim Sch G69 ... 100 B4
Chryston Rd Chryston G69 ... 100 B4
Kirkintilloch G69, G66 ... 80 B3
Chryston Sec Sch G69 ... 100 B4
Chuckie La PA5 ... 111 E3
Church Ave Cardross G82 ... 48 A4
Rutherglen G73 ... 138 B3
Stepps G33 ... 99 E3
Wishaw ML2 ... 166 A2
Church Cres Airdrie ML6 ... 103 F1
Hamilton ML3 ... 183 E3
Church Ct Ayr KA8 ... 236 A1
Dumbarton G82 ... 49 F2
Church Dr G66 ... 79 E3
Church Gr FK10 ... 10 A3
Church Hill PA1 ... 113 F3
Church La Carluke ML8 ... 187 F1
Coatbridge ML5 ... 122 A4
Denny FK6 ... 21 E2
Kilmarnock KA1 ... 227 F3
Kilsyth G65 ... 60 B4
Church Manse La PA11 ... 110 B4
Church Pl Ardrossan KA22 ... 205 E1
Caldercruix ML6 ... 104 C2
Falkirk FK2 ... 42 A3
Old Kilpatrick G60 ... 73 D3
Church Rd
Bridge Of W PA11 ... 110 C4
California FK1 ... 66 C3
Clarkston G76 ... 157 F3
Glasgow G46 ... 136 B1
Muirhead G69 ... 100 B4
Quarriers Village PA11 ... 89 F1
Rhu G84 ... 15 E3
Wishaw ML2 ... 166 B3
Church St Alexandria G83 ... 27 F2
Alloa FK10 ... 10 A4
Blantyre G72 ... 161 F4
Clydebank G81 ... 74 A2
Coatbridge ML5 ... 122 A4
Dumbarton G82 ... 24 B1
Falkirk FK2 ... 24 B1
Glasgow G11 ... 96 B1
Glasgow, Muirhead G69 ... 120 B2
Gourock PA19 ... 44 C4
Hamilton ML3 ... 162 C2
Harthill ML7 ... 127 E3
High Bonnybridge FK4 ... 40 B2
Irvine KA12 ... 219 D1
Johnstone PA5 ... 111 F2
Kilbarchan PA10 ... 111 D2
Kilmarnock KA3 ... 222 C1
Kilsyth G65 ... 60 B4
Kilwinning KA13 ... 207 F2
Larkhall ML9 ... 185 D1
Lochwinnoch PA12 ... 129 E1
Motherwell ML1 ... 142 C3
Port Glasgow PA14 ... 47 E1
Stenhousemuir FK5 ... 23 F2
Troon KA10 ... 229 E1
Uddingston G71 ... 140 C3
Church View
Cambuslang G72 ... 139 D4
Coatbridge ML5 ... 121 E2
Church View Ct G65 ... 33 E1
Church View Gdns ML4 ... 142 A3
Church Wlk FK6 ... 21 F1
Churchill Ave
East Kilbride G74 ... 159 F1
Johnstone PA5 ... 131 E4
Kilwinning KA13 ... 208 A2
Churchill Cres Ayr KA8 ... 239 E4
Bothwell G71 ... 141 D2
Churchill Dr
Ardrossan KA22 ... 205 E2
Bishopton PA7 ... 72 A2
Bridge Of A FK9 ... 2 A3
Glasgow G11 ... 95 F2
Churchill Pl PA10 ... 111 D2
Churchill Sq G84 ... 17 D1
Churchill Way G64 ... 77 F1
Circus Dr G31 ... 117 F3
Circus Pl G31 ... 117 F3
Circus Place La G31 ... 117 F3
Citadel Ct Ayr KA7 ... 235 F1
Citadel Pl Ayr KA7 ... 235 F1
Citadel Way KA10 ... 229 F2
Citizen La G1 ... 241 D2
Citrus Cres G71 ... 141 E4
Cityford Cres G73 ... 137 F4
Cityford Dr G73 ... 137 F3
Civic St G4 ... 97 D1
Civic Way G66 ... 58 C1
Clachan Dr G51 ... 115 F4
Clachan Rd G84 ... 16 A2
Clachan The ML2 ... 165 D2
Clackmannan Coll of F Ed
FK10 ... 10 A4
Clackmannan Rd FK10 ... 10 B3
Claddens Pl G66 ... 79 F2
Claddens Quadrant G22 ... 97 E3
Claddens St G22 ... 97 D3
Claddoch Cotts G82 ... 25 E3
Cladence Gr G75 ... 180 C3
Clair Rd G64 ... 78 C1
Claire St ML2 ... 165 E3
Clairinch Gdns PA4 ... 94 B1
Clairmont Gdns G3 ... 240 A4
Clamp Rd ML2 ... 164 B2

Clamps Gr G74 ... 181 D4
Clamps Terr G74 ... 181 D4
Clamps Wood G74 ... 181 D4
Clannald Pl FK1 ... 41 F1
Clanrye Dr ML5 ... 122 A2
Clapperhow Rd ML1 ... 143 D1
Clare St G21 ... 98 A1
Claremont FK10 ... 9 F4
Claremont Ave G66 ... 79 D4
Claremont Cres KA13 ... 207 E2
Claremont Dr
Bridge Of A FK9 ... 2 B4
Milngavie G62 ... 55 D1
Claremont Gdns G62 ... 55 D1
Claremont High Sch G74 ... 181 E4
Claremont Ind Est FK10 ... 10 A3
Claremont Pass G3 ... 240 A4
Claremont Pl Glasgow G3 ... 96 C1
Glasgow G3 ... 240 A4
Claremont Prim Sch FK10 ... 9 F4
Claremont St
Bonnybridge FK4 ... 39 F3
Glasgow G3 ... 116 C4
Claremont Terr G3 ... 240 A4
Claremont Terrace La G3 ... 240 A4
Claremount Ave G46 ... 136 B1
Clarence Dr Glasgow G11 ... 96 A2
Paisley PA1 ... 114 A2
Clarence Gdns G11 ... 96 A2
Clarence La G12 ... 96 A2
Clarence St Clydebank G81 ... 74 B1
Greenock PA15 ... 45 F3
Paisley PA1 ... 114 A3
Clarendon Pl Ayr KA7 ... 239 E3
3 Glasgow G20 ... 97 D1
Stirling FK8 ... 7 D4
Wishaw ML2 ... 164 C1
Clarendon Rd Stirling FK8 ... 7 D4
Wishaw ML2 ... 164 C1
Clarendon St G20 ... 97 D1
Clarinda Ave FK1 ... 41 D3
Clarinda Cres G66 ... 59 D1
Clarinda Pl ML1 ... 143 E2
Clarion Cres G13 ... 95 D4
Clarion Rd G13 ... 95 D4
Clark Cres KA20 ... 217 E4
Clark Dr KA12 ... 219 F2
Clark Pl
Newton Mearns G77 ... 156 A2
Saltcoats KA21 ... 206 A1
Torrance G64 ... 78 B4
Clark St Airdrie ML6 ... 123 D4
Bannockburn FK7 ... 7 D1
Clydebank G81 ... 73 F2
Johnstone PA5 ... 111 F2
Kilmarnock KA1 ... 227 F4
Paisley PA3 ... 113 E3
Renfrew PA4 ... 94 A2
Wishaw ML2 ... 165 F3
Clark Way ML4 ... 141 F4
Clarke Ave KA7 ... 238 C3
Clarkston Ave G44 ... 136 C2
Clarkston Dr ML6 ... 123 E4
Clarkston Prim Sch ML6 ... 123 E4
Clarkston Rd G44 ... 136 C2
Clarkston & Stamperland Sta
G76 ... 157 F4
Clarkwell Rd ML3 ... 161 F2
Clarkwell Terr ML3 ... 161 F2
Clathic Ave G61 ... 76 A2
Claud Rd PA3 ... 114 A3
Claude Ave G72 ... 139 F2
Claude St ML9 ... 185 D2
Clavens Rd G52 ... 114 C3
Claverhouse Pl PA2 ... 114 A2
Claverhouse Rd G52 ... 114 C4
Clavering St E PA1 ... 113 E3
Clavering St W PA1 ... 113 E2
Clay Cres Bellshill ML4 ... 142 B4
Kilmarnock KA3 ... 222 C1
Clay Rd ML4 ... 142 B4
Claycrofts Pl FK7 ... 7 D3
Clayhouse Rd G33 ... 99 F2
Claymore Dr Houston PA6 ... 111 E4
Stirling FK7 ... 7 E2
Claypotts Pl G33 ... 99 D1
Claypotts Rd G33 ... 99 D1
Clayslaps Rd G3 ... 96 B1
Clayslays View KA11 ... 228 A2
Claythorn Ave G40 ... 117 F3
Claythorn Ct G40 ... 241 F1
Claythorn Pk G40 ... 117 F3
Claythorn St G40 ... 241 F1
Claythorn Terr G40 ... 241 F1
Clayton Ave KA12 ... 219 E2
Clayton Path ML4 ... 142 A4
Clayton Terr 11 G31 ... 117 F4
Clearfield Ave ML3 ... 162 A2
Cleaves The FK10 ... 4 A3
Cleddans Cres G81 ... 74 B3
Cleddans Rd Clydebank G81 ... 74 B3
Kirkintilloch G66 ... 58 C1
Cleddans View
Clydebank G81 ... 74 B2
Glenmavis ML6 ... 102 C2
Cleddens Ct G64 ... 78 A1
Cleeves Ave KA24 ... 191 F3
Cleeves Quadrant G53 ... 135 D3
Cleeves Rd G53 ... 135 D3
Cleghorn Ave ML11 ... 215 D3
Cleghorn Rd ML11 ... 215 D3
Cleghorn St G22 ... 97 D2
Cleish Ave G61 ... 75 E4
Cleland La G5 ... 117 E3
Cleland Rd G74 ... 160 A2

Cleland Prim Sch ML1 .... 144 B1
Cleland Rd Cleland ML1 .... 144 A1
  Motherwell ML1 .... 143 E1
  Wishaw ML2 .... 165 D2
Cleland St G5 .... 117 E3
Cleland Sta ML1 .... 144 B1
Clelland Ave G64 .... 98 A4
Clem Attlee Gdns ML9 .... 185 D1
Clements Pl KA20 .... 206 C1
Clerkland Rd KA3 .... 195 E1
Clerwood St G32 .... 118 B3
Cleuch Ave FK10 .... 4 A1
Cleuch Dr FK12 .... 4 C4
Cleuch Gdns G76 .... 157 E4
Cleughearn Rd G75 .... 180 B1
Clevans Rd PA11 .... 110 B4
Cleveden Cres G12 .... 96 A3
Cleveden Crescent La
  G12 .... 96 A3
Cleveden Dr Glasgow G12 .... 96 B2
  Rutherglen G73 .... 138 B3
Cleveden Drive La G12 .... 96 B2
Cleveden Gdns G12 .... 96 B3
Cleveden La G12 .... 96 A3
Cleveden Pl G12 .... 96 A3
Cleveden Rd G12 .... 96 A3
Cleveden Sec Sch G12 .... 96 B3
Cleveland La G3 .... 240 A3
Cleveland St G3 .... 240 A3
Cliff Rd G3 .... 240 A4
Clifford Gdns G51 .... 116 A3
Clifford La G51 .... 116 B3
Clifford Pl **[3]** G51 .... 116 B3
Clifford Rd H'dn F? 7 D3
Clifford St G51 .... 116 B3
Clifton Pl Coatbridge ML5 .... 122 B3
  [1] Glasgow G3 .... 116 C4
Clifton Rd G46 .... 136 A2
Clifton St G3 .... 96 C1
Clifton Terr
  Cambuslang G72 .... 138 C2
  Johnstone PA5 .... 112 A1
Cliftonhill Stad
  (Albion Rovers & Hamilton
  Academicals FC's) ML5 .... 122 B3
Climie Pl KA3 .... 228 A4
Clincart Rd G42 .... 137 D4
Clincarthill Rd G73 .... 138 A4
Clippens Rd PA3 .... 112 A3
Clive St ML7 .... 146 C3
Cloak Rd PA13 .... 69 E2
Cloan Ave G15 .... 75 D1
Cloan Cres G64 .... 78 A2
Clober Farm La G62 .... 54 C2
Clober Prim Sch G62 .... 54 C1
Clober Rd G62 .... 55 D1
Cloberfield G62 .... 54 C2
Cloberfield Gdns G62 .... 54 C2
Cloberhill Rd G13 .... 75 E1
Cloch Brae PA19 .... 44 A3
Cloch Rd PA19 .... 43 F3
Cloch St G33 .... 119 D4
Clochbar Ave G62 .... 54 C2
Clochbar Gdns G62 .... 54 C1
Clochoderick Ave PA10 .... 111 D1
Clochranhill Rd ML7 .... 238 C1
Clockerhill Pl ML1 .... 143 F2
Cloister Ave ML6 .... 123 E2
Clonbeith St G33 .... 99 F1
Cloncaird KA13 .... 207 E1
Closeburn St G22 .... 97 E3
Cloth St G78 .... 134 B1
Clouden Rd G67 .... 62 A1
Cloudhowe Terr G72 .... 140 B1
Clouston Ct **[4]** G20 .... 96 C2
Clouston La G20 .... 96 C2
Clouston St G20 .... 96 C2
Clova Pl G71 .... 140 C3
Clova St G46 .... 135 F2
Clove Mill Wynd ML9 .... 184 C1
Clover Leaf Path G83 .... 27 F2
Cloverbank St G21 .... 98 A1
Clovergate G67 .... 77 F1
Cloverhill KA7 .... 239 E3
Cloverhill Pl G69 .... 100 B4
Cloverhill Terr G74 .... 159 F1
Cloverhill View G74 .... 159 E1
Cloves The FK11 .... 4 A3
Cluanie Ave ML7 .... 146 C3
Clune Brae PA14 .... 47 F1
Clune Park Prim Sch PA14 .... 47 F1
Clune Park St PA14 .... 47 F1
Clunie Pl Coatbridge ML5 .... 122 A2
  Wishaw ML2 .... 165 F3
Clunie Rd G52 .... 115 F2
Cluny Ave Bearsden G61 .... 76 A1
  Clydebank G81 .... 74 B4
Cluny Dr Bearsden G61 .... 76 A1
  Newton Mearns G77 .... 156 A3
  Paisley PA3 .... 114 A3
  Stenhousemuir FK5 .... 23 F2
Cluny Gdns Glasgow G14 .... 95 F2
  Glasgow, Baillieston G69 .... 120 A2
Cluny Villas G14 .... 95 F2
Clutha Pl G75 .... 180 A4
Clutha St G51 .... 116 B3
Clyde Ave Barrhead G78 .... 134 B1
  Bothwell G72 .... 140 C1
  Hamilton ML3 .... 163 E1
  Torrance G64 .... 78 A4
Clyde Cres Lanark ML11 .... 215 D2
  Larbert FK5 .... 23 D2
Clyde C Clydebank G81 .... 73 F3
  Dumbarton G82 .... 49 F2

Clyde Dr Bellshill ML4 .... 142 B2
  Shotts ML7 .... 147 D2
Clyde La ML1 .... 143 D2
Clyde Pl Ardrossan KA22 .... 205 E2
  Cambuslang G72 .... 139 E2
  Glasgow G5 .... 240 C1
  Johnstone PA5 .... 131 E4
  Kilmarnock KA1 .... 228 A3
  Motherwell ML1 .... 143 D2
  Troon KA10 .... 229 F3
Clyde Rd Gourock PA19 .... 44 C3
  Paisley PA3 .... 114 A4
Clyde Shopping Ctr G81 .... 74 A1
Clyde Sq PA15 .... 45 F3
Clyde St Carluke ML8 .... 187 F1
  Coatbridge ML5 .... 122 B4
  Falkirk FK1 .... 41 F3
  Glasgow G1 .... 241 D1
  Renfrew PA4 .... 94 B3
Clyde St E G84 .... 16 C1
Clyde Terr Ardrossan KA22 .... 205 E2
  Bothwell G71 .... 141 D1
  Motherwell ML1 .... 164 B1
Clyde Tower ML1 .... 163 F3
Clyde Valley Ave ML1 .... 163 F2
Clyde Valley Ctry Est ML8 .... 201 D1
Clyde Valley High Sch ML1 .... 186 A4
Clyde View Ashgill ML9 .... 200 A4
  Hamilton ML3 .... 162 A1
  Paisley PA2 .... 114 A1
Clyde View Ave KA20 .... 206 B1
Clyde View Ct G60 .... 72 B4
Clyde Way PA3 .... 114 A4
Clyde Wynd PA15 .... 45 E2
Clydebank Bsns Pk G81 .... 74 A1
Clydebank Coll G81 .... 74 A2
Clydebank High Sch G81 .... 74 A2
Clydebank Ind Est G81 .... 73 E1
Clydebank Sta G81 .... 74 A1
Clydebrae Dr G71 .... 162 A4
Clydebrae St G51 .... 116 A4
Clydeford Dr Glasgow G32 .... 118 C2
  Uddingston G71 .... 140 C4
Clydeford Rd G32 .... 139 D4
Clydeholm Rd G14 .... 95 E1
Clydeholm Terr G81 .... 94 B4
Clydemuir Prim Sch G81 .... 73 E2
Clydeneuk Dr G71 .... 140 B4
Clydesdale Ave
  Hamilton ML3 .... 183 E3
  Paisley PA3 .... 94 A1
  Wishaw ML2 .... 164 B1
Clydesdale Pl ML3 .... 183 E3
Clydesdale Rd ML4 .... 142 B2
Clydesdale St Hamilton ML3 .... 162 B2
  Larkhall ML9 .... 185 D2
  Motherwell ML1 .... 142 C2
Clydeside Expressway G3 .... 116 C4
Clydeside Ind Est G14 .... 95 F1
Clydeside Rd G73 .... 117 F1
Clydesmill Dr G32 .... 139 D4
Clydesmill Gr G32 .... 139 D4
Clydesmill Pl G32 .... 139 D4
Clydesmill Rd G32 .... 139 D4
Clydevale G71 .... 141 D1
Clydeview Bothwell G71 .... 141 E1
  Dumbarton G82 .... 49 F1
Clydeview Rd
  Greenock PA15 .... 46 A1
  Port Glasgow PA14 .... 68 C4
Clydeview Sch ML1 .... 163 E4
Clydeview Shopping Ctr
  G72 .... 139 E2
Clydeview Terr G32 .... 139 E4
Clydeway Ind Est **[8]** G3 .... 116 C4
Clynder Rd PA15 .... 46 B1
Clynder St G51 .... 116 A3
Clyth Dr G46 .... 136 B1
Co-operative Terr PA5 .... 112 A2
Coach Pl G65 .... 61 D1
Coach Rd G65 .... 60 C4
Coal Wynd FK7 .... 7 E1
Coalburn Rd G71 .... 141 D3
Coalburn St ML6 .... 83 F1
Coalgate FK10 .... 10 A3
Coalhall Ave ML1 .... 143 D1
Coalhill Pl KA12 .... 205 D2
Coalhill St G31 .... 118 A3
Coalpots Way FK10 .... 5 F2
Coatbank St ML5 .... 122 A3
Coatbank Way ML5 .... 122 A3
Coatbridge Central Sta
  ML5 .... 121 F4
Coatbridge Coll ML5 .... 122 A4
Coatbridge High Sch
  ML5 .... 121 F4
Coatbridge Ind Est ML5 .... 102 A1
Coatbridge Rd
  Coatbridge G69 .... 120 C3
  Glenboig ML5 .... 101 D2
  Glenboig, Garnqueen ML5 .... 101 F3
  Holytown ML6 .... 102 B2
Coatdyke Sta ML5 .... 122 B4
Coathill Hosp ML5 .... 122 A2
Coathill St ML5 .... 122 A2
Coats Cres G69 .... 120 A3
Coats Dr PA2 .... 113 D2
Coats Pl KA2 .... 225 F1
Coats St ML5 .... 122 A4
Coatshill Ave G72 .... 140 B1
Cobbett Rd ML1 .... 163 D3
Cobblebrae Cres FK2 .... 24 A1
Cobblerigg Way G71 .... 140 C3
Cobbleton Rd ML1 .... 142 C1
Cobden Rd G21 .... 97 F1

Cobden St Alva FK12 .... 5 D3
  Alva FK12 .... 5 D4
Cobham St PA15 .... 46 C1
Cobington Pl G33 .... 99 D1
Cobinshaw St G32 .... 119 D3
Coblecrook Gdns FK12 .... 4 C3
Coblecrook La FK12 .... 4 C3
Coblecrook Pl FK12 .... 4 C3
Coburg St **[3]** G5 .... 117 D3
Cochno Rd G81 .... 74 A4
Cochno St G81 .... 74 B1
Cochran St PA1 .... 113 F2
Cochrane Ave
  Dundonald KA2 .... 225 F1
  Falkirk FK2 .... 42 A2
Cochrane Castle Prim Sch
  PA5 .... 131 E4
Cochrane Cres FK12 .... 4 C4
Cochrane Ct G62 .... 76 B4
Cochrane Rd KA2 .... 225 F1
Cochrane Pl
  Helensburgh G84 .... 17 D1
  Prestwick KA9 .... 236 A4
Cochrane St Barrhead G78 .... 134 A1
  Bellshill ML4 .... 141 F3
  Falkirk FK2 .... 42 A2
  Glasgow G1 .... 241 D2
  Irvine KA12 .... 219 D1
  Kilbirnie KA25 .... 149 D1
Cochranemill Rd PA5 .... 111 E1
Cochranes The FK12 .... 5 D4
Cochrie Pl FK10 .... 4 B1
Cockburn Pl
  Coatbridge ML5 .... 121 F2
  Irvine KA11 .... 224 C3
Cockburn St FK5 .... 42 A2
Cockels Loan PA4 .... 94 A1
Cockenzie St G32 .... 119 D3
Cockhill Way ML4 .... 141 E3
Cocklebie Rd KA3 .... 195 E1
Cockmuir St G21 .... 98 A2
Cockrane Castle Prim Sch
  PA5 .... 131 E4
Coddington Cres ML1 .... 142 C4
Cogan Rd G43 .... 136 B3
Cogan St Barrhead G78 .... 134 A1
  Glasgow G43 .... 136 B4
Coila Ave KA9 .... 236 B3
Coire Loan ML7 .... 147 D2
Colbert St G40 .... 117 F2
Colbreggan Ct G81 .... 74 B3
Colbreggan Gdns G81 .... 74 B3
Colchester Dr G12 .... 96 A3
Coldgreen Ave KA25 .... 149 D1
Coldingham Ave G14 .... 94 C3
Coldstream Cres ML2 .... 165 E3
Coldstream Dr Paisley PA2 .... 113 D1
  Rutherglen G73 .... 138 B3
Coldstream Pl G21 .... 97 E2
Coldstream Rd G81 .... 74 A1
Coldstream St G72 .... 161 E4
Colebrooke Pl G12 .... 96 C2
Colebrooke St
  Cambuslang G72 .... 139 D3
  [7] Glasgow G12 .... 96 C2
Colebrooke Terr G12 .... 96 C2
Coleburn Ct KA11 .... 219 F3
Coleridge G75 .... 180 A4
Coleridge Ave G71 .... 141 D2
Colfin St G34 .... 100 B1
Colgrain Prim Sch G84 .... 25 D4
Colgrain St G20 .... 97 D3
Colgrave Cres G32 .... 118 C2
Colinbar Circ G78 .... 134 A1
Colinslee Ave PA2 .... 113 F1
Colinslee Cres PA2 .... 113 F1
Colinslee Dr PA2 .... 113 F1
Colinslie Rd G53 .... 135 E4
Colinton Pl G32 .... 119 D4
Colintraive Ave G33 .... 98 C2
Colintraive Cres G33 .... 98 C2
Coll G74 .... 181 E4
Coll Ave Port Glasgow PA14 .... 69 D4
  Renfrew PA4 .... 94 B1
Coll Gdns KA11 .... 225 D4
Coll of Nautical Studies
  G5 .... 117 E3
Coll Pl G21 .... 98 A1
Coll St G21 .... 98 A1
Colla Gdns G64 .... 78 B1
Collace Ave PA11 .... 110 B4
College Cres FK2 .... 24 B1
College Gate G61 .... 75 E3
College La G1 .... 241 E2
College Pk KA10 .... 229 F4
College St Dumbarton G82 .... 49 F2
  Glasgow G1 .... 241 E2
College Way G82 .... 49 F2
College Wynd KA1 .... 227 F4
Collenan Ave KA10 .... 230 A2
Collessie Dr G33 .... 99 E1
Collier St PA5 .... 111 F2
Colliers Rd FK7 .... 8 B3
Colliertree Rd ML6 .... 123 E4
Collina St G20 .... 96 B3
Collingwood Ct FK1 .... 41 F3
Collingwood Pl G84 .... 17 D1
Collingwood Terr PA19 .... 44 C3
Collins St G4 .... 241 E2
Collins St Clydebank G81 .... 74 B3
  Glasgow G4 .... 241 F2
Collylaw Rd FK10 .... 5 E2
Collylinn Rd G61 .... 75 F2

Colmonell Ave G13 .... 94 C4
Colonsay G74 .... 181 E4
Colonsay Ave
  Port Glasgow PA14 .... 69 D4
  Renfrew PA4 .... 94 B1
Colonsay Dr G77 .... 156 A3
Colonsay House KA9 .... 236 A3
Colonsay Pl KA3 .... 223 D3
Colonsay Rd Glasgow G52 .... 115 F3
  Paisley PA2 .... 133 E4
Colquhoun Ave G52 .... 115 D4
Colquhoun Ct G41 .... 116 B2
Colquhoun Dr
  Alexandria G83 .... 27 F4
  Bearsden G61 .... 75 F3
Colquhoun Park Prim Sch
  G61 .... 75 E2
Colquhoun Pk G52 .... 115 D4
Colquhoun Rd
  Kilmarnock KA3 .... 223 E1
  Milton G82 .... 50 C1
Colquhoun Sq G84 .... 16 B1
Colquhoun St
  Dumbarton G82 .... 50 A2
  Helensburgh G84 .... 16 B1
  Stirling FK7 .... 7 E3
Colquhoun Terr FK7 .... 7 E3
Colsnaur FK11 .... 4 A3
Colson Pl ML4 .... 142 B2
Colston Ave G64 .... 97 F4
Colston Dr G64 .... 97 F4
Colston Gdns Airdrie ML6 .... 123 E4
  Bishopbriggs G64 .... 97 F4
Colston Path G64 .... 97 F4
Colston Pl Airdrie ML6 .... 123 E4
  Bishopbriggs G64 .... 97 F4
Colston Rd Airdrie ML6 .... 123 E4
  Bishopbriggs G64 .... 97 F4
Colston Terr ML6 .... 123 E4
Colt Ave ML5 .... 101 F1
Colt Pl ML5 .... 122 A4
Colt Terr ML5 .... 122 A4
Coltmuir Cres G64 .... 97 F4
Coltmuir Dr G64 .... 97 F4
Coltmuir Gdns G64 .... 97 F4
Coltmuir St G22 .... 97 D3
Coltness Ave ML7 .... 166 C4
Coltness Dr ML4 .... 142 A2
Coltness High Sch ML2 .... 165 E2
Coltness La G33 .... 119 E3
Coltness Prim Sch ML2 .... 165 E3
Coltness Rd ML2 .... 165 E3
Coltness St G33 .... 119 E4
Coltpark Ave G64 .... 97 F4
Coltpark La G64 .... 97 F4
Coltsfoot Dr G53 .... 135 D2
Coltswood Ct ML5 .... 122 A4
Coltswood Rd ML5 .... 122 A4
Columba Cres ML1 .... 142 B1
Columba Path G72 .... 140 B1
Columba RC High Sch ML5 .... 122 A2
Columba St Glasgow G51 .... 116 A4
  Greenock PA16 .... 45 E2
  Helensburgh G84 .... 16 B1
Columbia Pl G75 .... 180 A4
Columbia Way G75 .... 180 A4
Columbine Way ML8 .... 201 F4
Colvend La G40 .... 117 F2
Colvend St G40 .... 117 F2
Colville Ct ML1 .... 143 E1
Colville Dr G73 .... 138 B3
Colvilles Pl G75 .... 181 D3
Colvilles Rd G75 .... 181 D3
Colwood Ave G53 .... 135 D2
Colwood Gdns G53 .... 135 D2
Colwood Pl G53 .... 135 D2
Colwood Sq G53 .... 135 D2
Colwyn Ct ML6 .... 103 D1
Colzium House G65 .... 36 C1
Colzium View G65 .... 60 C4
Combe Quadrant ML4 .... 141 F2
Comedie Rd G33 .... 99 F2
Comely Bank ML3 .... 161 F2
Comely Park Prim Sch FK1 .... 42 A2
Comely Park Terr **[5]** FK1 .... 42 A2
Comely Pl FK1 .... 42 A2
Comelypark La G31 .... 118 A3
Comelybank Rd G82 .... 49 E2
Comelypark Pl **[6]** G31 .... 118 A3
Comelypark St G31 .... 118 A3
Commerce St G5 .... 240 C1
Commercial Ct G5 .... 117 E3
Commercial Rd
  Barrhead G78 .... 134 B2
  Glasgow G5 .... 117 E3
Common Gn ML3 .... 162 C2
Commonhead Ave ML6 .... 102 C1
Commonhead La ML6 .... 102 C1
Commonhead Rd
  Glasgow G69 .... 120 C4
  Kilmarnock KA3 .... 228 A2
Commonhead St ML6 .... 102 C1
Commonside St ML6 .... 102 C1
Commonwealth Pl G75 .... 180 B4
Commore Ave G78 .... 134 B1
Commore Dr G13 .... 95 D4
Commore Pl G78 .... 154 B3
Community Ave ML4 .... 142 A1
Community Pl ML4 .... 142 A2
Community Rd ML4 .... 141 F3
Comrie Cres ML3 .... 161 F2
Comrie Rd G33 .... 99 D3
Comrie St G32 .... 119 D2
Cona St G46 .... 135 F2
Conan Ct G72 .... 139 E3

Condor Glen ML1 .... 142 C4
Condorrat Interchange
  G67 .... 82 B4
Condorrat Prim Sch G67 .... 82 A4
Condorrat Rd Airdrie ML6 .... 102 B3
Condorrat Ring Rd G67 .... 82 B4
Coneyhill Rd FK9 .... 2 A4
Coneypark Cres FK4 .... 38 B2
Coneypark St FK4 .... 38 B2
Congress Rd G3 .... 116 B4
Congress Way G3 .... 116 C4
Conifer Pl G66 .... 79 D3
Coningsby Pl FK10 .... 10 A3
Conisborough Path G33 .... 99 F1
Conisborough Rd G34 .... 100 A1
Coniston G75 .... 179 F3
Coniston Cres ML3 .... 183 E3
Coniston Dr ML4 .... 142 A2
Conistone Cres G69 .... 119 F2
Connal St G40 .... 118 A2
Connell Cres G62 .... 55 E1
Connell Ct G25 .... 149 D1
Conner Ave FK2 .... 24 A4
Conniston St G32 .... 118 C4
Connor Rd G78 .... 134 A2
Connor St ML6 .... 103 F1
Conon Ave G61 .... 75 E2
Conservation Pl ML2 .... 165 E1
Consett La G33 .... 119 E4
Consett St G33 .... 119 E4
Constable Rd FK7 .... 7 D3
Constarry Rd G65 .... 60 C2
Container Way PA15 .... 45 F3
Content Ave KA8 .... 239 D4
Content St KA8 .... 236 A1
Contin Pl G20 .... 96 B3
Conval Way PA4 .... 94 B1
Conval Way PA3 .... 113 E4
Conway Ct FK1 .... 41 F2
Coo La G76 .... 178 C3
Coodham Pl KA13 .... 207 E2
Cook Rd G83 .... 28 A4
Cook St G5 .... 117 D3
Coolgardie Gn **[10]** G75 .... 180 B4
Coolgardie Pl G75 .... 180 B4
Coolgardie Rd G46 .... 187 F2
Cooper's Well St G11 .... 96 B1
Cooperage Ct G14 .... 94 B3
Cooperage La FK1 .... 42 A3
Copeland Prim Sch G51 .... 116 A4
Copenhagen Ave G75 .... 180 C3
Copland Pl Alva FK12 .... 4 C4
  Glasgow G51 .... 116 A3
Copland Quadrant G51 .... 116 A3
Copland Rd G51 .... 116 A3
Coplaw St G42 .... 117 D2
Copperfield La G71 .... 141 D4
Coralmount Gdns G66 .... 79 F4
Coranbae Pl KA7 .... 238 A1
Corbett Ct G32 .... 118 C2
Corbett St G32 .... 119 D2
Corbie Pl G62 .... 54 B1
Corbiewood Dr FK7 .... 11 F4
Corbiston Way G67 .... 62 A1
Cordale Ave G82 .... 27 E1
Cordiner St G44 .... 137 D4
Cordon Rd KA3 .... 222 C2
Corentin Ct FK1 .... 42 B2
Corkerhill Gdns G52 .... 115 F2
Corkerhill Pl G52 .... 115 F1
Corkerhill Rd G52 .... 115 E2
Corkerhill Sta G52 .... 115 F1
Corlaich Ave G42 .... 137 F4
Corlaich Dr G42 .... 137 F4
Corlic St PA15 .... 46 A1
Corlic Way PA13 .... 89 E4
Cormack Ave G64 .... 57 E1
Cormorant Ave PA6 .... 111 E4
Corn Exchange Rd FK8 .... 7 D4
Corn St G4 .... 97 D1
Cornaig Rd G53 .... 135 D4
Cornalee Gdns G53 .... 135 D4
Cornalee Pl G53 .... 135 D4
Cornalee Rd G53 .... 135 D4
Cornelia St ML1 .... 142 A1
Cornelian Terr ML4 .... 142 A2
Cornhaddock St PA15 .... 45 F2
Cornhill Ct **[7]** G74 .... 159 F1
  East Kilbride G74 .... 159 F1
Cornhill Cres FK7 .... 7 D2
Cornhill Dr ML5 .... 121 F4
Cornhill St G21 .... 98 A3
Cornock Cres G81 .... 74 A2
Cornock St G81 .... 74 A2
Cornsilloch Brae ML9 .... 186 A2
Cornton Bsns Pk FK9 .... 2 A2
Cornton Cres FK9 .... 2 A3
Cornton Prim Sch FK9 .... 2 A2
Cornton Rd FK9 .... 2 A3
Cornwall Ave G73 .... 138 B3
Cornwall Ct **[7]** G74 .... 159 F1
  East Kilbride G74 .... 159 F1
Cornwall St G41 .... 116 B3
Cornwall St S G41 .... 116 B3
Cornwall St W **[10]** G74 .... 159 F1
Coronation Ave ML9 .... 199 D4
Coronation Cres ML9 .... 199 D4
Coronation Pl Gartcosh G69 .... 100 C4
  Larkhall ML9 .... 199 D4
  Skinflats FK2 .... 24 C2
Coronation Rd E ML1 .... 142 C2
Coronation Rd E ML1 .... 142 C2
Coronation Road Ind Est
  ML1 .... 142 C2
Coronation St Monkton KA3 .... 233 E3
  Wishaw ML2 .... 165 E2
Coronation Way G61 .... 76 A1

Corpach Pl G34 100 B1
Corporation St FK1 42 B2
Corpus Christi RC Prim Sch
Airdrie ML6 123 D2
Glasgow G13 95 E3
Corra Linn ML3 162 A2
Corran Ave G77 156 B3
Corran St G33 118 C4
Correen Gdns G61 75 D4
Corrie Ave FK5 23 F2
Corrie Brae G65 36 B1
Corrie Cres
Kilmarnock KA3 222 C2
Saltcoats KA21 205 F1
Corrie Ct ML3 161 F1
Corrie Dr Motherwell ML1 163 D4
Paisley PA1 114 C2
Corrie Gdns G75 180 A2
Corrie Gr G44 136 C2
Corrie House KA9 236 A3
Corrie Pl Falkirk FK1 41 E2
Helensburgh G84 16 C2
Kirkintilloch G66 79 F2
Troon KA10 229 F4
Corrie Rd G65 36 B1
Corrie View G68 81 F4
Corrie Way ML9 185 D1
Corrour Rd Glasgow G43 136 C4
Newton Mearns G77 156 B3
Corruna Ct ML8 188 A1
Corsankell Wynd KA21 205 F1
Corse Ave KA11 221 D1
Corse Dr G78 134 A2
Corse Pl KA2 226 C4
Corse Rd G52 114 C3
Corse St KA23 190 B3
Corsebar Ave PA2 113 E1
Corsebar Cres PA2 113 E1
Corsebar Dr PA2 113 E1
Corsebar La PA2 113 D1
Corsebar Rd PA2 113 D1
Corsebar Way PA2 113 E2
Corsefield Rd PA12 128 C1
Corseford Ave PA5 131 E4
Corseford Sch PA10 131 D4
Corsehill KA13 208 A2
Corsehill Dr KA23 190 A3
Corsehill Mount Rd KA11 225 D4
Corsehill Mount Rdbt
KA11 225 E4
Corsehill Pk Ayr KA7 238 C3
Irvine KA11 225 E4
Corsehill Pl Ayr KA7 238 C3
Glasgow G34 120 B4
Stewarton KA3 195 F1
Corsehill Prim Sch KA13 207 F2
Corsehill Rd KA7 238 C3
Corsehill St G34 120 B4
Corsehill Terr KA11 220 C1
Corsehillbank St KA3 195 E1
Corselet Rd G53 135 D2
Corserine Bank KA11 219 F2
Corserine Rd KA7 238 A1
Corsewall Ave G32 119 F2
Corsewall St ML5 121 F4
Corsford Dr G53 135 E3
Corsliehill Rd PA6 90 C4
Corsock Ave ML3 161 F1
Corsock St G31 118 B4
Corston St G33 118 B4
Cortachy Ave FK2 24 A2
Cortachy Pl G64 78 B1
Coruisk Dr G76 157 E4
Corunna St [6] G3 116 C4
Coshneuk Rd G33 99 D2
Cosy Neuk ML9 185 E1
Cottage Cres FK1 41 F3
Cottar St G20 96 C4
Cotter Dr KA3 228 B4
Cotton Ave PA3 112 A3
Cotton St Glasgow G40 118 A1
Paisley PA1 113 F2
Cotton Vale ML1 143 F1
Coulport Pl G84 16 A1
Coulter Ave
Coatbridge ML5 121 F4
Wishaw ML2 165 E4
Coulthard Dr KA9 236 B3
Countess St KA21 216 C4
County Ave G72 138 C4
County Dr ML11 215 E2
County Hospl FK10 10 A4
County Pl PA1 113 F3
County Sq PA1 113 F3
Couper Pl G4 241 E4
Couper St G4 241 E4
Coursington Cres ML1 164 A4
Coursington Gdns ML1 163 F4
Coursington Pl ML1 163 F4
Coursington Rd ML1 164 A4
Court Hill G84 15 D2
Court Rd PA14 47 E1
Courthill Alva FK12 5 D4
Bearsden G61 75 E3
Courthill Ave G44 137 D3
Courthill Cres G65 60 C4
Courthill Pl KA24 191 E4
Courthill St KA24 191 E4
Courtrai Ave G84 16 A1
Coustonholm Rd G43 136 B4
Couther Quadrant ML6 103 D1
Covanburn Ave ML3 162 C1
Cove Cres ML7 146 C3
Cove Pl G84 16 A1
Cove Rd PA19 44 C4
Coveland Dr G73 138 A2
Covenant Cres ML9 185 D1
Covenant Pl ML2 164 B1
Covenanter Rd ML7 127 E2
Covenanters Way ML2 186 B3
Coventry Dr G31 118 A4
Cow Wynd FK1 42 A2
Cowal Cres Gourock PA19 44 A3
Kirkintilloch G66 59 D1
Cowal Dr PA3 112 A3
Cowal St G20 96 B4
Cowal View PA19 44 A3
Cowan Cres Ayr KA8 236 B2
Barrhead G78 134 B2
Cowan La G12 96 C1
Cowan Rd G68 61 E1
Cowan St Bonnybridge FK4 40 A3
Glasgow G12 96 C1
Cowan Wilson Ave G72 161 E4
Cowan Wynd
Uddingston G71 141 D4
Wishaw ML2 186 B4
Cowane St FK8 7 D4
Cowans Row KA3 228 B4
Cowcaddens Rd G3 97 D1
Cowcaddens St G2 241 D3
Cowcaddens Underground
Sta G4 240 C4
Cowden Dr G64 78 A2
Cowden St G51 115 E4
Cowdenhill Cir G13 95 E4
Cowdenhill Pl G13 95 E4
Cowdenhill Rd G13 95 E4
Cowdray Cres PA4 94 B2
Cowgate G66 79 E4
Cowglen Hospl G53 135 E4
Cowglen Rd G53 135 E4
Cowie Prim Sch FK7 12 B4
Cowie Rd FK7 12 A4
Cowiehall Rd FK7 12 B4
Cowlairs Ind Est G22 97 E3
Cowlairs Rd [6] G21 97 F2
Coxdale Ave G66 79 D4
Coxhill St G21 97 E2
Coxithill Rd FK7 7 D2
Coxton Pl G33 99 E1
Coyle Pk KA10 229 F3
Coylebank KA9 236 B3
Coylton Cres ML3 161 F1
Coylton Rd G43 136 C3
Crabb Quadrant ML1 142 B1
Cragdale G74 159 E2
Craggan Dr G14 95 D3
Crags Ave PA2 113 F1
Crags Cres PA2 113 F1
Crags Rd PA2 113 F1
Cragwell Pk G76 158 C4
Craig Ave Alexandria G83 27 E4
Dalry KA24 191 D4
Craig Cotts KA2 226 B4
Craig Cres Kirkintilloch G66 80 A4
Stirling FK9 2 B2
Craig Ct FK9 2 A3
Craig Dr KA2 226 C4
Craig Gdns G77 156 B3
Craig Hill G75 180 B4
Craig Leith Rd FK7 7 E3
Craig Pl G77 156 A3
Craig Rd Glasgow G44 137 D3
Linwood PA3 111 F4
Neilston G78 154 B3
Troon KA10 229 D2
Craig St Airdrie ML6 122 C4
Blackridge EH48 107 F2
Blantyre G72 161 F4
Coatbridge ML5 121 F2
Craig View KA11 221 D1
Craigallian Ave
Cambuslang G72 139 E2
Milngavie G62 55 D2
Craiganour La G43 136 B3
Craigard Pl G73 138 B2
Craigash Quadrant G62 54 C2
Craigash Rd G62 54 C2
Craigbank FK10 5 E1
Craigbank Cres G76 178 C3
Craigbank Dr G53 135 D3
Craigbank Gr G76 178 C3
Craigbank Prim Sch
Alloa FK10 5 E1
Larkhall ML9 199 D4
Craigbank Rd ML9 199 D4
Craigbank Sch KA21 216 C4
Craigbank Sec Sch G53 135 E4
Craigbank St ML9 185 D1
Craigbanzo St G81 74 B4
Craigbarnet Ave G64 78 A4
Craigbarnet Cres G33 99 D2
Craigbarnet Rd G62 54 B1
Craigbet Ave PA11 89 F1
Craigbet Cres PA11 89 F1
Craigbet Pl PA11 89 F1
Craigbo Ave G23 76 B1
Craigbo Ct G23 96 B4
Craigbo Dr G23 76 B1
Craigbo Pl G23 96 B4
Craigbo Rd G23 76 B1
Craigbo St G23 76 B1
Craigbog Ave PA5 131 E4
Craigburn Ave PA6 111 E4
Craigburn Cres PA6 111 E4
Craigburn Ct Ashgill ML9 185 F1
Falkirk FK1 41 F1
Craigburn Pl PA6 111 F4
Craigburn St ML3 183 E4
Craigdene Dr KA20 206 C1
Craigdhu Ave Airdrie ML6 123 F4
Milngavie G62 54 C1
Craigdhu Prim Sch G62 75 F4
Craigdhu Rd Bearsden G61 75 F4
Milngavie G62 54 C1
Craigdonald Pl PA5 111 F2
Craigellan Rd G43 136 B3
Craigelvan Ave G67 81 F3
Craigelvan Ct G67 81 F3
Craigelvan Dr G67 81 F3
Craigelvan Gdns G67 81 F3
Craigelvan Gr G67 81 F3
Craigelvan Pl G67 81 F3
Craigelvan View G67 81 F3
Craigenbay Cres G66 79 F3
Craigenbay Rd G66 79 F3
Craigenbay St G21 98 A2
Craigencart Ct G81 73 F3
Craigend Cres G62 54 C1
Craigend Dr ML5 121 E2
Craigend Dr W G62 54 C1
Craigend Pl G13 95 F3
Craigend Rd
Cumbernauld G67 81 F3
East Kilbride G75 179 F1
Stirling FK7 7 D2
Troon KA10 232 C4
Craigend St G13 95 F3
Craigend View G67 81 F3
Craigend Visitor Ctr G62 54 C4
Craigendmuir Rd G33 99 F2
Craigendmuir St G33 98 B1
Craigendon Oval PA2 133 E3
Craigendon Rd PA2 133 E3
Craigendoran Ave G84 25 C4
Craigendoran Sta G84 25 C4
Craigends Ave PA11 89 F2
Craigends Dr PA10 111 D2
Craigends Pl PA11 89 F2
Craigends Rd
Glengarnock KA14 170 A3
Houston PA6 111 F4
Craigenfeoch Ave PA5 111 E1
Craigenhill Rd ML8 203 D3
Craigenlay Ave G63 31 E2
Craigens Rd ML1,ML6 124 B2
Craigfaulds Ave PA2 113 D1
Craigfell Ct ML3 161 F1
Craigfern Dr G63 31 E2
Craigfin Ct KA9 236 B3
Craigflower Ave G53 135 D2
Craigflower Gdns G53 135 D2
Craigflower Rd G53 135 D2
Craigford Dr FK7 7 E1
Craigforth Cres FK8 1 C1
Craighalbert Rd G68 61 E2
Craighalbert Rdbt G68 61 E2
Craighalbert Way G68 61 E2
Craighall Pl KA7 239 D1
Craighall Quadrant G78 154 B3
Craighall Rd G4 97 D1
Craighall St FK8 1 C1
Craighaw St G81 74 B4
Craighead Ave Glasgow G33 98 B2
Milton Of C G65 58 B3
Craighead Dr G62 54 B1
Craighead Prim Sch G65 58 B3
Craighead Rd
Bishopton PA7 72 A1
Milton Of C G65 58 B3
Craighead Sch ML3 162 A4
Craighead St ML6 123 F4
Craighead Way G78 134 A1
Craighill Dr G76 157 E3
Craighill Gr G76 157 E3
Craighill View EH48 107 F2
Craighirst Dr G81 74 A4
Craighirst Rd G62 54 B1
Craighlaw Ave G76 157 E1
Craighlaw Dr G76 157 E1
Craigholm Rd KA7 239 E4
Craigholme PA6 91 E1
Craigholme Sch G41 116 B2
Craighorn FK11 4 A3
Craighorn Dr FK1 41 F1
Craighorn Rd FK12 4 C3
Craighouse St G33 99 D1
Craighton Gdns G65 57 F4
Craigie Ave Ayr KA8 239 D4
Kilmarnock KA1 227 F2
Craigie Coll of Ed KA8 239 E4
Craigie Ct FK5 23 D1
Craigie Dr G77 156 C2
Craigie La [7] ML9 185 D2
Craigie Lea KA8 239 D4
Craigie Pk G66 79 F3
Craigie Pl Crosshouse KA2 226 C4
Kilmarnock KA1 227 F2
Craigie Rd Ayr KA8 236 A1
Hurlford KA1 228 C3
Kilmarnock KA1 227 F1
Kilmarnock, Riccarton KA1 227 F2
Craigie St Glasgow G42 117 D1
Prestwick KA9 236 A4
Craigie Way KA8 239 E4
Craigiebar Dr PA2 133 E4
Craigieburn Gdns G20 96 A4
Craigieburn Rd G67 61 F1
Craigiehall Ave PA8 93 D4
Craigiehall Cres PA8 93 D4
Craigiehall Pl G51 116 B3
Craigiehall St G51 116 C3
Craigiehall Way PA8 93 D4
Craigieknowes St PA15 46 B2
Craigielea Cres G62 54 C1
Craigielea Ct PA4 94 B2
Craigielea Dr PA3 113 E3
Craigielea Pk PA4 94 B2
Craigielea Prim Sch PA3 113 D3
Craigielea Rd
Clydebank G81 73 F4
Renfrew PA4 94 B2
Craigielea St G31 118 A4
Craigielinn Ave PA2 133 E4
Craigievar Ave FK2 24 A2
Craigievar Pl G77 156 A3
Craigievar St G33 99 E1
Craiginn Ct EH48 107 E2
Craiginn Terr EH48 107 E2
Craiglea Ave KA2 226 C4
Craiglea Ct EH48 107 E2
Craiglea Pl ML6 123 E4
Craiglea Terr ML6 103 F2
Craiglee G75 180 C3
Craigleith FK10 5 F2
Craigleith Ave FK1 41 F1
Craigleith St G32 118 C3
Craiglinn Park Rd G68 61 D1
Craiglinn Rdbt G68 61 D1
Craiglockhart St G33 99 E1
Craiglomond Gdns G83 27 E4
Craiglynn Gdns G83 27 F4
Craigmaddie Gdns G64 78 A4
Craigmaddie Rd G64 56 A1
Craigmaddie Terrace La [17]
G3 96 C1
Craigmark Pl KA11 219 F3
Craigmarloch Ave G64 78 A4
Craigmarloch Rdbt G68 61 E2
Craigmarloch View G63 31 D2
Craigmillar Ave G62 55 D2
Craigmillar Pl FK5 23 F2
Craigmillar Rd G42 137 D4
Craigmochan Ave ML6 102 C1
Craigmont Dr G20 96 C3
Craigmont St G20 96 C3
Craigmore Rd G61 75 D4
Craigmore St G31 118 B3
Craigmore Wynd [10] ML9 185 D2
Craigmount Ave PA2 133 E3
Craigmount St G66 79 E4
Craigmuir Cres G52 114 C3
Craigmuir Gdns G72 161 D3
Craigmuir Pl G52 114 C3
Craigmuir Rd
Blantyre G72 161 D3
Glasgow G52 114 C3
Craigmuschat Rd PA19 44 C4
Craignaw Pl KA11 220 A1
Craigneil Dr KA9 236 B4
Craigneil St G33 99 F1
Craigneith Ct G74 160 C2
Craignethan Castle ML9 200 C1
Craignethan Cres ML9 200 B2
Craignethan Rd
Carluke ML8 187 F2
Rutherglen G46 157 D4
Craigneuk Ave ML6 123 E3
Craigneuk St ML1 164 B3
Craignure Cres ML6 123 F4
Craignure Rd G73 138 A2
Craigomus Cres FK11 3 F3
Craigpark G31 118 A4
Craigpark Ave KA9 236 A3
Craigpark Dr G31 118 A4
Craigpark Sch KA8 236 B1
Craigpark St G81 74 B4
Craigpark Way G71 141 D4
Craigs Ave G81 74 B3
Craigs Pl KA21 217 D4
Craigs The PA16 45 E4
Craigsdow Rd KA10 229 F3
Craigsheen Ave G76 158 B4
Craigshiel Pl KA7 238 B2
Craigside Ct G68 81 F4
Craigside Rd G68 81 F4
Craigskeen Pl KA9 236 B3
Craigson Pl ML6 123 F3
Craigspark KA22 205 E2
Craigstewart Cres KA7 238 B1
Craigston Ave KA7 239 E3
Craigston Pl PA5 111 F1
Craigston Rd PA5 111 F1
Craigstone View G65 60 C4
Craigthornhill Rd ML10 198 A3
Craigton Ave
Barrhead G78 134 C1
Milngavie G62 54 C1
Craigton Cotts G62 54 B3
Craigton Cres Alva FK12 4 C3
Newton Mearns G77 156 A3
Craigton Dr Barrhead G78 134 C1
Glasgow G51 115 F3
Newton Mearns G77 156 B3
Craigton Gdns G62 54 C1
Craigton Ind Est G52 115 F3
Craigton Pl Blantyre G72 140 B1
Glasgow G51 115 F3
Craigton Prim Sch G52 115 F3
Craigton Rd Glasgow G51 115 F4
Kilbirnie KA25 170 A4
Milngavie G62 54 C2
Neilston G77 155 D2
Craigton St G81 74 B4
Craigvale Cres ML6 123 F4
Craigvicar Gdns G32 119 E2
Craigview FK10 5 E1
Craigview Ave PA5 111 F1
Craigview Rd ML1 163 F4
Craigview Terr PA5 111 E1
Craigward FK10 10 A3
Craigweil Pl KA7 238 C4
Craigweil Rd KA7 238 C4
Craigwell Ave G73 138 B3
Craiksland Pl KA10 230 A2
Crail St G31 118 B3
Cramalt Ct KA11 220 A2
Crammond Ave ML5 121 E2
Cramond Ave PA4 94 C1
Cramond Ct FK1 42 A1
Cramond Pl KA11 219 F1
Cramond St G5 117 F1
Cramond Terr G32 119 D3
Cramond Way KA11 219 F1
Cranberry Moss Rd
Kilwinning KA13 207 E1
Kilwinning KA13 207 E2
Cranberry Rd KA13 207 D1
Cranborne Rd G12 96 A3
Cranbrooke Dr G20 96 B4
Crandleyhill Rd KA9 236 A3
Cranesbill Ct KA7 239 D2
Crannog Rd G82 50 C1
Crannog Way KA13 207 E2
Cranston St G3 240 A2
Cranworth La G12 96 B2
Cranworth St G12 96 B2
Crarae Ave G61 75 F1
Crathes Ave FK5 24 A2
Crathes Ct G44 136 C2
Crathie Ct ML8 187 F2
Crathie Dr Ardrossan KA22 205 E1
Denny FK6 21 E2
Glasgow G11 96 A1
Glenmavis ML6 102 C2
Crathie Quadrant ML2 165 D3
Crathie Rd KA3 222 C1
Crauford Ave KA23 190 C2
Craufurd Cres KA15 171 F2
Craufurdland Rd KA3 223 D3
Craven Gr KA11 219 F3
Craw Pl PA12 129 E1
Craw Rd PA2 113 E2
Crawberry Rd PA15 46 A1
Crawford Ave
Kirkintilloch G66 79 F2
Prestwick KA9 236 B3
Crawford Cres
Blantyre G72 140 B1
Uddingston G71 140 C4
Crawford Dr
East Kilbride G74 160 A1
Glasgow G15 75 D1
Helensburgh G84 16 C2
Crawford Hill G74 160 A1
Crawford Rd Houston PA6 91 E1
Milngavie G62 54 C2
Crawford Sq FK2 14 B2
Crawford St Glasgow G11 96 A1
Hamilton ML3 162 A3
Motherwell ML1 163 E3
Port Glasgow PA14 47 E1
Crawforddyke Prim Sch
ML8 202 A4
Crawfurd Ave G73 138 A3
Crawfurd Dr PA3 113 D3
Crawfurd Gdns G73 138 B2
Crawfurd Rd G73 138 A2
Crawfurd St PA15 45 F3
Crawfurdland Pl KA2 221 E1
Crawfurds View PA12 129 E2
Crawhin Gdns PA15 45 E2
Crawriggs Ave G66 79 E3
Creamery Rd ML2 165 E1
Crebar Dr G78 134 B1
Crebar St G46 135 F2
Credon Dr Airdrie ML6 123 D2
Crosshouse KA2 226 C4
Credon Gdns G73 138 B2
Cree Ave G64 78 B1
Cree Gdns G32 118 C3
Cree Pl G75 159 D1
Creebank Pl KA10 229 F3
Creelshaugh Rd KA3 213 D2
Creighton Gr G74 159 F1
Creigton Ct KA3 223 D3
Creinch Dr G83 19 F1
Creran Ct Hamilton ML3 162 A1
Prestwick KA9 236 B3
Creran Dr Denny FK6 39 E3
Renfrew PA4 94 A2
Creran Path [12] ML2 165 F3
Crescent Rd G13 95 D3
Crescent St PA15 46 A2
Crescent The
Clarkston G76 158 A3
Clydebank G81 73 F2
Longriggend ML6 84 B1
Stewarton KA3 195 F1
Cresswell La G12 96 B2
Cresswell Pl G77 156 C1
Cresswell St [5] G12 96 B2
Cressy St G51 115 F4
Crest Ave G13 95 D4
Crestlea Ave PA2 133 F4
Creteil Ct FK1 42 B2
Creveul Ct G83 27 F3
Crichton Ave KA24 191 D4
Crichton Ct G45 137 F1
Crichton Pl G21 97 F2
Crichton St Coatbridge ML5 122 A4
Glasgow G21 97 F2
Cricketfield La PA6 91 D2
Crieff Ave ML6 123 E1
Criffel Pl Kilmarnock KA1 228 A2
Motherwell ML1 143 E2
Criffell Gdns G32 119 E2
Criffell Rd G32 119 E2
Crimea St G2 240 B2
Crimond Pl Kilsyth G65 36 A1
Shieldhill FK1 66 C4
Crinan Cres ML5 101 E1
Crinan Gdns G64 78 B1
Crinan Pl Ardrossan KA22 205 E3
Bellshill ML4 142 A2
Coatbridge ML5 101 E1

Crinan Rd G64 .... 78 B1
Crinan St G31 .... 118 A4
Crindledyke Cres ML2 ... 166 A3
Cringate Gdns FK7 .... 7 F1
Cripps Ave G81 .... 74 B1
Crisswell Cl PA16 .... 44 B1
Crisswell Cres PA16 .... 44 B1
Crocus Bank KA7 .... 239 E2
Crocus Gr KA12 .... 219 E2
Croe Pl KA1 .... 228 A2
Croft Ml M9 .... 184 C1
Croft Pl ML9 .... 184 C2
Croft Rd Balmore G64 .... 77 F4
  Cambuslang G72 .... 139 D3
  East Kilbride G75 .... 180 C4
  Larkhall ML9 .... 184 C2
Croft St Alexandria G83 ..... 27 F2
  Kilmarnock KA1 .... 222 C1
Croft Terr KA11 .... 220 C1
Croft Way PA4 .... 94 C1
Croft Wynd G71 .... 141 D3
Croft's Rd FK10 .... 4 A2
Croftbank Ave G71 .... 141 D1
Croftbank Cres
  Bothwell G71 .... 141 D1
  Uddingston G71 .... 140 C3
Croftbank Gate G71 .... 141 D1
Croftbank St 🆂 G21 .... 97 F2
Croftburn Dr G44 .... 137 E2
Croftcot Ave ML4 .... 141 F2
Croftcroighn Rd G33 .... 99 D1
Croftcroighn Sch G33 .... 99 F1
Croftend Ave G44 .... 137 F3
Croftend La G44 .... 137 F3
Croftfoot Cres G45 .... 138 A2
Croftfoot Dr G45 .... 137 F2
Croftfoot Pl Denny FK6 ...... 21 E2
  Gartcosh G69 .... 101 D3
Croftfoot Quadrant G45 ... 137 F2
Croftfoot Rd G44 .... 137 F2
Croftfoot Sch G44 .... 137 F3
Croftfoot St G45 .... 138 A2
Croftfoot Sta G44 .... 137 F3
Croftfoot Terr G45 .... 137 F2
Crofthead KA11 .... 220 A2
Crofthead Ave KA3 .... 223 D3
Crofthead Cotts G76 .... 154 B4
Crofthead Cres ML4 .... 141 F2
Crofthead Ct Irvine KA11 ... 220 A2
  Stirling FK8 .... 2 A1
  Stonehouse ML9 .... 198 C1
Crofthead Dr G65 .... 33 E1
Crofthead Pl Bellshill ML4 ... 141 F2
  Newton Mearns G77 ..... 156 C2
Crofthead Rd Ayr KA7 ...... 239 E3
  Kilmaurs KA3 .... 222 A4
  Prestwick KA9 .... 233 E1
  Stirling FK8 .... 2 A1
Crofthead St G71 .... 140 C3
Crofthill Ave G71 .... 140 C3
Crofthill Rd G44 .... 137 F2
Crofthouse Dr G44 .... 137 F2
Croftmont Ave G44 .... 137 F2
Croftmoraig Ave G69 .... 81 D2
Crofton Ave G44 .... 137 E2
Croftpark Cres G72 .... 161 F3
Croftpark Rd G81 .... 74 A4
Croftpark St ML4 .... 142 A3
Croftshaw Rd FK12 .... 5 D4
Croftside Ave G44 .... 137 F2
Croftspar Ave G32 .... 119 E3
Croftspar Dr G32 .... 119 E3
Croftspar Gr G32 .... 119 E3
Croftspar Pl G32 .... 119 E3
Croftwood G64 .... 78 A2
Croftwood Ave G44 .... 137 E2
Croftwood Rd ML3 .... 162 B1
Crogal Cres ML6 .... 123 E1
Cromalt Ave G75 .... 180 A2
Cromalt Cres G61 .... 75 E4
Cromarty Ave
  Bishopbriggs G64 .... 78 B1
  Glasgow G43 .... 136 C3
Cromarty Cres G61 .... 75 F4
Cromarty Gdns G76 .... 137 D1
Cromarty Pl Chryston G69 ... 80 B1
  East Kilbride G74 .... 160 B2
Cromarty Rd ML6 .... 120 A2
Crombie Gdns G69 .... 120 C3
Cromdale Rd
  Kilmarnock KA1 .... 228 A2
  Port Glasgow PA14 .... 69 D3
Cromdale St G51 .... 115 F4
Cromer St G20 .... 96 C3
Cromer Ct G82 .... 50 B2
Cromer Way PA3 .... 113 E4
Crompton Ave G44 .... 137 D3
Crompton Way KA12 ...... 219 F2
Cromwell Dr FK1 .... 42 B2
Cromwell La 🆂 G20 .... 97 D1
Cromwell Rd Ayr KA7 ...... 235 F1
  Falkirk FK1 .... 42 B2
Cromwell Rd W FK1 .... 42 B2
Cromwell St G20 .... 97 D1
Crona Dr ML3 .... 161 F2
Cronberry Quadrant G52 ... 114 C2
Cronberry Terr G52 .... 114 C2
Cronin Pl ML4 .... 142 A4
Cronulla Pl G65 .... 60 C4
Crookedshields Rd
  G72, G74 .... 160 A4
Crookfur Cottage Homes
  G77 .... 156 B3
Crookfur Prim Sch G77 ... 156 B4
Crookfur Rd G77 .... 156 B3

Crookhill Dr PA12 .... 129 E2
Crookhill Gdns PA12 .... 129 E2
Crookston Ave G52 .... 115 D2
Crookston Castle G53 ..... 115 D1
Crookston Castle Sec Sch
  G53 .... 115 D1
Crookston Ct G52 .... 115 D2
Crookston Dr G52 .... 114 C2
Crookston Gdns G52 ...... 114 C2
Crookston Gr G52 .... 115 D2
Crookston Path G52 .... 114 C2
Crookston Pl G52 .... 114 C2
Crookston Quadrant G52 . 115 D2
Crookston Rd G53 .... 135 D4
Crookston Sta PA52 ...... 114 C2
Crookston Terr G52 .... 115 D2
Crookstonhill Path G52 ... 114 C2
Crophill FK10 .... 5 E1
Crosbie Ct KA10 .... 232 B4
Crosbie Dr Paisley PA2 .... 132 C4
  West Kilbride KA23 ..... 190 B2
Crosbie La G20 .... 96 B4
Crosbie Pl KA10 .... 232 C4
Crosbie Rd KA10 .... 232 C4
Crosbie St G20 .... 96 B4
Crosbie Terr KA9 .... 236 B4
Crosbie Wood PA2 .... 113 D1
Cross KA15 .... 171 D4
Cross Arthurlie Sch G78 .. 134 A2
Cross Arthurlie St G78 .... 134 A2
Cross Brae FK1 .... 66 B3
Cross Gates ML4 .... 142 A2
Cross Key's Cl ML11 .... 215 D2
Cross Rd PA2 .... 113 D1
Cross Shore St PA15 .... 46 A3
Cross St Falkirk FK2 .... 24 A1
  Glasgow G32 .... 119 E1
  Paisley PA1 .... 113 E2
Cross Stone Pl ML1 .... 163 F3
Cross The Dalry KA24 ..... 191 E4
  Glasgow G1 .... 241 E1
  🆂 Kilmarnock KA1 ...... 227 F4
  Prestwick KA9 .... 233 E1
  Stewarton KA3 .... 211 E4
  Stonehouse ML9 .... 198 C1
Crossart St ML7 .... 125 D1
Crossbank Ave G42 .... 117 F1
Crossbank Dr G42 .... 117 E1
Crossbank Rd G42 .... 117 E1
Crossbank Terr G42 .... 117 E1
Crossburn KA7 .... 238 A1
Crossburn Ave G62 .... 54 C1
Crossburn Dr KA10 .... 230 A2
Crossburn La KA10 .... 230 A2
Crossburn Terr KA10 ..... 230 A2
Crossclyde View ML8 ..... 201 E1
Crossdene Rd KA2 .... 226 C4
Crossdykes G66 .... 80 A4
Crossen La ML8 .... 188 A1
Crossflat Cres PA1 .... 114 A3
Crossford Dr G23 .... 76 C1
Crossgate G66 .... 58 B1
Crossgates PA7 .... 72 A2
Crossgates Ave ML1 ..... 144 A2
Crossgates St ML9 .... 184 C2
Crosshill Ave Glasgow G42 . 117 D1
  Kirkintilloch G66 .... 79 E3
Crosshill Dr Deland ML1 .. 144 A2
  Rutherglen G73 .... 138 A3
Crosshill Pl PA14 .... 68 C4
Crosshill Rd Bishopbriggs G64 78 C3
  Port Glasgow PA14 ...... 68 C3
  Port Glasgow, Boglestone
  PA14 .... 68 C4
Crosshill St Airdrie ML6 ... 122 C4
  Coatbridge ML5 .... 121 D2
  Lennoxtown G65 .... 33 E1
  Motherwell ML1 .... 163 F3
Crosshill Sta G42 .... 117 D1
Crosshill Wynd KA3 .... 223 E3
Crosshouse Hospl KA2 ... 222 A1
Crosshouse Prim Sch
  KA2 .... 221 F1
  East Kilbride G75 .... 180 A3
Crosshouse Rd
  Clachan of C G65 .... 33 D2
  East Kilbride G75 .... 180 A3
  Kilmaurs KA3 .... 222 A1
Crossing La ML9 .... 200 A2
Crosslaw Ave ML11 ...... 215 E2
Crosslee Cres PA16 .... 91 E1
Crosslee Pk PA6 .... 111 E4
Crosslee Rd PA11 .... 111 D4
Crosslee St G52 .... 115 E3
Crosslees Dr G46 .... 135 F2
Crosslees Pk G46 .... 135 F2
Crosslees Rd G46 .... 135 F1
Crosslet Ave G82 .... 50 B2
Crosslet Ct G82 .... 50 B2
Crosslet Rd G82 .... 50 A2
Crosslee Terr 🆂 G51 ..... 116 A4
Crossmill Ave G78 .... 134 B2
Crossmyloof Gdns G41 ... 116 B1
Crossmyloof Sta G41 ..... 116 C1
Crosspoint Dr G23 .... 76 C1
Crossroads KA24 .... 170 B2
Crossslee Rd G53 .... 115 D1
Crossveggate Bsns Pk G62 55 E1
Crossveggate G62 .... 55 D1
Crossview Ave G69 .... 120 B3
Crossview Pl G69 .... 120 B3
Crossways PA6 .... 91 E1
Crossveggate G62 .... 55 D1
Crovie Rd G53 .... 135 D4
Crow Ave ML1 .... 143 D3
Crow Rd Glasgow G11 ...... 96 A1
  Lennoxtown G65 .... 33 D3
  Stonehouse ML9 .... 198 C1

Crow Wood Rd G69 .... 100 A4
Crow Wood Terr G69 ..... 100 A4
Crow-Wood Cres ML6 ... 123 D1
Crow-Wood Rd ML6 ...... 123 D1
Crowflat View G71 .... 121 E1
Crowflats Rd G71 .... 140 C3
Crowhill Cres ML6 .... 102 C1
Crowhill Rd G64 .... 97 F4
Crowhill St G22 .... 97 E3
Crowlin Cres G33 .... 119 D4
Crown Ave G81 .... 74 A2
Crown Cir 🔟 G12 .... 96 B2
Crown Gdns Alloa FK10 .... 9 F4
  Glasgow G12 .... 96 B2
Crown Rd N G12 .... 96 B2
Crown Rd S G12 .... 96 B2
Crown St Ayr KA8 .... 235 F1
  Calderbank ML6 .... 123 D2
  Coatbridge ML5 .... 122 B4
  Glasgow G5, G42 .... 117 E3
  Glasgow, Gorbals G1, G5 117 E3
  Greenock PA15 .... 45 F3
Crown Terr G12 .... 96 B2
Crownest Loan FK5 .... 23 F1
Crownhall Pl G32 .... 119 E3
Crownhall Rd G32 .... 119 E3
Crownpoint Rd G40 .... 117 F3
Crowood Dr ML6 .... 123 E4
Croy G74 .... 159 E2
Croy Ave G77 .... 157 D3
Croy Pl G21 .... 98 B3
Croy Rd Coatbridge ML5 . 121 F2
  Glasgow G21 .... 98 B3
Croy Sta G68 .... 60 C2
Cruachan Ave Paisley PA2 . 133 F4
  Renfrew PA4 .... 94 B1
  Stirling FK9 .... 2 A2
Cruachan Ct FK1 .... 42 B1
Cruachan Dr Barrhead G78 . 134 B1
  Newton Mearns G77 .... 156 C2
Cruachan Pl KA1 .... 228 A2
Cruachan Rd Bearsden G61 . 75 D4
  Rutherglen G73 .... 138 B2
Cruachan St G46 .... 135 F2
Cruachan Way G78 .... 134 B1
Cruckburn Wynd FK7 .... 6 C2
Cruden St G51 .... 115 F3
Cruickshank Dr FK1 .... 66 B3
Cruikshank's Ct FK6 .... 21 F1
Crum Ave G46 .... 136 A2
Crum Cres FK7 .... 7 E1
Crumhielden Gdns
  KA10 .... 230 A2
Crummock Gdns KA15 ... 150 B1
Crummock St KA15 ...... 150 B1
Crusader Ave G13 .... 75 E1
Crusader Cres KA3 .... 211 E4
Cubie St G40 .... 117 F3
Cubrieshaw Dr KA23 ..... 190 B2
Cubrieshaw St KA23 ..... 190 B3
Cuckoo Way ML1 .... 143 D3
Cuff Cres KA15 .... 171 D4
Cuilhill Rd G69 .... 121 D4
Cuillin Ct FK1 .... 42 B1
Cuillin Pl Irvine KA11 ..... 220 A2
  Kilmarnock KA1 .... 228 A2
Cuillin Way G78 .... 134 B1
Cuillins Ave PA14 .... 68 C3
Cuillins The
  Moodiesburn G69 .... 81 D2
  Uddingston G71 .... 120 C1
Cuilmuir Terr G65 .... 60 C2
Cuilmuir View G65 .... 60 C2
Cuilt Pl G63 .... 31 D2
Cuilts Rd G63 .... 30 A2
Culbin Dr G13 .... 95 D4
Cullen ML8 .... 73 D2
Cullen La 🆂 G75 .... 180 C4
Cullen Pl G71 .... 141 D4
Cullen Rd East Kilbride G75 . 180 B4
  Motherwell ML1 .... 163 E3
Cullen St Alexandria G83 ... 27 E4
  Glasgow G32 .... 119 D2
Cullion Way G22 .... 97 E2
Cullins Rd G73 .... 138 B2
Culloch Rd Bearsden G61 ... 75 E4
  Slamannan FK1 .... 86 A1
Culloden Dr G67 .... 82 C1
Culloden Pl KA3 .... 223 D2
Culloden St G31 .... 118 A4
Culmore Pl FK1 .... 42 C1
Culrain Gdns G32 .... 119 D3
Culrain St G32 .... 119 D3
Culross Hill G74 .... 159 E1
Culross Pl Coatbridge ML5 . 121 F4
  East Kilbride G74 .... 159 E1
Culross St G32 .... 119 E2
Culross Way G69 .... 81 D2
Cult Rd G66 .... 79 F2
Cultenhove Cres FK7 .... 6 C2
Cultenhove Pl FK7 .... 7 D2
Cultenhove Rd FK7 .... 6 C2
Cultfield Path ML1 .... 144 B1
Cults St G51 .... 115 F3
Culvain Ave G61 .... 75 D4
Culvain Pl FK1 .... 42 B1
Cuizean ML6 .... 104 B2
Culzean Ave
  Coatbridge ML5 .... 121 F2
  Prestwick KA9 .... 236 B4
Culzean Cres Glasgow G69 120 A2
  Kilmarnock KA3 .... 228 B4
  Newton Mearns G77 .... 157 D2
Culzean Dr East Kilbride G74 159 E2
  Glasgow G32 .... 119 E2
  Gourock PA19 .... 43 F3
  Motherwell ML1 .... 143 E1

Culzean Pl
  East Kilbride G74 .... 159 E2
  Kilwinning KA13 .... 207 E1
  Stenhousemuir FK5 ...... 23 E2
Culzean Rd KA7 .... 238 B2
Cumberland Arc 🔳 G5 .... 117 E2
Cumberland Ct KA12 .... 16 A2
Cumberland Pl
  Coatbridge ML5 .... 121 E2
  🔳 Glasgow G5 .... 117 E2
Cumberland Rd
  Greenock PA16 .... 44 C2
  Rhu G84 .... 15 E3
Cumberland St Glasgow G5 117 E2
  Glasgow, Laurieston G5 . 117 D3
Cumberland Terr G84 ...... 15 E3
Cumberland Wlk PA16 .... 44 C2
Cumbernauld Coll G67 ... 61 F1
Cumbernauld High Sch G67 62 B1
Cumbernauld Prim Sch G67 62 A2
Cumbernauld Rd
  Chryston G69 .... 100 B4
  Cumbernauld G67 .... 81 E2
  Glasgow G31, G33 ...... 118 B4
  Longcroft FK4 .... 39 D2
  Moodiesburn G69 .... 81 D2
  Stepps G33 .... 99 E3
Cumbernauld Sta G67 ..... 83 D4
Cumbrae G74 .... 160 B1
Cumbrae Ave PA14 .... 69 D4
Cumbrae Cres ML5 .... 122 C3
Cumbrae Cres N G82 ...... 49 E3
Cumbrae Cres S G82 ...... 49 E3
Cumbrae Ct Clydebank G81 . 74 A1
  Greenock PA16 .... 45 D3
  Irvine KA11 .... 220 A2
Cumbrae Dr Falkirk FK1 ... 41 E2
  Kilmarnock KA3 .... 223 D3
  Motherwell ML1 .... 163 E4
Cumbrae House KA9 ...... 236 A3
Cumbrae Pl
  Coatbridge ML5 .... 122 C2
  Gourock PA19 .... 44 B3
  West Kilbride KA23 ...... 190 B2
Cumbrae Rd Paisley PA2 .. 133 F4
  Renfrew PA4 .... 94 B1
  Saltcoats KA21 .... 205 F1
Cumbrae St G33 .... 119 D4
Cumloden Dr G20 .... 96 B4
Cumming Dr G42 .... 137 D4
Cumming St G41 .... 116 B3
Cumnock Dr Airdrie ML6 . 123 D2
  Barrhead G78 .... 134 B1
  Hamilton ML3 .... 161 E1
Cumnock Rd G33 .... 98 C3
Cumroch Rd G65 .... 33 E1
Cunard Ct G81 .... 94 A4
Cunard Cres KA3 .... 211 E4
Cunghame Dr KA20 ...... 206 A1
Cunninghame Rd
  Ardrossan KA22 .... 205 E2
  Kilbarchan PA10 .... 111 D2
  Kilwinning KA13 .... 207 E1
  Rutherglen G73 .... 138 A4
Cunning Park Dr KA7 .... 238 B2
Cunningair Dr ML1 .... 163 F2
Cunningham Dr
  Clydebank G81 .... 73 F3
  Glasgow G46 .... 136 C2
  Harthill ML7 .... 127 E3
Cunningham Gdns FK2 .... 42 C3
Cunningham Rd KA7 ...... 239 E3
Cunningham Rd
  Paisley G52 .... 114 C4
  Stenhousemuir FK5 ...... 24 A2
  Stirling FK7 .... 7 E4
Cunningham St ML1 ...... 163 E3
Cunningham Watt Rd
  KA7 .... 195 E1
Cunninghame Dr KA11 ... 227 F2
Cunninghame Rd
  East Kilbride G74 .... 159 F1
  Irvine KA12 .... 224 A4
  Prestwick KA9 .... 236 B4
  Rutherglen G73 .... 138 B4
Cupar Dr PA16 .... 44 C2
Cuparhead Ave ML5 ...... 121 F2
Cuppleton Brae PA9 ...... 130 A1
Curfew Rd G13 .... 75 E1
Curle St G14 .... 95 E1
Curlew Cres PA16 .... 45 D2
Curlew La PA16 .... 45 D2
Curlew Pl PA5 .... 131 E4
Curling Cres G44 .... 137 E4
Curlinghaugh Cres ML2 . 165 E2
Curlingmire G75 .... 180 C4
Curran Ave ML2 .... 164 C1
Currie Ct KA12 .... 205 E1
Currie St G20 .... 96 C3
Curreiside Ave ML7 .... 146 C2
Curreiside Pl ML2 .... 164 B2
Curtecan Pl KA7 .... 238 C3
Curtis Ave G44 .... 137 E4
Curzon St G20 .... 96 C3
Cushenquarter Dr FK7 .... 12 B2
Custom House Quay Ret Pk
  PA15 .... 46 A3
Customhouse Pl PA15 .... 46 A3
Custonhall Pl FK6 .... 21 E1
Cut The G71 .... 140 C2
Cuthbert Pl KA3 .... 223 D1
Cuthbert St G71 .... 141 D4
Cuthbertson Prim Sch G42 117 D2
Cuthbertson St G42 ...... 117 D2
Cuthelton Dr G31 .... 118 C2
Cuthelton St G31 .... 118 B2
Cuthelton Terr G31 .... 118 B2
Cutsburn Pl KA3 .... 211 F4
Cutsburn Rd KA3 .... 211 F4

Cutstraw Rd KA3 .... 211 F4
Cuttyfield Pl FK2 .... 24 B2
Cypress Ave Beith KA15 ... 150 B1
  Blantyre G72 .... 140 B1
  Uddingston G71 .... 141 D4
Cypress Cres G75 .... 180 B3
Cypress Ct
  East Kilbride G75 .... 180 B3
  Hamilton ML3 .... 162 C1
  Kirkintilloch G66 .... 79 D3
Cypress Gdns KA11 .... 219 F3
Cypress Pl G75 .... 180 B3
Cypress St G22 .... 97 E3
Cyprus Ave PA5 .... 112 A1
Cyprus St G81 .... 114 A2

Daer Ave PA4 .... 94 C1
Daer Way ML3 .... 162 A2
Daer Wlk ML9 .... 199 D4
Daffodil Way ML1 .... 163 F4
Dairsie Gdns G64 .... 98 B4
Dairsie House Sch G43 .. 136 C3
Daisy St G42 .... 137 D4
Daisybank KA14 .... 170 B3
Dakala Ct ML2 .... 165 D1
Dakota Way PA4 .... 94 B1
Dalbeth Pl G32 .... 118 C1
Dalbeth Rd G32 .... 118 C1
Dalblair Rd KA7 .... 238 C4
Dalcharn Pl G34 .... 120 A4
Dalcross St G11 .... 96 B1
Dalcruin Gdns G69 .... 81 D2
Dalderse Ave FK2 .... 42 A3
Daldowie Ave G32 .... 119 E2
Daldowie Rd G71 .... 120 A1
Daldowie St ML5 .... 121 F2
Dale Ave G75 .... 180 B3
Dale Cres KA12 .... 219 E2
Dale Ct ML2 .... 164 B1
Dale Dr ML1 .... 143 D2
Dale Path G40 .... 117 F2
Dale St G40 .... 118 A2
Dale Way G73 .... 138 A2
Daleview Dr G76 .... 157 E3
Daleview Gr G76 .... 157 E3
Dalfoil Ct PA1 .... 114 C2
Dalgain Ct KA11 .... 220 A3
Dalgarroch Ave G81 ...... 94 C4
Dalgarven Mews KA3 .... 223 E3
Dalgleish Ave G81 .... 73 F3
Dalgleish Ct FK8 .... 7 D4
Dalgraig Cres G72 .... 140 B1
Dalhousie Gdns G64 .... 78 A1
Dalhousie House G64 ...... 78 A1
Dalhousie La G15 .... 240 B4
Dalhousie Rd PA10 .... 111 D1
Dalhousie St G3 .... 240 C4
Dalilea Dr G34 .... 100 B1
Dalilea Pl G34 .... 100 B1
Dalintober St G5 .... 240 B1
Daljarrock KA13 .... 207 D1
Dalkeith Ave
  Bishopbriggs G64 .... 78 A2
  Glasgow G41 .... 116 A2
Dallas Ct KA10 .... 229 E1
Dallas La KA10 .... 229 E1
Dallas Pl KA10 .... 229 E1
Dallas Rd KA10 .... 229 E1
Dalmacoulter Rd ML6 ... 103 D2
Dalmahoy Cres PA11 .... 163 B3
Dalmahoy St G32 .... 118 C4
Dalmahoy Way KA13 .... 207 D2
Dalmailing Ave KA11 .... 220 A1
Dalmally St G20 .... 96 C2
  Greenock PA15 .... 46 C3
Dalmarnock Ct G40 ...... 118 A2
Dalmarnock Prim Sch G40 118 A2
Dalmarnock Rd G40 ...... 118 A1
Dalmarnock Road Trad Est
  G40 .... 118 A1
Dalmarnock Sta G40 ..... 118 A2
Dalmary Dr PA1 .... 114 A3
Dalmellington Ct
  East Kilbride G74 .... 159 E1
  Hamilton ML3 .... 162 C1
Dalmellington Dr G74 ... 159 E1
Dalmellington Rd Ayr KA7 239 E2
  Glasgow G53 .... 115 D1
Dalmeny Ave G46 .... 136 B2
Dalmeny Dr G78 .... 134 A1
Dalmeny Rd ML3 .... 162 B1
Dalmeny St G5 .... 117 F1
Dalmilling Cres KA8 ..... 236 B1
Dalmilling Dr KA8 .... 236 C1
Dalmilling Rd KA8 .... 236 C1
Dalmoak Rd G82 .... 48 B3
Dalmoak Rd PA15 .... 27 F2
Dalmonach Rd G83 .... 27 F3
Dalmore Cres G84 .... 16 A2
Dalmore Dr FK12 .... 4 C3
Dalmore Pl KA11 .... 219 F3
Dalmuir Sta G81 .... 73 F2
Dalness St G32 .... 119 D2
Dalnottar Ave G60 .... 73 D3
Dalnottar Dr G60 .... 73 D3
Dalnottar Gdns G60 .... 73 D3
Dalnottar Hill Rd G60 ...... 73 D3
Dalnottar Terr G60 .... 73 D3
Dalreoch Ave G69 .... 120 B3
Dalreoch Ct G82 .... 49 E2
Dalreoch Path G69 .... 120 B3
Dalreoch Sta G82 .... 49 E3

Dalreoch Sta G82 ...... 49 F2
Dalriada Cres ML1 ...... 142 B1
Dalriada Dr G64 ...... 78 B4
Dalriada Rd PA6 ...... 44 B2
Dalriada St G40 ...... 118 B2
Dalry Gdns ML3 ...... 161 E1
Dalry La KA2 ...... 205 E2
Dalry Prim Sch KA24 ...... 191 D4
Dalry Rd Ardrossan KA22 ...... 205 E2
  Beith KA15 ...... 171 D4
  Kilbirnie KA25 ...... 177 A4
  Kilwinning KA13 ...... 207 E2
  Saltcoats KA21 ...... 206 A1
  Stewarton KA3 ...... 195 E1
  Uddingston G71 ...... 141 D4
Dalry Sta KA24 ...... 191 E4
Dalrymple Ct Irvine KA12 ...... 219 F2
  Kirkintilloch G66 ...... 79 E4
Dalrymple Dr
  East Kilbride G74 ...... 159 F1
  Irvine KA12 ...... 219 F2
  Newton Mearns G77 ...... 157 D2
Dalrymple Pl KA12 ...... 219 E2
Dalrymple St PA15 ...... 46 A3
Dalserf Cres G46 ...... 136 A1
Dalserf Path ML9 ...... 185 E1
Dalserf St G33 ...... 118 A3
Dalserf Prim Sch ML9 ...... 199 F4
Dalsetter Ave G15 ...... 75 D1
Dalsetter Pl G15 ...... 75 D1
Dalshannon Pl G67 ...... 82 A4
Dalshannon Rd G67 ...... 82 A4
Dalshannon View G67 ...... 82 A4
Dalshannon Way G67 ...... 82 A4
Dalsholm Rd G20 ...... 96 A4
Dalskeith Ave PA3 ...... 113 D3
Dalskeith Cres PA3 ...... 113 D3
Dalskeith Rd PA3 ...... 113 D3
Dalswinton St G34 ...... 120 B4
Dalton Ave G81 ...... 74 C1
Dalton Hill ML3 ...... 161 F1
Dalton St G31 ...... 118 C3
Dalveit Gdns G83 ...... 27 F4
Dalvait Rd G83 ...... 27 F4
Dalveen Ct G78 ...... 134 B1
Dalveen Dr G71 ...... 140 C4
Dalveen Quadrant ML5 ...... 122 B3
Dalveen St G32 ...... 118 C3
Dalveen Way G73 ...... 138 B2
Dalwhinnie Ave G72 ...... 140 B1
Dalwood Rd KA9 ...... 236 A4
Daly Gdns G72 ...... 140 C1
Dalzell Ave ML1 ...... 164 A2
Dalzell City Pk ML1 ...... 163 F2
Dalzell Dr ML1 ...... 164 A2
Dalziel Dr G41 ...... 116 B2
Dalziel High Sch ML1 ...... 163 E3
Dalziel Rd G52 ...... 114 C4
Dalziel St Hamilton ML3 ...... 162 A3
  Motherwell ML1 ...... 163 F4
Damhead Rd KA1 ...... 227 F2
Dampark KA3 ...... 195 E4
Damshot Cres G53 ...... 135 E4
Damshot Rd G53 ...... 135 E4
Damside G48 ...... 235 F1
Danby Rd G69 ...... 119 F2
Danes Ave [1] G14 ...... 95 E2
Danes Cres G14 ...... 95 E2
Danes Dr G14 ...... 95 E2
Danes La N [3] G14 ...... 95 E2
Danes La S G14 ...... 95 E2
Daniel McLaughlin Pl G66 ...... 58 C1
Dankeith Dr KA1 ...... 231 E2
Dankeith Rd KA1 ...... 231 E2
Darg Rd KA20 ...... 217 E4
Dargarvel Ave G41 ...... 116 A2
Dargavel Rd Bishopton PA7 ...... 72 A2
  Erskine PA8 ...... 72 C1
Dark Brig Rd ML8 ...... 201 D1
Darkwood Cres PA3 ...... 113 D3
Darkwood Ct PA3 ...... 113 D3
Darkwood Dr PA3 ...... 113 D3
Darleith Rd Alexandria G83 ...... 27 F4
  Cardross G82 ...... 26 A1
Darleith St G32 ...... 118 C3
Darley Cres KA10 ...... 229 E1
Darley Mains Rd G53 ...... 135 E2
Darley Pl Hamilton ML3 ...... 183 D4
  Troon KA10 ...... 229 E1
Darley Rd G68 ...... 61 F3
Darlington View KA3 ...... 195 F1
Darluith Rd PA3 ...... 111 F3
Darmeid Pl ML7 ...... 147 D2
Darmule Dr KA13 ...... 207 E3
Darnaway Ave G33 ...... 99 E1
Darnaway Dr G33 ...... 99 E1
Darnaway St G33 ...... 99 E1
Darndaff Rd PA15 ...... 46 A1
Darngaber Gdns ML3 ...... 183 F2
Darngaber Rd ML3 ...... 183 F2
Darngavil Rd ML6 ...... 103 F3
Darnick St G21 ...... 98 A1
Darnley Cres G64 ...... 77 F2
Darnley Dr KA1 ...... 227 F3
Darnley Gdns G41 ...... 116 C1
Darnley Ind Est G53 ...... 135 D3
Darnley Path G46 ...... 135 F3
Darnley Pl G41 ...... 116 C1
Darnley Prim Sch No 1
  G53 ...... 135 E2
Darnley Rd Barrhead G78 ...... 134 C2
  Glasgow G41 ...... 116 C1
Darnley St Glasgow G41 ...... 116 C2
  Stirling FK8 ...... 7 D4
Darnshaw Cl KA11 ...... 220 B3
Darrach Dr FK6 ...... 21 D1

Darragh Gn ML2 ...... 166 A3
Darroch Ave PA19 ...... 44 C4
Darroch Dr Erskine PA8 ...... 72 C2
  Gourock PA19 ...... 44 C4
Darroch Way G67 ...... 62 A2
Dartford St G22 ...... 97 D2
Dartmouth Ave PA19 ...... 44 C3
Darvel Cres PA1 ...... 114 C2
Darvel Dr G77 ...... 157 D3
Darvel St G53 ...... 134 C3
Darwin Pl G81 ...... 73 E2
Darwin Rd G75 ...... 180 B4
Dava St G51 ...... 116 A4
Davaar G74 ...... 160 B1
Davaar Dr Coatbridge ML5 ...... 121 E4
  Kilmarnock KA3 ...... 223 D3
  Motherwell ML1 ...... 142 B1
  Paisley PA2 ...... 133 F4
Davaar Pl G77 ...... 156 B3
Davaar Rd Greenock PA16 ...... 44 B2
  Renfrew PA4 ...... 94 B1
Davaar St G40 ...... 118 A2
Daven Loan [10] ML2 ...... 165 F3
Davarr Pl FK1 ...... 41 E2
Dave Barrie Ave ML9 ...... 184 C3
Daventry Dr G12 ...... 96 A3
Davey St PA15 ...... 45 E3
David Dale Ave KA3 ...... 211 E4
David Gage St KA13 ...... 207 F3
David Livingstone Ctr G72 ...... 140 C1
David Livingstone Meml
  Prim Sch G72 ...... 140 B1
David Orr St KA1 ...... 222 C1
David Pl Glasgow G69 ...... 119 F2
  Paisley PA3 ...... 114 A4
David St Coatbridge ML5 ...... 122 B4
  Glasgow G40 ...... 118 A3
  Salsburgh ML7 ...... 125 D1
David Way PA3 ...... 114 A4
David's Cres KA13 ...... 207 E1
David's Loan FK2 ...... 24 B1
Davidson Ave KA14 ...... 170 B3
Davidson Cres G65 ...... 59 F2
Davidson Dr PA19 ...... 44 C4
Davidson Gdns G14 ...... 95 F2
Davidson La Pl Ayr KA8 ...... 236 A1
  Glasgow G32 ...... 119 E3
Davidson Quadrant G81 ...... 73 F4
Davidson Rd G83 ...... 27 F4
Davidson St Airdrie ML6 ...... 122 C4
  Bannockburn FK7
  Clydebank G81 ...... 94 C4
  Coatbridge ML5 ...... 122 A2
  Glasgow G40 ...... 118 A2
Davidston Pl G66 ...... 79 F2
Davieland Rd G46 ...... 136 A3
Davies Dr G83 ...... 27 F3
Davies Quadrant ML1 ...... 142 B1
Davington Dr ML3 ...... 161 E1
Daviot St G51 ...... 115 E3
Dawsholm Ind Est G20 ...... 96 A4
Dawson Ave East Kilbride G74 ...... 9 F4
  East Kilbride G75 ...... 159 D1
Dawson Park Sch FK7 ...... 24 A1
Dawson Pl G4 ...... 97 D2
Dawson Rd G4 ...... 97 D2
Dawson St PA3 ...... 114 A4
De Morville Pl KA15 ...... 171 D4
De Walden Terr KA23 ...... 223 D1
Deacons Rd G65 ...... 60 C4
Deaconsbank Ave G46 ...... 135 F1
Deaconsbank Cres G46 ...... 135 E1
Deaconsbank Gr G46 ...... 135 E1
Dealston Rd G78 ...... 134 A2
Dean Castle Ctry Pk KA3 ...... 223 D2
Dean Cres Chryston G69 ...... 80 B1
  Hamilton ML3 ...... 162 B1
  Stirling FK8 ...... 2 B2
Dean Ct KA3 ...... 222 C1
Dean La KA3 ...... 223 D1
Dean Park Ave G71 ...... 141 D1
Dean Park Dr G72 ...... 139 E2
Dean Park Rd PA4 ...... 94 C1
Dean Pl KA2 ...... 226 C4
Dean Rd Kilbirnie KA25 ...... 149 D1
  Kilmarnock KA3 ...... 223 D2
Dean St Bellshill ML4 ...... 142 A3
  Clydebank G81 ...... 74 B1
  Kilmarnock KA3 ...... 223 D1
  Stewarton KA3 ...... 195 F1
Dean Terr KA3 ...... 223 D2
Deanbank Sch ML5 ...... 101 E1
Deanbrae St G71 ...... 140 C3
Deanfield Quadrant G52 ...... 114 C3
Deanhill La KA3 ...... 223 D2
Deans Ave G72 ...... 139 E2
Deanside Rd G52 ...... 115 D4
Deanston Dr G41 ...... 136 C4
Deanston Pl ML5 ...... 122 B2
Deanstone Wlk ML5 ...... 122 B1
Deanwood Ave G44 ...... 136 C2
Deanwood Rd G44 ...... 136 C2
Deas Rd ML7 ...... 146 B3
Dechmont Ave G72 ...... 139 F2
  Motherwell ML1 ...... 163 E4
Dechmont Cotts G72 ...... 139 F2
Dechmont Gdns G72 ...... 140 A1
Dechmont Pl G72 ...... 139 E2
Dechmont Rd G71 ...... 120 C1
Dechmont St Glasgow G31 ...... 118 B2
  Hamilton ML3 ...... 162 B1
Dechmont View
  Bellshill ML4 ...... 141 F2
  Uddingston G71 ...... 141 D4

Dee Ave Kilmarnock KA1 ...... 228 A2
  Paisley PA2 ...... 112 C1
  Renfrew PA4 ...... 94 C2
Dee Dr PA2 ...... 112 C1
Dee Path Larkhall ML9 ...... 199 D4
  Motherwell ML1 ...... 143 D3
Dee Pl East Kilbride G75 ...... 179 F3
  Johnstone PA5 ...... 131 E4
Dee St Coatbridge ML5 ...... 101 E1
  Glasgow G33 ...... 118 B4
  Greenock PA16 ...... 45 D3
  Shotts ML7 ...... 146 B3
Dee Terr ML3 ...... 183 D4
Deedes St ML6 ...... 122 B3
Deep Dale G74 ...... 159 E2
Deepdene Rd Bearsden G61 ...... 75 E1
  Chryston G69 ...... 80 C1
Deer Park Ave KA20 ...... 217 F4
Deer Park Ct ML3 ...... 183 E4
Deer Park Pl ML3 ...... 183 F4
Deerdykes Ct N G68 ...... 81 F3
Deerdykes Ct S G68 ...... 81 F3
Deerdykes Pl G68 ...... 81 F3
Deerdykes Rd G68 ...... 81 E3
Deerdykes View G68 ...... 81 E3
Deerpark Pl ML3 ...... 5 F1
Deerpark Prim Sch FK10 ...... 5 F1
Deeside Dr ML8 ...... 188 A2
Deeside Pl ML5 ...... 122 B2
Delfie Dr PA16 ...... 45 D2
Delhi Ave G81 ...... 73 E2
Delkens Gr ML1 ...... 143 E1
Dellburn St ML1 ...... 164 A3
Dellingburn St PA15 ...... 46 A2
Delny Pl G33 ...... 119 F4
Delph Rd FK10 ...... 4 B1
Delphwood Cres FK10 ...... 4 B1
Delves Pk ML11 ...... 215 D2
Delves Rd ML11 ...... 215 D2
Delvin Rd G44 ...... 137 D3
Denbak Ave ML9 ...... 162 A1
Denbeck St G32 ...... 118 C3
Denbrae St G32 ...... 118 C3
Denewood Ave PA2 ...... 133 E4
Denham St G22 ...... 97 D2
Denholm Cres G75 ...... 180 C4
Denholm Dr Glasgow G46 ...... 136 B1
  Wishaw ML2 ...... 165 E3
Denholm Gdns
  Greenock PA16 ...... 45 E3
  Quarter ML3 ...... 183 F2
Denholm Gn [5] G75 ...... 180 C4
Denholm St PA16 ...... 45 E3
Denholm Terr
  Greenock PA16 ...... 45 E3
  Hamilton ML3 ...... 161 F2
Denholm Way KA15 ...... 171 D4
Denmark St G22 ...... 97 E2
Denmilne Gdns G34 ...... 120 B4
Denmilne Path G34 ...... 120 B4
Denmilne Rd G34 ...... 120 B4
Denmilne St G34 ...... 120 B4
Denniston Pl ML1 ...... 215 E3
Dennistoun Cres G84 ...... 25 D4
Dennistoun Rd PA14 ...... 70 B4
Dennistoun St ML4 ...... 142 A3
Denny High Sch FK6 ...... 39 F4
Denny Prim Sch FK6 ...... 21 E1
Denny Rd
  Dennyloanhead FK4 ...... 39 F3
  Larbert FK5 ...... 23 D1
Dennyholm Wynd KA25 ...... 149 D1
Denovan Rd FK6 ...... 21 F2
Dentdale G74 ...... 159 E2
Deramore Ave G46 ...... 157 D4
Derby St G3 ...... 116 C4
Derby Terrace La [6] G3 ...... 116 C4
Deroran Pl FK8 ...... 6 C3
Derrywood Rd G65 ...... 58 B3
Dervaig Gdns ML6 ...... 84 B2
Derwent Ave FK1 ...... 41 F1
Derwent Dr ML5 ...... 101 E1
Derwent St G22 ...... 97 D2
Derwentwater G75 ...... 179 F3
Despard Ave G32 ...... 119 F2
Despard Gdns G32 ...... 119 F2
Deveron Ave G46 ...... 136 B1
Deveron Cres ML3 ...... 161 F2
Deveron Rd Bearsden G61 ...... 75 E1
  East Kilbride G74 ...... 160 A1
  Kilmarnock KA1 ...... 143 D3
  Motherwell ML1 ...... 143 D3
  Troon KA10 ...... 229 E2
Deveron St Coatbridge ML5 ...... 101 E1
  Glasgow G33 ...... 98 B1
Devilla Ct KA9 ...... 236 B4
Devine Dr ML2 ...... 166 A3
Devlin Gr G72 ...... 161 F4
Devol Ave PA14 ...... 47 D1
Devol Cres G53 ...... 135 D4
Devol Rd PA14 ...... 68 B3
Devon Ct FK10 ...... 4 A1
Devon Dr Bishopton PA7 ...... 72 B2
  Tullibody FK10 ...... 4 C2
Devon Gdns
  Bishopbriggs G64 ...... 77 F2
  Carluke ML8 ...... 187 F1
Devon Pl Glasgow G42 ...... 117 D2
  Tullibody FK10 ...... 4 A1
Devon Rd Alloa FK10 ...... 10 B3
  Greenock PA16 ...... 44 B2
Devon St G5 ...... 117 D2
Devon Village FK10 ...... 5 F2
Devon Way ML1 ...... 163 D3

Devon Wlk G68 ...... 81 F4
Devonbank FK10 ...... 5 F2
Devondale Ave G72 ...... 140 B1
Devonhill Ave ML3 ...... 183 E4
Devonport Pk G75 ...... 180 A4
Devonshire Gardens La [2]
  G12 ...... 96 A2
Devonshire Gdns [1] G12 ...... 96 A2
Devonshire Terr G12 ...... 96 A2
Devonshire Terrace La
  G12 ...... 96 A2
Devonview Pl ML6 ...... 122 C3
Devonview Sch ML6 ...... 122 C3
Devonview St ML6 ...... 122 C3
Devonway FK10 ...... 10 C3
Dewar G71 ...... 121 D1
Dewar Wlk ML8 ...... 201 D1
Dewshill Cotts ML7 ...... 126 A2
Dhuhill Dr E G84 ...... 16 C2
Diamond St ML4 ...... 142 A2
Diana Ave G13 ...... 95 D4
Diana Quadrant ML1 ...... 143 D3
Diana Vernon Ct G84 ...... 25 C4
Dick Cres KA12 ...... 219 E3
Dick Ct ML3 ...... 198 C1
Dick Institute Mus KA1 ...... 228 A4
Dick Quad G82 ...... 48 A4
Dick Rd KA1 ...... 228 A4
Dick St G20 ...... 96 C2
Dick Terr KA12 ...... 219 E3
Dickburn Cres FK4 ...... 39 E1
Dickens Ave G81 ...... 74 A2
Dickens Gr ML1 ...... 143 E1
Dickies Wells FK12 ...... 5 E4
Dickson Dr KA12 ...... 219 E3
Dickson Sq ML1 ...... 144 A1
Dickson St ML9 ...... 185 E1
Diddup Dr KA20 ...... 206 A1
Differ Ave G65 ...... 59 F1
Dillichip Cl G83 ...... 27 F1
Dillichip Gdns G83 ...... 27 F2
Dillichip Loan G83 ...... 27 F2
Dillichip Terr G83 ...... 27 F2
Dilwara Ave G14 ...... 95 F1
Dimity St PA5 ...... 111 F2
Dimsdale Cres ML2 ...... 165 E1
Dimsdale Rd ML2 ...... 165 E1
Dinard Dr G46 ...... 136 B2
Dinart St G34 ...... 98 B1
Dinduff St G34 ...... 100 B1
Dingwall Dr PA16 ...... 44 C2
Dinmont Ave PA2 ...... 112 C1
Dinmont Cres ML1 ...... 142 B1
Dinmont Pl [1] G41 ...... 116 C1
Dinmont Rd G41 ...... 116 B1
Dinmont Way PA2 ...... 112 C1
Dinmurchie Rd KA10 ...... 229 F3
Dinwiddie St G21 ...... 98 B1
Dinyra Pl ML5 ...... 101 E3
Dippin Pl ML1 ...... 205 F1
Dipple Ct KA25 ...... 149 D2
Dipple Pl G15 ...... 75 D1
Dipple Rd KA25 ...... 149 D2
Dipple View KA25 ...... 149 D2
Dirleton Dr Glasgow G41 ...... 136 C4
  Paisley PA2 ...... 113 D1
Dirleton Gate G61 ...... 75 E1
Dirleton Gdns FK10 ...... 9 F3
Dirleton La G12 ...... 96 A2
Dirrans Terr KA13 ...... 207 F1
Ditton Dr KA1 ...... 227 F2
Divernia Way G78 ...... 155 E4
Diverswell FK10 ...... 4 B3
Divert Rd PA19 ...... 44 B3
Divert Wlk PA19 ...... 44 B3
Dixon Ave Dumbarton G82 ...... 49 F2
  Glasgow G42 ...... 117 D1
Dixon Dr G82 ...... 49 E1
Dixon Pl G74 ...... 159 D2
Dixon Rd Glasgow G42 ...... 117 E1
  Helensburgh G84 ...... 16 C2
Dixon St Coatbridge ML5 ...... 122 A2
  Glasgow G1 ...... 240 C1
  Glasgow G3 ...... 162 B2
  Paisley PA1 ...... 113 F2
Dixons Blazes Ind Est
  G42, G5 ...... 117 E2
Doake Ave FK5 ...... 23 E1
Dobbie's Loan G4 ...... 241 D4
Dobbie's Loan Pl G4 ...... 241 E3
Dobbies St ML5 ...... 187 D3
Dochart Ave PA4 ...... 94 C1
Dochart Dr ML5 ...... 101 E1
Dochart Pl KA1 ...... 42 B1
Dochart St G33 ...... 98 C1
Dock Breast PA15 ...... 46 A3
Dock Rd KA22 ...... 205 D1
Dock St Clydebank G81 ...... 94 B4
  Falkirk FK2 ...... 24 B1
Dockhead Pl KA21 ...... 216 C4
Dockhead St KA21 ...... 216 C4
Dodhill Pl G13 ...... 95 D3
Dodside Gdns G32 ...... 119 E2
Dodside Pl G32 ...... 119 E2
Dodside Rd G77 ...... 155 F2
Dodside St G32 ...... 119 E2
Dolan St G69 ...... 120 A3
Dollar Park G71 ...... 42 A4
Dollar Pk [4] ML1 ...... 164 A2
Dollar Pl ML1 ...... 42 A3
Dollar Pk ML1 ...... 164 A2
Dollar Terr G20 ...... 96 B4
Dollin Aquacentre G72 ...... 159 F1
Dolphin Rd G41 ...... 116 B1
Dominica Av [4] G75 ...... 159 D1
Don Ave PA4 ...... 94 C1

Don Ct ML3 ...... 183 D4
Don Dr PA2 ...... 112 C1
Don Path ML9 ...... 199 D4
Don Pl PA5 ...... 131 E4
Don St Glasgow G33 ...... 98 B1
  Greenock PA16 ...... 45 E3
Donald Cres KA10 ...... 229 E2
Donald Terr ML3 ...... 162 B1
Donald Way G71 ...... 141 D4
Donald's Ct PA15 ...... 46 A3
Donaldfield Rd PA11 ...... 110 A4
Donaldson Ave Kilsyth G65 ...... 60 C4
  Saltcoats KA21 ...... 216 C4
  Stevenston KA20 ...... 206 C1
Donaldson Cres G66 ...... 79 E4
Donaldson Dr Irvine KA12 ...... 219 E2
  Kilmarnock KA3 ...... 223 E2
  Renfrew PA4 ...... 94 B2
Donaldson Gn G71 ...... 141 D4
Donaldson Pl Airdrie ML6 ...... 123 D4
  Cambusbarron FK7 ...... 6 B3
  Kirkintilloch G66 ...... 79 E4
Donaldson Rd
  Kilmarnock KA3 ...... 223 E2
  Larkhall ML9 ...... 185 E1
Donaldson St
  Hamilton ML3 ...... 162 A3
  Kirkintilloch G66 ......
Donaldswood Pk PA2 ...... 133 E4
Donaldswood Rd PA2 ...... 133 E4
Doncaster St G20 ...... 97 D2
Dongola Rd KA7 ...... 239 D4
Donnelly Way ML2 ...... 164 B2
Donnies Brae G78 ...... 154 C4
Doo'cot Brae FK10 ...... 10 A4
Doon Ave KA9 ...... 236 A3
Doon Cres G61 ...... 75 E2
Doon Ct KA12 ...... 219 E1
Doon Pl Kilmarnock KA1 ...... 228 A2
  Kirkintilloch G66 ...... 58 C1
  Saltcoats KA21 ...... 206 A2
  Symington KA1 ...... 231 E2
Doon Rd KA3 ...... 229 F3
Doon Rd G66 ...... 59 D1
Doon Side G67 ...... 62 A1
Doon St Clydebank G81 ...... 74 B2
  [2] Larkhall ML9 ...... 185 E1
  Motherwell ML1 ...... 164 A2
Doon Way G66 ...... 59 D1
Doonfoot Ct G74 ...... 159 E1
Doonfoot Gdns G74 ...... 159 E1
Doonfoot Prim Sch KA7 ...... 238 C2
Doonfoot Rd Ayr KA7 ...... 238 C2
  Glasgow G43 ...... 136 B3
Doonholm Pl KA7 ...... 238 C1
Doonholm Rd KA7 ...... 238 C1
Dora St G40 ...... 117 F2
Dorain Rd ML1 ...... 143 E2
Dorchester Ave G12 ...... 96 A3
Dorchester Ct G12 ...... 96 A3
Dorchester Pl G12 ...... 96 A3
Dorian Dr G76 ...... 157 E4
Dorlin Rd G33 ...... 99 F3
Dormanside Ct G53 ...... 115 D2
Dormanside Gate G53 ...... 115 D2
Dormanside Rd G53 ...... 115 E2
Dornal Ave G13 ...... 94 C4
Dornal Dr KA10 ...... 229 F3
Dornford Ave G32 ...... 119 F2
Dornford Rd G32 ...... 119 F2
Dornie Cl KA3 ...... 195 E1
Dornie Dr G32 ...... 139 D4
Dornie Path [2] ML7 ...... 165 F3
Dornoch Ave G46 ...... 136 B1
Dornoch Ct Bellshill ML4 ...... 142 A3
  Kilwinning KA13 ...... 207 D2
Dornoch Pk KA7 ...... 238 C3
Dornoch Pl
  Bishopbriggs G64 ...... 78 B1
  Chryston G69 ...... 80 B1
  East Kilbride G74 ...... 159 E1
  Motherwell ML3 ...... 143 D3
Dornoch St G40 ...... 117 F3
Dornoch Way Airdrie ML6 ...... 122 C3
  Cumbernauld G68 ...... 62 A3
Dorrator Rd FK1 ...... 41 F3
Dorset Rd PA16 ...... 44 C2
Dorset Sq G3 ...... 240 A3
Dorset St G3 ...... 240 A3
Dosk Ave G13 ...... 94 C4
Dosk Pl G13 ...... 94 C4
Double Edges Rd G78 ...... 154 B3
Dougalston Ave G62 ...... 55 D1
Dougalston Cres G62 ...... 55 D1
Dougalston Gdns N G62 ...... 55 D1
Dougalston Gdns S G62 ...... 55 D1
Dougalston Rd G23 ...... 76 C1
Douglas Acad G62 ...... 54 B2
Douglas Ave Dalry KA24 ...... 191 E3
  Elderslie PA5 ...... 112 A1
  Glasgow G46 ...... 136 B1
  Glasgow, Carmyle G32 ...... 119 D1
  Kirkintilloch G66 ...... 79 E3
  Langbank PA14 ...... 70 B4
  Prestwick KA9 ...... 236 A3
  Rutherglen G73 ...... 138 B3
Douglas Cres Airdrie ML6 ...... 123 D3
  Bishopton PA7 ...... 72 C2
  Hamilton ML3 ...... 183 E3
  Uddingston G71 ...... 141 D4
Douglas Ct G66 ...... 79 E3
  Troon KA10 ...... 229 E3

Douglas Dr Ashgill ML9 ...... 199 F4
Bellshill ML4 .... 142 B2
Bothwell G71 .... 141 D1
Cambuslang G72 ...... 138 C3
Clydebank G15 .... 74 C1
East Kilbride G75 .... 179 F4
Glasgow G69 .... 119 F3
Helensburgh G84 ..... 16 B2
Newton Mearns G77 ... 156 C3
Stirling FK7 .... 7 E2
Douglas Dr E G84 .... 16 C2
Douglas Gdns
 Bearsden G61 .... 75 F2
 Glasgow G46 .... 136 B1
 Kirkintilloch G66 ... 79 E3
 Uddingston G71 ..... 140 C3
Douglas La Ayr KA7 ... 238 C4
 Glasgow G2 .... 240 B3
Douglas Muir Dr G62 . 54 B1
Douglas Muir Gdns G62 . 54 B2
Douglas Muir Pl G62 . 54 B2
Douglas Muir Rd
 Clydebank G81 ..... 74 B4
 Milngavie G62 ..... 54 B1
Douglas Park Cres G61 . 76 A3
Douglas Park La ML3 . 162 B2
Douglas Pl Bearsden G61 . 75 F3
 Coatbridge ML5 .... 121 F3
 Hamilton ML3 ...... 183 E3
 Kirkintilloch G66 .. 79 E3
 Stenhousemuir FK5 . 23 F2
Douglas Rd Dumbarton G82 . 50 A2
 Renfrew PA4 .... 114 A4
Douglas St Airdrie ML6 . 123 D3
 Ayr KA7 .... 238 C4
 Bannockburn FK7 ... 7 F1
 Blantyre G72 ...... 161 E3
 Carluke ML8 .... 187 F1
 Glasgow G2 .... 240 B3
 Hamilton ML3 ...... 162 B2
 Kilmarnock KA1 .... 227 F4
 Larkhall ML9 ...... 185 D2
 Milngavie G62 ..... 55 D1
 Motherwell ML1 .... 163 E3
 Paisley PA1 .... 113 E3
 Stirling FK8 ...... 2 A1
 Uddingston G71 .... 141 D4
 Wishaw ML2 .... 186 B4
Douglas St Glasgow G41 . 116 C1
 Renfrew PA3 .... 93 F1
 Stirling FK7 ...... 6 C3
Douglas View ML5 .... 121 F2
Douglasdale G74 ..... 159 E1
Doughiehill Pl PA14 . 68 B4
Doughiehill Rd PA14 . 68 B4
Dougray Pl G78 ..... 134 B1
Dougrie Dr G45 ..... 137 E2
Dougrie Gdns G45 ... 137 F2
Dougrie Pl G45 ..... 137 F2
Dougrie Rd G45 ..... 137 E2
Dougrie St G45 ..... 137 F2
Dougrie Terr G45 ... 137 E2
Doune Cres
 Bishopbriggs G64 ... 78 A2
 Chapelhall ML6 .... 123 E1
 Newton Mearns G77 . 156 C3
 Stenhousemuir FK5 . 24 A2
Doune Gardens La G20 . 96 C2
Doune Gdns Glasgow G20 . 96 C2
 Gourock PA19 ...... 44 A3
Doune Quadrant G20 . 96 C2
Doune Terr ML5 ..... 101 E1
Doura Dr KA11 ...... 219 F3
Doura Pl KA12 ...... 219 E3
Dove Pl G75 .... 179 F3
Dove St G53 .... 135 D3
Dove Wynd ML4 ..... 141 F4
Dovecot G43 .... 136 B4
Dovecot La Kilwinning KA13 . 207 F2
 Lanark ML11 .... 215 D2
Dovecot Pl FK10 .... 4 A2
Dovecot Rd FK10 ... 4 A2
Dovecote View G66 . 79 F4
Dovecothall St G78 . 134 B2
Dovecotwood G65 .. 36 B1
Dovehill FK10 ..... 10 A4
Doveholm G82 ..... 50 A3
Doveholm Ave G82 . 50 A3
Dover St Coatbridge ML5 . 101 E1
 Glasgow G3 .... 240 A3
Dowan Pl FK7 ..... 6 C3
Dowan Rd G62 .... 55 F1
Dowanfield Rd G67 . 61 F1
Dowanhill Prim Sch G11 . 96 B1
Dowanhill St G11 .. 96 B1
Dowanside La G12 . 96 B2
Dowanside Rd G12 . 96 B2
Downcraig Dr G45 . 137 E1
Downcraig Gr G45 . 137 E1
Downcraig Rd G45 . 137 E1
Downcraig Terr G45 . 137 E2
Downfield Dr ML3 . 183 D4
Downfield Gdns G72 . 140 C1
Downfield St G32 .. 118 C2
Downhill St G12 ... 96 B2
Downie St ML3 .... 183 F1
Downiebrae Rd G73 . 118 A1
Downs Cres FK10 .. 9 F3
Downs St G21 ..... 97 F3
Dowrie Cres G53 .. 135 D3
Draffan Rd ML9 ... 200 A1
Draffen Ct ML1 ... 163 F4
Draffen St ML1 ... 163 F4
Drake St G40 ..... 117 F3

Drakemire Ave G45 ... 137 E2
Drakemire Dr G45 ... 137 E2
Dreghorn Prim Sch KA11 . 220 B1
Dreghorn Rd KA11 ... 225 E3
Dreghorn St G31 .... 118 B4
Dreisling Rd PA15 .. 45 F2
Drimnin Rd G33 ..... 99 F3
Drip Rd FK8 .... 1 C1
Drive David Gray G66 . 59 D1
Drive Rd G51 .... 115 F4
Drochil St G34 ..... 100 A1
Dromore St G66 .... 79 E4
Drossie Rd FK1 ..... 42 A2
Drove Hill G68 ..... 61 D2
Drove Loan FK6 .... 39 F3
Drove Loan Cres FK6 . 39 F4
Druid Dr KA13 ..... 207 F2
Drum Mains Pk G68 . 81 E4
Drumadoon Dr G84 . 16 C1
Drumaling Terr G65 . 57 F4
Drumbathie Rd ML6 . 123 E4
Drumbeg Dr G53 ... 135 D3
Drumbeg Pl G53 ... 135 D3
Drumbeg Terr G62 . 54 B1
Drumbottie Rd G21 . 98 A3
Drumbreck Pl G66 . 79 F4
Drumbreck Rd G62 . 54 B1
Drumby Cres G76 .. 157 E4
Drumby Dr G76 .... 157 E4
Drumcarn Dr G62 .. 54 C1
Drumcavel Rd G69 . 100 C4
Drumchapel Gdns G15 . 75 D1
Drumchapel High Sch G15 . 75 D2
Drumchapel Hospl G15 . 75 D1
Drumchapel Pl G15 . 75 D1
Drumchapel Rd G15 . 75 D1
Drumchapel Sh Ctr G81 . 74 C2
Drumchapel Sta G15 . 75 D1
Drumclair Ave FK1 . 86 A3
Drumclair Pl ML6 .. 123 E4
Drumclog Ave G62 . 55 D2
Drumclog Gdns G33 . 98 C3
Drumclog Pl KA3 .. 223 D2
Drumcross Rd Bowling G60 . 72 B2
 Glasgow G53 ...... 115 E1
Drumduff G75 ..... 180 B3
Drumellan Rd KA7 . 239 D1
Drumelzier Ct KA11 . 220 A2
Drumfin Ave ML6 .. 104 C2
Drumfork Ct G84 .. 25 C4
Drumfork Rd G84 . 25 D4
Drumfrochar Pl PA15 . 45 F2
Drumfrochar Rd PA15 . 45 F2
Drumgarve Ct G84 . 16 B1
Drumgelloch St ML6 . 123 E4
Drumgelloch Sta ML6 . 123 E4
Drumgray Gdns ML6 . 83 E1
Drumgray La ML6 .. 83 E1
Drumhead Pl G32 . 118 C1
Drumhead Rd G32 . 118 C1
Drumhill G66 ..... 59 D1
Drumilaw Cres G73 . 138 A3
Drumilaw Rd G73 . 138 A3
Drumilaw Way G73 . 138 A3
Drumillan Hill PA16 . 44 B1
Drumkinnon Rd G83 . 27 E4
Drumlaken Ave G23 . 76 B1
Drumlaken Ct G23 . 76 B1
Drumlaken Path G23 . 76 B1
Drumlaken Pl G23 . 76 B1
Drumlaken St G23 . 76 B1
Drumlanford Rd KA10 . 229 F3
Drumlanrig Pl
 G34 .... 120 A4
Drumlanrig Quadrant
 G34 .... 120 A4
Drumley Ave KA6 .. 237 F3
Drumleyhill Dr KA1 . 228 C3
Drumlin Dr G62 ... 76 A4
Drumloch Gdns G75 . 180 C3
Drumlochy Rd G33 . 99 D1
Drummilling Ave KA23 . 190 B3
Drummilling Dr KA23 . 190 B3
Drummilling Rd KA23 . 190 B3
Drummond Ave G73 . 137 F4
Drummond Cres KA8 . 236 C1
Drummond Dr
 Paisley PA1 .... 114 B2
 Wishaw ML2 .... 165 D1
Drummond Hill G74 . 160 A2
Drummond House G67 . 62 A2
Drummond La FK8 . 7 D3
Drummond Pl
 Blackridge EH48 ... 107 E2
 Bonnybridge FK4 .. 40 A4
 East Kilbride G74 . 160 A2
 Falkirk FK1 ...... 41 F2
 Kilmarnock KA3 ... 223 E1
 Stirling FK8 ..... 7 D3
Drummond Place La FK8 . 7 D3
Drummond St PA16 . 45 E2
Drummond Way G77 . 156 A3
Drummore Ave ML5 . 122 B2
Drummore Dr FK5 . 23 D2
Drummore Sch G15 . 75 E2
Drummuir Foot KA11 . 220 A3
Drumnessie Ct G68 . 81 F4
Drumnessie Rd G68 . 81 F4
Drumnessie View G68 . 81 F4
Drumover Dr G31 . 118 C3
Drumoyne Ave G51 . 115 F4
Drumoyne Cir G51 . 115 F3
Drumoyne Dr G51 . 115 F4
Drumoyne Pl G51 . 115 F3
Drumoyne Prim Sch G51 . 115 F4
Drumoyne Quadrant G51 . 115 F3

Drumoyne Rd G51 ... 115 F4
Drumoyne Sq G51 ... 115 F4
Drumpark Specl Sch ML5 . 121 D3
Drumpark St
 Coatbridge ML5 .... 121 E2
 Glasgow G46 ...... 135 F2
 Stirling FK7 ...... 7 D2
Drumpellier Ave
 Coatbridge ML5 ... 121 E3
 Cumbernauld G67 .. 82 B4
 Glasgow G69 ...... 120 A2
Drumpellier Cres ML5 . 121 E3
Drumpellier Ct G67 . 82 B4
Drumpellier Ctry Pk ML5 . 121 E4
Drumpellier Gdns G67 . 82 B4
Drumpellier Gr G67 . 82 B4
Drumpellier Pl
 Cumbernauld G67 .. 82 B4
 Glasgow G69 ...... 120 A2
Drumpellier Rd G69 . 120 A2
Drumpellier St G33 . 98 B1
Drumreoch Dr G42 . 137 F4
Drumreoch Pl G42 . 137 F4
Drumriggend Rd FK1 . 85 E2
Drumry Prim Sch G15 . 74 C2
Drumry Rd G81 .... 74 B2
Drumry Rd E G15 .. 74 C1
Drumry Sta G81 ... 74 B1
Drums Ave PA3 .... 113 E3
Drums Cres PA3 ... 113 E3
Drums Rd G53 .... 115 D2
Drums Terr PA16 .. 45 D4
Drumsack Ave G69 . 100 B4
Drumsargard Rd G73 . 138 B3
Drumshangie St ML6 . 103 D1
Drumshantie Rd PA19 . 44 C3
Drumshantie Terr PA19 . 44 C4
Drumshaw Dr G32 . 139 E4
Drumslea PA16 .... 45 E4
Drumtrocher St G65 . 60 B4
Drumvale Dr G69 .. 80 C1
Drury La G46 ..... 45 D4
Drury St G2 ...... 240 C2
Dryad St G46 ..... 135 F3
Drybridge Rd KA2 . 225 F1
Dryburgh Ave Denny FK6 . 21 E1
 Paisley PA2 .... 113 D1
 Rutherglen G73 ... 138 A4
Dryburgh Gdns G20 . 96 C2
Dryburgh Hill G74 . 159 E1
Dryburgh La G74 .. 159 E1
Dryburgh Pl
 Coatbridge ML5 ... 121 F4
 Kirkintilloch G66 . 79 F4
Dryburgh Rd Bearsden G61 . 75 E3
 Wishaw ML2 ...... 165 D2
Dryburgh St ML3 .. 162 A3
Dryburgh Way G72 . 161 E4
Dryburgh Wlk G69 . 81 D2
Dryden St G46 .... 115 D3
Drygate G4 .... 241 F2
Drygate St ML9 ... 185 D2
Drygrange Rd G33 . 99 E1
Drymen Pl G66 .... 79 E2
Drymen Rd Balloch G83 . 19 F1
 Bearsden G61 ..... 75 F2
Drymen St G52 .... 115 F3
Drynoch Pl G22 ... 97 D4
Drysdale St Alloa FK10 . 10 A3
 Glasgow G14 ...... 94 C3
Duart Ave KA9 .... 236 B4
Duart Cres KA9 ... 236 B4
Duart Dr East Kilbride G74 . 159 E2
 Elderslie PA5 ..... 112 B1
 Newton Mearns G77 . 157 D3
Duart St G20 ..... 96 B4
Dubbs Rd Kilwinning KA13 . 207 D1
 Port Glasgow PA14 . 68 A4
 Stevenston KA20 .. 206 C1
Dubs Rd G78 ...... 134 C2
Dubton St G34 .... 100 A1
Duchal Rd PA13 ... 89 E4
Duchal St PA14 ... 68 A4
Duchall Pl G14 ... 95 D2
Duchess Ct ML3 .. 163 D1
Duchess Dr G84 .. 16 A2
Duchess Palace G73 . 138 B4
Duchess Pl G73 ... 138 B4
Duchess Rd G73 .. 118 B1
Duchray Dr PA1 .. 114 C2
Duchray La G33 .. 98 B1
Duchray St G33 .. 98 B1
Ducraig St G32 .. 119 D3
Duddingston Ave KA13 . 207 D2
Dudhope St G33 .. 99 E1
Dudley Dr Coatbridge ML5 . 101 E1
 Glasgow G12 ..... 96 A2
Dudley La G12 ... 96 A2
Duff Cres FK8 ... 1 C1
Duff Pl Kilmarnock KA3 . 223 E2
 Saltcoats KA21 .. 206 A1
Duff St PA15 .... 46 A3
Duffus Pl G32 ... 139 E4
Duffus St G34 ... 100 A1
Duffus Terr G32 . 139 E4
Duguid St KA21 .. 206 A1
Duich Gdns G23 . 76 C1
Duisdale Rd G32 . 139 E4
Duke St Alva FK12 . 5 F1
 Bannockburn FK7 . 7 E1
 Denny FK6 ...... 21 E1
 Glasgow G31 .... 118 A3
 Hamilton ML3 ... 162 C2
 Larkhall ML9 ... 185 D2
 Motherwell ML1 . 163 F4
 Paisley PA2 .... 113 F1
 Wishaw ML2 .... 165 F3

Duke Street Sta G31 ... 118 A4
Duke Terr KA9 ...... 236 A1
Duke's Rd G73 ..... 138 B3
Dukes Gate G71 .... 140 C2
Dukes Pl ML3 ...... 183 E3
Dukes Rd Coatbridge G69 . 120 C3
 Troon KA10 .... 229 D2
Dullatur Rdbt G68 . 61 F3
Dulnain St G72 .... 139 F3
Dulsie Rd G21 ..... 98 B3
Dumbain Cres G83 . 28 A4
Dumbain Rd G83 .. 20 A1
Dumbarton Acad G82 . 50 A2
Dumbarton Central Sta
 G82 .... 49 F2
Dumbarton Cottage Hospl
 G82 .... 49 F3
Dumbarton East G82 . 50 A2
Dumbarton Joint Hospl
 G82 .... 49 E2
Dumbarton Rd Bowling G60 . 72 B4
 Clydebank G60, G81 . 73 E2
 Glasgow G14 ..... 94 C3
 Glasgow, Partick G11 . 96 A1
 Milton G82 ...... 50 C1
 Stirling FK8 .... 6 C3
Dumbreck Ave G41 . 116 A2
Dumbreck Ct G41 . 116 A2
Dumbreck Pl G41 . 116 A2
Dumbreck Rd G41 . 116 A2
Dumbreck Sq G41 . 116 A2
Dumbreck Sta G41 . 116 B2
Dumbreck Terr G65 . 59 F4
Dumbrock Cres G63 . 31 E2
Dumbrock Dr G63 . 31 D2
Dumbrock Rd G63 . 31 E2
Dumbuck Cres G82 . 50 B1
Dumbuck Gdns G82 . 50 A1
Dumbuck Rd G82 . 50 B2
Dumbuie Ave G82 . 50 A2
Dumfries Cres ML6 . 122 C3
Dumfriespark KA6 . 237 D1
Dumgoyne Ave G62 . 54 C1
Dumgoyne Ct ML6 . 103 D1
Dumgoyne Dr G61 . 75 E4
Dumgoyne Gdns G62 . 54 C1
Dumgoyne Pl G76 . 157 E4
Dumyat Ave FK10 . 4 A1
Dumyat Dr FK1 ... 41 F2
Dumyat Rd Alva FK12 . 4 C3
 Menstrie FK11 ... 3 F3
Dumyat St FK10 .. 4 C1
Dun Pk G66 ...... 79 F4
Dunagoil Rd G45 . 137 E1
Dunagoil St G45 . 137 F1
Dunalastair Dr G33 . 99 F3
Dunalistair Dr G33 . 99 D3
Dunan Pl G33 .... 119 F4
Dunard Ct ML8 ... 187 F2
Dunard Rd G73 .. 138 A4
Dunard St G20 ... 96 C2
Dunard Way PA3 . 113 E4
Dunaskin St G11 . 96 B1
Dunavon Pl ML5 . 122 B2
Dunbar Ave
 Coatbridge ML5 . 121 E2
 Johnstone PA5 .. 131 F4
 Rutherglen G73 . 138 B4
 Stenhousemuir FK5 . 23 F2
Dunbar Dr ML1 .. 164 A2
Dunbar Gate FK6 . 21 F2
Dunbar Hill G74 . 159 E1
Dunbar Pl G74 .. 159 E1
Dunbar Rd PA2 .. 113 D1
Dunbeath Ave G77 . 156 C3
Dunbeith Pl G20 . 96 B3
Dunbeth Ave ML5 . 122 A4
Dunbeth Ct ML5 . 122 A4
Dunbeth Rd ML5 . 122 A4
Dunblane Dr G74 . 159 F1
Dunblane Pl
 Coatbridge ML5 . 121 F2
 East Kilbride G74 . 159 F1
Dunblane St G4 .. 240 C4
Dunbrach Rd G68 . 61 E2
Dunbritton Rd G82 . 50 B2
Duncairn Ave FK4 . 39 F3
Duncan Ave Falkirk FK2 . 24 A2
 Glasgow G14 .... 95 E2
Duncan Ct Kilmarnock KA3 . 223 E2
 Motherwell ML1 . 142 B1
Duncan Dr KA12 . 219 E1
Duncan Graham St ML9 . 185 D2
Duncan La N G14 . 95 E2
Duncan La S G14 . 95 E2
Duncan McIntosh Rd G68 . 62 B4
Duncan Rd Helensburgh G84 . 16 C2
 Kilmarnock KA3 .. 223 E2
Duncan St Bonnybridge FK4 . 39 F3
 Clydebank G81 ... 74 A2
 Greenock PA15 ... 45 F3
Duncan's Ct ML11 . 215 D2
Duncanrig Secd Sch G75 . 159 E1
Duncansby Rd G33 . 119 E4
Duncarnock Ave G78 . 154 C4
Duncarnock Cres G78 . 154 C4
Duncarron Ind Est FK6 . 21 F1
Duncarron Pl FK6 . 21 E1
Dunchattan Gr KA10 . 229 F1
Dunchattan Pl G31 . 117 F4

Dunchattan St G31 ... 117 F4
Dunchattan Way KA10 . 229 F1
Dunchurch Rd PA1 ... 114 B3
Dunclutha Dr G71 ... 141 D1
Dunclutha St G40 ... 118 A1
Duncolm Pl G62 .... 54 B1
Duncombe Ave G81 . 74 A4
Duncombe St G20 .. 96 B4
Duncombe View G81 . 74 B2
Duncraig Cres PA5 . 131 E4
Duncruin Dr G64 ... 77 F1
Duncruin St G20 ... 96 B4
Duncruin Terr G20 . 96 B4
Duncryne Ave G32 . 119 F2
Duncryne Gdns G32 . 119 F2
Duncryne Pl G64 .. 97 F4
Duncryne Rd
 Alexandria G83 ... 27 F3
 Balloch G83 ..... 20 C4
 Glasgow G32 .... 119 E2
Dundaff Ct FK6 ... 21 E1
Dundaff Hill G68 . 61 E1
Dundarroch St FK5 . 23 D1
Dundas Ave G64 .. 78 A4
Dundas Cotts FK4 . 39 D1
Dundas Ct G74 ... 159 F1
Dundas La G1 .... 241 D3
Dundas Pl G74 ... 159 F1
Dundas St G1 .... 241 D3
Dundas Wlk KA3 . 223 E2
Dundashill G4 ... 97 D2
Dundasvale Ct G4 . 240 C4
Dundee Ct FK2 ... 42 A4
Dundee Dr G52 .. 115 D2
Dundee Pl FK2 ... 42 A4
Dundonald Ave PA5 . 111 E1
Dundonald Castle KA2 . 225 F1
Dundonald Cres
 Newton Mearns G77 . 157 D2
 Troon KA11 ...... 224 C1
Dundonald Ct KA4 . 222 D3
Dundonald Dr ML3 . 183 E4
Dundonald Pl G78 . 154 B4
Dundonald Prim Sch KA2 . 225 F1
Dundonald Rd Glasgow G12 . 96 B2
 Irvine KA11 ...... 224 C1
 Kilmarnock KA1 .. 227 E4
 Paisley PA3 ..... 114 A4
 Troon KA10 ..... 229 F2
Dundonald St G72 . 161 E4
Dundrennan Rd G42 . 136 C4
Dundyvan La ML2 . 165 D1
Dundyvan Rd ML5 . 121 F3
Dundyvan St ML2 . 165 D1
Dundyvan Way ML5 . 121 F3
Dunearn St G4 ... 96 C1
Dunearn Pl PA2 .. 114 A2
Dunearn Wynd ML9 . 185 D1
Dunedin Ct G75 . 180 A4
Dunedin Dr G75 . 180 A4
Dunedin Rd ML9 . 185 D1
Dunedin Terr G81 . 94 B4
Dunellan Ave G69 . 81 D1
Dunellan Cres G69 . 81 D1
Dunellan Dr G81 . 74 A4
Dunellan Gdns G69 . 81 D1
Dunellan Rd G62 . 54 B1
Dunellan St G52 . 115 F3
Dungavel Gdns ML3 . 183 F4
Dungavel Rd KA1 . 228 A2
Dungeonhill Rd G34 . 120 B4
Dunglass Ave
 East Kilbride G74 . 159 F2
 Glasgow G14 .... 95 E2
Dunglass La G N G14 . 95 E2
Dunglass La S G14 . 95 E2
Dunglass Pl Milngavie G62 . 54 C2
 Newton Mearns G77 . 156 A3
Dunglass Rd PA7 . 72 B1
Dunglass Sq G74 . 159 F2
Dunglass View G63 . 31 E2
Dungoil Ave G68 . 61 D2
Dungoil Rd G66 . 79 F2
Dungourney Dr PA16 . 45 E4
Dungoyne St G20 . 96 B4
Dunholme Pk G81 . 73 E2
Dunipace Prim Sch FK6 . 21 E2
Dunira St G32 ... 118 C2
Dunivaig St G33 . 119 F4
Dunkeld Ave G73 . 138 A4
Dunkeld Dr G61 . 76 A2
Dunkeld Gdns G64 . 78 A1
Dunkeld La G69 . 81 D1
Dunkeld Pl Coatbridge ML5 . 121 F2
 Hamilton ML3 ... 161 F2
 Newton Mearns G77 . 157 D2
Dunkeld St ML1 . 163 F3
Dunkenny Pl G15 . 74 C2
Dunkenny Rd G15 . 74 C2
Dunlin G12 ..... 96 B3
Dunlin Cres PA6 . 91 E1
Dunlin Ct ML4 .. 141 F4
Dunlop Cres Ayr KA8 . 236 B1
 Bothwell G71 ... 141 D1
Dunlop Ct ML11 . 215 D2
Dunlop Gr G71 .. 121 D1
Dunlop Pl Airdrie ML6 . 103 D1
 Milngavie G62 .. 54 C2
Dunlop Prim Sch KA3 . 195 D4
Dunlop Rd Barrmill KA15 . 172 A2
 Lugton KA3 .... 173 E3
 Stewarton KA3 .. 195 E1

Dunlop St Cambuslang G72 .. 139 F3
Fenwick KA3 .... 213 D2
Glasgow G1 .... 241 D1
Greenock PA16 .... 45 E2
Kilmarnock KA1 .... 222 C1
Linwood PA3 .... 112 B3
Renfrew PA4 .... 94 B2
Stewarton KA3 .... 195 F1
Dunlop Terr KA8 .... 236 B1
Dunmar Cres FK10 .... 4 C1
Dunmar Dr FK10 .... 4 C1
Dunmore Dr G62 .... 76 B4
Dunmore St Clydebank G81 .... 94 B4
Dunn Mews KA1 .... 227 E4
Dunn St Clydebank G81 .... 73 E2
Clydebank, Dalmuir G81 .... 73 F2
Glasgow G40 .... 118 A2
Greenock PA15 .... 45 F2
Paisley PA1 .... 114 A2
Dunn Terr ML7 .... 127 F3
Dunnachie Dr ML3 .... 121 D2
Dunnet Ave ML6 .... 102 C3
Dunnett Ave KA1 .... 228 A4
Dunnichen Gdns G64 .... 78 B1
Dunnikier Wlk G68 .... 60 C1
Dunning PF K2 .... 24 B1
Dunning St G31 .... 118 B2
Dunnolar Wlk ML2 .... 165 F3
Dunnottar Cres G74 .... 159 E2
Dunnottar Dr FK5 .... 23 F2
Dunnottar St
   Bishopbriggs G64 .... 78 B1
   Glasgow G33 .... 99 D1
Dunnottar Ave ML5 .... 156 C3
Dunollie Gdns KA3 .... 223 D3
Dunolly Dr G77 .... 156 C3
Dunolly St G21 .... 98 A1
Dunoon Ave KA3 .... 222 C2
Dunottar Ave ML5 .... 122 A1
Dunphail Dr G34 .... 100 B1
Dunphail Rd G34 .... 100 B4
Dunragit St G31 .... 118 B4
Dunrobin Ave
   Elderslie PA5 .... 112 B1
   Stenhousemuir FK5 .... 23 F3
Dunrobin Cres G74 .... 159 E2
Dunrobin Ct G74 .... 159 E2
Dunrobin Dr
   East Kilbride G74 .... 159 E2
   Gourock PA19 .... 43 F3
Dunrobin PA15 .... 121 F4
Dunrobin Prim Sch ML6 .... 123 F4
Dunrobin Rd ML6 .... 123 F4
Dunrobin St G31 .... 118 A3
Dunrod Hill G74 .... 159 F2
Dunrod St G32 .... 119 D2
Duns Cres ML2 .... 165 E4
Duns Path ML5 .... 122 B2
Dunscore Brae ML3 .... 161 F1
Dunside Dr G53 .... 135 D3
Dunsiston Rd ML6 .... 124 A2
Dunskaith Pl G34 .... 120 B4
Dunskaith St G34 .... 120 B4
Dunskey Rd KA3 .... 223 D3
Dunsmore Rd PA7 .... 72 A2
Dunsmuir St G51 .... 116 A4
Dunster Gdns G64 .... 78 A2
   8 .... 78 B2
Dunswin Ave G81 .... 73 F2
Dunsyre Pl G23 .... 76 C1
Dunsyre St G33 .... 118 C4
Duntarvie Ave G34 .... 120 B4
Duntarvie Cl G34 .... 120 B4
Duntarvie Cres G34 .... 120 B4
Duntarvie Dr G34 .... 120 A4
Duntarvie Gdns G34 .... 120 B4
Duntarvie Pl G34 .... 120 A4
Duntarvie Quadrant G34 .... 120 B4
Duntarvie Rd G34 .... 120 B4
Duntarvie Ave G13 .... 95 D3
Duntarvie Ct G78 .... 134 B2
Duntiblae Rd 80 A4
Duntiglennan Rd G81 .... 74 A3
Duntilland Ave ML7 .... 127 F4
Duntilland Rd Airdrie ML6 ... 124 C4
   Salsburgh ML7 .... 125 E3
Duntocher Rd
   Bearsden G61 .... 75 D3
   Clydebank G81 .... 74 A2
   Clydebank, Radnor Pk G81 .. 74 A2
Duntonknoll KA12 .... 219 E2
Duntreath Ave G15, G13 .... 74 C1
Duntreath Dr G15 .... 74 C1
Duntreath Gdns G15 .... 74 C1
Duntreath Gr G15 .... 74 C1
Duntreath Terr G65 .... 60 B4
Duntroon Pl ML4 .... 142 A2
Duntroon St G31 .... 118 A4
Dunure Courts KA13 .... 207 E2
Dunure Cres FK4 .... 40 A3
Dunure Dr Hamilton ML3 ... 161 F1
   Kilmarnock KA3 .... 228 A4
   Newton Mearns G77 .... 157 D3
   Rutherglen G73 .... 137 E3
Dunure Pl Coatbridge ML5 ... 121 F2
   Kilmarnock KA3 .... 223 D3
   Newton Mearns G77 .... 157 D2
Dunure Rd KA7 .... 238 B1
Dunure St Bonnybridge FK4 .. 40 A3
   Glasgow G20 .... 96 B4
Dunvegan Ave 102 C2
Dunvegan Ave
   Coatbridge ML5 .... 101 E1
   Elderslie PA5 .... 112 B1
   Stenhousemuir FK5 .... 23 F2
Dunvegan Ct FK10 .... 10 A3

Dunvegan Dr
   Bishopbriggs G64 .... 78 A2
   Falkirk FK2 .... 24 B1
   Newton Mearns G77 .... 157 D3
   Stirling FK9 .... 2 A2
Dunvegan Pl
   Bonnybridge FK4 .... 39 F3
   East Kilbride G74 .... 159 E2
   Irvine KA12 .... 219 E3
   Uddingston G71 .... 140 B4
Dunvegan Quadrant PA4 .... 94 A2
Dunwan Ave G13 .... 94 C4
Dunwan Pl G13 .... 94 C4
Dura Rd ML7 .... 167 E3
Durban Ave Clydebank G81 .. 73 E2
   East Kilbride G75 .... 180 A2
Durham Rd PA16 .... 44 C3
Durisdeer Dr ML3 .... 161 F1
Durness Ave G61 .... 76 A2
Duror St G32 .... 119 D3
Duris Gdns G32 .... 119 E2
Durrockstock Cres PA2 ...... 132 C4
Durrockstock Rd PA2 .... 132 C4
Durrockstock Way PA2 ...... 132 C4
Durward G74 .... 160 A2
Durward Ave G41 .... 116 B1
Durward Cres PA2 .... 112 C1
Durward Ct Glasgow G41 ... 116 B1
   Motherwell ML1 .... 142 B1
Durward Way ML7 .... 112 C1
Duthie Rd PA19 .... 45 D4
Duthil St G51 .... 115 E3
Dyce Ave ML6 .... 122 C2
Dyce La G11 .... 96 A1
Dyer's La G1 .... 241 E1
Dyers' Wynd PA1 .... 113 F3
Dyfrig St Blantyre G72 .... 161 E4
   Shotts ML7 .... 146 C3
Dyke Rd G13 .... 95 D4
Dyke St Coatbridge ML5 .... 122 B2
   Glasgow G69 .... 120 B3
Dykebar Ave G13 .... 95 D3
Dykebar Cres PA2 .... 114 A1
Dykebar Hospl PA2 .... 134 A1
Dykehead Cres ML6 .... 102 C1
Dykehead Dr G65 .... 60 C3
Dykehead La G33 .... 119 E4
Dykehead Prim Sch ML7 .... 146 C3
Dykehead Rd Airdrie ML6 .. 103 D2
   Bargeddie G69 .... 121 D3
   Cumbernauld G68 .... 61 E3
   Queenzieburn G65 .... 59 F4
Dykehead Sq ML3 .... 161 E2
Dykehead St G33 .... 119 E4
Dykemuir Pl G21 .... 98 A2
Dykemuir Quadrant G21 ... 98 A2
Dykemuir St G21 .... 98 A2
Dykeneuk Rd PA14 .... 68 B4
Dykes Pl KA21 .... 205 F1
Dykes The KA25 .... 170 A4
Dykesfield Pl KA21 .... 205 F1
Dykesmains Prim Sch 205 F2
Dysart Way ML6 .... 124 A3
Eagle Cres G61 .... 75 D3
Eagle St G4 .... 97 E1
Eaglesham Ct 1 G51 .... 116 C3
Eaglesham Path ML5 .... 101 E3
Eaglesham Pl 2 G51 .... 116 C3
Eaglesham Prim Sch G76 .. 178 C2
Eaglesham Rd
   Clarkston G76 .... 157 F3
   East Kilbride G75 .... 179 E4
   Newton Mearns G77 .... 156 B2
Earl Ave ML6 .... 103 D3
Earl Dr KA2 .... 225 F1
Earl Haig Rd G52 .... 114 C4
Earl La G14 .... 95 E2
Earl Of Mar Ct FK10 .... 10 A3
Earl Pl Bridge Of W PA11 ... 110 B3
   Glasgow G14 .... 95 E2
Earl St G14 .... 95 D2
Earl View ML1 .... 143 D2
Earl's Gate G71 .... 140 C2
Earl's Hill G68 .... 61 D2
Earlbank Ave G14 .... 95 E2
Earlbank La N G14 .... 95 E2
Earlbank La S G14 .... 95 E2
Earls Ct KA10 .... 10 A3
Earls Way KA7 .... 238 B1
Earlsburn Ave FK7 .... 7 D2
Earlsburn Rd G66 .... 79 F2
Earlscourt G69 .... 80 C1
Earlshill Dr Bannockburn FK7 .. 7 F1
   Howwood PA9 .... 130 C3
Earlspark Ave G43 .... 136 C3
Earlston Ave KA1 .... 227 F2
Earlston Cres ML5 .... 122 B2
Earn Ave Bearsden G61 .... 76 A2
   Bellshill ML4 .... 141 F3
   Renfrew PA4 .... 94 C1
Earn Cres ML2 .... 165 D1
Earn Ct FK10 .... 10 A3
Earn Gdns ML9 .... 199 D4
Earn Loan ML1 .... 143 D3
Earn Pl Denny FK6 .... 39 E3
   Kilmarnock KA1 .... 228 A3
Earn Rd
   Newton Mearns G77 .... 156 B4
   Troon KA10 .... 229 F2
Earn St G33 .... 98 C1
Earn Terr ML7 .... 146 C3

Earncraig Gn KA11 .... 220 A2
Earnhill Rd PA16 .... 44 B3
Earnock Ave ML1 .... 163 E1
Earnock H Sch ML3 .... 162 A1
Earnock Rd ML3 .... 161 F1
Earnock St Glasgow G33 ..... 98 B2
   Hamilton ML3 .... 162 A2
Earnside St G32 .... 119 D2
Easdale G74 .... 181 D4
Easdale Dr G32 .... 119 D2
Easdale Path ML5 .... 101 E3
Easdale Pl G77 .... 156 A3
Easdale Rise ML3 .... 161 F2
East Academy St ML2 .... 165 D1
East Ave Carluke ML8 .... 187 E1
   Hamilton G72 .... 161 F3
   Motherwell ML1 .... 143 D1
   Plains ML6 .... 104 A2
   Renfrew PA4 .... 94 B2
East Barns St G81 .... 94 B4
East Bath La G2 .... 241 D3
East Blackhall St PA15 ...... 46 A2
East Boreland Pl FK6 .... 21 F1
East Bowhouse Head
   KA11 .... 220 A3
East Bowhouse Way
   KA11 .... 220 A3
East Breast PA15 .... 46 A3
East Bridge St FK1, G2 ...... 42 A2
East Broomlands KA11 ...... 220 A1
East Buchanan St PA1 ...... 113 F3
East Burnside St G65 .... 60 B4
East Campbell St G1 .... 241 F1
East Castle St FK10 .... 10 A3
East Crawford St ML6 .... 46 B2
East Dean St ML4 .... 142 A3
East Dr ML1 .... 23 E1
East Faulds Rd ML11 .... 215 F3
East Fulton Prim Sch PA3 .. 111 F3
East Gargieston Ave KA1 .. 227 E3
East Gate Glenboig ML5 .... 101 E4
   Wishaw ML2 .... 165 E2
East George St ML5 .... 122 A4
East Glebe Terr ML3 .... 162 A1
East Greenlees Ave G72 ... 139 E2
East Greenlees Cres G72 .. 139 E2
East Greenlees Dr G72 ..... 139 E2
East Greenlees Gr G72 ..... 138 C2
East Greenlees Rd G72 ..... 139 E2
East Hallhill Rd G33 .... 120 B3
East Hamilton St
   Greenock PA15 .... 46 B2
   Wishaw ML2 .... 165 D1
East High St Airdrie ML6 .. 123 D4
   Kirkintilloch G66 .... 58 B1
East India Breast PA15 ..... 46 A3
East Kilbride Rd
   Rutherglen G73, G72 .... 138 C2
   Thorntonhall G74 .... 158 B2
East Kilbride Sta G74 ...... 159 F1
East Kirkland KA24 .... 191 E4
East La PA1 .... 114 A2
East Lennox Dr G84 .... 16 C2
East Link Rd FK9 .... 2 B3
East Machan St ML9 .... 185 D1
East Main St ML7 .... 127 F3
East Mains FK11 .... 4 A3
East Mains Rd G64 .... 159 F2
East Milton Gr G75 .... 159 D1
East Milton Prim Sch G75 .. 179 E4
East Montrose St G84 ...... 16 C1
East Murrayfield FK7 .... 7 F1
East Netherton St KA1 ..... 227 F4
East Park Cres KA3 .... 222 A4
East Park Pl KA3 .... 222 A4
East Park Rd KA8 .... 236 A2
East Plean Prim Sch FK7 ... 12 B2
East Rd Irvine KA12 .... 219 E1
   Kilbarchan PA10 .... 111 D2
   Motherwell ML1 .... 143 D2
   Port Glasgow PA14 .... 68 C4
   Prestwick KA9 .... 236 B3
East Rossdhu Dr G84 .... 16 C2
East Scott Terr ML3 .... 162 B1
East Shaw St
   Greenock PA15 .... 45 F3
   Kilmarnock KA3 .... 227 F3
East Springfield Terr G64 .. 98 A4
East Stirling St FK11 .... 5 D4
East Station Ind Est ML9 .. 185 D2
East Stewart Pl ML5 .... 122 B3
East Stewart St
   Coatbridge ML5 .... 122 B3
   Greenock PA15 .... 46 A2
East Stirling St FK11 .... 5 D4
East Thomson St G81 .... 94 B4
East Thornlie St ML2 .... 165 D1
East Union St KA10 .... 229 E2
East Vennel KA10 .... 10 A3
East Wellbrae Cres ML3 ... 162 A1
East Wellington St G31 .... 118 B3
East William St PA15 .... 46 B2
East Woodside Ave KA1 ... 69 D4
Eastbank Acad G32 .... 119 D2
Eastbank Dr G32 .... 119 D3
Eastbank Prim Sch G32 ... 119 E3
Eastburn Dr FK1 .... 42 B2
Eastburn Rd G21 .... 98 A3
Eastcote Ave G14 .... 95 F2
Eastcroft G73 .... 138 A4
Eastcroft Terr G21 .... 98 A2
Eastend ML2 .... 129 E2
Eastend Ave ML1 .... 143 D1
Easter Carmuirs
   Prim Sch FK1 .... 41 D3

Easter Cornton Rd FK9 .... 2 A2
Easter Craigs G31 .... 118 A4
Easter Cres ML2 .... 165 F2
Easter Garngaber Rd G66 .. 79 F3
Easter Livilands FK7 .... 7 E2
Easter Mews G71 .... 140 C3
Easter Queenslie Rd G33 .. 119 F4
Easter Rd Clarkston G76 ... 158 A3
   Shotts ML7 .... 146 B3
Easter Wood Cres G71 .... 121 E1
Easterepeens Ave G66 .... 79 E4
Easterhill Pl G32 .... 118 C2
Easterhill Rd G84 .... 16 C2
Easterhill St G32 .... 119 D1
Easterhouse Pl G34 .... 120 B4
Easterhouse Quadrant
   G34 .... 120 B4
Easterhouse Rd G34 .... 120 B4
Easterhouse Sta G69 ...... 120 B3
Easterhouse Sta G69 ...... 120 B3
Eastern Ave FK10 .... 4 C3
Eastern Cres KA25 .... 170 A4
Easterton Ave G76 .... 158 A3
Easterton Cres FK7 .... 12 C4
Easterton Dr FK7 .... 12 C4
Easterton Gr FK7 .... 12 C4
Eastfield Ave G72 .... 138 C3
Eastfield Cres G82 .... 50 A1
Eastfield Pl G82 .... 50 A1
Eastfield Prim Sch G68 .... 61 D1
Eastfield Rd
   Caldercruik ML6 .... 105 D3
   Cumbernauld G68 .... 202 A4
   Cumbernauld G68 .... 61 E2
   Glasgow G21 .... 97 F2
Eastgate G69 .... 81 F1
Easthall Prim Sch G34 ..... 119 F4
Eastlea Pl ML6 .... 123 D3
Eastmuir Specl Sch G33 .. 119 D3
Eastmuir St Wishaw ML2 .. 165 F3
   Wishaw ML2 .... 165 F3
Easton Ct FK8 .... 2 A1
Easton Dr FK1 .... 41 F4
Easton Pl ML5 .... 122 A3
Eastside G66 .... 58 B1
Eastside Ind Est G66 .... 58 B1
Eastvale Pl G3 .... 116 B4
Eastwood Ave
   Glasgow G41 .... 136 B4
   Glasgow, Giffnock G46 .... 136 B1
   Irvine KA12 .... 219 E2
Eastwood Cres G46 .... 135 F2
Eastwood Dr ML2 .... 166 A3
Eastwood High Sch G77 .. 156 C4
Eastwood La G84 .... 25 C4
Eastwood Rd G69 .... 80 C1
Eastwood Toll G46 .... 136 A1
Eastwood View G72 .... 139 F3
Eastwood Way ML9 .... 185 D2
Eastwoodmains Rd
   Clarkston G76 .... 157 E4
   Giffnock G46 .... 157 D4
Eastwood Bank PA10 ...... 111 E1
Ebenezer Pl FK1 .... 66 C3
Ebroch Dr G65 .... 60 C4
Ebroch Pk G65 .... 60 C4
Eccles Ct FK7 .... 7 D2
Eccles St G22 .... 97 F3
Eckford St G32 .... 119 D2
Edata Gr G22 .... 97 E3
Edderton Pl G34 .... 120 A4
Eddington Dr G77 .... 156 B2
Eddleston Pl G72 .... 139 F3
Eddlewood Ct G33 .... 120 A4
Eddlewood Path G33 ...... 119 F4
Eddlewood Rd G33 .... 119 F4
Eden Ct KA13 .... 207 D2
Eden Dr G75 .... 179 F3
Eden Gdns G75 .... 179 F3
Eden La G33 .... 98 B1
Eden Pk G72 .... 139 D2
Eden Pl Cambuslang G72 .. 139 E3
   Renfrew PA4 .... 94 C1
Eden Rd FK10 .... 10 A3
Eden St G33 .... 98 B1
Edenhall Ct G77 .... 156 B1
Edenhall Gr G77 .... 156 B1
Edenkill Pl G63 .... 31 E2
Edenside G68 .... 62 A4
Edenwood St G31 .... 118 C3
Edgam Dr G52 .... 115 E3
Edgefauld Ave G21 .... 97 F2
Edgefauld Pl G21 .... 97 F3
Edgefauld Rd Glasgow G21 .. 97 F2
   Glasgow G21 .... 98 A2
Edgehill La G11 .... 96 A2
Edgehill Rd Bearsden G61 .. 75 F3
   Glasgow G11 .... 96 A2
Edgemont Pk ML3 .... 183 E4
Edgemont St G41 .... 136 C4
Edinbarnet Prim Sch G81 .. 74 B4
Edinbeg Ave G42 .... 137 F4
Edinbeg Pl G42 .... 137 F4
Edinburgh Dr PA19 .... 43 F3
Edinburgh Rd Glasgow G33 .. 98 C1
   Harthill ML7 .... 127 E3
   Motherwell ML1 .... 143 E4
Edington Gdns G69 .... 80 C2
Edington St G4 .... 97 D1
Edison St G52 .... 114 C4
Ediston Rd KA9 .... 236 A4
Edmiston Ave KA9 .... 236 A4
Edmiston Dr Glasgow G51 .. 116 A3
   Linwood PA3 .... 112 A3

Edmonstone Dr G65 .... 60 B4
Edmonton Terr G75 .... 180 B4
Edmund Kean G74 .... 160 B3
Edrom Ct G32 .... 118 C3
Edrom Path G32 .... 118 C3
Edrom St G32 .... 118 C3
Edward Ave Renfrew PA4 .. 94 C2
   Stenhousemuir FK5 .... 23 F2
Edward Pl FK8 .... 2 B1
Edward Dr FK2 .... 16 B2
Edward Pl FK2 .... 24 C2
Edward Rd FK2 .... 2 A1
Edward St Clydebank G81 .. 94 B4
   Coatbridge G69 .... 120 C3
   Hamilton ML3 .... 162 B1
   Kilsyth G65 .... 36 B1
   Motherwell ML1 .... 163 E3
Edwin St G51 .... 116 B3
Edzell Ct G14 .... 95 E1
Edzell Gdns Airdrie ML6 .. 123 E1
   Newton Mearns G77 ...... 156 C2
Edzell Pl G14 .... 95 E2
Edzell Rd G14 .... 95 E2
Edzell Row KA13 .... 207 D2
Edzell St Coatbridge ML5 .. 121 E2
   Glasgow G14 .... 95 E1
Egidia Ave G46 .... 136 B1
Egilsay Cres G22 .... 97 F4
Egilsay Pl G22 .... 97 F4
Egilsay St G22 .... 97 F4
Egilsay Terr G22 .... 97 F4
Eglinton Park Visitor Ctr
   KA12 .... 219 E4
Eglinton Cres KA10 .... 229 E1
Eglinton Ct Glasgow G5 .. 117 D3
Eglinton Ctry Pk KA13 .... 208 A1
Eglinton Dr Eaglesham G76 .. 178 C2
Eglinton Gate G46 .... 136 B1
Eglinton Interchange
   KA12 .... 219 D4
Eglinton Pl Ayr KA7 .... 235 F1
   Kilwinning KA13 .... 207 F2
   Saltcoats KA21 .... 216 C4
Eglinton Rd KA22 .... 205 D2
Eglinton Sq KA22 .... 205 E2
Eglinton St Beith KA15 .... 171 D4
   Glasgow G5 .... 122 A4
   Irvine KA12 .... 219 D4
   Saltcoats KA21 .... 216 C4
Eglinton Terr G21 .... 235 F1
Eglinton Wlk G76 .... 178 C2
Egmont Pk G75 .... 180 A4
Eider Ave G75 .... 180 A3
Eider Gr G75 .... 180 A3
Eildon Dr G78 .... 134 B1
Eildon Cres ML6 .... 123 F1
Eildon Dr G78 .... 134 B1
Eildon Rd G66 .... 79 F4
Eileen Gdns G64 .... 78 A1
Eilt Wlk 8 ML2 .... 165 F3
Elba Ct KA8 .... 236 A1
Elba Gdns KA8 .... 236 A1
Elba La G31 .... 118 B3
Elcho St G40 .... 117 F3
Elder Ave KA15 .... 171 E4
Elder Cottage Hospl G51 .. 115 F4
Elder Cres G72 .... 139 F2
Elder St G51 .... 141 D4
Elder Park Prim Sch G51 .. 115 F4
Elder St G51 .... 115 F4
Elderbank G61 .... 75 F2
Elderpark Gdns G51 .... 115 F4
Elderpark Gr G51 .... 115 F4
Elders Way ML2 .... 165 F2
Elderslie Cres KA1 .... 227 F2
Elderslie Hospl PA5 .... 112 B1
Elderslie St G3 .... 240 A3
Eldin Pl Bridge Of W PA11 .. 110 C3
   Elderslie PA5 .... 112 B1
Eldon Gdns G61 .... 96 A1
Eldon Pl PA16 .... 44 C4
Eldon St Glasgow G3 ...... 96 C1
   Greenock PA16 .... 45 E4
Eldrig Pl KA7 .... 238 C1
Eldon Dr FK7 .... 7 E2
Elgin Gdns G76 .... 157 F4
Elgin Pl Airdrie ML6 .... 122 C4
   East Kilbride G74 .... 159 F2
   Falkirk FK1 .... 42 B2
   Kilsyth G65 .... 36 B1
Elgin Rd G61 .... 75 F4
Elgin Terr ML3 .... 161 F2
Elgin Way ML4 .... 142 A3
Elibank St G33 .... 99 D1
Elie St G11 .... 96 B1
Elim Dr FK11 .... 5 D4
Eliot Cres ML3 .... 162 B1
Eliot Terr ML3 .... 162 B1
Elizabeth Ave Larbert FK5 .. 23 E1
   Milton Of G65 .... 58 A3
Elizabeth Cres Falkirk FK1 .. 41 D3
   Glasgow G46 .... 136 B1
Elizabeth Quadrant ML1 .. 142 C3
Elizabeth St Glasgow G51 .. 116 B3
   Stirling FK8 .... 7 D3
Elizabeth Wynd ML3 .... 183 E4

Elizabethan Way PA4 ... 94 B1
Ella Gdns ML4 ... 142 B2
Ellangowan Rd
　Glasgow G41 ... 136 B4
　Milngavie G62 ... 55 D1
Ellergreen Rd G61 ... 75 F2
Ellerslie St PA5 ... 112 A2
Ellesmere St G22 ... 97 D2
Elliot Ave Glasgow G46 ... 136 B2
　Paisley PA2 ... 132 C4
Elliot Cres G74 ... 160 A1
Elliot Dr G46 ... 136 B2
Elliot Pl Glasgow G3 ... 116 C4
　Hamilton ML9 ... 200 A2
Elliot St G3 ... 116 C4
Elliot Terr FK2 ... 42 A4
Ellis St Coatbridge ML5 ... 122 A3
　Kilmarnock KA1 ... 227 F4
Ellis Way ML1 ... 163 F3
Elisland East Kilbride G74 ... 160 C2
　Kirkintilloch G66 ... 59 D1
Ellisland Ave G81 ... 74 B2
Ellisland Cres G73 ... 137 F3
Ellisland Dr Blantyre G72 ... 161 D3
　Kilmarnock KA3 ... 228 B4
　Kirkintilloch G66 ... 59 D1
Ellisland Pl Ayr KA7 ... 239 D3
　Saltcoats KA21 ... 206 A2
Ellisland Rd Clarkston G76 ... 157 F3
　Cumbernauld G67 ... 62 A1
　Glasgow G43 ... 136 B3
Ellisland Sq KA7 ... 239 D3
Ellisland Wynd ML1 ... 143 E2
Elsimuir Farm Rd G69 ... 120 B2
Elsimuir Pl G69 ... 120 B2
Elsimuir Rd G69 ... 120 B2
Elsimuir St ML5 ... 121 F2
Elliston Ave G53 ... 135 E3
Elliston Cres G53 ... 135 E3
Elliston Dr G53 ... 135 E3
Elliston Pl PA9 ... 130 C3
Elliston Rd PA9 ... 130 C3
Ellon Dr PA3 ... 112 A3
Ellon Way PA3 ... 114 A4
Ellrig G75 ... 180 B3
Elm Ave Kirkintilloch G66 ... 79 E3
　Renfrew PA4 ... 94 B2
Elm Bank Bishopbriggs G64 ... 78 A1
　Kirkintilloch G66 ...
Elm Cres G71 ... 141 E4
Elm Ct ML3 ... 183 F2
Elm Dr Cambuslang G72 ... 139 E3
　Chapelhall ML6 ... 123 F2
　Cumbernauld G67 ... 62 C2
　Johnstone PA5 ... 112 A1
Elm Gdns Bearsden G61 ... 75 F3
　Troon KA10 ... 230 A1
Elm Gr Alloa FK10 ... 10 B3
　Langbank PA14 ... 70 B4
　Larbert FK5 ... 23 E1
Elm La E G14 ... 95 E2
Elm La W G14 ... 95 E2
Elm Pk KA22 ... 205 E2
Elm Pl G75 ... 180 B3
Elm Quadrant ML6 ... 123 E4
Elm Rd Bridge Of W PA11 ... 110 C4
　Clydebank G81 ... 74 A3
　Dumbarton G82 ... 49 F2
　Motherwell ML1 ... 143 D3
　Paisley PA2 ... 114 A1
　Rutherglen G73 ... 138 A2
Elm St Blantyre G72 ... 161 F4
　Clarkston G76 ... 157 F3
　Coatbridge ML5 ... 122 B3
　Glasgow G14 ... 95 E2
　Lennoxtown G65 ... 57 F4
　Motherwell ML1 ... 163 E4
　Stirling FK8 ... 1 C1
Elm Terr PA19 ... 44 C3
Elm View ML4 ... 142 B2
Elm Way G72 ... 139 F2
Elm Wlk FK5 ... 75 F3
Elmbank FK11 ... 4 A2
Elmbank Ave
　Kilmarnock KA1 ... 228 A4
　Uddingston G71 ... 141 D4
Elmbank Cres
　Dennyloanhead FK4 ... 39 E3
　Glasgow G2 ... 240 B3
　Hamilton ML3 ... 162 A2
Elmbank Dr Alexandria G83 ... 27 F3
　Kilmarnock KA1 ... 228 A4
　Larkhall ML9 ... 185 E1
Elmbank Rd Langbank PA14 ... 70 B4
　Stirling FK7 ... 7 D2
Elmbank St Ayr KA8 ... 236 A2
　Bellshill ML4 ... 142 A2
　Glasgow G2 ... 240 B3
　Glasgow G2 ... 240 B3
Elmbank Street La G2 ... 240 B3
Elmbank Terr KA12 ... 219 E2
Elmfoot St G5 ... 117 E1
Elmhurst ML1 ... 163 E2
Elmira Rd G69 ... 100 B4
Elmore Ave G44 ... 137 D3
Elms Pl Beith KA15 ... 150 A1
　Stevenston KA20 ... 206 C1
Elms The G44 ... 137 D2
Elmslie Ct G69 ... 120 B2
Elmvale Prim Sch G22 ... 97 F3
Elmvale Row G21 ... 97 F3
Elmvale St G21 ... 97 F3
Elmway ML9 ... 185 D3
Elmwood Ave Glasgow G11 ... 95 F2
　Newton Mearns G77 ... 156 C3

Elmwood Ct G71 ... 141 D1
Elmwood Gdns G66 ... 79 D3
Elmwood La G14 ... 95 F2
Elmwood Rd ML7 ... 147 D1
Elphin St G23 ... 76 B1
Elphinstone Cres Airth FK2 ... 14 C2
　East Kilbride G75 ... 180 C3
Elphinstone Mews PA13 ... 89 E4
Elphinstone Pl G51 ... 116 B4
Elphinstone Rd G46 ... 157 D4
Elrig Rd G43 ... 137 D3
Elsinore Path G75 ... 180 C3
Elspeth Gdns G64 ... 78 B1
Elswick Dr ML6 ... 105 D2
Eltham St G22 ... 97 D2
Elvan Pl G75 ... 179 F4
Elvan St Glasgow G32 ... 118 C3
　Motherwell ML1 ... 163 E3
Elvan Tower ML1 ... 163 F3
Embo Dr G13 ... 95 D3
Emerald Terr ML4 ... 142 A2
Emerson Rd G64 ... 78 A1
Emerson Rd W G64 ... 78 A1
Emerson St G20 ... 97 D3
Emily Dr ML1 ... 163 F2
Emma Jay Rd ML4 ... 142 A3
Empress Dr G84 ... 16 B2
Empress Rd G84 ... 15 E3
Endfield Ave G12 ... 96 A3
Endrick Bank G64 ... 78 A2
Endrick Dr Balloch G83 ... 19 F1
　Bearsden G61 ... 75 F2
　Denny PA6 ... 39 F3
　Paisley PA1 ... 114 A3
Endrick Gdns G62 ... 54 C1
Endrick Pl FK7 ... 7 D2
Endrick Rd PA15 ... 46 A1
Endrick St G21 ... 97 E2
Endrick Way G83 ... 27 F3
Engelen Dr FK10 ... 10 A3
Engels St G83 ... 27 F4
Englewood Ave KA8 ... 236 A3
English St ML2 ... 165 D4
Ennerdale G74 ... 159 E3
Ennisfree Rd G72 ... 161 E4
Ensay St G22 ... 97 E4
Enterkin St G32 ... 118 C2
Enterkine KA13 ... 207 D1
Eribol Wlk ML1 ... 143 E2
Eriboll Pl G22 ... 97 D4
Eriboll St G22 ... 97 D4
Ericht Pl ML7 ... 146 C3
Ericht Rd G43 ... 136 B3
Eriska Ave G14 ... 95 D3
Eriskay Ave Hamilton ML3 ... 161 F1
　Newton Mearns G77 ... 156 A3
　Port Glasgow PA14 ... 69 D4
Eriskay Cres G77 ... 156 A3
Eriskay Ct Falkirk FK1 ... 42 B1
　Irvine KA11 ... 225 E4
Eriskay Dr G60 ... 73 E3
Eriskay Pl Kilmarnock KA3 ... 223 D3
　Old Kilpatrick G60 ... 73 E3
Ermelo Gdns G75 ... 180 A2
Erradale St G22 ... 97 D4
Errogie St G34 ... 120 A4
Erskine View G60 ... 73 D3
Erskine Ave G41 ... 116 A2
Erskine Cres ML6 ... 122 C3
Erskine Ct ML0 ... 123 E4
Erskine Ferry Rd G60 ... 73 D3
Erskine Hospl PA7 ... 72 C3
Erskine Pl
　Clackmannan FK10 ... 10 C3
　Kilmarnock KA3 ... 223 D3
　Saltcoats KA21 ... 216 C4
Erskine Rd G46 ... 157 D3
Erskine Sq G52 ... 114 C4
Erskine St Alloa FK10 ... 10 A4
　Alva FK12 ... 5 D4
Erskine Way ML7 ... 146 C2
Erskinefauld Rd PA3 ... 112 A3
Ervie St G34 ... 120 B4
Escart Rd ML8 ... 187 F2
Esdaile Ct ML1 ... 143 D2
Esk Ave PA4 ... 94 C1
Esk Dale G74 ... 159 E2
Esk Dr PA2 ... 112 C1
Esk Rd Kilmarnock KA1 ... 228 A2
　Troon KA10 ... 229 F3
Esk St G14 ... 94 C3
Esk Way PA2 ... 112 C1
Eskbank St G32 ... 119 D3
Eskdale G74 ... 157 D3
Eskdale Dr G73 ... 138 B4
Eskdale Rd G61 ... 75 E1
Eskdale St G42 ... 117 D1
Esmond St G3 ... 96 B1
Espedair St PA2 ... 113 F2
Esperanto Rd KA9 ... 236 C4
Espieside Cres ML5 ... 121 E4
Esplanade Ayr KA7 ... 238 C4
　Greenock PA16 ... 45 E4
　Prestwick KA9 ... 233 D1
Essenside Ave G15 ... 75 E1
Essex Dr G14 ... 95 F3
Essex La G14 ... 95 F2
Essex Rd PA16 ... 44 C2
Esslemont Ave G14 ... 95 E2
Esson Pl KA3 ... 223 D2
Estate Ave FK1 ... 42 B2
Estate Quadrant G32 ... 139 E4
Estate Rd G32 ... 119 E1
Etive Ave Bearsden G61 ... 76 A2
　Hamilton ML3 ... 162 A1
Etive Cres
　Bishopbriggs G64 ... 78 A1
　Cumbernauld G67 ... 82 A3

Etive Ct Clydebank G81 ... 74 B3
　Cumbernauld G67 ... 82 A3
Etive Dr Airdrie ML6 ... 123 E3
　Bishopton PA7 ... 72 B1
　Cumbernauld G67 ... 82 A3
　Glasgow G46 ... 136 B1
Etive Pl Cumbernauld G67 ... 82 B3
　Irvine KA12 ... 219 E3
　Stirling FK9 ... 2 A2
Etive St Glasgow G32 ... 119 D3
　Wishaw ML2 ... 165 D1
Etna St ML9 ... 147 D2
Eton Ct FK2 ... 42 B4
Etna Ind Est ML2 ... 164 B2
Etna Rd FK2 ... 42 B4
Etna St ML2 ... 164 B2
Eton La G12 ... 96 C1
Etrick Ave ML4 ... 142 A4
Etterick Wynd G72 ... 161 E4
Ettrick Ave PA4 ... 94 C1
Ettrick Cres
　Kilmarnock KA3 ... 222 C2
　Rutherglen G73 ... 138 B4
Ettrick Ct
　Cambuslang G72 ... 139 F2
　Falkirk FK1 ... 42 B1
Ettrick Dr Bearsden G61 ... 75 E4
　Bishopton PA7 ... 72 B1
Ettrick Hill G74 ... 160 A2
Ettrick Oval PA2 ... 132 C4
Ettrick Pl Ayr KA8 ... 236 A2
　Glasgow G43 ... 136 B4
　Kilmarnock KA3 ... 222 C2
Ettrick Sq G67 ... 61 F1
Ettrick St ML2 ... 165 D3
Ettrick Terr PA5 ... 131 E4
Euchan Pl KA10 ... 229 F3
Eurocentral Rail Terminal
　ML1 ... 142 B4
Evan Cres G46 ... 136 B1
Evan Dr G46 ... 136 B1
Evans St FK5 ... 23 E2
Evanton Dr G46 ... 135 F2
Evanton Pl G46 ... 135 F2
Evelyn Terr KA13 ... 207 F1
Everard Ct G21 ... 97 F4
Everard Dr G21 ... 97 F3
Everard Pl G21 ... 97 F4
Everard Quadrant G21 ... 97 F3
Everglades The G69 ... 100 A4
Eversley St G32 ... 119 D2
Everton Rd G53 ... 115 E1
Ewart Cres ML3 ... 162 A1
Ewart Terr ML3 ... 162 A1
Ewenfield Ave KA7 ... 239 D2
Ewenfield Gdns KA7 ... 239 D2
Ewenfield Pk KA7 ... 238 C2
Ewenfield Rd KA7 ... 239 D2
Ewing Ave KA7 ... 239 D2
Ewing Ct Hamilton ML3 ... 183 E4
　Stirling FK7 ... 7 E2
Ewing Dr FK2 ... 42 A4
Ewing Pl Falkirk FK2 ... 42 A4
　Glasgow G31 ... 118 B3
Ewing St Kilbarchan PA10 ... 111 D2
　Rutherglen G73 ... 138 A4
Ewing Way KA3 ... 211 E4
Ewing Wlk G62 ... 55 E1
Excelsior St ML2 ... 164 B2
Exchange Pl G1 ... 241 D2
Exeter Dr G11 ... 96 A1
Exeter La G11 ... 96 A1
Exeter St ML5 ... 122 A3
Exhibition Centre Sta G3 ... 116 C4
Exmouth Pl PA19 ... 44 C3
Eynort St G22 ... 97 D4
Eyrepoint Ct G33 ... 119 D4

Factory Rd ML1 ... 163 F3
Fagan Ct G72 ... 140 C1
Faifley Prim Sch G81 ... 74 B4
Faifley Rd G81 ... 74 B4
Failford Pl KA3 ... 223 D2
Fair Oaks G76 ... 158 C4
Fair View Dr ML11 ... 214 A2
Fair Way G82 ... 48 A4
Fairbairn Cres G46 ... 136 A1
Fairbairn St G60 ... 118 A2
Fairburn St G32 ... 118 C2
Fairfax Ave G44 ... 137 E3
Fairfield FK10 ... 5 E1
Fairfield Ave FK4 ... 40 A3
Fairfield Ct G76 ... 157 F3
Fairfield Dr Clarkston G76 ... 157 F3
　Renfrew PA4 ... 94 B1
Fairfield Gdns G51 ... 115 F4
Fairfield Pk KA7 ... 238 C4
Fairfield Pl Bothwell G71 ... 141 D1
　East Kilbride G74 ... 159 E1
　Falkirk FK2 ... 42 A3
　Glasgow G51 ... 115 F4
　Hamilton ML3 ... 162 C1
Fairfield Rd KA7 ... 238 C4
Fairfield Sch FK10 ... 5 D1
Fairford Dr G67 ... 82 B4
Fairgreen Pl FK7 ... 11 F4
Fairhaven KA10 ... 229 F4
Fairhaven Rd G23 ... 96 B4
Fairhaven Sq KA13 ... 207 D2
Fairhill Ave Glasgow G53 ... 135 E4
　Hamilton ML3 ... 162 B1
Fairhill Cres ML3 ... 162 B1
Fairhill Pl ML3 ... 183 E4
Fairhill Rd ML3 ... 7 D1
Fairholm Ave ML3 ... 163 E1

Fairholm St Glasgow G32 ... 118 C2
　Larkhall ML9 ... 184 C2
Fairley St G51 ... 116 A3
Fairlie G74 ... 159 E2
Fairlie Ave KA1 ... 227 E4
Fairlie Dr Falkirk FK1 ... 41 E3
　Irvine KA11 ... 220 A3
Fairlie Gdns FK1 ... 41 E3
Fairlie Park Dr G11 ... 96 A1
Fairlie St FK1 ... 41 E3
Fairlie View KA2 ... 226 C3
Fairmount Dr FK10 ... 5 D1
Fairrie St PA15 ... 46 B2
Fairview Ct G62 ... 55 D1
Fairway G61 ... 75 E3
Fairway Ave PA2 ... 133 C4
Fairways Irvine KA12 ... 219 D4
　Larkhall ML9 ... 185 E2
　Stewarton KA3 ... 211 F4
Fairways Pl KA4 ... 40 A4
Fairways View G81 ... 74 B3
Fairweather Pl G77 ... 156 B2
Fairyburn Rd FK10 ... 9 F4
Fairyhill Pl KA1 ... 227 F3
Fairyhill Rd KA1 ... 227 F3
Fairyknowe Gdns G71 ... 141 D1
Faith Ave PA11 ... 89 F1
Falcon Cres PA16 ... 45 D3
Falcon Dr FK5 ... 23 D2
Falcon La PA16 ... 45 D3
Falcon Rd PA5 ... 131 E4
Falcon Terr G20 ... 96 B4
Falcon Terrace La G20 ... 96 B4
Falconbridge Rd G74 ... 160 B2
Falconer Ct FK7 ... 7 E2
Falconer St PA14 ... 47 E1
Falconer Terr ML3 ... 162 B1
Falfield St G5 ... 117 D2
Falkirk Coll of F & H Ed
　Flexible Learning Ctr
　FK2 ... 42 C3
Falkirk District Royal
　Infmry FK1 ... 42 A2
Falkirk High Sch FK1 ... 41 F2
Falkirk High Sta FK1 ... 42 A2
Falkland Ave G77 ... 157 D3
Falkland Cres G64 ... 98 B4
Falkland Dr G74 ... 159 E1
Falkland La G12 ... 96 A2
Falkland Park Rd KA8 ... 236 A2
Falkland Pk G74 ... 159 E1
Falkland Pl Ayr KA8 ... 236 A2
　Coatbridge ML5 ... 122 A2
　East Kilbride G74 ... 159 E1
　Stenhousemuir FK5 ... 23 F2
Falkland Rd KA8 ... 236 A2
Falkland St G12 ... 96 A2
Fallin Prim Sch FK7 ... 8 B3
Falloch Pl ML2 ... 165 F3
Falloch Rd Bearsden G61 ... 75 E1
　Glasgow G42 ... 137 D4
　Milngavie G62 ... 54 C2
Fallside Ave G71 ... 141 E3
Fallside Rd G71 ... 141 D2
Falmouth Dr PA19 ... 44 C3
Falside Ave PA2 ... 113 F1
Falside Rd Glasgow G32 ... 119 D1
　Paisley PA2 ... 113 E1
Falstaff G74 ... 160 B3
Fancy Farm Pl PA16 ... 44 C2
Fancy Farm Rd PA16 ... 45 D2
Fara St G23 ... 96 C4
Faraday Ave ML2 ... 165 E2
Faransay Pl KA3 ... 223 D3
Fardalehill View KA2 ... 221 F1
Farden Pl KA9 ... 236 B3
Farie St G73 ... 138 A4
Farlands View KA23 ... 190 B2
Farm Cres ML1 ... 143 F2
Farm Ct G71 ... 141 D2
Farm La ML4 ... 141 F2
Farm Pk G66 ... 79 E2
Farm Rd Blantyre G72 ... 140 B1
　Clydebank G81 ... 73 E2
　Clydebank, Duntocher G81 ... 74 A4
　Cowie FK7 ... 12 B4
　Fallin FK7 ... 8 B3
　Glasgow G41 ... 116 A3
　Hamilton ML3 ... 161 F2
　Kilmarnock KA3 ... 222 C2
　Port Glasgow PA14 ... 68 C4
Farm St Falkirk FK2 ... 24 A1
　Motherwell ML1 ... 163 E4
Farm Terr ML3 ... 161 F2
Farm Cross G73 ... 118 E1
Farmeloan Rd G73 ... 138 A4
Farmfield Terr KA23 ... 190 B3
Farmgate Sq ML4 ... 141 F2
Farmington Ave G32 ... 119 E3
Farmington Gate G32 ... 119 E3
Farmington Gdns G32 ... 119 E3
Farmington Gr G32 ... 119 E3
Farndale G74 ... 159 E2
Farne Dr G44 ... 137 E2
Farnell St G4 ... 97 E1
Farquhar Rd PA14 ... 47 D1
Farquhar Sq FK10 ... 107 E4
Farquharson Way FK1 ... 41 F1
Farrell Pl KA1 ... 236 A1
Farrier Ct PA5 ... 111 F2
Faskally Ave G64 ... 77 F2
Faskally Wlk ML2 ... 165 F3

Faskin Cres G53 ... 134 C4
Faskin Pl G53 ... 134 C4
Faskin Rd G53 ... 134 C4
Faskine Ave Airdrie ML6 ... 122 C3
　Calderbank ML6 ... 123 D1
Faskine Cres ML6 ... 122 C3
Fasque Pl G15 ... 74 C2
Fastnet St G33 ... 119 D4
Fauldhouse St G5 ... 117 E2
Faulds G69 ... 120 B3
Faulds Gdns G69 ... 120 B3
Faulds Park Rd PA19 ... 43 F3
Faulds St ML5 ... 121 F2
Fauldshead Rd PA4 ... 94 B2
Fauldspark Cres G69 ... 120 B3
Fauldswood Cres PA2 ... 113 D1
Fauldswood Dr PA2 ... 113 D1
Faulkner Gr ML1 ... 164 C4
Fearnan Pl PA16 ... 45 D2
Fearnmore Rd G20 ... 96 B4
Fearnoch KA9 ... 236 B3
Fellhill St KA7 ... 239 D3
Fells The G65 ... 57 F4
Fellsview Ave G66 ... 58 C1
Felton Pl G13 ... 94 C4
Fencedyke Prim Sch
　KA11 ... 220 A2
Fencedyke Way KA11 ... 220 A2
Fendoch St G32 ... 119 D2
Fenella St G32 ... 119 D3
Fennsbank Ave G73 ... 138 B2
Fenton St FK10 ... 10 B4
Fenwick Dr Barrhead G78 ... 134 B1
　Hamilton ML3 ... 183 F4
Fenwick Pl G46 ... 136 A1
Fenwick Prim Sch KA3 ... 213 D2
Fenwick Rd Glasgow G46 ... 136 B2
　Kilmaurs KA3 ... 222 B4
Fenwickland Ave KA7 ... 239 D2
Fenwickland Pl KA7 ... 239 D2
Ferclay St G81 ... 74 B4
Fereneze Ave
　Glasgow G13 ... 95 D4
　Hamilton ML3 ... 161 F2
Fereneze Dr PA2 ... 133 E4
Fereneze Rd G78 ... 154 B4
Fergus Ave PA3 ... 113 D3
Fergus Ct G20 ... 96 C2
Fergus Dr Glasgow G20 ... 96 C2
　Greenock PA16 ... 45 D2
　Paisley PA3 ... 113 D3
Fergus Gdns ML3 ... 162 C1
Fergus La G20 ... 96 C2
Fergus Pl PA16 ... 45 D2
Fergus Rd PA16 ... 45 D2
Fergushill Rd KA13 ... 208 A2
Ferguslie PA1 ... 113 D2
Ferguslie Park Cres PA3 ... 113 D3
Ferguslie Park Ave PA3 ... 113 D3
Ferguslie Prim Sch PA3 ... 113 D3
Ferguslie Wlk PA1 ... 113 D2
Ferguson Ave
　Milngavie G62 ... 55 D1
　Prestwick KA9 ... 236 B4
　Renfrew PA4 ...
Ferguson Dr Denny FK6 ... 21 E1
　Falkirk FK2 ... 24 A3
　Motherwell ML1 ... 163 F2
Ferguson Gr FK4 ... 40 A3
Ferguson St Ayr KA8 ... 236 B2
　Johnstone PA5 ... 111 F2
　Renfrew PA4 ... 94 B2
　Stirling FK8 ... 1 C1
Fergusson Pl G74 ... 160 B3
Fergusson Rd G67 ... 61 F1
Fergusson Terr G65 ... 58 B3
Fergusson Rd G61 ... 75 F2
Fern Ave Bishopbriggs G64 ... 98 A4
　Erskine PA8 ... 93 D4
　Kirkintilloch G66 ... 79 E3
Fern Brae KA7 ... 238 C3
Fern Dr G78 ... 134 A2
Fern Gr G69 ... 101 D3
Fern La G13 ... 95 F3
Fern Lea Gr FK2 ... 24 B2
Fern Pl KA1 ... 227 E4
Fern St ML1 ... 164 A2
Fernan St G32 ... 118 C3
Fernbank Ave G72 ... 139 E2
Fernbank St G21 ... 97 F3
Fernbrae Ave G73 ... 138 B2
Fernbrae Way G73 ... 138 A2
Ferncroft Dr G44 ... 137 E3
Ferndale ML9 ... 185 D1
Ferndale Ct G23 ... 96 B4
Ferndale Dr G23 ... 96 B4
Ferndale Gdns G23 ... 96 B4
Ferndale Pl G23 ... 96 B4
Ferness Oval G21 ... 98 B4
Ferness Pl G21 ... 98 B4
Ferness Rd G21 ... 98 B4
Ferneze Cres ML3 ... 161 F2
Ferneze Gr G46 ... 96 A3
Fernhill Grange G71 ... 141 D1
Fernhill Rd G73 ... 138 A2
Fernhill Sch G73 ... 138 B2
Fernie Gdns G20 ... 96 C4
Ferniegair Ave G84 ... 16 A1
Fernieshaw Rd ML1 ... 144 C1
Fernlea G61 ... 75 F2
Fernleigh Pl G69 ... 80 C1
Fernleigh Rd G43 ... 136 B3
Fernside Wlk ML3 ... 162 C1
Fernslea Ave G72 ... 161 E4

erry Loan G83 .... 27 F3
erry Orch FK9 .... 2 B1
erry Rd Bishopton PA7 .... 72 A4
Bothwell G71 .... 141 D1
Cardross G82 .... 48 A3
Glasgow G3 .... 96 A1
Renfrew PA4 .... 94 B3
Rosneath G84 .... 15 D2
South Alloa FK7 .... 9 F2
Stirling FK9 .... 2 B1
Iddingston G71 .... 140 C3
rryden Ct G14 .... 95 F1
rryden St G14 .... 95 F1
rsit St G43 .... 136 B3
tlar Dr Glasgow G44 .... 137 E3
Kilmarnock KA3 .... 223 D3
tlar Rd PA11 .... 110 B4
ttercairn Ave G15 .... 74 C2
ttercairn Gdns G46 .... 78 B1
tlar St G43 .... 118 C4
tdison Pl KA9 .... 236 C3
ddoch Ct ML2 .... 165 F4
dra St G33 .... 118 D1
eld Gr G76 .... 157 F3
eld Rd Clarkston G76 .... 157 F3
Clydebank G81 .... 74 B4
arkhall ML9 .... 185 D1
eld St ML3 .... 162 B1
elden Pl G40 .... 118 A3
elden St G40 .... 118 A3
eldhead Dr G43 .... 136 A3
eldhead Sq G43 .... 136 A3
eldings The KA3 .... 195 E4
elds La PA6 .... 91 D2
fe Ave Airdrie ML6 .... 123 D3
Glasgow G52 .... 115 D2
fe Cres G71 .... 141 D1
fe Ct G71 .... 141 D1
fe Dr Greenock PA16 .... 44 B3
Motherwell ML1 .... 142 B1
fe Rd PA4 .... 94 B1
fth Ave Airdrie ML6 .... 123 E4
Glasgow G12 .... 95 F3
Millerston G33 .... 99 D3
Renfrew PA4 .... 94 B1
fth Rd G72 .... 161 F3
fty Pitches Pl G52, G51 .... 115 E4
fty Pitches Rd G52 .... 115 D4
fty Pk PA2 .... 114 A1
naven Gdns G61 .... 75 E4
nch Dr G13 .... 95 D4
nch Pl Johnstone PA5 .... 131 E4
Kilmarnock KA1 .... 228 B4
nch Pl PA8 .... 73 D1
ndhorn Ave Paisley PA2 .... 112 C1
Renfrew PA4 .... 94 B2
ndhorn Ct G15 .... 179 E4
ndhorn Pl
East Kilbride G75 .... 179 F4
Falkirk FK1 .... 42 B1
Troon KA10 .... 229 F3
ndhorn Rd KA9 .... 233 F2
ndhorn St G33 .... 118 B4
ndlay St Kilsyth G65 .... 60 B4
ndlay's Brae KA21 .... 216 C4
ndochty PA8 .... 73 D2
ndochty St G33 .... 99 F1
ngal La G20 .... 96 B4
ngal St G20 .... 96 B4
ngalton Rd G77 .... 155 F3
ngask St G32 .... 119 E2
nglas Ave PA4 .... 114 A1
nglen Gdns G62 .... 54 C1
nglen Pl G13 .... 135 D3
nglen Ave G78 .... 134 B1
nhaven St G32 .... 118 C2
nistere Ave FK1 .... 42 A2
nlarig Ct FK5 .... 23 F2
nlarig St G34 .... 120 B4
nlas Ave KA7 .... 239 D2
nlas St G22 .... 97 E2
nlay Ave KA24 .... 191 E4
nlay Dr Glasgow G31 .... 118 A4
Linwood PA3 .... 111 F3
nlay Rise G62 .... 76 B3
nnart Rd ML6 .... 163 F3
nnart St Glasgow G40 .... 117 F2
Greenock PA16 .... 45 E3
nneston La PA15 .... 46 A2
nnart Rd ML6 .... 163 F3
nnart Sq G40 .... 117 F2
nneston Way PA15 .... 46 A2
nnick Glen KA7 .... 239 D2
nnie Terr Gourock PA19 .... 44 B3
Low Wynd ML1 .... 164 A2
nnieston Sq G33 .... 116 C4
nnieston St G33 .... 116 C4
nsbay St G51 .... 115 F3
intaig La ML2 .... 165 F2
ntrie Terr ML1 .... 161 F2
ntry Ave PA7 .... 133 F4
ntry Cres
Barrhead G78 .... 134 B1
Bishopbriggs G64 .... 78 B1

Fintry Dr G44 .... 137 E4
Fintry Gdns G61 .... 75 E4
Fintry Pl
East Kilbride G75 .... 180 A2
Irvine KA11 .... 220 A1
Fintry Rd PA15 .... 46 A1
Fintry Terr KA11 .... 220 A2
Fintry Wlk KA11 .... 220 A1
Fir Bank KA7 .... 113 F4
Fir Bank Ave ML9 .... 185 D1
Fir Ct Cambuslang G72 .... 139 F2
Coatbridge ML5 .... 121 F2
Fir Dr G75 .... 180 A3
Fir Gr G71 .... 141 E4
Fir La FK5 .... 23 E1
Fir Park St ML1 .... 163 F2
Fir Pk (Motherwell FC) ML1 .... 163 F2
Fir Pl Cambuslang G72 .... 139 E3
Cleland ML1 .... 144 A1
Glasgow G69 .... 120 A2
Johnstone PA5 .... 112 A1
Kilmarnock KA1 .... 227 E4
Fir St PA15 .... 46 C1
Fir Terr PA19 .... 44 B3
Fir View ML6 .... 123 D1
Firbank Ave G64 .... 78 A4
Firbank Terr G78 .... 134 C1
Firdon Cres G15 .... 75 D1
Firhill Ave ML6 .... 122 C3
Firhill Rd G20 .... 233 E3
Firhill Pk (Partick Thistle FC) G20 .... 97 D2
Firhill Rd G20 .... 97 D2
Firhill St G20 .... 97 D2
Firlee G75 .... 179 E4
Firpark Rd G64 .... 98 A4
Firpark Sch ML1 .... 163 F2
Firpark St G31 .... 117 F4
Firpark Terr Cambusbarron FK7 .... 6 B3
Glasgow G31 .... 117 F4
Firs Cres FK7 .... 7 E1
Firs Entry FK7 .... 7 E1
Firs Pk (East Stirlingshire FC) FK2 .... 42 B3
Firs Rd FK10 .... 4 A2
Firs St FK2 .... 42 B3
Firs The Bannockburn FK7 .... 7 E1
Glasgow G44 .... 137 D2
First Ave Alexandria G83 .... 27 F3
Bearsden G61 .... 76 B2
Dumbarton G82 .... 50 B1
Glasgow G44 .... 136 C1
Irvine KA12 .... 219 D2
Kirkintilloch G66 .... 79 E1
Millerston G33 .... 99 D2
Renfrew PA4 .... 94 B1
Uddingston G71 .... 140 C4
First Gdns G41 .... 116 A2
First Rd G72 .... 161 E3
First St G71 .... 140 C4
First Terr G81 .... 74 A2
Firth Cres PA19 .... 44 B3
Firth Gdns KA10 .... 229 E4
Firth Rd KA10 .... 229 E4
Firth View Terr KA22 .... 205 E2
Firthview Terr G82 .... 49 E2
Firtree Pl ML2 .... 166 A3
Firtree Rd ML2 .... 166 A3
Firwood Cts G77 .... 156 C2
Firwood Dr G44 .... 137 E3
Firwood Rd G77 .... 156 C2
Fischer Gdns PA3 .... 112 C3
Fischcross Prim Sch FK10 .... 5 E2
Fisher Ave Kilsyth G65 .... 60 B4
Paisley PA3 .... 112 A2
Fisher Cres G81 .... 74 A3
Fisher Ct Glasgow G31 .... 117 F4
Knockentiber KA2 .... 221 F2
Fisher Dr PA3 .... 112 C2
Fisher St ML9 .... 185 D1
Fisher Way ML1 .... 112 C2
Fishers Rd PA4 .... 94 B3
Fisherwood Rd G81 .... 73 F3
Fishescoates Ave G73 .... 138 B3
Fishescoates Gdns G73 .... 138 B3
Fitzalan Dr PA3 .... 94 A1
Fitzalan Rd PA4 .... 94 A1
Fitzroy La G3 .... 116 C4
Fitzroy Pl G3 .... 116 C4
Five Roads KA13 .... 208 A2
Five Ways Rd ML9 .... 200 B2
Flakefield G74 .... 159 D1
Flanders St G81 .... 74 B4
Flatterton La PA16 .... 44 B1
Flatterton Rd PA16 .... 44 B1
Flax Mill Rd ML7 .... 127 F3
Flax Rd G71 .... 141 D3
Flaxfield Gr ML1 .... 142 B1
Flaxmill Ave ML2 .... 164 B2
Fleck Ave KA21 .... 206 A1
Fleet Ave PA4 .... 94 C1
Fleet St G32 .... 119 D2
Fleming Ave Chryston G69 .... 100 B4
Clydebank G81 .... 94 B4
Fleming Cres KA21 .... 206 A2
Fleming Ct Carluke ML8 .... 187 F1
Clydebank G81 .... 74 A1
Hamilton ML3 .... 161 F2
Motherwell ML1 .... 164 A2
Fleming Dr Stenhousemuir FK5 .... 24 A2
Stewarton KA3 .... 211 E4
Fleming Gdns FK1 .... 41 F3

Fleming Pl Blackridge EH48 .... 107 F2
East Kilbride G75 .... 180 C4
Fleming Rd Bellshill ML4 .... 142 A4
Bishopton PA7 .... 72 A2
Cumbernauld G67 .... 61 F1
Houston PA6 .... 91 D1
Fleming St Glasgow G31 .... 118 A3
Kilmarnock KA1 .... 227 F3
Paisley PA3 .... 113 F4
Fleming Terr KA12 .... 219 D3
Fleming Way Hamilton ML3 .... 161 F1
15 Larkhall ML9 .... 185 E1
Flemington Ind Est G72 .... 139 F2
Flemington St G21 .... 97 E1
Flenders Ave G76 .... 157 E3
Flenders Rd G76 .... 157 E3
Fletcher Ave PA19 .... 44 C4
Fleurs Ave G41 .... 116 A2
Fleurs Rd G41 .... 116 A2
Flinders Pl G75 .... 180 A4
Flint Cres FK7 .... 12 B4
Flint Mill La PA15 .... 46 A1
Flloyd St ML5 .... 121 F4
Floors Rd G76 .... 157 E1
Floors St PA5 .... 111 F1
Floorsburn Cres PA5 .... 111 F1
Flora Gdns G64 .... 78 B1
Florence Dr Glasgow G46 .... 136 B1
Kilmacolm PA13 .... 89 D4
Florence Gdns G73 .... 138 B2
Florence St Glasgow G5 .... 117 E3
Greenock PA15 .... 45 D2
Florida Ave G42 .... 137 D4
Florida Cres G42 .... 137 D4
Florida Dr G42 .... 137 D4
Florida Gdns G69 .... 120 A3
Florida Sq G42 .... 137 D4
Florida St G42 .... 137 D4
Florish Rd PA8 .... 93 F4
Flowerdale Pl G53 .... 135 D2
Flowerhill Ind Est ML6 .... 123 D4
Flowerhill St ML6 .... 123 D4
Flures Ave PA8 .... 93 F4
Flures Cres PA8 .... 93 F4
Flures Dr PA8 .... 93 F4
Flures Pl PA8 .... 93 F4
Fochabers Dr G52 .... 115 E3
Fogo Pl G20 .... 96 B3
Foinaven Rd ML3 .... 183 F2
Foot Of Lone Rd ML11 .... 214 A3
Footfield Rd ML4 .... 141 F2
Forbes Cres FK5 .... 23 E1
Forbes Ct FK2 .... 42 C3
Forbes Dr Ayr KA8 .... 236 B2
3 Glasgow G40 .... 117 F3
Motherwell ML1 .... 142 B1
Forbes Pl Kilmarnock KA3 .... 223 D1
Paisley PA1 .... 113 F2
Forbes Rd Alloa FK10 .... 4 C3
Forbes St Alloa FK10 .... 4 C3
Glasgow G40 .... 117 F3
Stirling FK8 .... 2 A1
Forbes Wlk KA3 .... 223 D1
Ford Ave KA11 .... 225 E4
Ford Rd Bonnybridge FK4 .... 40 A3
Glasgow G12 .... 96 B2
Newton Mearns G77 .... 156 B2
Fordneuk St G40 .... 118 A3
Fordoun St G34 .... 120 B4
Fordyce Ct G77 .... 156 B2
Fordyce St G11 .... 96 A1
Fore Row ML3 .... 162 C2
Fore St Glasgow G14 .... 95 E2
Port Glasgow PA14 .... 47 E1
Forebraes FK10 .... 10 A4
Foregate Sq KA1 .... 222 C1
Foregate The KA1 .... 222 C1
Forehill Prim Sch KA7 .... 239 E3
Forehill Rd KA7 .... 239 E3
Forehouse Rd PA10 .... 110 B2
Foremount Terrace La
10 G12 .... 96 B2
Forest Ave ML3 .... 183 E3
Forest Dr Bearsden G61 .... 75 D4
Bellshill ML4 .... 142 B2
Bothwell G71 .... 141 D2
Forest Gdns G66 .... 79 D2
Forest Gr KA3 .... 223 D3
Forest Kirk ML8 .... 202 A4
Forest La ML3 .... 183 E3
Forest Pl Crossford ML8 .... 201 E1
Kirkintilloch G66 .... 79 D2
Paisley PA2 .... 113 F1
Forest Rd Cumbernauld G67 .... 62 C3
Larkhall ML9 .... 185 D2
Forest View G67 .... 62 A4
Forest Walks G65 .... 57 D3
Forest Way KA7 .... 239 E3
Forester Gr FK10 .... 4 C1
Forestfield Gdns ML6 .... 105 D2
Foresthall Cres G21 .... 98 A2
Foresthall Dr G21 .... 98 A2
Forfar Ave G52 .... 115 D2
Forfar Cres G64 .... 98 B4
Forfar Rd PA16 .... 44 C2
Forgan Gdns G64 .... 98 B4
Forge Pl G21 .... 98 A1
Forge Rd Airdrie ML6 .... 123 F3
Ayr KA8 .... 236 B2
Forge Sh Ctr The G31 .... 118 B3
Forge St Glasgow G21 .... 98 A1
Kilmarnock KA1 .... 222 C2
Forge Vennal KA13 .... 207 E2
Forgewood Path ML6 .... 123 F3
Forgewood Rd ML1 .... 142 B1

Forglen Cres FK9 .... 2 A3
Forglen Rd FK9 .... 2 A3
Forgue St Glasgow G34 .... 100 A1
Formby Dr G23 .... 76 B1
Forres Ave G46 .... 136 B2
Forres Cres ML4 .... 142 A3
Forres Gate G46 .... 136 B1
Forres Quadrant ML2 .... 165 D3
Forres St Blantyre G72 .... 161 E3
Glasgow G23 .... 76 C1
Forrest Gate ML3 .... 162 A1
Forrest Pl ML7 .... 127 F3
Forrest Rd
Forrestfield ML6 .... 106 A1
Lanark ML11 .... 215 D3
Salsburgh ML7 .... 126 A3
Stirling FK8 .... 2 A1
Forrest St Airdrie ML6 .... 123 E4
Blantyre G72 .... 161 F4
Glasgow G40 .... 118 A3
Shotts ML7 .... 146 C3
Forrester Ct 1 G64 .... 97 F4
Forrester Pl FK7 .... 7 E1
Forrestfield Cres G77 .... 156 C3
Forrestfield Gdns G77 .... 156 C3
Forrestfield Rd ML6 .... 106 A1
Forrestfield St G21 .... 98 A1
Forrestlea Rd ML8 .... 202 A4
Forsa Ct G75 .... 180 B2
Forsyth Ct KA11 .... 215 E2
Forsyth Gr PA16 .... 45 D3
Forsyth St Airdrie ML6 .... 123 D4
Greenock PA16 .... 45 D3
Fort Matilda Pl PA16 .... 45 C4
Fort Matilda Sta PA16 .... 45 C4
Fort Matilda Terr PA16 .... 45 C4
Fort St Ayr KA7 .... 235 F1
Motherwell ML1 .... 163 E4
Fortacre Pl KA11 .... 220 A3
Forteviot Ave G69 .... 120 B3
Forteviot Pl G69 .... 120 B3
Forth Ave Larbert FK5 .... 23 D2
Paisley PA2 .... 112 C1
Forth Cres Alloa FK10 .... 10 B3
East Kilbride G75 .... 179 F4
Stirling FK8 .... 2 B2
Forth Ct East Kilbride G75 .... 179 F4
Stirling FK8 .... 2 B2
Forth Gr FK9 .... 179 F4
Forth Pl Johnstone PA5 .... 131 E4
Kilmarnock KA1 .... 228 A3
Larkhall ML9 .... 199 D4
Forth Rd Bearsden G61 .... 75 E1
Torrance G64 .... 78 A4
Forth St Cambus FK10 .... 9 D4
Clydebank G81 .... 94 B4
Fallin FK7 .... 8 B2
Glasgow G41 .... 116 C2
Greenock PA16 .... 45 D3
Stirling FK8 .... 2 B2
Forth Terr ML3 .... 183 D4
Forth View FK8 .... 2 A1
Forthbank Ind Est FK10 .... 10 A2
Forthbank
(Stirling Albion FC) FK7 .... 7 F4
Forthvale FK11 .... 4 A3
Forthview FK7 .... 7 E1
Forthview FK1 .... 41 F1
Kirkintilloch G66 .... 79 F4
Forties Cres G46 .... 136 A3
Forties Gdns G46 .... 136 A3
Forties Rd PA6 .... 111 E4
Forties Way G46 .... 136 A3
Fortieth Ave G75 .... 180 C3
Fortingale Ave G12 .... 96 B3
Fortingale Pl G12 .... 96 B3
Fortingall Rd G72 .... 161 F3
Fortissat Ave ML7 .... 146 B3
Fortissat Rd ML7 .... 126 A1
Fortrose St G11 .... 96 A1
Fortuna Ct FK1 .... 42 A4
Forum Sh Ctr The PA15 .... 45 F3
Fossil Gr G66 .... 59 D1
Foswell Pl G15 .... 74 C3
Fotheringay La G41 .... 116 B1
Fotheringay Rd G41 .... 116 C1
Fotheringham Rd KA8 .... 239 D4
Foulburn Rd ML7 .... 145 E1
Foulis La G13 .... 95 F3
Foulis St G13 .... 95 F3
Foulsykes Rd ML2 .... 165 F2
Foundry La G78 .... 134 B1
Foundry Loan FK5 .... 23 D1
Foundry Rd
Bonnybridge FK4 .... 40 A3
Cleland ML1 .... 144 B1
Shotts ML7 .... 146 C3
Foundry St FK2 .... 42 A4
Foundry Wynd KA13 .... 207 E2
Fountain Cres PA4 .... 93 E3
Fountain Dr PA4 .... 93 E2
Fountain Rd FK9 .... 2 A4
Fountainwell Ave G21 .... 97 E2
Fountainwell Dr G21 .... 97 E1
Fountainwell Pl G21 .... 97 E1
Fountainwell Rd G21 .... 97 F1
Fountainwell Sq G21 .... 97 F1
Fountainwell Terr G21 .... 97 F1
Four Acres Dr KA3 .... 222 A4
Four Windings PA6 .... 91 D1
Fourth Ave Dumbarton G82 .... 50 B1
Kirkintilloch G66 .... 79 E1
Millerston G33 .... 99 D2
Renfrew PA4 .... 94 B1
Fourth Gdns G41 .... 116 A2

Fourth Rd G71 .... 161 F3
Fourth St G71 .... 120 C1
Fowlds St KA1 .... 227 F4
Fowlis Dr G77 .... 156 B3
Fox Gr ML1 .... 163 D4
Fox St Glasgow G1 .... 240 C1
Greenock PA16 .... 45 E4
Foxbar Cres PA2 .... 132 C4
Foxbar Dr Glasgow G13 .... 95 D3
Paisley PA2 .... 132 C4
Foxbar Rd PA2 .... 132 C4
Foxes Gr G66 .... 79 F3
Foxglove Pl Ayr KA7 .... 239 E2
Glasgow G53 .... 135 D2
Foxhills Pl G23 .... 76 C1
Foxley St G32 .... 119 E1
Foyers Terr G21 .... 98 A2
Franchi Dr FK5 .... 23 F3
Francis St 7 G5 .... 117 D2
Frankfield Rd G33 .... 99 F3
Frankfield St G33 .... 98 C1
Frankfort St G41 .... 116 C1
Franklin Pl G75 .... 159 D1
Franklin St G40 .... 117 F2
Fraser Ave Bishopton PA7 .... 72 A2
Dumbarton G82 .... 50 B2
Johnstone PA5 .... 112 A1
Newton Mearns G77 .... 156 C3
Rutherglen G73 .... 138 B4
Troon KA10 .... 229 E3
Fraser Cres ML3 .... 162 A1
Fraser Gdns G66 .... 79 D4
Fraser Pl FK9 .... 2 A2
Fraser St Cambuslang G72 .... 138 C3
Cleland ML1 .... 144 A1
Fraser Wlk KA3 .... 223 E2
Frazer Ave G84 .... 16 A2
Frazer St G40 .... 118 A3
Frederick St ML5 .... 121 F4
Freeland Cres G53 .... 135 D3
Freeland Ct G53 .... 135 D3
Freeland Dr
Bridge Of W PA11 .... 90 B1
Glasgow G53 .... 135 D3
Renfrew PA4 .... 93 E3
Freeland La 8 G75 .... 180 C4
Freeland Pl G66 .... 79 E4
Freeland Rd PA8 .... 93 D4
Freelands Cres G60 .... 73 E3
Freelands Ct G81 .... 73 E2
Freelands Pl G60 .... 73 E3
Freelands Rd G60 .... 73 E3
Freesia Ct ML1 .... 163 F3
French St Clydebank G81 .... 73 F2
Glasgow G40 .... 117 F2
Renfrew PA4 .... 94 A1
Wishaw ML2 .... 165 D2
Freuchie St G34 .... 120 A4
Friar Ave G64 .... 78 A2
Friar's Dene ML11 .... 214 C2
Friar's La ML11 .... 214 C2
Friar's Wynd ML11 .... 214 C2
Friars Croft Irvine KA12 .... 219 D1
Friars Lawn KA13 .... 207 E2
Friars Pl G13 .... 95 F4
Friars St FK8 .... 7 D4
Friars Way ML6 .... 123 E2
Friarscourt Ave G13 .... 95 E4
Friarscourt Rd G69 .... 80 A1
Friarsfield Rd ML11 .... 214 C2
Friarton Rd G43 .... 136 C3
Friendship Gdns FK2 .... 24 B2
Friendship Way PA4 .... 94 B1
Frobisher Ave FK1 .... 41 F1
Frobisher Pl G84 .... 17 D1
Frood St ML1 .... 142 B1
Fruin Ave G77 .... 156 C3
Fruin Pl G22 .... 97 E2
Fruin Rd G15 .... 74 C1
Fruin Rise ML3 .... 161 F1
Fruin St G22 .... 97 E2
Fudstone Dr KA25 .... 170 A4
Fulbar Ave PA4 .... 94 B2
Fulbar Cres PA2 .... 112 C1
Fulbar Ct PA4 .... 94 B2
Fulbar Gdns PA2 .... 112 C1
Fulbar La PA4 .... 94 B2
Fulbar Rd Glasgow G52 .... 115 E4
Paisley PA2 .... 112 C2
Fulbar St PA4 .... 94 B2

Fullarton Ave
Dundonald KA2 .... 225 F1
Glasgow G32 .... 119 D1
Troon KA10 .... 229 F1
Fullarton Ct KA10 .... 229 F1
Fullarton Dr KA10 .... 229 D1
Fullarton Pl
Coatbridge ML5 .... 121 D2
Stevenston KA20 .... 217 E4
Troon KA10 .... 230 A2
Fullarton Rd
Cumbernauld G68 .... 61 F3
Glasgow G32 .... 139 D4
Prestwick KA9 .... 233 F1
Fullarton Rdbt KA12 .... 219 D1
Fullarton St Ayr KA7 .... 238 C4
Coatbridge ML5 .... 121 F2
Irvine KA12 .... 219 D1
Kilmarnock KA1 .... 222 C1
Fullers Gate G81 .... 74 B4
Fullarton Ctyd KA10 .... 230 A1
Fullerton Dr KA23 .... 190 A2

Fullerton La PA15 .... 46 C2
Fullerton Sq KA22 .... 205 E1
Fullerton St PA1 .... 113 E4
Fullerton Terr PA3 .... 113 F4
Fulmar Ct ⁴ G64 .... 97 F4
Fulmar Pk G74 .... 159 E2
Fulton PI PA3 .... 131 E3
Fulshaw Cres KA8 .... 236 C1
Fulshaw Ct KA9 .... 236 B3
Fulton Cres PA10 .... 111 D2
Fulton Dr PA6 .... 111 F4
Fulton Gdns PA6 .... 111 F4
Fulton Rd G62 .... 55 D1
Fulton St G13 .... 95 F4
Fulton's La KA3 .... 222 C1
Fulwood Ave Glasgow G13 .... 94 C4
  Linwood PA3 .... 112 A3
Fulwood Pk Ind Est ML3 .... 162 A2
Fulwood Pl G13 .... 94 C4
Furlongs The ML3 .... 162 C3
Furnace Ct KA11 .... 228 C3
Furnace Rd ML3 .... 183 F2
Fyfe Park Terr PA14 .... 47 F1
Fyfe Shore Rd PA14 .... 47 F1
Fyffe Park Rd PA14 .... 47 F1
Fyne Ave ML4 .... 141 F3
Fyne Cres ML9 .... 184 C3
Fyne Ct ML3 .... 162 A1
Fyne La ML7 .... 146 C3
Fyne Way ML1 .... 143 D3
Fyneart St KA1 .... 165 F2
Fynloch Pl G81 .... 73 F4
Fyvie Ave G43 .... 136 A3
Fyvie Cres PA15 .... 123 F3

Gaberston Ave FK10 .... 10 B4
Gabriel St PA15 .... 46 A1
Gadburn Sch G21 .... 98 B3
Gadie Ave PA4 .... 94 C1
Gadie St G33 .... 118 B4
Gadloch Ave G66 .... 79 E1
Gadloch Gdns G66 .... 79 E2
Gadloch St G22 .... 97 E3
Gadloch View G66 .... 79 E1
Gadsburn Ct G21 .... 98 B3
Gadshill St G21 .... 97 F1
Gael St PA16 .... 45 E2
Gagarin Terr KA13 .... 207 F1
Gailes Pk G72 .... 140 C1
Gailes Pl KA1 .... 227 F2
Gailes Rd
  Cumbernauld G68 .... 61 F3
  Irvine KA11 .... 224 B2
  Troon KA10 .... 229 E4
Gailes St G40 .... 118 A2
Gain Rd G67, ML5 .... 82 A1
Gain & Shankburn Rd
  G67 .... 82 B1
Gainburn Ct G67 .... 81 F3
Gainburn Cres G67 .... 81 F3
Gainburn Gdns G67 .... 81 F3
Gainburn Pl G67 .... 81 F3
Gainburn View G67 .... 82 A3
Gainford Pl KA3 .... 222 C2
Gainside Rd ML5 .... 101 D3
Gair Cres Carluke ML8 .... 188 A2
  Wishaw ML2 .... 165 D1
Gair Rd ML8 .... 188 A3
Gair Wynd ML7 .... 147 D2
Gairbraid Ave G20 .... 96 B3
Gairbraid Ct G20 .... 96 B3
Gairbraid Pl G20 .... 96 B3
Gairbraid Terr G69 .... 121 D3
Gairdoch Dr FK2 .... 24 B2
Gairdoch St FK2 .... 42 A4
Gairloch Gdns G69 .... 59 D1
Gaitskell Ave G83 .... 27 E4
Gala Ave PA4 .... 94 C1
Gala Cres ML2 .... 165 D3
Gala St G33 .... 98 C1
Galbraith Cres ML8 .... 187 D3
Galbraith Dr Glasgow G51 .... 115 F4
  Milngavie G62 .... 75 F4
Galdenoch St G33 .... 99 D1
Gallacher Ave PA2 .... 113 D1
Gallacher Cres G83 .... 19 F1
Gallacher Ct Pa1 .... 113 E3
Gallacher Way G72 .... 27 E1
Gallahill Ave PA4 .... 69 D4
Gallamuir Dr FK7 .... 12 B2
Gallamuir Rd FK7 .... 12 B3
Gallan Ave G23 .... 76 C1
Gallion Wlk KA1 .... 227 F4
Galloway Ave Ayr KA8 .... 236 B1
  Hamilton ML3 .... 183 E4
Galloway Ct KA11 .... 42 A3
  Irvine KA11 .... 220 A3
Galloway Dr Hamilton ML3 ... 183 E3
  Rutherglen G73 .... 138 A2
Galloway Pl KA21 .... 216 C4
  East Kilbride G74 .... 160 B2
Galloway St Falkirk FK1 .... 42 A3
  Glasgow G21 .... 97 F3
Galloway Wynd ML3 .... 183 E4
Gallowflat St G73 .... 138 A4
Gallowgate G1, G4, G40 .... 117 F3
Gallowhill ML9 .... 185 D1
Gallowhill Ave G66 .... 79 E3
Gallowhill Gr G66 .... 79 E4
Gallowhill Prim Sch PA3 ...... 114 A4
Gallowhill Rd
  Carmunnock G76 .... 158 C4
  Kirkintilloch G66 .... 79 E3
  Lanark ML11 .... 215 D2
  Paisley PA3 .... 114 A3

Galrigside Rd KA1 .... 227 E4
Galston Ave G77 .... 157 D3
Galston Ct ML3 .... 183 F4
Galston Rd KA1 .... 228 C3
Galston St G53 .... 134 C4
Galt Ave KA12 .... 219 E2
Galt Pl G75 .... 180 B4
Galt St PA15 .... 46 B2
Gambeson Cres FK7 .... 7 E2
Gameshill View KA3 .... 211 F4
Gamrie Dr G53 .... 135 D4
Gamrie Gdns G53 .... 135 D4
Gamrie Rd G53 .... 135 D4
Gannochy Dr G64 .... 78 B1
Gantock Cres G33 .... 119 D4
Ganton Ct KA13 .... 207 D2
Garden Ct KA8 .... 235 F1
Garden Pl KA10 .... 229 F2
Garden Square La KA13 .... 207 F2
Garden Sq Ayr KA8 .... 235 F1
  Falkirk FK1 .... 42 B3
  Kilmarnock KA3 .... 222 C1
Garden Terr FK1 .... 42 B3
Garden Veteran's Cotts
  PA8 .... 72 C3
Gardenhall G75 .... 179 F4
Gardenhall Ct G75 .... 179 F4
Gardenside ML4 .... 142 A2
Gardenside Ave
  Glasgow G32 .... 139 D2
  Uddingston G71 .... 140 C3
Gardenside Cres G32 .... 139 D4
Gardenside Pl G32 .... 139 D4
Gardenside Rd ML3 .... 162 B1
Gardenside St G71 .... 140 C3
Gardner St KA9 .... 236 B4
Gardner Gr G71 .... 141 D4
Gardner St G11 .... 96 A1
Gardrum Gdns FK1 .... 66 B4
Gardrum Pl KA3 .... 222 C2
Gardyne St G14 .... 100 A1
Gare Rd G84 .... 141 D4
Garelet Pl KA11 .... 220 A1
Gareloch Ave PA2 .... 113 D1
Garelochhead Sta 28 C2
Gareloch Cl PA15 .... 46 A1
Gareloch Cres PA16 .... 102 C1
Gareloch La PA14 .... 68 B4
Garelochh Rd
  Greenock PA15 .... 46 A2
  Port Glasgow PA14 .... 68 C4
  Rhu G84 .... 15 F2
Garfield Ave ML4 .... 142 B3
Garfield Dr ML4 .... 142 B2
Garfield St G31 .... 118 A3
Garforth Rd G69 .... 119 F2
Gargieston Prim Sch KA2 ..... 227 E3
Gargrave Ave G69 .... 119 F2
Garion Dr G13 .... 95 D3
Garliestion Rd G33 .... 119 F3
Garmouth Ct ³ G51 .... 116 A4
Garmouth Gdns ⁴ G51 .... 116 A4
Garmouth St G51 .... 115 F4
Garnet St G33 .... 240 B4
Garnetbank Prim Sch G3 ..... 240 B4
Garnethill St G3 .... 240 B4
Garngaber Ave G66 .... 79 E3
Garngaber Ct G66 .... 79 F3
Garngrew Rd FK4 .... 38 C2
Garnhall Farm Rd G68 .... 62 C4
Garnie Ave PA8 .... 93 E4
Garnie La PA8 .... 93 E4
Garnie Oval PA8 .... 73 E1
Garnie Pl PA8 .... 73 E1
Garnieland Rd PA8 .... 73 E1
Garnkirk La G33 .... 99 F3
Garnock Acad KA25 .... 149 D1
Garnock Ct Irvine KA12 .... 219 E1
  Kilbirnie KA25 .... 191 E4
Garnock Pk G74 .... 160 A1
Garnock Rd
  Kilmarnock KA1 .... 228 A3
  Stevenston KA20 .... 217 E4
Garnock St Dalry KA24 .... 191 E4
  Glasgow G21 .... 97 F1
  Kilbirnie KA25 .... 149 D1
Garnock View KA13 .... 207 F2
Garnockside KA14 .... 170 A3
Garpel Way PA12 .... 129 E1
Garrallan KA13 .... 207 E1
Garrawy Rd G84 .... 16 C1
Garrel Gr G65 .... 36 B1
Garrell Ave G65 .... 36 B1
Garrell Gr G65 .... 36 B1
Garrell Pl G65 .... 60 B4
Garrell Rd G65 .... 60 B4
Garrell Way
  Cumbernauld G67 .... 61 F1
  Kilsyth G65 .... 60 B4
Garrier Pl KA1 .... 222 B1
Garrier Rd KA11 .... 220 C1
Garrioch Cres ³ G20 .... 96 B3
Garrioch Dr G20 .... 96 B3
Garrioch Gate ⁷ G20 .... 96 B3
Garrioch Quadrant ⁴ G20 ...... 96 B3
Garrioch Rd G20 .... 96 B3
Garriochmill Rd G20 .... 96 C2
Garrion Bsns Pk ML2 .... 186 A4
Garrion Pl ML9 .... 185 F1
Garrion St ML2 .... 186 B3
Garrison Pl FK1 .... 42 A3
Garrowhill Dr G69 .... 119 F3
Garrowhill Halt G69 .... 119 F3
Garrowhill Prim Sch G69 ...... 120 A3
Garry Ave G61 .... 76 A1
Garry Dr PA2 .... 113 D1
Garry Pl Falkirk FK1 .... 42 B1
  Kilmarnock KA1 .... 228 A3
  Troon KA10 .... 229 F3

Garry St G44 .... 137 D4
Garry Way ML7 .... 146 C3
Garryhorn KA9 .... 236 B3
Garscadden Prim Sch G13 ..... 94 C4
Garscadden Rd G15 .... 75 D1
Garscadden Rd S
  Glasgow G15 .... 94 C4
  Glasgow G15 .... 95 D4
Garscadden Sta G14 .... 95 D3
Garscadden View G81 .... 74 B2
Garscube Cross G4 .... 97 D1
Garscube Rd G4, G20 .... 97 D1
Garshake Ave G82 .... 50 B3
Garshake Rd G82 .... 50 B3
Garshake Terr G82 .... 50 B3
Gartartan Rd PA1 .... 114 C3
Gartcarron Hill G68 .... 61 E2
Gartcloss Rd ML5 .... 101 E1
Gartcluth Gdns PA7 .... 11 F4
Gartconnel Dr G61 .... 75 F3
Gartconnell Gdns G61 .... 75 F3
Gartconnell Rd G61 .... 75 F3
Gartconner Ave G66 .... 80 A4
Gartconner Prim Sch G66 ...... 80 A4
Gartcosh Prim Sch G69 .... 100 C2
Gartcosh Rd ML5 .... 100 C1
Gartcosh Wlk ML4 .... 141 F3
Gartcows Ave FK1 .... 42 A2
Gartcows Cres FK1 .... 42 A2
Gartcows Dr FK1 .... 42 A2
Gartcows Gdns FK1 .... 41 F2
Gartcows Pl FK1 .... 42 A2
Gartcows Rd FK1 .... 42 A2
Gartcraig Rd G33 .... 118 C4
Garten Dr ML7 .... 147 D2
Gartferry Ave G69 .... 80 C1
Gartferry Rd G69 .... 80 C1
Gartferry St G21 .... 98 A2
Gartfield St ML6 .... 123 D3
Gartgill Rd ML5 .... 101 F1
Garth St G1 .... 241 D2
Garthamlock
  Prim Sch G33 .... 99 E1
Garthamlock Rd G33 .... 99 F1
Garthamlock Sec Sch G34 ..... 99 F1
Garthill Gdns FK1 .... 41 F2
Garthill Rd FK1 .... 41 F2
Gartland Dr
  Ardrossan KA22 .... 205 E2
  Glasgow G31 .... 118 A4
Gartland La PA1 .... 113 F3
Gartlea Ave ML6 .... 123 D4
Gartlea Rd ML6 .... 123 D4
Gartleahill ML6 .... 123 D3
Gartliston Rd ML5 .... 101 F2
Gartliston Terr G69 .... 121 D3
Gartloch Rd G66, G33 .... 100 A4
Gartly St G44 .... 136 C2
Gartmore Gdns G71 .... 140 C4
Gartmore La G69 .... 81 D1
Gartmore Rd PA1 .... 114 B2
Gartmore Terr G72 .... 138 A2
Gartness Dr ML6 .... 123 F2
Gartness Rd ML6 .... 124 A2
Gartocher Dr G32 .... 119 E3
Gartocher Rd G32 .... 119 E3
Gartocher Terr G32 .... 119 E3
Gartons Rd G21 .... 98 B2
Gartsherrie Ave ML5 .... 101 F3
Gartsherrie Ind Est ML5 ...... 101 F3
Gartsherrie Prim Sch
  ML5 .... 121 F4
Gartsherrie Rd ML5 .... 121 F4
Gartshore Cres G65 .... 59 F1
Gartshore Gdns G68 .... 62 C1
Garturk St Coatbridge ML5 .. 122 A2
  Glasgow G42 .... 117 D1
Garvald Ct G40 .... 118 A2
Garvald La FK6 .... 21 E4
Garvald Rd FK6 .... 39 E4
Garvald St Glasgow G40 ...... 118 A2
  Greenock PA15 .... 46 B2
Garvally Cres FK10 .... 10 A4
Garve Ave G44 .... 137 D3
Garvel Cres G33 .... 119 F3
Garvel Dr PA15 .... 45 E2
Garvel Pl G62 .... 54 B1
Garvel Rd Glasgow G33 .... 119 F3
  Milngavie G62 .... 54 C1
Garvel Sch for the Deaf
  PA16 .... 44 C3
Garven Ct KA1 .... 228 A4
Garven Rd KA20 .... 217 F3
Garvie Ave PA19 .... 44 C3
Garvin Lea ML4 .... 142 A4
Garvock Dr Glasgow G43 ..... 136 A3
  Greenock PA15 .... 45 E2
Garwhitter Dr G62 .... 55 D1
Gas St PA5 .... 112 A2
Gaskin Path G33 .... 99 F3
Gask House Sch G64 .... 97 F4
Gask Pl G13 .... 94 C4
Gaskin Path G33 .... 99 F3
Gasworks Rd ML8 .... 187 E2
Gatehead Pl PA10 .... 111 D2
Gatehouse St G32 .... 119 E3
Gates Rd PA12 .... 129 E2
Gateshead Pl PA10 .... 111 D2
Gateside PA10 .... 219 F3
Gateside Ave
  Bonnybridge Fk4 .... 40 B3
  Cambuslang G72 .... 139 E3
  Greenock PA16 .... 45 D4
  Kilsyth G65 .... 60 A4

Gateside Cres
  Airdrie ML6 .... 123 D4
  Barrhead G78 .... 134 A1
Gateside Gdns PA16 .... 45 D2
Gateside Gr PA16 .... 45 D2
Gateside Pk G65 .... 60 A4
Gateside Pl KA1 .... 227 F2
Gateside Prim Sch KA15 ..... 171 F4
Gateside Rd
  Barrhead G78 .... 134 A1
  Stirling FK7 .... 7 D2
  Wishaw ML2 .... 164 C2
Gateside Sch for the Deaf
  PA2 .... 133 E4
Gateside St Glasgow G31 ..... 118 A3
  Hamilton ML3 .... 162 C2
  West Kilbride KA23 .... 190 B3
Gateway The G74 .... 160 A2
Gaughan Quadrant ML1 ...... 163 E3
Gauldry Ave G52 .... 115 E2
Gauze St PA1 .... 113 F3
Gavell Rd G65 .... 60 A4
Gavin St Motherwell ML1 .... 163 F3
Gavinburn Gdns G60 .... 73 D4
Gavinburn Pl G60 .... 73 D4
Gavinburn Sch G60 .... 72 C4
Gavinburn St G60 .... 73 D4
Gavins Rd Alloa FK10 .... 4 C1
  Clydebank G81 .... 74 A3
Gavinton St G44 .... 136 C3
Gayne Dr ML5 .... 101 E3
Gean Ct G67 .... 62 C2
Gean Rd FK10 .... 9 F4
Gearholm Rd KA7 .... 238 B2
Geary St G23 .... 76 C1
Geddes Hill G74 .... 160 A2
Geddes Rd G21 .... 98 B4
Geelong Gdns G65 .... 33 E1
Geils Ave G82 .... 50 B1
Geils Quadrant G82 .... 50 B1
Geilsland Rd KA13 .... 171 E4
Geilsland Residential Sch
  KA15 .... 171 E4
Geirston Pk G82 .... 48 B4
Geirston Rd KA25 .... 148 C1
Gelston St G32 .... 119 D2
Gemini Gr ML1 .... 143 D3
Gemmel Pl G77 .... 156 B2
Gemmell Cres KA8 .... 236 B1
Gemmell Way ML9 .... 199 A4
General Roy Way ML8 .... 202 B4
Generals Gate G71 .... 140 C3
Gentle Row G81 .... 73 F3
George Aitken Ct KA22 .... 205 E2
George Ave G81 .... 74 B2
George Cres G81 .... 74 B2
George Ct ML1 .... 162 A3
George Gray St G73 .... 138 B4
George La PA1 .... 113 F2
George Mann Terr G73 .... 138 A2
George Pl PA1 .... 113 F2
George Rd PA19 .... 44 C3
George Reith Ave G12 .... 95 F3
George Sq Ayr KA8 .... 236 A1
  Glasgow G2 .... 241 D2
  Greenock PA15 .... 45 E3
George St Airdrie ML6 .... 122 C4
  Alexandria G83 .... 27 F2
  Alva FK12 .... 5 D3
  Ayr KA8 .... 236 A1
  Barrhead G78 .... 134 A2
  Chapelhall ML6 .... 123 E2
  Falkirk FK2 .... 42 A3
  Glasgow G1 .... 241 D2
  Glasgow, Baillieston G69 ... 120 A2
  Hamilton ML3 .... 162 A3
  Helensburgh G84 .... 16 C1
  Hownwood PA9 .... 130 C3
  Johnstone PA5 .... 111 F2
  Larbert FK5 .... 23 F2
  Laurieston FK2 .... 42 C2
  Motherwell ML1 .... 163 F2
  Motherwell, New Stevenston
    ML1 .... 143 D2
  Paisley PA1 .... 113 F2
  Stevenston KA20 .... 217 E4
George Street La G83 .... 27 F2
George Terr KA12 .... 219 E2
George Way ⁸ ML9 .... 185 D2
George's Ave KA8 .... 236 A2
Gerald Terr FK5 .... 23 F2
Gerard Pl ML4 .... 142 A4
Gertrude Pl G78 .... 134 A1
Ghillies La ML1 .... 142 B1
Gibb St Chapelhall ML6 .... 123 E1
  Cleland ML1 .... 144 A1
Gibbhan Pl FK6 .... 39 F4
Gibbon Cres G74 .... 160 B2
Gibbshill Pl ML7 .... 127 E3
Gibshill Rd PA15 .... 46 C1
Gibson Ave G82 .... 50 A2
Gibson Cres PA5 .... 111 F1
Gibson La PA13 .... 69 E1
Gibson Quadrant ML1 .... 142 B1
Gibson Rd PA4 .... 94 B1
Gibson St Dumbarton G82 ..... 50 A2
  Glasgow G4 .... 241 F1
  Glasgow, Kelvingrove G12 .. 96 C1
  Greenock PA15 .... 46 C1
  Kilmarnock KA1 .... 222 B1
  Salsburgh ML7 .... 125 D1
Gibsongray St FK2 .... 42 B3
Giffen Rd KA21 .... 217 D4
Giffnock Park Ave G46 .... 136 B2
Giffnock Prim Sch G46 .... 136 B1
Giffnock Sta G46 .... 136 B2

Gifford Dr G52 .... 115 D3
Gifford Wynd PA2 .... 112 C3
Gigha Cres KA11 .... 220 A3
Gigha Gdns ML8 .... 202 A4
Gigha La KA11 .... 220 A3
Gigha Pl KA11 .... 220 A3
Gigha Quadrant ML2 .... 164 C3
Gigha Terr KA11 .... 220 A3
Gigha Wynd KA11 .... 220 A3
Gilbert St G3 .... 116 B4
Gilbertfield Path G33 .... 99 D3
Gilbertfield Pl G33 .... 99 D3
Gilbertfield Rd G72 .... 139 F2
Gilbertfield St G33 .... 99 D3
Gilburn Pl ML7 .... 146 C2
Gilchrist Dr FK1 .... 41 F2
Gilchrist St ML5 .... 122 A4
Gilchrist Way ML2 .... 165 E1
Gilderdale Le G74 .... 159 E3
Gilfillan Ave KA21 .... 206 A3
Gilfillan Pl Falkirk FK2 .... 24 B3
  Overtown ML2 .... 186 B4
Gilfillan Way PA2 .... 132 C4
Gilhill St G20 .... 96 B4
Gill Pk FK6 .... 21 F2
Gill Rd ML2 .... 186 B3
Gillbank Ave ML8 .... 187 E3
Gillbank La ⑥ ML9 .... 185 E3
Gilliburn Rd PA13 .... 89 E4
Gilliespie Dr G84 .... 16 B3
Gillespie Pl FK7 .... 7 D3
Gillespie Terr FK7 .... 12 B3
Gillies Cres G74 .... 160 B3
Gillies Ct ML6 .... 123 F4
Gillies Pl FK7 .... 7 E2
Gillies Hill FK7 .... 6 B1
Gillies La G69 .... 120 B2
Gillies St KA10 .... 229 E2
Gillsburn Gdns KA3 .... 223 D3
Gilmartin Rd PA3 .... 111 F3
Gilmerton St G32 .... 119 D2
Gilmour Ave
  Clydebank G81 .... 74 A3
  Thornliebank G74 .... 158 A2
Gilmour Cres
  Eaglesham G76 .... 178 C3
  Rutherglen G73 .... 137 F4
Gilmour Dr ML3 .... 161 F2
Gilmour Pl Bellshill ML4 ...... 141 F2
  Coatbridge ML5 .... 121 F4
  Glasgow G5 .... 117 E3
Gilmour St Alexandria G83 ... 27 E2
  Clydebank G81 .... 74 B2
  Eaglesham G76 .... 178 C3
  Greenock PA15 .... 46 B3
  Kilmarnock KA1 .... 222 C1
  Paisley PA1 .... 113 F3
  Stewarton KA3 .... 195 F1
Gilmourton Cres G77 .... 156 B2
Gilroy Cl ML11 .... 215 E2
Gilshochill Sta G23 .... 96 C4
Gimmerscroft Cres KA3 ...... 123 F2
Girdle Gate KA11 .... 219 F2
Girdle Toll KA11 .... 220 A1
Girthon St G32 .... 119 E2
Girvan St G33 .... 118 B4
Glade The ML9 .... 185 D3
Gladney Ave G13 .... 94 C4
Gladsmuir Rd G52 .... 115 D3
Gladstone Ave
  Barrhead G78 .... 134 A1
  Johnstone PA5 .... 131 E4
Gladstone Ct ML3 .... 162 A3
Gladstone Pl FK8 .... 7 D3
Gladstone Rd
  Saltcoats KA21 .... 217 D4
  Sterhousemuir FK5 .... 23 E2
Gladstone St
  Bellshill ML4 .... 142 A3
  Clydebank G81 .... 73 F1
  ⑪ Glasgow G4 .... 97 D1
Glaive Ave FK7 .... 7 E2
Glaive Rd G13 .... 75 F1
Glamis Ave Carluke ML8 ..... 187 F1
  East Kilbride G74 .... 159 F2
  Eldersie PA5 .... 112 A3
  Newton Mearns G77 .... 156 C2
Glamis Dr PA16 .... 45 D3
Glamis Gdns G64 .... 78 A2
Glamis Pl PA16 .... 45 D3
Glamis Rd G31 .... 118 B2
Glanderston Ave
  Barrhead G78 .... 134 C1
  Newton Mearns G77 .... 156 A2
Glanderston Ct G13 .... 95 D4
Glanderston Dr G13 .... 95 D4
Glanderston Gate G77 .... 155 E2
Glanderston Rd G77 .... 155 E1
Glasgow Acad G12 .... 96 C2
Glasgow Bot Gdns G12 .... 96 C2
Glasgow Caledonian Univ
  G4 .... 241 D4
Glasgow Caledonian
  Univ Park Campus G3 .... 96 C1
Glasgow Coll of
  Building & Printing G5 ...... 117 E2
Glasgow Coll of
  Building & Printing
  (Annexe) G31 .... 118 C2
Glasgow Coll of
  Building & Printing
  (David Dale Bldg) G40 ...... 117 F2
Glasgow Coll of
  Building & Printing
  (Bridgeton Annexe) G40 ... 117 F2
Glasgow Dental Hospl G2 .... 240 B2

Glasgow & Edinburgh Rd
Calderbank ML1, ML6 .... 123 D1
Coatbridge G71, ML5 .... 120 E2
Glasgow G69 .... 120 B3
Motherwell ML1 .... 144 A4
Glasgow La KA22 .... 205 E1
Glasgow Rd
Bannockburn FK7 .... 11 E4
Blantyre G72 .... 161 F4
Cambuslang G73, G72 .... 138 C3
Cambuslang, Silverbank G72 138 C1
Clarkston G76 .... 157 E1
Clydebank G81 .... 94 B4
Clydebank, Hardgate G81 .... 74 B3
Coatbridge ML5 .... 121 E3
Cumbernauld G67 .... 82 B4
Cumbernauld, Kildrum G67 .. 62 A2
Denny FK6 .... 21 F1
Dumbarton G82 .... 50 B1
Eaglesham G76 .... 178 C4
East Kilbride G72, G74 .... 160 A4
Falkirk FK1 .... 41 E3
Glasgow G69 .... 120 A2
Glasgow, Barrhead G53 ...... 134 B2
Glasgow, Muirhead KA3 ...... 223 E3
Kilsyth G65 .... 60 A4
Kirkintilloch G66 .... 79 D4
Lanark ML11 .... 214 C2
Longcroft FK4 .... 39 E2
Milngavie G62 .... 55 D1
Paisley PA1 .... 114 B2
Port Glasgow PA14 .... 47 F1
Renfrew PA4 .... 94 C1
Rutherglen G73 .... 117 F1
Stirling FK7 .... 7 D1
Strathblane G63 .... 31 D2
Uddingston G71 .... 140 C4
Wishaw ML2 .... 164 C2
Glasgow Sch of Art G3 ...... 240 B3
Glasgow St
Ardrossan KA22 .... 205 E1
Glasgow G12 .... 96 C1
Helensburgh G84 .... 16 B1
Rutherglen G73 .... 138 A4
Kilbirnie KA25 .... 149 D4
Glasgow Univ (Annexe)
G13 .... 95 F4
Glasgow Vennel KA12 .... 219 E1
Glasgow Zoo G71 .... 120 B1
Glassel Rd G34 .... 100 B1
Glasserton Pl G43 .... 136 C3
Glasserton Rd G43 .... 136 C3
Glassford Rd ML3 .... 198 B3
Glassford St Glasgow G1 .... 241 D2
Milngavie G62 .... 55 D1
Motherwell ML1 .... 164 A2
Glasshouse Loan FK10 .... 10 A3
Glassock Rd KA3 .... 222 C3
Glaudhall Ave G69 .... 100 C4
Glazert Pl G65 .... 58 A3
Glebe Ave Bothwell G71 ..... 141 D1
Carmunnock G76 .... 158 B4
Coatbridge ML5 .... 121 E2
Irvine KA11 .... 225 E4
Kilmarnock KA1 .... 228 A4
Stirling FK8 .... 7 D4
Glebe Cres Airdrie ML6 ...... 123 E4
Alva FK12 .... 5 D4
Ayr KA8 .... 235 F1
East Kilbride G74 .... 159 F1
Hamilton ML3 .... 162 B1
Stirling FK8 .... 7 D4
Glebe Ct Beith KA15 .... 171 D4
Glasgow G4 .... 241 E3
Kilmacolm PA13 .... 89 E4
Glebe Dr ML11 .... 215 D2
Glebe Gdns
Alexandria G83 .... 27 F2
Houston PA6 .... 91 D1
Glebe Hollow G71 .... 141 D1
Glebe La G77 .... 156 B2
Glebe Pk G82 .... 50 A3
Glebe Pl Cambuslang G72 .. 139 D3
Rutherglen G73 .... 137 F4
Saltcoats KA21 .... 216 C4
Glebe Prim Sch KA12 .... 219 E1
Glebe Rd Ayr KA8 .... 235 F1
Beith KA15 .... 171 D4
Kilmacolm PA13 .... 89 E4
Newton Mearns G77 .... 156 B2
Glebe St Bellshill ML4 .... 141 F3
Denny FK6 .... 21 F1
East Kilbride G74 .... 159 F1
Falkirk FK1 .... 42 A3
Glasgow G4 .... 241 E4
Glasgow G4 .... 241 F3
Hamilton ML3 .... 162 B1
Kilwinning KA13 .... 207 F2
Renfrew PA4 .... 94 B2
Saltcoats KA21 .... 216 C4
Glebe Terr Alva FK10 .... 10 A3
Fenwick KA3 .... 213 D2
Glebe The Alva FK12 .... 5 D4
Bothwell G71 .... 141 D1
Irvine KA11 .... 225 E4
Lanark ML11 .... 214 C2
Glebe Wynd G71 .... 141 D1
Glebefield Rd G84 .... 15 F3
Glebelands Way KA15 .... 171 D4
Gleddoch Rd G52 .... 114 C3
Gleddstane Rd PA7 .... 72 A2
Glen Affric G74 .... 160 A1
Glen Affric Ave G53 .... 135 E2
Glen Affric Pl KA1 .... 227 E3
Glen Affric Way ML6 .... 123 E1
Glen Afton Ct KA1 .... 227 E3
Glen Alby Pl G53 .... 135 E2

Glen Almond G74 .... 160 B1
Glen Arroch G74 .... 160 A1
Glen Ave Balloch G83 .... 28 A4
Chryston G69 .... 80 C1
Glasgow G32 .... 119 D3
Gourock PA19 .... 44 C3
Neilston G78 .... 154 C4
Port Glasgow PA14 .... 47 D1
Glen Avon Dr G61 .... 123 E1
Glen Bervie G74 .... 160 A1
Glen Brae
Bridge Of W PA11 .... 110 B4
Falkirk FK1 .... 42 A2
Glen Cally G74 .... 160 A1
Glen Cannich G74 .... 160 A1
Glen Carron G74 .... 160 A1
Glen Clova G74 .... 160 A1
Glen Clova Dr G68 .... 61 E2
Glen Clunie G74 .... 160 B1
Glen Clunie Ave G53 .... 135 E2
Glen Clunie Dr G53 .... 135 E2
Glen Clunie Pl G53 .... 135 E2
Glen Cona Dr G53 .... 135 E3
Glen Cova Gdns KA2 .... 227 E3
Glen Creran Cres G78 .... 154 B3
Glen Cres Falkirk FK1 .... 42 A1
Glasgow G13 .... 94 C4
Stevenston KA20 .... 206 B1
Glen Dr Coatbridge ML5 ..... 121 E3
Motherwell ML1 .... 160 B2
Glen Derry G74 .... 160 B2
Glen Dessary G74 .... 181 D4
Glen Devon G74 .... 160 B1
Glen Doll G74 .... 160 A1
Glen Doll Rd G78 .... 154 A3
Glen Douglas Dr G68 .... 61 E2
Glen Douglas Pl PA16 .... 45 E2
Glen Douglas Rd PA16 ...... 45 E2
Glen Douglas Way PA16 .... 45 E2
Glen Dr Helensburgh G84 .. 16 B2
Motherwell ML1 .... 143 D3
Glen Dye G74 .... 160 A1
Glen Eagles G74 .... 160 A1
Glen Esk G74 .... 160 B1
Glen Esk Dr G53 .... 135 E2
Glen Etive Pl G73 .... 138 C1
Glen Falloch G74 .... 160 A1
Glen Falloch Cres G78 ...... 154 B3
Glen Farg G74 .... 160 B1
Glen Farrar G74 .... 160 A1
Glen Farrar Wlk KA22 .... 227 E3
Glen Feshie G74 .... 181 D4
Glen Finlet Rd G78 .... 154 B3
Glen Fruin Dr ML9 .... 185 E1
Glen Fruin Pl ML6 .... 123 E1
Glen Fruin Rd PA16 .... 45 E2
Glen Fyne Rd G68 .... 61 D2
Glen Gairn G74 .... 160 B1
Glen Gairn Cres G78 .... 154 B3
Glen Garrell Pl G65 .... 36 B1
Glen Garry G74 .... 181 D4
Glen Gdns Elderslie PA5 .... 112 B2
Falkirk FK1 .... 42 A2
Glen Ger East Kilbride G75 . 180 B4
Kilsyth G65 .... 36 B1
Glen Isla G74 .... 160 B1
Glen Isla Ave G78 .... 154 B3
Glen Kinglas Ave PA16 ...... 45 E1
Glen Kinglas Rd PA16 .... 45 E1
Glen La Paisley PA1 .... 113 F3
Uplawmoor G78 .... 153 D2
Glen Lednock Dr G68 .... 61 D2
Glen Lee G74 .... 160 B1
Glen Lethnot G74 .... 160 A1
Glen Livet Pl G53 .... 135 E2
Glen Lochay Gdns G68 ...... 61 D2
Glen Loy Pl G53 .... 135 E2
Glen Luce Dr G32 .... 119 E2
Glen Luss Gdns G68 .... 61 D2
Glen Luss Pl ML5 .... 122 B2
Glen Luss Rd PA16 .... 45 E1
Glen Luss Way PA16 .... 45 E1
Glen Lyon G74 .... 160 B1
Glen Lyon Cres KA2 .... 227 E3
Glen Lyon Ct G68 .... 61 D2
Glen Lyon Rd G78 .... 154 B3
Glen Mallie G74 .... 160 B1
Glen Mark G74 .... 160 B1
Glen Mark Rd G78 .... 154 B3
Glen Markie Dr G53 .... 135 E2
Glen More G74 .... 160 A1
Glen Moriston Rd
Cumbernauld G68 .... 61 D2
Glasgow G53 .... 135 E2
Glen Moy G74 .... 160 B1
Glen Muir Rd G78 .... 154 B3
Glen Nevis G74 .... 181 D4
Glen Nevis Pl
Kilmarnock KA1 .... 227 E3
Rutherglen G73 .... 138 B1
Glen Ochil Rd ML6 .... 123 E1
Glen Ogilvie G74 .... 160 B1
Glen Ogle St G32 .... 119 E2
Glen Orchy Ct G68 .... 61 D3
Glen Orchy Dr
Cumbernauld G68 .... 61 D2
Glasgow G53 .... 135 E2
Glen Orchy Pl
Chapelhall ML6 .... 123 E1
Cumbernauld G68 .... 61 D2
Glasgow G53 .... 135 E2
Kilmarnock KA2 .... 227 E3
Glen Orrin Ave KA2 .... 227 E3
Glen Orrin Pl KA2 .... 227 E3
Glen Prosen G74 .... 160 B1
Glen Quoich G74 .... 160 B2
Glen Rannoch Dr ML6 .... 123 E1

Glen Rd Airdrie ML6 .... 123 F3
Bishopton PA7 .... 72 A2
Caldercruix ML6 .... 104 C2
East Kilbride G74 .... 158 C3
Glasgow G32 .... 119 D4
Lennoxtown G65 .... 33 D1
Motherwell ML1 .... 143 E4
Old Kilpatrick G60 .... 73 D3
Glen Rd Plean FK7 .... 12 B1
Shotts ML7 .... 146 C2
Torwood FK5 .... 22 B4
West Kilbride KA23 .... 190 B3
Wishaw ML2 .... 165 D2
Glen Rinnes Dr G78 .... 154 B3
Glen Rosa Gdns G68 .... 61 D2
Glen Roy Dr G78 .... 154 B3
Glen Sannox Dr G68 .... 61 D2
Glen Sannox View G68 ...... 61 D2
Glen Sax Dr PA4 .... 94 C1
Glen Shee G74 .... 160 B1
Glen Shee Ave G53 .... 154 B3
Glen Shee Cres ML6 .... 123 E1
Glen Shiel Cres KA2 .... 227 E3
Glen Shirva Rd G65 .... 59 F2
Glen St Barrhead G78 .... 134 B2
Cambuslang G72 .... 139 E2
Glasgow G4 .... 45 E4
Motherwell ML1 .... 142 C1
Paisley PA3 .... 113 F3
Glen Tanner G74 .... 160 B1
Glen Tarbert Dr G78 .... 154 B3
Glen Tennet G74 .... 160 B1
Glen Terr FK6 .... 21 E1
Glen Trool Wlk KA2 .... 227 E4
Glen Truim View KA2 .... 227 E3
Glen Turret G74 .... 160 B1
Glen Tye Rd FK7 .... 7 E3
Glen Urquhart G74 .... 160 A1
Glen View
Cumbernauld G67 .... 62 B2
Dennyloanhead FK4 .... 39 E3
Hamilton ML3 .... 183 E4
Glenacre Cres G71 .... 140 C4
Glenacre Dr Airdrie ML6 .... 123 E3
Glasgow G45 .... 137 E2
Glenacre Quadrant G45 .... 137 E2
Glenacre Rd G67 .... 82 C4
Glenacre St G45 .... 137 E2
Glenacre Terr G45 .... 137 E2
Glenafeoch Rd ML8 .... 188 A1
Glenafton View ML3 .... 183 D4
Glenallan Cres KA7 .... 238 B1
Glenallan Terr ML1 .... 142 B1
Glenallan Way PA2 .... 132 C4
Glenalmond Rd G73 .... 138 B2
Glenalmond St G32 .... 119 D2
Glenan Gdns G84 .... 16 B1
Glenapp Ave PA2 .... 114 A1
Glenapp Pl KA13 .... 207 E1
Glenapp Quadrant KA1 ..... 228 A4
Glenapp Rd PA2 .... 114 A1
Glenapp St G41 .... 116 C2
Glenarklet Dr PA2 .... 114 A1
Glenarn Rd G84 .... 15 F2
Glenartney PA6 .... 91 E3
Glenartney Rd G69 .... 80 B1
Glenashdale Way PA2 .... 114 A1
Glenavon Ct KA3 .... 162 A1
Glenavon Rd G20 .... 96 B4
Glenbank Ave G66 .... 79 E2
Glenbank Dr G46 .... 135 F1
Glenbank Rd G66 .... 79 E2
Glenbarr St G21 .... 97 F1
Glenbervie Ave FK5 .... 23 D2
Glenbervie Cres
Cumbernauld G68 .... 61 F3
Larbert FK5 .... 23 D2
Glenbervie Dr
Kilwinning KA13 .... 207 D2
Larbert FK5 .... 23 D2
Glenbervie Pl Glasgow G23 76 C1
Gourock PA19 .... 44 A3
Newton Mearns G77 .... 156 A3
Glenbervie Wynd KA12 ..... 224 B4
Glenbo Dr FK6 .... 39 F4
Glenboig Farm Rd ML5 ...... 101 F3
Glenboig New Rd ML5 .... 101 F3
Glenboig Rd Gartcosh G69 101 D4
Glenboig ML5 .... 101 E3
Glenboig Ct ML1 .... 42 A2
Glenbrae La ML15 .... 46 A1
Glenbrae Rd Greenock PA15 46 A1
Port Glasgow PA14 .... 68 B4
Glenbride Rd KA23 .... 190 B2
Glenbrittle Dr PA2 .... 114 A1
Glenbrittle Way PA2 .... 114 A1
Glenbuck Ave G33 .... 98 C3
Glenbuck Dr G33 .... 98 C3
Glenburn Ave
Cambuslang G72 .... 138 C3
Chryston G69 .... 80 C1
Glasgow G69 .... 120 B3
Motherwell ML1 .... 143 E2
Glenburn Cres
Milton Of Camp G65 .... 58 B3
Paisley PA2 .... 133 E4
Uddingston G71 .... 141 E4
Glenburn Dr PA13 .... 69 E1
Glenburn Gdns
Bishopbriggs G64 .... 77 F1
Glenboig ML5 .... 101 E3
Glenburn Ind Est KA9 .... 236 C4

Glenburn La Glasgow G20 .. 96 C4
Kilmacolm PA13 .... 69 E1
Glenburn Rd Ayr KA9 .... 236 C4
Glenburn Rd Bearsden G61 75 F3
East Kilbride G74 .... 159 D2
Glenburn Pl ML4 .... 142 A3
Glasgow G46 .... 136 A1
Hamilton ML3 .... 162 A2
Kilmacolm PA13 .... 69 E1
Paisley PA2 .... 133 E4
Prestwick KA9 .... 236 C4
Glenburn Sch PA16 .... 44 C2
Glenburn St Glasgow G20 .. 96 C4
Port Glasgow PA14 .... 47 D1
Glenburn Terr Carluke ML8 . 201 F4
Motherwell ML1 .... 143 E1
Glenburn Way G44 .... 158 C2
Glenburnie Pl G34 .... 120 B3
Glenbuck Wynd ML9 .... 185 D2
Glenburnie Pl G34 .... 119 F4
Glencairn Ave ML2 .... 164 B2
Glencairn Dr Chryston G69 . 80 C1
Glasgow G41 .... 116 C1
Rutherglen G73 .... 137 F4
Glencairn Gdns
Cambuslang G72 .... 139 E3
Glasgow G41 .... 116 C1
Glencairn Ind Est KA1 .... 227 F3
Glencairn La G41 .... 116 C1
Glencairn Prim Sch
Motherwell ML1 .... 163 F3
Stevenston KA20 .... 217 E4
Glencairn Rd Ayr KA7 .... 239 E3
Cumbernauld G67 .... 62 B1
Dumbarton G82 .... 49 F2
Greenock PA16 .... 44 C2
Kilmacolm PA13 .... 89 E4
Langbank PA14 .... 70 B4
Paisley PA3 .... 114 A4
Glencairn Ret Pk KA1 .... 227 F3
Glencairn Sq KA1 .... 227 F3
Glencairn St Falkirk FK1 .... 41 D3
Larkhall ML9 .... 185 D2
Kirkintilloch G66 .... 79 E4
Motherwell ML1 .... 163 F3
Saltcoats KA21 .... 216 C4
Stevenston KA20 .... 206 C1
Stirling FK7 .... 7 D2
Glencairn Terr KA3 .... 222 A4
Glencalder Cres ML4 .... 142 B2
Glencally Ave PA2 .... 114 A1
Glencart Gr PA10 .... 111 E1
Glencleland Rd ML2 .... 164 B2
Glenclora Dr PA2 .... 114 A1
Glencloy St G22 .... 96 C4
Glenclune Ct PA13 .... 89 E4
Glencoats Dr PA3 .... 113 D2
Glencoe Dr ML1 .... 143 D3
Glencoe Pl Glasgow G13 .... 95 F4
Hamilton ML3 .... 183 D4
Glencoe Rd Carluke ML8 ... 202 A4
Rutherglen G73 .... 138 B2
Stirling FK8 .... 2 A1
Glencoe St G13 .... 95 F4
Glenconner Dr KA7 .... 239 D3
Glenconner Pl KA7 .... 239 D3
Glenconner Rd KA7 .... 239 D3
Glenconner Way G66 .... 59 D1
Glenconner Rd ML9 .... 199 D4
Glencorse Rd PA2 .... 113 D1
Glencorse St G32 .... 118 C4
Glencraig St ML6 .... 122 C4
Glencroft Ave G71 .... 140 C4
Glencroft Rd G44 .... 137 F3
Glencryan Rd G67 .... 62 A1
Glencryan Sch G67 .... 82 C4
Glendale Ave ML6 .... 123 E3
Glendale Cres Ayr KA7 ...... 239 E2
Bishopbriggs G64 .... 98 B4
Glendale Dr G64 .... 98 B4
Glendale Pl Ayr KA7 .... 239 D2
Bishopbriggs G64 .... 98 B4
Glasgow G31 .... 118 A3
Glendale Prim Sch G41 ..... 116 C2
Glendale St G31 .... 118 A3
Glendaruel Ave G61 .... 76 A2
Glendaruel Rd G73 .... 138 C1
Glendarvel Gdns G22 .... 97 E2
Glendee Gdns PA4 .... 94 B1
Glendee Rd PA4 .... 94 B1
Glendentan Rd PA11 .... 110 B3
Glendevon Pl Clydebank G81 73 F2
Hamilton ML3 .... 183 D4
Glendevon Sq G33 .... 99 D1
Glendevon Way KA11 .... 220 A3
Glendinning Pl G76 .... 178 B2
Glendinning Rd G13 .... 75 F1
Glendoick Pl G77 .... 156 A3
Glendorch Ave ML2 .... 165 E3
Glendore St G14 .... 95 F1
Glendoune Rd G76 .... 157 F3
Glendower Way PA2 .... 132 C4
Glenduffhill Rd G69 .... 119 F3
Gleneagles Ave
Cumbernauld G68 .... 62 A3
Kilwinning KA13 .... 207 E2
Gleneagles Dr
Bishopbriggs G64 .... 78 A2
Gourock PA19 .... 44 A3
Newton Mearns G77 .... 157 D2
Gleneagles Gate G77 .... 157 D2
Gleneagles Gdns G64 .... 78 A2
Gleneagles La N G14 .... 95 E2
Gleneagles La S G14 .... 95 E2
Gleneagles Pk G74 .... 159 E1
Gleneagles Pl KA2 .... 224 C4
Gleneagles Cres G66 .... 59 D1

Glenelg Path ML5 .... 101 E3
Glenelg Quadrant G34 .... 100 B1
Glenelm Pl ML4 .... 142 A3
Glenesk Cres G53 .... 135 E2
Glenfarg Cres G61 .... 76 A2
Glenfarg Rd Hamilton ML3 .. 183 D4
Rutherglen G73 .... 138 A2
Glenfarg St G20 .... 97 D1
Glenfarm Rd ML1 .... 143 F2
Glenfield Ave PA2 .... 133 F4
Glenfield Cres PA2 .... 133 F3
Glenfield Gdns KA1 .... 227 F3
Glenfield Pl KA1 .... 227 F3
Glenfield Rd
East Kilbride G75 .... 181 D3
Paisley PA2 .... 133 F3
Glenfinlas St G84 .... 16 C1
Glenfinnan Dr
Bearsden G61 .... 76 B2
Glasgow G20 .... 96 B3
Glenfinnan Pl G20 .... 96 B3
Glenfinnan Rd G20 .... 96 B3
Glenfruin Cres PA2 .... 114 A1
Glenfruin Rd G72 .... 161 E4
Glenfuir Rd FK1 .... 41 F3
Glenfuir St FK1 .... 41 E3
Glengarnock Prim Sch
KA14 .... 170 A4
Glengarnock Sta KA14 .... 170 B3
Glengarnock Workshops
KA14 .... 170 B4
Glengarriff Rd ML4 .... 142 A4
Glengarry Cres FK1 .... 41 F2
Glengarry Dr G52 .... 115 E3
Glengavel Cres G33 .... 98 C3
Glengavel Gdns ML2 .... 165 E4
Glengowan Prim Sch
Caldercruix ML6 .... 105 C2
Larkhall ML9 .... 185 D2
Glengowan Rd
Bridge Of W PA11 .... 110 B4
Caldercruix ML6 .... 105 D2
Glengyre St G34 .... 100 B1
Glenhead Cres
Clydebank G81 .... 74 A4
Glasgow G22 .... 97 E3
Glenhead Prim Sch G67 .... 62 C3
Glenhead Rd Clydebank G81 74 A3
Kirkintilloch G66 .... 79 E2
Glenhead St G22 .... 97 E3
Glenholme Ave PA2 .... 113 D1
Glenhove Rd G67 .... 62 A1
Glenhuntly Rd PA14 .... 47 E1
Glenhuntly Terr G14 .... 95 D3
Gleniffer Ave G13 .... 94 C3
Gleniffer Braes Ctry Pk
PA2 .... 133 D3
Gleniffer Cres PA5 .... 112 B1
Gleniffer Ct ML6 .... 101 D1
Gleniffer Dr G78 .... 134 A3
Gleniffer High Sch PA2 ...... 133 D4
Gleniffer Rd Paisley PA2 .... 132 B2
Renfrew PA4 .... 114 A4
Uplawmoor G78 .... 152 B2
Gleniffer View
Clydebank G81 .... 74 B2
Neilston G78 .... 154 B4
Gleninver Rd PA16 .... 45 D2
Glenisla Ave G69 .... 81 D2
Glenisla St G31 .... 118 B2
Glenkirk Dr G15 .... 75 D1
Glenlea Prim Sch ML3 .... 162 A3
Glenlee St ML3 .... 161 F3
Glenleith Pl KA11 .... 220 B1
Glenlivet Pl KA11 .... 220 B1
Glenlivet Rd G78 .... 154 B3
Glenlora Dr G53 .... 135 D4
Glenlora Terr G53 .... 135 D4
Glenluce Gdns G69 .... 81 D2
Glenluce Terr G74 .... 160 A4
Glenluggie Rd G66 .... 80 A4
Glenlui Ave G73 .... 138 A3
Glenlyon Ct ML3 .... 183 D4
Glenlyon Gr KA11 .... 219 F3
Glenlyon Pl G73 .... 138 B2
Glenmalloch Ph PA5 .... 112 B2
Glenmanor Ave G69 .... 80 C1
Glenmanor Prim Sch G69 .. 80 C1
Glenmanor Rd G69 .... 80 C1
Glenmare Ave G66 .... 80 A4
Glenmavis Cres ML8 .... 188 A1
Glenmavis Ct ML8 .... 188 A1
Glenmavis Rd ML6 .... 102 C1
Glenmavis St G4 .... 240 C4
Glenmore Ave
Alexandria G83 .... 27 E3
Bellshill ML4 .... 142 A2
Glasgow G42 .... 137 F4
Glenmore Dr FK4 .... 39 F3
Glenmore Rd ML1 .... 143 E2
Glenmoss Ave PA8 .... 72 C1
Glenmount Pl KA7 .... 238 A1
Glenmuir Ct KA8 .... 236 B1
Glenmuir Cres G53 .... 135 D3
Glenmuir Dr G53 .... 135 D3
Glenmuir Pl KA8 .... 236 B1
Glenmuir Rd KA8 .... 236 B1
Glenmuir Wynd KA8 .... 236 B1
Glenochil Pk FK10 .... 4 C2
Glenochil Rd FK10 .... 4 C2
Glenochil Terr FK10 .... 4 C2
Glenoran La ML9 .... 185 D2
Glenorchard Rd G64 .... 56 B1
Glenorchy St G78 .... 154 B3
Glenpark ML6 .... 123 F3

Glenpark Ave
Glasgow G46 .... 136 A1
Prestwick KA9 .... 236 B3
Glenpark Dr PA14 .... 47 D1
Glenpark Gdns G72 .... 138 C4
Glenpark Pl KA7 .... 239 D2
Glenpark Rd PA12 .... 129 E2
Glenpark St Glasgow G31 .. 118 A3
Wishaw ML2 .... 165 D2
Glenpark Terr G72 .... 138 C4
Glenpath G82 .... 50 B2
Glenpatrick Rd PA5 .... 112 B1
Glenraith Path G33 .... 99 D2
Glenraith Rd G33 .... 99 D1
Glenraith Sq G33 .... 99 D2
Glenraith Wlk G33 .... 99 E1
Glenriddel Rd KA7 .... 239 D3
Glenriddet Ave KA25 ...... 170 A4
Glenshee St G31 .... 118 B2
Glenshee Terr ML3 .... 183 D4
Glenshiel Ave PA2 .... 114 A1
Glenshira Ave PA2 .... 114 A1
Glenside Ave G53 .... 115 D1
Glenside Cres KA23 .... 190 B3
Glenside Dr G73 .... 138 C3
Glenside Gr KA23 .... 190 B3
Glenside Rd
Dumbarton G82 .... 50 B3
Port Glasgow PA14 .... 68 B4
Glenspean Pl ML5 .... 122 B3
Glenspean St G43 .... 136 B3
Glenspean St G43 .... 136 B3
Glentanar Pl G22 .... 97 D4
Glentanar Rd G22 .... 97 D4
Glentanar Rd G73 .... 138 B2
Glentore Quadrant ML6 ... 103 D1
Glentrool Gdns
Glasgow G22 .... 97 E2
Moodiesburn G69 .... 81 D2
Glenturret St G32 .... 119 D2
Glentyan Ave PA10 .... 111 D2
Glentyan Dr G53 .... 135 D3
Glentyan Terr G53 .... 135 D4
Glentye Gdns FK1 .... 41 F1
Glenview Airdrie ML6 ...... 123 E3
Denny FK6 .... 21 D2
Kirkintilloch G66 .... 79 E4
Larkhall ML9 .... 184 C2
Menstrie FK11 .... 4 A3
West Kilbride KA23 .... 190 B2
Glenview Ave Bonnybridge FK4 38 C2
Caldercruix ML6 .... 105 D2
Glenview Cres G69 .... 81 D2
Glenview Dr FK1 .... 41 F1
Glenview Pl G72 .... 140 B1
Glenview St ML6 .... 102 C2
Glenview Terr PA15 .... 45 E2
Glenville Ave G46 .... 136 A2
Glenville Gate G76 .... 158 A3
Glenville Terr G76 .... 158 A3
Glenward Ave G65 .... 57 F4
Glenwell St ML6 .... 102 C2
Glenwinnel Rd FK12 .... 4 C4
Glenwood Ave ML6 .... 123 E2
Glenwood Bsns Ctr G45 ... 137 F2
Glenwood Cres G66 .... 79 D3
Glenwood Dr G46 .... 135 F1
Glenwood Gdns G66 .... 79 D3
Glenwood Path G45 .... 137 F2
Glenwood Pl Glasgow G45 . 137 F2
Kirkintilloch G66 .... 79 D3
Glenwood Rd G66 .... 79 D3
Glenyards Rd FK4 .... 40 A1
Glidden Ct ML2 .... 186 B4
Glorat Ave G65 .... 57 F4
Gloucester Ave
Clarkston G76 .... 157 E4
Rutherglen G73 .... 138 B3
Gloucester St G5 .... 117 D3
Glowrorum Dr FK6 .... 39 F4
Glynwed Ct FK2 .... 42 B4
Goatfell View KA10 .... 229 F4
Gockston Rd PA3 .... 113 E4
Goddard Pl ML2 .... 166 A3
Godfrey Ave FK6 .... 21 E1
Godfrey Cres FK5 .... 23 E1
Gogar Loan FK9 .... 3 E3
Gogar Pl Glasgow G33 .... 118 C4
Stirling FK7 .... 7 E1
Gogar St G33 .... 118 C4
Goil Ave ML4 .... 141 E3
Goil Way ML1 .... 143 D3
Goldberry Ave G14 .... 95 D3
Goldcraig Ct KA11 .... 220 A3
Goldenacre Pl ML6 .... 103 F2
Goldenberry Ave KA23 .... 190 B2
Goldenhill Prim Sch G81 .. 74 A3
Goldenlee View PA6 .... 111 D4
Goldie Pl KA20 .... 206 B1
Goldie Rd G71 .... 141 D2
Golf Ave Bellshill ML4 .... 142 A2
Stevenston KA20 .... 217 F3
Golf Course Rd Balmore G64 77 E4
Bridge Of W PA11 .... 110 B4
Golf Cres KA10 .... 229 E1
Golf Ct G44 .... 136 C1
Golf Dr Clydebank G15 .... 74 C1
Paisley PA1 .... 114 B2
Port Glasgow PA14 .... 68 B4
Golf Gdns ML9 .... 185 E1
Golf Pl Bellshill ML4 ..... 142 A2
Greenock PA16 .... 45 E4
Helensburgh G84 .... 17 D1
Irvine KA12 .... 219 D3
Troon KA10 .... 229 E1

Golf Rd Bishopton PA7 ..... 72 A2
Clarkston G76 .... 157 E4
Gourock PA19 .... 44 B3
Rutherglen G73 .... 138 A2
Golf View G81 .... 73 F2
Golffields Rd KA12 .... 219 E1
Golfhill Dr Alexandria G83 . 27 F3
Glasgow G31 .... 118 A4
Helensburgh G84 .... 16 C1
Golfhill Prim Sch G31 .... 117 F4
Golfhill Quadrant ML6 .... 103 D1
Golfhill Rd ML2 .... 164 C2
Golfhill Sch ML6 .... 102 C1
Golfloan KA3 .... 211 F4
Golfview G61 .... 75 E3
Golfview Dr ML5 .... 121 E4
Golfview Pl ML5 .... 121 E3
Golspie Ave ML6 .... 122 C2
Golspie St G51 .... 116 A4
Good Shepherd Sch G32 ... 118 C1
Goodview Gdns ML9 .... 185 E1
Goosecroft Rd FK8 .... 7 D4
Goosedubbs G1 .... 241 D1
Gooseholm Cres G82 .... 50 A3
Gooseholm Rd G82 .... 50 A3
Gopher Ave G71 .... 141 D4
Gorbals Cross
Glasgow G5 .... 117 E3
Larkhall ML9 .... 185 D2
Gorbals St G1, G5 .... 117 E3
Gordon Ave Bishopton PA7 . 72 A2
Glasgow G69 .... 119 F3
Glasgow, Netherlee G44 .... 136 C1
Paisley G52 .... 114 C4
Gordon Cres
Bridge Of A FK9 .... 2 A4
Newton Mearns G77 .... 156 C3
Stirling FK8 .... 1 C1
Gordon Ct ML6 .... 123 F4
Gordon Dr Alloa FK10 ..... 10 B4
East Kilbride G74 .... 160 A2
Glasgow G44 .... 136 C2
Gordon La G1 .... 240 C2
Gordon Pl Bellshill ML4 ... 141 F1
Falkirk FK1 .... 42 A3
Gordon Rd Glasgow G44 ... 136 C1
Hamilton ML3 .... 161 F2
Gordon St Ayr KA8 .... 236 A2
Glasgow G1 .... 240 C2
Greenock PA15 .... 46 C2
Paisley PA1 .... 113 F2
Gordon Terr Ayr KA8 ...... 239 D4
Blantyre G72 .... 140 B1
Hamilton ML3 .... 162 A2
Gorebridge St G32 .... 118 C4
Goremire Rd ML8 .... 202 A4
Gorget Ave G13 .... 75 E1
Gorget Pl G13 .... 75 E1
Gorget Quadrant G13 ..... 75 E1
Gorrie St FK6 .... 21 E1
Gorse Cres PA11 .... 110 C4
Gorse Pk KA7 .... 239 E2
Gorse Pl G71 .... 141 D4
Gorsehall St ML1 .... 144 A1
Gorsewood G64 .... 77 F1
Gorstan Pl G20 .... 96 B3
Gorstan St G23 .... 96 B4
Goschen Terr KA8 .... 236 A1
Gosford La G14 .... 95 D2
Gottries Rd KA12 .... 219 D1
Goudie St PA3 .... 113 E4
Gough St G33 .... 118 B4
Goukscroft Pk KA7 .... 238 B2
Gould St KA8 .... 236 B1
Gourlay G74 .... 160 B3
Gourlay Dr ML2 .... 186 B3
Gourlay St Glasgow G21 .. 97 F2
1 Glasgow, Springburn G21 . 97 F2
Gourock High Sch PA19 ... 44 B4
Gourock Prim Sch PA19 ... 44 C4
Gourock St G5 .... 117 D2
Gourock Sta PA19 .... 44 C4
Govan St G83 .... 27 E3
Govan High Sch G51 ...... 115 F4
Govan Rd Glasgow G51 .... 115 F4
Glasgow, Plantation G51 ... 116 B3
Govan Underground Sta
G51 .... 116 A4
Govanhill St G42 .... 117 D1
Gowan Ave FK2 .... 42 A3
Gowan Brae ML6 .... 105 D3
Gowan La FK2 .... 42 A3
Gowanbank Gdns PA5 ...... 111 F1
Gowanbank Prim Sch G53 .. 135 D3
Gowanbank Rd KA7 .... 239 D1
Gowanbrae G66 .... 79 E3
Gowanhill Gdns FK8 ...... 1 C1
Gowanlea Ave G15 .... 75 D1
Gowanlea Dr
Glasgow G46 .... 136 B2
Slamannan FK1 .... 86 A3
Gowanlea Terr G71 .... 141 D4
Gowanside Pl ML8 .... 187 E1
Gower St KA7 .... 239 D2
Gower St G41 .... 116 B2
Gower Terr G41 .... 116 B3
Gowkhall Ave ML1 .... 143 F2
Gowkhouse Rd PA13 .... 89 F4
Goyle Ave G15 .... 75 E2
Grace Ave G69 .... 120 C3
Grace St G3 .... 240 A2
Gracie Cres FK7 .... 8 B4
Gradion Pl FK1 .... 42 A2
Graeme Ct ML1 .... 142 B1
Graeme High Sch FK1 ..... 42 B2
Graeme Pl FK1 .... 41 F1
Graffham Ave G46 .... 136 C2
Grafton Pl G1 .... 241 D3

Graham Ave
Cambuslang G72 .... 139 E3
Clydebank G81 .... 74 A2
East Kilbride G74 .... 159 F1
Hamilton ML3 .... 183 E4
Larbert FK5 .... 23 D2
Stirling FK9 .... 2 B2
Graham Cres G82 .... 48 A4
Graham Dr G62 .... 54 C1
Graham Pl Ashgill ML9 ... 185 F1
Helensburgh G84 .... 17 D1
Kilmarnock KA3 .... 223 E1
Kilsyth G65 .... 36 B1
Graham Rd Crossford ML8 . 201 D1
Dumbarton G82 .... 49 E2
Graham Sq G31 .... 117 F3
Graham St Airdrie ML6 ... 123 D4
Barrhead G78 .... 134 B2
Bridge Of A FK9 .... 2 A4
Greenock PA16 .... 45 E3
Hamilton ML3 .... 162 C2
Johnstone PA5 .... 111 F1
Motherwell ML1 .... 143 D3
Wishaw ML2 .... 165 D1
Graham Terr Airth FK2 .... 14 B2
Bishopbriggs G64 .... 98 A4
Stewarton KA3 .... 195 E1
Grahamfield Pl KA15 ..... 171 D4
Grahams Ave PA12 .... 129 E2
Grahams Rd FK2 .... 42 A3
Grahamsdyke Cres FK4 .... 40 A2
Grahamsdyke Rd
Bonnybridge FK4 .... 40 A2
Kirkintilloch G66 .... 58 C1
Grahamshill Ave ML6 ..... 123 E4
Grahamshill St ML6 ...... 123 E4
Grahamston Ave KA14 .... 170 A4
Grahamston Cres PA2 .... 134 B4
Grahamston Ct PA2 ...... 134 B4
Grahamston Pk G78 ...... 134 A3
Grahamston Pl PA2 .... 134 B4
Grahamston Rd G78, PA2 .. 134 B3
Grahamston Sta FK1 ..... 42 A3
Graigleith View FK10 .... 4 B2
Graignestock Pl **3** G40 . 117 F3
Graignestock St G40 ..... 117 F3
Graigside PI G68 .... 81 F4
Graitney Cres ML1 .... 143 F1
Grammar School Sq ML3 .. 162 C2
Grampian Ave PA2 .... 133 E4
Grampian Cres
Chapelhall ML6 .... 123 F1
Glasgow G32 .... 119 D2
Grampian Ct KA11 .... 220 A2
Grampian Dr G75 .... 180 A2
Grampian Pl G32 .... 119 D2
Grampian Rd
Kilmarnock KA1 .... 228 A2
Port Glasgow PA14 .... 69 D3
Stirling FK7 .... 7 E1
Wishaw ML2 .... 164 C2
Grampian St G32 .... 119 D2
Grampian Way
Barrhead G78 .... 134 B1
Bearsden G61 .... 75 D4
Cumbernauld G68 .... 61 D1
Gran St G81 .... 94 C4
Granary Rd FK2 .... 42 A4
Granary Sq FK2 .... 42 A4
Granby La G12 .... 96 B2
Grandtully Dr G12 .... 96 B3
Grange Acad KA1 .... 227 E4
Grange Ave Ayr KA7 ...... 239 D1
Falkirk FK2 .... 42 A3
Milngavie G62 .... 55 D1
Wishaw ML2 .... 164 C1
Grange Ct ML11 .... 214 C3
Grange Dr FK2 .... 42 A3
Grange Gdns Bothwell G71 . 141 D1
Bridge Of A FK9 .... 2 B4
Grange Pl Alexandria G83 . 27 F3
Kilmarnock KA1 .... 227 F4
Grange Rd Alloa FK10 ..... 9 F3
Bearsden G61 .... 75 F3
Bridge Of A FK9 .... 2 B3
Glasgow G42 .... 117 D1
Stevenston KA20 .... 206 B1
Grange St Kilmarnock KA1 . 227 F4
Motherwell ML1 .... 164 A2
Grange Terr KA1 .... 227 E4
Grangemouth Rd FK2 ..... 42 C3
Grangemuir Rd KA9 .... 236 A4
Grangeneuk Gdns G68 .... 61 E1
Granger Rd Balloch G83 ... 27 E4
Kilmarnock KA3 .... 227 F3
Grangeview FK5 .... 23 E1
Grant Cres G82 .... 27 E1
Grant Ct Airdrie ML6 .... 123 E4
Hamilton ML3 .... 183 E4
Grant Pl Coatbridge ML5 .. 122 B2
Kilmarnock KA3 .... 223 E1
Stirling FK9 .... 2 A2
Grant St Alloa FK10 ...... 9 F3
Glasgow G3 .... 240 A4
Greenock PA15 .... 46 B2
Helensburgh G84 .... 16 B1
Grantholm Ave ML1 .... 143 D3
Grantlea Gr G32 .... 119 E2
Grantlea Terr G32 .... 119 E2
Grantley Gdns G41 .... 136 B4
Grantley St G41 .... 136 B4
Grantoftem Path G75 .... 180 C3
Granton St G5 .... 117 F1
Grantown Ave ML6 .... 123 F3
Grantown Gdns ML6 ...... 102 C3
Grants Ave PA2 .... 113 E1
Grants Way PA2 .... 113 E1

Granville St Clydebank G81 . 74 A2
Glasgow G3 .... 240 A3
Helensburgh G84 .... 16 C1
Grasmere G75 .... 179 F3
Grasmere Ct ML3 .... 183 E3
Grassyards Intc KA3 ..... 223 E2
Grassyards Rd KA3 .... 223 E1
Grathellen Ct ML1 .... 164 A4
Gray Cres KA12 .... 224 B4
Gray Dr G61 .... 75 F2
Gray St Alexandria G83 ... 27 F3
Cleland ML1 .... 144 A1
Glasgow G3 .... 96 B1
Greenock PA15 .... 46 A2
Kirkintilloch G66 .... 80 A4
Larkhall ML9 .... 185 D2
Prestwick KA9 .... 236 B4
Shotts ML7 .... 147 D2
Gray's Cl ML11 .... 214 B2
Gray's Rd G71 .... 141 D3
Grayshill Rd G68 .... 81 F3
Graystale Rd FK7 .... 7 D2
Graystonelee Rd ML7 .... 146 B3
Graystones KA11 .... 207 F3
Great Dovehill G1, G4 ... 241 E1
Great George La G12 ..... 96 B2
Great Hamilton St PA2 ... 113 F1
Great Kelvin La G12 ..... 96 C1
Great Western Rd
Clydebank G15, G13 .... 74 B2
Glasgow G12 .... 96 B2
Great Western Terr **14** ... 96 B2
Great Western Terrace La **13**
G12 .... 96 B2
Green Ave KA12 .... 219 E2
Green Bank KA24 .... 191 E4
Green Bank Rd G68 .... 61 E1
Green Dale ML2 .... 165 E3
Green Farm Rd PA3 ...... 112 A3
Green Gdns ML1 .... 144 B1
Green Loan ML1 .... 143 D2
Green Pl Bothwell G71 .... 161 D1
Calderbank ML6 .... 123 D1
Green Rd Paisley PA2 .... 113 D2
Rutherglen G73 .... 138 A4
Green St Ayr KA8 .... 235 F1
Bothwell G71 .... 141 D1
Clydebank G81 .... 74 A2
Glasgow G40 .... 117 F3
Saltcoats KA21 .... 216 C4
Stonehouse ML9 .... 198 C1
Green Street La Bsns Pk
KA8 .... 235 F1
Green The Alva FK12 ..... 5 D4
Glasgow G40 .... 117 F2
Greenacre Ct FK7 .... 7 F1
Greenacre Pl FK7 .... 7 F1
Greenacres
Ardrossan KA22 .... 205 F2
Motherwell ML1 .... 163 E3
Greenacres View ML1 .... 163 E3
Greenan Ave G42 .... 137 F4
Greenan Gr KA7 .... 238 A2
Greenan Pk KA7 .... 238 A2
Greenan Rd Ayr KA7 ..... 238 B2
Kilmarnock KA1 .... 228 A2
Greenan Terr KA9 .... 236 B4
Greenan Way KA7 .... 238 A2
Greenbank G72 .... 161 E4
Greenbank Ave G46 ...... 157 D4
Greenbank Dr PA2 .... 133 E4
Greenbank Gdns G76 ..... 157 E3
Greenbank Pl FK1 .... 41 E2
Greenbank Rd
Falkirk FK1 .... 41 E2
Irvine KA12 .... 219 E1
Greenbank St G73 .... 138 A4
Greenbank Terr ML8 ..... 187 F1
Greencraig Ave FK1 ..... 66 B3
Greendyke St G1 .... 241 E1
Greenend Ave PA5 .... 111 E1
Greenend Pl G32 .... 119 E4
Greenend View ML4 ...... 141 F3
Greenfarm Rd G77 .... 156 A3
Greenfaulds Cres G67 ... 83 D4
Greenfaulds Rd
Cumbernauld G67 .... 82 C4
Cumbernauld G67 .... 83 D4
Greenfaulds Sta G67 .... 82 C4
Greenfield Ave Ayr KA7 .. 238 B1
Glasgow G32 .... 119 D4
Greenfield Cres ML2 .... 165 E2
Greenfield Dr Irvine KA12 . 219 E1
Wishaw ML2 .... 165 E2
Greenfield Pl G32 .... 119 D3
Greenfield Quadrant ML1 . 143 F2
Greenfield Rd
Carluke ML8 .... 187 F2
Clarkston G76 .... 157 F3
Glasgow G32 .... 119 D3
Hamilton ML3 .... 162 A3
Greenfield St Alloa FK10 .. 10 A4
Bonnybridge FK4 .... 40 A3
Glasgow G51 .... 115 F4
Wishaw ML2 .... 165 E2
Greenfields Hgh Sch G67 . 82 B4
Greenfoot KA13 .... 207 F2
Greengairs Ave G51 ..... 115 E4
Greengairs Prim Sch ML6 . 83 F1
Greengairs Rd ML6 ...... 83 F1
Greenhall Pl G72 .... 161 E3
Greenhead FK12 .... 5 D3

Greenhead Ave
Dumbarton G82 .... 50 A1
Stevenston KA20 .... 206 C2
Greenhead Gdns G82 ...... 50 A1
Greenhead Rd
Bearsden G61 .... 75 F3
Dumbarton G82 .... 50 B1
Inchinnan PA4 .... 93 E1
Lennoxtown G65 .... 57 F4
Wishaw ML2 .... 165 E3
Greenhead St G40 .... 117 F2
Greenhill G64 .... 98 B1
Greenhill Ave
Gartcosh G69 .... 100 C3
Glasgow G46 .... 136 B1
Greenhill Bsns Pk PA3 ... 113 E4
Greenhill Cres
Elderslie PA3, PA5 .... 112 B3
Linwood PA3, PA5 .... 112 B3
Greenhill Ct
Bonnybridge FK4 .... 40 A4
Irvine KA11 .... 220 A3
Rutherglen G73 .... 138 A3
Greenhill Dr PA3 .... 112 B3
Greenhill Prim Sch ML5 .. 122 A4
Greenhill Rd
Blackridge EH48 .... 107 F2
Bonnybridge FK4 .... 40 A4
Cleland ML1 .... 144 C2
Paisley PA3 .... 113 E4
Rutherglen G73 .... 138 A3
Greenhill St G73 .... 138 A3
Greenhill St KA22 .... 221 F2
Greenhills Cres G75 ..... 180 A3
Greenhills Prim Sch G75 . 180 B4
Greenhills Rd G75 .... 180 B3
Greenholm Ave
Clarkston G76 .... 157 F3
Uddingston G71 .... 140 C4
Greenholm St KA1 .... 227 F1
Greenholme Ct G44 ...... 137 D3
Greenholme St G44 ...... 137 D3
Greenhorn's Well Ave FK1 . 41 F2
Greenhorn's Well Cres
FK1 .... 41 F2
Greenhorn's Well Dr FK1 .. 41 F2
Greenknowe Dr ML8 ...... 186 C1
Greenknowe Rd G43 ...... 136 A3
Greenknowe St ML2 ...... 166 A3
Greenlaw Ave Paisley PA1 . 114 A2
Wishaw ML2 .... 165 E2
Greenlaw Cres PA1 ...... 114 A2
Greenlaw Dr
Newton Mearns G77 .... 156 B3
Paisley PA1 .... 114 A2
Greenlaw Ind Est PA3 .... 113 F3
Greenlaw Rd Glasgow G14 . 94 C2
Newton Mearns G77 .... 156 B3
Greenlea Rd G69 .... 100 A4
Greenlea St G13 .... 95 F3
Greenlees Ct KA24 ...... 191 D4
Greenlees Gdns G72 ..... 138 C2
Greenlees Gr ML5 .... 122 B3
Greenlees Rd G72 .... 139 D2
Greenloan Ave G51 ...... 115 E4
Greenloan View ML9 ..... 185 D3
Greenmoss ML4 .... 142 B3
Greenmount G22 .... 97 D4
Greenmount Dr FK1 ...... 66 B4
Greenock Acad PA16 ..... 45 E4
Greenock Ave G44 .... 137 D3
Greenock Central Sta PA15 . 46 A2
Greenock High Sch PA16 .. 44 B3
Greenock Rd Bishopton PA7 . 71 E3
Greenock PA14 .... 46 C3
Inchinnan PA4 .... 93 E3
Langbank PA14 .... 70 B4
Paisley PA3 .... 113 E4
Port Glasgow PA14 .... 47 F3
Greenock West Sta PA15 .. 45 F2
Greenrig G71 .... 140 C3
Greenrig Rd ML11 .... 214 A3
Greenrig St G33 .... 98 B2
Greenrigg Cotts ML7 .... 127 F2
Greenrigg Rd G67 .... 62 A3
Greenrigg St G71 .... 140 C3
Greens Ave G66 .... 79 E4
Greens Cres G66 .... 79 E4
Greens Rd G67 .... 82 C3
Greenshields Rd G69 .... 120 A3
Greenside KA11 .... 220 A2
Greenside Ave
Kilbirnie KA25 .... 170 A4
Prestwick KA9 .... 236 B4
Springside KA11 .... 220 C3
Greenside Cl ML11 ...... 215 D2
Greenside Cres G33 ..... 98 C2
Greenside Pl G61 .... 75 E4
Greenside Rd
Carmunnock G76 .... 158 C4
Clydebank G81 .... 74 A4
Motherwell ML1 .... 143 E4
Wishaw ML2 .... 165 E1
Greenside St Alloa FK10 .. 10 A3
Glasgow G33 .... 99 D3
Motherwell ML1 .... 143 F2
Greenside Terr KA11 .... 221 D1
Greenside Way KA11 ..... 220 A2
Greentowers Rd ML11 ... 214 C3
Greentree Dr G69 .... 119 F2
Greentree Pk KA7 .... 239 E2
Greenview Prim Sch G77 . 117 F2
Greenview St G43 .... 136 B4
Greenville Ct FK1 .... 41 F1
Greenway La G72 .... 161 E3

Greenways Ave PA2 113 D1
Greenways Ct PA2 113 D1
Greenwood Acad KA11 220 A1
Greenwood Ave
Cambuslang G72 139 F3
Chryston G69 80 C1
Stirling FK8 7 D4
Greenwood Cres ML5 122 B3
Greenwood Ct G76 157 F4
Greenwood Dr
Bearsden G61 76 A2
Johnstone PA5 131 F4
Greenwood Intc KA11 224 C4
Greenwood Quadrant G81 .. 74 B1
Greenwood Rd
Clarkston G76 157 E4
Irvine KA11 220 B1
Greenwood St ML7 146 C3
Greenyards Intc G67 62 B1
Greer Quadrant G81 74 A2
Grenada Pl G75 159 D1
Grenadier Gdns ML1 163 E2
Grendon Ct FK8 7 D3
Grendon Gdns FK8 7 D3
Grenville Dr G72 138 C2
Grenville Rd PA19 44 C3
Greta Meek La G65 58 B3
Gretna St G40 118 A2
Grey Pl PA15 45 F3
Greyfriars Rd G71 140 B4
Greyfriars St G32 118 C4
Greygoran FK10 5 E1
Greystone Ave G73 138 B3
Greystone Bauks ML11 214 C2
Greywood St G13 95 F4
Grier Pl ML9 184 C1
Griers Wlk KA11 225 E3
Grierson Cres FK7 6 B3
Grierson La G33 118 B4
Grierson St G33 118 B4
Grieve Croft G72 140 C1
Grieve Rd Cumbernauld G67 .. 62 A2
Greenock PA16 45 D3
Griffen Ave PA3 112 C3
Griffin Dock Rd KA8 235 F1
Griffin Pl ML4 142 A4
Griffiths St FK1 42 A2
Griffiths Way ML8 186 C2
Griqua Terr G71 141 D1
Grodwell Dr FK12 4 C4
Grogarry Rd G15 75 D2
Grosvenor Cres 10 G12 96 B2
Grosvenor Crescent La 12
G12 96 B2
Grosvenor La Glasgow G12 .. 96 B2
Greenock PA15 46 B2
Grosvenor Rd PA15 46 B2
Grosvenor Terr 13 G12 96 B2
Grougar Dr KA3 223 D2
Grougar Rd KA3 228 B4
Grove Cres Falkirk FK2 24 A1
Larkhall ML9 185 E1
Grove Park Gdns G20 97 D1
Grove Pk G66 79 E2
Grove St FK6 21 E1
Grove The Bishopton PA7 72 A2
Bridge Of W PA11 110 C3
Kilbarchan PA10 111 D2
Neilston G78 154 B3
Rutherglen G46 157 D4
Grove Way ML4 141 F2
Grove Wood G71 121 E1
Grove Wynd ML1 143 D2
Groveburn Ave G46 136 A2
Grovepark Ct G20 97 D1
Grovepark Pl G20 97 D1
Grovepark St G20 97 D2
Groves The G64 98 B4
Grovewood Bsns Ctr ML4 .. 141 F4
Grudie St G34 120 A4
Gryfe Rd Bridge Of W PA11 .. 110 B4
Port Glasgow PA14 68 C4
Gryfe St PA15 46 A1
Gryfebank Ave PA6 91 F1
Gryfewood Cres PA6 91 F1
Gryffe Ave Bridge Of W PA11 . 90 B1
Renfrew PA4 94 A3
Gryffe Cres PA2 112 C1
Gryffe Gr PA11 110 B4
Gryffe High Sch PA6 91 D1
Gryffe Rd PA13 89 E4
Gryffe St G44 137 D4
Guildford St G33 99 E1
Guiltreehill KA7 239 D1
Gullane Cres G68 61 F3
Gullane Ct Hamilton ML3 183 D4
Irvine KA12 224 B4
Gullane Pl KA13 207 D2
Gullane St G11 96 A1
Gulliland Ave KA2 225 F1
Gulliland Pl KA12 219 E1
Gullin Dr KA9 236 C3
Gunn Quadrant ML4 141 F2
Guthrie Dr G71 121 D1
Guthrie Pl East Kilbride G74 . 159 F1
Rhu G84 15 E2
Torrance G64 57 E1
Guthrie Rd KA21 217 D4
Guthrie St Glasgow G20 96 B3
Hamilton ML3 162 B2
Guy Mannering Rd G84 25 D4
Gyle Pl ML2 165 F2

Habbieauld Rd KA3 222 A4
Haberlea Ave G53 135 E2
Haberlea Gdns G53 135 E1
Haddington Gdns KA11 220 A3
Haddow Gr 6 G71 141 D4
Haddow St ML3 162 C2
Hadrian Terr ML1 163 E4
Hagart Rd PA6 91 D1
Hagen Dr ML1 143 F1
Hagg Cres PA5 111 F2
Hagg Pl PA5 111 F2
Hagg Rd PA5 111 F1
Haggs Castle G41 116 B1
Haggs La G41 116 B1
Haggs Rd G41 116 B1
Haggswood Ave G41 116 B1
Haghill Prim Sch G31 118 A4
Haghill Rd G31 118 B4
Hagholm Rd ML11 215 F4
Hagmill Cres ML5 122 B1
Hagmill Rd ML5 122 A1
Hagthorn Ave KA25 170 A4
Haig Ave FK8 2 A1
Haig Dr G69 119 F2
Haig St Glasgow G21 98 A2
Greenock PA15 45 F3
Hailes Ave G32 119 E3
Haining Ave KA1 228 A3
Haining Rd PA4 94 B2
Haining The PA4 94 B1
Hairmyres Dr G75 179 F4
Hairmyres Hospl G75 179 F4
Hairmyres Pk G75 179 F4
Hairmyres Rdbt G75 158 C1
Hairmyres St G42 117 E1
Hairmyres Sta G75 158 C1
Hairst St PA4 94 B2
Halbeath Ave G15 74 C2
Halbert St G41 116 C1
Halberts Cres FK7 7 D1
Haldane Ave FK9 2 A3
Haldane Ct G83 27 F4
Haldane La 29 G14 95 E2
Haldane Pl G75 180 C4
Haldane Prim Sch G83 27 F4
Haldane St G14 95 E2
Haldane Terr G83 19 F1
Halfemerke Prim Sch G74 160 A2
Halfmerk N G74 160 A1
Halfmerk S G74 160 A1
Halfway St KA23 190 B3
Halgreen Ave G15 74 C2
Halifax Way 7 PA4 94 B1
Halkett Cres G83 27 F4
Hall Bar Gdns ML8 201 F2
Hall La KA10 230 A2
Hall Pl ML11 215 D2
Hall Rd Nemphlar ML11 214 A3
Rhu G84 15 E3
Hall St Alexandria G83 27 F2
Clydebank G81 74 A1
Hamilton ML3 162 B1
Motherwell ML1 143 D2
Renton G82 49 E4
Hallbrae St G33 98 C1
Hallcraig St ML6 123 D4
Halley Dr G13 94 C4
Halley Pl G13 94 C4
Halley Sq G13 94 C4
Halley St G13 94 C4
Hallforest St G33 99 D1
Hallglen Prim Sch FK1 42 A1
Hallglen Rd FK1 42 A1
Hallglen Terr FK1 42 A1
Hallgraig Pl ML8 187 E1
Hallhill Cres G33 119 F3
Hallhill Rd Glasgow G32 119 D3
Glasgow, Barlanark G33 119 F3
Glasgow, Garrowhill G69 120 A3
Johnstone PA5 131 E4
Halliburton Cres G34 119 F4
Halliburton Terr G34 120 A4
Hallidale Cres PA4 94 C1
Hallinan Gdns ML2 164 C1
Hallpark FK10 10 B4
Hallrule Dr G52 115 E3
Halls Vennal KA8 235 F1
Hallside Ave G72 139 F3
Hallside Bvd G72 139 F2
Hallside Cres G72 139 F3
Hallside Dr G72 139 F3
Hallside Gdns ML2 165 F2
Hallside Pl G5 117 E2
Hallside Prim Sch G72 139 F2
Hallside Rd G72 139 F2
Hallside St PA9 130 C3
Hallydown Dr G13 95 E3
Halpin Cl ML4 141 E3
Halton Gdns G69 119 F2
Hamersley Pl G75 180 A4
Hamilcomb Rd ML4 142 A2
Hamill Dr G65 60 C4
Hamilton Ave Glasgow G41 . 116 B2
Stenhousemuir FK5 23 F2
Hamilton Cres Ayr KA7 239 D4
Bearsden G61 75 F4
Bishopton PA7 71 F2
Cambuslang G72 139 E3
Coatbridge ML5 122 A3
Renfrew PA4 94 B3
Stevenston KA20 206 C1
Hamilton Ct KA3 222 A4
Hamilton Dr Airdrie ML6 103 D1
Blantyre G72 161 D3
Bothwell G71 141 D1
Cambuslang G72 139 D3
Erskine PA8 72 C2
Falkirk FK1 42 A2
Glasgow G12 96 C2
Glasgow, Giffnock G46 136 B1
Motherwell ML1 163 F2
Stirling FK9 2 B2
Hamilton Gate PA15 45 F3
Hamilton Gdns KA3 195 F1
Hamilton Gram Sch ML3 ... 162 B2
Hamilton Int Tech Pk G72 161 E3
Hamilton Park Ave G12 96 C2
Hamilton Pl
East Kilbride G75 180 C4
Hamilton ML3 183 E3
Motherwell ML1 143 D2
Motherwell, Whittagreen
ML1 143 E2
Hamilton Rd Bellshill ML4 141 F2
Blantyre G72 161 D3
Bothwell G71 141 D1
Cambuslang G72 139 E2
East Kilbride G72, G74 160 B3
Glasgow G32 119 E1
Larbert FK2 23 E3
Larkhall ML9 184 C3
Motherwell ML1 163 E3
Rutherglen G73 138 B4
Hamilton Sch for the Deaf
ML3 162 A1
Hamilton St Carluke ML8 187 F1
Clydebank G81 94 B4
Dumbarton G82 50 A2
Falkirk FK1 41 E3
Glasgow G42 117 E1
Kilwinning KA13 207 F2
Larkhall ML9 185 D2
Paisley PA3 113 F3
Saltcoats KA21 216 C4
Hamilton Terr G81 94 B4
Hamilton View G71 141 D4
Hamilton Way
Greenock PA15 45 F3
Prestwick KA9 233 E1
Hamiltonhill Cres G22 97 D2
Hamiltonhill Rd G22 97 D2
Hamlet G74 160 A3
Hampden Dr G42 137 D4
Hampden La G42 137 D4
Hampden Pk
(Queen's Park FC) G42 ... 137 E4
Hampden Terr G42 137 D4
Hampden Way 11 PA4 94 B1
Hangingshaw Pl G42 137 E4
Hanover Cl G42 137 D4
Hanover Ct Glasgow G1 241 D3
Paisley PA1 114 A3
Hanover Gdns
Bishopbriggs G64 78 A1
Paisley PA1 113 E2
Hanover St Glasgow G1 241 D2
Helensburgh G84 25 C4
Hanson St G31 117 F4
Hapland Ave G53 115 E1
Hapland Rd G53 115 E1
Happyhills KA23 190 B3
Haran Rd G83 19 F1
Harbour Ind Est KA22 205 E1
Harbour La PA3 113 F3
Harbour Pl KA22 205 D1
Harbour Rd
Ardrossan KA22 216 A4
Irvine KA12 219 D1
Paisley PA3 113 F3
Troon KA10 229 D2
Harbour St
Ardrossan KA22 216 A4
Ayr KA7 235 F1
Irvine KA12 219 D1
Saltcoats KA21 216 C4
Harburn Pl Glasgow G23 76 C1
Glasgow, Yoker G14 94 C3
Harcourt Dr G31 118 A4
Hardacres ML11 215 D3
Hardgate Dr G51 115 E4
Hardgate Gdns G51 115 E4
Hardgate Pl G51 115 E4
Hardgate Rd G51 115 E4
Hardie Ave G73 138 B4
Hardie Cres FK7 8 B2
Hardie Ct FK7 7 E2
Hardie St Alexandria G83 27 E4
Blantyre G72 161 E4
Hamilton ML3 162 A1
Motherwell ML1 163 F4
Hardmuir Gdns G66 58 C1
Hardmuir Rd G66 58 C1
Hardridge Ave G52 115 F1
Hardridge Pl G52 115 F1
Hardridge Rd G52 115 F1
Hardy Hill G84 17 D1
Harebell Pl KA7 239 D2
Harefield Dr G14 95 D3
Harelaw Ave Barrhead G78 . 134 B1
Glasgow G44 136 C2
Neilston G78 154 B3
Port Glasgow PA14 68 B4
Harelaw Cres PA2 133 E4
Hareleeshill Prim Sch ML9 185 E1
Hareleeshill Rd ML9 185 E1
Hareshaw Dr KA3 223 D3
Hareshaw Gdns KA3 223 D3
Hareshaw Rd ML1 144 B2
Harestanes Gdns G66 59 D1
Harestanes Ind Est ML8 201 F3
Harestanes Prim Sch G66 ... 59 D1
Harestanes Rd ML8 201 F2
Harestone Cres ML2 165 E1
Harestone Rd ML2 165 E1
Harhill St G51 116 A4
Harkins Ave G72 161 E4
Harkness Ave G65 58 A3
Harland Cotts G14 95 E2
Harland St G14 95 E2
Harlaw Gdns G64 78 B1
Harley Ct FK2 42 A4
Harley Pl KA21 205 F1
Harley St G51 116 B3
Harling Dr KA10 229 E1
Harmetray St G22 97 E3
Harmony Ct G51 116 A4
Harmony Pl G51 116 A4
Harmony Row 1 G51 116 A4
Harmony Sq G51 116 A4
Harmsworth St G11 95 F1
Harper Cres ML2 165 F2
Harperland Dr KA1 227 E4
Harport St G46 135 F2
Harriet Pl G43 136 A3
Harriet Rd KA3 223 D1
Harriet St G73 138 A4
Harrington Rd G74 159 F1
Harris Cl G77 156 A3
Harris Cres G60 73 D3
Harris Ct Alloa FK10 10 A3
Irvine KA11 225 E4
Harris Dr G60 73 D3
Harris Gdns G60 73 E3
Harris Pl KA3 223 D3
Harris Quadrant ML2 165 F3
Harris Rd Glasgow G23 76 C1
Old Kilpatrick G60 73 E3
Port Glasgow PA14 69 D4
Harris Terr KA11 225 E4
Harrison Dr G51 116 A3
Harrison Pl FK1 41 F3
Harrow Ct G15 74 C2
Harrow Pl G15 74 C2
Hart St Clydebank G81 74 B4
Glasgow G31 118 C3
Linwood PA3 112 B3
Hart Wynd FK7 7 F1
Hartfield Cres G78 154 C4
Hartfield Ct G82 50 A2
Hartfield Gdns G82 50 A2
Hartfield Rd KA7 238 C3
Hartfield Terr Paisley PA2 .. 114 A1
Shotts ML7 167 D4
Harthall KA8 236 C1
Harthill Rd EH48 107 E1
Hartlaw Cres G52 115 D3
Hartree Ave G13 94 C4
Hartshill Prim Sch ML7 127 F3
Hartstone Pl G53 135 D4
Hartstone Rd G53 135 D4
Hartstone Terr G53 135 D4
Hartwood Gdns ML7 146 A1
Hartwood Hospl ML7 145 F2
Hartwood Rd ML7 145 F1
Hartwood Sta ML7 145 F2
Hartwoodhill Hospl ML7 146 A2
Harvest Dr ML1 163 E2
Harvey Gdns KA22 205 E2
Harvey Sq PA12 129 E1
Harvey St Ardrossan KA22 205 E2
Glasgow G4 97 E1
Harvey Terr PA12 129 E1
Harvey Way ML4 142 B4
Harvey Wynd FK8 2 A1
Harvie Ave G77 156 B3
Harvie St G51 116 B3
Harwood Gdns G69 81 D2
Harwood St G32 118 C4
Hastie St G3 96 B1
Hastings G75 180 A4
Hatfield Ct PA13 89 E4
Hatfield Dr G12 96 A3
Hathaway Dr G46 136 A1
Hathaway La G20 96 C3
Hathaway St G20 96 C3
Hathersage Ave G69 120 A3
Hathersage Dr G69 120 A3
Hathersage Gdns 11 G69 .. 120 A3
Hatton Gdns G52 115 D2
Hatton Pl ML1 143 E1
Hatton Terr ML1 143 E1
Hattonhill ML1 143 E1
Hattonrigg Rd ML4 142 A4
Haugh Gdns FK2 24 A1
Haugh Pl ML3 162 C1
Haugh Rd Glasgow G3 116 B4
Kilsyth G65 60 B4
Stirling FK9 2 A1
Haugh St FK2 24 A1
Haughburn Pl G53 135 D4
Haughburn Rd G53 135 D4
Haughburn Terr G53 135 E4
Haughton Ave G65 60 C4
Haughview Rd ML1 163 D3
Haupland Rd KA22 205 D3
Havelock La G11 96 B1
Havelock Pk G75 159 D1
Havelock Pl G84 16 C1
Havelock St Glasgow G11 96 B1
Helensburgh G84 16 C1
Haven Pk G75 179 F3
Havoc Rd G82 49 E2
Hawbank Rd G74 159 D2
Hawbank Rdbt G75 159 D1
Hawick Ave PA2 113 D1
Hawick Cres ML9 185 D1
Hawick Dr ML5 122 B2
Hawick St Glasgow G13 94 C4
Wishaw ML2 165 E3
Hawkhead Ave PA2 114 B1
Hawkhead Hospl PA2 114 B1
Hawkhead Rd PA1 114 A2
Hawkhead Sta PA1 114 A2
Hawkhill Ave KA8 236 A1
Hawkhill Avenue La KA8 .. 236 A1
Hawkhill Dr KA20 206 C1
Hawkhill Pl KA20 206 C1
Hawkhill Rd FK10 10 B3
Hawksland Wlk ML3 162 C1
Hawkwood G75 180 B3
Hawkwood Rd ML6 102 C2
Hawley Rd FK1 42 B2
Hawthorn Ave
Bearsden G61 76 A4
Bishopbriggs G64 98 A4
Dumbarton G82 49 D3
Erskine PA8 93 F4
Johnstone PA5 112 A1
Kirkintilloch G66 79 E3
Prestwick KA9 236 B4
Wishaw ML2 166 B3
Hawthorn Cres
Beith KA15 171 D4
Erskine PA8 93 F4
Fallin FK7 8 B2
Stirling FK8 1 C1
Hawthorn Ct
Clarkston G76 157 F3
Kilwinning KA13 207 F1
Hawthorn Dr Airdrie ML6 123 E3
Ayr KA7 239 E2
Banknock FK4 38 C1
Barrhead G78 155 E4
Coatbridge ML5 122 B3
Denny FK6 21 E2
Falkirk FK1 41 F2
Fallin FK7 8 B2
Harthill ML7 127 F3
Motherwell ML1 143 D2
Shotts ML7 147 E2
Stevenston KA20 206 C2
Wishaw ML2 165 E2
Hawthorn Gdns
Bellshill ML4 142 B2
Cambuslang G72 139 F2
Clarkston G76 157 F3
Larkhall ML9 185 E1
Prestwick KA9 236 B4
Hawthorn Gr ML8 186 C3
Hawthorn Hill ML3 162 C1
Hawthorn Pl Blantyre G72 ... 161 F4
Shotts ML7 167 D4
Troon KA10 229 E2
Hawthorn Prim Sch G22 97 E2
Hawthorn Quadrant G22 97 E3
Hawthorn Rd
Clarkston G76 157 F3
Cumbernauld G67 62 C2
Erskine PA8 93 F4
Hawthorn Sq KA1 227 E4
Hawthorn St Clydebank G81 .. 74 A2
Glasgow G22 97 E3
Torrance G64 57 E1
Hawthorn Terr
East Kilbride G75 180 A3
Uddingston G71 141 D4
Hawthorn Way Erskine PA8 .. 93 F4
Milton Of C G65 58 B3
Hawthorn Wlk G72 138 B3
Hawthornden Gdns G23 76 C1
Hawthorne Pl Gourock PA19 . 44 A3
Larbert FK5 23 E1
Hawthornhill Rd G82 49 E3
Hay Ave PA7 72 B2
Hay Dr PA5 112 A2
Hay Hill KA8 236 C1
Hay St PA15 45 F2
Hayburn Cres G11 96 A2
Hayburn Gate G11 96 A1
Hayburn La G11 96 A2
Hayburn St G11 96 A1
Hayes Gr G83 27 F3
Hayfield FK2 42 B4
Hayfield Rd FK2 42 B4
Hayfield St G5 117 E2
Hayfield Terr FK6 39 F4
Hayhill Rd G74 179 E4
Hayle Gdns G69 80 C2
Haylnn St G14 95 F1
Haymarket St G32 118 C4
Hayock Prim Sch KA20 206 C1
Hayocks Rd KA20 206 C1
Haypark Rd FK6 39 E3
Haysholm Sch KA12 219 F2
Haystack Pl G66 79 F2
Hayston Cres G22 97 D3
Hayston Rd
Cumbernauld G68 61 F2
Kirkintilloch G66 79 D4
Hayston St G22 97 D3
Hayward Ave ML8 202 B4
Hayward Ct ML8 202 B4
Haywood St G22 97 E3
Hazel Ave Ardrossan KA22 ... 205 E2
Bearsden G61 76 A4
Dumbarton G82 49 D3
Glasgow G44 136 C2
Johnstone PA5 112 A1
Kilmarnock KA1 227 E4
Kirkintilloch G66 79 E3
Hazel Bank G65 58 A2
Hazel Cres FK6 21 E2
Hazel Dene G64 98 A4
Hazel Gdns ML1 163 F2
Hazel Gr Falkirk FK2 42 B4
Kilwinning KA13 208 A2
Kirkintilloch G66 79 E3
Law ML8 186 C3
Hazel Path ML1 144 A1
Hazel Pk ML3 162 C1
Hazel Rd Banknock FK4 38 C1
Cumbernauld G67 62 B2
Hazel Terr Gourock PA19 44 B3
Uddingston G71 141 D4

Hazel Wood ML2 .... 165 E3
Hazelbank Motherwell ML1 . 143 D3
  Plains ML6 .... 103 F2
Hazelbank Gdns FK8 .... 2 A1
Hazelbank Wlk ML6 .... 122 B4
Hazeldean Cres ML2 .... 165 E3
Hazelden Rd G77 .... 177 E4
Hazelden Sch of Equitation
  G77 .... 156 B1
Hazeldene La 29 ML9 .... 185 C1
Hazelhead G74 .... 160 A1
Hazella Dr G46 .... 136 C2
Hazelmere Rd PA13 .... 89 D4
Hazelton ML1 .... 163 E3
Hazelwood Ave
  Bridge Of W PA11 .... 110 C4
  Newton Mearns G77 .... 156 C2
  Paisley PA2 .... 132 C4
Hazelwood Dr G72 .... 161 E4
Hazelwood Gdns G73 .... 138 B2
Hazelwood La PA11 .... 110 B4
Hazelwood Rd Ayr KA7 .... 238 C3
  Bridge Of W PA11 .... 110 B3
  Glasgow G41 .... 116 B2
Hazlitt Pl G20 .... 97 D3
Hazlitt St G20 .... 97 D3
Head of Muir Prim Sch FK6 ... 39 E3
Head St KA15 .... 171 E4
Headhouse Ct G75 .... 180 B4
Headhouse Gn G75 .... 180 C4
Headlands Gr KA15 .... 171 E4
Headlesscross Rd ML7 .... 147 F1
Headrigg Gdns KA23 .... 190 B3
Headrigg Rd KA23 .... 190 B3
Headsmuir Ave ML8 .... 187 E1
Healthcare International
  (HCI) G81 .... 73 F1
Heath Ave Bishopbriggs G64 . 98 A4
  Kirkintilloch G66 .... 79 E2
Heath Rd ML9 .... 185 D2
Heathcliffe Ave G72 .... 140 B1
Heathcot Ave G15 .... 74 C1
Heathcot Pl G15 .... 74 C1
Heather Ave Alexandria G83 .. 27 F3
  Barrhead G78 .... 134 A3
  Bearsden G61 .... 75 F4
  Clydebank G81 .... 44 A4
  Motherwell ML1 .... 143 D3
  Shieldhill FK1 .... 66 B3
Heather Dr G66 .... 79 D2
Heather Gdns G66 .... 79 D2
Heather Gr 10 G75 .... 180 C4
Heather Pk KA7 .... 239 E2
Heather Pl ML6 .... 105 D3
Heather Pl Johnstone PA5 .... 112 A1
  Kilmarnock KA1 .... 227 E4
  Kirkintilloch G66 .... 79 D2
Heather Rd ML1 .... 214 A3
Heather Row ML6 .... 187 F2
Heather St ML6 .... 105 D3
Heather View G65 .... 33 F1
Heather Way ML1 .... 143 D2
Heatherbank Wlk ML6 .... 122 B4
Heatherbrae G64 .... 77 F1
Heatherdale Gdns FK6 .... 39 F4
Heatherhouse Ind Est
  KA12 .... 224 A4
Heatherhouse Rd KA12 .... 224 A4
Heatherstane Bank KA11 ..... 220 B1
Heatherstane Way KA11 ...... 220 B1
Heathery Knowe G75 .... 180 C4
Heathery Knowe Prim Sch
  G75 .... 180 C4
Heathery Lea Ave ML5 .... 122 B2
Heathery Rd ML2 .... 164 C2
Heatheryknowe Rd
  Coatbridge G69 .... 120 C4
  Glasgow G69 .... 120 C4
Heathfield ML2 .... 186 A4
Heathfield Ave G69 .... 81 D1
Heathfield Dr G62 .... 55 D2
Heathfield Ind Est KA8 .... 236 B2
Heathfield Prim Sch KA8 ..... 236 A3
Heathfield Rd KA8 .... 236 B2
Heathfield St G33 .... 119 E4
Heathpark KA8 .... 236 B3
Heathside Rd G46 .... 136 B3
Heathwood Dr G46 .... 136 A2
Hecla Ave G15 .... 74 C2
Hecla Pl G15 .... 74 C2
Hecla Sq G15 .... 74 C2
Hector Rd G41 .... 136 B4
Hedges The FK1 .... 41 F3
Heggies Ave PA14 .... 69 D4
Heights Rd EH48 .... 107 E2
Helen St G51 .... 116 A3
Helen Way G81 .... 27 F1
Helen Wynd ML9 .... 185 D1
Helen's Terr KA13 .... 207 F1
Helena Pl G76 .... 157 F4
Helensburgh Central Sta
  G84 .... 16 B1
Helensburgh Dr G13 .... 95 F3
Helensburgh Upper Sta G84 16 B2
Helenslea G71 .... 139 F2
Helenslea Pl ML4 .... 141 F2
Helenslee Cres G82 .... 49 E2
Helenslee Ct G82 .... 49 E2
Helenslee Rd
  Dumbarton G82 .... 49 E2
  Langbank PA14 .... 70 B4
Helenvale Ct G31 .... 118 B3
Helenvale St G31 .... 118 B3
Helmsdale Ave G72 .... 140 B2
Helmsdale Ct G72 .... 139 E3
Helmsdale Dr PA5 .... 112 B2

Hemlock St G13 .... 95 F4
Hemmingen Ct ML8 .... 187 F2
Hemphill View KA2 .... 221 F2
Henderland Dr G61 .... 75 F1
Henderland Rd G61 .... 75 F1
Henderson Ave Alloa FK10 .... 10 A4
  Cambuslang G72 .... 139 F3
Henderson Pl FK12 .... 5 D4
Henderson Rd KA10 .... 229 E1
Henderson St Airdrie ML6 .... 123 D4
  Bridge Of A PA9 .... 2 A4
  Clydebank G81 .... 94 C4
  Coatbridge ML5 .... 121 F3
  Glasgow G20 .... 96 C2
  Paisley PA1 .... 113 E3
Henderson Terr PA19 .... 44 C3
Hendry St FK2 .... 42 A4
Hennings The FK10 .... 5 E1
Henrietta St G14 .... 95 E2
Henry Bell Gn 8 G75 .... 180 C4
Henry Bell St G84 .... 16 C1
Henry St Alva FK12 .... 5 D3
  Barrhead G78 .... 134 A2
Hepburn Hill ML3 .... 183 E4
Hepburn Rd G52 .... 115 D4
Hepburn Way KA11 .... 220 B4
Herald Ave G13 .... 75 E1
Herald Gr ML1 .... 163 E2
Herald St KA2 .... 216 A4
Herald Way 7 PA4 .... 94 B1
Herbert St G20 .... 96 C2
Herbertshire St FK6 .... 21 F1
Herbertson Cres KA12 .... 219 E2
Herbertson Gr G72 .... 140 B1
Herbertson St
  Blantyre G72 .... 161 F4
  8 Glasgow G5 .... 117 D3
Hercules Way PA4 .... 94 B1
Herdshill Ave FK1 .... 66 B3
Heriot Ave PA2 .... 132 C4
Heriot Cres G64 .... 78 A2
Heriot Prim Sch PA2 .... 132 C4
Heriot Rd G66 .... 79 E2
Heritage Ct G77 .... 156 C3
Heritage Dr FK2 .... 24 A2
Heritage View ML5 .... 121 F4
Heritage Way ML5 .... 121 F4
Herma St G23 .... 96 C4
Hermes Way ML4 .... 142 C3
Hermiston Ave G32 .... 119 E3
Hermiston Pl Glasgow G32 .. 119 E3
  Motherwell ML1 .... 143 D3
Hermiston Rd G32 .... 119 D3
Hermitage Acad G84 .... 25 D4
Hermitage Ave G13 .... 95 E3
Hermitage Cres ML5 .... 122 A2
Hermitage Prim Sch G84 ..... 16 B1
Hermitage Rd FK9 .... 2 C3
Herndon Ct G77 .... 157 D3
Heron Ct G81 .... 74 A3
Heron Pl PA5 .... 131 E4
Heron Rd PA6 .... 45 D2
Heron Way PA4 .... 94 B1
Heronswood KA13 .... 207 F3
Herries Rd G41 .... 116 B1
Herriet St G41 .... 116 C2
Herriot Ave KA25 .... 149 D2
Herriot St ML5 .... 121 F4
Herschell St G13 .... 95 F3
Hertford Ave G12 .... 96 A3
Hervey St KA10 .... 30 A4
Hestan Pl KA3 .... 223 D3
Heugh St FK1 .... 42 A2
Hewett Cres PA6 .... 91 E1
Hexham Gdns G41 .... 116 B1
Heyford St FK7 .... 6 B3
Heys St G78 .... 134 B1
Hibernia St PA16 .... 45 E2
Hickman St G42 .... 117 E1
Hickory Cres G71 .... 141 E4
Hickory St G22 .... 97 F3
High Avon St ML9 .... 184 C2
High Banton Rd G65 .... 37 E2
High Barholm PA10 .... 111 D2
High Barrwood Rd G65 .... 60 C4
High Beeches G76 .... 158 C4
High Blantyre Prim Sch
  G72 .... 161 D4
High Blantyre Rd G72, ML3 161 F3
High Burnside Ave ML5 ...... 121 F3
High Calside PA2 .... 113 F2
High Carnegie Rd PA14 ...... 68 C4
High Coats ML5 .... 122 A4
High Common Rd G74 .... 181 D4
High Craigends G65 .... 60 C4
High Dykes Prim Sch G83 ... 28 A1
High Flender Rd G76 .... 157 E3
High Glencairn St KA1 .... 227 F4
High Graighall Rd G4 .... 97 D1
High Kirk View PA5 .... 111 F1
High Mains Ave G82 .... 50 B2
High Meadow ML8 .... 188 B1
High Mill Rd ML8 .... 188 A1
High Overton St ML9 .... 200 B2
High Parks Cres ML3 .... 183 E3
High Parksail PA8 .... 93 E4
High Patrick St ML3 .... 162 C2
High Pleasance ML9 .... 185 D2
High Rd Ayr KA8 .... 236 A1
  Motherwell ML1 .... 163 F4
  Paisley PA2 .... 113 E2
  Saltcoats KA21 .... 216 A4
  Stevenston KA20 .... 206 B1
High Row G64 .... 78 A3
High Sch of Glasgow
  (Jun Sch) G61 .... 75 E2
High Sch of Glasgow The
  G13 .... 95 F3

High St Airdrie ML6 .... 122 C4
  Airth FK2 .... 14 B2
  Alloa FK10 .... 10 A3
  Ayr KA7 .... 238 C4
  Bonnybridge FK4 .... 40 A3
  Carluke ML8 .... 187 F1
  Clackmannan FK10 .... 10 C2
  Dumbarton G82 .... 49 F2
  Falkirk FK1 .... 42 A3
  Glasgow G1 .... 241 E2
  Greenock PA15 .... 45 F3
  Irvine KA12 .... 219 E1
  Johnstone PA5 .... 111 F2
  Kilbirnie KA25 .... 149 D2
  Kilmacolm PA13 .... 69 E1
  Kilmarnock KA3 .... 223 D1
  Lanark ML11 .... 215 D2
  Lochwinnoch PA12 .... 129 E1
  Motherwell ML1 .... 143 F2
  Neilston G78 .... 154 C4
  Paisley PA1 .... 113 F2
  Renfrew PA4 .... 94 C2
  Rutherglen G73 .... 138 A4
  Shotts ML7 .... 146 C2
  Slamannan FK1 .... 86 A4
  Stewarton KA3 .... 195 F1
High Station Rd FK1 .... 42 A2
High Street Sta G1 .... 241 E2
High View Gr FK1 .... 66 B3
High Whitehills Rd G75 ...... 180 C3
Highburgh Ave ML11 .... 215 D2
Highburgh Ct ML11 .... 215 D2
Highburgh Dr G73 .... 138 B3
Highburgh Rd G12 .... 96 B1
Highcraig Ave PA5 .... 111 E1
Highcroft Ave G44 .... 137 E3
Highcross Ave ML5 .... 121 E2
Highet Gdns G42 .... 219 D2
Highet St ML4 .... 222 C1
Highfield Ave
  Kilmarnock KA3 .... 223 D2
  Kirkintilloch G66 .... 58 C1
  Paisley PA2 .... 133 E4
  Prestwick KA9 .... 236 B4
Highfield Cres
  Motherwell ML1 .... 164 A4
  Paisley PA2 .... 133 E4
Highfield Ct G66 .... 58 C1
Highfield Dr
  Clarkston G76 .... 157 E4
  Glasgow G12 .... 96 A3
  Rutherglen G73 .... 138 B2
  Stevenston KA20 .... 206 C1
Highfield Gr G66 .... 58 C1
Highfield Pl
  East Kilbride G71 .... 159 F2
  Glasgow G12 .... 96 A3
  Irvine KA11 .... 219 F3
Highfield Rd Ayr KA7 .... 239 D2
  Kirkintilloch G66 .... 58 C1
  Larkhall ML9 .... 185 D2
Highfield St KA13 .... 207 F2
Highholm Ave PA14 .... 47 D1
Highholm Prim Sch PA14 .... 47 E1
Highholm St PA14 .... 47 D1
Highland Ave G72 .... 161 E4
Highland Dr FK5 .... 23 E2
Highland Dykes Cres FK4 .... 40 A3
Highland Dykes Dr FK4 .... 40 A3
Highland La G51 .... 116 B4
Highland Pk G65 .... 36 B1
Highland Pk G65 .... 36 B1
Highland Rd G62 .... 55 D1
Highlanders' Acad Prim Sch
  PA15 .... 45 F2
Highmain Prim Sch ML8 .... 187 F1
Highmill Rd ML8 .... 162 A1
Highthorne Cres KA23 .... 190 C3
Hilary Cres KA7 .... 239 D3
Hilary Dr G69 .... 119 F3
Hilda Cres G33 .... 98 C2
Hill Ave G77 .... 156 B2
Hill Cres G76 .... 157 F3
Hill Dr G76 .... 178 C2
Hill House Rd FK6 .... 39 F4
Hill House The G84 .... 16 C2
Hill Interchange KA11 .... 219 F3
Hill La KA22 .... 205 E1
Hill Pk FK10 .... 10 A4
Hill Pl Alloa FK10 .... 10 A4
  Ardrossan KA22 .... 205 E1
  Bellshill ML4 .... 141 F2
  Motherwell ML1 .... 143 E1
  Stevenston KA20 .... 206 C3
Hill Rd Cumbernauld G67 .... 61 F1
  Harthill ML7 .... 127 E3
  Howwood PA9 .... 130 C3
  Kilsyth G65 .... 36 B1
  Netherburn ML9 .... 199 F3
  Stonehouse ML9 .... 198 C1
Hill St Alexandria G83 .... 27 E3
  Alloa FK10 .... 10 A4
  Ardrossan KA22 .... 205 E1
  Caldercruix ML6 .... 104 C3
  Chapelhall ML6 .... 123 E1
  Dumbarton G82 .... 49 E2
  Glasgow G3 .... 240 B4
  Greenock PA15 .... 46 A2
  Hamilton ML3 .... 161 F2
  Irvine KA12 .... 219 E1
  Kilmarnock KA3 .... 222 C1
  Larkhall ML9 .... 185 D1
  Saltcoats KA21 .... 216 C4
  Stirling FK7 .... 7 D2
  Wishaw ML2 .... 165 D2
Hill Street Ind Est KA22 .... 205 E1
Hill Terr ML1 .... 143 E1

Hill View East Kilbride G75 .. 180 C4
  Milton G82 .... 50 C1
Hill View Rd ML11 .... 214 A2
Hill's Trust Prim Sch G51 .. 116 A4
Hillary Ave G73 .... 138 B3
Hillary Rd FK5 .... 23 F1
Hillbank Rd KA3 .... 222 C2
Hillbank St G83 .... 27 F2
Hillcrest Carmunnock G76 .. 158 B4
  Chryston G69 .... 100 B4
  Stewarton KA3 .... 211 F4
Hillcrest Ave
  Clydebank G81 .... 74 A4
  Coatbridge ML5 .... 122 B3
  Cumbernauld G67 .... 82 C4
  Glasgow G44 .... 136 C2
  Glasgow, Carmyle G32 ...... 139 D4
  Paisley PA2 .... 133 E3
  Wishaw ML2 .... 164 C2
Hillcrest Ct G67 .... 62 C1
Hillcrest Dr Alloa FK10 .... 10 B3
  Newton Mearns G77 .... 157 D3
  Stevenston KA20 .... 206 C1
Hillcrest Pl Denny FK6 .... 39 E4
  Kilwinning KA13 .... 207 F2
Hillcrest Rd Bearsden G61 ... 75 F2
  Falkirk FK1 .... 41 F1
  Glasgow G32 .... 139 E4
  Queenzieburn G65 .... 59 F4
  Uddingston G71 .... 141 D4
Hillcrest St G62 .... 55 D1
Hillcrest Terr G71 .... 141 D2
Hillcrest View ML9 .... 185 D2
Hillcroft Terr 6 G64 .... 97 F4
Hillend Cres Clarkston G76 . 157 E3
  Clydebank G81 .... 73 F4
Hillend Dr PA15 .... 46 B2
Hillend Pl PA15 .... 46 B2
Hillend Rd Clarkston G76 .... 157 E3
  Glasgow G22 .... 97 D4
  Rutherglen G73 .... 138 A3
Hillfoot Houston PA6 .... 111 F4
  Renton G82 .... 27 E1
Hillfoot Ave Bearsden G61 ... 75 F3
  Dumbarton G82 .... 50 B2
  Rutherglen G73 .... 138 A4
  Wishaw ML2 .... 165 E4
Hillfoot Cres Ayr KA7 .... 239 D3
  Wishaw ML2 .... 165 E4
Hillfoot Dr Bearsden G61 .... 75 F3
  Coatbridge ML5 .... 121 E3
  Glasgow G69 .... 100 C3
  Wishaw ML2 .... 165 E4
Hillfoot Gdns
  Uddingston G71 .... 140 C4
  Wishaw ML2 .... 165 E4
Hillfoot Rd Airdrie ML6 ..... 123 D3
  Ayr KA7 .... 239 E3
Hillfoot St G31 .... 118 A4
Hillfoot Sta G61 .... 76 A3
Hillfoot Terr ML8 .... 188 A1
Hillfoots Rd FK9 .... 2 C2
Hillhead Ave Banknock FK4 .. 38 C2
  Carluke ML8 .... 188 A1
  Chryston G69 .... 80 C1
  Motherwell ML1 .... 143 D1
  Rutherglen G73 .... 138 A2
Hillhead Cres
  Hamilton ML3 .... 161 F2
  Motherwell ML1 .... 143 D1
Hillhead Dr Airdrie ML6 .... 123 D3
  Falkirk FK1 .... 41 F1
  Motherwell ML1 .... 143 D1
Hillhead High Sch G12 .... 96 C1
Hillhead Pl G73 .... 138 A2
Hillhead Prim Sch
  Glasgow G12 .... 96 B2
  Kilmarnock KA3 .... 222 C2
  Kirkintilloch G66 .... 79 F4
Hillhead Rd Glasgow G21 ... 98 B4
  Kirkintilloch G66 .... 58 C1
  Stevenston KA20 .... 206 C2
Hillhead Sq KA3 .... 222 C2
Hillhead St Glasgow G12 .... 96 B1
  Milngavie G62 .... 55 D1
Hillhead Terr ML3 .... 161 F2
Hillhead Underground Sta
  G12 .... 96 B2
Hillhouse Cres ML3 .... 161 F2
Hillhouse Farm Gate
  ML11 .... 214 C3
Hillhouse Farm Rd ML11 ... 214 C2
Hillhouse Gate ML8 .... 202 B4
Hillhouse Gdns KA10 .... 229 E3
Hillhouse Pk Ind Est ML3 .. 161 F2
Hillhouse Pl KA13 .... 195 E1
Hillhouse Rd
  Hamilton ML3 .... 161 F2
  Troon KA10 .... 229 E3
Hillhouse St G21 .... 98 A3
Hillhouse Terr ML3 .... 161 F2
Hillhouseridge Rd ML7 ..... 146 B3
Hillington East Sta G52 ..... 115 D3
Hillington Gdns G52 .... 115 D2
Hillington Ind Est
  Glasgow G52 .... 115 D4
  Paisley PA3 .... 114 B4
Hillington Park Cir G52 ..... 115 D3
Hillington Prim Sch G52 .... 115 D3
Hillington Quadrant G52 ... 115 D3
Hillington Rd
  Glasgow G52 .... 94 C1
  Renfrew G52 .... 94 C1
Hillington Rd S G52 .... 115 D3
Hillington Terr G52 .... 115 D3
Hillington West Sta G52 ... 114 C4
Hillkirk Pl G21 .... 97 F2
Hillkirk St G21 .... 97 F2

Hillmoss KA3 .... 222 A4
Hillneuk Ave G61 .... 76 A3
Hillneuk Dr G61 .... 76 A3
Hillocks Pl KA10 .... 229 F4
Hillpark KA6 .... 237 F3
Hillpark Ave PA2 .... 113 E1
Hillpark Cres FK7 .... 7 E1
Hillpark Dr
  Bannockburn FK7 .... 7 E1
  Glasgow G43 .... 136 B3
  Kilmarnock KA3 .... 222 C1
Hillpark Rise KA13 .... 207 D2
Hillpark Sec Sch G43 .... 136 B3
Hillrigg ML6 .... 83 E1
Hillrigg Ave ML6 .... 123 E4
Hillsborough Rd G69 .... 119 F3
Hillshaw Foot KA11 .... 220 B1
Hillshaw Gn KA11 .... 220 B1
Hillside Alloa FK10 .... 5 E1
  Croy G65 .... 60 C2
  Houston PA6 .... 91 E1
  West Kilbride KA23 .... 190 B2
Hillside Ave Alexandria G83 .. 27 F2
  Bearsden G61 .... 75 F3
  Clarkston G76 .... 157 E4
  Kilmacolm PA13 .... 69 E1
Hillside Cotts Dalry KA24 .. 191 F4
  Glenboig ML5 .... 101 F3
Hillside Cres
  Coatbridge ML5 .... 121 F2
  Hamilton ML3 .... 162 B1
  Motherwell ML1 .... 142 B4
  Neilston G78 .... 154 B4
  Prestwick KA9 .... 236 B4
Hillside Ct Glasgow G46 .... 135 F2
  Stevenston KA20 .... 217 E4
Hillside Dr Barrhead G78 .. 134 A2
  Bearsden G61 .... 76 A3
  Bishopbriggs G64 .... 78 A1
  Blackridge EH48 .... 107 E2
  Port Glasgow PA14 .... 47 D1
Hillside Gardens La
  6 G11 .... 96 A2
Hillside Gr G78 .... 134 A1
Hillside Pk G81 .... 74 A3
Hillside Pl Blackridge EH48 . 107 E2
  Motherwell ML1 .... 143 E2
Hillside Quadrant G43 ...... 136 A3
Hillside Rd Barrhead G78 ... 134 A2
  Cardross G82 .... 26 A1
  Glasgow G43 .... 136 A3
  Gourock PA19 .... 44 B4
  Greenock PA15 .... 46 A1
  Neilston G78 .... 154 B4
  Paisley PA2 .... 114 A1
Hillside St KA20 .... 217 E4
Hillside Terr Alloa FK10 ...... 10 A4
  Hamilton ML3 .... 162 B1
  Milton Of C G65 .... 58 A3
Hillswick Cres G22 .... 97 D4
Hilltop Ave ML4 .... 142 A4
Hilltop Cres PA19 .... 44 C3
Hilltop Pl KA7 .... 239 E3
Hilltop Rd Chryston G69 ..... 80 C1
  Gourock PA19 .... 44 C3
Hillview Banton G65 .... 37 E2
  Greengairs ML6 .... 83 F1
Hillview Ave Kilsyth G65 ..... 60 C4
  Lennoxtown G65 .... 57 F4
Hillview Cotts G65 .... 59 F2
Hillview Cres Bellshill ML4 . 142 A4
  Larkhall ML9 .... 185 D1
  Uddingston G71 .... 140 C4
Hillview Dr 11 Blantyre G72 . 140 B1
  Bridge Of A PA9 .... 2 A3
  Clarkston G76 .... 157 F4
  Helensburgh G84 .... 16 B2
Hillview Gdns G64 .... 98 B4
Hillview Pl Chryston G76 ... 157 F4
  Fallin FK7 .... 8 B2
  Newton Mearns G77 .... 156 B2
Hillview Rd
  Bridge Of W Blantyre G72 . 140 B1
  Bridge Of A PA9 .... 2 A3
  Clarkston G76 .... 157 F4
  Helensburgh G84 .... 16 B2
Hillview Gdns G64 .... 98 B4
Hillview Pl Chryston G76 ... 157 F4
Hilton Ct G60 .... 73 D3
Hilton Cres FK10 .... 10 B4
Hilton Ct Ardrossan KA21 .. 205 F2
  Bishopbriggs G64 .... 78 A2
Hilton Gdns G13 .... 95 F4
Hilton Pk G64 .... 77 F2
Hilton Rd Alloa FK10 .... 10 B4
  Bishopbriggs G64 .... 78 A2
Hilton Sq G62 .... 54 C1
Hilton Terr
  Bishopbriggs G64 .... 77 F2
  Cambuslang G72 .... 138 C2
  Fallin FK7 .... 8 B2
  Glasgow G13 .... 95 F4
Hiltonbank St ML2 .... 162 A2
Hindog Pl KA24 .... 191 D4
Hindsland Rd ML9 .... 185 D1
Hinshaw St G20 .... 97 D2
Hinshelwood Dr G51 .... 116 A3
Hinshelwood Pl G51 .... 116 A3
Hirsel Pl G71 .... 141 D1
Hirst Cres FK7 .... 8 B2
Hirst Ct FK7 .... 8 B2
Hirst Gdns ML7 .... 146 B3
Hirst Rd ML7 .... 126 B2
Hirstrigg Cotts ML7 .... 126 A2
Hobart Cres G81 .... 73 E3
Hobart Quadrant ML2 ..... 165 F3
Hobart Rd G75 .... 180 B4
Hobart St G22 .... 97 D2

Hobden St G21 ..... 98 A2
Hoddam Ave G45 ..... 138 A2
Hoddam Terr G45 ..... 138 A2
Hodge St FK1 ..... 42 A2
Hoey Dr ML2 ..... 186 B4
Hogan Ct G81 ..... 73 F3
Hoga Way ML1 ..... 143 F1
Hogarth Ave Glasgow G32 ..... 118 B4
 Saltcoats KA21 ..... 205 F1
Hogarth Cres G32 ..... 118 B4
Hogarth Ct G83 ..... 27 F3
Hogarth Dr G32 ..... 118 B4
Hogarth Gdns G32 ..... 118 B4
Hogg Ave PA5 ..... 111 F1
Hogg Rd ML6 ..... 123 E2
Hogg St ML6 ..... 123 D4
Hogganfield St G33 ..... 98 B1
Holbourne Pl FK11 ..... 4 A4
Hole Farm Rd PA16 ..... 45 F2
Holeburn La G43 ..... 136 B3
Holeburn Rd G43 ..... 136 B3
Holehills Dr ML6 ..... 103 D1
Holehills Pl ML6 ..... 103 D1
Holehouse Brae G78 ..... 154 B4
Holehouse Dr Glasgow G13 ..... 95 D3
 Kilbirnie KA25 ..... 149 D2
Holehouse Rd
 Eaglesham G76 ..... 178 C3
 East Kilbride G74 ..... 159 D4
 Kilmarnock KA3 ..... 228 A4
Holehouse Terr G78 ..... 154 B4
Holland St G2 ..... 240 B3
Hollandbush Ave FK4 ..... 38 C2
Hollandbush Cres FK4 ..... 38 C2
Hollandhurst Rd ML3 ..... 183 E4
Hollandhurst Rd ML5 ..... 101 F1
Hollinwell Rd G23 ..... 76 B1
Hollow Pk KA7 ..... 239 D1
Hollowglen Rd G32 ..... 119 D3
Hollows Ave PA2 ..... 132 C4
Hollows Cres PA2 ..... 132 C4
Holly Ave Milton Of C G65 ..... 58 A3
 Stenhousemuir FK5 ..... 23 F2
Holly Bank KA7 ..... 239 E3
Holly Dr Dumbarton G82 ..... 49 D3
 Glasgow G21 ..... 98 A2
Holly Gr Banknock FK4 ..... 38 C1
 Bellshill ML4 ..... 142 C3
Holly Pl Johnstone PA5 ..... 132 A4
Holly St Airdrie ML6 ..... 123 E3
 Clydebank G81 ..... 74 A2
Hollybank Pl G72 ..... 139 D2
Hollybank St G21 ..... 98 A1
Hollybrook Pl G42 ..... 117 D1
Hollybrook Sch G42 ..... 117 D1
Hollybrook St G42 ..... 117 D1
Hollybush Ave PA2 ..... 133 D4
Hollybush Pl KA3 ..... 223 D3
Hollybush Rd G52 ..... 114 C3
Hollymount G61 ..... 75 F1
Holm Ave Paisley PA2 ..... 113 F1
 Uddingston G71 ..... 140 C4
Holm Cres KA3 ..... 213 D2
Holm Crest ML8 ..... 201 D1
Holm Gdns ML4 ..... 142 B2
Holm La G74 ..... 159 F1
Holm Pl Larkhall ML9 ..... 184 C1
 Linwood PA3 ..... 112 A4
Holm Rd ML6 ..... 201 D1
Holm St Carluke ML8 ..... 187 E1
 Glasgow G2 ..... 240 C2
 Motherwell ML1 ..... 143 D2
 Stewarton KA3 ..... 211 F4
Holmbank Ave G41 ..... 136 B4
Holmbrae Ave G71 ..... 140 C4
Holmbrae Rd G71 ..... 140 C4
Holmbyre Rd G45 ..... 137 E1
Holmbyre Terr G45 ..... 137 E1
Holmes Ave PA4 ..... 94 B1
Holmes Cres KA1 ..... 227 E3
Holmes Farm Rd KA1 ..... 227 E3
Holmes Quadrant ML4 ..... 142 A2
Holmes Rd KA1 ..... 227 E3
Holmes Village KA1 ..... 227 E3
Holmfauld Rd G51 ..... 95 F1
Holmfauldhead Dr G51 ..... 115 F4
Holmfauldhead Pl G51 ..... 115 F4
Holmfield G66 ..... 79 F4
Holmhead KA25 ..... 170 A4
Holmhead Cres G44 ..... 137 D3
Holmhead Pl G44 ..... 137 D3
Holmhead Rd G44 ..... 137 D3
Holmhill Ave G72 ..... 139 D2
Holmhills Dr G72 ..... 138 C2
Holmhills Gdns G72 ..... 138 C2
Holmhills Gr G72 ..... 138 C2
Holmhills Pl G72 ..... 138 C2
Holmhills Rd G72 ..... 138 C2
Holmhills Terr G72 ..... 138 C2
Holmlands Pl KA1 ..... 227 E3
Holmlea Dr KA1 ..... 227 F3
Holmlea Prim Sch G44 ..... 137 D3
Holmlea Rd G44 ..... 137 D4
Holmpark PA7 ..... 72 A2
Holmquarry Rd KA1 ..... 227 F3
Holms Ave KA11 ..... 220 B1
Holms Cres PA8 ..... 72 C1
Holms Pl G69 ..... 100 C4
Holms Rd KA14 ..... 170 A3
Holmscroft Ave PA15 ..... 45 F2
Holmscroft St PA15 ..... 45 F3
Holmscroft Way PA15 ..... 45 F2
Holmston Cres KA7 ..... 239 E4
Holmston Dr KA7 ..... 239 E3
Holmston Prim Sch KA7 ..... 239 E4
Holmston Rd KA7 ..... 239 E4

Holmwood Ave G72 ..... 140 B1
Holmwood Ave G71 ..... 140 C4
Holmwood Gdns G71 ..... 140 C3
Holmwood Gr G44 ..... 137 D2
Holton Cres FK10 ..... 5 E1
Holton Sq FK10 ..... 5 E1
Holy Cross High Sch ML3 ..... 162 C2
Holy Cross Prim RC Sch
 G42 ..... 117 D1
Holy Cross Prim Sch G65 ..... 60 C2
Holy Cross RC Prim Sch
 PA16 ..... 45 D3
Holy Family Prim Sch G66 ..... 79 D3
Holy Family RC Prim Sch
 Bellshill ML4 ..... 142 B3
 Port Glasgow PA14 ..... 69 D4
Holy Trinity Episcopal
 Prim Sch FK8 ..... 7 D4
Holyknowe Cres G65 ..... 57 F4
Holyknowe Rd G65 ..... 57 F4
Holyoake St G31 ..... 228 C4
Holyrood Cres G20 ..... 96 C1
Holyrood Pl FK5 ..... 23 F2
Holyrood Quadrant G20 ..... 96 C1
Holyrood Sec RC Sch G42 ..... 117 E1
Holyrood St ML3 ..... 162 A3
Holytown Prim Sch ML1 ..... 143 D3
Holytown Rd ML4 ..... 142 C3
Holytown Sta ML1 ..... 143 D3
Home Farm Cotts FK6 ..... 39 F3
Home Farm Rd KA7 ..... 239 D1
Home St ML1 ..... 215 E2
Homer Pl ML4 ..... 142 C3
Homestead The FK8 ..... 6 B4
Homeston Ave G71 ..... 141 D2
Homoeopathic Hospl G12 ..... 96 A3
Honeybank Cres ML8 ..... 188 A2
Honeybog Rd G52 ..... 114 C3
Honeycomb Pl ML9 ..... 200 B2
Honeyman Cres ML1 ..... 215 E2
Honeysuckle La G83 ..... 27 F4
Honeysuckle Pk KA7 ..... 239 D1
Honeywell Cres ML6 ..... 123 F1
Hood Ct G84 ..... 16 C1
Hood St Clydebank G81 ..... 74 B1
 Greenock PA15 ..... 45 F3
Hookney Terr FK6 ..... 21 E1
Hope Ave PA11 ..... 89 F1
Hope Cres ML9 ..... 185 D2
Hope St Ayr KA7 ..... 238 C4
 Bellshill ML4 ..... 142 B3
 Carluke ML8 ..... 188 A1
 Falkirk FK1 ..... 42 A3
 Glasgow G2 ..... 240 C3
 Greenock PA15 ..... 45 F2
 Hamilton ML3 ..... 162 C2
 Helensburgh G84 ..... 25 C4
 Lanark ML11 ..... 215 D2
 Motherwell ML1 ..... 163 F4
 Stirling FK8 ..... 1 C1
 Wishaw ML2 ..... 166 A2
Hopefield Ave G12 ..... 96 B3
Hopehill Gdns G20 ..... 97 D2
Hopehill Rd G20 ..... 97 D2
Hopeman PA3 ..... 135 F2
Hopeman Ave G46 ..... 135 F2
Hopeman Dr G46 ..... 135 F2
Hopeman Path G46 ..... 135 F3
Hopeman Rd G46 ..... 135 F2
Hopeman St G46 ..... 135 F2
Hopepark Terr FK6 ..... 39 F3
Hopetoun Bank KA11 ..... 220 B1
Hopetoun Dr FK9 ..... 2 A4
Hopetoun Pl G23 ..... 76 C1
Hopetoun Terr G21 ..... 98 A2
Hopkin's Brae G66 ..... 58 B1
Horatius St ML1 ..... 142 A1
Hornal Rd Bothwell G71 ..... 141 D2
 Uddingston G71 ..... 140 C2
Hornbeam Dr G81 ..... 74 A2
Hornbeam Rd
 Cumbernauld G67 ..... 62 C3
 Uddingston G71 ..... 141 D4
Horndean Cres G33 ..... 99 E1
Horndean Ct G64 ..... 78 A2
Horne St G22 ..... 97 E4
Hornock Rd ML5 ..... 101 F1
Hornshill Dr ML1 ..... 144 A1
Hornshill Farm Rd G33 ..... 99 F3
Hornshill St G21 ..... 98 A2
Horsburgh Ave G65 ..... 36 B1
Horsburgh St G33 ..... 99 E1
Horse Shoe Rd G61 ..... 75 F3
Horsewood Rd PA11 ..... 110 B4
Horslet St ML5 ..... 121 E2
Horslethill Rd G12 ..... 96 B2
Horsley Brae ML2 ..... 186 A2
Horton Pl G84 ..... 17 D2
Hospital Rd ML2 ..... 186 A4
Hospital St ML5 ..... 122 A2
Hospitland Dr ML11 ..... 215 E2
Hotspur St G20 ..... 96 C2
Houldsworth Cres ML7 ..... 167 D4
Houldsworth La G3 ..... 116 C4
Houldsworth St G3 ..... 240 A3
House O' Muir Rd ML7 ..... 126 A2
Househillmuir Cres G53 ..... 135 E3
Househillmuir La G53 ..... 135 E4
Househillmuir Pl G53 ..... 135 D3
Househillmuir Rd G53 ..... 135 D3
Househillwood Cres G53 ..... 135 D3
Househillwood Rd G53 ..... 135 D3
Housel Ave G13 ..... 95 D4
Houston Cres KA24 ..... 191 D4
Houston Pl Elderslie PA5 ..... 112 B1
 Glasgow G5 ..... 116 C3

Houston Rd
 Bridge Of W PA11 ..... 90 B1
 Houston PA6 ..... 91 D1
 Inchinnan PA3, PA4, PA6 ..... 92 B2
 Kilmacolm PA13 ..... 89 F4
Houston St Glasgow G5 ..... 116 C3
 Greenock PA16 ..... 45 F3
 Hamilton ML3 ..... 162 B1
 Renfrew PA4 ..... 94 B2
 Wishaw ML2 ..... 165 E1
Houston Terr G74 ..... 159 E1
Houstonfield Quadrant
 PA6 ..... 91 D1
Houstonfield Rd PA6 ..... 91 D1
Houstoun Ct PA5 ..... 111 F2
Houstoun Sq PA5 ..... 111 F2
Howacre ML11 ..... 214 C3
Howard Ave G74 ..... 160 A3
Howard Ct
 East Kilbride G74 ..... 160 A3
 Kilmarnock KA3 ..... 227 F4
Howard Park Dr KA1 ..... 227 F4
Howard St Falkirk FK1 ..... 41 F2
 Glasgow G1 ..... 241 D1
 Kilmarnock KA3 ..... 227 F4
 Larkhall ML9 ..... 185 E1
 Paisley PA1 ..... 114 A2
Howat Cres KA12 ..... 219 F2
Howat St G51 ..... 116 A4
Howatshaws Rd G82 ..... 50 A3
Howburn Cres ML7 ..... 127 F3
Howburn Rd ML7 ..... 127 E3
Howden Ave
 Kilwinning KA13 ..... 207 F2
 Motherwell ML1 ..... 143 E4
Howden Dr PA3 ..... 112 A3
Howden Pl ML1 ..... 143 D3
Howe Gdns G71 ..... 141 D4
Howe Rd G65 ..... 60 B4
Howes St ML5 ..... 122 A2
Howetown FK10 ..... 5 E3
Howford Rd G52 ..... 115 D2
Howford Sch G53 ..... 115 D1
Howgate KA13 ..... 207 E2
Howgate Ave G15 ..... 74 C2
Howgate Rd ML3 ..... 183 E4
Howgate St Ctr FK1 ..... 42 A2
Howie Bldgs G76 ..... 157 F4
Howie Cres G84 ..... 15 D2
Howie's Pl ML1 ..... 41 D2
Howieshill Ave G72 ..... 139 D3
Howieshill Rd G72 ..... 139 D3
Howlands Rd FK7 ..... 7 D2
Howletnest Rd ML6 ..... 162 C1
Howmore St G5 ..... 123 E3
Hownow Lea ML1 ..... 164 A2
Howson Lea ML1 ..... 164 A2
Howson View ML1 ..... 163 D4
Howth Dr G13 ..... 95 F4
Howth Terr G13 ..... 95 F4
Howwood Prim Sch PA9 ..... 131 D3
Hoylake Pk G71 ..... 140 C1
Hoylake Pl G72 ..... 76 C1
Hoylake Sq KA13 ..... 207 E2
Hozier Cres G71 ..... 140 C4
Hozier Pl ML9 ..... 185 D2
Hozier Pl G71 ..... 141 D2
Hozier St Carluke ML8 ..... 187 F1
 Coatbridge ML5 ..... 122 A2
Hudson Pl KA9 ..... 233 E1
Hudson Terr G75 ..... 180 B4
Hudson Way G75 ..... 180 B4
Hudspeth Ct G83 ..... 27 E4
Hugh Murray Dr G72 ..... 139 E3
Hugh Watt Pl KA3 ..... 222 A4
Hughenden Dr G12 ..... 96 A2
Hughenden Gdns G12 ..... 96 A2
Hughenden La G12 ..... 96 A2
Hughenden Rd G12 ..... 96 A2
Hugo St G20 ..... 96 C3
Hulks Rd ML6 ..... 83 E2
Humbie Ct G77 ..... 156 C1
Humbie Gate G77 ..... 156 C1
Humbie Gr G77 ..... 156 C2
Humbie Lawns G77 ..... 156 C1
Humbie Rd Eaglesham G76 ..... 178 B4
 Newton Mearns G77 ..... 156 C1
Hume Cres FK9 ..... 2 A3
Hume Ct FK9 ..... 2 A3
Hume Dr Bothwell G71 ..... 141 D2
 Uddingston G71 ..... 140 C4
Hume Pl G75 ..... 180 B4
Hume Rd G67 ..... 62 A1
Hume St G81 ..... 74 A1
Hunt Hill G68 ..... 60 B1
Hunter Ave KA22 ..... 205 E1
Hunter Cres KA10 ..... 236 C4
Hunter Dr KA11 ..... 219 D3
Hunter Gdns Bonnybridge FK4 ..... 40 A3
 Denny FK6 ..... 21 E1
Hunter High Sch G74 ..... 160 B1
Hunter Pl Kilbarchan PA10 ..... 111 D1
 Kilwinning KA13 ..... 208 A2
 Milngavie G62 ..... 54 C1
 Shotts ML7 ..... 146 C3
 Stenhousemuir FK2 ..... 24 A2
Hunter Prim Sch G74 ..... 160 B1
Hunter Rd Crosshouse KA2 ..... 221 F1
 Hamilton ML3 ..... 162 A3
 Milngavie G62 ..... 54 C2
 Rutherglen G73 ..... 118 B1
Hunter St Airdrie ML6 ..... 103 D1
 Bellshill ML4 ..... 142 A3
 East Kilbride G74 ..... 159 F1
 Glasgow G4 ..... 241 F2
 Paisley PA1 ..... 113 F3
 Prestwick KA9 ..... 236 B4
 Shotts ML7 ..... 146 B3

Hunter's Ave Ayr KA8 ..... 236 A2
 Dumbarton G82 ..... 50 B2
Hunter's Cl ML11 ..... 215 D2
Hunter's Ct KA7 ..... 238 C3
Hunterfield Dr PA2 ..... 138 C3
Hunterhill Ave PA2 ..... 113 F2
Hunterhill Rd PA2 ..... 113 F2
Hunterian Mus G12 ..... 96 B2
Hunterlees Rd ML10 ..... 198 A2
Hunters Hill Ct G22 ..... 97 F3
Hunters Pl PA15 ..... 45 F3
Huntersfield Rd PA5 ..... 111 E1
Huntershill Rd G64 ..... 97 F4
Huntersill St G21 ..... 97 F3
Hunterston Rd KA23 ..... 190 B3
Hunthill La G72 ..... 161 D3
Hunthill Pl G76 ..... 158 A3
Hunthill Rd G72 ..... 161 D4
Hunting Lodge Gdns ML3 ..... 163 D1
Huntingdon Rd G21 ..... 97 F1
Huntingdon Sq G21 ..... 97 F1
Huntingtower Rd G69 ..... 119 F2
Huntley Cres FK8 ..... 1 C1
Huntly Ave Bellshill ML4 ..... 142 A3
 Glasgow G46 ..... 136 B1
Huntly Ct Bishopbriggs G64 ..... 98 A4
Huntly Dr Bearsden G61 ..... 75 F4
 Cambuslang G72 ..... 139 D2
 Coatbridge ML5 ..... 121 E2
 Greenock PA16 ..... 44 C2
Huntly Gdns G12 ..... 96 B2
Huntly Path G69 ..... 81 D1
Huntly Pl Kilmarnock KA3 ..... 223 E1
Huntly Quadrant ML2 ..... 165 D3
Huntly Rd Glasgow G12 ..... 96 B2
 Paisley G52 ..... 114 C4
Huntly Terr Paisley PA2 ..... 114 A1
 Port Glasgow PA14 ..... 47 D1
 Shotts ML7 ..... 147 D2
Hurlawcrook Rd G75 ..... 180 C1
Hurlet Cotts G53 ..... 134 C3
Hurlet Rd PA2, G53 ..... 134 B4
Hurlford Ave G13 ..... 94 C4
Hurlford Rd KA1 ..... 228 A3
Hurly Hawkin G64 ..... 98 B4
Hurworth St FK1 ..... 41 F2
Hutcheson Rd G46 ..... 136 A1
Hutcheson St G1 ..... 241 D2
Hutchesons' Gram Sch
 Glasgow G42 ..... 117 D1
 Glasgow, Crossmyloof G41 ..... 116 C1
Hutchison Pl G72 ..... 139 F2
Hutchinson Pl ML2 ..... 186 B4
Hutchison Town Ct
 G5 ..... 117 E2
Hutchison Pl G5 ..... 76 A1
Hutchison Pl ML5 ..... 121 F3
Hutchison St ML3 ..... 162 B1
Hutton ML4 ..... 142 A3
Hutton Dr G51 ..... 115 F4
Hutton Pk KA10 ..... 10 B4
Huxley St G20 ..... 96 C3
Hyacinth Way ML8 ..... 201 F4
Hydepark St G3 ..... 240 A2
Hyndal Ave G53 ..... 115 E1
Hyndford Pl ML11 ..... 215 D2
Hyndford Rd ML11 ..... 215 E1
Hyndland Ave G11 ..... 96 A1
Hyndland Rd G12 ..... 96 A2
Hyndland Sec Sch G12 ..... 96 A2
Hyndland St G11 ..... 96 A1
Hyndland Sta G12 ..... 96 A2
Hyndlee Dr G52 ..... 115 E3
Hyndman Rd KA23 ..... 190 B2
Hyndshaw Rd Carluke ML8 ..... 188 A2
 Law ML2 ..... 187 E4
Hyndshaw View ML8 ..... 187 D2
Hyslop Pl G81 ..... 74 A2
Hyslop St KA20 ..... 206 C1
Hyslop St ML6 ..... 122 C4

Iain Dr G61 ..... 75 E3
Iain Rd G61 ..... 75 E3
Ian Smith Ct G81 ..... 94 A4
IBM Sta PA16 ..... 44 B1
Ibrox Ind Est G51 ..... 116 B3
Ibrox Prim Sch G51 ..... 116 A3
Ibrox St G51 ..... 116 A3
Ibrox Sta G51 ..... 116 A3
Ibrox Stad (Rangers FC)
 G51 ..... 116 A3
Ibrox Terr G51 ..... 116 A3
Ibroxholm Ave G51 ..... 116 A3
Ibroxholm Oval G51 ..... 116 A3
Ibroxholm Pl G51 ..... 116 A3
Ida Quadrant ML4 ..... 141 F3
Iddesleigh Ave G62 ..... 55 D1
Ilay Ave G61 ..... 96 A4
Ilay Ct G61 ..... 96 A4
Ilay Rd G61 ..... 96 A4
Imlach Pl ML1 ..... 163 E3
Imperial Dr ML6 ..... 122 C3
Inch Garve G74 ..... 160 B1
Inch Keith G74 ..... 160 B1
Inch Marnock G74 ..... 160 B1
Inch Murrin G74 ..... 160 B1
Inchbrae Rd G52 ..... 115 E2
Inchcolm Gdns G69 ..... 81 D2
Inchconnachan Ave G83 ..... 19 F1
Inchcruin Pl G15 ..... 74 C2
Inchfad Dr G15 ..... 74 C2
Inchfad Rd G83 ..... 19 F1

Inchgotrick Rd KA1 ..... 227 F2
Inchgower Gr G84 ..... 15 E3
Inchgreen St PA14 ..... 46 C1
Inchholm La G11 ..... 95 F1
Inchinnan St G11 ..... 95 F1
Inchinnan Bsns Pk PA4 ..... 93 D2
Inchinnan Ind Est PA4 ..... 93 D3
Inchinnan Prim Sch PA4 ..... 93 E4
Inchinnan Rd Bellshill ML4 ..... 141 F4
 Paisley PA3 ..... 113 F4
 Renfrew PA4 ..... 94 A2
Inchkeith Pl Falkirk FK1 ..... 42 A1
 Glasgow G32 ..... 119 D4
Inchlaggan Pl G15 ..... 74 C2
Inchlee St G14 ..... 95 F1
Inchlonaig Dr G83 ..... 19 F1
Inchmoan Pl G15 ..... 74 C2
Inchmurrin Ave G66 ..... 80 A4
Inchmurrin Cres G83 ..... 19 F1
Inchmurrin Dr
 Kilmarnock KA3 ..... 223 D3
 Rutherglen G73 ..... 138 B1
Inchmurrin Gdns G73 ..... 138 B1
Inchmurrin Pl G73 ..... 138 B1
Inchna FK11 ..... 4 A3
Inchneuk Rd ML5 ..... 101 F3
Inchoch St G33 ..... 99 F1
Inchrory Pl G15 ..... 74 C2
Inchwood Ct G68 ..... 82 A4
Inchwood Pl G68 ..... 82 A4
Inchwood Rd G68 ..... 82 A4
Incle St PA1 ..... 113 F3
Ingale Ave KA9 ..... 236 C4
India Dr PA4 ..... 93 E3
India St Alexandria G83 ..... 27 F3
 Glasgow G2 ..... 240 B3
Industry St G66 ..... 79 E4
Inga St G20 ..... 96 C4
Ingerbreck Ave G73 ..... 138 B2
Ingleby Dr G31 ..... 118 A4
Ingleby Pl G78 ..... 154 C4
Inglefield Ct ML6 ..... 123 D4
Inglefield St G42 ..... 117 D1
Ingleneuk Ave G33 ..... 99 D3
Ingleside G66 ..... 79 E3
Inglestone Ave G46 ..... 136 A1
Ingleston St PA15 ..... 46 B2
Inglewood Cres G46 ..... 136 A1
 East Kilbride G75 ..... 180 A4
Inglewood Pl G75 ..... 180 A4
Inglewood Rd PA16 ..... 9 F4
Inglis Dr FK2 ..... 24 B1
Inglis Pl G75 ..... 180 C4
Inglis St Glasgow G31 ..... 118 A3
 Wishaw ML2 ..... 164 B1
Inglison Dr PA7 ..... 71 F2
Ingram Pl KA3 ..... 222 D2
Ingram St G1 ..... 241 D2
Inishail Rd G33 ..... 99 E1
Inkerman Pl KA1 ..... 222 C1
Inkerman Rd G52 ..... 114 C3
Innellan Dr KA3 ..... 223 C1
Inner City Trad Est G4 ..... 241 E4
Innerleithen Dr ML2 ..... 165 E3
Innermanse Quadrant
 ML1 ..... 143 F3
Innerpeffray Dr FK2 ..... 24 A2
Innerwick Dr G52 ..... 115 D3
Innerwood Rd KA13 ..... 207 F3
Innes Ct G74 ..... 159 F2
International Ave G72 ..... 161 E2
Inver Ct FK2 ..... 24 A1
Inver Rd G33 ..... 119 F4
Inverallan Ct FK9 ..... 1 C4
Inverallan Dr FK9 ..... 1 C4
Inverallan Rd FK9 ..... 1 C4
Inveraray Dr G64 ..... 78 A2
Inveraray Pl FK5 ..... 23 F3
Inveravon Dr ML1 ..... 163 E3
Inverbervie PA8 ..... 73 D1
Invercanny Dr G15 ..... 75 D2
Invercanny Pl G15 ..... 75 D2
Invercargill G75 ..... 180 A4
Invercloy Pl KA3 ..... 222 C2
Inverclyde Gdns G73 ..... 138 C2
Inverclyde Royal Hospl
 PA16 ..... 44 C2
Invercree Wlk ML5 ..... 101 E3
Inveresk Pl ML5 ..... 122 A4
Inveresk Quadrant G32 ..... 119 D3
Inveresk St G32 ..... 119 D3
Inverewe Ave G46 ..... 135 E1
Inverewe Dr G46 ..... 135 E1
Inverewe Gdns G46 ..... 135 E1
Inverewe Pl G46 ..... 135 E1
Inverewe Way G77 ..... 156 A3
Invergarry Ave G46 ..... 135 E1
Invergarry Ct G46 ..... 135 E1
Invergarry Dr G46 ..... 135 E1
Invergarry Gdns G46 ..... 135 E1
Invergarry Gr G46 ..... 135 E1
Invergarry Pl G46 ..... 135 E1
Invergarry Quad G46 ..... 135 F1
Invergarry Vw G46 ..... 135 F1
Inverglas Ave PA4 ..... 94 C1
Invergordon Ave G43 ..... 136 C4
Invergyle Dr G52 ..... 115 E3
Inverkar Dr KA7 ..... 238 B2
Inverkar Rd KA7 ..... 239 D3
Inverkip Dr ML7 ..... 146 C3
Inverkip Rd Gourock PA16 ..... 44 B1
 Greenock PA16 ..... 45 E2
Inverkip St PA15 ..... 45 F3
Inverlair Ave G43 ..... 136 C3

Inverleith St G32 .... 118 C4
Inverleven Pl KA11 ...... 219 F4
Inverlochy St G33 .... 99 E1
Inverness St G51 .... 115 F3
Inveroran Dr G61 .... 76 A2
Invershiel Rd G23 .... 76 C1
Invershin Dr 6 G20 ...... 96 B3
Inverurie St G21 .... 97 E2
Invervale Ave ML6 .... 123 F3
Inzievar Terr G32 .... 119 D1
Iona ML6 .... 123 E3
Iona Ave G74 .... 160 A2
Iona Cres Gourock PA19 .. 44 B3
  Old Kilpatrick G60 .... 73 E3
Iona Ct KA11 .... 225 E4
Iona Dr PA2 .... 133 E4
Iona Gdns G60 .... 73 E3
Iona La G69 .... 81 D1
Iona Path G72 .... 161 E4
Iona Pl Coatbridge ML5 .. 101 E1
  Falkirk FK1 .... 42 A1
  Irvine KA11 .... 225 E4
  Kilmarnock KA3 .... 223 D3
  Old Kilpatrick G60 .... 73 E3
Iona Quadrant ML2 .... 165 F2
Iona Rd Port Glasgow PA14 . 69 D4
  Renfrew PA4 .... 94 B1
  Rutherglen G73 .... 138 C2
  Wishaw ML2 .... 165 F3
Iona Ridge ML3 .... 161 F1
Iona St Glasgow G51 ..... 116 A4
  Greenock PA16 .... 45 E2
  Motherwell ML1 .... 142 B1
Iona Way Kirkintilloch G66 . 80 A4
  Stepps G33 .... 99 F2
Iona Wlk PA19 .... 44 B3
Iona Wynd G83 .... 27 F1
Iris Ave G45 .... 138 A2
Iris Ct KA7 .... 239 E2
Irongray St G31 .... 118 B4
Irvine Cres ML5 .... 122 B4
Irvine Ctr KA12 .... 219 D1
Irvine Gdns G65 .... 58 A3
Irvine Ind Est KA12 ..... 224 A4
Irvine Mains Cres KA12 .. 219 E2
Irvine Maritime Mus
  KA12 .... 219 D1
Irvine Pl Kilsyth G65 ... 36 A1
  Stirling FK8 .... 7 D4
Irvine Rd Crosshouse KA2 . 221 F1
  Irvine KA13 .... 219 D4
  Kilmarnock KA2 .... 222 B1
  Kilmaurs KA3 .... 222 A4
  Kilwinning KA13 .... 207 F1
Irvine Royal Acad KA12 .. 219 D3
Irvine St Glasgow G40 ... 118 A2
  Glenmavis ML6 .... 102 C2
Irvine Sta KA12 .... 219 D1
Irvine Terr ML3 .... 183 E4
Irving Ave G81 .... 74 A3
Irving Ct Clydebank G81 . 74 A3
  Falkirk FK1 .... 42 A3
Irving Quadrant G81 ..... 74 A3
Irwin St PA15 .... 46 C1
Isabella Gdns ML3 .... 163 E1
Isla Ave ML2 .... 165 F3
Island Rd G67 .... 82 B4
Island View KA22 .... 205 D2
Islands Cres FK1 .... 42 A1
Islay ML6 .... 123 F3
Islay Ave Port Glasgow PA14 . 69 D4
  Rutherglen G73 .... 138 C2
Islay Cres Clydebank G60 . 73 E3
  Paisley PA2 .... 133 E4
  Saltcoats KA21 .... 205 F1
Islay Ct Hamilton ML3 ... 161 F1
  Irvine KA11 .... 225 E4
Islay Dr
  Newton Mearns G77 .... 156 A3
  Old Kilpatrick G60 .... 73 E3
Islay Gdns Carluke ML8 .. 202 A4
  Larkhall ML9 .... 185 D2
Islay Pl KA3 .... 223 D3
Islay Quadrant ML2 ...... 164 C1
Islay Rd G60 .... 80 A4
Isle Of Pin Rd KA10 ..... 230 A1
Isobel Mair Sch G76 ..... 136 B1
Ivanhoe G74 .... 160 B2
Ivanhoe Cres ML2 .... 165 E2
Ivanhoe Ct ML8 .... 187 E1
Ivanhoe Dr Kirkintilloch G66 . 79 F4
  Saltcoats KA21 .... 206 A1
Ivanhoe Pl
  Motherwell ML1 .... 143 D3
  Stirling FK6 .... 2 A1
Ivanhoe Rd
  Cumbernauld G67 .... 82 C4
  Glasgow G13 .... 95 E4
  Paisley PA2 .... 132 C1
Ivanhoe Way PA2 .... 112 C1
Ivy Cres PA19 .... 44 C3
Ivy Gr ML5 .... 122 A3
Ivy Pl Ayr KA7 .... 239 E3
  Blantyre G72 .... 161 E4
  Motherwell ML1 .... 143 D2
Ivy Rd G71 .... 141 E4
Ivy Terr ML1 .... 143 D3
Ivy Way ML6 .... 123 F2
Ivybank Ave G72 .... 139 E2
Ivybank Cres PA14 .... 47 D1
Ivybank Rd PA14 .... 47 D1
Izatt St FK10 .... 10 A4

Jack St Hamilton ML3 .... 183 E4
  Motherwell ML1 .... 164 A2

Jack's Rd Bothwell G71 .. 141 D3
  Saltcoats KA21 .... 205 F1
Jacks View KA23 .... 190 B3
Jackson Ct ML5 .... 122 A3
Jackson Pl Carluke ML8 .. 187 F2
  Renton G82 .... 27 E1
Jackson St ML5 .... 122 A4
Jackton Rd G75 .... 179 E3
Jacob Pl FK1 .... 42 A2
Jacob's Ladder Way ML2 .. 186 B3
Jacobs Dr PA19 .... 44 B3
Jagger Gdns G69 .... 119 F2
Jail Wynd FK8 .... 7 D4
Jamaica Dr G75 .... 159 D1
Jamaica La PA15 .... 45 F3
Jamaica St Glasgow G1 ... 240 C1
  Greenock PA15 .... 45 F3
James Aiton Prim Sch G72 . 139 D3
James Brown Ave KA8 ..... 236 C2
James Campbell Rd KA8 ... 239 E4
James Cres KA12 .... 219 E2
James Croft Dr FK1 ...... 41 F1
James Dempsey Ct ML5 .... 121 F3
James Dempsey Gdns
  ML5 .... 121 F3
James Dunlop Gdns G64 ... 98 A4
James Gray St G41 .... 136 C4
James Hamilton Acad KA3 . 223 E1
James Hamilton Dr ML4 ... 142 A3
James Hamilton Heritage Pk
  G74 .... 159 E2
James Healy Dr ML3 ...... 183 E4
James Hemphill Ct G65 ... 57 F4
James Leeson Ct G65 ..... 58 B3
James Little St KA1 ..... 227 F4
James McFarlane Sch
  KA22 .... 205 E2
James Miller Cres KA21 .. 217 D4
James Morrison St G1 .... 241 E1
James Nisbet St G21 ..... 97 F1
James Reid Sch KA21 ..... 206 A1
James St Alexandria G83 . 27 F3
  Alva FK12 .... 5 D3
  Ayr KA8 .... 236 A1
  Bannockburn FK7 .... 7 E1
  Bellshill ML4 .... 141 F4
  Carluke ML8 .... 187 F1
  Dalry KA24 .... 191 D4
  Falkirk FK2 .... 42 A3
  Glasgow G40 .... 117 F2
  Haggs FK4 .... 39 D2
  Helensburgh G84 .... 16 B1
  Laurieston FK2 .... 42 C2
  Motherwell ML1 .... 163 E4
  Prestwick KA9 .... 236 A3
  Stenhousemuir FK5 ..... 23 E1
  Stirling FK8 .... 2 A1
James Sym Cres KA1 ...... 227 F3
James View ML1 .... 142 C2
James Watt Ave G75 ...... 181 D4
James Watt Coll PA15 .... 45 F3
James Watt Pl G74 .... 159 D2
James Watt Rd G62 .... 54 C2
James Watt St G2 .... 240 B2
James Watt Way PA15 ..... 46 B2
James Wilson Pl ML8 ..... 201 D1
Jamestown Prim Sch G83 .. 27 F4
Jamieson Ave FK5 .... 23 F2
Jamieson Ct Clydebank G81 . 74 A4
  6 Glasgow G42 .... 117 D1
Jamieson Dr G74 .... 160 B2
Jamieson Gdns ML7 .... 146 C3
Jamieson Pl KA3 .... 223 D3
Jamieson St G42 .... 117 E1
Jamieson Way KA15 .... 171 D4
Jane Ct ML9 .... 185 D1
Jane Rae Gdns G81 .... 94 B4
Jane's Brae G67 .... 82 C4
Jane's Brae Intc G67 .... 82 C4
Janebank Ave G72 .... 139 E2
Janefield Ave PA5 .... 111 F1
Janefield Pl Bath KA15 .. 150 A1
  Blantyre G72 .... 161 E3
  Lennoxtown G65 .... 33 E1
Janefield St G31 .... 118 B3
Janesmith St ML2 .... 164 B2
Jardine St G20 .... 96 C2
Jardine Terr Gartcosh G69 . 100 C3
  Greenock PA16 .... 45 F4
Jarvie Ave ML6 .... 104 A1
Jarvie Cres G65 .... 60 B4
Jarvie Pl FK2 .... 42 A4
Jarvie Way PA2 .... 132 C4
Jasmine Pl G67 .... 82 A3
Jasmine Rd KA1 .... 227 E4
Jasmine Way ML8 .... 201 D1
Java St ML1 .... 142 B1
Jean Armour Dr G81 ...... 74 B2
Jean Armour La KA11 ..... 44 C2
Jean Armour Pl KA21 ..... 206 A1
Jean Armour Terr PA16 ... 44 C2
Jean St PA14 .... 47 D1
Jeanette Ave ML3 .... 183 E4
Jeanie Deans Dr G84 ..... 25 D4
Jedburgh Ave G73 .... 138 A4
Jedburgh Dr PA2 .... 133 D4
Jedburgh Gdns 6 G20 ..... 96 C2
Jedburgh Pl Coatbridge ML5 . 121 F2
  East Kilbride G74 ..... 159 F1
Jedburgh St Blantyre G72 . 161 E4
  Wishaw ML2 .... 165 E4
Jedworth Ave G15 .... 75 E2
Jedworth Ct G61 .... 75 F3
Jedworth Rd G15 .... 75 D2
Jeffrey Pl G65 .... 36 B1
Jeffrey St KA1 .... 227 F3
Jellicoe Pl G84 .... 17 D1

Jellico St G81 .... 73 F2
Jellyholm Rd FK10 .... 10 C4
Jennie Lee Dr ML2 .... 186 A4
Jennys Well Ct PA2 ...... 114 A1
Jennys Well Rd PA2 ...... 114 A1
Jermond Dr KA12 .... 219 E3
Jervis Pl G84 .... 17 D1
Jervis Terr G75 .... 180 A4
Jerviston Ct ML1 .... 143 D1
Jerviston Rd Glasgow G33 . 99 E1
  Motherwell ML1 .... 143 D1
Jerviston St
  Motherwell ML1 .... 163 F4
  Motherwell, New Stevenston
  ML1 .... 143 D2
Jerviswood ML1 .... 143 D1
Jerviswood Dr ML11 ...... 215 E4
Jerviswood Rd ML11 ...... 215 D2
Jessie St G42 .... 117 E1
Jessiman Sq PA4 .... 94 A1
Jimmy Sneddon Way ML1 ... 142 B1
Joanna Terr G72 .... 161 E4
Jocelyn Sq G1 .... 241 D1
Jockshorn Terr KA3 ...... 222 B3
John Bassy Dr FK4 .... 38 B2
John Bosco RC Sec Sch
  G5 .... 117 E2
John Bowman Gdns ML4 .... 142 A3
John Brannan Way ML4 .... 141 E3
John Brogan Pl KA21 ..... 217 D4
John Brown Pl G69 .... 100 B4
John Burnside Dr G81 .... 74 B4
John Cambell Ct PA19 .... 44 C4
John Cambell St PA19 .... 44 C4
John Davidson Dr FK6 .... 21 E2
John Dickie St KA1 ...... 222 C1
John Ewing Gdns ML9 ..... 185 D2
John Finnie St KA1 ...... 227 F4
John Galt Prim Sch KA12 . 219 D3
John Gregor Pl PA22 ..... 129 E1
John Hendry Rd G71 ...... 141 D2
John Jarvis Sq G65 ...... 36 B1
John Knox La ML3 .... 161 F2
John Knox St
  Clydebank G81 .... 94 B4
  Glasgow G4 .... 241 F2
John Lang St PA5 .... 112 A2
John Logie Baird Prim Sch
  G84 .... 17 D1
John McEwan Way G64 ..... 78 A4
John Murray Ct ML1 ...... 163 F2
John Murray Dr FK9 ...... 2 A4
John Ogilvie RC H Sch
  ML3 .... 161 F2
John Paul Acad G23 ...... 76 B1
John Rushforth Pl FK8 ... 1 C1
John Smith Ct ML6 .... 122 C4
John Smith Way ML7 ...... 146 B3
John St Ayr KA8 .... 239 D4
  Barrhead G78 .... 134 A2
  Bellshill ML4 .... 142 A3
  Blantyre G72 .... 161 F4
  Carluke ML8 .... 187 F1
  Falkirk FK1 .... 42 A4
  Glasgow G1 .... 241 D2
  Gourock PA19 .... 44 C4
  Greenock PA15 .... 46 A2
  Haggs FK4 .... 39 D2
  Hamilton ML3 .... 162 C2
  Helensburgh G84 .... 16 B1
  Kirkintilloch G66 ..... 58 B1
  Larkhall ML9 .... 185 D1
  Renton G82 .... 49 E4
  Stirling FK8 .... 7 D4
  Wishaw ML2 .... 164 B2
John Street La G44 ...... 136 B3
John Street Prim Sch G84 . 17 F2
John Wheatley Coll G32 .. 119 D3
John Wheatley Coll
  (Easterhouse Campus)
  G34 .... 120 A4
John Wilson Dr G65 ...... 36 A1
John Wilson St PA15 ..... 46 B1
John Wood St PA14 .... 47 F1
John Wright Sports Ctr The
  G74 .... 160 A2
Johnsburn Dr G53 .... 135 D3
Johnsburn Rd G53 .... 135 D3
Johnshaven PA8 .... 73 D1
Johnshaven St G43 .... 136 B4
Johnshill PA12 .... 129 E2
Johnson Ct G84 .... 16 C1
Johnson Dr G72 .... 139 D3
Johnston Ave
  Clydebank G81 .... 94 B4
  Kilsyth G65 .... 60 B4
Johnston Dr KA10 .... 229 E3
Johnston Pl FK6 .... 21 E1
Johnston Rd G69 .... 101 D3
Johnston St Airdrie ML6 . 123 D4
  Bannockburn FK7 .... 7 E1
  Greenock PA15 .... 45 E4
  Paisley PA1 .... 113 F2
Johnston Terr PA16 ...... 45 E4
Johnstone Ave G52 .... 115 D4
Johnstone Dr G73 .... 138 A4
Johnstone High Sch PA5 .. 131 E4
Johnstone Hospl PA5 ..... 111 F2
Johnstone La ML8 .... 188 A1
Johnstone Rd ML3 .... 162 C1
Johnstone St Alva FK12 .. 5 D3
  Bellshill ML4 .... 142 B3
  Menstrie FK11 .... 3 F3
Johnstone Sta PA5 .... 112 A1

Johnstone Terr G65 ...... 59 F2
Joiners La KA3 .... 195 D4
Jones Ave FK5 .... 41 E4
Jones Wynd ML1 .... 143 F1
Jonquil Way ML8 .... 201 F4
Joppa St G33 .... 118 C4
Jordan St G14 .... 95 E1
Jordanhill Coll Sch G13 . 95 E3
Jordanhill Cres G13 ..... 95 E3
Jordanhill Dr G13 .... 95 E3
Jordanhill La G13 .... 95 F3
Jordanhill Sta G11 ...... 95 F2
Jordanvale Ave G14 ...... 95 E1
Jowitt Ave G81 .... 74 B1
Jubilee Bank G66 .... 79 E2
Jubilee Ct G52 .... 114 C4
Jubilee Dr KA3 .... 195 F1
Jubilee Gdns G61 .... 75 F3
Jubilee Pl KA3 .... 195 F1
Jubilee Rd FK6 .... 21 F2
Jubilee Terr PA5 .... 111 E1
Julian Ave G12 .... 96 B2
Julian La G12 .... 96 B2
Juniper Ave G75 .... 180 B3
Juniper Ct G66 .... 79 D3
Juniper Dr G66 .... 58 A2
Juniper Gn KA7 .... 239 E3
Juniper Gr ML3 .... 162 C1
Juniper Pl Glasgow G32 .. 119 F2
  Johnstone PA5 .... 132 A4
  Uddingston G71 .... 141 E4
Juniper Rd G71 .... 141 E4
Juniper Terr G32 .... 119 F2
Juniper Wynd ML1 .... 143 D3
Juno La PA16 .... 44 B2
Juno St ML1 .... 142 B1
Juno Terr PA16 .... 44 B2
Jupiter La PA16 .... 44 B2
Jupiter Pl G84 .... 15 D3
Jupiter St ML1 .... 142 B1
Jupiter Terr PA16 .... 44 B2
Jura G74 .... 181 D4
Jura Ave PA4 .... 94 B1
Jura Ct Glasgow G52 ..... 115 F3
  Irvine KA11 .... 225 E4
Jura Dr Blantyre G72 .... 140 B2
  Kirkintilloch G66 ..... 80 A4
  Old Kilpatrick G60 .... 73 E3
Jura Gdns Carluke ML8 ... 202 A4
  Hamilton ML3 .... 162 A1
  Larkhall ML9 .... 185 D2
  Old Kilpatrick G60 .... 73 E3
Jura Pl Old Kilpatrick G60 . 73 E3
  Troon KA10 .... 229 F4
Jura Quadrant ML2 .... 164 C1
Jura Rd Old Kilpatrick G60 . 73 E3
  Paisley PA2 .... 133 E4
Jura St Glasgow G52 ..... 115 F3
  Greenock PA16 .... 45 E2
Jura Wynd ML5 .... 101 E3
Jutland Ct G84 .... 15 D3

Kaim Dr G53 .... 135 E3
Kairnhill Ct ML11 .... 214 C2
Kames Ct KA11 .... 220 A3
Kames Rd ML7 .... 146 C3
Kane St ML1 .... 198 C1
Karadale Gdns ML9 .... 185 D2
Karol Path G4 .... 97 D1
Karrienair Rd G64 .... 78 B1
Katewell Ave G15 .... 74 C2
Katherine St ML6 .... 123 F4
Kathleen Ps G84 .... 16 A2
Katrine Ave
  Bishopbriggs G64 ...... 78 A1
  Uddingston ML4 .... 141 E3
Katrine Cres ML6 .... 102 C1
Katrine Dr
  Newton Mearns G77 .... 157 D2
  Paisley PA2 .... 113 D1
Katrine Pl Cambuslang G72 . 139 D3
  Coatbridge ML5 .... 101 E4
Katrine Rd G72 .... 139 E3
  Irvine KA12 .... 219 E3
Katrine Rd Greenock PA15 . 46 A2
  Shotts ML7 .... 146 C3
Katrine Way 6 G71 .... 141 D2
Katrine Wynd ML1 .... 143 D3
Katriona Path 6 ML9 ..... 185 E1
Kay Gdns ML1 .... 163 D3
Kay Park Cres KA3 .... 223 D1
Kay Park Gr KA3 .... 223 D1
Kay Park Terr KA3 .... 223 D1
Kay St G21 .... 97 F2
Kaystone Rd G15 .... 75 D1
Keal Ave G15 .... 95 D4
Keal Cres G15 .... 95 D4
Keal Dr G15 .... 95 D4
Keal Pl G15 .... 95 D4
Keane Path ML1 .... 164 A2
Kearn Ave G15 .... 75 D1
Kearn Pl G15 .... 75 D1
Keats Pk G71 .... 141 E3
Keil Cres G82 .... 49 E2
Keil Sch G82 .... 49 E2
Keilarsbrae FK10 .... 5 D1
Keir Ave G15 .... 2 A1
Keir Cres ML1 .... 165 D2
Keir Dr G64 .... 77 F1
Keir Gdns FK9 .... 2 A4
Keir Hardie Ave
  Laurieston FK2 .... 42 C2
  Motherwell ML1 .... 143 D3
Keir Hardie Cres KA13 ... 208 A2

Keir Hardie Ct G64 ...... 78 A1
Keir Hardie Dr
  Ardrossan KA22 .... 205 D2
  Bellshill ML4 .... 141 F2
  Kilbirnie KA25 .... 149 D1
  Kilsyth G65 .... 60 B4
Keir Hardie Meml Prim Sch
  ML1 .... 143 E2
Keir Hardie Pl
  Bellshill ML4 .... 141 F2
  Saltcoats KA21 .... 206 A1
Keir Hardie Rd Alva FK12 . 5 E4
  Larkhall ML9 .... 185 E3
  Stevenston KA20 .... 206 C1
Keir Hardie St PA15 ..... 46 C1
Keir St Bridge Of A FK9 . 2 A4
  Glasgow G41 .... 116 C2
Keir's Wlk G72 .... 139 D3
Keith Ave Glasgow G46 ... 136 B2
  Stirling FK7 .... 7 E2
Keith Ct G11 .... 96 B1
Keith Pl KA3 .... 223 E1
Keith Quadrant ML2 ...... 165 D3
Keith St Bellshill ML4 .. 142 A3
  Glasgow G11 .... 96 B1
Kelburne Cres ML4 .... 141 F3
Kelbourne St G20 .... 96 C2
Kelbourne St G20 .... 96 C2
Kelburn Cres KA1 .... 227 F2
Kelburn St G78 .... 134 A1
Kelburn Terr PA14 .... 48 A1
Kelburne Gdns
  Glasgow G80 .... 120 A2
  Paisley PA1 .... 114 A3
Kelburne Oval PA1 .... 114 A3
Kelhead Ave
  Glasgow G52 .... 114 C3
  Paisley PA1 .... 114 C2
Kelhead Dr G52 .... 114 C3
Kelhead Path G52 .... 114 C3
Kelhead Pl G52 .... 114 C3
Kellas St G51 .... 116 A4
Kellie Gr G74 .... 159 E2
Kellie Path FK10 .... 10 A4
Kelliebank FK10 .... 9 F3
Kellock Ave ML5 .... 121 E2
Kellock Cres ML5 .... 121 E2
Kells Pl G15 .... 74 C2
Kelly Pk FK5 .... 21 F2
Kelly St PA16 .... 45 E3
Kelly's La ML8 .... 188 A1
Kelso Ave
  Bridge Of W PA11 ..... 110 B4
  Paisley PA2 .... 113 D1
  Rutherglen G73 .... 138 A4
Kelso Cres ML2 .... 165 D3
Kelso Dr Carluke ML8 .... 188 B1
  East Kilbride G74 ..... 160 B2
Kelso Gdns G69 .... 80 C2
Kelso Pl G14 .... 94 C3
Kelso St G13 .... 94 C3
Kelso Quadrant ML5 ...... 121 F4
Kelton St G32 .... 119 D2
Kelvin Ct Glasgow G12 ... 96 A3
  Kirkintilloch G66 ..... 58 B1
Kelvin Dr Airdrie ML6 ... 123 F4
  Barrhead G78 .... 134 B1
  Bishopbriggs G64 ...... 78 A1
  Chryston G69 .... 80 C1
  East Kilbride G75 ..... 180 C4
  Glasgow G20 .... 96 B3
  Kirkintilloch G66 ..... 79 D4
  Shotts ML7 .... 147 D2
Kelvin Gdns Hamilton ML3 . 161 F2
  Kilsyth G65 .... 60 B4
Kelvin Hall Transport Mus
  G3 .... 96 B1
Kelvin Park S G75 .... 181 D2
Kelvin Pl G75 .... 181 D4
Kelvin Rd Bellshill ML4 . 142 A4
  Cumbernauld G67 .... 83 D4
  East Kilbride G75 ..... 181 D3
  Milngavie G62 .... 54 C2
  Uddingston G71 .... 140 C4
Kelvin Rd N G67 .... 83 D4
Kelvin St G65 .... 96 B1
Kelvin South Bsns Pk G75 . 180 C2
Kelvin St ML5 .... 122 B3
Kelvin Terr G65 .... 59 F2
Kelvin View Torrance G64 . 78 B4
Kelvin Way
  1 Bellshill G71 ...... 141 D2
  Glasgow G3, G12 .... 96 C1
  Kilsyth G65 .... 36 B1
  Kirkintilloch G66 ..... 79 D4
Kelvinbridge Rdbt G64 ... 78 A4
Kelvinbridge Underground Sta
  G4 .... 96 C1
Kelvindale G64 .... 57 E1
Kelvindale Gdns G20 ..... 96 B3
Kelvindale Pl 11 G20 .... 96 B3
Kelvindale Prim Sch G12 . 96 B3
Kelvindale Rd G12 .... 96 B3
Kelvingrove Mus & Art Gall
  G3 .... 96 B1
Kelvingrove St G3 .... 116 C4
Kelvinhall Underground Sta
  G11 .... 96 B1
Kelvinhaugh Pl G3 .... 116 B4
Kelvinhaugh Prim Sch G3 . 116 B4
Kelvinhaugh St G3 .... 116 B4
Kelvinhead Rd G65 .... 37 F1

Kelvinside Acad G12 96 B2
Kelvinside Ave G20 96 C2
Kelvinside Cres G65 37 F2
Kelvinside Dr G20 96 C2
Kelvinside Gardens La 7
G20 96 C2
Kelvinside Gdns G20 96 C2
Kelvinside Gdns E G20 96 C2
Kelvinside Terr S 9 G20 96 C2
Kelvinside Terr W 8 G20 96 C2
Kelvinvale G66 58 B1
Kelvinview Ave FK4 38 C1
Kemp Ave PA3 94 A1
Kemp Ct Ardrossan KA21 205 F2
Hamilton ML3 162 C2
Kemp St 8 Glasgow G21 97 F2
Hamilton ML3 162 C2
Kemper Ave FK1 42 B2
Kempock Pl PA19 44 C4
Kempock St Glasgow G40 118 B2
Gourock PA19 44 C4
Kempsthorn Cres G53 115 D1
Kempsthorn Rd G53 115 D1
Ken Rd KA1 228 A3
Kenbank Cres PA11 110 B4
Kenbank Rd PA11 110 B4
Kendal Ave Glasgow G12 96 A3
Glasgow, Giffnock G46 136 B2
Kendal Dr G12 96 A3
Kendal Rd G75 179 F3
Kendoon Ave G15 74 C2
Kenilburn Ave ML6 103 D1
Kenilburn Cres ML6 103 D1
Kenilworth G74 160 C2
Kenilworth Ave
Glasgow G41 136 B4
Helensburgh G84 25 D4
Paisley PA2 132 C4
Wishaw ML2 165 D2
Kenilworth Cres
Bearsden G61 75 E3
Bellshill ML4 142 A3
Greenock PA16 45 E2
Hamilton ML3 161 F2
Kenilworth Ct
Carluke ML8 187 F1
Motherwell ML1 143 D3
Kenilworth Dr
Airdrie ML6 123 E4
Laurieston FK2 42 C2
Saltcoats KA21 206 A1
Kenilworth Rd
Bridge Of A FK9 2 A4
Kirkintilloch G66 79 F4
Lanark ML11 215 D2
Kenilworth Way PA2 112 C1
Kenmar Gdns G71 140 C4
Kenmar Rd ML3 162 A3
Kenmar Terr ML3 162 A3
Kenmore KA10 229 E2
Kenmore Ave KA9 236 B3
Kenmore Dr PA16 45 D2
Kenmore Gdns G61 76 A3
Kenmore Pl Greenock PA16 45 D2
Troon KA10 229 F2
Kenmore Rd
Cumbernauld G67 62 A1
Kilmacolm PA13 89 E4
Kenmore St G32 119 D3
Kenmore Way ML8 187 F2
Kenmuir Ave G32 119 F2
Kenmuir Rd G32 139 E4
Kenmuir St
Coatbridge ML5 121 E2
Falkirk FK1 41 D3
Kenmuiraid Pl ML4 141 F2
Kenmuirhill Rd G32 119 E1
Kenmure Ave G64 77 F1
Kenmure Cres G64 77 F1
Kenmure Dr G64 77 F1
Kenmure Gdns G64 77 F1
Kenmure La G64 77 F1
Kenmure Pl FK5 23 F2
Kenmure Rd G46 157 D3
Kenmure St G41 116 C2
Kenmure View PA9 130 C3
Kenmure Way G73 138 A2
Kennard St FK2 42 B3
Kennedar Dr G51 115 F4
Kennedy Ave G65 60 A2
Kennedy Ct Glasgow G46 136 B2
Kilmarnock KA3 223 E2
Kennedy Dr Airdrie ML6 122 C4
Helensburgh G84 16 B2
Kilmarnock KA3 223 E2
Kennedy Gdns ML2 186 A4
Kennedy Path G4 241 E3
Kennedy Rd
Saltcoats KA21 205 F1
Troon KA10 229 D1
Kennedy St Glasgow G4 241 E3
Kilmarnock KA1 227 F3
Wishaw ML2 165 E2
Kennedy's La PA15 46 A2
Kennelburn Rd ML6 123 E1
Kenneth Rd ML1 163 E3
Kennihill ML6 103 D1
Kennihill Quadrant ML6 103 D1
Kenningknowes Rd FK7 6 C3
Kennishead Ave G46 135 F3
Kennishead Path G46 135 F3
Kennishead Pl G46 135 F3
Kennishead Rd G53 135 E3
Kennishead Sta G46 135 F3
Kennisholm Ave G46 135 F3
Kennisholm Path G46 135 F3
Kennisholm Pl G46 135 F3
Kennoway Dr G11 95 F1
Kennyhill Sch G31 118 B4
Kennyhill Sq G31 118 A4
Kenshaw Ave ML9 199 D4
Kenshaw Pl ML9 199 D4
Kensington Dr G46 136 B1
Kensington Gate 21 G12 96 B2
Kensington Gate La 22 G12 96 B2
Kensington Rd G12 96 B2
Kent Ct G84 17 D2
Kent Dr Helensburgh G84 17 D2
Rutherglen G73 138 B3
Kent Pl G75 179 F3
Kent Rd Alloa FK10 9 F4
Glasgow G3 240 A3
Stirling FK7 7 D3
Kent St G40 241 F1
Kentallen Rd G33 119 F3
Kentigern Terr G64 98 A4
Kentmere Cl G75 180 A3
Kentmere Dr G75 180 A3
Kentmere Pl G75 180 A3
Keppel Dr G44 137 F3
Keppoch St G21 97 E2
Keppochhill Dr G21 97 E2
Keppochhill Pl G21 97 E1
Keppochhill Rd G21 97 E2
Keppochhill Way G21 97 E1
Keppock Pl FK1 41 F1
Ker Rd G62 54 C2
Ker St PA15 45 F3
Kerelaw Ave KA20 206 C1
Kerelaw Rd KA20 206 B1
Kerelaw Sch KA20 206 B1
Kerfield Pl G15 74 C2
Kerr Ave KA21 217 D4
Kerr Cres Haggs FK4 39 D2
Hamilton ML3 162 B1
Kerr Dr Irvine KA12 219 E1
Motherwell ML1 163 E3
Kerr Gdns G71 141 D4
Kerr Pl Denny FK6 21 E1
Glasgow G40 117 F3
Irvine KA12 219 E1
Kerr Rd KA3 223 E1
Kerr St Barrhead G78 134 A1
Blantyre G72 161 F4
Glasgow G40 117 F3
Kirkintilloch G66 79 E4
Paisley PA3 113 E3
Kerrera Pl G33 119 E3
Kerrera Rd G33 119 E3
Kerrix Rd KA1 231 D1
Kerrmuir Ave KA1 228 C3
Kerrs La KA21 216 C4
Kerry Pl G15 74 C2
Kerrycroy Ave G42 137 E4
Kerrycroy Pl G42 137 E4
Kerrycroy St G42 137 E4
Kerrydale St G40 118 A2
Kerrylamont Ave G42 137 F4
Kerse Ave KA24 191 F4
Kerse Gdns FK2 42 C3
Kerse Gn Rd FK10 10 C3
Kerse La FK1 42 B3
Kerse Pl FK1 42 B3
Kerse Rd FK7 7 E3
Kersebonny Rd FK8 6 B4
Kersepark KA7 239 D1
Kershaw St ML2 186 B4
Kersie Rd FK7 9 D2
Kersie Terr FK7 9 F2
Kersland Cres KA1 228 C3
Kersland Dr G62 55 D1
Kersland Foot KA11 219 F3
Kersland Gait KA3 211 F4
Kersland La
1 Glasgow G12 96 B2
Milngavie G62 55 D1
Kersland Rd KA14 170 B3
Kersland Sch PA2 114 B1
Kersland St G12 96 B2
Kerswinning Ave KA25 170 A4
Kessington Dr G61 76 A2
Kessington Rd G61 76 A2
Kessock Dr G22 97 D2
Kessock Pl G22 97 D2
Kestrel Cres PA16 45 D3
Kestrel Ct G81 74 A3
Kestrel Pl Greenock PA16 45 D3
Johnstone PA5 131 E4
Kestrel Rd G13 95 E3
Keswick Dr ML3 183 E3
Keswick Rd G75 179 F3
Kethers La ML1 163 E4
Kethers St ML1 163 E3
Keverkae FK10 9 F3
Kevoc Cotts KA6 237 D3
Kew Gdns G71 141 D4
Kew La G12 96 B2
Kew Terr G12 96 B2
Keynes Sq ML4 142 B2
Keystone Ave G62 76 A4
Keystone Quadrant G62 76 A4
Keystone Rd G62 76 A4
Kibble Sch The PA3 113 E4
Kibbleston Rd PA10 130 C4
Kidsneuk KA12 219 D3
Kidsneuk Gdns KA12 219 D3
Kidston Dr G84 16 A1
Kier Hardie Ct KA15 171 D4
Kierhill Rd G68 61 E1
Kilallan Ave PA11 90 B1
Kilallan Rd PA6 90 B3
Kilbarchan Prim Sch PA10 111 D2
Kilbarchan Rd
Bridge Of W PA11 110 C3
Johnstone PA10, PA5 111 E1
Kilbarchan St 2 G5 117 D3
Kilbean Dr FK1 41 F1
Kilbeck Gdns G61 75 E4
Kilbeg Terr G46 135 E2
Kilberry St G21 98 A1
Kilbirnie Pl G5 117 D2
Kilbirnie St G5 117 D2
Kilbirnie Terr FK6 21 E2
Kilblain St PA15 45 F3
Kilbowie Pl ML6 123 E3
Kilbowie Prim Sch G81 74 A2
Kilbowie Rd Clydebank G81 74 A2
Cumbernauld G67 62 A1
Kilbrandon Cres KA7 238 A1
Kilbrandon Way KA7 238 A1
Kilbrannan Ave KA21 205 F1
Kilbrannan Dr PA16 45 D2
Kilbreck La ML1 143 E2
Kilbrennan Dr Falkirk FK1 41 D2
Motherwell ML1 163 D4
Kilbrennan Rd PA3 112 A3
Kilbride Dr G84 16 C2
Kilbride Rd KA3 195 E1
Kilbride St G5 117 E1
Kilbride View G71 141 D4
Kilburn Gr G72 140 B1
Kilburn Pl G13 95 D3
Kilchattan Dr G44 137 E4
Kilchoan Rd G33 99 E1
Kilcloy Ave G15 75 D2
Kilcreggan View PA15 46 B1
Kildale Rd PA12 129 D1
Kildale Way G73 137 F4
Kildare Dr ML11 215 D2
Kildare Pl ML11 215 D2
Kildare Rd ML11 215 D2
Kildary Ave G44 137 D3
Kildary Rd G44 137 D3
Kildean Hospl FK8 1 C1
Kildean Sch FK8 1 C1
Kildermorie Rd G34 120 A4
Kildonan Ct ML2 165 F4
Kildonan Dr Glasgow G11 96 A1
Helensburgh G84 16 C1
Kildonan House KA9 236 A3
Kildonan Pl
Motherwell ML1 163 E4
Saltcoats KA21 205 F1
Kildonan St ML5 122 A4
Kildrostan St G41 116 C1
Kildrum Prim Sch G67 62 B2
Kildrum Rd G67 62 B2
Kildrum South Rdbt G67 62 A1
Kildrummy Ave FK5 23 F2
Kildrummy Pl G74 159 E2
Kilearn Rd PA3 114 A4
Kilearn Sq PA3 114 A4
Kilearn Way PA3 114 A4
Kilfinan Rd ML7 146 B3
Kilfinan St G22 97 D4
Kilgarth St ML5 121 E2
Kilgraston Rd PA11 110 B3
Kilkerran KA13 207 D2
Kilkerran Dr Glasgow G33 98 C3
Troon KA10 229 E4
Killearn Dr PA1 114 C2
Killearn Rd PA15 46 A1
Killearn St G22 97 E2
Killermont Ave G61 76 A1
Killermont Ct G61 76 A2
Killermont Mdws G72 140 C1
Killermont Pl KA13 207 D2
Killermont Prim Sch G61 76 A2
Killermont Rd G61 76 A1
Killermont St G1 241 D3
Killermont View G20 76 A1
Killiegrew Rd G41 116 B1
Killin Dr PA3 111 F3
Killin Pl Greenock PA16 45 D2
Troon KA10 229 F2
Killin St G32 119 D2
Killoch Ave PA3 113 D3
Killoch Dr Barrhead G78 134 B1
Glasgow G13 95 D3
Killoch Pl KA11 219 F2
Killoch Rd PA3 113 D3
Killoch Way Irvine KA11 219 F2
Paisley PA3 113 D3
Kilmacolm Pl PA15 46 B1
Kilmacolm Prim Sch PA13 89 E4
Kilmacolm Rd
Bridge Of W PA11 90 A2
Greenock PA15 46 A1
Houston PA6 91 D2
Port Glasgow PA14 69 D3
Kilmahew Ave G82 26 A1
Kilmahew Ct
Ardrossan KA22 205 E1
Cardross G82 26 A1
Kilmahew Dr G82 26 A1
Kilmahew Gr G82 26 A1
Kilmahew St KA22 205 E1
Kilmailing Rd G44 137 D3
Kilmair Pl G20 96 B3
Kilmaluag Terr G46 135 E2
Kilmannan Gdns G62 54 C2
Kilmany Ct KA22 205 E1
Kilmany Dr G32 118 C3
Kilmany Gdns G32 118 C3
Kilmardinny Ave G61 75 F3
Kilmardinny Cres G61 76 A3
Kilmardinny Dr G61 75 F3
Kilmardinny Gate G61 75 F3
Kilmardinny Gr G61 75 F3
Kilmarnock Acad KA1 228 A4
Kilmarnock Coll KA3 223 D1
Kilmarnock Coll
(Bank Street Campus)
KA12 219 E2
Kilmarnock Rd
Crosshouse KA2 222 A1
Dundonald KA2 225 F1
Glasgow G43 136 B4
Kilmaurs KA3 222 B3
Monkton KA9 233 F3
Springside KA11 221 D1
Symington KA1 231 E2
Troon KA10 229 F3
Kilmarnock Sta KA1 222 C1
Kilmarnock Tech Coll KA3 228 A4
Kilmartin La ML8 187 F2
Kilmartin Pl G46 135 F2
Kilmaurs Dr G46 136 C2
Kilmaurs Prim Sch KA3 222 A4
Kilmaurs Rd
Crosshouse KA2 221 F1
Fenwick KA3 212 C1
Kilmarnock KA3 222 C2
Kilmaurs St G51 115 F3
Kilmaurs Sta KA3 222 A4
Kilmeny Cres ML2 165 E3
Kilmeny Terr KA22 205 E1
Kilmichael Ave ML2 166 A3
Kilmorie Dr G73 137 F4
Kilmory Ave G71 141 D4
Kilmory Ct
East Kilbride G75 180 B2
Falkirk FK1 41 E2
Kilmory Dr G77 156 C3
Kilmory Gdns ML8 188 A2
Kilmory Pl Kilmarnock KA3 222 C2
Troon KA10 229 F3
Kilmory Rd Carluke ML8 202 A4
Saltcoats KA21 205 F1
Kilmory Wlk KA3 195 E1
Kilmuir Cres G46 135 E2
Kilmuir Dr G46 135 F2
Kilmuir Rd Glasgow G46 135 F2
Uddingston G71 120 C1
Kilmun Rd PA15 46 A2
Kilmun St G20 96 B4
Kiln Ct KA12 219 E1
Kilnbank Cres KA7 239 E4
Kilnburn Rd ML1 163 E4
Kilncadzow Rd ML8 202 C4
Kilncraigs Ct FK10 10 B3
Kilncraigs Rd FK10 10 B3
Kilnford Cres KA2 225 E1
Kilnford Dr KA2 225 F1
Kilnknowie Cotts PA9 131 D3
Kilns Pl FK2 41 F3
Kilns Rd FK1 42 A3
Kilnside Rd PA1 114 A2
Kilnwell Quadrant ML1 163 E4
Kiloran Gr G77 156 A2
Kiloran St G46 135 F2
Kilpatrick Ave PA2 113 D1
Kilpatrick Cres PA2 133 E4
Kilpatrick Ct Irvine KA11 220 A2
Old Kilpatrick G60 73 D3
Kilpatrick Dr Bearsden G61 75 E4
East Kilbride G75 180 A2
Erskine PA8 73 D2
Renfrew PA4 114 A4
Kilpatrick Gdns G76 157 E4
Kilpatrick Pl KA11 220 A1
Kilpatrick Sta G60 73 D3
Kilpatrick View G82 50 A2
Kilpatrick Way 9 G71 141 D4
Kilrig Ave KA13 207 F2
Kilruskin Dr KA23 190 B2
Kilsyth Acad G65 36 B1
Kilsyth Cres KA11 220 A2
Kilsyth Prim Sch G65 60 B4
Kilsyth Rd Banknock FK4 38 B2
Kirkintilloch G66 58 C1
Queenzieburn G65 59 F4
Kilsyth Wlk KA11 220 A2
Kiltarie Cres ML6 123 F3
Kiltearn Rd G33 119 F4
Kiltongue Cotts ML6 122 B4
Kilvaxter Dr G46 135 F2
Kilwinning Acad KA13 207 E2
Kilwinning Cres ML3 161 F1
Kilwinning Rd Dalry KA24 191 D4
Irvine KA12 219 D3
Stevenston KA20 206 C1
Stewarton KA3 211 E4
Kilwinning Sta KA13 207 E2
Kilwynet Way PA3 114 A4
Kimberley Gdns G75 180 B4
Kimberley St Clydebank G81 73 F3
Wishaw ML2 164 B2
Kinalty Rd G44 137 D3
Kinarvie Cres G53 134 C4
Kinarvie Pl G53 134 C4
Kinarvie Rd G53 134 C4
Kinarvie Terr G53 134 C4
Kinbuck St G22 97 E2
Kincaid Dr G65 33 E1
Kincaid Field G65 58 B3
Kincaid Gdns G72 139 D3
Kincaid St PA16 45 D4
Kincaid Way G65 58 B3
Kincaidston Dr KA7 239 E2
Kincaidston Prim Sch KA7 239 D2
Kincardine Dr G64 98 B4
Kincardine Pl
Bishopbriggs G64 98 B4
East Kilbride G74 160 B2
Kincardine Rd FK2 24 B2
Kincardine Sq G33 99 E1
Kincath Ave G73 138 B2
Kinclaven Ave G15 75 D2
Kincraig St G51 115 E3
Kinellan Rd G61 75 F1
Kinellar Dr G14 95 D3
Kinfauns Dr Glasgow G15 75 D2
Newton Mearns G77 156 C3
King Edward La G13 95 F3
King Edward Rd G13 95 F3
King Edward St G83 27 F3
King George Ct PA4 94 C1
King George Gdns PA4 94 C1
King George Park Ave PA4 94 C1
King George Pl PA4 94 C1
King George Way PA4 94 C1
King O' Muirs Ave FK10 4 C2
King Pl G69 121 D3
King St Ayr KA8 236 A1
Clydebank G81 94 B4
Coatbridge ML5 121 F3
Falkirk FK2 42 B3
Fallin FK7 8 B2
Glasgow G1 241 D1
Gourock PA19 44 C4
Greenock PA15 45 F3
Hamilton ML3 162 A2
Kilmarnock KA1 227 F4
Kilsyth G65 60 B4
Kilwinning KA13 207 F2
Larkhall ML9 185 D2
Paisley PA1 113 E3
Port Glasgow PA14 47 E1
Renton G82 27 E1
Rutherglen G73 138 A4
Shotts ML7 146 C2
Stenhousemuir FK5 23 F2
Stirling FK8 7 D4
Stonehouse ML9 198 C1
Wishaw ML2 165 D1
Wishaw, Newmains ML2 166 A3
King St E G84 16 C1
King Street La Kilsyth G65 60 B4
Rutherglen G73 138 A4
King's Cres
Cambuslang G72 139 D3
Carluke ML8 188 A1
Helensburgh G84 16 C1
King's Ct KA15 150 A1
King's Dr Cumbernauld G68 61 F3
Glasgow G40 117 F2
Newton Mearns G77 157 D2
King's Gdns G77 157 D2
King's Glen Prim Sch PA15 46 B1
King's Inch Rd PA4 94 C2
King's Park Ave G44 137 E3
King's Park Prim Sch G44 137 E3
King's Park Rd
Glasgow G44 137 D4
Stirling FK8 7 D4
King's Park Sec Sch G44 137 E3
King's Park Sta G44 137 E3
King's Pk Rd FK8 6 C3
King's Pl G22 97 D3
King's Rd Beith KA15 150 A1
Elderslie PA5 112 A1
King's View G68 61 F3
King's Way G82 49 E3
Kingarth La G42 117 D1
Kingarth St Glasgow G42 117 D1
Hamilton ML3 183 E4
Kingcase Ave KA9 236 A3
Kingcase Prim Sch KA9 236 A3
Kingfisher Dr G13 94 C4
Kinghorn Dr G44 137 E4
Kinghorn La G44 137 E4
Kinglas Rd G61 75 E1
Kings Cres PA5 112 B2
Kings Ct Alloa FK10 10 A4
Ayr KA8 236 A1
8 Falkirk FK1 42 A2
Stenhousemuir FK5 23 E1
Kings Dr ML1 142 C2
Kings Myre ML11 215 E2
Kings Park Hospl FK7 6 C3
Kings Pk G64 57 E1
Kingsacre Rd G44 137 E4
Kingsbarns Dr G44 137 E4
Kingsborough Gate 4 G12 96 A2
Kingsborough Gdns G12 96 A2
Kingsborough La G12 96 A2
Kingsborough La E G12 96 A2
Kingsbrae Ave G44 137 E4
Kingsbridge Cres G44 137 E3
Kingsbridge Dr G44 137 F3
Kingsburgh Dr PA1 114 A3
Kingsburn Dr G73 138 A3
Kingsburn Gr G73 138 A3
Kingscliffe Ave G44 137 E3
Kingscourt Ave G44 137 E3
Kingscroft Rd KA9 236 A4
Kingsdale Ave G44 137 E4
Kingsdyke Ave G44 137 E4
Kingseat Pl FK1 41 F2
Kingsford Ave G44 136 C2
Kingsford Ct G77 156 B3
Kingsgate Ret Pk G74 160 A3
Kingsheath Ave G73 137 F3
Kingshill Ave G68 60 C1
Kingshill Dr G44 137 E3
Kingshill Rd ML7 167 D4
Kingshill View ML8 187 D2
Kingshouse Ave G44 137 E3
Kingshurst Ave G44 137 E3
Kingsknowe Dr G73 137 F3
Kingsland Cres G52 115 D3
Kingsland Dr G52 115 E3
Kingsland La G52 115 E3
Kingslea Rd PA6 91 D1
Kingsley Ave Glasgow G42 117 D1
Stenhousemuir FK5 23 F2

Kingsley Ct G71 .... 141 D4
Kingslynn Dr G44 .... 137 E3
Kingsmuir Dr G73 .... 137 F3
Kingstables La FK8 .... 7 D4
Kingston Ave Airdrie ML6 ... 123 E4
  Neilston G78 .... 154 B3
  Uddingston G71 .... 141 D4
Kingston Flats G65 .... 36 B1
Kingston Gr PA7 .... 72 A2
Kingston Ind Est G5 .... 116 C3
Kingston Pl G81 .... 73 E2
Kingston Rd Bishopton PA7 ... 72 A2
  Kilsyth G65 .... 36 B1
  Neilston G78 .... 154 B3
Kingston St G5 .... 240 C1
Kingsway Dalry KA24 .... 191 D4
  East Kilbride G74 .... 160 A2
  Glasgow G14 .... 95 D3
  Gourock PA19 .... 44 B3
  Kilsyth G65 .... 36 B1
  Kirkintilloch G66 .... 59 D1
Kingsway Ct G14 .... 95 D3
Kingswell Ave KA3 .... 223 D3
Kingswell Pk FK10 .... 10 B4
Kingswood Dr G44 .... 137 E4
Kingswood Rd PA7 .... 71 F2
Kingussie Ave KA3 .... 115 E1
Kingussie Dr G44 .... 137 E3
Kiniver Dr G15 .... 75 D1
Kinkell Gdns G66 .... 59 D1
Kinloch Ave
  Cambuslang G72 .... 139 D2
  Linwood PA3 .... 112 A3
  Stewarton KA3 .... 195 E1
Kinloch Dr ML1 .... 142 B1
Kinloch La PA16 .... 44 C2
Kinloch Rd Kilmarnock KA1 .. 228 A3
  Newton Mearns G77 .... 156 B3
  Renfrew PA4 .... 94 A1
Kinloch St G40 .... 118 B2
Kinloch Terr PA16 .... 44 C2
Kinloss Pl G74 .... 159 F1
Kinmount Ave G44 .... 137 D4
Kinnaird Ave Falkirk FK2 ...... 24 A2
  Newton Mearns G77 .... 157 D3
Kinnaird Cres G61 .... 76 A2
Kinnaird Dr Linwood PA3 .... 112 A3
  Stenhousemuir FK5 .... 23 F2
Kinnaird Pl G64 .... 98 A4
Kinnear Rd G40 .... 118 A2
Kinneil Pl ML3 .... 161 F1
Kinnell Ave G52 .... 115 E2
Kinnell Cres G52 .... 115 E2
Kinnell Pl G52 .... 115 E2
Kinnier Rd KA21 .... 217 D4
Kinnin Brae KA23 .... 190 B2
Kinning Park Ind Est G5 ... 116 C3
Kinning Park
  Underground Sta G41 ... 116 B3
Kinning St G5 .... 117 D3
Kinnis Vennel KA13 .... 207 E2
Kinnoul Gdns G61 .... 75 F2
Kinnoull Pl G72 .... 161 E4
Kinnoull Rd KA8 .... 228 A2
Kinpurnie Rd PA1 .... 114 B3
Kinross Ave Glasgow G52 .. 115 D2
  Port Glasgow PA14 .... 47 E1
Kinross Pk G74 .... 160 B2
Kinsail Dr G52 .... 114 C3
Kinstone Ave G14 .... 95 D3
Kintail Gdns G66 .... 59 D1
Kintessack Pl G64 .... 78 B1
Kintillo Dr G13 .... 95 D3
Kintore Pk ML3 .... 183 D4
Kintore Rd G43 .... 136 C3
Kintore Tower G72 .... 138 C2
Kintra St G51 .... 116 A4
Kintyre Ave PA5 .... 112 A2
Kintyre Cres
  Newton Mearns G77 .... 156 B3
  Plains ML6 .... 104 A2
Kintyre Gdns G66 .... 59 D1
Kintyre Pl FK1 .... 41 E2
Kintyre Rd G72 .... 161 E4
Kintyre St G21 .... 98 A1
Kintyre Terr PA16 .... 44 B2
Kintyre Wynd ML8 .... 187 F2
Kipland Wlk KA3 .... 122 B3
Kippen Dr G76 .... 158 A3
Kippen St Airdrie ML6 ...... 122 C4
  Glasgow G22 .... 97 E3
Kipperoch Rd G82 .... 49 D4
Kippford Pl ML6 .... 123 F1
Kippford St G32 .... 119 E2
Kipps Ave ML6 .... 122 C4
Kirk Ave FK5 .... 23 F1
Kirk Cres G60 .... 73 D4
Kirk Glebe Neilston G78 .... 154 C4
  Stewarton KA3 .... 211 E4
Kirk La Bearsden G61 .... 75 F3
  Glasgow G43 .... 136 B4
Kirk O' Shotts Prim Sch
  ML7 .... 125 E2
Kirk Path ML7 .... 167 D4
Kirk Pl Bearsden G61 .... 75 F3
  Cumbernauld G67 .... 82 A4
  Uddingston G71 .... 140 C3
Kirk Port KA7 .... 238 C4
Kirk Rd Bearsden G61 .... 75 F3
  Beith KA15 .... 171 D4
  Carluke ML8 .... 187 F1
  Carmunnock G76 .... 158 B4
  Dalserf ML9 .... 186 A1
  Houston PA6 .... 91 E1
  Motherwell ML1 .... 143 E4

Kirk Rd continued
  Shotts ML7 .... 146 C2
  Wishaw ML2 .... 165 E2
Kirk St Carluke ML8 .... 187 F1
  Coatbridge ML5 .... 121 F3
  Milngavie G62 .... 54 C1
  Motherwell ML1 .... 163 F4
  Prestwick KA9 .... 233 E1
  Stonehouse ML9 .... 198 C1
Kirk Vennel KA12 .... 219 E1
Kirk View KA15 .... 171 D4
Kirk Wynd 2 Falkirk FK1 .... 42 A2
  Stirling FK7 .... 7 D2
Kirkaig Ave PA4 .... 94 C1
Kirkbean Ave G73 .... 138 A2
Kirkbrae FK10 .... 10 C2
Kirkbride Terr FK7 .... 12 B2
Kirkbriggs Gdns G73 .... 138 A3
Kirkbriggs Way G73 .... 138 A3
Kirkburn FK1 .... 86 A4
Kirkburn Ave G72 .... 139 D2
Kirkburn Dr G63 .... 31 E2
Kirkburn Rd G63 .... 31 E2
Kirkcaldy Rd G41 .... 116 B1
Kirkconnel Ave
  Cumbernauld G68 .... 60 C1
  Glasgow G13 .... 94 C3
Kirkconnel Dr G73 .... 137 F3
Kirkcudbright Pl G74 .... 160 B2
Kirkdale Dr G52 .... 115 F2
Kirkdene Ave G77 .... 157 D3
Kirkdene Bank G77 .... 157 D3
Kirkdene Cres G77 .... 157 D3
Kirkdene Gr G77 .... 157 D2
Kirkdene Pl G77 .... 157 D3
Kirkfield Bank Way ML3 ... 162 A2
Kirkfield Prim Sch ML1 .... 214 B2
Kirkfield Rd Bothwell G71 ... 141 D2
  Kirkfieldbank ML11 .... 214 B2
Kirkfield Terr ML2 .... 165 E2
Kirkfield Wynd PA9 .... 130 C3
Kirkfieldbank Brae ML11 .. 214 C2
Kirkford KA3 .... 211 F4
Kirkford Rd G69 .... 80 C1
Kirkgate Alloa FK10 .... 10 A3
  Irvine KA12 .... 219 E1
  Saltcoats KA21 .... 216 C4
  Wishaw ML2 .... 165 F2
Kirkhall Gdns KA22 .... 205 E1
Kirkhall Pl FK6 .... 21 F1
Kirkhall Rd ML1 .... 143 E3
Kirkhill KA13 .... 207 E1
Kirkhill Ave G72 .... 139 D2
Kirkhill Cres Neilston G78 . 154 C4
  Prestwick KA9 .... 236 A3
Kirkhill Dr G20 .... 96 B3
Kirkhill Gate G77 .... 157 D2
Kirkhill Gdns G72 .... 139 D2
Kirkhill Gr G72 .... 139 D2
Kirkhill Pl 10 Glasgow G20 . 96 B3
  Wishaw ML2 .... 165 E1
Kirkhill Prim Sch G77 ...... 157 D3
Kirkhill Rd Gartcosh G69 .. 100 C3
  Newton Mearns G77 .... 157 D3
  Uddingston G71 .... 140 C4
  Wishaw ML2 .... 164 B1
Kirkhill St ML2 .... 164 B1
Kirkhill Sta G72 .... 139 D2
Kirkhill Terr G72 .... 139 D2
Kirkholm Ave KA8 .... 236 A2
Kirkhope Dr G15 .... 75 D1
Kirkhouse Ave G63 .... 31 E2
Kirkhouse Cres G63 .... 31 E2
Kirkhouse Rd G63 .... 31 E2
Kirkinner Rd G32 .... 119 E2
Kirkintilloch High Sch G66 . 80 A4
Kirkintilloch Ind Est G66 .. 58 B1
Kirkintilloch Rd
  Bishopbriggs G64 .... 78 B3
  Kirkintilloch G66 .... 58 A4
  Kirkintilloch, Waterside G66 .. 80 B4
Kirkland Ave
  Kilmarnock KA3 .... 222 C2
  Strathblane G63 .... 31 E2
Kirkland Cres KA24 .... 191 D4
Kirkland Dr FK6 .... 21 D1
Kirkland Gdns KA3 .... 222 B3
Kirkland La KA3 .... 211 E3
Kirkland La G83 .... 27 F2
Kirkland Rd Dunlop KA3 ... 195 D4
  Glengarnock KA14 .... 170 A4
Kirkland St Glasgow G20 ... 96 C2
  Motherwell ML1 .... 163 E4
Kirkland Terr KA11 .... 220 C1
Kirklandholm KA9 .... 236 B3
Kirklandneuk Prim Sch
  PA4 .... 94 A2
Kirklandneuk Rd PA4 .... 94 A2
Kirklands Cres
  Bothwell G71 .... 141 D2
  Kilsyth G65 .... 60 B4
Kirklands Hospl G71 .... 141 D2
Kirklands Rd ML11 .... 215 D2
Kirklandside Hospl KA1 ... 228 B3
Kirkle Dr G77 .... 157 D3
Kirklea Gdns PA3 .... 113 D3
Kirklee Cir G12 .... 96 B2
Kirklee Gardens La G12 ...... 96 B2
Kirklee Gdns G12 .... 96 B2
Kirklee Pl G12 .... 96 B2
Kirklee Quadrant 45 G12 .. 96 B2
Kirklee Quadrant La G12 .... 96 B2
Kirklee Rd Glasgow G12 ...... 96 B2
  Motherwell ML1 .... 143 E2
Kirklee Terr G12 .... 96 B2
Kirklee Terrace La G12 ...... 96 B2
Kirklee Terrace Rd 41
  G12 .... 96 B2

Kirkliston St G32 .... 118 C3
Kirkmichael Ave 9 G11 ..... 96 A2
Kirkmichael Gdns 8 G11 ... 96 A2
Kirkmichael Rd G84 .... 16 C1
Kirkmuir Dr
  Rutherglen G73 .... 138 A2
  Stewarton KA3 .... 195 E1
Kirkness St ML6 .... 123 D4
Kirknethan ML2 .... 164 B1
Kirknewton St G32 .... 119 D3
Kirkoswald G74 .... 160 B2
Kirkoswald Dr G81 .... 74 B2
Kirkoswald Rd
  Glasgow G43 .... 136 B3
  Motherwell ML1 .... 143 F2
Kirkpatrick Cres G83 .... 27 E4
Kirkpatrick St G40 .... 118 A3
Kirkriggs Ave G73 .... 138 A3
Kirkriggs Prim Sch G73 .... 138 A3
Kirkshaws Ave ML5 .... 121 F2
Kirkshaws Pl ML5 .... 121 F2
Kirkshaws Prim Sch ML5 .. 121 F2
Kirkshaws Rd ML5 .... 121 F2
Kirkslap FK6 .... 21 F1
Kirkstall Gdns G44 .... 78 A2
Kirkstone G77 .... 157 D3
Kirkstone Cl G75 .... 179 F3
Kirkstyle Ave ML8 .... 187 F1
Kirkstyle Cres Airdrie ML6 . 102 C1
Kirkstyle La G65 .... 158 B4
Kirkstyle Ct KA11 .... 220 A3
Kirkstyle La G65 .... 154 C4
Kirkstyle Pl ML6 .... 102 B2
Kirkstyle Prim Sch KA1 .... 228 A3
Kirkstyle Rd ML6 .... 99 F4
Kirkton Erskine PA8 .... 73 D4
  Erskine, North Barr PA8 ... 73 D2
Kirkton Ave Barrhead G78 . 134 A1
  Blantyre G72 .... 161 E3
  Carluke ML8 .... 187 F1
  Glasgow G13 .... 95 D3
  West Kilbride KA23 .... 190 B2
Kirkton Cres Cardross G82 . 26 A1
  Coatbridge ML5 .... 122 B2
Kirkton Ct
  Glasgow G13 .... 95 D3
  Milton Of C G65 .... 58 B3
Kirkton Ct Carluke ML8 .... 187 F1
  Eaglesham G76 .... 178 C2
Kirkton Dr G76 .... 178 C3
Kirkton Gate G74 .... 159 F1
Kirkton Moor Rd G76 ...... 178 B2
Kirkton Pl G74 .... 159 F1
Kirkton Pl Blantyre G72 .... 161 E3
  Coatbridge ML5 .... 122 B2
  East Kilbride G74 .... 159 F1
  Falkirk FK2 .... 24 B2
  Fenwick KA3 .... 213 D2
Kirkton Prim Sch ML8 ...... 187 F1
Kirkton Rd
  Cambuslang G72 .... 139 D3
  Cardross G82 .... 26 A1
  Dumbarton G82 .... 49 E2
  Fenwick KA3 .... 213 D2
  Kilmarnock KA3 .... 222 C3
  Kilmaurs KA3 .... 222 B3
  Neilston G78 .... 154 C3
Kirkton St ML8 .... 187 F1
Kirkton Terr G65 .... 32 C2
Kirktonfield Rd G78 .... 154 C4
Kirktonholm Cres G74 ...... 159 E1
Kirktonholm Prim Sch
  G74 .... 159 E1
Kirktonholme Rd G74 .... 159 E1
Kirktonside G78 .... 134 A1
Kirkvale Cres G77 .... 157 D3
Kirkvale Ct G77 .... 157 D3
Kirkvale Dr G77 .... 157 D3
Kirkview G67 .... 82 A3
Kirkview Ave ML7 .... 125 E1
Kirkview Cres G77 .... 156 C2
Kirkview Ct G67 .... 82 A3
Kirkview Gdns G71 .... 140 C4
Kirkville Pl G15 .... 75 D1
Kirkwall G67 .... 62 A3
Kirkwall Ave G72 .... 140 B2
Kirkwall Rd PA16 .... 44 C2
Kirkway FK2 .... 14 B2
Kirkwell Rd G44 .... 137 D3
Kirkwood Ave G81 .... 74 C1
Kirkwood Pl ML5 .... 121 F3
Kirkwood Quadrant G81 .... 74 B1
Kirkwood Rd G71 .... 140 C4
Kirkwood St
  Coatbridge ML5 .... 121 F3
  Glasgow G51 .... 116 B3
  Rutherglen G73 .... 138 A4
Kirkwood Sta ML5 .... 121 E3
Kirn Dr PA19 .... 44 B3
Kirn Rd KA3 .... 222 C1
Kirn St G20 .... 96 B4
Kirriemuir G74 .... 160 B2
Kirriemuir Ave G52 .... 115 E2
Kirriemuir Gdns G64 .... 78 B1
Kirriemuir Pl G52 .... 115 E2
Kirriemuir Rd G64 .... 78 B1
Kirstie Pl G83 .... 27 F1
Kirtle Dr PA4 .... 94 C1
Kirtle Pl G75 .... 179 F4
Kishorn Pl G33 .... 99 E1
Kitchener St ML2 .... 165 D2
Kittoch Pl 14 G74 .... 159 F1
Kittoch Sch G75 .... 180 B3
Kittoch St G74 .... 159 F1
Kittochside Rd G76 .... 158 C3
Kittyshaw Rd KA24 .... 191 D4
Klondyke Ct ML1 .... 143 D2

Knapdale St G22 .... 97 D4
Knights Gate G71 .... 140 C3
Knights Way FK6 .... 21 E1
Knightsbridge St G13 .... 95 E4
Knightscliffe Ave G13 .... 95 E4
Knightswood Ct G13 .... 95 E3
Knightswood Hospl G13 ... 95 E3
Knightswood Prim Sch G13 . 95 E4
Knightswood Rd G13 .... 95 E4
Knightswood Sec Sch G13 . 95 E3
Knightswood Terr G72 ..... 140 C1
Knivysbridge Pl ML4 .... 141 F2
Knock Jargon Ct KA21 ..... 205 F2
Knock Way PA3 .... 114 A4
Knockbuckle Ave PA13 ...... 69 D1
Knockbuckle Rd PA13 .... 89 E4
Knockburn Prim Sch G21 .. 98 B4
Knockburnie Rd G71 .... 141 D2
Knockember Rd KA11 ...... 221 D1
Knockhall St G33 .... 99 F1
Knockhill Dr G44 .... 137 D4
Knockhill Rd PA4 .... 94 A1
Knocklaw Mount KA3 ...... 222 C2
Knocklaw Rd KA3 .... 222 C2
Knockmarloch Dr KA1 ..... 227 F2
Knocknair St PA14 .... 68 C4
Knockrivoch Gdns KA22 .. 205 F2
Knockrivoch Pl KA22 .... 205 F2
Knockrivoch Wynd KA22 .. 205 F2
Knockside Ave PA2 .... 133 E4
Knoll Croft Rd ML7 .... 147 D2
Knoll Pk KA7 .... 238 C2
Knollpark Dr G76 .... 157 E3
Knowe Cres ML1 .... 143 E2
Knowe Rd Chryston G69 ... 100 B4
  Greenock PA15 .... 46 A2
  Paisley PA3 .... 114 A4
Knowe St G62 .... 54 C1
Knowe The Alloa FK10 .... 5 E1
  Troon KA10 .... 229 F4
Knoweholm Rd FK10 .... 4 A2
Knowehead Dr G71 .... 140 C3
Knowehead Gdns G71 ..... 140 C3
Knowehead Rd
  Clachan of C G65 .... 32 C2
  Hurlford KA1 .... 228 C3
  Kilmarnock KA1 .... 227 F2
  Wishaw ML2 .... 165 E1
Knoweholm KA7 .... 238 B1
Knowenoble St ML1 .... 144 A1
Knowes Ave G77 .... 156 C3
Knowes Rd G77 .... 156 C3
Knowetap St G20 .... 96 C4
Knowetop Ave ML1 .... 163 F2
Knowetop Cres G82 .... 49 E3
Knowhead Gdns 5 G41 ... 116 C2
Knowhead Terr 6 G41 .... 116 C2
Knowstop Prim Sch ML1 .. 163 F2
Knox Ave PA11 .... 110 B4
Knox Pl
  Newton Mearns G77 .... 156 A2
  Saltcoats KA21 .... 206 A1
Knox St Airdrie ML6 .... 123 D4
  Paisley PA1 .... 113 E2
Knoxland Prim Sch G82 .... 50 A2
Knoxland Sq G82 .... 50 A1
Knoxland St G82 .... 50 A1
Knoxville Rd KA25 .... 149 D1
Kronborg Way G71 .... 180 C3
Kyle Acad KA7 .... 239 E4
Kyle Ave Cowie FK7 .... 12 C4
  Springside KA11 .... 225 D2
Kyle Cres KA10 .... 230 A2
Kyle Ct G72 .... 139 D3
Kyle Ct G72 .... 138 C4
Kyle Dr Glasgow G52 .... 136 C2
  Troon KA10 .... 229 E3
Kyle Gr ML1 .... 143 D2
Kyle Quadrant
  Motherwell ML1 .... 143 E2
  Wishaw ML2 .... 164 C1
Kyle Rd G67 .... 62 A2
Kyle Sq G73 .... 137 F3
Kyle St Ayr KA7 .... 238 C4
  Glasgow G4 .... 241 D4
  Motherwell ML1 .... 143 E3
  Prestwick KA9 .... 236 B4
Kyle Terr G82 .... 49 D3
Kyleakin Dr G72 .... 140 A1
Kyleakin Gdns G72 .... 135 E2
Kyleakin Terr G46 .... 135 E2
Kylemore Cres ML1 .... 142 B1
Kylemore La PA16 .... 44 C2
Kylemore Terr PA16 .... 44 C2
Kylepark Ave G71 .... 140 B3
Kylepark Cres G71 .... 140 B4
Kylepark Dr G71 .... 140 B4
Kylerhea Rd G46 .... 135 E2
Kyleshill St KA13 .... 207 F2
Kyleswell St KA13 .... 207 F2
La Belle Allee 18 G3 .... 96 C1
La Belle Pl G3 .... 96 C1
Laberge Gdns ML1 .... 143 D2
Laburnum Ave Beith KA15 . 171 D4
  East Kilbride G75 .... 180 B3
Laburnum Cres ML2 .... 165 D3
Laburnum Ct G75 .... 180 B3
Laburnum Dr G66 .... 58 A3
Laburnum Gdns G66 .... 79 D3
Laburnum Gr
  Coatbridge ML5 .... 122 A3
  Kirkintilloch G66 .... 79 D3
  Stirling FK8 .... 7 D3
  Troon KA10 .... 229 E2
Laburnum Lea ML3 .... 162 C1
Laburnum Pl PA5 .... 132 A4

Laburnum Rd Ayr KA7 ..... 239 E3
  Banknock FK4 .... 38 C1
  Cumbernauld G67 .... 62 B1
  Glasgow G51 .... 116 B2
  Kilmarnock KA1 .... 227 E4
  Uddingston G71 .... 141 E4
Laburnum St PA15 .... 46 C1
Lachlan Cres PA8 .... 72 C1
Lacy St PA1 .... 114 A2
Ladder Ct G75 .... 180 A2
Lade Ct FK5 .... 41 E4
Lade Mill FK7 .... 7 E1
Lade Rd FK4 .... 40 A3
Lade Terr G52 .... 115 D2
Lade The G83 .... 27 F3
Ladeside KA3 .... 222 B4
Ladeside Cl G77 .... 156 B3
Ladeside Cres KA25 .... 23 F1
Ladeside Ct KA25 .... 170 A4
Ladeside Dr Johnstone PA5 . 111 F1
  Kilsyth G65 .... 60 B4
Ladeside Prim Sch FK5 ..... 41 E4
Ladeside Rd KA3 .... 222 B4
Ladhope Pl G13 .... 94 C4
Lady Alice Prim Sch PA16 . 45 E2
Lady Anne Cres ML6 .... 123 E3
Lady Anne St G14 .... 94 C3
Lady Isle Cres G71 .... 140 C3
Lady Jane Gate G71 .... 140 C2
Lady La PA1 .... 113 E2
Lady Margaret Dr KA10 ... 230 A1
Lady Mary Wlk ML3 .... 162 C1
Lady Watson Gdns ML3 ... 162 A1
Lady Wilson St ML6 .... 123 D4
Lady's Gate G83 .... 16 C4
Ladyacre KA13 .... 207 F2
Ladyacre Rd ML11 .... 215 D2
Ladyacres PA4 .... 93 E3
Ladybank G68 .... 61 F3
Ladybank Ct 11 G74 .... 159 F1
Ladybank Dr G52 .... 115 F2
Ladybank Gdns G74 .... 159 F1
Ladybank Pl 18 G74 .... 159 F1
Ladyburn Bsns Ctr PA15 ... 46 C2
Ladyburn Ct KA11 .... 219 F3
Ladyburn St Greenock PA15 . 46 B2
  Paisley PA1 .... 114 A2
Ladyford Ave KA13 .... 207 F2
Ladyha Ct KA11 .... 220 A3
Ladyhill Dr G69 .... 120 A2
Ladykirk Cres
  Glasgow G52 .... 115 D3
  Paisley PA2 .... 113 F2
Ladykirk Dr G52 .... 115 E3
Ladyland Dr KA25 .... 236 B4
Ladyland Dr KA25 .... 149 D2
Ladyloan Ave G15 .... 74 C2
Ladyloan Ct G81 .... 74 C2
Ladyloan Gdns G81 .... 74 C2
Ladymuir Circ PA8 .... 72 C1
Ladymuir Cres G53 .... 135 E4
Ladysgate Ct FK2 .... 24 A2
Ladysmill FK2 .... 42 B3
Ladysmill Ind Est FK2 .... 42 B3
Ladysmith Dr G75 .... 180 A2
Ladysmith Rd KA25 .... 149 D1
Ladysmith St ML2 .... 164 B2
Ladysneuk Rd FK9 .... 2 B1
Ladyton G83 .... 27 F2
Ladyton Prim Sch G83 ...... 28 A2
Ladywell Ct FK5 .... 23 D2
Ladywell Dr FK10 .... 4 A2
Ladywell Pl FK10 .... 4 A2
Ladywell Prim Sch ML1 .... 163 E4
Ladywell Rd ML1 .... 163 E4
Ladywell St G4 .... 241 F2
Ladywood G62 .... 55 D1
Lagan Rd ML8 .... 188 A1
Laggan Ave ML2 .... 147 D2
Laggan House KA9 .... 236 A3
Laggan Quadrant ML6 ..... 102 C1
Laggan Rd Airdrie ML6 .... 102 C1
  Bishopbriggs G64 .... 78 A1
  Glasgow G43 .... 136 B3
  Newton Mearns G77 .... 156 B4
Laggan Terr PA4 .... 94 A2
Laggan Way ML2 .... 165 F4
Laggary Ct G84 .... 15 F3
Laggary Rd G84 .... 15 F3
Laidlaw Ave ML1 .... 142 C2
Laidlaw Gdns G71 .... 120 C1
Laidlaw St G5 .... 240 B1
Laidon Rd ML6 .... 102 C1
Laidon Wlk 3 ML2 .... 165 F3
Laigh Ct KA15 .... 150 A1
Laigh Mount KA7 .... 238 C1
Laigh Rd Beith KA15 .... 150 A1
  Newton Mearns G77 .... 157 E3
Laighcartside St PA5 .... 112 A2
Laighdykes Rd KA21 .... 216 B3
Laighlands Rd G71 .... 141 D1
Laighmuir St G71 .... 140 C3
Laighpark Ave PA7 .... 72 A2
Laighstonehall Rd ML3 ... 162 A1
Laighstonehall Rd ML3 ... 162 A1
Laightoun Ct G67 .... 82 A3
Laightoun Dr G67 .... 82 A3
Laightoun Gdns G67 .... 82 A3
Lainshaw ML3 .... 207 E1
Lainshaw Ave KA1 .... 227 F2
Lainshaw Dr G45 .... 137 D1
Lainshaw Prim Sch KA3 ... 211 E4
Lainshaw St KA3 .... 211 E4
Laird Gr G71 .... 141 D4
Laird Pl G40 .... 117 F2

Laird St Coatbridge ML5 122 A4
Greenock PA15 45 F3
Laird Weir KA22 205 E2
Laird's Hill Ct G65 60 A4
Laird's Hill Pl G65 60 A4
Lairds Gate G71 140 B3
Lairds Hill G67 61 F1
Lairdsland Prim Sch G66 79 E4
Lairg Dr G72 140 B1
Lairhills Rd G75 180 C4
Lake Ave ML11 215 E1
Lakefield Ct G72 161 E3
Lamb St Glasgow G22 97 D3
Hamilton ML3 162 C2
Lambert Terr FK10 10 B4
Lamberton Ave FK7 7 E2
Lamberton Dr G52 115 E3
Lamberton Gdns KA11 220 B3
Lamberton Rd KA3 195 E1
Lambhill Quadrant 5
G41 116 C3
Lambhill St G41 116 B3
Lambie Cres G77 156 B3
Lambie Ct KA21 216 C4
Lamerton Rd G67 62 B1
Lamford Dr KA7 238 B1
Lamington Rd G52 115 D3
Lamlash Cres G33 119 D4
Lamlash Pl
East Kilbride G75 180 A2
Glasgow G33 119 D4
Helensburgh G84 16 C1
Motherwell ML1 163 E4
Lamlash Prim Sch G33 119 D4
Lamlash Sq G33 119 E4
Lammer Wynd 32 ML9 185 E1
Lammerknowes Rd G65 37 F2
Lammermoor G74 160 C2
Lammermoor Ave G52 115 E2
Lammermoor Cres G66 79 F4
Lammermoor Dr G67 82 C4
Lammermoor Gdns G66 79 F4
Lammermoor Prim Sch
ML2 165 D3
Lammermoor Rd G66 79 F4
Lammermoor Terr ML2 165 D2
Lammermuir Ct KA11 220 A2
Lammermuir Dr PA2 133 F4
Lammermuir Gdns G61 75 E4
Lammermuir Pl ML1 143 D3
Lammermuir Rd KA1 228 A2
Lammermuir Way ML6 123 F1
Lammermuir Wynd ML9 184 C3
Lamond View FK5 23 E1
Lamont Ave PA7 72 B2
Lamont Cres Fallin FK7 8 B3
Renton G82 27 E1
Lamont Dr KA12 224 B4
Lamont Pl KA12 224 B4
Lamont Rd G21 98 A3
Lanark Ave ML6 123 D2
Lanark Gram Sch ML11 215 D2
Lanark Ind Est ML11 215 F3
Lanark Moor Ctry Pk ML11 215 F2
Lanark Mus ML11 214 C2
Lanark Prim Sch ML11 215 D3
Lanark Rd Carluke ML8 202 A2
Larkhall ML9 185 E3
Netherburn ML8 200 B4
Lanark St G1 241 E1
Lanark Sta ML11 215 D2
Lancaster Ave Beith KA15 171 D4
Chapelhall ML6 143 F4
Motherwell ML1 143 F4
Lancaster Cres G12 96 B2
Lancaster Crescent La
G12 96 B2
Lancaster Rd G64 78 A2
Lancaster Terr 31 G12 96 B2
Lancaster Terrace La 30
G12 96 B2
Lancaster Way 4 PA4 94 B1
Lancefield Quay G3 240 A2
Lancefield St G3 240 A2
Landemer Dr G73 138 A3
Landressy Pl G40 117 F2
Landressy St G40 117 F2
Landsborough Ct KA21 205 F1
Landsborough Dr KA3 223 D2
Landsborough Pl KA20 206 C1
Landsdowne Gdns ML3 162 C2
Landsdowne Rd ML9 185 E1
Lane The G68 61 E3
Lanfine Rd PA1 114 B2
Lanfine Terr KA11 219 F3
Lanfine Way KA11 220 A3
Lang Ave Bishopton PA7 72 B2
Renfrew PA4 94 B1
Lang Pl PA5 111 F2
Lang Rd KA10 229 F4
Lang St PA1 114 A2
Langa St G20 96 C4
Langbank Dr PA13 69 F1
Langbank Prim Sch PA14 70 A4
Langbank Rise PA13 69 F1
Langbank St 1 G5 117 D3
Langbank Sta PA14 70 B4
Langbar Cres G33 119 F4
Langbrae Sch G66 79 D3
Langbyres Rd ML1 144 B1
Langcraig Rd KA1 227 F1
Langcraigs Ct PA2 133 E4
Langcraigs Dr PA2 133 E3
Langcraigs Prim Sch PA2 133 E4
Langcraigs Terr PA2 133 E3
Langcroft Ave KA9 233 F1
Langcroft Dr G72 139 E2
Langcroft Pl G51 115 E4
Langcroft Rd G51 115 E4
Langcroft Terr G51 115 E4
Langdale East Kilbride G74 159 E2
Newton Mearns G77 157 D3
Langdale Ave G33 98 C2
Langdale Rd G69 80 C1
Langdale St G33 98 C2
Langdales Ave G68 61 E1
Langfaulds Cres G81 74 B3
Langfaulds Prim Sch G15 74 C2
Langford Dr G53 135 D2
Langford Pl G53 135 D2
Langhill Dr G68 61 E2
Langhill Pl FK6 21 E1
Langholm G75 179 F3
Langholm Cres ML2 165 D3
Langholm Ct G69 81 D1
Langholm Dr PA3 112 B3
Langlands Ave
East Kilbride G75 180 C2
Glasgow G51 115 E4
Langlands Brae KA1 222 C1
Langlands Ct
East Kilbride G75 180 C2
Glasgow G51 115 F4
Langlands Dr
East Kilbride G75 180 C2
Glasgow G51 115 E4
Langlands Pl G75 180 C2
Langlands Rd
East Kilbride G75 180 C2
Glasgow G51 115 F4
Langlands Sch G51 115 F4
Langlands St KA1 222 C1
Langlands Terr G82 50 A3
Langlands-Seafar Intc
G67 82 C4
Langlea Ave G72 138 B2
Langlea Ct G72 138 C2
Langlea Dr G72 138 C3
Langlea Gdns G72 138 C3
Langlea Gr G72 138 C2
Langlea Rd G72 138 C2
Langlees Ave G77 157 D3
Langlees Prim Sch FK2 42 A4
Langlees St FK2 24 B1
Langley Ave G13 95 D4
Langloan Cres ML5 121 F3
Langloan Pl ML5 121 F3
Langloan Prim Sch ML5 121 F3
Langloan St ML5 121 F3
Langmuir Ave
Kirkintilloch G66 58 C1
Perceton KA11 220 B3
Langmuir Ct KA11 220 B3
Langmuir Rd
Bargeddie G69 121 D3
Kirkintilloch G66 59 D1
Langmuir Way G69 121 D3
Langmuirhead Rd G66 79 E1
Langness Rd G33 119 D4
Langoreth Ave ML3 161 F1
Langrig Rd Glasgow G21 98 A2
Newton Mearns G77 156 B2
Langshaw Cres ML8 187 F1
Langshot St 4 G51 116 B3
Langside Ave
Glasgow G41 136 C4
Kilmarnock KA1 227 F2
Uddingston G71 141 E3
Langside Coll Annexe G73 138 A3
Langside Coll F Ed G42 137 D4
Langside Ct G71 141 D1
Langside Dr
Blackridge EH48 107 D2
Glasgow G43 136 C3
Kilbarchan PA10 111 D1
Langside Gdns G42 137 D4
Langside La G42 117 D1
Langside Pk PA10 111 D1
Langside Pl Glasgow G41 136 C4
Kilbirnie KA25 149 D1
Langside Prim Sch G41 136 C4
Langside Rd Bothwell G71 141 D1
Glasgow G42 137 D4
Langside St G81 74 C3
Langside Sta G43 136 C3
Langside Terr PA14 68 B4
Langstile Pl G52 114 C3
Langstile Rd G52 114 C3
Langton Cres
Barrhead G78 134 B1
Glasgow G53 115 E1
Langton Gate G77 156 B3
Langton Gdns G69 119 F2
Langton Pl G77 156 B3
Langton Rd G53 115 E1
Langtree Ave G46 136 A1
Lanrig Pl G69 100 B4
Lanrig Rd G69 100 B4
Lansbury Gdns PA3 113 E4
Lansbury St G83 27 F4
Lansbury Terr ML9 185 E1
Lansdowne Cres
Glasgow G20 96 C1
Shotts ML7 147 D2
Lansdowne Crescent La
G3 240 A4
Lansdowne Dr G68 61 F2
Lansdowne Rd KA8 236 A2
Lantana Gr ML1 163 E4
Lanton Dr G52 115 D3
Lanton Rd G43 136 C3
Lappin St G81 94 B4
Laputa Pl KA1 227 F2
Larbert High Sch FK5 23 F1
Larbert High Sch (Annexe)
FK5 23 F1
Larbert Rd FK4 40 A3
Larbert St G4 240 C4
Larbert Sta FK5 23 E1
Larbert Village Prim Sch
FK5 23 D1
Larch Ave Bishopbriggs G64 98 A4
Kirkintilloch G66 79 E3
Larch Cres G66 79 E3
Larch Ct Blantyre G72 161 E4
Cumbernauld G67 62 C2
East Kilbride G75 180 A3
Larch Dr Banknock FK4 38 C1
East Kilbride G75 180 A3
Larch Gr Cumbernauld G67 62 C2
Hamilton ML3 162 C1
Milton Of C G65 58 A3
Motherwell ML1 143 D3
Stenhousemuir FK5 23 F2
Larch House KA9 236 A3
Larch Pl East Kilbride G75 180 A3
Johnstone PA5 132 A4
Kilmarnock KA1 227 E4
Uddingston G71 141 E4
Larch Rd Cumbernauld G67 62 C2
Glasgow G41 116 A2
Larch Terr KA15 171 E4
Larches The Alloa FK10 10 A4
Moodiesburn G69 81 D2
Larchfield Ave Glasgow G14 95 D2
Newton Mearns G77 156 C3
Larchfield Cres ML2 165 E3
Larchfield Ct G77 156 B2
Larchfield Dr G73 138 B2
Larchfield Gdns ML2 165 E3
Larchfield Gr ML2 165 E4
Larchfield La ML7 147 D1
Larchfield Pl Glasgow G14 95 D2
Wishaw ML2 165 E3
Larchfield Rd G61 75 F1
Larchgrove Ave G32 119 E3
Larchgrove Pl G32 119 E4
Larchgrove Rd G32 119 E4
Larchwood Rd KA7 239 E2
Larchwood Terr G78 155 E4
Larghill La KA7 239 D3
Largie Rd G43 136 C3
Largo Pl G51 115 F4
Largs Ave KA3 223 D2
Largs Rd KA25 148 B1
Larkfield Dr G72 161 E3
Larkfield Gr PA16 44 C2
Larkfield Ind Est PA16 44 B3
Larkfield Prim Sch PA16 44 C2
Larkfield Rd Greenock PA16 44 C2
Kirkintilloch G66 79 F3
Larkfield St 15 G42 117 D2
Larkhall Acad ML9 184 C1
Larkhall Ind Est ML9 199 D4
Larkin Gdns PA3 113 E4
Larkin Way ML4 141 F4
Larksfield Dr ML8 202 A4
Larkspur Dr G74 159 E2
Larkspur Way ML8 201 F4
Lashley Gr ML2 186 B4
Lasswade St G14 94 C3
Latherton Dr 7 G20 96 B3
Latimer Gdns G52 115 D2
Latta Ct KA9 236 B3
Latta St G82 50 A2
Lauchlin Pl G66 80 A4
Lauchope Rd ML1 143 E4
Lauchope St ML6 123 F1
Laudedale La G12 96 A2
Lauder Cres ML2 165 D3
Lauder Ct KA3 223 E2
Lauder Dr Linwood PA3 112 A3
Rutherglen G73 138 B3
Lauder Gdns Blantyre G72 140 B1
Coatbridge ML5 122 B2
Lauder Gn G74 160 A2
Lauder La ML3 161 F2
Lauder St 9 G5 117 D2
Lauderdale Dr G77 156 B2
Lauderdale Gdns G12 96 A2
Laudervale Gdns G83 27 E4
Laughland Dr ML1 143 E2
Laughlanglen Rd KA7 239 D2
Laundry La G33 99 E3
Lauranne Pl ML4 141 F3
Laurel Ave Clydebank G81 73 E2
Kirkintilloch G66 79 E3
Laurel Bank Ayr KA7 239 E2
Hamilton ML3 183 E4
Laurel Ct East Kilbride G75 180 B3
Falkirk FK1 41 E3
Laurel Dr East Kilbride G75 180 B3
29 Larkhall ML9 185 E1
Wishaw ML2 164 C2
Laurel Gdns
Chapelhall ML6 123 F1
Uddingston G71 140 C4
Laurel Gr Bonnybridge FK4 39 F2
Greengairs ML6 83 F1
Laurel La ML9 185 E1
Laurel Park Sch G12 96 B1
Laurel Pl Bonnybridge FK4 39 F2
East Kilbride G75 180 B3
Glasgow G11 96 A1
Kilmarnock KA1 227 E4
Laurel Sq FK4 38 C1
Laurel St G11 96 A1
Laurel Way G78 134 A2
Laurel Wlk G73 138 B2
Laurelbank ML5 122 A4
Laurelbank Ave FK4 40 A2
Laurelbank Rd
Chryston G69 100 A4
Glasgow G32 139 E4
Laurelhill Gdns FK8 6 C3
Laurelhill Pl FK8 7 D3
Laurels The
Newton Mearns G77 156 B3
Tullibody FK10 4 A1
Lauren View ML6 122 C4
Lauren Way PA2 113 D1
Laurence Dr G61 75 E3
Laurencecroft Rd FK8 2 A1
Laurenstone Terr G74 160 A2
Laurie Ct G71 141 D4
Laurieland Ave KA2 221 F1
Laurieston Ct KA2 225 F1
Laurieston Rd G5 117 E3
Laurieston Way G73 138 A2
Lauriston Ct KA22 205 E1
Lauriston Gr G77 156 A3
Lauriston Way KA3 223 D3
Lavelle Dr ML5 122 B4
Lavender Dr G75 180 B3
Lavender La ML8 201 F4
Laverock Ave
Greenock PA15 45 E2
Hamilton ML3 163 D1
Laverock Rd ML6 103 D2
Laverock Terr G69 80 C1
Laverockhall ML11 215 D3
Laverockhall St G21 97 F2
Law Brae KA23 190 B3
Law Dr ML1 143 E2
Law Hospl ML8 187 E4
Law Pl G74 159 F3
Law Prim Sch ML8 187 D3
Law Rdbt G74 159 F2
Law St G40 118 A3
Law View ML2 186 B3
Lawer Pl KA11 220 A2
Lawers Cres KA1 228 A2
Lawers Dr G61 75 E4
Lawers La ML1 143 E2
Lawers Pl PA16 45 D2
Lawers Rd Glasgow G43 136 A3
Kilmarnock KA1 228 A2
Renfrew PA4 94 B1
Lawfield Ave
Newton Mearns G77 157 D3
West Kilbride KA23 190 C2
Lawhill Ave G45 137 E2
Lawhill Rd Law ML8 187 D2
Symington KA1 231 E2
Lawhope Mill Rd ML6 123 F2
Lawmarnock Cres PA11 110 B4
Lawmarnock Rd PA11 110 B4
Lawmoor Ave G5 117 E2
Lawmoor Pl G5 117 E1
Lawmoor Rd G5 117 E2
Lawmoor St G5 117 E2
Lawmuir Cres G81 74 C4
Lawmuir Pl ML4 142 A1
Lawmuir Prim Sch ML4 142 A2
Lawmuir Rd Bellshill ML4 142 A2
Law ML8 186 C3
Lawn Pk G62 55 E1
Lawn St PA1 113 F3
Lawrence Ave
Glasgow G46 136 B1
Helensburgh G84 25 D4
Lawrence Dr G83 19 F1
Lawrence St G11 96 B1
Lawrie St Glasgow G11 96 A1
Stonehouse ML9 198 C1
Wishaw ML2 165 F3
Lawrie Way 24 ML9 185 E1
Lawson Ave ML1 163 F2
Lawson Dr KA22 205 E2
Lawson St Ayr KA8 236 A1
Kilmarnock KA1 228 A4
Laswell FK10 5 F2
Lawthorn Rdbt KA11 220 A3
Laxdale Dr FK6 39 E4
Laxford Ave G44 137 D2
Laxford Pl ML5 122 B2
Laxford Rd PA8 72 C1
Laxford Way ML1 143 E2
Laxton Dr G66 79 F2
Le Froy Gdns G75 180 B4
Le Froy La G75 180 B4
Lea Ave G78 154 B4
Leabank Ave PA2 133 F4
Leadburn Rd G21 98 B2
Leadburn St G32 118 C4
Leader St G33 98 B1
Leadhills Rd KA1 228 A2
Leaend Rd ML6 102 C1
Leander Cres Bellshill ML4 142 C3
Renfrew PA4 94 C1
Learigg Rd ML6 104 A2
Learmont Pl G62 54 C1
Learmonth St FK1 42 A2
Leathem Pl ML2 164 B1
Leathen Pl PA8 72 C1
Leaveret Lea KA3 228 B4
Leckethill Ave G68 81 F4
Leckethill Ct G68 81 F4
Leckethill Pl G68 81 F4
Leckethill View G68 81 F4
Leckie Dr ML3 162 B2
Leckie Pl G83 27 F3
Leckie St G41 136 B4
Ledaig St G31 118 B4
Ledard Rd G42 137 D4
Ledcameroch Cres G61 75 F2
Ledcameroch Pk G61 75 E2
Ledcameroch Rd G61 75 F2
Ledgate G66 58 B1
Ledgowan Pl G20 96 B4
Ledi Ave FK10 4 A1
Ledi Dr G61 75 D4
Ledi Path ML1 143 E2
Ledi Pl FK1 66 C4
Ledi Rd G43 136 B3
Ledi View FK9 2 A2
Ledmore Dr G15 74 C2
Ledmore Pl FK1 42 C1
Lednock Rd Glasgow G52 115 D3
Stepps G33 99 E3
Ledrish Ave G83 19 F1
Lee Ave G33 98 C1
Lee Cres G64 98 A4
Lee Pl ML4 142 B2
Leebank Dr G44 136 C1
Leeburn Ave PA6 91 E1
Leechford ML11 215 D3
Leechlee Rd ML3 162 C2
Leefield Dr G44 136 C1
Leehill Rd G21 97 F4
Leesburn Pl G74 159 F2
Leeside Rd G21 97 F4
Leesland G71 141 D4
Leeward Circ G75 159 D1
Leeward Pk KA7 239 D1
Leewood Dr G44 137 D1
Lefroy St ML5 121 F4
Legbrannock Ave ML1 143 E3
Legbrannock Cres ML1 143 E2
Legbrannock Rd ML1 143 F3
Leggaston Dr G53 135 E2
Leglen Wood Cres G33 98 B3
Leglen Wood Dr G33 98 B3
Leglen Wood Rd G33 98 B3
Leicester Ave G12 96 A3
Leighton St Glasgow G20 96 C3
Wishaw ML2 165 D1
Leitch St PA15 46 C2
Leitchland Rd PA2 132 B4
Leith Pl FK6 39 E4
Leith St G33 118 B4
Leithland Ave G53 115 D1
Leithland Prim Sch G53 115 D1
Leithland Rd G53 115 D1
Leman Dr PA6 111 E4
Leman Gr PA6 111 E4
Lembert Dr G76 157 E4
Lemmon St PA15 45 E2
Lendal Pl G75 179 F3
Lendale La G64 78 A2
Lendalfoot Gdns ML3 161 E1
Lendel Pl G51 116 B3
Lendrick Ave FK1 41 F1
Lenihall Dr G45 137 F1
Lenihall Terr G45 137 F1
Lennox Ave Bishopton PA7 72 A2
Coatbridge ML5 121 F4
Glasgow G14 95 E2
Milngavie G62 55 D1
Stirling FK7 7 D2
Lennox Castle Hospl G65 32 C1
Lennox Cres
Bishopbriggs G64 97 F4
Kilmarnock KA1 222 B1
Lennox Dr Bearsden G61 75 F3
Clydebank G81 74 B4
Prestwick KA9 236 B3
Lennox Gdns G14 95 E2
Lennox La E G14 95 E2
Lennox La W
20 Glasgow G14 95 E2
9 Glasgow G14 95 E2
Lennox Pl G81 73 F2
Lennox Rd Cumbernauld G67 61 F1
Dumbarton G82 50 A2
Lennoxtown G65 33 E1
Milton G82 50 C1
Lennox St Alexandria G83 27 F3
Dumbarton G82 50 A2
Glasgow G20 96 B4
Renton G82 49 E4
Wishaw ML2 165 F2
Lennox Terr PA3 114 A4
Lennoxtown Prim Sch G65 57 E4
Lentran St G34 120 B4
Lenwood Gdns G83 27 F2
Leny St G20 96 C2
Lenzie Acad G66 79 E3
Lenzie Hospl G66 79 F2
Lenzie Moss Prim Sch G66 79 D3
Lenzie Pl G22 97 F3
Lenzie Prim Sch G66 79 E3
Lenzie Rd Kirkintilloch G66 79 E4
Stepps G33 99 E3
Lenzie St G21 97 F3
Lenzie Sta G66 79 E2
Lenzie Terr G21 97 F3
Lenziemill Rd G67 83 D4
Leperstone Ave
Kilmacolm PA13 69 E1
Port Glasgow PA14 68 C4
Leperstone Rd PA13 69 E1
Lerwick Pl KA3 223 D3
Lesley Pl KA20 206 C1
Lesley Quadrant ML4 142 A1
Leslie Ave Bishopton PA7 72 A2
Newton Mearns G77 156 C4
Leslie Cres KA7 239 D3
Leslie Pl KA3 223 D1
Leslie Rd Glasgow G41 116 C2
Kilmarnock KA3 223 D1
Leslie St Glasgow G41 116 C2
Motherwell ML1 163 F4
Leslie Terr KA9 236 B4
Lesmahagow Rd ML11 214 A2
Lesmuir Dr G14 95 D3
Lesmuir Pl G14 94 C3

Lestrange Terr FK12 ... 5 D4
Letham Cotts FK2 ... 24 B4
Letham Ct G43 ... 136 C3
Letham Dr Bishopbriggs G64 ... 98 B4
  Glasgow G43 ... 136 C3
Letham Grange G68 ... 62 A3
Letham Oval G64 ... 98 B4
Letham Terrs FK2 ... 14 B1
Lethamhill Cres G33 ... 98 C1
Lethamhill Pl G33 ... 98 C1
Lethamhill Rd G33 ... 98 C1
Lethbridge Pl ◆ G75 ... 180 B4
Letherby Dr G44 ... 137 D4
Letheron Dr ML2 ... 165 D3
Lethington Ave G41 ... 136 C4
Lethington Pl G41 ... 136 C4
Lethington Rd G46 ... 157 D4
Letterfearn Rd G23 ... 76 C1
Letterickhills Cres G72 ... 139 F2
Lettoch St ⊡ K11 ... 116 A4
Levanne Gdns PA19 ... 43 F3
Levanne Pl PA19 ... 43 F3
Leven Ave Bishopbriggs G64 ... 78 A1
  Kilmarnock KA3 ... 223 D2
Leven Ct Alloa FK10 ... 10 B3
  Barrhead G78 ... 134 A3
  Dumbarton G82 ... 49 F2
  Hurlford KA1 ... 228 C3
Leven Dr Bearsden G61 ... 75 F2
  Hamilton ML3 ... 183 D4
  Hurlford KA1 ... 228 C3
Leven Path ML1 ... 143 E4
Leven Pl Erskine PA8 ... 72 C1
  Greenock PA15 ... 46 B1
  Irvine KA12 ... 219 E3
  Kilmarnock KA3 ... 223 D2
  Shotts ML7 ... 146 C3
Leven Quadrant ML6 ... 102 C1
Leven Rd Coatbridge ML5 ... 101 E1
  Greenock PA15 ... 46 B1
  Langbank PA14 ... 70 B4
  Troon KA10 ... 229 F3
Leven Sq PA4 ... 94 A2
Leven St Alexandria G83 ... 27 F2
  Dumbarton G82 ... 50 A2
  Falkirk FK2 ... 42 A4
  Glasgow G41 ... 116 C2
  Motherwell ML1 ... 163 F2
  Renton G82 ... 49 E4
Leven Terr ML1 ... 143 E1
Leven Valley Ent Pk G82 ... 49 E2
Leven Way
  East Kilbride G75 ... 179 F3
  Paisley PA2 ... 112 C1
Levenbank Gdns G83 ... 27 F4
Levencroft Mews G83 ... 27 F2
Levenford Terr G82 ... 49 E2
Levengrove Ct G82 ... 49 E2
Levengrove Terr G82 ... 49 F2
Levenhowe Pl G83 ... 27 F4
Levenhowe Rd G83 ... 27 F4
Lever Rd G84 ... 16 C2
Levern Cres G78 ... 134 A1
Levern Gdns G78 ... 134 A2
Levern Prim Sch G53 ... 135 D3
Levern Rd G53 ... 134 C3
Leverndale Hospl
Leverndale G53 ... 115 D1
  Paisley G53 ... 114 C1
Leverndale Ind Ctr G53 ... 134 C4
Leverside Ave
  Barrhead G78 ... 134 A1
  Glasgow G53 ... 135 E4
Leverside Cres G53 ... 135 E4
Leverside Rd G53 ... 135 E4
Lewis Ave Renfrew PA4 ... 94 B1
  Wishaw ML2 ... 165 F3
Lewis Cres Irvine KA12 ... 219 F1
  Johnstone PA10 ... 111 E1
  Old Kilpatrick G60 ... 73 E3
Lewis Ct Alloa FK10 ... 10 A3
  Falkirk FK2 ... 42 A1
Lewis Dr Kilmarnock KA3 ... 223 D3
  Old Kilpatrick G60 ... 73 E3
Lewis Gdns Bearsden G61 ... 75 D3
  Old Kilpatrick G60 ... 73 E3
Lewis Gr G60 ... 73 E3
Lewis Pl Airdrie ML6 ... 123 E3
  Newton Mearns G77 ... 156 A3
  Old Kilpatrick G60 ... 73 E3
Lewis Rd Greenock PA16 ... 45 E2
  Port Glasgow PA14 ... 69 D4
Lewis Rise KA11 ... 220 A1
Lewis Terr KA11 ... 220 A1
Lewis Wynd KA11 ... 220 A1
Lewiston Dr G23 ... 76 B1
Lewiston Pl G23 ... 76 B1
Lewiston Rd G23 ... 76 B1
Lexwell Rd PA7 ... 112 C3
Leyden Ct G20 ... 96 C3
Leyden Gdns G20 ... 96 C3
Leyden St G20 ... 96 C3
Leys Pk ML3 ... 162 A2
Leys The G64 ... 98 A4
Libary Gdns G72 ... 138 C3
Libberton Way ML3 ... 162 A2
Liberator Dr KA8 ... 236 C2
Liberton St G33 ... 118 C4
Liberty Ave G69 ... 121 D3
Liberty Path G72 ... 161 E4
Liberty Rd Bellshill ML4 ... 142 A2
  Caldercruix ML6 ... 105 D3
Libo Ave Glasgow G53 ... 115 E1
  Uplawmoor G78 ... 153 D2

Libo Pl PA8 ... 72 C1
Library La G46 ... 135 F2
Library Rd ML2 ... 165 D2
Lichtenfels Gdns KA9 ... 236 C4
Lickprivick Rd G75 ... 180 A3
Liddel Rd G67 ... 61 F1
Liddell Gr G75 ... 180 B4
Liddell St G32 ... 119 E1
Liddells Ct G44 ... 98 A4
Liddesdale Pl G22 ... 97 F4
Liddesdale Rd G22 ... 97 F4
Liddesdale Sq G22 ... 97 F4
Liddesdale Terr G22 ... 97 F4
Liddesdale Pass G22 ... 97 F4
Liddoch Way G73 ... 137 F4
Liff Gdns G64 ... 98 B4
Liff Pl G34 ... 100 B1
Lifnock Ave KA1 ... 228 C3
Lightburn Hospl G12 ... 119 D4
Lightburn Pl G32 ... 119 D4
Lightburn Rd
  Cambuslang G72 ... 139 F2
  Glasgow G31 ... 118 B3
Lilac Ave Clydebank G81 ... 73 E3
  Cumbernauld G67 ... 62 C3
Lilac Cres G71 ... 141 E4
Lilac Ct G67 ... 62 C3
Lilac Gdns G64 ... 98 A4
Lilac Hill Cumbernauld G67 ... 62 C3
  Hamilton ML3 ... 162 C1
Lilac Pl Cumbernauld G67 ... 62 C3
  Kilmarnock KA1 ... 227 F4
Lilac Way ML1 ... 143 D3
Lilac Wynd G72 ... 139 F2
Lily St G40 ... 118 A2
Lilybank Ave Airdrie ML6 ... 103 D1
  Cambuslang G72 ... 139 E2
  Muirhead G69 ... 100 B4
Lilybank Gardens La G12 ... 96 B1
Lilybank Gdns La G12 ... 96 B1
Lilybank Gdns G12 ... 96 B1
Lilybank Rd
  Port Glasgow PA14 ... 47 D1
  Prestwick KA9 ... 236 A3
Lilybank Sch PA14 ... 47 D1
Lilybank St ML3 ... 162 B2
Lilybank Terr G12 ... 96 B1
Lilybank Terrace La G12 ... 96 B1
Lime Cres Airdrie ML6 ... 123 E4
  Cumbernauld G67 ... 62 C2
Lime Gr Blantyre G72 ... 140 B1
  Kirkintilloch G66 ... 79 E3
  Larbert FK5 ... 23 E1
Lime La ⊡ G14 ... 95 E2
Lime Loan ML1 ... 143 D2
Lime Pl KA1 ... 227 E4
  Falkirk FK1 ... 41 D2
Lime St Glasgow G14 ... 95 E2
  Greenock PA15 ... 45 F2
Limecraigs Ave PA2 ... 133 E4
Limecraigs Cres PA2 ... 133 E4
Limecraigs Rd PA2 ... 133 E4
Limegrove St ML4 ... 142 A4
Limekiln Rd Ayr KA8 ... 236 A2
Limekilns St G81 ... 74 B4
Limekilnbarn Rd ML3 ... 183 E2
Limekilns Rd G67 ... 82 C3
Limekilns St G81 ... 74 B4
Limelands Quadrant
  ML6 ... 104 C2
Limerigg Prim Sch ML6 ... 86 B1
Limes The G44 ... 137 D3
Limeside Ave G73 ... 138 B4
Limeside Gdns G73 ... 138 B4
Limetree Ave G71 ... 141 E4
Limetree Cres G77 ... 156 B2
Limetree Ct ML3 ... 162 A3
Limetree Dr G81 ... 74 B2
Limetree Quadrant G71 ... 141 E4
Limetree Wlk G65 ... 58 A2
Limeview Ave PA2 ... 133 D4
Limeview Cres PA2 ... 133 D4
Limeview Rd PA2 ... 133 D4
Limeview Way PA2 ... 133 D4
Limonds Ct KA8 ... 236 A1
Limonds Wynd KA8 ... 236 A1
Limpetlaw ML11 ... 215 D3
Linacre Dr G32 ... 119 E3
Linacre Gdns G32 ... 119 E3
Linburn Pl G52 ... 115 D3
Linburn Rd Erskine PA8 ... 72 C1
  Glasgow G52 ... 114 C3
Linburn Sch G52 ... 114 B3
Linclive Intc PA3 ... 112 B3
Linclive Terr PA3 ... 112 B3
Lincluden Path ◪ G41 ... 116 C2
Lincoln Ave Glasgow G13 ... 95 D3
  Uddingston G71 ... 120 C1
Lincoln Rd PA16 ... 44 B2
Lincuan Ave G46 ... 157 E4
Lindams G71 ... 140 C3
Linden Ave Denny FK6 ... 21 E2
  Stirling FK7 ... 7 E3
  Wishaw ML2 ... 165 F2
Linden Dr Banknock FK4 ... 38 C1
  Clydebank G81 ... 74 A3
Linden Lea Hamilton ML3 ... 162 A2
  Milton Of Campsie G65 ... 58 A3
Linden Pl G13 ... 95 F4
Linden St G13 ... 95 F4
Linden Way G13 ... 95 F4
Lindores Ave G73 ... 138 B4
Lindores Dr G73 ... 159 E1
Lindores Pl G74 ... 159 E1

Lindores St G42 ... 137 D4
Lindrick Dr G23 ... 76 C1
Lindsay Ave Kilbirnie KA25 ... 149 D2
  Saltcoats KA21 ... 205 F1
Lindsay Dr Glasgow G12 ... 96 A3
  Kilmarnock KA3 ... 223 E2
  Stirling FK9 ... 2 A3
Lindsay Gdns G83 ... 27 F3
Lindsay Gr G74 ... 159 F1
Lindsay Loan ML11 ... 215 E3
Lindsay Pl
  East Kilbride G74 ... 160 A1
  Glasgow G12 ... 96 A3
  Johnstone PA5 ... 112 A2
  Kirkintilloch G66 ... 79 E2
Lindsay Quadrant G83 ... 28 A4
Lindsay Rd G74 ... 159 F1
Lindsay St Ayr KA8 ... 236 B1
  Kilmarnock KA1 ... 227 F4
Lindsay Terr G65 ... 57 F4
Lindsaybeg Rd G69 ... 80 A1
Lindsayfield Ave G75 ... 180 B2
Lindsayfield Rd G75 ... 180 A2
Lindston Pl KA7 ... 239 D1
Lindum Cres ML1 ... 163 D4
Lindum St ML1 ... 163 D4
Lineside Wlk G84 ... 15 F3
Linfern Ave E KA1 ... 228 B4
Linfern Ave E KA1 ... 228 B4
Linfern Ave W KA1 ... 228 B4
Linfern Pl KA7 ... 239 D2
Linfern Rd G12 ... 96 B2
Linghope Pl ML2 ... 186 A3
Lingley Ave ML6 ... 123 D3
Linhope Pl G75 ... 179 F4
Linister Cres PA9 ... 130 C3
Links Ave Glasgow G44 ... 137 E2
  Glasgow, Mount Vernon G32 ... 119 E2
  Prestwick KA9 ... 233 D1
Links Rd Glasgow G44 ... 137 E2
Links View ML9 ... 185 E1
Linksview Rd ML1 ... 143 D1
Linkwood Ave G15 ... 74 C2
Linkwood Cres G15 ... 75 D2
Linkwood Ct G15 ... 220 A3
Linkwood Dr G15 ... 75 D2
Linkwood Pl Clydebank G15 ... 74 C2
  Irvine KA11 ... 220 A3
Linlithgow Gdns G32 ... 119 E3
Linlithgow Pl FK5 ... 23 F2
Linn Cres
  Kirkfieldbank ML11 ... 214 A2
  Paisley PA2 ... 133 E4
Linn Dr G44 ... 136 C2
Linn Gdns G68 ... 61 D1
Linn Glen G65 ... 57 F4
Linn Park Gdns PA5 ... 112 A1
Linn Park Ind Est G45 ... 137 D1
Linn Rd KA22 ... 205 E2
Linnburn Terr KA22 ... 205 D2
Linnet Ave PA5 ... 131 E4
Linnet Pl G13 ... 94 C4
Linnet Rd Bellshill ML4 ... 142 A2
Linnet Way PA6 ... 45 D2
Linnhe Ave
  Bishopbriggs G64 ... 78 A1
  Glasgow G44 ... 137 D2
  Hamilton ML3 ... 162 A1
Linnhe Cres ML2 ... 165 D1
Linnhe Ct ML9 ... 184 C3
Linnhe Dr G78 ... 134 A3
Linnhe Pl Blantyre G72 ... 140 B1
  Erskine PA8 ... 72 C1
Linnhead Dr G53 ... 135 E3
Linnhead Pl G14 ... 95 D2
Linnpark Ave G44 ... 136 C1
Linnpark Ct G44 ... 136 C1
Linnvale Prim Sch G81 ... 74 B1
Linnwell Cres PA2 ... 133 E4
Linrigg Rd ML1 ... 144 B4
Linside Ave PA1 ... 114 A2
Lint Brae KA3 ... 195 F1
Lint Riggs FK1 ... 42 A3
Lintfield Loan G71 ... 141 D2
Linthaugh Rd G53 ... 115 E2
Linthaugh Terr G53 ... 115 E1
Linthill ML3 ... 215 D3
Linthouse Bldgs G51 ... 115 F4
Linthouse Rd G51 ... 96 A1
Linthouse Vennel KA12 ... 219 D1
Lintie Rd ML1 ... 143 E2
Lintlaw G72 ... 140 B1
Lintlaw Dr G52 ... 115 D3
Lintmill Terr G78 ... 154 B3
Linton St G33 ... 118 C4
Linwhin Cres ML1 ... 110 C4
Linwood Ave
  Clarkston G76 ... 157 F4
  East Kilbride G74 ... 159 D1
Linwood High Sch PA3 ... 111 F3
Linwood Rd PA1 ... 112 C2
Linwood Terr ML3 ... 162 A2
Lion Bank G65 ... 58 B1
Lionthorn Rd FK1 ... 41 F1
Lipney FK11 ... 4 A2
Lisburn Rd KA8 ... 236 A2
Lismore Ave
  Motherwell ML1 ... 163 D4
  Port Glasgow PA14 ... 69 D4
  Renfrew PA4 ... 94 B1
Lismore Cres ML1 ... 42 A1
Lismore Dr Irvine KA11 ... 225 D4
  Linwood PA3 ... 111 F3
  Paisley PA2 ... 133 E4

Lismore Gdns PA10 ... 111 E1
Lismore Hill ML3 ... 161 E2
Lismore House KA9 ... 236 A3
Lismore Pl
  Moodiesburn G69 ... 81 D2
  Newton Mearns G77 ... 156 A3
Lismore Rd G12 ... 96 A3
Lismore Way KA11 ... 225 E4
Lissens Wlk KA13 ... 207 E3
Lister Ct FK9 ... 2 A3
Lister Gdns G76 ... 158 A3
Lister Pl G52 ... 115 D4
Lister Rd G52 ... 115 D4
Lister St Crosshouse KA2 ... 222 A1
  Glasgow G4 ... 241 E4
Lister Wlk ML4 ... 142 B4
Lithgow Ave
  Kirkintilloch G66 ... 79 F4
  Langbank PA14 ... 70 A4
Lithgow Cres PA2 ... 114 A1
Lithgow Dr ML1 ... 144 A1
Lithgow Pl G74 ... 159 D1
Little Bellsland Rd KA1 ... 228 A3
Little Denny Rd FK6 ... 21 E1
Little Dovehill G1 ... 241 E1
Little John Gdns ML2 ... 165 F2
Little St G3 ... 240 A2
Littlehill Prim Sch G33 ... 98 B2
Littlehill St G21 ... 98 A2
Littleholm Pl G81 ... 73 F2
Littlemill Ave G68 ... 60 C1
Littledale Ave PA2 ... 132 B4
Littlestane Rd KA11 ... 220 A3
Littlestane Rdbt KA11 ... 220 A3
Littlestane Rise KA11 ... 220 A3
Littleton Gdns PA8 ... 72 C1
Littleton Dr G23 ... 76 B1
Littleton St G23 ... 76 B1
Livingston Dr ML6 ... 104 A2
Livingston La G4 G71 ... 141 D2
Livingston Terr KA1 ... 195 D4
Livingstone Ave G52 ... 115 D4
Livingstone Bvd ML3 ... 161 E2
Livingstone Cres
  Blantyre G72 ... 140 B1
  East Kilbride G75 ... 180 B4
  Falkirk FK2 ... 42 C3
Livingstone Ct KA1 ... 227 F4
Livingstone Dr
  East Kilbride G75 ... 180 C4
  Laurieston FK2 ... 42 C1
Livingstone Gdns ML9 ... 185 D2
Livingstone Pk G65 ... 36 B1
Livingstone Pl ML6 ... 123 D4
Livingstone Quadrant
  ML7 ... 127 E2
Livingstone St
  Clydebank G81 ... 74 B1
  Hamilton ML3 ... 161 F2
Livingstone Terr KA12 ... 219 E3
Livinstone Pk G65 ... 36 A1
Lloyd Ave G32 ... 119 D1
Lloyd Dr ML1 ... 143 D1
Lloyd St Glasgow G31 ... 118 A4
  Motherwell ML1 ... 143 D1
  Rutherglen G73 ... 118 A1
Lloyd Wlk KA3 ... 195 D4
Lloyds St ML5 ... 122 A2
Llynallan Rd ML7 ... 127 D3
Loach Ave KA12 ... 219 E1
Loadingbank KA25 ... 170 A4
Loadingbank Ct KA25 ... 170 A4
Loan Lea Cres ML9 ... 185 E1
Loan Pl MK7 ... 127 F3
Loan The G62 ... 54 B2
Loanbank Quadrant G51 ... 115 F4
Loancroft Ave G69 ... 120 B2
Loancroft Gate G71 ... 140 C3
Loancroft Gdns G71 ... 140 C3
Loancroft Pl G69 ... 120 A2
Loanend Cotts G72 ... 139 F1
Loanfoot Ave Glasgow G13 ... 95 D4
  Kilmarnock KA1 ... 222 B1
  Neilston G78 ... 154 B3
Loanfoot Gdns FK7 ... 12 B2
Loanfoot Rd G72 ... 161 E2
Loanhead Ave
  Dennyloanhead FK4 ... 39 E3
  Linwood PA3 ... 112 A3
  Motherwell ML1 ... 143 E2
  Renfrew PA4 ... 94 B2
Loanhead Cres ML1 ... 143 E2
Loanhead La PA3 ... 112 A3
Loanhead Prim Sch KA1 ... 228 A4
Loanhead Rd
  Coatbridge ML5 ... 121 F2
  Glasgow G32 ... 118 C4
  Kilmarnock KA1 ... 228 A4
Loaning ⊡ ML9 ... 185 E1
Loaning The Ayr KA7 ... 239 E4
  Kirkintilloch G66 ... 79 E4
  Motherwell ML1 ... 163 E4
  Rutherglen G73 ... 157 D4
Loaninghead Dr G82 ... 50 A3
Lobnitz Ave PA4 ... 94 B2
Loccard Rd KA20 ... 206 B1
Loch Achray Gdns G32 ... 119 E2
Loch Achray St G32 ... 119 E2
Loch Assynt G74 ... 181 D4
Loch Awe G74 ... 181 D4
Loch Awe Pl ML5 ... 201 F2
Loch Awe G74 ... 181 D4

Loch Dr G84 ... 16 A1
Loch Goil G74 ... 160 A1
Loch Laidon St G32 ... 119 E2
Loch Laxford St G32 ... 181 D4
Loch Lea G66 ... 58 C1
Loch Long G74 ... 181 D4
Loch Maben G74 ... 181 D4
Loch Maree G74 ... 181 D4
Loch Meadie G74 ... 181 D4
Loch Naver G74 ... 181 D4
Loch Park Ave ML8 ... 201 F4
Loch Park Pl ML9 ... 185 D1
Loch Pk ML2 ... 165 E2
Loch Pl KA11 ... 110 B4
Loch Prim Sch G73 ... 138 B2
Loch Rd Bridge Of W PA11 ... 110 B4
  Chapelhall ML6 ... 123 E1
  Kirkintilloch G66 ... 79 F4
  Milngavie G62 ... 55 D2
  Stepps G33 ... 99 E2
Loch Shin G74 ... 181 D4
Loch St ML6 ... 123 D1
Loch Striven G74 ... 160 A1
Loch Torridon G74 ... 181 D4
Loch View
  Calderbank ML6 ... 123 D1
  Caldercruix ML6 ... 105 D3
Loch Voil St G32 ... 119 E2
Lochaber Cres ML7 ... 147 D2
Lochaber Dr
  Rutherglen G73 ... 138 B2
  Stenhousemuir FK5 ... 23 F2
Lochaber Path G72 ... 161 E4
Lochaber Pl G74 ... 159 F2
Lochaber Rd G61 ... 76 A1
Lochaber Wlk G65 ... 58 B4
Lochaline Ave PA2 ... 113 D1
Lochaline Dr G44 ... 137 D2
Lochalsh Cres G66 ... 58 B4
Lochalsh Dr PA2 ... 113 D1
Lochalsh Pl G72 ... 140 A1
Lochans The G84 ... 15 D2
Lochar Cres G53 ... 115 E1
Lochar Pl G75 ... 179 F4
Lochard Dr PA2 ... 113 D1
Lochay Pl KA10 ... 229 F3
Lochay St G32 ... 119 E2
Lochbrae FK10 ... 5 E1
Lochbrae Dr G73 ... 138 B2
Lochbridge Rd G34 ... 120 A4
Lochbroom Ct G77 ... 156 C3
Lochbroom Dr
  Newton Mearns G77 ... 156 C3
  Paisley PA2 ... 113 D1
Lochburn La ML6 ... 102 C2
Lochburn Cres G20 ... 96 C4
Lochburn Pass G20 ... 96 C4
Lochburn Rd G20 ... 96 C4
Lochcraig Ct KA11 ... 220 A2
Lochdochart Rd G34 ... 120 B4
Lochearn Cres
  Airdrie ML6 ... 102 C1
  Paisley PA2 ... 113 D1
Lochearnhead Rd G33 ... 99 E3
Lochend Ave G69 ... 100 C4
Lochend Cotts G60 ... 73 E2
Lochend Cres G61 ... 75 F2
Lochend Dr G61 ... 75 F2
Lochend Pl KA10 ... 229 F1
Lochend Rd Bearsden G61 ... 75 F2
  Coatbridge ML5 ... 101 D1
  Glasgow G34, G69 ... 100 B1
  Glengarnock KA14 ... 170 B4
  Troon KA10 ... 229 E1
Lochend Sec Sch G34 ... 100 B1
Lochend St ML1 ... 163 F3
Locher Ave PA6 ... 91 F1
Locher Cres PA6 ... 111 F4
Locher Gdns PA6 ... 111 F4
Locher Rd PA10 ... 110 C2
Locher Way PA6 ... 111 E4
Locherburn Ave PA6 ... 111 E4
Locherburn Gr PA6 ... 111 E4
Locherburn Pl PA6 ... 111 E4
Lochfauld Rd G23 ... 77 D1
Lochfield Cres PA2 ... 113 F1
Lochfield Dr PA2 ... 114 A1
Lochfield Prim Sch PA2 ... 113 F1
Lochfield Rd PA2 ... 114 A1
Lochgilp St G20 ... 96 B4
Lochgoin Ave G15 ... 74 C2
Lochgoin Prim Sch G15 ... 74 C2
Lochgreen Ave KA10 ... 229 F4
Lochgreen Hospl FK1 ... 41 F1
Lochgreen Pl
  Coatbridge ML5 ... 101 E1
  Hamilton ML3 ... 183 D4
  Kilmarnock KA1 ... 227 F2
Lochgreen Rd G33 ... 98 B2
Lochgreen St G33 ... 98 B2
Lochhead Ave Denny FK6 ... 21 F1
Lochiel Dr G65 ... 58 B3
Lochiel La G73 ... 138 B2
Lochiel Rd G46 ... 135 F2
Lochinch Pl G77 ... 156 A3
Lochinvar Rd PA14 ... 68 C4
Lochinvar Pl G67 ... 40 C4
Lochinver Cres PA2 ... 113 D1
Lochinver Dr G44 ... 137 D3
Lochinver Gr G72 ... 139 D3
Lochknowe St ML8 ... 201 F4
Lochlands Gr KA15 ... 171 E4
Lochlands Ind Est FK5 ... 41 D4
Lochlea ML2 ... 160 B2
Lochlea Ave Clydebank G81 ... 74 B2
  Troon KA10 ... 229 F2
Lochlea Dr KA7 ... 239 D3

Lochlea Rd Clarkston G76 .... 157 F3
Cumbernauld G67 .... 62 B2
Glasgow G43 .... 136 B3
Rutherglen G73 .... 137 F3
Saltcoats KA21 .... 206 A2
Lochlea Way ML1 .... 143 F2
Lochlee Loan 12 ML9 .... 185 E1
Lochleven La G42 .... 137 D4
Lochleven Rd G42 .... 137 D4
Lochlibo Ave G13 .... 94 C4
Lochlibo Cres G78 .... 134 A1
Lochlibo Ct KA11 .... 220 A3
Lochlibo Rd Barrhead G78 .... 134 A1
Burnhouse KA15 .... 172 C2
Irvine KA11, KA13 .... 209 E2
Lugton G78 .... 152 C1
Neilston G78 .... 154 C4
Lochlibo Terr G78 .... 134 A1
Lochlie Pl KA20 .... 206 C1
Lochlip Rd PA12 .... 129 E1
Lochmaben Dr FK5 .... 23 F2
Lochmaben Rd G52 .... 114 C2
Lochmaben Wynd KA3 .... 223 D3
Lochmaddy Ave G44 .... 137 D2
Lochnagar Dr G61 .... 75 D4
Lochnagar Rd KA1 .... 228 A2
Lochnagar Way 19 ML9 .... 185 E1
Lochore Ave PA3 .... 114 A4
Lochpark KA7 .... 238 B2
Lochpark Pl FK6 .... 21 F1
Lochranza Ct KA3 .... 223 D3
Lochranza Dr
East Kilbride G75 .... 180 A2
Helensburgh G84 .... 16 C1
Lochranza La G75 .... 180 B2
Lochranza Pl KA21 .... 206 A1
Lochridge Pl FK6 .... 21 E1
Lochshore East Ind Est
KA14 .... 170 B4
Lochshore South Ind Est
KA25 .... 170 A4
Lochside Bearsden G61 .... 75 F2
Gartcosh G69 .... 100 C3
Lochside Ct KA8 .... 236 A1
Lochside Rd Ayr KA8 .... 236 A1
Slamannan FK1 .... 86 B1
Lochside St 2 G41 .... 116 C1
Lochview Ave PA19 .... 45 D4
Lochview Cres G33 .... 98 C2
Lochview Dr G33 .... 98 C2
Lochview Gdns G33 .... 98 C2
Lochview Pl G33 .... 98 C2
Lochview Quadrant ML4 .... 141 F2
Lochview Rd Bearsden G61 .... 75 F2
Beith KA15 .... 170 C4
Coatbridge ML5 .... 101 E1
Port Glasgow PA14 .... 47 D1
Lochview Terr G69 .... 100 C3
Lochwinnoch Prim Sch
PA12 .... 129 E2
Lochwinnoch Rd PA13 .... 89 E4
Lochwinnoch Sta PA12 .... 150 C4
Lochwood Ct KA13 .... 207 E3
Lochwood Loan G69 .... 81 D2
Lochwood Pl KA11 .... 219 F3
Lochwood St G33 .... 98 C1
Lochy Ave PA4 .... 94 C1
Lochy Gdns G64 .... 78 A1
Lochy Pl PA8 .... 72 C1
Lochy St ML2 .... 165 D1
Lock Sixteen FK1 .... 41 E3
Lockerbie Ave G43 .... 136 C3
Locket Yett View ML4 .... 141 F3
Lockhart Ave G72 .... 139 E3
Lockhart Dr
Cambuslang G72 .... 139 E3
Lanark ML11 .... 214 C3
Lockhart Hospl ML11 .... 215 E2
Lockhart Pl Stonehouse ML9 .... 198 C2
Wishaw ML2 .... 165 F2
Lockhart St Carluke ML8 .... 187 F1
Glasgow G21 .... 98 A1
Hamilton ML3 .... 183 E3
Stonehouse ML9 .... 199 D2
Lockhart Terr G74 .... 160 A1
Locks St ML5 .... 122 B3
Locksley Ave
Cumbernauld G67 .... 82 C4
Glasgow G13 .... 95 E4
Locksley Cres G67 .... 82 C3
Locksley Ct G67 .... 82 C3
Locksley Pl G67 .... 82 C3
Locksley Rd
Cumbernauld G67 .... 82 C3
Paisley PA2 .... 112 C1
Lodge Cres PA13 .... 89 F4
Lodge Dr FK5 .... 23 F1
Lodge Gdns PA13 .... 69 F1
Lodge Gr PA13 .... 69 F1
Lodge Pk PA13 .... 69 F1
Logan Ave G77 .... 156 B3
Logan Ct KA10 .... 229 E2
Logan Dr Cumbernauld G68 .... 61 E2
Paisley PA3 .... 113 E3
Troon KA10 .... 229 E2
Logan Gdns ML1 .... 165 D4
Logan St Blantyre G72 .... 161 F4
Glasgow G5 .... 117 E2
Logan Tower G72 .... 139 F2
Logandale Ave ML2 .... 165 F3
Loganlea Dr ML1 .... 143 D1
Logans Prim Sch ML1 .... 163 D4
Logans Rd ML1 .... 163 E4
Loganswell Dr G46 .... 135 F1
Loganswell Gdns G46 .... 135 F1
Loganswell Pl G46 .... 135 F1
Loganswell Rd G46 .... 135 F1
Logie Dr FK5 .... 23 D2
Logie La FK9 .... 2 B4
Logie Pk G74 .... 160 A2
Logie Rd FK9 .... 2 B2
Logie Sq G74 .... 160 A2
Lomax St G33 .... 118 B4
Lomond G75 .... 180 C3
Lomond Ave Hurlford KA1 .... 228 C3
Port Glasgow PA14 .... 68 C4
Renfrew PA4 .... 94 A1
Lomond Cres Alexandria G83 .... 27 E4
Beith KA15 .... 150 B1
Bridge Of W PA11 .... 110 B4
Cumbernauld G67 .... 82 B4
Paisley PA2 .... 133 E4
Stenhousemuir FK5 .... 23 F2
Stirling FK9 .... 2 A2
Lomond Ct Alloa FK10 .... 10 B3
Barrhead G78 .... 134 B1
Cumbernauld G67 .... 82 B4
Dumbarton G82 .... 49 F2
Helensburgh G84 .... 16 C1
Lomond Dr Airdrie ML6 .... 102 C1
Alexandria G83 .... 27 E4
Bannockburn FK7 .... 7 F1
Barrhead G78 .... 134 A2
Bishopbriggs G64 .... 78 A2
Bothwell G71 .... 141 D2
Cumbernauld G67 .... 82 A4
Dumbarton G82 .... 50 A3
Falkirk FK2 .... 24 B1
Newton Mearns G77 .... 156 B4
Wishaw ML2 .... 165 D1
Lomond Gdns PA5 .... 112 B1
Lomond Gr G67 .... 82 B4
Lomond Ind Est G83 .... 27 F3
Lomond Pl Coatbridge ML5 .... 101 F1
Cumbernauld G67 .... 82 A4
Erskine PA8 .... 72 C1
Irvine KA12 .... 219 E3
Stepps G33 .... 99 F2
Lomond Prim Sch G84 .... 16 B1
Lomond Rd Alexandria G83 .... 27 E4
Balloch G83 .... 27 E4
Bearsden G61 .... 75 F1
Coatbridge ML5 .... 101 E1
Greenock PA15 .... 46 A2
Kilmarnock KA1 .... 228 A4
Kirkintilloch G66 .... 79 E3
Shotts ML7 .... 146 C3
Uddingston G71 .... 120 C1
Lomond Sec Sch G84 .... 16 B1
Lomond St Alloa FK10 .... 4 C1
Glasgow G22 .... 97 D3
Helensburgh G84 .... 16 C1
Lomond View
Cumbernauld G67 .... 82 B4
Hamilton ML3 .... 161 F1
Symington KA1 .... 231 E2
Lomond Way Denny FK6 .... 39 E3
Irvine KA11 .... 220 A2
Motherwell ML1 .... 143 D3
Lomond Wlk
5 Larkhall ML9 .... 185 D2
Motherwell ML1 .... 143 E2
Lomondside Ave G76 .... 157 E4
Lomondview Ind Est PA5 .... 111 F2
London Rd
Glasgow G31, G32, G40 .... 118 C1
Kilmarnock KA3 .... 228 A4
London Road Prim Sch
G40 .... 118 A2
London St Larkhall ML9 .... 185 D2
Renfrew PA4 .... 94 B3
Lonend PA1 .... 113 F2
Loney Cres FK6 .... 39 F4
Long Calderwood Prim Sch
G74 .... 160 B2
Long Crags View G82 .... 50 B3
Long Dr East Kilbride G75 .... 181 D4
Irvine KA11 .... 219 F3
Long Row Glasgow G69 .... 120 B3
Lanark ML11 .... 214 C1
Menstrie FK11 .... 4 A4
Longay Pl G22 .... 97 E4
Longay St G22 .... 97 E4
Longbank Dr KA7 .... 239 D2
Longbank Rd KA7 .... 239 D2
Longbar Ave KA14 .... 170 B3
Longcraigs Ave KA22 .... 205 E3
Longcroft Dr PA4 .... 94 B2
Longdales Ave FK2 .... 42 A4
Longdales Ct FK2 .... 42 A4
Longdales Pl FK2 .... 42 A4
Longdales Rd FK2 .... 42 A4
Longden St G81 .... 94 B4
Longdyke Pl FK2 .... 24 B2
Longfield Ave KA21 .... 205 F1
Longfield Pl KA21 .... 205 F1
Longford Ave KA13 .... 207 E1
Longford St G33 .... 118 B4
Longhill Ave KA7 .... 238 B1
Longlands Pk KA7 .... 238 C2
Longlands Prim Sch G67 .... 82 C4
Longlee G69 .... 120 A2
Longmeadow PA5 .... 111 E1
Longpark Ave KA3 .... 222 C1
Longriggend Rd ML6 .... 85 E1
Longrow Gdns KA11 .... 219 F4
Longstone Pl G33 .... 119 D4
Longstone Rd G33 .... 119 D4
Longwill Terr G67 .... 62 A2
Lonmay Rd G33 .... 119 E4
Lonsdale Ave G46 .... 136 B2
Loom Wlk PA10 .... 111 D2
Lora Dr G52 .... 115 F2
Loreny Dr KA1 .... 227 F1
Loreny Ind Est KA1 .... 227 F2
Loretto Pl G33 .... 118 C4
Loretto St G33 .... 118 C4
Lorien Ct KA8 .... 236 B2
Lorimar Pl FK2 .... 24 A1
Lorimer Cres G75 .... 180 B4
Lorn Ave G69 .... 100 B4
Lorn Dr G83 .... 19 F1
Lorn Pl G66 .... 59 E1
Lorne Arc KA7 .... 238 C4
Lorne Cres G64 .... 78 B1
Lorne Dr Linwood PA3 .... 112 A3
Motherwell ML1 .... 142 B1
Lorne Gdns Laurieston FK2 .... 42 C2
Salsburgh ML7 .... 125 D1
Lorne Pl ML5 .... 122 B3
Lorne Rd Larbert FK5 .... 23 E1
Paisley G52 .... 114 C4
Lorne St Glasgow G51 .... 116 B3
Hamilton ML3 .... 162 B2
Helensburgh G84 .... 16 B1
Lorne Street Prim Sch G51 .... 116 B3
Lorne Terr G72 .... 138 C2
Lornshill Acad FK10 .... 4 C1
Lornshill Cres FK10 .... 9 F4
Lorraine Gardens La 25 G12 .... 96 B2
Lorraine Gdns 24 G12 .... 96 B2
Lorraine Rd 23 G12 .... 96 B2
Lorraine Way G83 .... 27 F1
Loskin Dr G22 .... 97 D4
Losshill FK11 .... 4 A3
Lossie Cres PA4 .... 94 C1
Lossie St G33 .... 98 B1
Lothian Cres Paisley PA2 .... 113 E1
Stirling FK9 .... 2 B2
Lothian Dr G76 .... 157 E4
Lothian Gdns 3 G20 .... 96 C2
Lothian Rd Ayr KA7 .... 239 D4
Greenock PA16 .... 44 B2
Stewarton KA3 .... 211 E4
Lothian St G52 .... 114 C4
Lothian Way G74 .... 160 B2
Louburn EH48 .... 107 E2
Louden Hill Rd G33 .... 98 C3
Louden St ML6 .... 123 D4
Loudens Wlk FK6 .... 21 E3
Loudon G75 .... 180 C3
Loudon Gdns PA5 .... 112 A2
Loudon Rd G33 .... 99 D2
Loudon St ML2 .... 165 D3
Loudon Terr G61 .... 75 E4
Loudonhill Ave ML3 .... 183 F4
Loudoun Ave KA1 .... 228 A2
Loudoun Cres KA13 .... 207 D2
Loudoun Pl Crosshouse KA2 .... 226 C4
Symington KA1 .... 231 E2
Loudoun St KA3 .... 211 F4
Loudoun Terr KA9 .... 236 B4
Loudoun-Montgomery
Prim Sch KA12 .... 219 E1
Louise Gdns ML1 .... 142 C3
Louisville Ave ML2 .... 165 E3
Lounsdale Ave PA2 .... 113 D2
Lounsdale Cres PA2 .... 113 D1
Lounsdale Dr PA2 .... 113 D1
Lounsdale House PA2 .... 113 D1
Lounsdale Pl G14 .... 95 D2
Lounsdale Rd PA2 .... 113 D1
Lounsdale Way PA2 .... 113 D2
Lourdes Ave G52 .... 115 E2
Lourdes Ct G52 .... 115 E2
Lourdes Prim RC Sch G52 .... 115 E3
Lourdes Sec Sch G52 .... 115 E2
Lovat Ave G61 .... 75 F4
Lovat Dr G66 .... 79 D4
Lovat Path 3 ML9 .... 185 E1
Lovat Pl Paisley G52 .... 114 C4
Rutherglen G73 .... 138 B2
Love Ave PA11 .... 89 F1
Love St Kilwinning KA13 .... 208 A2
Paisley PA3 .... 113 F3
Lovers Loan FK12 .... 5 D4
Lovers Wlk FK8 .... 2 A1
Low Barholm PA10 .... 111 D1
Low Broadlie Rd G78 .... 154 B4
Low Church La 1 KA1 .... 227 F4
Low Craigends G65 .... 60 C4
Low Cres G81 .... 94 C4
Low Flender Rd G76 .... 157 E3
Low Glencairn St KA1 .... 227 F3
Low Green Rd KA12 .... 219 D1
Low Moss Ind Est G64 .... 78 A2
Low Parksail PA8 .... 93 E4
Low Patrick St ML3 .... 162 C2
Low Pleasance ML9 .... 185 D2
Low Rd Ayr KA8 .... 236 C2
Paisley PA2 .... 113 E2
Low Waters Rd ML3 .... 162 B1
Lower Auchingramont Rd
ML3 .... 162 C2
Lower Bourtree Dr G73 .... 138 B2
Lower Bouverie St PA14 .... 47 E1
Lower Bridge St FK8 .... 2 A1
Lower Castlehill FK8 .... 2 A1
Lower Mill Rd G76 .... 157 F3
Lower Millgate G71 .... 140 C3
Lower Stoneymollan Rd
G83 .... 27 E4
Lower Sutherland Cres
G84 .... 16 A2
Lowndes St G78 .... 134 B1
Lowther Ave G61 .... 75 E4
Lowther Bank KA11 .... 220 B1
Lowther Pl KA1 .... 228 A2
Lowther Terr 35 G12 .... 96 B2
Loyal Ave PA8 .... 72 C1
Loyal Gdns G61 .... 75 D4
Loyal Pl PA8 .... 72 C1
Loyne Dr PA4 .... 94 C1
Luath St G51 .... 116 A4
Lubas Ave G42 .... 137 E4
Lubas Pl G42 .... 137 E4
Lubnaig Dr PA8 .... 72 C1
Lubnaig Gdns G61 .... 75 E4
Lubnaig Pl ML6 .... 102 C1
Lubnaig Rd G43 .... 136 C3
Lubnaig Wlk ML1 .... 143 D3
Luce Ave KA1 .... 228 A3
Luckenhill Dr ML6 .... 84 B2
Luckiesfauld G78 .... 154 B3
Luckingsford Ave PA4 .... 93 E4
Luckingsford Dr PA4 .... 93 E4
Luckingsford Rd PA4 .... 93 E4
Lucy Brae G71 .... 140 C4
Ludgate FK10 .... 10 A3
Ludovic Sq PA5 .... 111 F2
Luffness Gdns G32 .... 119 D1
Lugar Ave KA11 .... 220 A3
Lugar Cres KA9 .... 236 A3
Lugar Dr G52 .... 115 F2
Lugar Pl Glasgow G44 .... 137 F3
Troon KA10 .... 229 F3
Lugar St ML5 .... 122 A4
Luggie Rd ML8 .... 187 F2
Luggie View G67 .... 82 A4
Luggiebank Pl G69 .... 121 D2
Luggiebank Rd
Kirkintilloch G66 .... 79 E4
Kirkintilloch, Eastside G66 .... 58 B1
Lugton Ct KA12 .... 219 E1
Lugton Rd KA3 .... 195 D4
Luing ML6 .... 123 F3
Luing Rd G52 .... 115 F3
Lumloch St G21 .... 98 A2
Lumsden La G3 .... 96 B1
Lumsden Pl KA20 .... 206 C1
Lumsden St G3 .... 96 B1
Lunan Dr G64 .... 98 B4
Lunan Pl G51 .... 115 F4
Lunar Path ML6 .... 123 E1
Luncarty Pl G32 .... 119 D2
Luncarty St G32 .... 119 D2
Lunderston Dr G53 .... 135 D4
Lundholm Rd KA20 .... 217 F4
Lundie Gdns G64 .... 98 B4
Lundie St G32 .... 118 C2
Lurg St PA14 .... 68 B4
Luss Ave PA15 .... 46 A1
Luss Brae ML3 .... 161 F1
Luss Pl PA15 .... 46 A1
Luss Rd Alexandria G83 .... 27 E4
Glasgow G51 .... 115 F4
Helensburgh G84 .... 17 D3
Lusset Glen G60 .... 73 D3
Lusset Rd G60 .... 73 D3
Lusshill Terr G71 .... 120 A1
Lybster Cres G73 .... 138 B2
Lychgate Rd FK10 .... 4 A1
Lye Brae G67 .... 62 A1
Lyell Ct G74 .... 159 F2
Lyell Gr G74 .... 159 F2
Lyle Cres PA7 .... 72 A2
Lyle Gr PA16 .... 45 D4
Lyle Pl Greenock PA16 .... 45 D4
Paisley PA2 .... 113 F1
Lyle Rd Airdrie ML6 .... 123 F4
Greenock PA16 .... 45 D4
Kilmacolm PA13 .... 89 E4
Lyle Sq G62 .... 54 C1
Lyle St PA15 .... 45 F2
Lylefoot Cres PA16 .... 45 D4
Lylefoot Pl PA16 .... 45 D4
Lylesland Ct PA2 .... 113 F1
Lylestone Terr KA13 .... 208 B4
Lyman Dr ML2 .... 165 E4
Lymburn Pl KA8 .... 239 D4
Lymburn St G3 .... 116 B4
Lymekilns Rd G74 .... 159 E2
Lyndale Pl G20 .... 96 B4
Lyndale Rd G20 .... 96 B4
Lyndhurst Gardens La
G20 .... 96 C2
Lyndhurst Gdns G20 .... 96 C2
Lyne Croft G64 .... 78 A2
Lyne St ML2 .... 165 D3
Lynedoch Cres G3 .... 240 A4
Lynedoch Crescent La G3 .... 96 C1
Lynedoch Ind Est PA15 .... 46 A2
Lynedoch Pl G3 .... 240 A4
Lynedoch St Glasgow G3 .... 240 A4
Greenock PA15 .... 45 F2
Lynedoch Terr G3 .... 240 A4
Lynmouth Pl PA19 .... 44 C3
Lynn Ave KA24 .... 191 E4
Lynn Ct ML9 .... 185 D1
Lynn Dr Eaglesham G76 .... 178 C3
Kilbirnie KA25 .... 149 D2
Milngavie G62 .... 55 E1
Lynn Wlk Balloch G83 .... 27 F4
Bothwell G71 .... 141 D3
Lynnburn Ave ML4 .... 142 A3
Lynne Dr G23 .... 76 C1
Lynnhurst G71 .... 140 C4
Lynnwood Rd ML2 .... 166 B3
Lynton Ave G46 .... 136 A1
Lyon Cres FK9 .... 2 A3
Lyon Rd Erskine PA8 .... 72 C1
Linwood PA5 .... 112 A2
Paisley PA2 .... 112 C1
Lyoncross Ave G78 .... 134 B2
Lyoncross Cres G78 .... 134 B2
Lyoncross Rd G53 .... 115 D1
Lyons Quadrant ML2 .... 164 B2
Lysa Vale Pl ML4 .... 141 F3
Lysander Way 9 PA4 .... 94 B1
Lytham Dr G23 .... 76 C1
Lytham Mdws G72 .... 140 C1
Lythgow Way ML11 .... 215 E3
Lyttelton G75 .... 180 A4

Mabel St ML1 .... 163 F3
Maberry Cl KA3 .... 195 E1
Maberry Pl KA10 .... 229 F3
Macadam Gdns ML4 .... 142 A3
Macadam Pl Ayr KA8 .... 236 A1
East Kilbride G75 .... 180 C4
Falkirk FK1 .... 41 E3
Irvine KA11 .... 219 F1
Kilmarnock KA3 .... 223 E1
Macadam Sq KA8 .... 236 A1
Macallan Pl KA11 .... 219 F4
Macallister Pl KA3 .... 223 E1
Macalpine Pl KA3 .... 223 E1
Macandrew Pl KA3 .... 223 E1
Macara Dr KA12 .... 219 F2
Macarthur Ave ML6 .... 102 B2
Macarthur Cres G74 .... 159 E2
Macarthur Ct G74 .... 159 E2
Macarthur Dr G74 .... 159 E2
Macarthur Gdns G74 .... 159 E2
Macaulay Pl G84 .... 16 A1
Macauley Pl KA3 .... 223 E1
Macbeth G74 .... 160 A3
Macbeth Dr KA3 .... 223 E1
Macbeth Gdns KA3 .... 223 E1
Macbeth Pl G31 .... 118 B2
Macbeth Rd Greenock PA16 .... 45 D3
Stewarton KA3 .... 211 E4
Macbeth St G31 .... 118 B2
Macbeth Wlk KA3 .... 223 E1
Maccabe Gdns G65 .... 57 F4
Maccallum Pl KA3 .... 223 E1
Maccrimmon Pk G74 .... 159 D2
Macdairmid Dr ML3 .... 183 D4
Macdonald Ave G74 .... 159 D2
Macdonald Cres G65 .... 60 A2
Macdonald Ct KA15 .... 171 D4
Macdonald Dr
Kilmarnock KA3 .... 223 E1
Stirling FK7 .... 7 D2
Macdonald Gdns KA3 .... 223 E1
Macdonald Gr ML4 .... 141 F1
Macdonald Pl KA3 .... 223 E1
Macdonald St
Motherwell ML1 .... 163 F3
Rutherglen G73 .... 138 A4
Macdonald Wlk G83 .... 27 F4
Macdougal Quadrant ML4 .... 141 F1
Macdougall Dr KA3 .... 223 E1
Macdougall St Glasgow G43 .... 136 B4
Greenock PA15 .... 46 B2
Macdowall St
Johnstone PA5 .... 111 F2
Paisley PA3 .... 113 E3
Macduff PA8 .... 73 D1
Macduff Pl G31 .... 118 B2
Macduff St G31 .... 118 B2
Mace Ct FK7 .... 7 E2
Mace Rd G13 .... 75 E1
Macewan Pl KA3 .... 228 B4
Macfarlane Cres FK1 .... 42 A3
Macfarlane Dr KA3 .... 223 E1
Macfarlane Rd G61 .... 76 A2
Macfie Pl G74 .... 159 D2
Macgregor Dr KA3 .... 228 B4
Machan Ave ML9 .... 185 D2
Machan Rd ML9 .... 185 D1
Machanhill ML9 .... 185 D1
Machanhill Prim Sch ML9 .... 185 D2
Machanhill View ML9 .... 185 D1
Machrie Ct FK1 .... 41 E2
Machrie Dr Glasgow G45 .... 137 F2
Helensburgh G84 .... 16 C2
Newton Mearns G77 .... 156 C3
Machrie Gn G75 .... 180 A2
Machrie Pl KA13 .... 207 E2
Machrie Rd Glasgow G45 .... 137 F2
Kilmarnock KA3 .... 222 C2
Motherwell ML1 .... 163 D4
Machrie St G45 .... 137 F2
Macinnes Pl KA3 .... 223 E1
Macintosh Pl
East Kilbride G75 .... 180 B4
Falkirk FK1 .... 42 A1
Kilmarnock KA3 .... 223 E1
Macintyre Pl KA3 .... 223 E1
Macintyre Rd KA9 .... 233 E1
Macintyre St G3 .... 240 A2
Macivor Cres G74 .... 159 D2
Macivor Pl KA3 .... 223 E1
Mack St ML6 .... 123 D4
Mackean St PA3 .... 113 E3
Mackeith St G40 .... 117 F2
Mackellar Pl KA3 .... 223 E1
Mackendrick Pl KA3 .... 228 B4
Mackenzie Dr
Johnstone PA10 .... 111 D1
Kilmarnock KA3 .... 223 D1
Mackenzie Gdns G74 .... 159 D2
Mackenzie Pl FK1 .... 42 A1
Mackenzie St PA15 .... 46 B2
Mackenzie Terr ML4 .... 142 A4
Mackie Ave
Port Glasgow PA14 .... 47 D1
Stewarton KA3 .... 195 E1
Mackie Pl KA3 .... 223 E1
Mackie St KA8 .... 236 B1
Mackie's Mill Rd PA5 .... 132 B4
Mackinlay Pl KA1 .... 228 A4
Mackinlay St G5 .... 117 D2
Mackinnon Dr KA3 .... 228 B4
Mackinnon Terr KA12 .... 219 F2
Mackintosh Pl KA11 .... 219 F1

Maclachlan Ave FK6 .... 21 E1
Maclachlan Pl G84 .... 16 C2
Maclachlan Rd G84 .... 16 C2
Maclaren Pl KA3 .... 228 B4
Maclaren Terr FK2 .... 24 A1
Maclay Ave PA10 .... 111 D1
Maclean Cres FK12 .... 5 E4
Maclean Ct
  East Kilbride G74 .... 159 D2
  Stirling FK7 .... 7 E2
Maclean Dr KA3 .... 223 D1
Maclean Gr G74 .... 159 D2
Maclean Pl G74 .... 159 D2
Maclean Sq G51 .... 116 C3
Maclean St Clydebank G81 .... 94 C4
  Glasgow G51 .... 116 B3
Maclean Terr FH48 .... 107 E2
Maclehose Rd G67 .... 62 B2
Maclellan Rd G78 .... 154 C3
Maclellan St G41 .... 116 B3
Macleod Cres G84 .... 16 A2
Macleod Dr
  Helensburgh G84 .... 16 B2
  Kilmarnock KA3 .... 228 B4
Macleod Pl
  East Kilbride G74 .... 160 A2
  Kilmarnock KA3 .... 228 B4
Macleod St G4 .... 241 F2
Macmillan Dr Gourock PA19 .. 44 B3
  Kilmarnock KA3 .... 223 E1
Macmillan Gdns G71 .... 121 D1
Macmillan Pl KA3 .... 223 E1
Macmillan St ML9 .... 184 C1
Macnab Pl KA3 .... 223 D1
Macnaughton Dr KA3 .... 223 E1
Macneil Pl KA3 .... 223 D1
Macneil Dr G74 .... 159 D2
Macneill Gdns G74 .... 159 D2
Macneill St ML9 .... 184 C2
Macneish Way G74 .... 159 E2
Macnicol Ct G74 .... 159 D2
Macnicol Pk G74 .... 159 D2
Macnicol Pl
  East Kilbride G74 .... 159 D2
  Kilmarnock KA3 .... 223 E1
Macphail Dr KA3 .... 223 E1
Macpherson Gdns KA3 .... 223 E1
Macpherson Pl G74 .... 159 E2
Macpherson Pl Falkirk FK1 ... 41 F1
  Kilmarnock KA3 .... 223 E1
Macpherson Wlk KA3 .... 223 E1
Macphie Rd G82 .... 50 B2
Macrae Dr KA9 .... 233 E1
Macrae Gdns G74 .... 159 E2
Macreadie Pl KA11 .... 220 B3
Macrimmon Pl G75 .... 180 C4
Macrobert Ave KA11 .... 220 A1
Mactaggart Rd G67 .... 82 C4
Madeira La PA16 .... 45 E4
Madeira St PA16 .... 45 E4
Madill Pl FK5 .... 23 F2
Madison Ave G44 .... 137 D3
Madison Path G72 .... 161 E4
Madras Pl Glasgow G40 .... 117 F2
  Neilston G78 .... 154 C4
Madras St G40 .... 117 F2
Mafeking St Glasgow G51 .... 116 A3
  Wishaw ML2 .... 164 B2
Mafeking Terr G78 .... 154 B4
Magdalen Way PA2 .... 132 C4
Maggie Wood's Loan FK1 ..... 41 F3
Magna St ML1 .... 163 D4
Magnolia Dr G72 .... 139 F2
Magnolia Gdns ML1 .... 143 E2
Magnolia Pl G71 .... 141 E4
Magnolia St ML2 .... 165 D3
Magnum L Ctr KA12 .... 218 C1
Magnus Cres G44 .... 137 D2
Magnus Rd PA6 .... 111 E4
Mahon Ct G69 .... 80 C1
Maid Morville Ave KA11 ...... 225 E4
Maidens G74 .... 159 E2
Maidens Ave G77 .... 157 D3
Maidland Rd G53 .... 135 E4
Maidpath East G74 .... 159 E1
Maidpath West G74 .... 159 E1
Mailerbeg Gdns G69 .... 80 C2
Mailie Wlk ML1 .... 143 E2
Mailing Ave G64 .... 78 B1
Main Gdns FK6 .... 37 F2
Maimhor Rd KA23 .... 190 B2
Main Rd Ayr KA8 .... 236 C1
  Cardross G82 .... 48 A4
  Crookedholm KA3 .... 228 C4
  Cumbernauld G67 .... 82 A4
  Elderslie PA5 .... 112 B2
  Fenwick KA3 .... 213 D2
  Gatehead KA2 .... 226 C3
  Kilbirnie KA25 .... 149 D1
  Langbank PA14 .... 70 B4
  Paisley PA2 .... 113 E2
  Rosneath G84 .... 15 D2
  Springside KA11 .... 220 C1
  Waterside KA3 .... 213 F2
Main St Airth FK2 .... 14 B2
  Alexandria G83 .... 27 F3
  Alexandria, Dalmonach G83 . 27 F3
  Alloa FK10 .... 5 A1
  Ayr KA8 .... 235 F1
  Balloch G83 .... 19 F1
  Bannockburn FK7 .... 7 F1
  Banton G65 .... 37 E2
  Barrhead G78 .... 134 B1
  Beith KA15 .... 150 A1
  Bellshill ML4 .... 142 A3

Main St continued
  Blackridge EH48 .... 107 E2
  Blantyre G72 .... 161 E3
  Bonnybridge FK4 .... 40 A3
  Bothwell G71 .... 141 D1
  Bridge Of W PA11 .... 110 B4
  Calderbank ML6 .... 123 E1
  Caldercruix ML6 .... 105 D2
  California FK1 .... 66 C3
  Cambus FK10 .... 9 D4
  Cambuslang G72 .... 139 D3
  Chapelhall ML6 .... 123 F2
  Chryston G69 .... 80 B1
  Clarkston G76 .... 157 F3
  Cleland ML1 .... 144 B1
  Coatbridge ML5 .... 122 B3
  Cowie FK7 .... 12 B4
  Cumbernauld G67 .... 62 A3
  Dalry KA24 .... 191 E4
  Drybridge KA11 .... 225 E3
  Drybridge, Dundonald
    KA11, KA2 .... 225 F1
  Dunlop KA3 .... 195 D4
  East Kilbride G74 .... 159 F1
  Falkirk FK1 .... 41 F3
  Falkirk, Bainsford FK2 .... 42 A4
  Falkirk, Carronshore FK2 .... 24 B2
  Fallin FK7 .... 8 C2
  Gateside KA15 .... 171 F4
  Glasgow G40 .... 117 F2
  Glasgow, Muirhead G69 ...... 120 B2
  Glasgow, Thornliebank G46 . 135 F2
  Glenboig ML5 .... 101 F3
  Glengarnock KA14 .... 170 A3
  Greenock PA15 .... 46 B2
  Hamilton G72 .... 161 F3
  Houston PA6 .... 91 D1
  Howwood PA9 .... 130 C3
  Irvine KA11 .... 220 B1
  Kilmaurs KA3 .... 222 B4
  Kilsyth G65 .... 60 B4
  Kilwinning KA13 .... 207 F2
  Larbert FK5 .... 23 E1
  Lennoxtown G65 .... 57 E4
  Lochwinnoch PA12 .... 129 E1
  Longriggend ML6 .... 85 D1
  Milngavie G62 .... 76 A4
  Monkton KA9 .... 233 E2
  Motherwell ML1 .... 143 D3
  Neilston G78 .... 154 B4
  Newarthill ML2 .... 186 B3
  Plains ML6 .... 104 A1
  Plean FK7 .... 12 B2
  Prestwick KA9 .... 236 B4
  Rutherglen G73 .... 138 A4
  Salsburgh ML7 .... 125 D1
  Shieldhill FK1 .... 66 B3
  Shotts ML7 .... 147 D2
  Slamannan FK1 .... 86 A4
  Stenhousemuir FK5 .... 23 F1
  Stevenston KA20 .... 206 B1
  Stevenston KA3 .... 211 E4
  Stirling FK7 .... 6 B3
  Stirling, St Ninians FK7 .... 7 D2
  Symington KA1 .... 231 E2
  Torrance G64 .... 78 A4
  Troon KA10 .... 230 A2
  Tullibody FK10 .... 4 A1
  Twechar G65 .... 59 F2
  Uddingston G71 .... 140 C3
  West Kilbride KA23 .... 190 B3
  Wishaw ML2 .... 165 D2
  Wishaw, Newmains ML2 ... 166 A2
Main St E FK11 .... 4 A3
Main St W FK11 .... 3 F3
Mainhead Terr G67 .... 62 A3
Mainhill Ave G69 .... 120 B3
Mainhill Dr G69 .... 120 B3
Mainhill Pl G69 .... 120 B3
Mainhill Rd G69 .... 120 C3
Mainholm Acad KA8 .... 236 B1
Mainholm Cres KA8 .... 236 B1
Mainholm Rd Ayr KA8 .... 239 F4
  Ayr, Braehead KA8 .... 236 B1
Mains Ave Beith KA15 .... 150 A1
  Glasgow G46 .... 136 A1
  Helensburgh G84 .... 16 A2
Mains Ct ML11 .... 215 E3
Mains Dr PA8 .... 73 E1
Mains Hill PA8 .... 73 D1
Mains Pl ML4 .... 142 A2
Mains Rd Beith KA15 .... 150 A1
  East Kilbride G74 .... 159 F3
  Harthill ML7 .... 127 F3
Mains River PA8 .... 73 E1
Mains Wood PA8 .... 73 E1
Mainscroft PA8 .... 73 E1
Mainshill Ave PA8 .... 73 D1
Mainshill Gdns PA8 .... 73 D1
Mair Ave KA24 .... 191 F4
Mair St G51 .... 116 C3
Maitland Ave FK7 .... 7 E1
Maitland Bank ML9 .... 185 E2
Maitland Cres FK7 .... 7 E1
Maitland Ct G84 .... 16 B1
Maitland Dr G64 .... 57 F2
Maitland Pl PA4 .... 94 A1
Maitland St Glasgow G4 ...... 240 C4
  Helensburgh G84 .... 16 B1
Majors Loan FK1 .... 42 A2
Majors Pl FK1 .... 42 A2
Malcolm Ct KA3 .... 195 F1
Malcolm Dr FK5 .... 23 F2
Malcolm Gdns G74 .... 159 E1
Malcolm Pl G84 .... 17 D1
Malcolm St ML1 .... 163 E3
Malin Pl G33 .... 118 C4
Mallaig Pl G51 .... 115 F4

Mallaig Rd Glasgow G51 ..... 115 F4
  Port Glasgow PA14 .... 68 C4
Mallaig Terr PA16 .... 44 C2
Mallard Cres
  East Kilbride G75 .... 180 A3
  Greenock PA16 .... 45 D3
Mallard La
  🖬 Bothwell G71 .... 141 D2
  Greenock PA16 .... 45 D3
Mallard Pl G75 .... 180 A3
Mallard St G72 .... 74 A3
Mallard Terr G75 .... 180 A3
Mallard Way ML4 .... 141 F4
Malleable Gdns ML1 .... 142 B1
Malletsheugh Rd G77 .... 156 A2
Malloch Cres PA5 .... 112 A1
Malloch Pl G74 .... 160 A1
Malloch St G20 .... 96 C3
Malov Ct G75 .... 180 C3
Malplaquet Ct ML8 .... 188 A1
Maltbarns St G20 .... 97 D2
Malvaig La G72 .... 161 E3
Malvern Ct G31 .... 118 A3
Malvern Way PA3 .... 113 E4
Mamberg Dr G51 .... 115 F4
Mamore Pl G43 .... 136 B3
Mamore St G43 .... 136 B3
Mamre Dr FK6 .... 66 C3
Manchester Dr G12 .... 96 A3
Mandela Ave FK2 .... 42 B4
Mandora Ct ML8 .... 188 A1
Manitoba Cres G75 .... 159 D1
Mannering G74 .... 160 B2
Mannering Ct G41 .... 136 B4
Mannering Rd
  Glasgow G41 .... 136 B4
  Paisley PA2 .... 132 C4
Mannering Way PA2 .... 112 C1
Mannfield Ave FK4 .... 39 F2
Mannofield G61 .... 75 F2
Manor Ave KA3 .... 223 D2
Manor Cres Gourock PA19 ... 44 C4
  Tullibody FK10 .... 4 A1
Manor Dr ML6 .... 122 C4
Manor Gate G77 .... 156 C2
Manor Loan FK13 .... 3 D2
Manor Pk ML3 .... 162 B1
Manor Powis Cotts FK11 .... 3 D2
Manor Rd Clydebank G15 .... 74 C1
  Gartcosh G69 .... 100 C3
  Glasgow G52 .... 95 F2
  Paisley PA2 .... 112 C1
Manor St FK1 .... 42 A2
Manor View
  Calderbank ML6 .... 123 D1
  Larkhall ML9 .... 185 E1
Manor Way G73 .... 138 B2
Manresa Pl 🖬 G4 .... 97 D1
Manse Ave Bearsden G61 .... 75 F3
  Bothwell G71 .... 141 D1
  Coatbridge ML5 .... 121 E2
Manse Brae Dalserf ML9 ...... 200 A4
  Glasgow G44 .... 137 D3
  Rhu G84 .... 15 D3
Manse Cres Houston PA6 ...... 91 D1
  Stirling FK7 .... 7 D2
Manse Ct Barrhead G78 ...... 134 B2
  Kilsyth G65 .... 60 B4
  Kilwinning KA13 .... 207 F2
  Law ML8 .... 187 D2
Manse Dr G83 .... 27 F4
Manse Gdns G83 .... 27 F4
Manse Pl Airdrie ML6 .... 123 D4
  Bannockburn FK7 .... 7 F1
  Falkirk FK1 .... 42 A2
  Slamannan FK1 .... 86 A4
Manse Rd Bearsden G61 ...... 75 F3
  Bowling G60 .... 72 B4
  Carmunnock G76 .... 158 B4
  Coatbridge G69 .... 120 C3
  Glasgow G32 .... 119 E2
  Kilsyth G65 .... 60 C4
  Lanark ML11 .... 214 C2
  Motherwell ML3 .... 163 F2
  Neilston G78 .... 154 C4
  Salsburgh ML7 .... 125 E1
  Shotts ML7 .... 147 D2
  Stonehouse ML9 .... 198 B1
  West Kilbride KA23 .... 190 B3
  Wishaw ML7 .... 166 A2
Manse St Coatbridge ML5 ... 121 F3
  Kilmacolm PA13 .... 89 F4
  Saltcoats KA21 .... 205 F1
  Stonehouse ML9 .... 198 B1
  Wishaw ML2 .... 166 A2

Mansel St G21 .... 98 A3
Mansefield Ave G72 .... 139 D2
Mansefield Cres G60 .... 73 D3
Mansefield Dr G71 .... 140 C3
Mansefield Rd G76 .... 157 E3
Mansefield Terr KA3 .... 195 D4
Mansel St G21 .... 98 A3
Mansewood Dr G85 .... 73 D1
Mansewood Rd G43 .... 136 A3
Mansfield Ave FK10 .... 5 B1
Mansfield Cres G76 .... 157 E3
Mansfield Rd Bellshill ML4 .. 141 F2
  Clarkston G76 .... 157 E3
  Lochwinnoch PA12 .... 129 E2
  Paisley G52 .... 114 C4
  Prestwick KA9 .... 236 A3
  Quarter ML3 .... 183 F3
Mansfield St G11 .... 96 B1
Mansfield Way KA11 .... 220 A3
Mansion Ave PA14 .... 69 D4

Mansion Ct G72 .... 139 D3
Mansion St
  Cambuslang G72 .... 139 D3
  Glasgow G22 .... 97 E3
Mansionhouse Ave G32 ...... 139 E4
Mansionhouse Dr G32 .... 119 E3
Mansionhouse Gdns G41 ... 136 C4
Mansionhouse Gr G32 .... 119 F2
Mansionhouse Rd
  Falkirk FK1 .... 41 E3
  Glasgow G32 .... 119 F2
  Glasgow, Langside G41 ... 136 C4
  Paisley PA1 .... 114 A3
Manson Ave KA9 .... 233 E1
Manson Pl G75 .... 181 D3
Manson Rd KA12 .... 219 F2
Manuel Ave KA15 .... 171 D4
Manuel Ct Irvine KA11 .... 225 E4
  Kilbirnie KA25 .... 170 A4
Manuel Terr KA11 .... 225 E4
Maple Ave Dumbarton G82 ... 49 D3
  Milton Of C G65 .... 58 A3
  Newton Mearns G77 .... 156 B2
  Stenhousemuir FK5 .... 23 F2
Maple Bank ML3 .... 162 C1
Maple Cres G72 .... 139 F2
Maple Ct Alloa FK10 .... 10 A3
  Coatbridge ML5 .... 121 F2
  Cumbernauld G67 .... 62 C3
Maple Dr Ayr KA7 .... 239 E3
  Barrhead G78 .... 155 E4
  Beith KA15 .... 150 A1
  Clydebank G81 .... 74 A3
  Johnstone PA5 .... 132 A4
  Kirkintilloch G66 .... 79 D3
  Larkhall ML9 .... 185 D3
Maple Gr East Kilbride G75 . 180 A3
  Troon KA10 .... 229 E2
Maple Pl Banknock FK4 .... 38 C1
  Denny FK6 .... 21 E2
  East Kilbride G75 .... 180 A3
  Kilmarnock KA1 .... 227 E4
  Uddingston G71 .... 141 E4
Maple Quadrant ML6 .... 123 D4
Maple Rd Cumbernauld G67 . 62 C3
  Glasgow G41 .... 116 A2
  Greenock PA16 .... 45 D2
  Motherwell ML1 .... 143 D3
Maple Terr
  East Kilbride G75 .... 180 A3
  Irvine KA12 .... 219 E2
Maple Way G72 .... 161 E4
Mar Ave PA7 .... 72 A2
Mar Dr G61 .... 75 F4
Mar Gdns G73 .... 138 B2
Mar Pl Alloa FK10 .... 10 A4
  Alloa, New Sauchie FK10 ..... 5 E1
  Stirling FK8 .... 7 D4
Mar St FK10 .... 10 A3
Marble Ave KA11 .... 220 B1
Marc St G41 .... 116 C1
Marchbank Gdns PA1 .... 114 B2
Marchburn Ave KA9 .... 236 C4
Marchdyke Cres KA1 .... 227 F2
Marches The Lanark ML11 .. 215 D3
  Stirling FK8 .... 7 D4
Marchfield G64 .... 77 F2
Marchfield Ave PA3 .... 113 F4
Marchfield Quadrant KA8 .. 236 A3
Marchfield Rd KA8 .... 236 A3
Marchglen Pl FK10 .... 5 B1
Marchglen Pl G51 .... 115 E4
Marchmont Ct KA1 .... 228 C4
Marchmont Gdns G64 .... 77 F1
Marchmont Rd KA7 .... 238 C3
Marchmont Road La KA7 ... 238 C3
Marchmont Terr 🖬 G12 .... 96 B2
Marchside Ct FK10 .... 5 E1
Mardale G74 .... 159 E2
Maree Ct KA10 .... 10 B3
Maree Dr Cumbernauld G67 . 82 A4
  Glasgow G52 .... 115 F2
Maree Gdns G64 .... 78 A1
Maree Pl KA2 .... 219 E4
Maree Rd PA2 .... 113 D1
Maree Way G72 .... 161 E4
Maree Wlk 🖬 ML2 .... 165 F3
Marfield St G32 .... 118 C3
Margaret Ave Haggs FK4 .... 39 D2
  Salsburgh ML7 .... 125 D1
Margaret Ct FK6 .... 21 F1
Margaret Dr Alexandria G83 . 27 E3
  Bonnybridge FK4 .... 40 A3
Margaret Pl ML4 .... 141 F3
Margaret Rd
  Bannockburn FK7 .... 7 E1
  Hamilton ML3 .... 162 A3
Margaret St
  Coatbridge ML5 .... 122 A2
  Gourock PA19 .... 44 C4
  Greenock PA16 .... 45 E4
Margaret Terr FK7 .... 8 A3
Margaret's Pl ML9 .... 185 D2
Margareta Bldgs G44 .... 137 D3
Margaretvale Dr ML9 .... 185 D1
Marguerite Ave G66 .... 79 E3
Marguerite Ct G66 .... 79 E3
Marguerite Gdns
  Bothwell G71 .... 141 D1
  Kirkintilloch G66 .... 79 E3
Marguerite Gr G66 .... 79 E3
Marguerite Pl Ayr KA7 .... 239 E2
  Milton Of C G65 .... 58 A3
Marian Dr ML1 .... 143 E1
Marigold Ave ML1 .... 163 F4
Marigold Sq KA2 .... 239 D2
Marigold Way ML8 .... 201 F4
Marina Ct ML4 .... 141 F2

Marina Rd KA9 .... 236 A4
Marine Cres G51 .... 116 C3
Marine Dr KA12 .... 223 A3
Marine Gdns G51 .... 240 A1
Marine View Ct KA10 .... 229 E1
Mariner Ave ML1 .... 41 D3
Mariner Dr FK1 .... 41 D3
Mariner Gdns FK1 .... 41 E3
Mariner Rd FK1 .... 41 E3
Mariner St FK1 .... 41 D3
Marion St ML4 .... 142 B3
Mariscat Rd G41 .... 116 C1
Marjory Dr PA3 .... 114 A4
Marjory Rd PA4 .... 94 A1
Market Ct G65 .... 60 B4
Market End ML11 .... 215 D2
Market Pl Carluke ML8 .... 187 F1
  Kilmacolm PA13 .... 89 E4
  Kilsyth G65 .... 60 B4
  Uddingston G71 .... 141 E4
Market Rd Carluke ML8 ...... 187 F1
  Kirkintilloch G66 .... 80 A4
  Uddingston G71 .... 141 E4
Market St G65 .... 60 B4
Market St Airdrie ML6 .... 123 D4
  Kilsyth G65 .... 60 B4
  Uddingston G71 .... 141 E4
Markethill Rd
  East Kilbride G74 .... 159 F3
  East Kilbride, East Mains
    G74 .... 159 F2
Markethill Rdbt G74 .... 159 F2
Markinch Rd PA14 .... 68 C3
Marlborough Ave G11 .... 95 F2
Marlborough Pk G9 .... 2 B2
Marlborough La N G11 .... 95 F2
Marlborough La S G11 .... 95 F2
Marlborough Pk G75 .... 180 A4
Marldon La G11 .... 95 F2
Marlepark KA7 .... 239 D2
Marley Way G65 .... 58 A3
Marlfield Gdns ML4 .... 142 A4
Marloch Ave PA14 .... 69 D3
Marlow St G41 .... 116 C3
Marlow Terr G41 .... 116 C2
Marmion Ave G84 .... 25 D4
Marmion Cres ML1 .... 142 B1
Marmion Dr G66 .... 79 F4
Marmion Pl G67 .... 82 C4
Marmion Rd
  Cumbernauld G67 .... 82 C4
  Paisley PA2 .... 132 C4
Marmion St FK2 .... 42 A4
Marne St G31 .... 118 A4
Marnoch Dr ML5 .... 101 E3
Marnock Way G69 .... 80 C1
Marnock Terr PA2 .... 114 A1
Marr Coll KA10 .... 229 E2
Marr Dr KA10 .... 229 E2
Marr's Wynd ML11 .... 215 E3
Marress Rd KA12 .... 219 D2
Marress Rdbt KA12 .... 219 D1
Marrswood Gn ML3 .... 162 A2
Marrwood Ave G66 .... 80 A3
Mars Rd PA16 .... 44 B1
Marschal Ct FK7 .... 7 E2
Marshall Gr ML3 .... 162 A2
Marshall La ML2 .... 165 D2
Marshall St Coatbridge ML5 121 F2
  Larkhall ML9 .... 185 D1
  Wishaw ML2 .... 164 C1
Marshall's La PA1 .... 113 F2
Marshill FK10 .... 10 A3
Marsmount Rd KA9 .... 233 F1
Mart St G1 .... 241 D1
Martha St G1 .... 241 D3
Martin Ave Balloch G83 .... 28 A4
  Irvine KA12 .... 219 E3
Martin Cres G69 .... 120 B3
Martin Ct ML3 .... 162 B2
Martin Pl ML1 .... 143 E2
Martin Sq KA21 .... 206 A1
Martin St Coatbridge ML5 .. 122 B4
  Glasgow G40 .... 117 F2
Martinside G75 .... 180 C3
Martlet Dr PA5 .... 131 E4
Martyn St ML6 .... 122 C3
Martyrs Pl G64 .... 98 A4
Marwick St G31 .... 118 A4
Mary Dr ML4 .... 141 F2
Mary Glen ML2 .... 165 E3
Mary Love Pl KA20 .... 206 A1
Mary Rae Rd ML4 .... 141 F2
Mary Russell Sch The
  PA2 .... 114 B1
Mary Sq G69 .... 120 C3
Mary St Greenock PA16 .... 45 E2
  Hamilton ML3 .... 162 B1
  Johnstone PA5 .... 112 A2
  Laurieston PA2 .... 42 C2
  Paisley PA2 .... 113 F1
  Port Glasgow PA14 .... 47 D1
Mary Stevenson Dr FK10 .... 10 A4
Mary Street Rdbt FK2 .... 42 C2
Mary Young Pl G76 .... 157 F3
Maryborough Ave KA9 ...... 236 A3
Maryborough Rd KA9 .... 236 A3
Maryfield Pl Ayr KA8 .... 236 A2
  Falkirk FK1 .... 41 D2
Maryfield Rd KA8 .... 236 A2
Maryhill Prim Sch G20 .... 96 B4
Maryhill Rd Bearsden G61 .... 76 A1
Maryhill Sta G20 .... 96 B3
Maryknowe Rd ML1 .... 143 E1
Maryland Dr G52 .... 115 F3
Maryland Gdns G52 .... 115 F3
Maryland Rd G82 .... 50 B3

Marypark Rd PA14 .... 70 A4
Maryston St G33 .... 98 B1
Maryville Ave G46 .... 136 B1
Maryville Gdns G46 .... 136 B1
Maryville View G71 .... 120 B1
Marywood Sq G41 .... 116 C1
Mashock Path ML8 .... 201 D1
Mason La ML1 .... 163 F3
Mason St Larkhall ML9 .... 185 E1
Motherwell ML1 .... 163 F3
Masonfield Ave G68 .... 61 E1
Masonhill Pl KA7 .... 239 E3
Masonhill Rd KA7 .... 239 E3
Masterton St G21 .... 97 E2
Mather Terr FK2 .... 42 C2
Matherton Ave G77 .... 157 D3
Matheson Wlk G83 .... 27 F4
Mathew Smith Ave KA1 .... 227 F3
Mathie Cres PA19 .... 44 C3
Mathieson Rd G73 .... 118 B1
Mathieson St PA1 .... 114 A3
Matilda Rd G41 .... 116 C2
Matthew McWhirter Pl
ML9 .... 185 D2
Matthew Pl KA13 .... 207 F3
Mauchline G74 .... 160 C2
Mauchline Ave G66 .... 59 D1
Mauchline Ct
Hamilton ML3 .... 161 E1
Kilmarnock KA3 .... 223 D3
Kirkintilloch G66 .... 59 D1
Mauchline La PA16 .... 44 C2
Mauchline Rd KA1 .... 228 C3
Mauchline St G5 .... 117 D2
Mauchline Terr PA16 .... 44 C2
Maukinfauld Ct G32 .... 118 B2
Maukinfauld Rd G32 .... 118 C2
Mauldslie Dr ML8 .... 187 D3
Mauldslie Pl ML9 .... 199 F4
Mauldslie Rd Carluke ML8 .. 187 D1
Law ML8 .... 186 C1
Mauldslie St Bellshill ML4 ... 142 A2
Coatbridge ML5 .... 122 A3
Glasgow G40 .... 118 A2
Maule Dr G11 .... 96 A1
Maunsheugh Rd KA3 .... 213 D2
Maurice Ave FK7 .... 7 E2
Mavis Bank
Bishopbriggs G64 .... 97 F4
Blantyre G72 .... 161 E4
Mavis Rd PA16 .... 45 D2
Mavisbank Ave FK1 .... 66 B3
Mavisbank Gdns
Bellshill ML4 .... 142 A3
Glasgow G51 .... 116 C3
Mavisbank Rd G51 .... 116 B3
Mavisbank Sch ML6 .... 122 C4
Mavisbank St Airdrie ML6 .. 122 C4
Wishaw ML2 .... 166 B3
Mavisbank Terr
Johnstone PA5 .... 111 F1
Paisley PA1 .... 113 F2
Mavor Ave G74 .... 160 A2
Mavor Rdbt G74 .... 159 F2
Maxholm Rd KA1 .... 227 F3
Maxton Ave G78 .... 134 A2
Maxton Cres Alva FK12 .... 5 E4
Wishaw ML2 .... 165 E3
Maxton Gr G78 .... 134 A2
Maxton Terr G72 .... 138 C2
Maxwell Ave Bearsden G61 ... 75 F1
Glasgow G69 .... 120 A3
Glasgow, Pollockshields G41 116 C2
Maxwell Cres G72 .... 161 E3
Maxwell Ct Beith KA15 .... 171 D4
Kilmarnock KA3 .... 223 E2
Maxwell Dr Erskine PA8 .... 72 C2
Glasgow G69 .... 120 A3
Glasgow, Pollockshields G41 116 B2
Maxwell Gdns Glasgow G41 116 B2
Hurlford KA1 .... 228 C3
Maxwell Gn KA11 .... 220 A2
Maxwell Gr G41 .... 116 B2
Maxwell La G41 .... 116 C2
Maxwell Oval 2 G41 .... 116 C2
Maxwell Park Sta G41 .... 116 B1
Maxwell Path 13 ML9 .... 185 E1
Maxwell Pl
Bridge Of W PA11 .... 110 B4
Coatbridge ML5 .... 121 F3
Glasgow G41 .... 117 D2
Kilsyth G65 .... 36 B1
Stevenston KA20 .... 206 C1
Stirling FK8 .... 7 D4
Maxwell Rd Bishopton PA7 .... 72 A2
Glasgow G41 .... 117 D2
Maxwell St Clydebank G81 ..... 73 F2
Glasgow G1 .... 241 D1
Glasgow G1 .... 241 D2
Glasgow, Biallieston G69 ..... 120 A2
Paisley PA3 .... 113 F3
Port Glasgow PA14 .... 47 F1
Maxwell Terr G41 .... 116 C2
Maxwellton Ave G74 .... 160 A2
Maxwellton Pl G74 .... 160 A2
Maxwellton Rd
East Kilbride G74 .... 160 B2
Paisley PA1 .... 113 D2
Port Glasgow PA14 .... 68 C3
Maxwellton St PA1 .... 113 E2
Maxwelton Prim Sch G74 160 A2
Maxwelton Rd G33 .... 98 B1
Maxwood Pl KA11 .... 220 A3
May Gdns ML3 .... 162 B3
May Rd PA2 .... 133 F4
May St ML3 .... 162 B3
May Terr Glasgow G42 .... 137 D4
Glasgow, Merrylee G46 .... 136 B2
Maybank La G42 .... 117 D1
Maybank St G42 .... 117 D1
Mayberry Cres G32 .... 119 E3
Mayberry Gdns G32 .... 119 E3
Mayberry Gr G32 .... 119 E3
Mayberry Pl G72 .... 161 E4
Maybole Cres G77 .... 157 D2
Maybole Dr ML6 .... 123 D2
Maybole Gdns ML3 .... 161 E1
Maybole Gr G77 .... 157 D2
Maybole Pl ML5 .... 122 B2
Maybole Rd Ayr KA7 .... 239 D2
Port Glasgow PA14 .... 68 C3
Maybole St G53 .... 134 C3
Mayfield Ave Clarkston G76 157 F4
Hurlford KA1 .... 228 C3
Mayfield Cres
Howwood PA9 .... 130 C3
Stevenston KA20 .... 206 B1
Mayfield Ct Howwood PA9 .. 130 C3
Stirling FK7 .... 7 D2
Mayfield Dr Howwood PA9 . 130 C3
Longcroft FK4 .... 39 D2
Mayfield Gr KA20 .... 206 B1
Mayfield Mews FK1 .... 41 F2
Mayfield Pl Carluke ML8 ..... 202 A4
Saltcoats KA21 .... 217 D4
Mayfield Prim Sch KA21 ... 206 A1
Mayfield Rd Hamilton ML3 ... 161 F2
Saltcoats KA21 .... 217 D4
Stevenston KA20 .... 206 B1
Mayfield St Glasgow G20 .... 96 C3
Stirling FK7 .... 7 D2
Mayne Ave FK9 .... 2 A3
Mayville St KA20 .... 206 B1
McAdam Ct KA9 .... 236 B3
McAlister Rd G83 .... 27 F3
McAlley Ct FK9 .... 1 C4
McAllister Ave ML6 .... 123 E4
McAllister Ct FK7 .... 7 E1
McAlpine St Glasgow G2 ..... 240 B2
Wishaw ML2 .... 165 D1
McArdle Ave ML1 .... 163 D4
McArthur Pk G66 .... 79 E4
McArthur St G43 .... 136 B4
McAslin Ct G4 .... 241 E3
McAslin St G4 .... 241 F3
McAuslan Pl G84 .... 16 C1
McBride Ave G66 .... 79 E4
McCall's Ave KA8 .... 236 A1
McCallum Ave G73 .... 138 A4
McCallum Cres PA19 .... 44 C4
McCallum Ct G74 .... 159 D2
McCallum Gdns ML4 .... 141 F1
McCallum Gr G74 .... 159 D2
McCallum Pl G74 .... 159 D2
McCallum Rd ML9 .... 185 D1
McCardel Way KA3 .... 211 F4
McCarrison Rd ML2 .... 166 A3
McCash Pl G66 .... 79 E4
McClue Ave PA4 .... 94 A2
McClue Rd PA4 .... 94 B2
McClurg Ct ML1 .... 163 F3
McColgan Pl KA8 .... 236 B2
McColl Ave G83 .... 27 E3
McColl Pl G83 .... 27 E3
McConnell Rd PA12 .... 129 D1
McCormack Gdns ML1 .... 143 F2
McCracken Ave PA4 .... 94 A1
McCracken Dr G71 .... 141 E4
McCreery St G81 .... 94 B4
McCulloch Ave G71 .... 141 E3
McCulloch La G83 .... 27 E4
McCulloch St G41 .... 116 C2
McDonald Ave PA5 .... 111 F1
McDonald Cres G81 .... 94 B4
McDonald Dr KA12 .... 219 E2
McDonald Pl
Motherwell ML1 .... 143 D3
Neilston G78 .... 154 C4
McDowall Ave KA22 .... 205 E1
McDowall Pl KA22 .... 205 E1
McEwan Dr G84 .... 16 C2
McEwan Gdns G74 .... 159 D2
McEwan Wlk G83 .... 27 F3
McEwans Way ML9 .... 198 B1
McFarlane Rd G83 .... 28 A4
McFarlane St Glasgow G4 ... 241 F1
Paisley PA3 .... 113 E4
McGavin Ave KA13 .... 208 A2
McGavin Way KA13 .... 207 E2
McGhee St G81 .... 74 A2
McGibney Dr KA12 .... 219 E1
McGill Prim Sch G53 .... 115 E1
McGillivray Ave KA21 .... 205 F1
McGowan Pl ML3 .... 162 A3
McGown St PA3 .... 113 E3
McGregor Ave Airdrie ML6 .. 123 E4
Balloch G83 .... 28 A4
Renfrew PA4 .... 94 A1
Stevenston KA20 .... 206 B1
McGregor Dr G82 .... 50 B2
Mcgregor Path ML5 .... 101 E3
McGregor Rd G67 .... 61 F1
McGregor St Clydebank G81 . 94 B4
Glasgow G51 .... 115 F3
Wishaw ML2 .... 164 B2
McGrigor Rd Milngavie G62 .. 54 C2
Stirling FK7 .... 7 D2
McHardy Cres KA15 .... 171 F2
McInnes Ct ML2 .... 165 D1
McInnes Pl ML2 .... 186 A4
McInnes St G83 .... 28 A4
McIntosh Ct 1 G31 .... 117 F4
McIntosh Quadrant ML4 .... 141 F1
McIntosh St G31 .... 117 F4
McIntosh Way ML1 .... 163 E3
McIntyre Pl PA2 .... 113 F1
McIntyre Terr G72 .... 139 D3
McInver St G72 .... 139 F3
McIsaac Rd KA21 .... 217 D4
McKay Cres PA5 .... 112 A1
McKay Gr ML4 .... 141 F3
McKay Pl East Kilbride G74 . 159 D2
Newton Mearns G77 .... 156 B2
McKechnie St G51 .... 116 A4
McKell Ct FK1 .... 42 A2
McKellar Ave KA22 .... 205 E1
McKenna Dr ML6 .... 122 C4
McKenzie Ave G81 .... 74 A2
McKenzie Dr G83 .... 19 F1
McKenzie St PA3 .... 113 E3
McKenzie's Cl ML11 .... 215 D2
McKerrell St PA1 .... 114 A3
McKillop Pl KA21 .... 205 F1
McKim Wlk G82 .... 49 E4
McKinlay Ave G83 .... 20 A1
McKinlay Cres Alloa FK10 ..... 10 B4
Irvine KA12 .... 219 D1
Mckinnon Pl KA21 .... 206 A1
McKnight Ave KA3 .... 213 F2
McLachlan Ave FK7 .... 7 D1
McLachlan St FK5 .... 23 E1
McLaren Ave PA4 .... 94 B1
McLaren Cres G20 .... 96 C4
McLaren Ct Glasgow G46 .... 136 A1
Stenhousemuir FK5 .... 23 E1
McLaren Gdns G20 .... 96 C4
McLaren Gr G74 .... 159 D2
McLaren Pl G44 .... 136 C1
McLaren Terr FK7 .... 7 D2
McLauchlan View ML7 .... 127 F3
McLaurin Cres PA5 .... 111 E1
McLean Cres G83 .... 19 F1
McLean Dr Bellshill ML4 .... 141 F1
Irvine KA11 .... 225 E4
McLean Gdns ML9 .... 198 C1
McLean Mus PA16 .... 45 F3
McLean Pl PA3 .... 113 E4
McLean St KA8 .... 236 B1
McLees La ML1 .... 163 D4
McLelland Dr
Kilmarnock KA1 .... 227 F4
Plains ML6 .... 104 A1
McLennan St G42 .... 137 D4
McLeod Rd G82 .... 50 B2
McLeod St PA15 .... 46 B2
McLuckie Dr KA13 .... 207 E2
McLuckie Pk KA13 .... 207 E2
McMahon Dr ML2 .... 166 A3
McMillan Cres KA15 .... 171 D4
McMillan Dr KA22 .... 205 D2
McMillan Pl KA11 .... 224 C3
McMillan Rd ML2 .... 164 B1
McMillan Way ML8 .... 186 C3
McNair St G32 .... 119 D3
McNaught Pl
Kilmaurs KA3 .... 222 A4
Renton G82 .... 27 E1
McNay Cres KA21 .... 206 A1
McNeil Ave G81 .... 74 C1
McNeil Dr ML1 .... 143 D4
McNeil Gdns G5 .... 117 E2
McNeil Pl ML2 .... 186 B4
McNeil St G5 .... 117 E2
McNeill Ave KA9 .... 233 E1
McPhail Ave ML1 .... 143 F3
McPhail St Glasgow G40 .... 117 F2
Greenock PA15 .... 46 B2
McPhater St G4 .... 240 C4
McPherson Cres ML6 .... 123 F1
McPherson Dr
Bothwell G71 .... 141 D2
Gourock PA19 .... 44 B4
Stirling FK8 .... 2 A1
McPherson La G83 .... 27 E4
McPherson St
Bellshill ML4 .... 142 B3
Glasgow G1 .... 241 E1
McShannon Gr ML4 .... 142 A2
McTaggart Ave FK6 .... 21 F1
McVean Pl FK4 .... 39 D2
Meadow Ave Blantyre G72 .. 161 E3
Irvine KA12 .... 219 E2
Meadow Ct Carluke ML8 .... 188 B1
Dumbarton G82 .... 49 F3
Meadow Gn FK10 .... 5 D1
Meadow La Bothwell G71 ... 141 D1
Renfrew PA4 .... 94 B3
Meadow Path ML6 .... 123 E1
Meadow Pk Alva FK12 .... 5 D3
Ayr KA7 .... 239 D3
Meadow Pl FK8 .... 2 B1
Meadow Rd
Braidwood ML8 .... 202 A2
Dumbarton G82 .... 50 A2
Glasgow G11 .... 96 A1
Motherwell ML1 .... 164 A3
Meadow St Coatbridge ML5 122 A2
Falkirk FK1 .... 42 B2
Meadow View
Cumbernauld G67 .... 62 B2
Plains ML6 .... 104 A2
Meadow Way G77 .... 156 B3
Meadow Wlk ML5 .... 122 A3
Meadowbank La
Prestwick KA9 .... 236 A4
Uddingston G71 .... 140 C3
Meadowbank Pl G77 .... 156 B3
Meadowbank St G82 .... 49 F2
Meadowburn G64 .... 78 A2
Meadowburn Ave
Kirkintilloch G66 .... 79 F3
Newton Mearns G77 .... 156 B3
Meadowburn Prim Sch
G64 .... 78 A2
Meadowburn Rd ML2 .... 165 E2
Meadowfield Pl ML2 .... 166 B3
Meadowfoot Rd KA23 .... 190 B2
Meadowforth Rd FK7 .... 7 E4
Meadowhead Ave
Chryston G69 .... 80 C1
Irvine KA11 .... 224 C2
Meadowhead Ind Est
KA11 .... 224 C3
Meadowhead Rd
Irvine KA11 .... 224 C2
Plains ML6 .... 103 F1
Wishaw ML2 .... 164 B2
Meadowhead Rdbt KA11 .. 224 C1
Meadowhill G77 .... 156 B3
Meadowhill St ML9 .... 185 D2
Meadowland Rd FK9 .... 2 A3
Meadowpark Dr KA7 .... 239 D3
Meadowpark St G31 .... 118 A4
Meadows Ave ML9 .... 185 D2
Meadows The Houston PA6 .. 91 F1
Kilwinning KA13 .... 207 E2
Meadowside Beith KA15 ..... 171 D4
Crookedholm KA3 .... 228 C4
Hamilton ML3 .... 183 E3
West Kilbride KA23 .... 190 B3
Meadowside Ave PA5 .... 112 B1
Meadowside Gdns ML6 ..... 123 E4
Meadowside Ind Est PA4 ..... 94 B3
Meadowside Pl ML6 .... 123 E4
Meadowside Rd G65 .... 59 F4
Meadowside St
Glasgow G11 .... 96 A1
Renfrew PA4 .... 94 B3
Meadowwell St G32 .... 119 D3
Meadside Ave PA10 .... 111 D2
Meadside Rd PA10 .... 111 D2
Mealkirk St G81 .... 74 B4
Mearns Castle High Sch
G77 .... 157 D2
Mearns Ct ML3 .... 183 F4
Mearns Prim Sch G77 .... 156 B2
Mearns Rd Motherwell ML1 . 163 E4
Newton Mearns G77 .... 156 B1
Mearns St PA15 .... 45 F2
Mearns Way G64 .... 78 B1
Mearnscroft Gdns G77 ..... 156 C2
Mearnscroft Rd G77 .... 156 C2
Mearnskirk Rd G77 .... 156 B1
Medine Ave KA15 .... 150 A1
Medine Ct KA15 .... 150 A1
Medlar Ct G72 .... 139 F2
Medlar Rd G67 .... 62 B1
Medrox Gdns G67 .... 81 F3
Medwin Ct G75 .... 179 F4
Medwin Gdns G75 .... 179 F4
Medwin St G72 .... 139 F3
Medwyn Pl FK10 .... 9 F3
Medwyn St G14 .... 95 E2
Meek Pl G72 .... 139 D3
Meeks Rd FK2 .... 42 A3
Meetinghouse La PA1 .... 113 F3
Megan St G40 .... 117 F2
Meikle Ave PA4 .... 94 B1
Meikle Bin Brae G65 .... 57 F4
Meikle Cres
Greengairs ML6 .... 103 E4
Hamilton ML3 .... 183 E4
Meikle Ct KA3 .... 195 F1
Meikle Drumgray Rd ML6 . 103 F4
Meikle Earnock Rd ML3 .... 183 D4
Meikle Pl KA11 .... 220 A3
Meikle Rd G53 .... 135 E4
Meiklehill Ct G66 .... 58 C1
Meiklehill Rd G66 .... 58 C1
Meiklem St ML4 .... 142 B3
Meiklerig Cres G53 .... 115 E1
Meikleriggs Dr PA2 .... 113 D1
Meiklewood Ave KA9 .... 233 E1
Meiklewood Rd
Glasgow G51 .... 115 E3
Kilmarnock KA3 .... 222 C3
Melbourne Ave
Clydebank G81 .... 73 E3
East Kilbride G75 .... 180 B4
Melbourne Ct G46 .... 136 B2
Melbourne Gn 7 G75 .... 180 B4
Melbourne Rd KA21 .... 216 C4
Melbourne St G31 .... 117 F3
Melbourne Terr KA21 .... 216 C4
Meldon Pl G51 .... 115 E4
Meldrum Gdns G41 .... 116 B1
Meldrum Mains ML6 .... 102 C2
Meldrum St G81 .... 94 B4
Melford Ave Glasgow G46 ... 136 B1
Kirkintilloch G66 .... 79 D4
Shotts ML7 .... 147 D2
Melford Gdns PA10 .... 111 E1
Melford Rd ML4 .... 141 F4
Melford Way PA3 .... 114 A4
Melfort Ave Clydebank G81 .... 74 B2
Glasgow G41 .... 116 A2
Melfort Dr FK7 .... 7 D2
Melfort Path ML2 .... 165 F4
Melfort Quadrant ML1 .... 143 E2
Melfort Rd ML3 .... 161 F1
Mellerstain Dr G14 .... 94 C3
Mellock Gdns FK1 .... 41 F1
Melness Pl G51 .... 115 E4
Melrose Ave
Chapelhall ML6 .... 123 E1
Coatbridge G69 .... 120 C3
Linwood PA3 .... 112 A3
Motherwell ML1 .... 143 D3
Paisley PA2 .... 113 D1
Rutherglen G73 .... 138 A4
Melrose Cres ML2 .... 165 D3
Melrose Ct G73 .... 138 A4
Melrose Gdns Glasgow G20 .. 96 C2
Twechar G65 .... 59 F2
Uddingston G71 .... 120 C1
Melrose Pl Blantyre G72 .... 140 B1
Coatbridge ML5 .... 121 F4
10 Falkirk FK1 .... 42 A2
Larkhall ML9 .... 185 D1
Melrose Prim Sch G67 .... 82 C4
Melrose Rd
Cumbernauld G67 .... 82 C4
Port Glasgow PA14 .... 68 C4
Melrose St 6 Glasgow G4 .... 97 D1
Hamilton ML3 .... 162 A3
Melrose Terr
East Kilbride G74 .... 159 F2
Hamilton ML3 .... 162 A3
Melvaig Pl G20 .... 96 B3
Melvick Pl G51 .... 115 E4
Melville Cres ML1 .... 163 F3
Melville Ct G1 .... 241 D1
Melville Dr ML1 .... 163 F3
Melville Gdns G64 .... 78 A1
Melville Pk G74 .... 160 A2
Melville Pl Bridge Of A FK9 ..... 2 A4
Carluke ML8 .... 187 F1
Melville St Falkirk FK1 .... 42 A3
Glasgow G41 .... 116 C2
Kilmarnock KA3 .... 228 A4
Melville Terr FK8 .... 7 D3
Melvinhall Rd ML11 .... 215 D3
Memel St G21 .... 97 F3
Memus Ave G52 .... 115 E2
Mennock Ct ML3 .... 161 F1
Mennock Dr G64 .... 78 A2
Mennock La KA10 .... 229 F3
Mennock St ML1 .... 144 B1
Menock Rd G44 .... 137 E3
Menstrie Castle FK11 .... 3 F3
Menstrie Pl FK11 .... 4 A3
Menstrie Prim Sch FK11 .... 4 A3
Menteith Ave G64 .... 78 A1
Menteith Ct FK10 .... 10 B3
Menteith Dr G73 .... 138 B1
Menteith Gdns G61 .... 75 E4
Menteith Loan ML1 .... 143 D3
Menteith Pl G73 .... 138 B1
Menteith Rd
Motherwell ML1 .... 163 F4
Stirling FK9 .... 2 A2
Menzies Dr Glasgow G21 .... 98 A3
Stirling FK8 .... 2 A1
Menzies Pl G21 .... 98 A3
Menzies Rd G21 .... 98 A3
Merchant La G1 .... 241 D1
Merchants Cl PA10 .... 111 D2
Merchiston Ave Falkirk FK2 .. 42 A4
Linwood PA3 .... 111 F3
Merchiston Gdns FK2 .... 42 A3
Merchiston Hospl PA5 .... 111 F3
Merchiston Ind Est FK2 .... 42 B4
Merchiston Rd Falkirk FK2 ... 42 A4
Falkirk, Grahamston FK2 .... 42 A3
Merchiston St G32 .... 118 C4
Merchiston Terr FK2 .... 42 A4
Mercury La PA16 .... 44 B2
Meredith Dr FK5 .... 23 F2
Merino Rd PA15 .... 45 F2
Merkins Ave G82 .... 50 A3
Merkland Ct Glasgow G11 ..... 96 A1
Kirkintilloch G66 .... 59 D1
Merkland Dr Falkirk FK1 .... 42 C1
Kirkintilloch G66 .... 80 A4
Merkland Pl G66 .... 59 D1
Merkland Rd Ayr KA7 .... 239 D1
Coatbridge ML5 .... 101 E1
Merkland Sch G66 .... 58 C1
Merkland St G11 .... 96 A1
Merkland Way G75 .... 180 B2
Merksworth Ave KA24 .... 191 E4
Merksworth High Sch PA3 113 E4
Merksworth Way PA1 .... 113 F4
Merlewood Rd KA23 .... 190 A2
Merlin Ave Bellshill ML4 .... 142 A4
Greenock PA16 .... 45 D3
Merlin La PA16 .... 45 D3
Merlin Way PA3 .... 114 A4
Merlinford Ave PA4 .... 94 C2
Merlinford Cres PA4 .... 94 C2
Merlinford Dr PA4 .... 94 C2
Merlinford Way PA4 .... 94 C2
Merrick Ave
Prestwick KA9 .... 233 E1
Troon KA10 .... 229 F2
Merrick Ct ML6 .... 103 D1
Merrick Gdns Bearsden G61 . 75 E4
Glasgow G51 .... 116 A3
Quarter ML3 .... 183 F2
Merrick Pl Irvine KA11 .... 220 A1
Symington KA1 .... 231 E2
Merrick Rd KA1 .... 228 A2
Merrick Terr G71 .... 141 D4
Merrick View KA3 .... 195 F1
Merrick Way G73 .... 138 A2
Merry St ML1 .... 163 F4
Merryburn Ave G46 .... 136 B2
Merrycrest Ave G46 .... 136 B2
Merrycroft Ave G46 .... 136 B2
Merryflats G65 .... 59 F2
Merrygreen Pl KA3 .... 195 F1
Merryland Pl G51 .... 116 B4
Merryland St G51 .... 116 B4
Merrylee Ave PA14 .... 68 C4
Merrylee Cres G46 .... 136 B3
Merrylee Park Ave G46 .... 136 B2
Merrylee Park Mews G46 . 136 B3

Merrylee Prim Sch G44 ... 136 C3
Merrylee Rd G43 ... 136 C4
Merrylees Rd G77 ... 161 E4
Merryston Ct ML5 ... 121 F3
Merrystone St ML5 ... 121 F4
Merryton Ave Glasgow G15 ... 75 D2
  Glasgow, Merrylee G46 ... 136 B2
Merryton Pl G15 ... 75 D2
Merryton Rd Larkhall ML9 ... 184 C3
  Motherwell ML1 ... 164 B1
Merryton St ML9 ... 184 C3
Merryvale Ave G46 ... 136 B2
Merryvale Pl G46 ... 136 B3
Merryvale Rd KA12 ... 219 E1
Merryvale Rdbt KA12 ... 219 E1
Merton Dr G52 ... 115 D3
Merville Cres FK1 ... 66 C3
Merville Terr FK1 ... 66 C3
Meryon Gdns G32 ... 119 E1
Meryon Rd G32 ... 119 E2
Metcalfe Pl KA11 ... 224 C3
Methil Rd PA14 ... 68 C3
Methil St G14 ... 95 E2
Methlan Pk G82 ... 49 E1
Methlick Ave ML6 ... 122 C2
Methuen Rd Paisley PA3 ... 114 A4
  Renfrew PA3 ... 93 F1
Methven Ave Bearsden G61 ... 76 A3
  Kilmarnock KA1 ... 227 F2
Methven Pl
  East Kilbride G74 ... 159 E1
  Kilmarnock KA1 ... 227 F2
Methven Rd G46 ... 157 D4
Methven St Clydebank G81 ... 73 F2
  Glasgow G31 ... 118 B2
Metropole La G1 ... 241 D1
Mews La Ayr KA7 ... 238 C4
  Greenock PA16 ... 45 E4
  Kilmarnock KA1 ... 227 F4
  Paisley PA3 ... 113 F4
Mey Pl G7 ... 156 A2
Mharie Pl G83 ... 27 F1
Michael McParland Dr
  G64 ... 78 A4
Michael Terr ML6 ... 123 E1
Micklehouse Oval **2** G69 ... 120 A3
Micklehouse Pl **1** G69 ... 120 A3
Micklehouse Rd G69 ... 120 A3
Micklehouse Wynd **3**
  G69 ... 120 A3
Mid Ave PA14 ... 68 C4
Mid Barrwood Rd G65 ... 60 C4
Mid Dykes Rd KA21 ... 205 F1
Mid Pk G75 ... 180 C4
Mid Rd Beith KA15 ... 150 A1
  Cumbernauld G67 ... 82 C3
  Eaglesham G76 ... 178 C2
Mid Rig KA11 ... 220 A2
Mid-Loan St ML8 ... 202 A2
Mid-Wharf St G4 ... 97 E1
Midas Pl ML4 ... 142 C3
Midcroft G64 ... 77 F2
Midcroft Ave G44 ... 137 F3
Middle Pk PA3 ... 113 E1
Middle Ward St G81 ... 74 B4
Middlefield G75 ... 180 C3
Middlefield Ind Ctr FK2 ... 42 B4
Middlefield Ind Est FK2 ... 42 C4
Middlefield Rd FK2 ... 42 B3
Middlefield Sch G11 ... 96 A2
Middlehouse Ct ML8 ... 187 E1
Middlemass Ct FK2 ... 42 A3
Middlemass Dr KA1 ... 228 A4
Middlemuir Ave G66 ... 79 E3
Middlemuir Rd
  Kirkintilloch G66 ... 79 E3
  Stirling FK7 ... 7 E3
Middlepart KA20 ... 206 B1
Middlepart Cres KA21 ... 206 A1
Middlepenny Pl PA14 ... 70 A4
Middlepenny Rd PA14 ... 70 A4
Middlerigg Rd G68 ... 61 E1
Middlesex Gdns **3** G41 ... 116 C3
Middlesex St G41 ... 116 C3
Middleton Ave ML9 ... 199 D4
Middleton Cres PA3 ... 113 D3
Middleton Dr
  Helensburgh G84 ... 25 C4
  Gourock PA19 ... 55 E1
Middleton La G84 ... 25 C4
Middleton Pk KA11 ... 220 A2
Middleton Rd Irvine KA11 ... 220 A2
  Linwood PA3 ... 112 B4
  Paisley PA3 ... 113 D3
Middleton St
  Alexandria G83 ... 27 E3
  Glasgow G51 ... 116 B3
Midfaulds Ave PA4 ... 94 C1
Midland St G1 ... 240 C2
Midlem Dr G52 ... 115 E3
Midlem Oval G52 ... 115 E3
Midlock St G51 ... 116 B3
Midlothian Dr G41 ... 116 B1
Midthorn Cres FK2 ... 42 C3
Midton Ave KA9 ... 236 A4
Midton Rd Ayr KA7 ... 238 C3
  Howwood PA9 ... 131 D3
  Kilmarnock KA1 ... 227 F1
  Prestwick KA9 ... 236 B4
Midton St G21 ... 97 F2
Midtown PA11 ... 89 F3
Migvie Pl G20 ... 96 B3
Milford G75 ... 180 A4

Milford St G33 ... 119 D4
Milgarholm Ave KA12 ... 219 E1
Milgarholm Rdbt KA12 ... 219 E1
Mill Ave KA3 ... 222 B4
Mill Brae Ayr KA7 ... 239 C4
  Bridge Of W PA12 ... 110 B4
Mill Brae Ct ML5 ... 121 E3
Mill Cres Glasgow G40 ... 117 F2
  Irvine KA12 ... 219 F2
  Torrance G64 ... 57 E1
Mill Ct Hamilton ML3 ... 162 B1
  Kilbirnie KA25 ... 149 D1
  Kilmarnock KA1 ... 228 A4
  Rutherglen G73 ... 138 A4
Mill Gr ML3 ... 162 A1
Mill Hill FK7 ... 6 B3
Mill Loan ML6 ... 123 D4
Mill of Gryffe Rd PA11 ... 110 B4
Mill Pk Dalry KA24 ... 191 E4
  Hamilton ML3 ... 162 B1
Mill Pl PA3 ... 112 A3
Mill Rd Airdrie ML6 ... 103 D1
  Alloa FK10 ... 10 A3
  Banton G65 ... 37 E2
  Bothwell G71 ... 141 D1
  Cambusbarron FK7 ... 6 B3
  Cambuslang G72 ... 139 E3
  Cardross G82 ... 26 A1
  Carluke ML8 ... 187 F1
  Clydebank G81 ... 94 B4
  Falkirk FK2 ... 24 B3
  Hamilton ML3 ... 162 B1
  Hartwood ML7 ... 145 F1
  Irvine KA12 ... 219 F1
  Kilbirnie KA25 ... 149 D1
  Motherwell ML1 ... 163 F4
  Queenzieburn G65 ... 59 F4
  Riggend ML6 ... 83 D1
  Wishaw ML7 ... 166 C3
Mill Rig G75 ... 180 B3
Mill Rise G66 ... 79 E2
Mill St Alloa FK10 ... 10 A3
  Ayr KA7 ... 239 D4
  Caldercruix ML6 ... 104 C3
  Glasgow G40 ... 117 F2
  Greenock PA15 ... 45 F2
  Kilmarnock KA1 ... 227 F4
  Paisley PA1 ... 113 F2
  Rutherglen G73 ... 138 A3
Mill Street Ind Est ML6 ... 123 D4
Mill Waulk KA3 ... 211 F4
Mill Way G66 ... 80 A4
Mill Wynd KA7 ... 238 C4
Millands Ave G72 ... 140 B1
Millar Pl
  High Bonnybridge FK4 ... 40 A2
  Stenhousemuir FK2 ... 24 A3
  Stirling FK8 ... 2 B1
Millar Rd KA21 ... 217 D4
Millar St Greenock PA15 ... 46 A1
  Paisley PA1 ... 113 F3
  Stonehouse ML9 ... 198 C1
Millar Terr G73 ... 118 A1
Millarbank St G21 ... 97 F2
Millars Pl G66 ... 79 E2
Millars Way FK10 ... 5 E1
Millarston Ave PA1 ... 113 D2
Millarston Dr PA1 ... 113 D2
Millbank Ave ML4 ... 142 B2
Millbank Rd
  Port Glasgow PA14 ... 68 B4
  Wishaw ML2 ... 164 C1
Millbeg Cres G33 ... 119 F3
Millbeg Pl G33 ... 119 F3
Millbrae Ave G69 ... 100 B4
Millbrae Cres
  Clydebank G81 ... 94 B4
  Glasgow G42 ... 136 C4
Millbrae Ct G42 ... 136 C4
Millbrae Gdns G42 ... 136 C4
Millbrae Rd G42 ... 136 C4
Millbrix Ave G14 ... 95 D3
Millbrook G74 ... 159 D1
Millbrook Pl FK11 ... 3 F3
Millburn Ave
  Clydebank G81 ... 94 C4
  Renfrew PA4 ... 94 C2
  Rutherglen G73 ... 138 A3
Millburn Cres G82 ... 50 A2
Millburn Ct G75 ... 179 F4
Millburn Dr PA14 ... 68 B4
  Renfrew PA4 ... 94 C2
Millburn Gdns G75 ... 179 F4
Millburn La **6** ML9 ... 185 E1
Millburn Pl ML9 ... 199 D4
Millburn Rd
  Alexandria G83 ... 27 E2
  Ashgill ML9 ... 199 D2
  Dumbarton G82 ... 50 A2
  Port Glasgow PA14 ... 68 B4
  Renfrew PA4 ... 94 B2
Millburn St Falkirk FK2 ... 42 B3
  Glasgow G21 ... 98 A1
  Lennoxtown G66 ... 57 F4
  Motherwell ML1 ... 163 F4
Millburn Terr KA11 ... 220 A3
Millburn Way
  East Kilbride G75 ... 179 F4
  Renfrew PA4 ... 94 C2
Millcroft Rd Airdrie ML6 ... 83 D2
  Cumbernauld G67 ... 82 C2
  Cumbernauld, Carbrain G67 ... 62 A1
  Rutherglen G73 ... 117 F1
Milldam Rd G81 ... 74 B4
Milldown Pl KA11 ... 220 B1
Miller Ct G82 ... 50 A2
Miller Field Pl ML3 ... 162 C2

Miller Pl Airth FK2 ... 14 C2
  Ardrossan KA22 ... 205 D2
  Harthill ML7 ... 127 F3
Miller Rd Ayr KA7 ... 238 C4
  Balloch G83 ... 27 F4
Miller Sq KA9 ... 233 E1
Miller St Carluke ML8 ... 188 A1
  Clydebank G81 ... 74 A1
  Coatbridge ML5 ... 122 A3
  Dumbarton G82 ... 50 A2
  Glasgow G1 ... 241 D2
  Glasgow, Baillieston G69 ... 120 A2
  Hamilton ML3 ... 162 C2
  Harthill ML7 ... 127 F3
  Johnstone PA5 ... 112 A2
  Larkhall ML9 ... 185 D2
  Wishaw ML7 ... 165 D2
Miller's Pl ML6 ... 123 D4
Millerfield Pl G40 ... 118 A2
Millerfield Rd G40 ... 118 A2
Millerslea Gdns G84 ... 16 C1
Millersneuk Ave G66 ... 79 E2
Millersneuk Cres G33 ... 99 D3
Millersneuk Dr G66 ... 79 E2
Millersneuk Prim Sch G66 ... 79 F2
Millersneuk Rd G66 ... 79 E2
Millerston St G31 ... 118 A3
Millfield Ave Erskine PA8 ... 72 C1
  Motherwell ML1 ... 163 F4
Millfield Cres PA8 ... 73 D1
Millfield Dr PA8 ... 73 D1
Millfield Gdns PA8 ... 73 D1
Millfield Hill PA8 ... 72 C1
Millfield La PA8 ... 72 C1
Millfield Meadows PA8 ... 72 C1
Millfield Pl PA8 ... 72 C1
Millfield View PA8 ... 72 C1
Millfield Wlk PA8 ... 73 D1
Millfield Wynd PA8 ... 72 C1
Millflats St FK2 ... 24 A1
Millford Dr PA3 ... 112 A3
Millfore Ct KA11 ... 220 A2
Millgate Ave G71 ... 140 C4
Millgate Ct G71 ... 140 C4
Millgate Rd ML3 ... 162 B1
Millglen Pl KA22 ... 205 E2
Millglen Rd KA22 ... 205 E2
Millhall Rd Eaglesham G76 ... 179 E2
  Stirling FK7 ... 7 E3
Millheugh ML9 ... 184 C1
Millheugh Brae ML9 ... 184 C1
Millheugh Pl G72 ... 161 E3
Millheugh Rd ML3 ... 198 C3
Millhill Ave KA3 ... 222 B4
Millhill Terr KA1 ... 222 C2
Millholm Rd G44 ... 137 D2
Millhouse Cres G20 ... 96 B4
Millhouse Dr G20 ... 96 B4
Millichen Rd G23 ... 76 C3
Millig St G84 ... 16 B2
Milliken Dr PA10 ... 111 E1
Milliken Park Rd PA10 ... 111 E1
Milliken Pk Sta PA5 ... 131 E4
Milliken Rd PA10 ... 111 E1
Millport Ave G44 ... 137 E4
Millport Rd PA14 ... 68 C3
Millroad Dr G40 ... 241 F1
Millroad Gdns **2** G40 ... 117 F3
Millroad St G40 ... 241 F1
Millrock Ct KA10 ... 229 E2
Millstream Cres ML6 ... 105 D2
Millstream Ct PA1 ... 113 F2
Millview G78 ... 134 B2
Millview Mdws G78 ... 154 B4
Millview Pl G53 ... 135 D2
Millview Terr G78 ... 154 B4
Millwood St ML1 ... 136 C4
Milnbank St G31 ... 118 A4
Milncroft Pl G33 ... 99 D1
Milncroft Prim Sch G33 ... 119 E4
Milncroft Rd G33 ... 99 D1
Milndavie Cres G63 ... 31 E2
Milndavie Rd G63 ... 31 E1
Milnepark Rd FK7 ... 11 F4
Milner La G13 ... 95 F3
Milner Rd G13 ... 95 F3
Milngavie Prim Sch G62 ... 55 D1
Milngavie Rd Bearsden G61 ... 76 A3
  Strathblane G63 ... 31 F3
Milngavie Sta G62 ... 55 D1
Milnpark Gdns **4** G41 ... 116 C3
Milnpark St G41 ... 116 C3
Milnwood Dr Bellshill ML4 ... 142 B2
  Motherwell ML1 ... 142 C1
Milovaig Ave G23 ... 76 B1
Milovaig St G23 ... 76 B1
Milrig Rd G73 ... 138 A4
Milroy Gdns ML4 ... 142 A4
Milton Ave Cambuslang G72 ... 138 C3
Milton Brae Milton G82 ... 50 C1
  Stirling FK7 ... 7 D1
Milton Cl FK6 ... 21 E2
Milton Cres
  Bannockburn FK7 ... 7 E1
  Carluke ML8 ... 187 F1
  Irvine KA11 ... 220 B1
  Troon KA10 ... 229 F3
Milton Ct Irvine KA11 ... 220 B1
  Milton G82 ... 50 C1
Milton Douglas Rd G81 ... 74 A3
Milton Dr
  7 Bishopbriggs G64 ... 97 F4
  Kilmarnock KA3 ... 223 E1
Milton Est G83 ... 27 F3
Milton Gdns
  Bannockburn FK7 ... 7 D1
  Uddingston G71 ... 140 C4

Milton Gr FK7 ... 7 E1
Milton Hill G82 ... 50 C1
Milton Mains Rd G81 ... 74 A3
Milton Pk Ayr KA7 ... 239 D2
Milton Pl KA9 ... 233 E1
Milton Pl FK6 ... 21 E2
Milton Prim Sch G82 ... 50 C1
Milton Quadrant KA25 ... 149 D2
Milton Rd Bannockburn FK7 ... 7 E1
  Bishopbriggs G64 ... 201 E4
  East Kilbride G74 ... 159 D1
  Irvine KA11 ... 220 B1
  Kilbirnie KA25 ... 149 D2
  Kilmarnock KA3 ... 223 F1
  Kirkintilloch G66 ... 58 B3
  Lennoxtown G65 ... 57 F4
  Port Glasgow PA14 ... 68 C3
Milton Row FK6 ... 21 F2
Milton Sec Sch G72 ... 97 F4
Milton St Airdrie ML6 ... 123 D4
  Carluke ML8 ... 187 F1
  Glasgow G4 ... 241 D4
  Glasgow G4 ... 97 E2
  Hamilton ML3 ... 162 A2
  Motherwell ML1 ... 163 F4
Milton Terr
  Bannockburn FK7 ... 7 D1
  Hamilton ML3 ... 162 A3
Milton View KA2 ... 226 C3
Miltonbank Prim Sch G22 ... 97 E4
Milverton Ave G61 ... 75 E4
Milverton Rd G46 ... 136 A1
Mimosa Rd PA11 ... 110 B4
Minard Rd Glasgow G41 ... 116 C1
  Port Glasgow PA14 ... 68 C4
  Shotts ML7 ... 146 B3
Minard Way G71 ... 141 D4
Minch Way ML6 ... 123 E3
Mincher Cres ML1 ... 163 F2
Mine Rd FK9 ... 2 A4
Minella Gdns ML4 ... 142 A4
Minerva La PA4 ... 94 A1
Minerva St G3 ... 116 C4
Minerva Terr PA4 ... 94 B2
Minerva Way G3 ... 116 C4
Mingarry La G20 ... 96 C2
Mingarry St G20 ... 96 C2
Mingulay Cres G22 ... 97 E4
Mingulay Pl G22 ... 97 F4
Mingulay St G22 ... 97 E4
Ministers Pk G53 ... 158 C2
Minmoir Rd G53 ... 134 C4
Minster Wlk G69 ... 120 C3
Minstrel Rd G13 ... 75 E1
Minthill Pl ML7 ... 127 C3
Minto Ave G73 ... 138 B2
Minto Cres G52 ... 115 F3
Minto Ct FK12 ... 5 D3
Minto Gdns FK12 ... 5 D3
Minto Pk ML2 ... 165 E3
Minto St Glasgow G52 ... 115 F3
  Greenock PA16 ... 45 E2
Mireton St **6** G22 ... 97 D3
Mirren Dr G81 ... 73 F4
Mirren's Shore PA14 ... 47 E1
Mirrlees Dr G12 ... 96 B2
Mirrlees La G12 ... 96 B2
Misk Knowes KA20 ... 217 F3
Mission La **1** FK1 ... 42 A2
Mitchell Ave
  Cambuslang G72 ... 139 F3
  Renfrew PA4 ... 94 A1
Mitchell Cres FK10 ... 9 F4
Mitchell Ct
  East Kilbride G74 ... 159 E1
  Kilmarnock KA1 ... 228 A4
Mitchell Dr Cardross G82 ... 48 A3
  Milngavie G62 ... 55 E1
  Rutherglen G73 ... 138 A3
Mitchell Gr G74 ... 159 E1
Mitchell Hill Rd G45 ... 137 F1
Mitchell La G1 ... 240 C2
Mitchell Pl Falkirk FK1 ... 41 F1
  Saltcoats KA21 ... 205 E1
Mitchell Rd G67 ... 62 A2
Mitchell St Airdrie ML6 ... 122 C4
  Beith KA15 ... 150 B1
  Coatbridge ML5 ... 121 E3
  Glasgow G1 ... 240 C2
  Greenock PA15 ... 46 C1
Mitchell Way G83 ... 27 F3
Mitchison Rd G67 ... 62 A2
Mitre Ct **2** G11 ... 95 F2
Mitre La G14 ... 95 F3
Mitre La W G14 ... 95 F3
Mitre Rd G14, G11 ... 95 F2
Moat Ave G13 ... 95 E4
Mochrum Ct KA9 ... 236 B3
Mochrum Rd G43 ... 136 C3
Modan Rd FK7 ... 7 D2
Moffat Ave FK2 ... 24 B2
Moffat Ct G75 ... 179 F4
Moffat Gdns G75 ... 179 F4
Moffat Pl Blantyre G72 ... 140 B1
  East Kilbride G75 ... 179 F4
Moffat Rd Airdrie ML6 ... 123 F4
  Prestwick KA9 ... 233 E2
Moffat St Glasgow G5 ... 117 E2
  Greenock PA15 ... 45 F3
Moffat View ML6 ... 104 A2
Moffathill ML6 ... 123 F3
Mogarth Ave PA2 ... 132 C4
Moidart Ave PA4 ... 94 A2
Moidart Cres G52 ... 115 F3
Moidart Ct G78 ... 134 A2

Moidart Pl G52 ... 115 F3
Moidart Rd Glasgow G52 ... 115 F3
  Port Glasgow PA14 ... 68 C4
Moir St Alloa FK10 ... 10 A1
  Glasgow G1 ... 241 E1
Molendinar St G1 ... 241 E1
Molendinar Terr G78 ... 154 B3
Mollanbowie Rd G83 ... 19 F1
Mollins Ct G68 ... 81 E3
Mollins Rd G68 ... 81 E3
Mollinsburn Rd
  Annathill G67, ML5 ... 81 F1
  Glenmavis ML6 ... 102 B3
Mollinsburn St G21 ... 97 F2
Mollison Ave ML7 ... 127 F3
Monach Gdns KA11 ... 225 D4
Monach Rd Glasgow G33 ... 119 E4
  Port Glasgow PA14 ... 69 D4
Monaeboork Pl G84 ... 25 C4
Monar Dr G22 ... 97 D2
Monar Pl G22 ... 97 D2
Monar St G22 ... 97 D2
Monar Way **5** ML2 ... 165 F3
Monart Pl G20 ... 96 C2
Moncks Rd FK1 ... 42 B2
Moncrieff Gdns G66 ... 79 E3
Moncrieff Ave G66 ... 79 E3
Moncrieff St PA3 ... 113 F3
Moncrieffe Rd ML6 ... 123 E2
Moncur Ct KA13 ... 207 E3
Moncur Rd KA13 ... 208 A2
Moncur St G40 ... 241 F1
Moness Dr G52 ... 115 F2
Money Gr ML1 ... 164 A2
Moniebrugh Cres G65 ... 36 C1
Moniebrugh Rd G65 ... 36 C1
Monifieth Ave G52 ... 115 E2
Monikie Gdns G64 ... 78 B1
Monkcastle Dr G72 ... 139 D3
Monkland Ave G66 ... 79 E3
Monkland La G66 ... 79 F3
Monkland St ML6 ... 123 D4
Monkland Terr ML5 ... 101 E3
Monkland View
  Calderbank ML6 ... 123 D1
  Uddingston G71 ... 121 D1
Monkland View Cres
  G69 ... 121 D3
Monklands KA10 ... 229 F4
Monklands District
  General Hospl ML6 ... 122 B4
Monkreddan Cres KA13 ... 207 E3
Monks La ML8 ... 201 F2
Monks Rd ML6 ... 123 E2
Monksbridge Ave G13 ... 75 E1
Monkscourt Ave ML6 ... 122 C4
Monkscroft Ave **7** G11 ... 96 A2
Monkscroft Ct G11 ... 96 A1
Monkscroft Gdns G11 ... 96 A1
Monkton Ct KA9 ... 233 E1
Monkton Dr G15 ... 75 E1
Monkton Gdns G77 ... 157 D2
Monkton Pl PA14 ... 68 C4
Monkton Prim Sch KA9 ... 233 E2
Monkton Rd KA9 ... 233 E1
Monktonhill Rd KA9 ... 233 D4
Monkwood Pl KA7 ... 239 D1
Monmouth Ave G12 ... 96 A3
Monreith Ave G61 ... 75 E1
Monreith Rd G43 ... 136 C3
Monreith Rd E G44 ... 137 D3
Monroe Dr G71 ... 120 C1
Monroe Pl G71 ... 120 C1
Montague La G12 ... 96 A2
Montague St G4 ... 96 C1
Montalto Ave ML1 ... 143 D1
Montclair Pl PA3 ... 112 A3
Montego Gn **8** G75 ... 159 D1
Monteith Dr G76 ... 158 A4
Monteith Gdns G76 ... 157 F4
Monteith Pl Blantyre G72 ... 161 F4
  Glasgow G40 ... 117 F3
  10 Glasgow G40 ... 117 F3
Monteith Row G40 ... 117 F3
Monteith Wlk ML7 ... 146 C3
Montfode Ct KA22 ... 205 E2
Montfode Dr KA22 ... 205 D2
Montford Ave G44 ... 137 F4
Montfort Pl FK1 ... 42 A2
Montgomerie Cres KA11 ... 216 C4
Montgomerie Pier Rd
  KA22 ... 205 D1
Montgomerie Rd
  Prestwick KA9 ... 233 D1
  Saltcoats KA21 ... 216 C4
Montgomerie St
  Ardrossan KA22 ... 205 E1
  Port Glasgow PA14 ... 47 E1
Montgomerie Terr
  Ayr KA7 ... 235 F1
  Kilwinning KA13 ... 208 A2
Montgomerieston Pl
  KA25 ... 149 D1
Montgomerieston St
  KA25 ... 149 D1
Montgomery Ave
  Beith KA15 ... 171 E4
  Coatbridge ML5 ... 121 F4
  Paisley PA3 ... 114 A4
Montgomery Cres
  Falkirk FK2 ... 24 A1
  Wishaw ML2 ... 185 F4
Montgomery Ct
  Eaglesham G76 ... 178 C2
  Kilbirnie KA25 ... 149 D1
Montgomery Dr
  Falkirk FK2 ... 24 A1
  Glasgow G46 ... 136 B1
  Kilbarchan PA10 ... 111 D2

Montgomery Pl
15 East Kilbride G74 159 F1
Kilmarnock KA3 222 C1
Larkhall ML9 185 D1
Montgomery Rd PA3 114 A4
Montgomery Sq G76 178 C2
Montgomery St
Cambuslang G72 139 F3
Eaglesham G76 178 C2
East Kilbride G74 159 F1
Falkirk FK2 42 C3
Glasgow G40 118 A2
Irvine KA12 219 D1
Kilmarnock KA3 222 C1
Larkhall ML9 185 D2
Montgomery Terr G65 58 B3
Montgomery Way FK9 2 A2
Montgomery Well FK2 24 A1
Montgomeryfield KA11 225 D4
Montgreenan View KA13 207 F2
Montraive St G73 118 B1
Montrave St G52 115 E2
Montreal Pk G75 159 E1
Montrose Ave
Glasgow G32 119 E1
Paisley G52 114 C4
Port Glasgow PA14 68 C3
Montrose Cres ML3 162 B2
Montrose Dr G61 75 F4
Montrose Gdns
Blantyre G72 140 B1
Kilsyth G65 36 B1
Milngavie G62 55 D2
Montrose Pl PA3 112 A3
Montrose Rd Paisley PA2 132 C4
Stirling FK9 2 B2
Montrose St Clydebank G81 74 B1
Glasgow G1 241 E2
Motherwell ML1 142 B1
Montrose Terr
Bishopbriggs G64 98 B4
Bridge Of W PA11 110 B4
Montrose Way FK4 39 E3
Monument Cres KA9 233 F1
Monument Rd KA7 238 C2
Monymusk Gdns G64 78 B1
Monymusk Pl G15 74 C3
Moodie Ct KA1 227 F3
Moodiesburn St G33 98 C1
Moor Park Cres KA9 236 B3
Moor Park Pl KA9 236 B3
Moor Pk KA9 236 B3
Moor Pl KA8 236 B2
Moor Rd Ayr KA8 236 B3
Cartland ML11 202 C1
Eaglesham G76 178 B2
Milngavie G62 55 D1
Strathblane G63 31 E1
Moorburn Ave G46 136 A2
Moorburn Pl PA3 111 F3
Moorcroft Dr ML6 123 F4
Moorcroft Rd G77 156 B2
Moore Dr Bearsden G61 75 F2
Helensburgh G84 25 D4
Moore Gdns ML3 183 F4
Moore St Glasgow G31 117 F3
Motherwell ML1 143 D2
Moorfield Ave
Kilmarnock KA1 227 E3
Port Glasgow PA14 68 B4
Moorfield Cres ML6 123 F4
Moorfield Ind Est KA2 227 D4
Moorfield La PA19 44 B3
Moorfield Pl KA2 226 B3
Moorfield Rd Blantyre G72 161 E3
Gourock PA19 44 B4
Prestwick KA9 236 B4
Moorfield Rdbt KA1 227 D4
Moorfoot G64 78 B1
Moorfoot Ave
Glasgow G46 136 A2
Paisley PA2 113 E1
Moorfoot Dr Gourock PA19 44 B3
Wishaw ML2 164 C2
Moorfoot Gdns G75 180 A2
Moorfoot Path PA2 133 E4
Moorfoot Pl KA11 220 A2
Moorfoot Prim Sch PA19 44 B3
Moorfoot St G32 118 C3
Moorfoot Way
Bearsden G61 75 E4
Irvine KA11 220 A2
Moorhill Cres G77 156 B2
Moorhill Rd G77 156 B2
Moorhouse Ave
Glasgow G13 94 C3
Paisley PA2 113 D1
Moorhouse St G78 134 B1
Moorland Dr ML6 123 F4
Moorpark Ave Airdrie ML6 123 F4
Muirhead G69 100 B4
Moorpark Dr G52 115 D3
Moorpark Ind Est KA20 217 E4
Moorpark Pl KA20 217 E4
Moorpark Prim Sch
Kilbirnie KA25 149 D2
Renfrew PA4 94 A1
Moorpark Rd E KA20 217 E4
Moorpark Rd W KA20 217 E4
Moorpark Sq PA4 94 A1
Moorside St ML8 188 A1
Morag Ave G72 140 B1
Moraine Ave G15 75 D1
Moraine Cir G15 75 D1
Moraine Dr Clarkston G76 157 E4
Glasgow G15 75 D1
Moraine Pl G15 75 D1
Morar Ave G81 74 A2
Morar Cres Airdrie ML6 102 C1
Bishopbriggs G64 77 F1
Bishopton PA7 72 B1
Clydebank G81 74 A2
Coatbridge ML5 101 E1
Morar Ct Clydebank G81 74 A2
Cumbernauld G67 82 A4
Hamilton ML3 162 A1
Morar Dr Bearsden G61 76 A2
Clydebank G81 74 A2
Cumbernauld G67 82 A4
Falkirk FK2 24 B1
Linwood PA3 112 A3
Paisley PA2 113 D1
Rutherglen G73 138 A2
Morar Pl East Kilbride G74 159 F2
Irvine KA12 219 E3
Newton Mearns G77 156 B4
Renfrew PA4 94 A2
Morar Rd Clydebank G81 74 A2
Glasgow G52 115 F3
Port Glasgow PA14 68 C4
Morar St ML2 165 D1
Morar Terr Rutherglen G73 138 B2
Uddingston G71 141 D4
Morar Way Motherwell ML1 143 E2
Shotts ML7 147 D2
Moravia Ave G71 141 D2
Moray Ave ML6 123 D3
Moray Dr Clarkston G76 157 F4
Torrance G64 57 D1
Moray Gate G71 140 C2
Moray Gdns Clarkston G76 157 F4
Cumbernauld G68 61 F3
Uddingston G71 140 C4
Moray Pl Bishopbriggs G64 78 B1
Blantyre G72 161 E3
Chryston G69 100 B4
Glasgow G41 116 C1
Kirkintilloch G66 59 D1
Linwood PA3 112 A3
Moray Quadrant ML4 142 A3
Moray Rd PA14 47 E1
Moray Way ML1 143 D3
Mordaunt St G40 118 A2
Moredun Cres G32 119 E4
Moredun Rd PA2 113 D1
Moredun St G32 119 E4
Morefield Rd G51 115 E4
Morgan Ct FK7 7 E2
Morgan Mews 17 G42 117 D2
Morgan St Hamilton ML3 162 B1
Larkhall ML9 184 C2
Morina Gdns G53 135 E2
Morion Rd G13 95 E4
Moriston Ct ML2 165 F3
Morland G74 160 B2
Morley Cres FK7 7 D2
Morley St G42 137 D4
Morna La G14 95 F1
Mornay Way ML7 146 B3
Morningside Prim Sch
ML2 166 A2
Morningside Rd ML2 166 B2
Morningside St G33 118 C4
Morrin Path G21 97 F2
Morrin St G21 97 F2
Morris Cres Blantyre G72 161 E4
Hurlford KA1 228 C3
Motherwell ML1 143 F1
Morris La KA3 223 D1
Morris Moodie Ave KA20 217 F4
Morris Rd KA9 233 E1
Morris St Greenock PA15 46 B2
Hamilton ML3 162 B1
Larkhall ML9 185 E1
Morris Terr FK8 7 D4
Morrishall Rd G74 160 B2
Morrishill Dr KA15 171 D4
Morrison Ave
Bonnybridge FK4 39 F3
Stevenston KA20 206 C1
Morrison Ct KA20 206 C1
Morrison Dr
Bannockburn FK7 7 E1
Lennoxtown G65 57 F4
Morrison Gdns Ayr KA8 239 D4
Torrance G64 78 B4
Morrison Pl KA3 223 E1
Morrison Quadrant G81 74 C1
Morrison Rd KA9 233 E2
Morrison St Clydebank G81 73 F3
Glasgow G5 240 B1
Morriston Cres PA4 94 C1
Morriston Park Dr G72 139 D3
Morriston St G72 139 D3
Morten Gdns G41 116 B1
Morton Ave KA7 239 D3
Morton Pl KA1 222 C1
Morton Rd Ayr KA7 239 D3
Stewarton KA3 211 E4
Morton St ML1 163 F4
Morven Ave
Bishopbriggs G64 78 B1
Blantyre G72 140 B1
Kilmarnock KA3 222 C2
Paisley PA2 133 E4
Morven Cres KA10 229 E1
Morven Ct Airdrie ML6 103 D1
Falkirk FK1 42 B1
Morven Dr Clarkston G76 157 E4
Linwood PA3 112 A3
Troon KA10 229 E2
Morven Gait PA8 93 F4
Morven Gdns G71 140 C4
Morven La G72 140 B1
Morven Rd Bearsden G61 75 F3
Cambuslang G72 138 C2
Morven St Coatbridge ML5 122 A4
Glasgow G52 115 F3
Morven Way 3 G71 141 D2
Morville Cres KA13 207 F3
Mosesfield St G21 97 F3
Moss Ave Caldercruix ML6 105 D3
Linwood PA3 112 A3
Moss Dr Barrhead G78 134 A3
Erskine PA8 93 D4
Irvine KA11 224 C3
Moss Heights Ave G52 115 E3
Moss Knowe G67 62 B1
Moss Path G69 119 F2
Moss Rd Airdrie ML6 123 D3
Bridge Of W PA11 110 C4
Cumbernauld G67 62 C2
East Kilbride G75 180 B2
Fallin FK7 8 B2
Glasgow G51 115 E4
Helensburgh G82 25 E2
Kilmacolm PA13 89 E4
Kirkintilloch G66 80 A4
Kirkintilloch, High Gallowhill
G66 79 D3
Linwood PA3 112 B4
Muirhead G69 100 B4
Port Glasgow PA14 68 C4
Wishaw ML2 165 F2
Moss Side Ave ML6 122 C4
Moss St PA1 113 F3
Moss-Side Ave ML8 187 E1
Moss-Side Rd G41 116 C1
Mossacre Rd ML2 165 E2
Mossband La ML7 146 C3
Mossbank Blantyre G72 161 E3
East Kilbride G75 179 F4
Prestwick KA9 236 C4
Mossbank Ave G33 98 C2
Mossbank Cres ML1 143 F2
Mossbank Dr G33 98 C2
Mossbank Rd ML2 165 E2
Mossbell Rd ML4 141 F3
Mossblown St ML9 184 C2
Mossburn Ave Balloch G83 19 F1
Harthill ML7 127 E3
Mossburn Rd ML2 165 E2
Mossburn St ML2 165 E1
Mosscastle Rd Glasgow G33 99 E1
Slamannan FK1 86 A4
Mossdale G74 159 E2
Mossdale Ct ML4 142 B3
Mossdale Gdns ML3 161 F1
Mossend Ave
Helensburgh G84 16 C1
Kilbirnie KA25 170 A4
Mossend La G33 119 E4
Mossend Pl G84 16 C1
Mossend St G33 119 E4
Mossgiel G75 180 A4
Mossgiel Ave Cowie FK7 12 B4
Kilmarnock KA3 228 B4
Rutherglen G73 138 A3
Stirling FK8 2 A1
Troon KA10 229 F2
Mossgiel Cres G76 157 F3
Mossgiel Dr Clydebank G81 74 B2
Irvine KA12 219 E2
Mossgiel Gdns
Kirkintilloch G66 58 C1
Uddingston G71 140 C4
Mossgiel La 7 ML9 185 E1
Mossgiel Pl Ayr KA7 239 D3
Rutherglen G73 138 A3
Stevenston KA20 206 C1
Mossgiel Rd
Ardrossan KA22 205 E2
Ayr KA7 239 D3
Cumbernauld G67 62 A1
Glasgow G43 136 B3
Glasgow G43 136 B4
Saltcoats KA21 206 A2
Mossgiel St FK1 41 D3
Mossgiel Terr G72 140 B1
Mossgiel Way ML1 143 E2
Mosshall Gr ML1 143 F2
Mosshall Rd ML1 143 E4
Mosshall St ML1 143 F2
Mosshead Prim Sch G61 75 F4
Mosshead Rd
Bearsden G61 76 A4
Kilmarnock KA1 228 A2
Mosshill Rd ML4 142 A4
Mosshouse FK7 6 C2
Mosside Pl KA3 222 C2
Mosside Rd KA8 236 B2
Mossland Dr ML2 165 E2
Mossland Rd G52 114 C4
Mosslands Rd PA1 113 F4
Mosslingal G75 180 C3
Mossmulloch G75 180 C3
Mossneuk Ave G75 179 F4
Mossneuk Cres ML2 165 E2
Mossneuk Dr
East Kilbride G75 179 F4
Paisley PA2 133 E4
Wishaw ML2 165 E2
Mossneuk Pk ML2 165 E2
Mossneuk Prim Sch G75 179 F4
Mossneuk Rd G75 180 A4
Mossneuk St ML5 121 F2
Mosspark Ave
Glasgow G52 115 F2
Milngavie G62 55 D2
Mosspark Bvd G52 115 F2
Mosspark Dr G52 115 F2
Mosspark La G52 115 F2
Mosspark Oval G52 115 F2
Mosspark Prim Sch G52 115 F2
Mosspark Rd
Coatbridge ML5 121 E4
Milngavie G62 55 D2
Mosspark Sq G52 115 F2
Mosspark Sta G52 115 E2
Mossvale Cres G33 99 E1
Mossvale La PA3 113 E3
Mossvale Path G33 99 E2
Mossvale Rd G33 99 E1
Mossvale Sq Glasgow G33 99 D1
Paisley PA3 113 E3
Mossvale St PA3 113 E4
Mossvale Terr G69 81 D2
Mossvale Way G33 99 E1
Mossvale Wlk G33 99 E1
Mossview Cres ML6 123 D3
Mossview La G52 115 E3
Mossview Quadrant G52 115 E3
Mossview Rd G33 99 F3
Mosswell Rd G62 55 D2
Mossyde Ave PA14 69 D4
Mossywood Ct G68 81 F4
Mossywood Pl G68 81 F4
Mossywood Rd G68 81 F4
Mote Hill ML3 162 C3
Mote View KA2 221 E1
Motehill Rd PA3 114 A4
Motherwell Coll ML1 163 F2
Motherwell Heritage Ctr
ML1 163 E4
Motherwell Rd
Bellshill ML4 142 A2
Hamilton ML3 163 D2
Motherwell ML1 144 A3
Motherwell, Carfin ML1 143 E1
Motherwell St ML6 123 E4
Motherwell Sta ML1 163 E4
Moulin Cir G52 115 D2
Moulin Pl G52 115 D2
Moulin Rd G52 115 D2
Moulin Terr G52 115 D2
Mount Annan Dr G44 137 D4
Mount Ave Kilmarnock KA1 227 E3
Symington KA1 231 E2
Mount Cameron Dr N
G74 181 D4
Mount Cameron Dr S
G74 181 D4
Mount Cameron Prim Sch
G74 181 D4
Mount Carmel Prim Sch
KA3 222 C3
Mount Charles Cres KA7 238 B1
Mount Florida Prim Sch
G42 137 D4
Mount Florida Sta G42 137 D4
Mount Harriet Ave G33 99 F3
Mount Harriet Dr G33 99 F3
Mount Hope FK9 2 B4
Mount Oliphant FK7 12 B4
Mount Oliphant Cres KA7 239 D3
Mount Oliphant Pl KA7 239 D3
Mount Pl KA1 227 E3
Mount Pleasant Cres G65 58 A3
Mount Pleasant Dr G60 73 D3
Mount Pleasant St PA15 45 F2
Mount St G20 96 C2
Mount Stewart St ML8 187 F1
Mount Stuart St G41 136 C4
Mount The KA7 239 D2
Mount Vernon Ave
Coatbridge ML5 121 F4
Glasgow G32 119 F2
Mount Vernon Prim Sch
G32 119 E2
Mount Vernon Sta G32 119 F1
Mount View KA11 220 B1
Mount Village KA1 227 E4
Mount William FK10 5 F1
Mountainblue St G31 118 A3
Mountblow Rd G81 73 E3
Mountblow Sch G81 73 F3
Mountgarrie Rd G51 115 E4
Mountherrick G75 180 C3
Mournian Way ML3 162 B1
Mousebank La ML11 214 C2
Mousebank Rd ML11 214 C3
Mousemill Rd ML11 214 B3
Mowbray G74 160 B2
Mowbray Ave G69 100 C3
Mowbray Ct FK7 7 E2
Moy Path 4 ML2 165 F3
Moyne Rd G53 115 D1
Muckcroft Rd G69 80 B2
Mudale Ct FK1 42 B1
Mugdock Ctry Pk G62 55 D3
Mugdock Rd G62 55 D2
Muir Cl KA3 195 E1
Muir Cres G83 27 E4
Muir Dr Irvine KA12 219 E2
Stevenston KA20 217 E4
Troon KA10 229 E3
Muir Drive Cotts KA20 217 E4
Muir Rd G82 50 B3
Muir St Alexandria G83 27 E4
Bishopbriggs G64 78 A1
Blantyre G72 161 E3
Coatbridge ML5 121 F4
Hamilton ML3 162 C2
Larkhall ML9 185 D2
Law ML8 186 C3
Motherwell ML1 163 E4
Renfrew PA4 94 B2
Stenhousemuir FK5 23 E1
Muir Street Prim Sch
ML1 163 E4
Muir Terr PA3 114 A4
Muiralehouse Rd FK7 11 F4
Muirbank Ave G73 137 F4
Muirbank Gdns G73 137 F4
Muirbrae Rd G73 138 A2
Muirbrae Way G73 138 A2
Muirburn Ave G44 136 C2
Muirburn Rd Beith KA15 150 A2
Stonehouse ML10 198 A1
Muircroft Dr ML1 144 A1
Muirdrum Ave G52 115 E2
Muirdyke Ave FK2 24 B2
Muirdyke Rd
Coatbridge ML6 102 A3
Coatbridge, Drumpellier ML5 121 E4
Muirdykes Ave
Glasgow G52 115 D3
Port Glasgow PA14 68 B4
Muirdykes Cres PA3 113 D3
Muirdykes Rd
Glasgow G52 115 D3
Paisley PA3 113 D3
Muiredge Ct G71 140 C3
Muiredge & Jersy Rd
Cleland ML1 145 D1
Shotts ML7, ML1 145 E4
Muiredge Prim Sch G71 141 D3
Muiredge Terr G69 120 A2
Muirend Ave G44 136 C3
Muirend Rd Cardross G82 48 A4
Glasgow G44 136 C2
Kilmarnock KA3 222 C3
Stirling FK7 7 D3
Muirend St KA25 149 D1
Muirend Sta G44 136 C2
Muirfield Cres G23 76 C1
Muirfield Ct Glasgow G44 136 C2
Irvine KA12 224 C4
Muirfield Mdws G72 140 C1
Muirfield Pl KA13 207 E2
Muirfield Rd
Cumbernauld G68 62 A3
Stenhousemuir FK5 23 F1
Muirhall Pl FK5 23 E2
Muirhall Rd FK5 23 E2
Muirhall Terr ML7 125 D1
Muirhead Ave FK2 42 A4
Muirhead Cotts G66 80 A4
Muirhead Dr Linwood PA3 112 A3
Motherwell ML1 143 F2
Muirhead Gate 4 G71 141 D4
Muirhead Gdns
Glasgow G69 120 B2
Salsburgh ML7 125 D1
Muirhead Pl ML7 127 E2
Muirhead Prim Sch KA10 229 F2
Muirhead Rd Glasgow G69 120 A2
Stenhousemuir FK5 23 F2
Muirhead St
Kirkintilloch G66 79 E4
Lochwinnoch PA12 129 E1
Muirhead Terr ML1 163 F2
Muirhead Way G64 78 B1
Muirhead-Braehead Rdbt
G67 62 A2
Muirhill Ave G44 136 C3
Muirhill Cres G13 95 D4
Muirhouse Ave
Motherwell ML1 164 A2
Wishaw ML2 166 A3
Muirhouse Dr ML1 164 B1
Muirhouse La 7 G75 180 C4
Muirhouse Pk G61 75 E4
Muirhouse Prim Sch ML1 164 A1
Muirhouse Rd ML1 164 A1
Muirhouse St 12 G41 117 D2
Muirkirk Dr Glasgow G13 95 F4
Hamilton ML3 161 E1
Muirlee Rd ML8 188 A1
Muirlees Cres G62 54 C1
Muirmadkin Rd ML4 142 A3
Muirmaillen Ave ML1 144 B1
Muirpark Ave PA4 94 B1
Muirpark Dr
Bishopbriggs G64 98 A4
Shieldhill FK1 66 B3
Muirpark Gdns FK10 4 C2
Muirpark Rd KA15 150 A1
Muirpark St G11 96 A1
Muirshiel Ave G53 135 E3
Muirshiel Cres G53 135 E3
Muirshiel Ctry Pk PA12 108 A2
Muirshiel La PA14 68 B4
Muirshiel Rd PA14 68 B4
Muirshot Rd ML9 185 D2
Muirside Ave Glasgow G32 119 F2
Kirkintilloch G66 80 A4
Muirside Ct KA13 207 E1
Muirside Pl
Kilwinning KA13 207 E1
21 Wishaw ML2 165 F3
Muirside Rd Glasgow G69 120 A2
Kilwinning KA13 207 E1
Tullibody FK10 4 B2
Muirside St G69 120 A2
Muirskeith Cres G44 137 D3
Muirskeith Pl G43 136 C3
Muirskeith Rd G43 136 C3
Muirton Dr G64 77 F2
Muirton Rd FK7 7 F3
Muirton Rdbt FK7 7 F4
Muiryfauld Dr G31 118 C3
Muiryhall St ML5 122 A4
Muiryhall St E ML5 122 B4
Mulben Cres G53 134 C4
Mulben Pl G53 134 C4
Mulben Terr G53 134 C4

Mulberry Dr G75 .... 180 B3
Mulberry Rd Glasgow G43 ... 136 B3
Uddingston G71 .... 121 E1
Mulberry Way G75 .... 180 B3
Mulberry Wynd G72 .... 139 F2
Muldron Terr ML7 .... 147 D1
Mulgrew Ave KA21 .... 206 A1
Mull Airdrie ML6 .... 123 E3
East Kilbride G74 .... 181 E4
Mull Ave Paisley PA2 .... 133 F4
Port Glasgow PA14 .... 69 D4
Renfrew PA4 .... 94 B1
Mull Cres KA11 .... 220 A1
Mull Ct Alloa FK10 .... 10 A3
Irvine KA11 .... 220 A1
Mull Pl KA11 .... 220 A1
Mull Quadrant ML2 .... 165 F3
Mull St G21 .... 98 A1
Mull Terr KA11 .... 220 A1
Mullardoch St G23 .... 76 B1
Mulvey Cres ML6 .... 122 C4
Mungalend FK2 .... 42 A4
Mungaland Ct FK2 .... 42 A4
Mungalhead Rd FK2 .... 42 A4
Mungo Pk G75 .... 180 B4
Mungo Pl G71 .... 121 D1
Munlochy Rd G51 .... 115 E4
Munnoch Cres KA22 .... 205 D3
Munro Ave Kilmarnock KA1 .. 222 B1
Stirling FK9 .... 2 A2
Munro Ct G81 .... 73 F3
Munro Dr Kilbirnie KA25 ..... 170 A4
Milton Of C G65 .... 58 A3
Munro Dr E G84 .... 16 C2
Munro Dr W G84 .... 16 B2
Munro Gdns FK2 .... 42 C2
Munro La G13 .... 95 F3
Munro La E G13 .... 95 F3
Munro Pl Alloa FK10 .... 9 F3
East Kilbride G74 .... 160 A2
Glasgow G13 .... 95 F3
Kilmarnock KA1 .... 222 C1
Saltcoats KA21 .... 206 A1
Munro Rd Glasgow G13 .... 95 F3
Stirling FK7 .... 7 D4
Munro St Alexandria G83 ...... 27 F3
Greenock PA16 .... 45 D2
Stenhousemuir FK5 .... 23 F2
Munro Wlk G32 .... 96 C2
Murano St G20 .... 96 C2
Murchie Dr KA9 .... 236 B3
Murchison Dr G75 .... 180 A4
Murchison Rd PA6 .... 91 E1
Murchland Ave KA3 .... 213 D2
Murchland Way KA12 .... 219 E2
Murdieston St PA15 .... 45 E2
Murdoch Cres KA20 .... 217 E4
Murdoch Ct KA21 .... 205 F2
Murdoch Dr G62 .... 76 B4
Murdoch Pl Irvine KA11 ..... 224 C3
Motherwell ML1 .... 142 C2
Murdoch Rd G75 .... 180 C4
Murdoch Sq ML4 .... 142 B4
Murdoch's Lone KA7 .... 238 C1
Murdostoun Cres ML7 .... 127 F3
Murdostoun Gdns ML2 ...... 165 D3
Murdostoun Terr ML1 .... 144 B3
Murdostoun View ML2 .... 165 F3
Mure Ave KA3 .... 223 D3
Mure Pl G78 .... 153 D2
Muriel Blue Ct PA19 .... 44 C4
Muriel La G78 .... 134 B2
Muriel St G78 .... 134 B2
Muriel Street Ind Est G78 .. 134 B2
Murnin Ct FK7 .... 7 E2
Murnin Rd FK4 .... 40 A2
Murnin Road Ind Est FK4 .... 40 A2
Murray Ave Kilsyth G65 .... 60 B4
Saltcoats KA21 .... 205 F1
Murray Ct ML3 .... 183 F4
Murray Dr ML9 .... 198 C1
Murray Gdns G65 .... 58 B3
Murray Gr G61 .... 75 D4
Murray Path G71 .... 140 C3
Murray Pl Ayr KA8 .... 236 B2
Barrhead G78 .... 134 B2
Bellshill ML4 .... 141 F4
Cambusbarron FK7 .... 6 B3
Dumbarton G82 .... 50 B2
Gourock PA19 .... 44 C3
Kilmarnock KA3 .... 223 E1
Stirling FK8 .... 7 D4
Murray Prim Sch G75 .... 180 C4
Murray Rd Bothwell G71 ... 141 D2
Law ML8 .... 186 C2
Murray Rd The G75 .... 180 C4
Murray Row The G75 .... 180 C4
Murray Sq The ID G75 .... 180 C4
Murray St Ayr KA8 .... 236 B1
Greenock PA16 .... 45 E3
Paisley PA3 .... 113 E3
Renfrew PA4 .... 94 B2
Murray Terr ML1 .... 163 D4
Murrayfield G64 .... 78 A2
Murrayfield Dr G61 .... 75 F1
Murrayfield Pl FK7 .... 7 E1
Murrayfield St G32 .... 118 C4
Murrayfield Terr FK7 .... 7 E1
Murrayhill G75 .... 180 B4
Murrayshall Rd FK7 .... 7 D2
Murrayside ML9 .... 198 B1
Murrin Ave G64 .... 78 B1
Murroch Ave G82 .... 50 B4
Murroch Cres G83 .... 28 A1
Murroes Rd G51 .... 115 E4

Mus of Education G5 .... 116 C3
Mus of Modern Art G5 .... 241 D2
Mus of Transport G3 .... 96 B1
Musgrove Pl G71 .... 180 B4
Muslin St G40 .... 117 F2
Muttonhole Rd ML3 .... 182 C4
Mybster Pl G51 .... 115 E4
Myers Cres G71 .... 141 D3
Mylne Pl FK2 .... 24 A1
Myothill Rd FK6 .... 39 E4
Myres Rd G53 .... 135 E4
Myreside Pl G32 .... 118 B3
Myreside St G32 .... 118 C3
Myreton FK11 .... 4 A3
Myreton Ave PA13 .... 89 E4
Myreton Dr FK7 .... 11 F4
Myreton Way FK1 .... 41 F2
Myretoungate FK12 .... 4 C3
Myrie Gdns G64 .... 78 A1
Myroch Pl G34 .... 100 B1
Myrtle Ave G66 .... 79 E3
Myrtle Bank KA15 .... 171 D4
Myrtle Dr Motherwell ML1 .. 143 D2
Wishaw ML2 .... 164 B2
Myrtle Hill La G42 .... 137 E4
Myrtle La ML9 .... 185 E1
Myrtle Pk G42 .... 137 E1
Myrtle Pl G42 .... 137 E4
Myrtle Rd Clydebank G81 ...... 73 E2
Uddingston G71 .... 141 D4
Myrtle Sq G64 .... 98 A4
Myrtle St G72 .... 140 B1
Myrtle View Rd G42 .... 137 E4
Myrtle Wlk G72 .... 138 C3
Myvot Ave G67 .... 82 A3
Myvot Rd G67 .... 82 A3

Nailer Rd Falkirk FK1 .... 41 F3
Stirling FK7 .... 7 D1
Nairn Ave Bellshill ML4 .... 142 A3
Blantyre G72 .... 140 B1
Nairn Ct KA3 .... 195 E1
Nairn Cres ML6 .... 123 D3
Nairn Ct Falkirk FK1 .... 42 B1
Kilwinning KA13 .... 207 D2
Nairn Dr PA16 .... 44 B3
Nairn Pl Clydebank G81 .... 73 F2
East Kilbride G74 .... 160 B2
Nairn Quadrant ML2 .... 165 D3
Nairn Rd PA16 .... 44 B2
Nairn St Blantyre G72 .... 161 E3
Clydebank G81 .... 73 F2
Glasgow G3 .... 96 B1
Larkhall ML9 .... 184 C1
Nairn Way G68 .... 62 A3
Nairnside Rd G21 .... 98 B4
Naismith Ct ML9 .... 198 C1
Naismith St G32 .... 139 E4
Naismith Wlk ML4 .... 142 B4
Nansen St G20 .... 97 D2
Napier Ave G82 .... 48 A4
Napier Cres
Dumbarton G82 .... 49 E2
Falkirk FK2 .... 42 A4
Napier Ct Cardross G82 .... 48 A4
Cumbernauld G68 .... 62 B4
Old Kilpatrick G60 .... 73 E3
Napier Dr G51 .... 116 A4
Napier Gdns PA3 .... 112 B3
Napier Hill G75 .... 180 C4
Napier La G75 .... 180 C4
Napier Pk G68 .... 62 B4
Napier Pl Cumbernauld G68 .. 62 B4
Falkirk FK2 .... 42 A4
Old Kilpatrick G60 .... 73 E3
Napier Rd Cumbernauld G68 .. 62 B4
Glasgow G51 .... 116 A4
Glasgow G52 .... 114 C4
Napier Sq ML4 .... 142 B4
Napier St Clydebank G81 ...... 94 B4
Glasgow G51 .... 116 A4
Johnstone PA5 .... 111 F2
Linwood PA3 .... 112 B3
Napier Terr G51 .... 116 A4
Napier Way G68 .... 62 B4
Napiershall La G20 .... 96 C1
Napiershall Pl ID G20 .... 96 C1
Napiershall St G20 .... 96 C1
Napierston Rd G83 .... 27 F3
Naproch Pl G77 .... 157 E3
Naseby Ave G11 .... 95 F2
Naseby La G11 .... 95 F2
Nasmyth Ave Bearsden G61 .. 75 D4
East Kilbride G75 .... 180 C4
Nasmyth Pl G75 .... 180 C4
Nasmyth Rd G52 .... 115 D4
Nasmyth Rd N G52 .... 115 D4
Nasmyth Rd S G52 .... 115 D4
Nassau Pl ID G75 .... 180 C4
Naver Ct ML7 .... 147 D2
Navar Pl PA2 .... 114 A1
Naver St G33 .... 98 C1
Navy Way G84 .... 15 D2
Naylor La ML6 .... 123 D4
Nasmyth Bank G75 .... 180 C4
Nebit The FK12 .... 4 C3
Needle Gn ML8 .... 187 F1
Neidpath G69 .... 120 A2
Neidpath Ave ML5 .... 122 A2
Neidpath Dr PA5 .... 21 F2
Neidpath Pl ML5 .... 122 A2
Neidpath Rd ML8 .... 187 F2
Neidpath Rd E G46 .... 157 D3
Neidpath Rd W G46 .... 157 D4
Neil Ave KA12 .... 219 E3
Neil St Greenock PA16 .... 45 D2
Renfrew PA4 .... 94 B3

Neilsland Dr Hamilton ML3 ... 183 E4
Motherwell ML1 .... 163 D3
Neilsland Oval G53 .... 115 E1
Neilsland Prim Sch ML3 ..... 162 A1
Neilsland Rd ML3 .... 183 E4
Neilsland Sq Glasgow G53 .. 135 E1
Hamilton ML3 .... 162 B1
Neilsland St ML3 .... 162 C1
Neilson St Bellshill ML4 ...... 142 A3
Falkirk FK1 .... 42 A2
Neilston Ave G53 .... 135 E3
Neilston High Sta G78 .... 154 B4
Neilston Pl G65 .... 36 A1
Neilston Prim Sch G78 ...... 154 C4
Neilston Rd Neilston G78 ... 154 C4
Paisley PA2 .... 113 F1
Uplawmoor G78 .... 153 D2
Neilvaig Dr G73 .... 138 B2
Neistpoint Dr G33 .... 119 D4
Nelson Ave ML5 .... 121 F2
Nelson Cres ML1 .... 164 A2
Nelson Mandela Pl G2 .... 241 D3
Nelson Pl Ayr KA8 .... 236 A1
Glasgow G69 .... 120 A2
Helensburgh G84 .... 17 D1
Stirling FK7 .... 7 E3
Nelson Rd Gourock PA19 .... 44 C2
Saltcoats KA21 .... 217 D4
Nelson St Glasgow G5 .... 117 D3
Glasgow, Baillieston G69 ... 120 A2
Greenock PA15 .... 45 F3
Kilmarnock KA1 .... 227 F4
Nelson Terr G74 .... 181 D4

Nemphlar Moor Rd
Crossford ML8, ML11 .... 201 E1
Nemphlar ML11 .... 214 A4
Nemphlar Rd ML11 .... 214 A3
Nemphlar Hill ML11 .... 214 C3
Neptune St G51 .... 116 A4
Neptune Way ML4 .... 142 C3
Nerston Rd G74 .... 159 F3
Ness Ave PA5 .... 131 E4
Ness Dr Blantyre G72 .... 140 C1
East Kilbride G74 .... 160 A1
Ness Gdns
Bishopbriggs G64 .... 78 A1
Larkhall ML9 .... 199 D4
Ness Pl KA10 .... 229 F3
Ness Rd Greenock PA16 .... 45 E3
Renfrew PA4 .... 94 A2
Ness St Glasgow G33 .... 98 C1
Wishaw ML2 .... 164 B3
Ness Terr ML3 .... 162 A1
Ness Way ML1 .... 143 D3
Nethan Ave ML2 .... 164 B1
Nethan Ct ML1 .... 162 B2
Nethan Glen ML8 .... 201 D1
Nethan Path ML9 .... 199 D4
Nethan Pl ML3 .... 183 E3
Nethan St Glasgow G51 ..... 116 A4
Motherwell ML1 .... 142 B3
Nethanfoot Brig Rd ML8 .... 201 D1

Nether Auldhouse Rd
G43 .... 136 B3
Nether Robertland
Prim Sch KA3 .... 195 F1
Netherbank Rd ML2 .... 164 B1
Netherblane G63 .... 31 D2
Netherbog Ave G82 .... 50 A2
Netherbog Rd G82 .... 50 A2
Netherburn Ave
Glasgow G44 .... 136 C1
Houston PA6 .... 91 E1
Netherburn Gdns PA6 .... 111 F4
Netherburn Prim Sch
ML9 .... 200 A2
Netherburn Rd ML9 .... 200 A4
Nethercairn Pl G77 .... 157 E3
Nethercairn Rd G43 .... 136 C1
Nethercliffe Ave G44 .... 136 C1
Nethercraigs Dr PA2 .... 133 E4
Nethercraigs Rd PA2 .... 133 D4
Nethercroy Rd G65 .... 60 C3
Netherdale G77 .... 157 D3
Netherdale Cres ML2 .... 164 B1
Netherdale Dr PA1 .... 114 C2
Netherdale Rd ML2 .... 164 C1
Netherfield St G31 .... 118 B3
Nethergate The FK12 .... 4 C3
Nethergreen Cres PA4 .... 94 A2
Nethergreen Wynd PA4 .... 94 A2
Netherhall Rd ML2 .... 164 B1
Netherhill Ave G44 .... 137 D1
Netherhill Cotts PA3 .... 114 A4
Netherhill Cres PA3 .... 114 A3
Netherhill Rd
Moodiesburn G69 .... 80 C1
Paisley PA3 .... 114 A4
Netherhill Way PA3 .... 114 A4
Netherhouse Ave
Coatbridge ML5 .... 121 F2
Kirkintilloch G66 .... 79 F2
Netherhouse Pl G34 .... 120 C4
Netherhouse Rd G69 .... 120 C4
Netherland Rd KA3 .... 211 F4
Netherlee Cres KA24 .... 169 D1
Netherlee Prim Sch G44 .... 136 C1
Netherlee Rd G44 .... 137 D1
Nethermains Prim Sch
FK6 .... 21 E1
Nethermains Rd Denny FK6 .. 21 E1
Kilwinning KA13 .... 207 F1
Milngavie G62 .... 76 A4
Nethermiln Rd KA23 .... 190 B2
Netherpark Ave G44 .... 137 D1

Netherplace Cres
Glasgow G53 .... 135 D4
Newton Mearns G77 .... 156 B2
Netherplace Rd
Glasgow G53 .... 135 D4
Newton Mearns G77 .... 156 A2
Netherton Ave FK4 .... 69 D4
Netherton Ct Glasgow G45 .. 137 E1
Newton Mearns G77 .... 157 D3
Netherton Dr G78 .... 134 C1
Netherton Hill G65 .... 57 D4
Netherton Ind Est ML2 ...... 164 C1
Netherton Oval G65 .... 33 D1
Netherton Prim Sch
Glasgow G45 .... 137 E1
Wishaw ML2 .... 164 C1
Netherton Rd
East Kilbride G75 .... 180 A2
East Kilbride, The Murray
G75 .... 180 B4
Glasgow G13 .... 95 F4
Newton Mearns G77 .... 156 C3
Wishaw ML2 .... 164 C1
Netherton St Glasgow G13 .. 95 F4
Harthill ML7 .... 127 E3
Wishaw ML2 .... 164 C1
Nethervale Ave G44 .... 137 D1
Netherview Rd G44 .... 137 D1
Netherway G44 .... 136 C1
Netherwood Ave G68 .... 81 F4
Netherwood Ct G68 .... 82 A4
Netherwood Gr G68 .... 82 A4
Netherwood Pl G68 .... 81 F4
Netherwood Rd
Cumbernauld G68 .... 81 F4
Motherwell ML1 .... 164 B2
Netherwood Way G68 .... 82 A4
Nethy Way PA4 .... 94 C1
Neucks The FK1 .... 87 D3
Neuk Ave Houston PA6 .... 91 E1
Muirhead G69 .... 100 B4
Neuk Cres PA6 .... 91 E1
Neuk The ML2 .... 164 C2
Neuk Way G32 .... 139 E4
Neukfoot La G78 .... 153 D2
Nevan Rd KA10 .... 229 F3
Neville G74 .... 160 B2
Nevis Ave ML3 .... 162 A1
Nevis Cres FK10 .... 10 A4
Nevis Ct G78 .... 134 B1
Nevis Dr G64 .... 57 D1
Nevis Pl Falkirk FK1 .... 42 B1
Kilmarnock KA1 .... 228 A2
Shotts ML7 .... 147 D2
Nevis Rd Bearsden G61 .... 75 D4
Glasgow G43 .... 136 A3
Renfrew PA4 .... 94 A1
Nevis Way Irvine KA11 .... 220 A2
Renfrew PA3 .... 93 F1
Nevison St Larkhall ML9 .... 185 D1
New Ashtree St ML2 .... 164 C2
New Ave PA9 .... 130 C3
New Bldgs ML1 .... 162 B2
New Bridge St KA7 .... 235 F1
New Carron Rd FK5 .... 24 A2
New City Rd Glasgow G4 ... 240 B4
Glasgow G4 .... 240 C4
New City Row G63 .... 31 D2
New Cordale Rd G82 .... 49 E2
New Cross ML3 .... 162 C2
New Dock La PA15 .... 46 A3
New Edinburgh Rd G71 ..... 140 C4
New England Rd KA21 .... 206 A1
New Gartcosh Rd ML5 .... 101 E3
New Hallglen Rd FK1 .... 42 A1
New Inchinnan Rd PA3 ..... 113 F4
New Kirk Rd G61 .... 75 F3
New La ML6 .... 123 D2
New Lairdsland Rd G66 .... 79 E4
New Lanark Prim Sch
ML11 .... 215 D1
New Lanark Rd ML11 .... 214 C1
New Line Rd FK7 .... 11 D4
New Luce Dr G32 .... 119 E2
New Mill Rd KA1 .... 228 A4
New Monkland Prim Sch
ML6 .... 102 C2
New Park St ML3 .... 162 B3
New Plymouth G75 .... 180 A4
New Rd Ayr KA8 .... 235 F1
Bannockburn FK7 .... 7 E1
Cambuslang G72 .... 139 F3
New Sneddon St PA3 .... 113 F3
New St Beith KA15 .... 171 D4
Blantyre G72 .... 161 E4
Bridge Of A FK9 .... 1 C4
Clydebank G81 .... 74 A3
Dalry KA24 .... 191 E4
Irvine KA12 .... 219 D1
Kilbarchan PA10 .... 111 D2
Kilmarnock KA1 .... 227 F3
Lochwinnoch PA12 .... 129 E1
Paisley PA1 .... 113 F2
Slamannan FK1 .... 86 A4
Stevenston KA20 .... 217 E3
Stewarton KA3 .... 195 E1
Stonehouse ML9 .... 198 C1

New Stevenston Prim Sch
ML1 .... 143 D1
New Stevenston Rd ML1 ... 143 D1
New Trows Rd ML9 .... 199 D4
New View Dr ML4 .... 141 F2
New View Pl ML4 .... 141 F2
New Wynd G1 .... 241 D1
Neward Cres KA9 .... 236 B3
Newark Dr G41 .... 116 C1
Newark Ave PA16 .... 45 E4
Newark Castle PA14 .... 47 E1

Newark Cres KA7 .... 238 A1
Newark Dr Glasgow G41 ... 116 C2
Paisley PA2 .... 133 E4
Wishaw ML2 .... 165 E3
Newark Pl ML2 .... 165 E3
Newark St Greenock PA16 ... 45 E4
Port Glasgow PA14 .... 47 E1
Newark Terr KA9 .... 236 B3
Newarthill Prim Sch ML1 .. 143 F2
Newarthill Rd ML1 .... 143 E1
Newbarns St ML8 .... 187 F2
Newbattle Ave ML6 .... 123 D1
Newbattle Ct G32 .... 119 D1
Newbattle Gdns G32 .... 119 D1
Newbattle Pl G32 .... 119 D1
Newbattle Rd G32 .... 119 D1
Newbiggin Cres FK10 .... 4 B1
Newbold Ave ID G21 .... 97 F4
Newburgh PA8 .... 73 D2
Newburgh St G43 .... 136 B4
Newcarron Ct FK2 .... 42 A4
Newcastleton Dr G23 .... 76 C1
Newcroft Dr G44 .... 137 E3
Newdyke Ave G66 .... 79 F4
Newdyke Rd G66 .... 79 F4
Newdykes Farm Rd KA9 .... 233 E1
Newdykes Rd KA9 .... 233 E1
Newfield Cres ML3 .... 162 A2
Newfield Dr KA2 .... 225 F1
Newfield La ID G71 .... 141 D2
Newfield Pl Dundonald KA2 .. 225 F1
Glasgow G46 .... 135 F1
Irvine KA11 .... 220 A3
Rutherglen G73 .... 137 F4
Newfield Sq G53 .... 135 D3
Newhall St G40 .... 117 F2
Newhaven Rd G33 .... 119 D4
Newhaven St G32 .... 119 D4
Newhills Rd G33 .... 119 F4
Newhouse FK8 .... 7 D3
Newhouse Dr Falkirk FK1 .... 41 F1
Kilbirnie KA25 .... 169 F4
Newhouse Ind Est ML1 ..... 143 E4
Newhouse Interchange
KA11 .... 224 C3
Newhouse Way KA11 .... 220 A3
Newhousemill Rd
East Kilbride G74 .... 181 E4
Hamilton ML3 .... 182 A4
Newhouses Rd G68 .... 61 D2
Newhut Rd ML1 .... 142 B1
Newington St G32 .... 118 C3
Newlands Dr
Hamilton ML3 .... 183 E4
Kilmarnock KA3 .... 222 C3
Newlands Gdns PA5 .... 112 B1
Newlands Pl
East Kilbride G74 .... 159 F1
Kilmarnock KA3 .... 222 C2
Tullibody FK10 .... 4 B2
Newlands Rd
Bannockburn FK7 .... 11 E4
East Kilbride G75 .... 179 F3
East Kilbride G75 .... 180 A4
Glasgow G43 .... 136 C3
Uddingston G71 .... 140 C4
Newlands St
Coatbridge ML5 .... 122 A2
Lanark ML11 .... 215 E2
Newlands Terr
Carluke ML8 .... 187 F1
Milton Of C G65 .... 58 B3
Newlandsfield Rd G43 .... 136 B4
Newlandsmuir Rd G75 ...... 180 A3
Newmains Ave PA4 .... 93 D3
Newmains Prim Sch
Renfrew PA4 .... 94 B1
Wishaw ML2 .... 166 A2
Newmains Rd PA4 .... 94 B1
Newmarket St FK1 .... 7 E1
Newmarket St Ayr KA7 ..... 238 C4
Falkirk FK1 .... 42 A2
Newmill & Canthill Rd
ML7 .... 146 A3
Newmill Gdns ML7 .... 125 F2
Newmill Rd Dunlop KA3 .... 195 E4
Glasgow G21 .... 98 B3
Newmills FK10 .... 4 A2
Newmoor Interchange
KA11 .... 219 F1
Newnham Rd PA1 .... 114 C2
Newpark Cres
Cambuslang G72 .... 139 D4
Stirling FK7 .... 7 E2
Newpark Rd FK7 .... 7 E2
Newrose Ave ML4 .... 142 B4
Newshot Dr PA8 .... 73 E1
Newstead Gdns G23 .... 76 C1
Newton Ave
Cambuslang G72 .... 139 E3
Elderslie PA5 .... 112 C2
Skinflats FK2 .... 24 C2
Newton Brae G72 .... 139 F3
Newton Ct G77 .... 156 B2
Newton Dr Elderslie PA5 ... 112 C2
Uddingston G71 .... 141 D4
Newton Gr G77 .... 156 B2
Newton Of Barr Rd G22 .... 129 D1
Newton on Ayr Sta KA8 ... 236 B2
Newton Park Ct KA1 .... 236 A1
Newton Pl Glasgow G3 ...... 240 A4
Newton Mearns G77 .... 156 C2
Newton Rd Bishopton PA7 .. 72 A2
Kirkintilloch G66 .... 79 F2

Newton St Coatbridge ML5 ... 121 F2
Glasgow G3 ... 240 B3
Greenock PA16 ... 45 E3
Kilbirnie KA25 ... 149 D1
Paisley PA1 ... 113 E2
Newton Sta G72 ... 139 F3
Newton Station Rd G72 ... 139 F3
Newton Terr Elderslie PA3 ... 112 C2
Glasgow G3 ... 240 A3
Greenock PA16 ... 45 E3
Newton Terrace La G3 ... 240 A3
Newton Trad Est G4 ... 236 A1
Newton Way PA3 ... 114 A4
Newton Wlk KA1 ... 228 A4
Newtongrange Ave G32 ... 119 D1
Newtongrange Gdns G32 ... 119 D2
Newtonhead KA11 ... 220 A3
Newtonlea Ave G77 ... 156 C2
Newtonshaw FK10 ... 5 E1
Newtown St G65 ... 60 B4
Newtyle Pl G64 ... 78 B1
Newtyle Rd PA1 ... 114 B2
Nicholas St G1 ... 241 E2
Nicholson St G5 ... 117 D3
Nicklaus Way ML1 ... 143 F4
Nicol Dr PA16 ... 45 D3
Nicol St Airdrie ML6 ... 103 E1
Greenock PA16 ... 45 D2
Nicolson Ct G33 ... 99 F3
Nicolson St PA15 ... 45 F3
Niddrie Rd G42 ... 117 D1
Niddrie Sq G42 ... 116 C1
Niddry St PA1 ... 113 F3
Nigel Gdns G41 ... 116 B1
Nigel St ML1 ... 163 E3
Nigg Pl G34 ... 120 A4
Nightingale Pl PA5 ... 131 E3
Nikitas Ave M19 ... 199 D4
Nile Ct KA7 ... 238 C4
Nile St PA15 ... 45 F2
Nimmo Dr G51 ... 115 F4
Nimmo Pl Carluke ML8 ... 187 F2
Wishaw ML2 ... 165 E2
Nimmo Rd PA16 ... 45 E2
Nimmo St PA16 ... 45 E2
Nineyard St KA21 ... 216 C4
Ninian Ave PA4 ... 111 E4
Ninian Rd ML6 ... 123 E3
Ninian's Rise G66 ... 79 F4
Ninian's Terr KA13 ... 207 F1
Nisbet Dr Denny FK6 ... 21 E1
Shotts ML7 ... 146 B3
Nisbet Pl ML6 ... 123 F1
Nisbett St ML6 ... 123 F1
Nith Ave PA2 ... 112 C1
Nith Dr Hamilton ML3 ... 183 D4
Renfrew PA4 ... 94 C1
Nith La ML2 ... 165 F3
Nith Path ML1 ... 144 A1
Nith Pl Johnstone PA5 ... 131 E4
Kilmarnock KA1 ... 228 A3
Nith Quadrant ML1 ... 143 E2
Nith St G33 ... 98 B1
Nithsdale G74 ... 160 B2
Nithsdale Cres G61 ... 75 E3
Nithsdale Cross G41 ... 116 B2
Nithsdale Dr G41 ... 116 C2
Nithsdale Rd
Ardrossan KA22 ... 205 E2
Glasgow G41 ... 116 B2
Nithsdale St Glasgow G41 ... 116 C1
Shotts ML7 ... 146 B3
Nitshill Prim Sch G53 ... 135 D2
Nitshill Rd G53 ... 135 E2
Nitshill Sta G53 ... 135 D3
Niven Ct KA3 ... 223 E2
Niven St G20 ... 96 B3
Noble Prim Sch ML4 ... 142 A4
Noble Rd ML4 ... 142 A3
Nobles Pl ML4 ... 141 F2
Nobles View ML4 ... 141 F2
Nobleston G81 ... 74 B3
Noldrum Ave G32 ... 139 E4
Noldrum Gdns G32 ... 139 E4
Noltmire Rd KA8 ... 236 B2
Noran Cres KA10 ... 229 F3
Norbreck Dr G46 ... 136 B2
Norby Rd G11 ... 95 F2
Noremac Way ML4 ... 141 F4
Norfield Dr G44 ... 137 D4
Norfolk Cres G64 ... 77 F2
Norfolk Ct G15 ... 117 D3
Norfolk House G74 ... 159 F1
Norfolk Rd PA16 ... 44 C2
Norfolk St G5 ... 117 D3
Norham St G41 ... 116 C1
Norman Cres KA12 ... 219 D3
Norman St G40 ... 117 F1
Norse La N G14 ... 95 E2
Norse La S G14 ... 95 E2
Norse Pl G14 ... 95 E2
Norse Rd G14 ... 95 E2
North Ave Cambuslang G72 ... 138 C3
Carluke ML8 ... 187 E1
Clydebank G81 ... 74 A1
Motherwell ML1 ... 143 D1
North Bank Pl G81 ... 94 B4
North Bank St G81 ... 94 B4
North Barr Ave PA8 ... 73 D2
North Barr Ave PA8 ... 73 D1
North Berwick Ave G68 ... 61 F3
North Berwick Cres G75 ... 180 A3
North Berwick Gdns G68 ... 61 F2
North Biggar Rd ML6 ... 123 D4
North Birbiston Rd G65 ... 57 F4
North Bridge St ML6 ... 122 C4

North British Rd G71 ... 140 C3
North Bute St ML5 ... 122 A2
North Caldeen Rd ML5 ... 122 B3
North Calder Dr ML6 ... 123 E3
North Calder Rd G71 ... 121 E1
North Campbell Ave G62 ... 54 C1
North Canal Bank G4 ... 97 E1
North Canal Bank St G4 ... 97 E1
North Carbrain Rd G67 ... 61 F1
North Castle St FK10 ... 10 A3
North Claremont La G62 ... 55 D1
North Claremont St
G3 ... 96 C1
North Corsebar Rd PA2 ... 113 E1
North Court La G1 ... 241 D2
North Crescent Ave KA21 ... 205 E2
North Crescent Rd KA22 ... 205 D2
North Croft St PA3 ... 113 F3
North Ct G1 ... 241 D2
North Dean Park Ave
G71 ... 141 D1
North Douglas St G81 ... 94 B4
North Dr Kilbirnie KA25 ... 170 A4
Linwood PA3 ... 112 A3
Troon KA10 ... 229 F2
North Dryburgh Rd G... 165 D3
North Dumgoyne Ave G62 ... 54 C2
North Elgin Pl G81 ... 94 B4
North Elgin St G81 ... 94 B4
North Erskine Pk G61 ... 75 E3
North Faulds Rd ML11 ... 215 F3
North Frederick St G1 ... 241 D3
North Gardner St G11 ... 96 A2
North Gargieston Rd KA1 ... 227 E3
North Glasgow Coll
Glasgow G21 ... 98 B3
Glasgow, Springburn G21 ... 98 A4
North Gower St G51 ... 116 B3
North Grange Rd G61 ... 75 F3
North Hamilton Pl KA1 ... 222 C1
North Hamilton St KA1 ... 222 C1
North Hanover St G1, G4 ... 241 D3
North Harbour Ind Est
KA8 ... 235 F1
North Harbour Rd KA8 ... 235 F1
North Iverton Park Rd
PA5 ... 112 A2
North Kelvinside Sec Sch
G20 ... 96 C2
North Kilmeny Cres ML2 ... 165 E3
North La PA3 ... 112 B3
North Lodge Ave ML1 ... 163 F2
North Lodge Rd PA4 ... 94 B2
North Main St
Alexandria G83 ... 27 E3
Falkirk FK2 ... 24 B2
North Moraine La G15 ... 75 E1
North Neuk KA10 ... 229 F4
North Newmoor Ind Est
KA11 ... 219 F1
North Orchard St ML1 ... 163 E4
North Park Ave Ayr KA8 ... 236 A2
Barrhead G78 ... 134 A2
Glasgow G46 ... 135 F2
North Portland St G1, G4 ... 241 E2
North Rd Bellshill ML4 ... 142 A4
Coatbridge ML5 ... 122 A1
Cumbernauld G68 ... 82 A4
Johnstone PA5 ... 111 F1
Port Glasgow PA14 ... 68 C4
West Kilbride KA23 ... 190 B3
North Shore Rd KA10 ... 229 E3
North & South Rd ML1 ... 144 C1
North St Alexandria G83 ... 27 F3
Alloa FK10 ... 10 A4
Dalry KA24 ... 191 E4
Falkirk FK2 ... 42 A4
Glasgow G3 ... 240 A3
Greenock PA16 ... 45 E4
Houston PA6 ... 91 D2
Larkhall ML9 ... 185 D2
Motherwell ML1 ... 163 F4
North Street Ind Est G83 ... 27 F3
North Vennel Irvine KA11 ... 220 A2
Lanark ML11 ... 215 D2
North View G61 ... 75 E1
North View Rd PA11 ... 110 C3
North Wallace St G4 ... 241 E4
North Wood Rd FK10 ... 4 B1
North Woodside Rd G20 ... 96 C2
Northacre KA13 ... 207 F3
Northacre Gr KA13 ... 207 E3
Northall Quadrant ML1 ... 143 D1
Northampton Dr G12 ... 96 A3
Northampton La G12 ... 96 A3
Northbank Ave
Cambuslang G72 ... 139 E3
Kirkintilloch G66 ... 79 E4
Northbank Rd G66 ... 79 E4
Northbank St G72 ... 139 E3
Northbrae Pl G13 ... 95 D3
Northburn Ave ML6 ... 103 D1
Northburn Pl ML6 ... 103 D2
Northburn Rd ML5 ... 102 B1
Northburn St ML6 ... 104 A1
Northcraig Rd KA3 ... 223 D2
Northcroft Rd G69 ... 80 C1
Northdown Pl KA7 ... 238 B2
Northend FK7 ... 2 B1
Northfield G75 ... 179 F4
Northfield Ave Ayr KA8 ... 236 A2
Port Glasgow PA14 ... 68 C4
Shotts ML7 ... 147 D1
Northfield Dr G83 ... 27 F3
Northfield Pl KA8 ... 236 A2

Northfield Rd Bonhill G83 ... 28 A3
Denny FK6 ... 21 E2
Kilsyth G65 ... 36 A1
Northfield St ML1 ... 163 F4
Northflat Pl ML8 ... 202 B4
Northgate Quadrant G21 ... 98 B3
Northgate Rd G21 ... 98 B4
Northinch Ct G14 ... 95 E1
Northinch St G14 ... 95 E1
Northland Ave G14 ... 95 E3
Northland Dr G14 ... 95 E3
Northland Gdns G14 ... 95 E3
Northland La G14 ... 95 E2
Northmuir Dr ML2 ... 165 E2
Northmuir Rd G15 ... 75 D2
Northpark St G20 ... 96 C2
Northumberland St G20 ... 96 C2
Northway G72 ... 140 B1
Northwood Dr ML2 ... 166 A3
Norton St FK12 ... 5 D4
Norval St G11 ... 96 A1
Norwich Dr G12 ... 96 A3
Norwood Ave Alloa FK10 ... 9 F4
Bonnybridge FK4 ... 40 A4
Kirkintilloch G66 ... 79 D4
Norwood Cres FK10 ... 9 F4
Norwood Ct G44 ... 40 A4
Norwood Dr G46 ... 136 A1
Norwood Gr FK10 ... 9 F4
Norwood Pk G61 ... 75 F2
Norwood Pl G61 ... 75 F2
Norwood Terr G71 ... 141 D4
Notre Dame High AC Sch
G12 ... 96 B2
Notre Dame Prim Sch
PA16 ... 45 E2
Notre Dame Prim AC Sch
G12 ... 96 B2
Nottingham Ave G12 ... 96 A3
Nottingham La G12 ... 96 A3
Novar Dr G12 ... 96 A2
Novar Gdns G64 ... 77 F1
Novar St ML3 ... 162 B1
Nuneaton St G40 ... 118 A2
Nuneaton Street Ind Est
G40 ... 118 A2
Nurseries Rd G69 ... 119 F3
Nursery Ave Erskine PA7 ... 72 C2
Kilmarnock KA1 ... 228 A4
Prestwick KA9 ... 236 A3
Nursery Bldgs ML11 ... 215 D1
Nursery Ct ML8 ... 187 F2
Nursery Dr ML9 ... 200 A4
Nursery Gr PA13 ... 69 E1
Nursery La Glasgow G41 ... 117 D1
Kilmacolm PA13 ... 69 E1
Nursery Pk ML8 ... 187 F1
Nursery Pl
Ardrossan KA22 ... 205 E1
Blantyre G72 ... 161 E3
Nursery Rd Ayr KA7 ... 239 D3
Falkirk FK1 ... 41 F2
Nursery St Glasgow G41 ... 117 D2
Helensburgh G84 ... 25 D4
Kilmarnock KA1 ... 227 F4
Nutberry Ct G42 ... 117 D1

O'Connor Ct KA21 ... 216 C4
O'Hare G83 ... 28 A4
O'Neil Ave G64 ... 98 A4
O'Neil Terr G83 ... 27 F2
O'Wood Ave ML1 ... 143 D3
Oak Ave Bearsden G62 ... 75 F4
East Kilbride G75 ... 180 A3
Oak Cres Glasgow G69 ... 120 A2
Plean FK7 ... 12 B2
Oak Dr Cambuslang G72 ... 139 E2
Fallin FK7 ... 8 B2
Kirkintilloch G66 ... 79 D3
Larbert FK5 ... 23 E2
Oak Fern Dr G74 ... 159 E2
Oak Fern Gr G74 ... 159 E2
Oak Lea ML3 ... 162 C1
Oak Mall The PA15 ... 45 F3
Oak Park ML1 ... 143 D3
Oak Pk Bishopbriggs G64 ... 78 A1
Motherwell ML1 ... 143 D3
Oak Pl Coatbridge ML5 ... 122 B3
East Kilbride G75 ... 180 A3
Kilmarnock KA1 ... 227 F4
Uddingston G71 ... 141 E4
Oak Rd Ardrossan KA22 ... 205 E2
Clydebank G81 ... 73 F3
Cumbernauld G67 ... 62 C2
Paisley PA2 ... 114 A4
Oak St Glasgow G2 ... 240 B2
Stirling FK8 ... 1 C1
Oak Wynd G72 ... 139 F2
Oakbank Ave ML1 ... 164 C1
Oakbank Dr G78 ... 155 F4
Oakbank Ind Est G20 ... 97 D2
Oakbank Rd PA14 ... 68 C4
Oakbank St ML6 ... 123 E4
Oakburn Ave G62 ... 54 C1
Oakburn Cres G62 ... 54 C1
Oakdene Ave
Bellshill ML4 ... 142 A4
Uddingston G71 ... 141 D4
Oakdene Cres ML1 ... 143 E2
Oakfield Ave G12 ... 96 C1
Oakfield Dr ML1 ... 163 F3
Oakfield La G12 ... 96 C1
Oakfield Prim Sch FK5 ... 46 B2
Oakfield Rd ML1 ... 163 F3
Oakgrove Prim Sch G4 ... 97 D1
Oakhill Ave G69 ... 119 F2
Oakland Dr KA20 ... 206 C1
Oaklands Ave KA12 ... 219 E2

Oaklea Cres G72 ... 161 E4
Oakleigh Dr PA16 ... 45 E4
Oakley Dr G44 ... 136 C2
Oakley Terr G31 ... 117 F4
Oaks The Glasgow G44 ... 137 D2
Johnstone PA5 ... 111 F1
Oakshaw Brae PA1 ... 113 E3
Oakshaw St E PA1 ... 113 F3
Oakshaw St W PA1 ... 113 E3
Oakshawhead PA1 ... 113 E3
Oakside Pl ML3 ... 183 E4
Oakwood Ave Ayr KA8 ... 236 C3
Paisley PA2 ... 113 D1
Oakwood Cres G34 ... 100 B1
Oakwood Dr Beith KA15 ... 171 D4
Coatbridge ML5 ... 121 E3
Glasgow G34 ... 100 B1
Newton Mearns G77 ... 156 C2
Oates Gdns ML1 ... 164 A2
Oatfield St G21 ... 98 A2
Oban Ct G20 ... 96 C2
Oban Dr G20 ... 96 C2
Oban La G20 ... 96 C2
Oban Terr PA16 ... 44 C2
Oberon FK10 ... 9 F4
Obiston Gdns G32 ... 119 D3
Obree Ave KA9 ... 236 C3
Observatory La G12 ... 96 B2
Observatory Rd G12 ... 96 B2
Ochil Cres FK8 ... 2 A3
Ochil Ct East Kilbride G75 ... 180 A2
Irvine KA11 ... 220 A2
Tullibody FK10 ... 4 B3
Ochil Dr Barrhead G78 ... 134 B1
Paisley PA2 ... 133 F4
Ochil Pl Glasgow G32 ... 119 D2
Kilmarnock KA1 ... 228 A2
Ochil Rd Alva FK12 ... 5 D4
Bearsden G61 ... 75 D4
Bishopbriggs G64 ... 78 B1
Menstrie FK11 ... 4 A4
Renfrew PA4 ... 94 A1
Stirling FK9 ... 2 B2
Ochil St Alloa FK10 ... 10 A4
Fallin FK7 ... 8 B2
Glasgow G32 ... 119 D2
Tullibody FK10 ... 4 B3
Wishaw ML2 ... 164 C2
Ochil View Denny FK6 ... 39 E4
Shieldhill FK1 ... 66 B4
Uddingston G71 ... 141 D4
Ochilmount FK7 ... 7 E1
Ochiltree Ave G13 ... 95 F4
Ochiltree Dr ML3 ... 161 F1
Ochiltree Pl G33 ... 223 D3
Ochiltree Terr FK1 ... 41 D3
Ochiview Alva FK12 ... 5 D4
Cowie FK7 ... 12 C3
Ochilview Pk
(Stenhousemuir FC) FK5 ... 23 E2
Ochville Terr FK10 ... 5 E2
Octavia Terr PA16 ... 45 E4
Odense Ct G75 ... 180 C4
Ogilface Cres EH48 ... 107 E1
Ogilvie Ct ML6 ... 123 F4
Ogilvie Pl Bridge Of A FK9 ... 2 A3
Glasgow G31 ... 118 B2
Kilmarnock KA3 ... 223 D2
Ogilvie Prim RC Sch G33 ... 119 F4
Ogilvie Rd FK8 ... 7 D3
Ogilvie St G31 ... 118 B2
Old Airbles Rd ML1 ... 163 E3
Old Aisle Rd G66 ... 79 F4
Old Auchans View KA2 ... 225 F1
Old Avon Rd ML3 ... 163 D1
Old Belldsdyke Rd FK5 ... 23 D2
Old Biggar Rd ML6 ... 83 D1
Old Bore Rd ML6 ... 123 F4
Old Bothwell Rd G71 ... 162 A4
Old Bridge of Weir Rd
Bridge Of W PA6 ... 90 C1
Houston PA6 ... 91 D1
Old Bridge Rd KA8 ... 236 C2
Old Bridge St Alloa FK10 ... 10 A3
Ayr KA7 ... 235 F1
Old Bridgend ML8 ... 187 F1
Old Caley Rd KA12 ... 219 E3
Old Castle Rd G44 ... 137 D3
Old Church Gdns G69 ... 121 D3
Old Coach Rd G74 ... 159 F2
Old Cotts PA2 ... 134 B4
Old Cross Airdrie ML6 ... 123 D4
Hamilton ML3 ... 162 C2
Old Dalmarnock Rd G40 ... 117 F2
Old Dalnottar Rd G60 ... 73 D3
Old Denny Rd FK5 ... 23 D2
Old Drove Rd FK7 ... 6 B3
Old Dumbarton Rd G3 ... 96 B1
Old Eastfield St ML7 ... 127 D3
Old Edinburgh Rd G71 ... 141 E4
Old Farm Rd KA8 ... 236 B2
Old Gartloch Rd G34 ... 100 C3
Old Glasgow Rd
Cumbernauld G67 ... 62 A2
Stewarton KA3 ... 195 F1
Uddingston G71 ... 140 C3
Uddingston, Kylepark G71 ... 140 B4
Old Govan Rd PA4 ... 94 C2
Old Greenock Rd
Bishopton PA7 ... 71 E3
Bishopton, Kingston PA7 ... 72 B1
Langbank PA14 ... 70 B3
Old Hillfoot Rd KA7 ... 239 D3
Old Humbie Rd G77 ... 156 C1
Old Inns Rdbt G67 ... 62 A3
Old Inverkip Rd PA16 ... 45 D2
Old Irvine Rd KA1 ... 227 F4

Old Lanark Rd
Carluke ML8, ML11 ... 202 A2
Carluke ML8 ... 202 A4
Old Largs Rd PA16 ... 45 E1
Old Loans Rd KA10 ... 230 B3
Old Luss Rd Balloch G83 ... 19 D1
Helensburgh G84 ... 16 C1
Old Manse Gdns ML5 ... 122 A4
Old Manse Rd Glasgow G32 ... 119 E3
Wishaw ML2 ... 164 C1
Old Military Rd G83 ... 20 C4
Old Mill Park Ind Est G66 ... 58 B1
Old Mill Rd Bothwell G71 ... 141 D1
Cambuslang G72 ... 139 E3
Clydebank G81 ... 74 A3
East Kilbride G74 ... 159 F1
Kilmarnock KA1 ... 228 A4
Paisley PA2 ... 113 D2
Shotts ML7 ... 146 A1
Uddingston G71 ... 140 C3
Old Mill View G65 ... 60 C2
Old Mill Wlk G83 ... 27 F4
Old Monkland Prim Sch
ML5 ... 121 E2
Old Monkland Rd ML5 ... 121 F2
Old Mugdock Rd G63 ... 31 E1
Old Playfield Rd G76 ... 158 B4
Old Quarry Rd
Cumbernauld G68 ... 81 E3
Stevenston KA20 ... 217 E4
Old Raise Rd KA21 ... 206 A1
Old Rd PA5 ... 112 B2
Old Redding Rd FK2 ... 42 C2
Old Renfrew Rd PA4, G51 ... 95 D1
Old Rome Way KA2 ... 226 C3
Old Rutherglen Rd G5 ... 117 E2
Old School Ct FK10 ... 4 A1
Old Schoolhouse La PA6 ... 91 D2
Old Shettleston Rd G32 ... 119 D3
Old Sneddon St PA3 ... 113 F3
Old St Clydebank G81 ... 74 A3
Kilmarnock KA1 ... 227 F3
Old Stable Row ML5 ... 122 A4
Old Town FK7 ... 7 D4
Old Union St ML6 ... 123 E1
Old Willowyard Rd KA15 ... 171 D4
Old Wishaw Rd ML8 ... 187 F2
Old Wood Rd G69 ... 120 A2
Old Woodwynd Rd KA13 ... 207 F2
Old Wynd G1 ... 241 D1
Oldbarhills TP Site PA2 ... 134 B4
Oldhall Dr PA13 ... 69 E1
Oldhall Rd PA1 ... 114 B3
Oldhall Rdbt KA11 ... 224 C3
Oldhall West Ind Est
KA11 ... 224 C3
Oilfard Ave G71 ... 141 D2
Oliphant Cres
Clarkston G76 ... 157 F3
Paisley PA2 ... 132 C4
Oliphant Ct KA3 ... 222 B4
Oliphant Oval PA2 ... 132 C4
Olive Bank G71 ... 121 E1
Olive Ct ML1 ... 143 D3
Olive Rd KA1 ... 227 E4
Olive St G33 ... 98 B2
Oliver Rd FK1 ... 42 B2
Olympia Arc G75 ... 180 C4
Olympia Ct G74 ... 180 C4
Olympia St G40 ... 117 F3
Olympia Way G75 ... 180 C4
Olympia Way G74 ... 159 F1
Omoa Rd ML1 ... 144 A1
Onich Pl ML7 ... 147 D2
Onslow G75 ... 180 B4
Onslow Dr G31 ... 118 A4
Onslow Rd G81 ... 74 B1
Onslow Sq G31 ... 118 A4
Ontario Pk G75 ... 159 D1
Ontario Pl G75 ... 159 D1
Onthank Dr KA3 ... 222 C2
Onyx St ML4 ... 142 A2
Open Shore PA15 ... 46 A3
Oran Gate G20 ... 96 C3
Oran Gdns G20 ... 96 C3
Oran Pl G20 ... 96 C2
Oran St G20 ... 96 C2
Orangefield PA15 ... 45 F3
Orangefield Dr KA9 ... 233 E1
Orangefield Ind Est KA9 ... 233 E1
Orangefield La PA15 ... 45 F3
Orbiston Ct ML1 ... 164 A3
Orbiston Dr Bellshill ML4 ... 142 A2
Clydebank G81 ... 74 B4
Orbiston Pl ML1 ... 164 A3
Orbiston Rd Bellshill ML4 ... 141 F2
Bellshill ML4 ... 142 A1
Orbiston Sq ML4 ... 141 F1
Orbiston St ML1 ... 163 F3
Orcades Dr G44 ... 137 E2
Orchard Ave Ayr KA7 ... 239 D3
Bothwell G71 ... 141 D1
Orchard Brae G66 ... 79 F2
Orchard Ct Glasgow G32 ... 139 D4
Glasgow, Orchard Pk G46 ... 136 A2
Glasgow G46 ... 136 A2
Orchard Field G66 ... 79 F2
Orchard Gate ML9 ... 185 D1
Orchard Gn G74 ... 160 A2
Orchard Gr Coatbridge ML5 ... 122 A3
Glasgow G46 ... 136 A2
Kilmacolm PA13 ... 89 E4
Kilwinning KA13 ... 207 F2

Orchard House Hospl FK8 ...... 2 A1
Orchard Park Ave G46 ...... 136 A2
Orchard Pk G46 ...... 136 B2
Orchard Pl Ayr KA7 ...... 239 D3
  Bellshill ML4 ...... 141 F2
  Hamilton ML3 ...... 162 B2
  Kilwinning KA13 ...... 207 F2
  Kirkintilloch G66 ...... 80 A4
Orchard Rd FK9 ...... 2 A3
Orchard St Carluke ML8 ...... 187 F1
  Falkirk FK1 ...... 42 A3
  Glasgow G69 ...... 119 F2
  Greenock PA15 ...... 46 A2
  Hamilton ML3 ...... 162 C2
  Kilmarnock KA3 ...... 222 C1
  Motherwell ML1 ...... 163 E4
  Paisley PA1 ...... 113 F2
  Renfrew PA4 ...... 94 B2
  West Kilbride KA23 ...... 190 B3
  Wishaw ML2 ...... 186 A3
Orchard The FK10 ...... 4 A1
Orchard View Dr ML11 ...... 214 A2
Orchardcroft FK8 ...... 7 D4
Orchardton Rd G68 ...... 81 E4
Orchardton Woods Ind Pk
  G68 ...... 81 E4
Orchy Ave G76 ...... 136 A1
Orchy Cres Airdrie ML6 ...... 123 E2
  Bearsden G61 ...... 75 E1
  Paisley PA2 ...... 112 C1
Orchy Ct G81 ...... 74 B3
Orchy Dr G44 ...... 136 C1
Orchy Gdns G76 ...... 136 A1
Orchy St G44 ...... 137 D3
Orchy Terr G74 ...... 160 A1
Orefield Pl G74 ...... 159 F2
Oregon Pl G5 ...... 117 E2
Orion Pl ML4 ...... 142 C3
Orion Way
  Cambuslang G72 ...... 139 D3
  Carluke ML8 ...... 187 E1
Orkney Ct FK10 ...... 10 A3
Orkney Dr KA3 ...... 223 D3
Orkney Pl Falkirk FK1 ...... 42 A1
  6 Glasgow G51 ...... 116 A4
Orkney Quadrant ML2 ...... 165 E2
Orkney St G51 ...... 116 A4
Orlando G74 ...... 160 B3
Orleans Ave G14 ...... 95 F2
Orleans La G14 ...... 95 F2
Ormiston Ave G14 ...... 95 E2
Ormiston Dr Alloa FK10 ...... 4 C1
  Hamilton ML3 ...... 183 E4
Ormiston La 12 G14 ...... 95 E2
Ormiston La N 6 G14 ...... 95 E2
Ormiston La S 5 G14 ...... 95 E2
Ormiston Pl KA11 ...... 220 B4
Ormonde Ave G44 ...... 136 C2
Ormonde Cres G44 ...... 136 C2
Ormonde Ct G44 ...... 136 C2
Ormonde Dr G44 ...... 136 C2
Ornsay St G22 ...... 97 E4
Oronsay Ave PA4 ...... 69 D3
Oronsay Cres Bearsden G61 ...... 76 A2
  Old Kilpatrick G60 ...... 73 E3
Oronsay Ct G60 ...... 73 E3
Oronsay Gdns G60 ...... 73 E3
Oronsay Pl G60 ...... 73 E3
Oronsay Sq G60 ...... 73 E3
Orr Sq PA1 ...... 113 F3
Orr St Glasgow G40 ...... 117 F3
  Paisley PA1 ...... 113 F2
  Paisley, Castlehead PA2 ...... 113 F3
Orr Terr Harthill ML7 ...... 127 E2
  Neilston G78 ...... 154 B3
Orton Pl G51 ...... 116 A3
Osborne Cres G74 ...... 158 A2
Osborne Gdns FK1 ...... 41 F2
Osborne St Clydebank G81 ...... 74 A2
  Falkirk FK1 ...... 41 F2
  Glasgow G1 ...... 241 D1
Oslie View KA3 ...... 195 F1
Osprey Dr Kilmarnock KA1 ...... 228 B4
  Uddingston G71 ...... 141 D4
Osprey Rd FK6 ...... 45 D2
Ossian Ave PA1 ...... 114 C3
Ossian Rd G43 ...... 136 C3
Oswald Ct KA8 ...... 236 A2
Oswald Dr KA9 ...... 233 E1
Oswald Gdns ML8 ...... 201 F2
Oswald La KA8 ...... 235 F1
Oswald Pl KA8 ...... 236 A3
Oswald Rd KA8 ...... 236 A3
Oswald St Falkirk FK1 ...... 42 A2
  Glasgow G1 ...... 240 C2
Oswald Wlk G12 ...... 76 B4
Otago La G12 ...... 96 C1
Otago La N G12 ...... 96 C1
Otago Pk G75 ...... 159 D1
Otago St G12 ...... 96 C1
Othello G74 ...... 160 A3
Ottawa Cres G81 ...... 73 E2
Otterburn Ave KA3 ...... 223 D2
Otterburn Dr G46 ...... 136 B1
Otterswick Pl G33 ...... 99 E1
Ottoline Dr KA10 ...... 229 F1
Oudenarde Ct ML8 ...... 188 A1
Our Holy Redeemer's
  RC Prim Sch G81 ...... 94 B4
Our Lady & St Francis
  Prim Sch G81 ...... 73 F2
Our Lady of Lourdes
  RC Prim Sch G75 ...... 180 B4
Our Lady of Peace
  RC Prim Sch PA3 ...... 112 A3

Our Lady of the Annunciation
  Prim RC Sch G43 ...... 136 C3
Our Lady of the Assumption
  Prim RC Sch G20 ...... 97 D3
Our Lady of the Missions
  Prim Sch G46 ...... 136 A1
Our Lady of the Rosary Sch
  G52 ...... 115 D2
Our Lady & St Francis
  RC Prim Sch ML1 ...... 143 E1
Our Lady & St Margaret's
  RC Prim Sch 116 C3
Our Lady & St Patricks
  High Sch G82 ...... 49 E2
Our Lady's RC High Sch
  Cumbernauld G67 ...... 61 E1
  Motherwell ML1 ...... 164 A2
Outdale Ave KA9 ...... 236 C4
Oval The Glasgow G76 ...... 136 C1
  Glenboig ML5 ...... 101 E3
Overbrae Pl G15 ...... 74 C3
Overburn Ave G82 ...... 49 F3
Overburn Cres G82 ...... 49 F3
Overburn Terr G82 ...... 50 A3
Overdale Ave G42 ...... 136 C4
Overdale Cres KA9 ...... 236 B3
Overdale Gdns G42 ...... 136 C4
Overdale Pl ML2 ...... 186 B3
Overdale St G42 ...... 136 C4
Overjohnstone Dr ML2 ...... 164 B2
Overlea Ave G73 ...... 138 B3
Overlee Rd G76 ...... 157 F4
Overmills Cres KA7 ...... 239 E4
Overmills Rd KA7 ...... 239 E4
Overnewton Pl G3 ...... 116 B4
Overnewton Sq G3 ...... 96 B1
Overnewton St G3 ...... 96 B1
Overton Cres Denny FK6 ...... 21 E1
  Greenock PA15 ...... 45 E2
  Johnstone PA5 ...... 112 A2
  West Kilbride KA23 ...... 190 B3
Overton Ct KA23 ...... 190 B3
Overton Dr KA23 ...... 190 B3
Overton Gdns PA13 ...... 69 F1
Overton Gr PA13 ...... 69 F1
Overton Hospl G82 ...... 50 C3
Overton Prim Sch PA16 ...... 45 E2
Overton Rd Alexandria G83 ...... 27 E2
  Cambuslang G72 ...... 139 E2
  Johnstone PA5 ...... 112 A1
  Netherburn ML9 ...... 200 B3
  Overton St Alexandria G83 ...... 27 F3
  Cambuslang G72 ...... 139 E2
Overtoun Ave G82 ...... 50 A2
Overtoun Dr Clydebank G81 ...... 73 F2
  Rutherglen G73 ...... 138 A4
Overtoun Rd G81 ...... 73 F2
Overtown Ave G53 ...... 135 D3
Overtown Prim Sch ML2 ...... 186 B4
Overtown Rd ML2 ...... 165 F1
Overtown St G31 ...... 118 A3
Overwood Dr
  Dumbarton G82 ...... 50 A2
  Glasgow G44 ...... 137 E3
Overwood Gr G82 ...... 50 A2
Owen Ave G75 ...... 180 B4
Owen Kelly Pl KA21 ...... 205 F1
Owen Pk G75 ...... 180 B4
Owen St ML1 ...... 163 F4
Owendale Ave ML4 ...... 142 A4
Oxford Ave PA19 ...... 45 D3
Oxford Dr PA3 ...... 112 A3
Oxford La Glasgow G5 ...... 117 D3
  Renfrew PA4 ...... 94 B2
Oxford Rd Greenock PA16 ...... 44 B2
  Renfrew PA4 ...... 94 B2
Oxford St Coatbridge ML5 ...... 121 F3
  Glasgow G5 ...... 240 C1
  Kirkintilloch G66 ...... 79 E4
Oxgang Pl G66 ...... 79 F4
Oxgang Prim Sch G66 ...... 79 F4
Oxhill Pl G82 ...... 49 E2
Oxhill Rd G82 ...... 49 E2
Oxton Dr G52 ...... 115 D3

Pacemuir La PA13 ...... 89 D4
Pacemuir Rd PA13 ...... 89 E4
Paddock St ML5 ...... 122 B2
Paddock The
  Clarkston G76 ...... 158 A3
  Perceton KA11 ...... 220 B3
Paddockholm North
  Ind Est KA25 ...... 149 D1
Paddockholm Rd KA25 ...... 149 D1
Paddockholm South
  Ind Est KA25 ...... 149 D1
Padruff Pl KA25 ...... 149 D1
Paidmyre Cres G77 ...... 156 B2
Paidmyre Gdns G77 ...... 156 B2
Paidmyre Rd G77 ...... 156 B2
Paisley Abbey PA1 ...... 113 F2
Paisley Canal Sta PA1 ...... 113 F2
Paisley (Gilmour St) Sta
  PA3 ...... 113 F3
Paisley Gram Sch PA1 ...... 114 A3
Paisley Maternity Hospl
  PA2 ...... 113 E1
Paisley Rd Barrhead G78 ...... 134 A2
  Glasgow G5 ...... 240 A1
  Renfrew PA4 ...... 94 B1
Paisley Rd W G52 ...... 115 E2
Paisley St James PA3 ...... 113 E3
Paisley St James Sta PA3 ...... 113 E3
Palace Grounds Rd ML3 ...... 162 C2
Palace of Art G52 ...... 115 F2
Palacecraig St ML5 ...... 122 A2
Paladin Ave G13 ...... 95 D4

Palermo St 3 G21 ...... 97 F2
Palladium Pl G14 ...... 95 E2
Palm Pl G71 ...... 121 E1
Palmer Ave G13 ...... 75 E1
Palmerston G75 ...... 180 A4
Palmerston Pl Glasgow G3 ...... 116 B4
  Johnstone PA5 ...... 131 E4
Pandora Way G71 ...... 141 D4
Pankhurst Pl G74 ...... 159 F1
Panmure St G20 ...... 97 D3
Panrock Ct KA10 ...... 229 E2
Pantonville Rd KA23 ...... 190 B2
Papermill Rd PA16 ...... 45 E1
Pappert G83 ...... 28 A2
Pardovan Pl FK1 ...... 41 F3
Paris Ave FK6 ...... 21 F1
Park Ave Balloch G83 ...... 19 F1
  Barrhead G78 ...... 134 A1
  Bishopton PA7 ...... 72 A1
  Carluke ML8 ...... 187 F2
  Dennyloanhead FK4 ...... 39 F3
  Dumbarton G82 ...... 50 A2
  Elderslie PA5 ...... 112 B1
  Glasgow G3 ...... 96 C1
  Greenock PA16 ...... 45 D4
  Kilwinning KA13 ...... 207 F2
  Kirkintilloch G66 ...... 79 E4
  Larkhall ML9 ...... 185 E1
  Milngavie G62 ...... 55 D1
  Motherwell, New Stevenston
  ML1 ...... 143 D3
  Park Bank PA8 ...... 73 D1
  Park Brae PA8 ...... 93 E4
  Park Burn Ct ML3 ...... 162 A3
  Park Burn Ind Est ML3 ...... 162 A3
  Park Cir Ayr KA7 ...... 238 C4
  Carluke ML8 ...... 187 F2
  Glasgow G3 ...... 240 A4
Park Circus La Ayr KA7 ...... 238 C4
  Glasgow G3 ...... 240 A4
Park Circus Pl G3 ...... 240 A4
Park Ct Beith KA15 ...... 171 E4
  Bishopbriggs G64 ...... 78 A2
  Clydebank G81 ...... 74 A2
  Glasgow G46 ...... 136 A2
Park Dr Bannockburn FK7 ...... 7 E1
  Bellshill ML4 ...... 142 A2
  Erskine PA8 ...... 93 D4
  Erskine, Park Mains PA8 ...... 73 E4
  Glasgow G3 ...... 240 A4
  Hamilton ML3 ...... 163 E1
  Lanark ML11 ...... 214 C2
  Rutherglen G73 ...... 138 A4
  Stenhousemuir FK5 ...... 23 E1
  Thorntonhall G74 ...... 158 B2
  Wishaw ML2 ...... 166 A3
Park Gardens La G3 ...... 96 C1
Park Gate Erskine PA8 ...... 93 D4
  Glasgow G3 ...... 240 A4
Park Gate Pl ML4 ...... 141 F3
Park Gdns Bannockburn FK7 ...... 7 E1
  Glasgow G3 ...... 96 C1
  Kilbarchan PA10 ...... 111 D2
Park Glade PA8 ...... 93 D4
Park Gn PA8 ...... 93 D4
Park Gr Cardross G82 ...... 48 A4
  Erskine PA8 ...... 93 E4
Park Hill PA8 ...... 73 D1
Park La Ardrossan KA22 ...... 205 E2
  Blantyre G72 ...... 161 F4
  Carluke ML8 ...... 187 F1
  Glasgow G40 ...... 117 F3
  Kilsyth G65 ...... 60 B4
  Kilwinning KA13 ...... 207 E3
  Stirling FK8 ...... 7 D4
Park Lea ML6 ...... 105 D2
Park Mains Sch PA8 ...... 73 D1
Park Moor PA8 ...... 93 D4
Park Pl Alloa FK10 ...... 10 B4
  Bellshill ML4 ...... 141 F2
  Glasgow G40 ...... 117 F3
  Johnstone PA5 ...... 112 A2
  Lanark ML11 ...... 214 C2
  Stirling FK7 ...... 6 C3
  Strathblane G63 ...... 31 D2
  Thorntonhall G74 ...... 158 B2
Park Prim Sch FK10 ...... 10 A3
Park Quadrant
  Glasgow G3 ...... 240 A4
  Wishaw ML2 ...... 166 A3
Park Rd Ardrossan KA22 ...... 205 E1
  Bargeddie G69 ...... 121 D3
  Bellshill ML4 ...... 142 A2
  Bishopbriggs G64 ...... 78 A1
  Blackridge EH48 ...... 107 F2
  Bridge Of W PA11 ...... 90 B1
  Calderbank ML6 ...... 123 D2
  Chryston G69 ...... 100 B4
  Clydebank G81 ...... 73 F2
  Falkirk FK2 ...... 24 A1
  Glasgow G4 ...... 96 C1

Park Rd continued
  Glasgow, Carmyle G32 ...... 139 E4
  Glasgow, Giffnock G46 ...... 136 A1
  Hamilton ML3 ...... 162 B2
  Inchinnan PA4 ...... 93 E4
  Johnstone PA5 ...... 111 F1
  Kilmacolm PA13 ...... 89 E4
  Menstrie FK11 ...... 4 A3
  Milngavie G62 ...... 55 D1
  Motherwell ML1 ...... 143 D1
  Paisley PA2 ...... 113 E1
  Saltcoats KA21 ...... 216 C4
  Shotts ML7 ...... 146 B3
Park Ridge PA8 ...... 93 E4
Park Sch Glasgow G3 ...... 96 C1
Park St Airdrie ML6 ...... 122 C4
  Alexandria G83 ...... 27 E3
  Alva FK12 ...... 5 D4
  Carluke ML8 ...... 187 F1
  Cleland ML1 ...... 144 A2
  Coatbridge ML5 ...... 122 A4
  Cowie FK7 ...... 12 C4
  Dumbarton G82 ...... 50 A2
  Falkirk FK1 ...... 42 A3
  High Bonnybridge FK4 ...... 40 B2
  Kilmarnock KA1 ...... 222 C1
  Kirkintilloch G66 ...... 80 A4
  Motherwell ML1 ...... 163 F3
  Motherwell, New Stevenston
  ML1 ...... 143 D2
Park St S G3 ...... 96 C1
Park Terr Ayr KA7 ...... 238 C4
  Cardross G82 ...... 48 A4
  East Kilbride G74 ...... 159 F1
  Glasgow G3 ...... 96 C1
  Gourock PA19 ...... 44 C4
  Stirling FK8 ...... 7 D3
  Tullibody FK10 ...... 4 A1
Park Terrace East La G3 ...... 240 A4
Park Terrace La G3 ...... 96 C1
Park Top PA8 ...... 73 E1
Park View Ardrossan KA22 ...... 205 E2
  Caldercruix ML6 ...... 105 D3
  Kilbarchan PA10 ...... 111 D2
  Kilbirnie KA25 ...... 149 D1
  Larkhall ML9 ...... 185 D1
  Paisley PA2 ...... 113 E1
Park Way KA7 ...... 62 A2
Park Winding PA8 ...... 93 E4
Park Wood PA8 ...... 73 E1
Parkandarroch Cres ML8 ...... 188 A1
Parkbrae Gdns G20 ...... 97 D3
Parkbrae Pl G20 ...... 97 D3
Parkburn Ave G66 ...... 79 E4
Parkburn Rd G65 ...... 36 B1
Parkdyke FK7 ...... 6 C3
Parkend Ave KA21 ...... 217 D4
Parkend Cres FK1 ...... 66 B3
Parkend Gdns KA21 ...... 217 D4
Parkend Rd KA21 ...... 217 D4
Parker Pl Kilsyth G65 ...... 60 B4
  Larkhall ML9 ...... 185 D2
Parkfield G75 ...... 180 C3
Parkfoot Ct FK1 ...... 42 A2
Parkfoot St G65 ...... 36 B1
Parkgate FK12 ...... 4 C3
Parkgrove Ave G46 ...... 136 B2
Parkgrove Terr 16 G3 ...... 96 C1
Parkgrove Terrace La G3 ...... 96 C1
Parkhall Rd G81 ...... 73 F2
Parkhall St G74 ...... 159 F1
Parkhall Terr G81 ...... 73 F3
Parkhead Ave KA13 ...... 207 F2
Parkhead Cross G31 ...... 118 B3
Parkhead Ct FK10 ...... 10 B4
Parkhead La ML6 ...... 123 D4
Parkhead Rd Alloa FK10 ...... 10 B4
  Falkirk FK1 ...... 42 A1
Parkhead St Airdrie ML6 ...... 123 D4
Parkhill Ave
  Crosshouse KA2 ...... 226 C4
  Port Glasgow PA14 ...... 69 D4
Parkhill Dr Dalry KA24 ...... 191 E4
  Lochwinnoch PA12 ...... 129 E2
  Rutherglen G73 ...... 138 A4
Parkhill Rd G43 ...... 136 B4
Parkholm La G5 ...... 116 C3
Parkhouse Dr KA25 ...... 149 D1
Parkhouse Gdns KA22 ...... 205 E1
Parkhouse Rd
  Ardrossan KA22 ...... 205 E1
  Glasgow G53 ...... 135 D2
Parkhouse Sch G22 ...... 97 E3
Parkhouse St G5 ...... 117 E3
Parkinch PA8 ...... 93 E4
Parkknowe Rd G74 ...... 238 C4
Parkknowe Rd Blantyre ML3 ...... 161 D1
  Glasgow G43 ...... 136 B2
Parkneuk St ML1 ...... 163 E4
Parknook Way 4 ML9 ...... 185 D2
Parks View ML3 ...... 183 D3
Parksail PA8 ...... 93 E4
Parksail Dr PA8 ...... 93 E4
Parkside G64 ...... 78 A1
Parkside Gdns G20 ...... 97 D3
Parkside La G20 ...... 97 D3
Parkside Pl G20 ...... 97 D3
Parkside Rd
  Motherwell ML1 ...... 163 D3
  Shotts ML7 ...... 146 B2
Parkthorn View KA2 ...... 225 F1
Parkvale Ave PA8 ...... 93 E4

Parkvale Cres PA8 ...... 93 F4
Parkvale Dr PA8 ...... 93 E4
Parkvale Gdns PA8 ...... 93 E4
Parkvale Pl PA8 ...... 93 E4
Parkvale Way PA8 ...... 93 E4
Parkview KA7 ...... 238 C1
Parkview Ave Falkirk FK1 ...... 41 F1
  Kirkintilloch G66 ...... 79 E4
Parkview Cres ML2 ...... 166 A2
Parkview Ct G66 ...... 79 E4
Parkview Dr
  Coatbridge ML5 ...... 121 F4
  Glasgow G33 ...... 99 F3
Parkview Prim Sch G20 ...... 96 B4
Parkville Dr G72 ...... 161 F3
Parkville Rd ML4 ...... 142 B4
Parkway Alloa FK10 ...... 10 A4
  Erskine PA8 ...... 93 D4
Parkway Ct ML5 ...... 121 F3
Parkway Pl ML5 ...... 121 F3
Parnell St ML6 ...... 122 C3
Parnie St G1 ...... 241 D1
Parry Terr G75 ...... 159 D1
Parsonage Row G1 ...... 241 E2
Parsonage Sq G4 ...... 241 E2
Parterre G74 ...... 219 E1
Partick Bridge St G11 ...... 96 B1
Partick St ML5 ...... 122 B3
Partick Sta (Underground)
  G11 ...... 96 A1
Partickhill Ave G11 ...... 96 A1
Partickhill Ct G11 ...... 96 A2
Partickhill Rd G11 ...... 96 A2
Partridge Rd PA16 ...... 45 D3
Patchy Pk ML9 ...... 199 D4
Paterson Ave KA12 ...... 219 F3
Paterson Cres KA12 ...... 219 E3
Paterson Dr
  Helensburgh G84 ...... 16 A2
  Shieldhill FK1 ...... 66 B3
Paterson Pl Bearsden G61 ...... 75 E4
  Bonnybridge FK4 ...... 40 B3
  Bridge Of A FK9 ...... 2 A3
Paterson St Ayr KA8 ...... 236 A2
  Glasgow G5 ...... 240 B1
  Motherwell ML1 ...... 163 F4
Paterson Terr G75 ...... 180 B4
Path The FK7 ...... 7 E1
Pather St ML3 ...... 165 D1
Pathfoot KA13 ...... 207 F2
Pathfoot Ave FK9 ...... 2 B4
Pathfoot Dr FK9 ...... 2 B4
Pathfoot Rd FK9 ...... 2 B3
Pathfoot View KA13 ...... 207 F2
Pathhead Gdns G33 ...... 98 C3
Pathhead Rd G76 ...... 158 B4
Patna Ct ML3 ...... 161 F1
Patna St G40 ...... 118 A2
Paton St Alloa FK10 ...... 10 A4
  Glasgow G31 ...... 118 A4
  Greenock PA16 ...... 45 E3
Patrick Ave KA20 ...... 206 B1
Patrick Dr FK1 ...... 66 C4
Patterson Dr ML8 ...... 187 D3
Patterton Dr G78 ...... 134 B1
Patterton Sta G77 ...... 156 B4
Patterton St G81 ...... 73 F2
Pattle Pl KA7 ...... 238 C1
Paul Dr FK7 ...... 14 C2
Pavilion Pl KA22 ...... 205 E1
Pavilion Rd KA7 ...... 238 C4
Pavilion View ML10 ...... 9 F4
Paxstone Cres ML7 ...... 127 F3
Paxstone Dr ML7 ...... 127 F3
Paxton Pl KA1 ...... 228 A4
Payne St G4 ...... 97 E1
Peace Ave Kilmarnock KA1 ...... 222 B1
  Quarriers Village PA11 ...... 89 F1
Peacock Ave PA2 ...... 112 C1
Peacock Cross ML3 ...... 162 B2
Peacock Cross Ind Est
  ML3 ...... 162 B2
Peacock Dr Hamilton ML3 ...... 162 B2
  Paisley PA2 ...... 112 C1
Peacock Loan ML8 ...... 187 F2
Pearce La G51 ...... 116 A4
Pearce St G51 ...... 116 A4
Pearl St ML4 ...... 142 A2
Pearson Ave FK4 ...... 39 E3
Pearson Dr PA4 ...... 94 B2
Pearson Pl
  Dennyloanhead FK4 ...... 39 E3
  Linwood PA3 ...... 112 A3
Peat Pl G53 ...... 135 D3
Peat Rd Bridge Of W PA11 ...... 110 C4
  Glasgow G53 ...... 135 D3
  Greenock PA15 ...... 45 E2
Peathill Ave G69 ...... 100 A4
Peathill Rd FK4 ...... 40 A3
Peathill St G21 ...... 97 E2
Peatland Quadrant KA1 ...... 228 A2
Peatland Rd KA1 ...... 228 A2
Pebbles Dr G73 ...... 138 B4
Peden Ave KA24 ...... 191 D4
Peden Pl KA12 ...... 219 F1
Peden St ML7 ...... 127 E3
Pedmyre La G76 ...... 158 B4
Peebles Path ML5 ...... 122 B2
Peebles St KA8 ...... 235 F1
Peel Brae G66 ...... 58 B1
Peel Ct G72 ...... 139 D3
Peel Glen Rd G15 ...... 75 D3
Peel La G11 ...... 96 A1
Peel Park Pl G74 ...... 158 C1
Peel Pl Bothwell G71 ...... 141 D2
  Coatbridge ML5 ...... 121 E3

Peel Rd G76 158 A1
Peel St Cardross G82 48 A4
Glasgow G11 96 A1
Peel View G81 74 B2
Pegasus Ave Carluke ML8 187 F1
Paisley PA3 112 C3
Pegasus Rd ML4 142 C3
Peggieshill Pl KA7 239 D3
Peggieshill Rd KA7 239 D3
Peile La PA16 45 E3
Peile St PA16 45 E3
Peiter Pl G72 161 E4
Pelstream Ave FK7 7 D2
Pemberton Valley KA7 239 D1
Pembroke G74 160 B2
Pembroke Rd PA16 44 B2
Pembroke St Glasgow G3 240 A3
Larbert FK5 23 E2
Penbreck Ct KA11 220 A3
Pencaitland Dr G32 119 D2
Pencaitland Gr G32 119 D2
Pencaitland Pl G23 76 C1
Pendeen Cres G33 119 F3
Pendeen Pl G33 119 F3
Pendeen Rd G33 119 F3
Penders La FK1 42 A3
Pendicle Cres G61 75 E2
Pendicle Rd G61 75 F2
Pendreich Way FK9 2 A2
Penfold Cres G75 180 B4
Penicuik St G32 118 B3
Penilee Rd PA1 114 C3
Penilee Sec Sch G52 114 C3
Penilee Terr G52 114 C3
Peninver Dr G51 115 F4
Penman Ave G73 137 F4
Pennan PA8 73 D2
Pennan Pl G14 95 D3
Penneld Rd G52 114 C3
Penniecroft Ave G82 50 B3
Pennyburn Prim Sch KA13 207 E1
Pennyburn Rd KA13 207 E1
Pennyfern Dr PA16 45 D2
Pennyfern Rd PA16 45 D2
Pennyroyal Ct G74 159 E2
Pennyvenie Way KA11 220 A3
Penrioch Dr G75 180 B2
Penrith Ave G46 136 B1
Penrith Dr G12 96 A3
Penrith Pl G75 179 F3
Penryn Gdns G32 119 E2
Penston Rd G33 119 E4
Pentland Ave Linwood PA3 112 A3
Port Glasgow PA14 68 C3
Pentland Cres
Larkhall ML9 184 C3
Paisley PA2 133 E4
Pentland Ct Airdrie ML6 103 D1
Barrhead G78 134 B1
Pentland Dr Barrhead G78 134 B1
Bishopbriggs G64 78 B1
Prestwick KA9 236 B3
Renfrew PA4 114 A4
Pentland Pl Bearsden G61 75 D4
Irvine KA11 220 A2
Pentland Rd Chryston G69 100 B4
East Kilbride G75 180 A2
Glasgow G43 136 B3
Kilmarnock KA1 228 A2
Wishaw ML2 164 C2
Penzance Way G69 80 C1
Peockland Gdns PA5 112 A2
Peockland Pl PA5 112 A2
People's Palace (Mus) G40 117 F3
Peploe Dr G74 160 B3
Perceton Rdbt KA11 220 A3
Perceton Row KA11 220 B2
Perchy View ML2 165 E1
Percy Dr G46 136 B1
Percy Rd PA4 94 A1
Percy St Glasgow G51 116 B3
Larkhall ML9 185 D2
Perran Gdns G69 80 C1
Perray Ave G82 49 D3
Perrays Dr G82 49 D2
Perth Ave ML6 123 D2
Perth Cres G81 73 E3
Perth St G3 240 A2
Peter Coats Building PA2 113 F2
Peter D.Stirling Rd G66 58 B1
Peter St KA12 219 D1
Peters Ave G83 20 A1
Petersburn Pl ML6 123 E3
Petersburn Prim Sch ML6 123 E3
Petersburn Rd ML6 123 E3
Petershill Ct G21 98 B2
Petershill Dr G21 98 B2
Petershill Pl G21 98 A2
Petershill Rd G21 98 A2
Peterson Dr G13 94 C4
Peterson Gdns G13 94 C4
Peterswell Brae FK7 7 F1
Petition Pl G71 141 D3
Pettigrew St G32 119 D3
Peveril Ave Glasgow G41 116 B1
Rutherglen G73 138 B3
Peveril Ct G73 138 B3
Pharonhill St G31 118 B3
Philip Dr FK5 23 E1
Philip Murray Rd ML4 141 E3
Philip Sq KA8 236 A1
Philip St FK2 42 A4
Philipshill Gate G74 158 C2
Philipshill Rd G76 158 C2
Phoenix Bsns Pk The PA3 112 C3
Phoenix Cres ML4 141 F4
Phoenix Pl Elderslie PA5 112 B2
Motherwell ML1 143 D2
Phoenix Rd ML4 142 C3
Phoenix Ret Pk The PA3 112 C3
Piazza Sh Ctr PA1 113 F3
Piccadilly St G3 240 A2
Picken St KA1 227 F3
Pickerstonhill ML1 143 F2
Picketlaw Dr G76 158 B4
Picketlaw Farm Rd G76 158 B4
Pier Rd Balloch G83 19 E1
Rhu G84 15 F2
Piershill St G32 118 C4
Piersland Pl KA11 220 A3
Pike Rd FK7 7 E2
Pikeman Rd G13 95 E4
Pilmuir Ave G44 136 C2
Pilrig St G32 118 C4
Pilton Rd G15 75 D2
Pine Ave G72 139 F2
Pine Brae KA7 239 E3
Pine Cl G67 62 C2
Pine Cres Cumbernauld G67 62 C2
East Kilbride G75 180 A3
Johnstone PA5 112 A1
Pine Ct Coatbridge ML5 121 F2
Cumbernauld G67 62 C2
East Kilbride G75 180 B3
Pine Gr Alloa FK10 10 B3
Calderbank ML6 123 D1
Cumbernauld G67 62 C2
Motherwell ML1 143 D3
Uddingston G71 141 D4
Pine House KA9 236 A3
Pine Lawn ML2 165 E3
Pine Pk ML3 162 C1
Pine Pl Cumbernauld G67 62 C2
Glasgow G5 117 E2
Pine Rd Clydebank G81 73 E2
Cumbernauld G67 62 C2
Dumbarton G82 49 F2
Kilmarnock KA1 227 E4
Pine St Airdrie ML6 123 E4
Greenock PA15 45 F2
Lennoxtown G65 57 F4
Paisley PA2 114 A1
Pine Wlk FK5 23 E1
Pineapple The FK2 14 A3
Pinelands G64 78 A2
Pines The G44 137 D2
Pinewood Ave G66 79 D3
Pinewood Ct
Dumbarton G82 50 B3
Kirkintilloch G66 79 D3
Pinewood Pl G66 79 D3
Pinewood Prim Sch G15 75 E2
Pinkerton Ave G73 137 F4
Pinkerton La PA4 94 B1
Pinkston Dr G21 97 F1
Pinkston Rd G21, G4 241 E4
Pinmore KA13 207 E1
Pinmore Pl G53 134 C3
Pinmore St G53 134 C3
Pinwherry Dr G33 98 C3
Pinwherry Pl G71 141 D2
Piper Ave PA6 111 E4
Piper Rd Airdrie ML6 123 E3
Houston PA6 111 E4
Piperhill KA7 239 D1
Pirleyhill Dr FK1 66 B3
Pirleyhill Gdns FK1 42 A1
Pirnhall Rd FK7 11 D4
Pirnie Pl G65 60 B4
Pirnmill Ave
East Kilbride G75 180 A2
Motherwell ML1 163 D4
Pirnmill Pl G84 16 C1
Pirnmill Rd KA21 205 F1
Pit Rd Bellshill ML4 141 F3
Kirkintilloch G66 80 B4
Pitcairn Cres G75 179 F4
Pitcairn Gr G75 180 A4
Pitcairn Pl G75 179 F4
Pitcairn St G31 118 C2
Pitcairn Terr ML3 162 A2
Pitcaple Dr G43 136 A3
Pitfairn Rd FK10 5 F2
Pitlochry Dr Glasgow G52 115 E2
Larkhall ML9 185 E1
Pitmedden Rd G64 78 B1
Pitmilly Rd G15 75 E2
Pitreavie Ct ML3 183 D4
Pitreavie Pl G33 99 E1
Pitt St G2 240 B3
Pitt Terr FK8 7 D3
Place Of Bonhill G82 27 E2
Place View KA25 149 D1
Pladda Ave Irvine KA11 220 A1
Port Glasgow PA14 69 D4
Pladda Cres KA11 220 A1
Pladda Ct KA11 220 A1
Pladda Dr KA9 236 B3
Pladda Rd Renfrew PA4 94 B1
Saltcoats KA21 205 F1
Pladda St ML1 163 D4
Pladda Terr KA11 220 A1
Pladda Way G84 16 C1
Pladda Wynd KA11 220 A1
Plains Prim Sch ML6 104 A1
Plaintrees Ct PA2 113 F1
Plan View KA25 149 D2
Plane Pl G71 121 E1
Planetree Pl PA5 112 A1
Planetree Rd G81 74 A3
Plant St G31 118 B3
Plantation Ave ML1 143 D3
Plantation Park Gdns 5 G51 116 B3
Plantation Sq G51 116 C3
Plateau Dr KA10 229 F4
Platthorn Dr G74 159 F1
Platthorn Rd G74 159 F1
Players Rd FK7 7 E4
Playfair St G40 118 A2
Playingfield Cres KA2 221 F1
Playingfield Rd KA2 221 F1
Plaza The 1 G74 159 F1
Pleaknowe Cres G69 80 C1
Pleamuir Pl G68 61 E1
Plean Ctry Pk FK7 12 A1
Plean St G14 95 D3
Pleasance FK1 42 A2
Pleasance Ct 13 FK2 42 A2
Pleasance Gdns FK1 42 A2
Pleasance Rd FK2 42 A2
Pleasance Sq 12 FK1 42 A2
Pleasance St G43 136 B4
Pleasantfield Rd KA9 236 A3
Pleasantside Ave PA14 69 D4
Plotcock Rd ML3 198 B4
Plover Dr G75 180 A3
Plover Pl PA5 131 E4
Plusgarten Loan ML2 165 F4
Plymouth Ave PA19 44 C3
Pochard Way ML4 141 F4
Poet's View G66 79 F4
Poindfauld Terr G82 50 A2
Pointhouse Rd G3 116 B4
Pokelly Pl KA3 195 F1
Polbae Cres G76 178 C3
Poles Rd KA3 213 D2
Polkemmet Dr ML7 127 F3
Polkemmet La ML7 127 F3
Polkemmet Rd ML7 127 F3
Pollick Ave G78 153 D2
Pollick Farm La G78 153 D1
Pollock Ave
Eaglesham G76 178 C3
Hamilton ML3 162 A2
Pollock Cres KA13 207 F1
Pollock House G43 135 F4
Pollock Rd Bearsden G61 76 A2
Newton Mearns G77 156 B2
Pollock St Bellshill ML4 142 B3
Motherwell ML1 163 F4
Pollockshields East Sta G41 117 D2
Pollok Ave G43 136 A4
Pollok Ctry Pk G43 116 A1
Pollok Dr G64 77 F1
Pollok La G74 160 A2
Pollok Pl G74 160 A2
Pollokshaws East Sta G43 136 B4
Pollokshaws Rd G41 117 D2
Pollokshaws West Sta G43 136 A4
Pollokshields Prim Sch G41 116 C2
Pollokshields Prim Sch Annexe (Infs) G41 116 C2
Pollokshields West Sta G41 116 C1
Polmadie Ave G5 117 E1
Polmadie Ind Est G5 117 F1
Polmadie Rd G42, G5 117 E1
Polmadie St G42 117 E1
Polmaise Ave FK7 7 D2
Polmaise Cres FK7 8 B3
Polmaise Ct FK7 7 D2
Polmaise Rd
Cambusbarron FK7 6 C2
Stirling FK7 6 C3
Polnoon Ave G13 95 D3
Polnoon Dr G76 178 C3
Polnoon St G76 178 B2
Polo Ave KA10 229 F1
Polo Gdns KA10 229 F1
Polquhap Ct G53 135 D4
Polquhap Gdns G53 135 D4
Polquhap Pl G53 135 D4
Polson Dr PA5 111 F1
Polsons Cres PA2 113 E1
Polwarth La G12 96 A2
Polwarth St G12 96 A2
Pomona Pl ML3 161 F1
Pompee Rd FK10 5 D1
Poplar Ave Bishopton PA7 72 A1
Glasgow G11 95 F2
Johnstone PA5 112 A1
Newton Mearns G77 156 C2
Poplar Cres PA7 72 A1
Poplar Ct ML5 121 F2
Poplar Dr Clydebank G81 73 F3
Kirkintilloch G66 79 D3
Milton Of C G65 58 B3
Poplar Gdns G75 180 B3
Poplar Pl Blantyre G72 140 B1
Gourock PA19 44 B3
Motherwell ML1 143 D2
Uddingston G71 141 E4
Poplar Rd G82 49 F2
Poplar St Airdrie ML6 123 E4
Greenock PA15 46 C1
Poplar Way Ayr KA7 239 E3
Cambuslang G72 139 F2
Poplars The Bearsden G61 75 E4
Tullibody FK10 4 A1
Poplin St G40 118 A2
Porchester St G33 99 E1
Port Dundas Ind Est G4 97 E1
Port Dundas Pl G2 241 D3
Port Dundas Rd G4 241 D4
Port Glasgow High Sch PA14 69 D3
Port Glasgow Ind Est PA14 68 C4
Port Glasgow Rd
Greenock PA15 46 C2
Kilmacolm PA13 69 D1
Port Glasgow Sta PA14 47 E1
Port St Glasgow G3 240 A2
Stirling FK8 7 D4
Portal Rd G13 95 E4
Portdownie FK1 41 E3
Portencross Rd KA23 190 B3
Porter St 1 G51 116 B3
Porterfield Rd
Kilmacolm PA13 89 F4
Renfrew PA4 94 A2
Porters La ML6 123 E1
Porters Well G71 140 C3
Portessie PA8 73 D1
Porthlethen PA8 73 D1
Porting Cross Pl KA3 223 D3
Portland Ave KA12 224 A4
Portland Brae KA1 228 C3
Portland Ct KA1 228 C3
Portland Pk ML3 162 C1
Portland Pl Hamilton ML3 162 C1
Irvine KA12 224 A4
Kilmarnock KA1 227 F4
Lanark ML11 215 D2
Stevenston KA20 217 E4
Portland Place Ind Est KA20 217 E4
Portland Rd
Cumbernauld G68 61 F3
Irvine KA12 224 A4
Kilmarnock KA1 227 F4
Paisley PA2 114 A2
Portland Rdbt KA12 219 D1
Portland Sq ML3 162 C1
Portland St
Coatbridge ML5 122 A4
Kilmarnock KA1 222 C1
Troon KA10 229 E2
Portland Terr KA10 229 D1
Portland Wynd 2 ML9 185 D2
Portman St G41 116 C3
Portmark Ave KA7 238 B1
Portmarnock Dr G23 96 C4
Porton Pl PA7 72 A2
Portpatrick Rd G60 72 C4
Portreath Rd G69 80 C2
Portree Terr PA16 44 C2
Portsmouth Dr PA19 44 C3
Portsoy PA8 73 D1
Portsoy Ave G13 94 C4
Portsoy Pl G13 94 C4
Portugal St G5 117 D3
Portwell ML3 162 C2
Possil Cross G22 97 E2
Possil Rd G4 97 D2
Possilpark & Parkhouse Sta G22 97 D3
Postgate ML3 162 C2
Posthill FK10 5 E1
Potassels Rd G69 100 B4
Potrail Pl ML3 162 A2
Potter Cl G32 118 C2
Potter Gr G32 118 C2
Potter Pl Glasgow G32 118 C2
Skinflats FK2 24 C2
Potter St G32 118 C2
Potterhill Ave PA2 133 F4
Potterhill Rd G53 115 D1
Potters Wynd ML11 215 E3
Pottery Pl KA3 222 C1
Pottery St PA15 46 C2
Pottis Rd FK7 7 E2
Potts Way ML1 142 B1
Powbrone G75 180 C3
Powburn Cres G71 140 B4
Powfoot St G31 118 B3
Powforth Cl ML9 184 C2
Powgree Cres KA15 171 E3
Powmill Rd KA9 233 E1
Powrie St G33 99 E2
Prentice La 5 G71 141 D4
Prentice Rd ML1 163 D3
President Kennedy Dr FK7 12 B2
Preston Pl Glasgow G42 117 D1
Gourock PA19 44 B4
Preston St G42 117 D1
Prestonfield G62 54 C1
Prestonfield Ave KA13 207 D2
Prestwick Acad KA9 233 E1
Prestwick Airport Sta KA9 233 D2
Prestwick Ct G68 61 F2
Prestwick Int Airport KA9 233 F1
Prestwick Pl G77 157 D2
Prestwick Rd KA8 236 A2
Prestwick St G53 135 D3
Prestwick Sta KA9 233 D1
Pretoria Ct G75 180 A2
Pretoria Rd FK5 23 D1
Priestfield Ind Est G72 161 E3
Priestfield St G72 161 E3
Priesthill Ave G53 135 E3
Priesthill Cres G53 135 E3
Priesthill & Darnley Sta G53 135 E3
Priesthill Rd G53 135 E3
Priestknowe Rdbt G74 159 F1
Prieston Rd PA11 110 B4
Primrose Ave
Bellshill ML4 142 A4
Larkhall ML9 199 D4
Primrose Cres ML1 163 F3
Primrose Ct 21 G14 95 E2
Primrose Pk KA7 239 E2
Primrose Pl Alloa FK10 10 A3
Cumbernauld G67 82 A3
Kilmarnock KA1 222 B1
Saltcoats KA21 206 A1
Uddingston G71 141 E4
Primrose St Alloa FK10 10 A4
Bonnybridge FK4 40 A3
Glasgow G14 95 E2
Primrose Way ML8 201 F4
Prince Albert Rd G12 96 B2
Prince Albert Terr G84 16 B1
Prince Edward St 2 G42 117 D1
Prince of Wales Gdns G20 96 B4
Prince Pl ML2 166 A3
Prince's Gdns G12 96 A2
Prince's Pl 20 G12 96 B2
Prince's Terr G12 96 B2
Princes Ct KA8 236 A1
Princes Gate Bothwell G71 140 C2
Rutherglen G73 138 A4
Princes Mall 8 G74 159 F1
Princes Pk PA8 72 C2
Princes Pl KA22 205 D1
Princes Sq Barrhead G78 134 B2
3 East Kilbride G74 159 F1
Troon KA10 229 E2
Princes Square Shop Ctr G1 241 D2
Princes St
Ardrossan KA22 205 D1
Caldercruix ML6 105 D3
California FK1 66 C3
Falkirk FK1 42 A3
Greenock PA15 45 F3
Kilmarnock KA1 227 F4
Motherwell ML1 163 F4
Port Glasgow PA14 47 E1
Rutherglen G73 138 A4
Stirling FK8 7 D4
Princes St E G84 16 C1
Princess Anne Quadrant ML1 142 C3
Princess Cres PA1 114 A3
Princess Ct
Helensburgh G84 16 B1
Kilmarnock KA1 228 A2
Princess Dr G69 121 D3
Princess Rd ML1 142 C2
Princess Sq 25 ML2 165 F3
Princess St FK4 40 A3
Princess Way G84 15 D2
Printers Land G76 158 A3
Priorwood Rd G77 156 A2
Priory Ave PA3 114 A4
Priory Dr G71 140 B4
Priory Gate ML2 186 A4
Priory Pl Cumbernauld G68 60 C1
Glasgow G13 95 E4
Priory Rd G13 95 E4
Priory St G72 161 E4
Priory Terr ML2 164 B1
Procession Rd PA2 133 E3
Professors' Sq G12 96 B1
Progress Dr ML6 105 D3
Promenade KA8 236 A2
Prosen St G32 118 C2
Prospect Ave
Cambuslang G72 138 C3
Uddingston G71 140 C4
Prospect Ct G72 161 E3
Prospect Dr ML9 199 F4
Prospect Rd
Cumbernauld G68 61 E3
Glasgow G41 136 B4
Prospect St FK1 41 F3
Prospecthill Cir G42 117 E1
Prospecthill Cres G42 137 F4
Prospecthill Dr G42 137 E4
Prospecthill Pl
Glasgow G42 137 F4
Greenock PA15 45 F2
Prospecthill Rd Falkirk FK1 42 A1
Glasgow G42 137 E4
Saltcoats KA21 206 A1
Prospecthill Sq G42 137 E4
Prospecthill St PA15 45 F2
Provan Hall G34 99 F1
Provan Rd G33 118 B4
Provand Hall Cres G69 120 A2
Provanhall Prim Sch G34 100 A1
Provanhill St G21 97 F1
Provanmill Rd G33 98 C1
Provost Cl PA5 111 F2
Provost Driver Ct PA4 94 C1
Provost Gate ML9 185 D2
Provost Hunter Ave FK12 5 E4
Pullar Ave FK9 2 A3
Pullar Ct FK9 2 A3
Pundeavon Ave KA25 149 D2
Purdie G74 160 B3
Purdie St ML3 162 A3
Purdon St G11 96 A1
Putyan Ave KA24 191 D4
Pyatshaw Rd ML9 185 D1

Quadrant Rd G43 136 C3
Quadrant The G76 157 F4
Quail Rd KA8 236 A2
Quakerfield FK7 7 F1
Quarrelton Rd PA5 111 F1
Quarrier St PA15 46 B2
Quarrolhall Cres FK2 24 A2
Quarry Ave G72 139 F2
Quarry Brae Prim Sch G31 118 B3

Quarry Dr Kilmacolm PA13 ...... 69 E1
Kirkintilloch G66 .... 79 F4
Quarry Knowe
Bannockburn FK7 .... 11 F4
Dumbarton G82 .... 49 B3
Rhu G84 .... 15 F3
Quarry La Dumbarton G82 ...... 49 F2
Eaglesham G76 .... 178 B2
Lennoxtown G65 .... 33 E1
Quarry Pk G75 .... 180 C4
Quarry Pl Alloa FK10 .... 10 B4
Cambuslang G72 .... 138 C3
Dumbarton G82 .... 49 E3
Hamilton ML3 .... 162 C2
Shotts ML7 .... 146 B3
Quarry Rd Airdrie ML6 .... 103 D1
Barrhead G78 .... 134 A2
Cambusbarron FK7 .... 6 B3
East Kilbride G75 .... 180 B3
Irvine KA12 .... 219 E2
Larkhall ML9 .... 185 D1
Paisley PA2 .... 113 F1
Port Glasgow PA14 .... 68 C4
Shotts ML7 .... 146 B3
Quarry St Coatbridge ML5 ..... 122 B4
Hamilton ML3 .... 162 C2
Johnstone PA5 .... 111 F1
Larkhall ML9 .... 185 D1
Motherwell ML1 .... 143 D2
Shotts ML7 .... 165 D2
Quarrybank PA10 .... 111 E1
Quarrybrae Ave G76 .... 157 E4
Quarrybrae Gdns G71 .... 141 E3
Quarrybrae St G31 .... 118 C3
Quarryknowe Lanark ML11 ... 215 D2
Rutherglen G73 .... 137 F4
Quarryknowe Pl ML4 .... 141 F2
Quarryknowe St
Clydebank G81 .... 74 C4
Glasgow G31 .... 118 C3
Quarryside St ML6 .... 102 C2
Quarrywood Ave G21 .... 98 B2
Quarrywood Rd G21 .... 98 B2
Quarter Prim Sch ML3 .... 183 F2
Quay (Leisure Complex) The
G5 .... 240 A1
Quay Pend G82 .... 49 F2
Quay Rd G73 .... 118 A1
Quay Road N G73 .... 118 A1
Quay St Dumbarton G82 .... 49 F2
Saltcoats KA21 .... 216 C4
Quebec Dr G75 .... 159 E1
Quebec Gn G75 .... 159 E1
Quebec Wynd G72 .... 139 E4
Queen Elizabeth Ave G52 .. 114 C4
Queen Elizabeth Ct ML1 ... 163 E4
Queen Elizabeth Sq 🅱
G5 .... 240 A1
Queen Margaret Acad
KA7 .... 239 E2
Queen Margaret Ct 🅱 G20 .. 96 C2
Queen Margaret Dr G20 ...... 96 C2
Queen Mary Ave
Clydebank G81 .... 74 B1
Glasgow G42 .... 117 D1
Queen Mary St G40 .... 118 A2
Queen Mother's Hospl The
G3 .... 96 B1
Queen Rd KA12 .... 219 E3
Queen Sq G41 .... 116 C1
Queen St Alexandria G83 .... 27 E2
Alloa FK10 .... 10 A4
Alva FK12 .... 5 D4
Ayr KA8 .... 236 A1
Bannockburn FK7 .... 7 E1
Falkirk FK2 .... 42 B3
Fallin FK7 .... 8 B2
Glasgow G1 .... 241 D2
Hamilton ML3 .... 162 A3
Helensburgh G84 .... 16 B2
🅹 Kilmarnock KA1 .... 227 F4
Kilwinning KA13 .... 208 A2
Kirkintilloch G66 .... 79 F4
Motherwell ML1 .... 163 F4
Paisley PA1 .... 113 E2
Renfrew PA4 .... 94 B2
Rutherglen G73 .... 138 A4
Stirling FK8 .... 7 D4
Stonehouse ML9 .... 198 C1
Queen St Sta G1 .... 241 D3
Queen Street St G1 .... 241 D3
Queen Victoria Dr G14 ...... 95 E2
Queen Victoria Gate G13 ... 95 E3
Queen Victoria St ML6 ...... 122 C4
Queen's Ave Bridge of A FK9 .. 2 A3
Cambuslang G72 .... 139 D3
Queen's Court G84 .... 25 C4
Queen's Cres Carluke ML8 .. 188 A1
Chapelhall ML6 .... 123 E2
Coatbridge G69 .... 120 C3
Falkirk FK1 .... 41 F3
🅶 Glasgow G4 .... 97 D1
Queen's Ct Bridge Of A FK9 .. 1 C4
Milngavie G62 .... 76 A4
Queen's Dr Alexandria G83 ... 27 E2
Ardrossan KA22 .... 205 E2
Cumbernauld G68 .... 61 F3
Glasgow G42 .... 117 D1
Kilmarnock KA1 .... 228 A3
Larbert FK5 .... 23 E1
Monkton KA9 .... 233 E3
Troon KA10 .... 229 E3

Queen's Drive La G42 .... 117 D1
Queen's Gate G76 .... 157 F4
Queen's Gdns G12 .... 96 B2
Queen's La FK9 .... 2 A4
Queen's Park Ave G42 .... 117 D1
Queen's Park Sta G42 .... 117 D1
Queen's Pl Glasgow G12 .... 96 B2
Kilwinning KA13 .... 208 A2
Queen's Quadrant KA8 ...... 236 A1
Queen's Rd Eldersie PA5 ..... 112 B1
Stirling FK8 .... 6 C4
Queen's St California FK1 ...... 66 C3
Cleland ML1 .... 144 A1
Queen's Terr KA7 .... 238 C4
Queen's Terrace La KA7 ..... 238 C4
Queens Cres Bellshill ML4 .. 141 F2
Motherwell ML1 .... 142 C2
Queens Ct FK5 .... 23 E2
Queens Dr Bishopton PA7 .... 72 B2
Denny FK6 .... 21 F2
Falkirk FK1 .... 41 F3
Hamilton ML3 .... 183 E3
Queens Point G84 .... 15 D4
Queens Terr KA9 .... 233 D1
Queens Way Alexandria G83 .. 27 E2
Torrance G64 .... 78 A4
Queensbank Ave G69 .... 100 C4
Queensberry Ave
Bearsden G61 .... 75 F4
Clarkston G76 .... 157 F4
Queensborough Gdns 🅸
G12 .... 96 A2
Queensby Ave 🇳 G69 .... 120 A3
Queensby Dr G69 .... 120 A3
Queensby Pl G69 .... 120 B3
Queensby Rd G69 .... 120 A3
Queensdale Ave ML9 .... 199 D4
Queensdale Rd ML9 .... 199 D4
Queensferry St G5 .... 117 F1
Queenshaugh Dr FK8 .... 2 B1
Queenside Cres PA8 .... 72 C1
Queensland Ct G52 .... 115 E3
Queensland Dr G52 .... 115 E3
Queensland Gdns G52 .... 115 E3
Queensland La E G52 .... 115 E3
Queensland La W G52 .... 115 E3
Queenslie Ind Est G33 ...... 119 E4
Queenslie St G33 .... 98 B1
Queensway
East Kilbride G74 .... 159 E1
Gourock PA19 .... 44 B3
Queenzieburn Ind Est 59 F4
Quendale Dr G32 .... 118 C2
Quentin St G41 .... 116 C1
Quinton Gdns G69 .... 120 A3

Raasay Cres PA2 .... 123 F3
Raasay Dr PA2 .... 133 E4
Raasay Gdns G77 .... 156 A3
Raasay Pl G22 .... 97 E4
Raasay St G22 .... 97 E4
Racecourse Rd KA7 .... 238 C3
Racecourse View Ayr KA7 .. 238 C3
Hamilton ML3 .... 162 C3
Rachan St G34 .... 100 B1
Radleigh Sch G76 .... 157 E4
Radnor St G81 .... 74 A2
Rae Ct FK2 .... 24 B2
Rae St FK5 .... 23 E2
Raeberry St G20 .... 96 C1
Raebog Cres ML6 .... 102 C1
Raebog Rd ML6 .... 102 C2
Raeburn Ave G74 .... 160 A2
Raeburn Cres ML3 .... 161 F2
Raeburn Pl G74 .... 160 A2
Raeburn Wlk ML4 .... 142 A4
Raes Rd ML8 .... 201 D4
Raeside Ave G77 .... 156 B2
Raeswood Dr G53 .... 134 C4
Raeswood Pl G53 .... 135 D4
Raeswood Rd G53 .... 134 C4
Raewell Cres ML4 .... 141 F2
Rafford St G51 .... 116 A4
Raggithill Ave KA6 .... 237 F3
Raglan St Alexandria G83 .... 27 F2
Glasgow G4 .... 97 D1
Raglan Street La G83 .... 27 F2
Railway Rd ML6 .... 122 B4
Raise St KA21 .... 216 C4
Raith Ave Glasgow G44,G45 .. 137 E2
Prestwick KA9 .... 236 C4
Raith Dr ML4 .... 142 A2
Raith Rd KA12 .... 213 D2
Raith Terr KA9 .... 236 C4
Raithburn Ave
Glasgow G45 .... 137 E2
Kilmarnock KA3 .... 222 C2
Raithburn Rd G45 .... 137 E2
Ralston Ave G52 .... 114 C2
Ralston Ct G52 .... 114 C2
Ralston Dr
Crookedholm KA3 .... 228 B4
Glasgow G52 .... 114 C2
Ralston Path G52 .... 114 C2
Ralston Pl G52 .... 114 C2
Ralston Prim Sch G52 .... 114 C3
Ralston Rd Barrhead G78 ... 134 B1
Bearsden G61 .... 75 F3
Ralston St Airdrie ML6 ...... 122 C4
Larkhall ML9 .... 185 D1
Ralstonyards Rd KA3 .... 228 C4
Ram St G32 .... 118 C3
Ramage Rd ML8 .... 188 A1
Ramillies Ct ML8 .... 188 A1
Ramoth ML11 .... 214 B2
Rampart Ave G13 .... 95 D4

Ramsay Ave Johnstone PA5 .. 111 F1
Laurieston FK2 .... 42 C2
Ramsay Cres PA10 .... 111 D1
Ramsay Ct G77 .... 156 C2
Ramsay Hill G74 .... 160 A2
Ramsay Pl Coatbridge ML5 .. 121 E3
Johnstone PA5 .... 111 F1
Stirling FK8 .... 2 A1
Ramsay St G81 .... 73 F2
Ramsey Tullis Ave FK10 ...... 4 B1
Ramsey Tullis Dr FK10 .... 4 B1
Ramsey Wynd ML4 .... 142 A4
Ramstane Pl KA11 .... 220 B3
Ranald Gdns G73 .... 138 B2
Randolph Ave G69 .... 137 D1
Randolph Cres FK7 .... 7 E1
Randolph Ct G76 .... 7 D3
Randolph Dr G76 .... 136 C1
Randolph Gdns Denny FK6 .. 21 E1
Glasgow G76 .... 136 C1
Randolph La G11 .... 95 F2
Randolph Pl FK7 .... 7 E1
Randolph Rd Glasgow G11 .. 95 F2
Stirling FK8 .... 7 D3
Randolph Terr FK7 .... 7 D2
Randyford Rd FK2 .... 42 B3
Randyford St FK2 .... 42 C3
Ranfurly Ct PA11 .... 110 B4
Ranfurly Dr G68 .... 61 F2
Ranfurly Pl PA11 .... 110 B4
Ranfurly Rd
Bridge Of W PA11 .... 110 C3
Glasgow G52 .... 114 C3
Range Ave ML1 .... 164 B2
Range Pl ML3 .... 162 C1
Range Rd ML1 .... 164 A2
Range Road Ind Est ML2 .. 164 B2
Range St ML1 .... 164 A2
Rangehouse Rd G75 .... 180 C3
Ranken Dr KA12 .... 219 E2
Rankin Cres
Dennyloanhead FK4 .... 39 E3
Greengairs ML6 .... 83 F1
Rankin Ct KA3 .... 223 E2
Rankin Dr G77 .... 156 B3
Rankin Rd ML2 .... 165 F2
Rankin St Carluke ML8 ...... 187 F1
Greenock PA15 .... 46 A2
Rankine Ave G75 .... 181 D4
Rankine Pl
East Kilbride G75 .... 181 D4
Johnstone PA5 .... 111 F2
Rankine St PA5 .... 111 F2
Rannoch Ave
Bishopbriggs G64 .... 78 A1
Coatbridge ML5 .... 101 E1
Hamilton ML3 .... 162 A1
Newton Mearns G77 .... 156 B4
Rannoch Ct KA3 .... 195 E1
Rannoch Ct Alloa FK10 .... 10 B3
Cumbernauld G67 .... 82 A3
Hamilton G72 .... 161 F3
Rannoch Dr Bearsden G61 .. 76 A2
Cumbernauld G67 .... 82 A3
Kirkintilloch G66 .... 59 D1
Renfrew PA4 .... 94 B2
Wishaw ML2 .... 165 D1
Rannoch Gdns G64 .... 78 B1
Rannoch Gn G74 .... 159 F2
Rannoch Pl Irvine KA12 ..... 219 E3
Paisley PA2 .... 114 A2
Shieldhill FK1 .... 66 B2
Shotts ML7 .... 146 C3
Stenhousemuir FK5 .... 23 F2
Rannoch Rd Airdrie ML6 .... 102 C1
Johnstone PA5 .... 131 F4
Kilmacolm PA13 .... 89 E4
Uddingston G71 .... 120 C1
Rannoch St G44 .... 137 D3
Rannoch Terr ML9 .... 185 E1
Rannoch Way 🇳 G71 .... 141 D2
Rannock La G69 .... 81 D1
Raploch Ave G14 .... 95 D2
Raploch Cres G81 .... 74 B4
Raploch La G14 .... 95 D2
Raploch Prim Sch FK8 .... 1 C1
Raploch Rd Larkhall ML9 .. 184 C2
Stirling FK8 .... 1 C1
Raploch St ML9 .... 184 C2
Rashieburn PA8 .... 73 D1
Rashieglen PA8 .... 73 D1
Rashiehill PA8 .... 73 D1
Rashiehill Rd FK1 .... 86 A3
Rashielee Ave PA8 .... 73 D1
Rashielee Prim Sch PA8 ..... 73 D1
Rashielee Rd PA8 .... 73 D1
Rashley Sq KA22 .... 205 E2
Rathlin Ave KA1 .... 227 F2
Rathlin House KA9 .... 236 A3
Rathlin St G51 .... 116 A4
Rathlin Terr G82 .... 49 E3
Ratho Dr Cumbernauld G68 .. 61 F3
Glasgow G21 .... 97 F2
Ratho Pk ML3 .... 183 D4
Ratho St PA15 .... 46 B2
Rattray PA8 .... 73 D2
Rattray St G32 .... 118 C2
Ravel Row G31 .... 118 B3
Ravel Wynd G71 .... 141 D4
Ravelston Rd G61 .... 75 F2
Ravelston St G32 .... 118 C3
Raven Rd PA16 .... 45 D3
Raven Wynd ML2 .... 165 D2
Ravens Ct 🔎 G5 .... 97 F4
Ravenscliffe Dr G46 .... 136 A2
Ravenscourt G74 .... 158 B1
Ravenscraig Ave PA2 .... 113 E1

Ravenscraig Ct ML4 .... 142 A3
Ravenscraig Dr G53 .... 135 E3
Ravenscraig Hospl PA16 ..... 45 D2
Ravenscraig Prim Sch
PA16 .... 44 C2
Ravenscraig Rd KA3 .... 211 E4
Ravenscraig Terr G53 .... 135 E3
Ravenshall Rd G41 .... 136 B4
Ravenshill Dr ML1 .... 144 B1
Ravenspark Hospl KA12 ... 219 D3
Ravenstone Dr G46 .... 136 B3
Ravenswood Ave PA2 ...... 132 C4
Ravenswood Dr G41 .... 116 B1
Ravenswood Prim Sch
G69 .... 82 C4
Ravenswood Rd G69 .... 120 B3
Rawyards Ave ML6 .... 103 D1
Raymond Pl G75 .... 159 E1
Rayne Pl G15 .... 75 D2
Ream Ave ML6 .... 123 F3
Reay Ave Cardross G82 ...... 48 A4
Red Bridge Ct ML5 .... 122 A4
Red Cross House KA12 .... 219 E1
Red Deer Rd G75 .... 180 B4
Red Fox Dr G83 .... 27 F4
Red Gables Sq KA22 .... 205 D2
Red Rd Glasgow G21 .... 98 A2
Red Row G21 .... 27 E1
Red Road Ct G21 .... 98 A2
Redan St G40 .... 117 F3
Redbrae Rd Falkirk FK1 ...... 41 E3
Kirkintilloch G66 .... 79 F4
Redburn G83 .... 28 A1
Redburn Ave G46 .... 157 D4
Redburn Caravan Pk
KA12 .... 219 D4
Redburn Ct G62 .... 62 C3
Redburn Ind Est KA12 ..... 219 E4
Redburn Pl
Cumbernauld G67 .... 62 C3
Irvine KA12 .... 219 D3
Redburn Rd
Blackridge EH48 .... 107 D1
Cumbernauld G67 .... 62 C3
Redburn Rdbt KA12 .... 219 D4
Redcastle Sq G33 .... 99 E1
Redcliffe Dr G75 .... 180 A4
Redclyffe Gdns G84 .... 16 B2
Reddance Terr KA24 .... 191 E4
Redden St FK2 .... 42 C1
Redding Ave KA3 .... 222 C2
Redding Rd FK2 .... 42 C2
Rederech Cres ML3 .... 161 F1
Redford St G33 .... 118 B4
Redgate Pl G14 .... 95 D2
Redgauntlet Rd G84 .... 25 D4
Redgrave G74 .... 160 B3
Redhall Rd ML7 .... 147 D2
Redhill Rd G68 .... 61 E2
Redhills View G65 .... 57 F4
Redholme ML9 .... 185 D1
Redhouse La ML8 .... 187 F2
Redhurst Cres PA2 .... 133 E4
Redhurst La PA2 .... 133 E4
Redhurst Way PA2 .... 133 E4
Redlands La G12 .... 96 B2
Redlands Rd
🅰 Glasgow G12 .... 96 B2
Tullibody FK10 .... 4 A2
Redlands Terr 🅱 G12 .... 96 B2
Redlands Terrace La 🅴
G12 .... 96 B2
Redlawood Pl G72 .... 140 A3
Redlawood Rd G72 .... 140 A3
Redmire Cres ML7 .... 167 D4
Redmoss Rd Clydebank G81 .. 73 F4
Milton Of C G65 .... 58 A3
Redmoss St G22 .... 97 D3
Rednock St G22 .... 97 E2
Redpath Dr Glasgow G52 .. 115 E3
Stenhousemuir FK2 .... 24 A2
Redwell Pl FK10 .... 9 F4
Redwing Gdns ML2 .... 165 D1
Redwood Ave G74 .... 158 C1
Redwood Cres
Bishopton PA7 .... 72 B2
Cambuslang G72 .... 139 F2
East Kilbride G74 .... 158 C1
Uddingston G71 .... 141 E4
Redwood Ct
Cumbernauld G67 .... 139 F2
East Kilbride G75 .... 179 F4
Redwood Dr
East Kilbride G74 .... 158 C1
Glasgow G21 .... 98 A2
Redwood Gr ML6 .... 122 A3
Redwood Pl
East Kilbride G74 .... 158 C1
Kirkintilloch G66 .... 79 D3
Uddingston G71 .... 141 E4
Redwood Rd
Cumbernauld G67 .... 62 C2
Motherwell ML1 .... 143 D3
Reedlands Dr FK6 .... 39 E4
Reedloch Dr KA10 .... 229 F4
Reelick Ave G13 .... 94 C4
Reelick Quadrant G13 ...... 94 C4
Reema Rd ML4 .... 142 A3
Reen Pl G71 .... 141 D2
Reform St KA15 .... 150 A1
Regal Ct KA24 .... 191 E4
Regal Gr ML7 .... 146 C2

Regency Way
Hamilton ML3 .... 163 D1
Motherwell ML1 .... 142 C2
Regent Moray St G3 .... 96 B1
Regent Park Sq G41 .... 116 C1
Regent Pl G80 .... 79 E2
Regent St Clydebank G81 .... 73 F2
Greenock PA15 .... 45 F2
Kirkintilloch G66 .... 79 E4
Paisley PA1 .... 114 A3
Regents Gate G72 .... 140 B2
Register Ave ML4 .... 142 A2
Register Rd G65 .... 60 C4
Regwood St G41 .... 136 B4
Reid Ave Bearsden G61 ...... 76 A3
Linwood PA3 .... 112 A3
Reid Gr ML1 .... 164 A2
Reid Kerr Coll PA3 .... 113 F3
Reid Kerr Coll Annexe The
PA3 .... 113 F3
Reid Pl G40 .... 117 F2
Reid St Airdrie ML6 .... 103 D1
Coatbridge ML5 .... 122 A4
Glasgow G40 .... 117 F2
Hamilton ML3 .... 163 F3
Rutherglen G73 .... 138 A4
Salsburgh ML7 .... 125 D1
Reid Terr KA21 .... 217 D4
Reid's Ave G74 .... 206 B3
Reidvale St G31 .... 118 A3
Reilly Gdns FK4 .... 40 A2
Reilly Rd
High Bonnybridge FK4 .... 40 A2
Houston PA6 .... 91 E4
Reith Dr G75 .... 180 B4
Rennes Pl ML4 .... 142 C3
Renfield La G2 .... 240 C2
Renfield St Glasgow G2 .... 240 C3
Renfrew PA4 .... 94 B2
Renfrew Ct G2 .... 241 D3
Renfrew High Sch PA4 ...... 94 B1
Renfrew La G2 .... 240 C3
Renfrew Rd
Glasgow PA4, G51 .... 95 D1
Paisley PA3 .... 113 F3
Renfrew St
Coatbridge ML5 .... 121 E2
Glasgow G2 .... 240 C3
Rennie Pl East Kilbride G74 .. 159 D2
Saltcoats KA21 .... 216 C4
Rennie Rd G65 .... 42 A2
Renshaw Dr G52 .... 115 D3
Renshaw Rd Bishopton PA7 .. 72 A2
Eldersie PA5 .... 112 B1
Renton Prim Sch G82 .... 27 E1
Renton Rd Dumbarton G82 .. 49 E3
Greenock PA15 .... 46 B1
Renton St G4 .... 241 D4
Renton St G22 .... 97 E2
Renwick Pl ML1 .... 215 E3
Renwick Way KA9 .... 236 B3
Reservoir Rd PA19 .... 44 C3
Resipol Rd G33 .... 99 F3
Reston Dr G52 .... 115 D3
Reuther Ave G73 .... 138 A4
Revoch Dr G13 .... 95 D4
Reynolds Ave G75 .... 181 D4
Reynolds Path ML2 .... 165 E1
Rhannan Rd G44 .... 137 D3
Rhannan Terr G44 .... 137 D3
Rhindhouse Pl G69 .... 120 B3
Rhindhouse Rd G69 .... 120 B3
Rhindmuir Ave G69 .... 120 B3
Rhindmuir Cres G69 .... 120 B3
Rhindmuir Ct G69 .... 120 B3
Rhindmuir Dr G69 .... 120 B3
Rhindmuir Gdns G69 .... 120 B3
Rhindmuir Path G69 .... 120 B3
Rhindmuir Pl G69 .... 120 B3
Rhindmuir Rd G69 .... 120 B3
Rhindmuir View G69 .... 120 B3
Rhindmuir Wynd G69 ...... 120 B3
Rhinds St ML5 .... 121 E2
Rhindsdale Cres G69 .... 120 B3
Rhodders Gr FK12 .... 5 D4
Rhu Prim Sch G84 .... 15 E3
Rhu Quad ML2 .... 186 B3
Rhu Rd Lower
Helensburgh G84 .... 16 A1
Rhu G84 .... 15 F2
Rhu Road Higher G84 .... 16 A2
Rhu-Ellen Ct G84 .... 15 E2
Rhyber Ave ML11 .... 215 D3
Rhymer St G21 .... 97 F1
Rhymie La G12 .... 119 D2
Rhymiebank ML9 .... 198 B1
Rhynie Dr G51 .... 116 A3
Riach Gdns ML1 .... 142 B1
Ribblesdale G74 .... 159 F2
Riccarton G75 .... 180 A4
Riccarton Rd KA1 .... 228 B3
Riccarton St G42 .... 117 E1
Riccartsbar Ave PA2 .... 113 E2
Rice Way ML1 .... 164 A2
Richard St Renfrew PA4 ...... 94 B2
Richard Quadrant G81 .... 74 A3
Richard St G22 .... 240 B2
Richardland Pl KA1 .... 228 A4
Richardland Rd KA1 .... 227 F4
Richardson Ave KA1 .... 228 C3
Richie Ave G80 .... 48 A4
Richmond Ave G76 .... 157 F4
Richmond Ct G73 .... 138 B4

Richmond Dr
Bishopbriggs G64 .... 78 A2
Linwood PA3 .... 112 A4
Rutherglen G73, G72 .... 138 B4
Rutherglen, Cambuslang
G73, G72 .... 138 C3
Richmond Gdns G69 .... 100 A4
Richmond Gr G73 .... 138 B4
Richmond Park Sch G5 .... 117 E2
Richmond Pl G73 .... 138 B4
Richmond Rd G73 .... 138 B4
Richmond St Clydebank G81 .. 74 B1
Glasgow G1 .... 241 E2
Richmond Terr KA2 .... 225 F1
Riddell St Clydebank G81 .. 74 B2
Coatbridge ML5 .... 122 B4
Riddon Ave G81 .... 94 C4
Riddon Pl G13 .... 94 C4
Riddrie Cres G33 .... 118 C4
Riddrie Knowes G33 .... 118 C4
Riddrievale Ct G33 .... 98 C1
Riddrievale St G33 .... 98 C1
Ridgepark Dr ML11 .... 214 C3
Ridgepark Sch ML11 .... 214 C3
Ried Ct KA3 .... 228 C4
Rig St KA3 .... 211 E4
Rigby St G32 .... 118 C3
Rigfoot KA11 .... 220 A3
Rigghead A3 .... 211 E4
Rigghead Ave G67 .... 62 A3
Riggs The Milngavie G62 ... 55 D2
Prestwick KA9 .... 233 E1
Riggside Rd G33 .... 99 E1
Righead Gate 2 G42 .... 159 F1
Righead Ind Est ML4 .... 141 E4
Righead Rd G75 .... 159 E1
Riglands Way PA4 .... 94 B2
Riglaw Pl G13 .... 95 D4
Rigmuir Rd G51 .... 115 E3
Rigwoodie Pl KA7 .... 238 C1
Rimmon Cres ML7 .... 146 C3
Rimsdale St G40 .... 118 A3
Ring Rd FK10 .... 10 A4
Ringford St G21 .... 97 F2
Ripon Dr G12 .... 96 A3
Risk St Clydebank G81 ..... 73 F2
Dumbarton G82 .... 49 F2
Ristol Rd G13 .... 95 D3
Ritchie Cres PA5 .... 112 B2
Ritchie Ct KA3 .... 223 E1
Ritchie Pk PA5 .... 112 A2
Ritchie Pl G77 .... 156 B2
Ritchie St 21 Glasgow G5 .. 117 D2
West Kilbride KA23 .... 190 B3
Wishaw ML2 .... 164 B2
Ritchie's Cl ML11 .... 215 D2
River Ct KA5 .... 149 D1
River Rd G32 .... 119 D1
River St Ayr KA8 .... 235 F1
Falkirk FK2 .... 24 A1
River Terr KA8 .... 235 F1
River View G82 .... 48 A4
River Wlk KA13 .... 207 F3
Riverbank Dr ML4 .... 142 B2
Riverbank Pl KA1 .... 228 A4
Riverbank St G43 .... 136 B4
Riverbank View FK6 .... 7 E4
Riverdale Gdns ML3 .... 162 C1
Riverford Rd Glasgow G43 .. 136 B4
Rutherglen G73 .... 118 B1
Riversdale La G14 .... 95 D2
Riverside Balloch G83 ...... 27 F4
Houston PA6 .... 91 D1
Milngavie G62 .... 55 D1
Riverside Bsns Pk KA11 .. 224 C4
Riverside Dr FK8 .... 2 B1
Riverside Gdns G76 .... 157 F3
Riverside La G82 .... 49 F2
Riverside Gr G44 .... 137 D1
Riverside Pl Ayr KA8 .... 239 D4
Cambuslang G72 .... 139 F3
Riverside Prim Sch FK8 ... 1 A1
Riverside Rd
Eaglesham G76 .... 178 C4
Glasgow G43 .... 136 C4
Greenock PA15 .... 46 A2
Irvine KA11 .... 220 B1
Kilbirnie KA25 .... 149 D1
Kirkfieldbank ML11 .... 214 B2
Larkhall ML9 .... 199 D4
Stewarton KA3 .... 211 F4
Riverside Terr G76 .... 157 F3
Riverside View FK10 .... 10 A2
River Way KA11 .... 224 C4
Riverside Wlk ML1 .... 163 F4
Riverton Gr G75 .... 180 A4
Riverview Dr G5 .... 240 B1
Riverview Gdns G5 .... 240 B1
Riverview Pl G5 .... 240 B1
Roaden Ave PA2 .... 132 C4
Roaden Rd PA2 .... 132 C4
Roadhead PA12 .... 150 C4
Roadmeetings Hospl ML8 . 202 B4
Roadside G67 .... 62 A3
Roadside Pl ML6 .... 103 E4
Robb Terr G66 .... 80 A3
Robert Bruce Ct KA5 .... 23 D1
Robert Burns Ave
Clydebank G81 .... 74 B2
Hamilton ML3 .... 143 F2
Robert Burns Ct KA15 ..... 150 A1
Robert Burns Quadrant
ML4 .... 141 F3
Robert Creighton Pl KA3 .. 222 C1
Robert Dick Ct FK10 .... 4 B1
Robert Gibson Gdns ML5 . 122 A3
Robert Hardie Ct FK5 ...... 23 E1
Robert Kinmond Ave FK10 .. 4 B1

Robert Knox Ave FK10 ...... 4 B1
Robert Noble Pl KA1 .... 222 B1
Robert Owen Prim Sch
ML11 .... 215 E2
Robert Smellie Cres ML9 .. 185 D1
Robert Smillie Memorial
Prim Sch ML9 .... 185 D1
Robert St Glasgow G51 .... 116 B4
Port Glasgow PA14 .... 47 F1
Shotts ML7 .... 146 C2
Robert Stewart Pl KA1 ..... 222 C1
Robert Templeton Dr G72 . 139 D3
Robert W Service Ct KA13 .. 207 F1
Robertland Rigg KA3 .... 195 F1
Robertland Sq KA3 .... 211 F4
Roberton Ave G41 .... 116 B1
Roberton St ML6 .... 123 F2
Roberts Quadrant ML4 ..... 142 A2
Roberts St Clydebank G81 . 73 F2
Wishaw ML2 .... 165 D2
Robertson Ave FK4 .... 40 A3
Robertson Cres Ayr KA8 .. 236 B1
Neilston G78 .... 154 B4
Saltcoats KA21 .... 217 D4
Robertson Dr Bellshill ML4 .. 142 A2
East Kilbride G74 .... 160 A1
Robertson La G2 .... 240 C2
Robertson Pl
Kilmarnock KA1 .... 228 A4
Stirling FK7 .... 7 D2
Robertson St Airdrie ML6 .. 122 C4
Alva FK12 .... 5 D4
Barrhead G78 .... 134 A1
Glasgow G1, G2 .... 240 C2
Greenock PA15 .... 45 F3
Hamilton ML3 .... 161 F3
Robertson Terr G69 .... 120 B3
Robin Pl ML2 .... 165 D2
Robin Rd PA4 .... 45 D3
Robin Way G32 .... 139 E4
Robroyston Ave G33 .... 98 C2
Robroyston Rd
Bishopbriggs G64 .... 78 C1
Glasgow G33 .... 98 B2
Glasgow G33 .... 98 B2
Glasgow, Robroyston G33 . 98 C3
Kirkintilloch G66 .... 79 E4
Robshill Ct G77 .... 156 B2
Robsland Ave KA7 .... 238 C3
Robslee Cres G46 .... 136 A2
Robslee Dr G46 .... 136 A2
Robslee Prim Sch G46 .... 136 A1
Robslee Rd G46 .... 136 A1
Robson Gr 4 G42 .... 117 D2
Rochdale Pl G66 .... 79 E4
Roche Way KA24 .... 191 E4
Rochsoles Dr ML6 .... 103 D4
Rochsolloch Farm Cotts
ML6 .... 122 C4
Rochsolloch Prim Sch
ML6 .... 122 C3
Rochsolloch Rd ML6 .... 122 B3
Rock Dr PA10 .... 111 D1
Rock St G4 .... 97 D2
Rockall Dr G44 .... 137 E2
Rockbank Pl Clydebank G81 . 74 B3
Glasgow G40 .... 118 A3
Rockbank St G40 .... 118 A3
Rockburn Cres ML4 .... 142 A3
Rockburn Dr G76 .... 157 E4
Rockcliffe St G40 .... 117 F2
Rockfield Pl G21 .... 98 B3
Rockfield Rd G21 .... 98 B3
Rockhampton Ave G75 .... 180 A4
Rockliffe Path ML6 .... 123 F1
Rockmount Ave
Barrhead G78 .... 134 B1
Glasgow G46 .... 136 A2
Rockville Ct KA21 .... 217 D4
Rockrose Pk KA7 .... 239 D2
Rockwell Ave PA2 .... 133 E4
Rodding The ML11 .... 215 D3
Roddinghead Rd G46 ...... 157 D3
Rodger Ave G77 .... 156 B2
Rodger Dr G73 .... 138 A3
Rodger Pl G73 .... 138 A3
Rodil Ave G44 .... 137 E2
Rodney Pl G84 .... 17 D1
Rodney Rd PA19 .... 44 C3
Rodney St G4 .... 97 D1
Roebank Dr G78 .... 134 B1
Roebank Rd KA15 .... 150 B1
Roebank St G31 .... 118 A4
Roffey Park Rd PA1 .... 114 B3
Rogart St G40 .... 117 F3
Rogerfield Prim Sch G34 . 120 B4
Rogerfield Rd G34 .... 120 B4
Rogers Ct ML9 .... 198 B1
Rokeby La G12 .... 96 C2
Roland Cres G77 .... 156 C2
Roman Ave Bearsden G61 . 75 F3
Glasgow G15 .... 75 D1
Roman Cres G60 .... 72 C4
Roman Ct Bearsden G61 .. 75 F3
Kirkintilloch G66 .... 215 F4
Roman Dr Bearsden G61 .. 75 F3
Bellshill ML4 .... 142 A2
Falkirk FK1 .... 41 E3
Roman Gdns G61 .... 75 F3
Roman Hill Rd G81 .... 74 A4
Roman Pl ML4 .... 141 F2
Roman Rd Ayr KA7 .... 238 C1
Bearsden G61 .... 75 F3
Bonnybridge FK4 .... 40 A2
Clydebank G81 .... 74 A3
Kirkintilloch G66 .... 79 E4
Motherwell ML1 .... 163 F4
Roman Way G71 .... 141 E3

Romney Ave G44 .... 137 E2
Rona Ave PA14 .... 69 D4
Rona Pl KA3 .... 223 D3
Rona St G21 .... 98 A1
Rona Terr G72 .... 138 C2
Ronades Rd PA2 .... 42 A4
Ronald Cres FK5 .... 23 D1
Ronald Pl FK8 .... 7 D4
Ronaldsay Ct KA11 .... 225 D4
Ronaldsay Dr G64 .... 78 B1
Ronaldsay Pl G67 .... 82 B4
Ronaldsay St G22 .... 97 E4
Ronaldshaw Pk KA7 .... 238 C3
Ronay St Glasgow G22 .... 97 E4
Wishaw ML2 .... 165 F3
Rook Rd PA16 .... 45 D3
Rooksdell Ave PA2 .... 113 E1
Ropework La G1 .... 241 D1
Rorison Pl ML9 .... 185 F1
Rosa Burn Ave G75 .... 180 A2
Rosa Pl KA21 .... 206 A1
Rose Cres Gourock PA19 . 44 B3
Hamilton ML3 .... 161 F2
Rose Dale G64 .... 98 A4
Rose Knowe Rd G42 .... 137 E4
Rose Mount Ct ML4 .... 123 E4
Rose Pl G74 .... 160 B2
Rose St Alloa FK10 .... 4 C1
Bonnybridge FK4 .... 40 A3
Cumbernauld G67 .... 82 A3
Glasgow G3 .... 240 C4
Greenock PA16 .... 45 E2
Kirkintilloch G66 .... 79 E4
Motherwell ML1 .... 164 A3
Rose Terr Denny FK6 .... 21 E1
Stenhousemuir FK5 .... 23 F2
Roseacre La ML9 .... 185 D1
Rosebank Ave
Blantyre G72 .... 140 C1
Falkirk FK1 .... 41 F3
Kirkintilloch G66 .... 79 F4
Rosebank Cres KA7 .... 238 C3
Rosebank Dr
Cambuslang G72 .... 139 E2
Uddingston G71 .... 141 E4
Rosebank Gdns Alloa FK10 .. 5 E1
Irvine KA11 .... 219 F4
Rosebank La 10 G71 .... 141 E4
Rosebank Pl Falkirk FK1 .. 41 F3
Hamilton ML3 .... 162 A2
Kilmarnock KA3 .... 222 C1
Rosebank Rd Bellshill ML4 . 142 A4
Wishaw ML2 .... 186 B3
Rosebank Sch KA7 .... 239 D3
Rosebank Terr
Bargeddie G69 .... 121 D2
Kilmacolm PA13 .... 89 E4
Rosebay Pk KA7 .... 239 D1
Roseberry La ML6 .... 123 F2
Roseberry Pl ML3 .... 162 A2
Roseberry Rd ML6 .... 123 F2
Roseberry St G5 .... 117 F1
Roseberry Pl FK8 .... 2 A2
Roseburn Ct G67 .... 62 C3
Rosedale G74 .... 159 E2
Rosedale Ave PA2 .... 132 B4
Rosedale Dr G69 .... 120 A2
Rosedale Gdns
Glasgow G20 .... 96 B4
Helensburgh G84 .... 16 C1
Rosedale St ML11 .... 214 C1
Rosedene Terr ML4 .... 142 A3
Rosefield Gdns G71 .... 140 C3
Rosegreen Cres ML4 .... 142 A4
Rosehall Ave ML5 .... 122 A2
Rosehall High Sch ML5 ... 121 F2
Rosehall Ind Est ML5 ...... 122 A1
Shotts ML7 .... 146 B2
Rosehall Terr Falkirk FK1 . 42 A2
Wishaw ML2 .... 164 C1
Rosehill Dr G67 .... 82 A3
Rosehill Rd G64 .... 78 B4
Roseholm Ave KA12 .... 219 F1
Roselea ML6 .... 104 C2
Roselea Dr G62 .... 55 D2
Roselea Gdns G13 .... 95 F4
Roselea Pl G72 .... 140 B1
Roselea Rd G71 .... 140 C4
Roselea St ML9 .... 185 D2
Rosemary Cres G74 .... 159 E2
Rosemary Pl G74 .... 159 E2
Rosemead Terr FK1 .... 66 C3
Rosemount
Cumbernauld G68 .... 61 F3
Kilwinning KA13 .... 207 E1
Rosemount Ave G77 .... 156 B1
Rosemount Ct G77 .... 156 B1
Rosemount Gate G84 ...... 16 C1
Rosemount La G72 .... 161 F4
21 Larkhall ML9 .... 185 E1
Rosemount Mdws G71 .... 140 C1
Rosemount Pl PA19 .... 44 A3
Rosemount St G21 .... 117 F4
Rosendale Way G72 .... 161 F4
Roseneath Dr G84 .... 16 A1
Roseneath Gate G74 .... 159 E2
Roseneath Prim Sch G84 . 15 D2
Rosenheath St ML6 .... 104 B1
Roseness Pl G33 .... 119 D4
Rosepark Ave G71 .... 141 E3
Rosepark Cotts ML5 .... 121 F1
Rosevale Cres
Bellshill ML4 .... 142 B2
Hamilton ML3 .... 162 A1
Rosevale Rd G61 .... 75 F2

Rosevale Sch G22 .... 97 E4
Rosevale St G11 .... 96 A1
Rosewood Ave
Bellshill ML4 .... 142 A4
Paisley PA2 .... 113 D1
Rosewood Path ML4 .... 141 F3
Rosewood St G13 .... 95 F4
Roslea Dr G31 .... 118 A4
Roslin Ct G13 .... 89 E4
Roslin St PA15 .... 46 A3
Roslin Tower G72 .... 138 C2
Roslyn Dr G69 .... 120 C3
Rosneath Rd
Port Glasgow PA14 .... 68 B4
Rosneath G84 .... 15 D1
Rosneath St G51 .... 116 A4
Ross Ave Kirkintilloch G66 . 79 F4
Renfrew PA4 .... 94 A1
Ross Cres Falkirk FK1 ..... 41 E3
Motherwell ML1 .... 163 E3
Ross Ct FK7 .... 7 D2
Ross Dr Airdrie ML6 .... 122 C2
Motherwell ML1 .... 163 E3
Uddingston G71 .... 121 E1
Ross Gdns ML1 .... 163 E3
Ross Hall Pl PA4 .... 94 B2
Ross Pl G73 .... 138 B2
Ross Rd KA21 .... 205 F1
Ross St Ayr KA8 .... 236 B1
Coatbridge ML5 .... 122 A4
Glasgow G40 .... 241 E1
Paisley PA1 .... 114 A2
Ross Terr ML3 .... 163 E1
Ross Wlk KA3 .... 223 D1
Rossbank Rd PA14 .... 47 D1
Rossdale G46 .... 136 B1
Rossendale Ct G43 .... 136 B4
Rossendale Rd G43 .... 136 B4
Rosshall Ave PA1 .... 114 A2
Rossendale Rd G43 .... 136 B4
Rosshall Hospl G52 .... 115 D2
Rosshill Ave G52 .... 114 C3
Rosshill Rd G52 .... 114 C3
Rossie Cres G64 .... 98 B4
Rossie Gr G77 .... 156 A3
Rossland Cres PA7 .... 72 A2
Rossland Pl PA7 .... 72 B1
Rosslea Dr G46 .... 136 B1
Rosslyn Ave
East Kilbride G74 .... 160 A2
Rutherglen G73 .... 138 B4
Rosslyn Ct ML3 .... 162 A2
Rosslyn Pl KA8 .... 236 A2
Rosslyn Rd Ashgill ML9 ... 199 F4
Bearsden G61 .... 75 D3
Rosslyn Terr 3 G12 .... 96 B2
Rossvail Sch FK1 .... 41 E3
Rostan Rd G43 .... 136 B3
Rosyth Rd G5 .... 117 F1
Rosyth St G5 .... 117 F1
Rotherwick Dr PA1 .... 114 C2
Rotherwood Ave
Glasgow G13 .... 75 E1
Paisley PA2 .... 132 C4
Rotherwood Pl G13 .... 75 E1
Rotherwood Way PA2 ...... 132 C4
Rothes Dr G23 .... 96 B4
Rothes Pl G23 .... 76 B1
Rothesay Cres ML5 .... 122 A2
Rothesay Pl
Coatbridge ML5 .... 122 A2
East Kilbride G74 .... 159 F1
Kilmarnock KA3 .... 222 C2
Rothesay Rd PA16 .... 44 C2
Rothesay St G75 .... 180 C4
Rottenrow Glasgow G4 .... 241 E2
Glasgow G4 .... 241 F2
Rottenrow E G4 .... 241 E2
Roughburn Rd FK9 .... 2 A3
Roughcraig St ML6 .... 103 D1
Roughlands Cres FK2 ..... 24 A2
Roughlands Dr FK2 .... 24 A2
Roughlea Pl G77 .... 156 A2
Roughrigg Rd ML6 .... 124 B3
Rouken Glen Pk G46 .... 135 F1
Rouken Glen Rd G46 .... 136 A1
Roukenburn St G46 .... 135 F2
Round Riding Rd G82 ...... 50 A2
Roundel The Falkirk FK2 .. 42 B4
Wishaw ML2 .... 165 E1
Roundelwood FK10 .... 5 F2
Roundhill Dr PA1 .... 114 C2
Roundhouse The 12 B4
Roundknowe Rd G71 ...... 120 B1
Rowallan Gdns G11 .... 96 A2
Rowallan La G46 .... 135 F2
Rowallan La E G11 .... 96 A2
Rowallan Rd G46 .... 135 F2
Rowallan Dr
Bannockburn FK7 .... 11 F4
Kilmarnock KA3 .... 223 D2
Rowallan Gdns ML4 .... 141 F3
Rowallan La Clarkston G76 . 157 F4
Rowallan Rd G46 .... 135 F2
Rowallan St ML6 .... 16 A2
Rowallan Terr G33 .... 99 D3
Rowan Ave Milton Of C G65 . 58 B3
Renfrew PA4 .... 94 B2
Rowan Cres Ayr KA7 .... 239 E3
Falkirk FK1 .... 41 D2
Kirkintilloch G66 .... 79 E3
Rowan Ct Bannockburn FK7 . 7 F1
Cambuslang G72 .... 139 E2
Rowan Dr Bankhead FK4 .. 38 C1
Bearsden G61 .... 76 A4
Clydebank G81 .... 73 F2
Dumbarton G82 .... 49 D2
Rowan Gate PA2 .... 113 F1
Rowan Gdns G41 .... 116 A2
Rowan Gr ML3 .... 183 F2

Rowan House KA9 .... 236 A3
Rowan La ML1 .... 143 D1
Rowan Pl Beith KA15 .... 171 E4
Blantyre G72 .... 161 E4
Cambuslang G72 .... 139 E3
Coatbridge ML5 .... 121 F2
Kilmarnock KA1 .... 227 E4
Troon KA10 .... 229 E2
Rowan Rd Cumbernauld G67 . 62 B2
Glasgow G41 .... 116 A2
Linwood PA3 .... 111 F4
Rowan Rise ML3 .... 162 C1
Rowan St Beith KA15 .... 171 E4
Greenock PA16 .... 45 E3
Paisley PA2 .... 113 F1
Wishaw ML2 .... 165 D3
Rowan Tree La KA1 .... 219 E2
Rowanbank Pl ML6 .... 122 B4
Rowanbank Rd KA9 .... 236 C4
Rowand Ave G46 .... 136 B2
Rowandale Ave G69 .... 120 A2
Rowanden Ave ML4 .... 142 A3
Rowanhill Pl KA1 .... 227 E4
Rowanlea ML6 .... 103 F2
Rowanlea Ave PA2 .... 132 C4
Rowanlea Dr G46 .... 136 B2
Rowanpark Dr G78 .... 134 A3
Rowans Gdns G71 .... 141 D2
Rowans The Alloa FK10 ... 5 E1
Bishopbriggs G64 .... 77 F1
Rowanside Terr KA22 ...... 205 E2
Rowantree Ave
Motherwell ML1 .... 143 E4
Rutherglen G73 .... 138 A3
Uddingston G71 .... 141 E4
Rowantree Gdns
Irvine KA11 .... 220 A3
Rutherglen G73 .... 138 A3
Rowantree Pl
Johnstone PA5 .... 111 F1
Larkhall ML9 .... 185 E1
Lennoxtown G65 .... 57 F4
Rowantree Rd PA5 .... 112 A1
Rowantree Terr
Lennoxtown G65 .... 57 F4
Motherwell ML1 .... 143 D3
Rowantreehill Rd PA13 .... 89 F4
Rowanwood Cres ML5 ..... 121 E3
Rowena Ave G13 .... 75 E1
Rowmore Quays G84 ...... 15 F2
Roxburgh Ave PA15 .... 45 F2
Roxburgh Dr Bearsden G61 . 75 F4
Coatbridge ML5 .... 122 B2
Roxburgh Pk G74 .... 159 F1
Roxburgh Pl Blantyre G72 . 161 E4
Stenhousemuir FK5 .... 23 E2
Roxburgh Rd Hurlford KA1 . 228 C3
Paisley PA2 .... 132 B4
Roxburgh St Glasgow G12 . 96 B2
Greenock PA15 .... 45 F3
Roxburgh Way PA15 .... 97 E2
Roy St G21 .... 97 E2
Roy Young Ave G83 .... 28 A4
Royal Alexandra Hospl
PA2 .... 113 E1
Royal Bank Pl G1 .... 241 D2
Royal Cres G3 .... 116 C4
Royal Dr ML3 .... 163 D1
Royal Exchange Ct G1 .... 241 D2
Royal Exchange Sq G1 ... 241 D2
Royal Gdns G85 .... 7 D4
Royal Hospl Yorkhill
(For Sick Children) G3 .... 96 B1
Royal Inch Terr PA4 .... 94 B3
Royal Infmy G4 .... 241 F3
Royal Maternity &
Women's Hospl G1 .... 241 E2
Royal Samaritan Hospl
For Women G42 .... 117 D2
Royal Scottish Acad of
Music & Drama G3 .... 240 C3
Royal Scottish National
Hospl The FK5 .... 22 C2
Royal St PA19 .... 44 C4
Royal Terrace La G3 .... 96 C1
Royellen Ave ML3 .... 161 F1
Royston Rd G21, G33 ...... 98 B2
Royston Sq G21 .... 241 F4
Roystonhill G21 .... 97 F1
Rozelle KA7 .... 238 C1
Rozelle Ave Glasgow G15 . 75 D2
Newton Mearns G77 .... 156 A2
Rozelle Dr G77 .... 156 A2
Rozelle Pl G77 .... 156 A2
Rozelle Terr KA7 .... 239 D1
Rubie Cres KA12 .... 219 E1
Rubislaw Dr G61 .... 75 F2
Ruby St G40 .... 118 A2
Ruchazie Pl G33 .... 118 C4
Ruchazie Prim Sch G33 .. 99 D1
Ruchazie Rd G32, G33 .... 118 C4
Ruchill Hospl (Infectious
diseases) G20 .... 97 D3
Ruchill Pl G20 .... 96 C3
Ruchill Prim Sch G20 ...... 96 C3
Ruchill St G20 .... 96 C3
Rue End St PA15 .... 46 A3
Ruel St G44 .... 137 D4
Rufflees Ave G78 .... 134 B2
Rugby Ave G13 .... 95 D4
Rugby Pk (Kilmarnock FC)
KA1 .... 227 E4

Rugby Rd KA1 .... 227 E4
Rulley View FK6 .... 21 E2
Rullion Pl G33 .... 118 C4
Rumford Pl KA3 .... 223 E3
Rumford St G40 .... 117 F2
Rumlie The FK1 .... 86 A3
Runciman Pl G74 .... 160 A2
Rundell Dr G65 .... 58 B3
Rupert St G4 .... 96 C1
Rushyhill St G21 .... 96 A4
Ruskie Rd FK9 .... 2 A2
Ruskin La G12 .... 96 C2
Ruskin Pl Glasgow G12 .... 96 C2
　Kilsyth G65 .... 60 B4
Ruskin Sq G64 .... 78 A1
Ruskin Terr Glasgow G12 .... 96 C2
　Rutherglen G73 .... 118 A1
Russel St FK2 .... 42 A3
Russell Colt St ML5 .... 122 A4
Russell A KA3 .... 223 E2
Russell Dr Alexandria G83 .... 27 E4
　Ayr KA8 .... 236 A1
　Bearsden G61 .... 75 F3
　Dalry KA24 .... 191 E4
Russell Gdns
　Newton Mearns G77 .... 156 B2
　🔟 Uddingston G71 .... 141 D4
Russell La ML2 .... 165 D1
Russell Pl Clarkston G76 .... 158 A3
　East Kilbride G75 .... 180 B4
　Linwood PA3 .... 111 F3
Russell Rd Clydebank G81 ..... 73 F4
　Lanark ML11 .... 215 D3
Russell St Ayr KA8 .... 236 A1
　Bellshill ML4 .... 142 B3
　Chapelhall ML6 .... 123 F1
　Hamilton ML3 .... 162 A3
　Johnstone PA5 .... 112 A2
　Paisley PA3 .... 113 E4
　Wishaw ML2 .... 165 D1
Rutherford Ave
　Bearsden G61 .... 75 D4
　Kirkintilloch G66 .... 80 A3
Rutherford Ct
　Bridge Of A FK9 .... 2 A4
　Clydebank G81 .... 74 A1
Rutherford Grange G66 .... 79 E3
Rutherford La G75 .... 180 C4
Rutherford Sq G75 .... 180 C4
Rutherglen Ind Est G73 .... 118 A1
Rutherglen Rd G5 .... 117 F1
Rutherglen Sta G73 .... 138 A4
Ruthven Ave G46 .... 136 B1
Ruthven La 🔟 Glasgow G12 .. 96 B2
　Glenboig ML5 .... 101 E3
Ruthven Pl
　Bishopbriggs G64 .... 98 B4
　Troon KA10 .... 229 F2
Ruthven St G12 .... 96 B2
Rutland Cres G51 .... 116 C3
Rutland Pl G51 .... 116 C3
Ryan Rd G64 .... 78 A1
Ryan Way G73 .... 138 B2
Ryat Dr G77 .... 156 B3
Ryat Gn G77 .... 156 B3
Ryatt Linn PA8 .... 72 C1
Rydal Gr G75 .... 179 F3
Rydal Pl G75 .... 179 F3
Rydal Rd G75 .... 179 F3
Ryden Mains Rd ML6 .... 102 B2
Rye Cres G21 .... 98 A3
Rye Rd G21 .... 98 B3
Rye Way PA2 .... 112 C1
Ryebank Rd G21 .... 98 B3
Ryecroft Dr G69 .... 120 A3
Ryedale Pl G15 .... 75 D2
Ryefield Ave
　Coatbridge ML5 .... 121 E4
　Johnstone PA5 .... 111 F1
Ryefield Pl PA5 .... 111 F1
Ryefield Rd G21 .... 98 A3
Ryehill Pl G21 .... 98 B3
Ryehill Rd G21 .... 98 B2
Ryemont Rd G21 .... 98 B3
Ryeside Pl KA24 .... 169 C1
Ryeside Rd G21 .... 98 A2
Rylands KA9 .... 236 B3
Rylands Dr G32 .... 119 E2
Rylands Gdns G32 .... 119 F2
Rylees Cres G52 .... 114 C3
Rylees Pl G52 .... 114 C3
Rylees Rd G52 .... 114 C3
Rysland Ave G77 .... 156 C3
Rysland Cres G77 .... 156 C3
Rysland Dr KA13 .... 213 D2
Ryvra Rd G13 .... 95 E3

Sachelcourt Ave PA7 .... 72 A1
Sackville Ave G13 .... 95 F3
Sackville La G13 .... 95 F3
Sacred Heart High Sch
　PA2 .... 114 B1
Sacred Heart Prim Sch
　Cumbernauld G67 .... 62 A1
　Gourock PA16 .... 44 C2
Sacred Heart RC Prim Sch
　Bellshill ML4 .... 142 A2
　Glasgow G40 .... 117 F2
Saddell Rd G15 .... 75 D2
Saffronhall Cres ML3 .... 162 B2
Saffronhall La ML3 .... 162 B2
Sainford Cres FK2 .... 24 A1
St Abb's Dr PA2 .... 113 D1
St Agatha's Prim Sch G66 .. 80 A4
St Agnes' Prim Sch G23 ...... 96 C4

St Aidan's RC High Sch
　ML2 .... 165 D2
St Aidan's RC Prim Sch
　ML2 .... 165 E3
St Aidan's RC Sch G31 ...... 118 B3
St Albert's RC Prim Sch
　G41 .... 116 C2
St Aloysius Coll G3 .... 240 B4
St Aloysius' Prim Sch G22 ... 97 F3
St Aloysius RC Prim Sch
　ML6 .... 123 F1
St Ambrose Sch ML5 .... 121 F4
St Ambrose's Prim Sch
　G22 .... 97 F4
St Andrew St PA15 .... 46 A2
St Andrew's Acad KA21 .... 205 F1
St Andrew's Ave
　Bishopbriggs G64 .... 77 F1
　Prestwick KA9 .... 236 B3
St Andrew's Brae G82 .... 50 A3
St Andrew's Coll G61 .... 75 E4
St Andrew's Cres
　Dumbarton G82 .... 50 A3
　Paisley PA3 .... 113 E4
St Andrew's Cross G41 ..... 117 D2
St Andrew's Ct FK5 .... 23 D2
St Andrew's Dr Airth FK2 ... 14 A4
　Glasgow G41 .... 116 B2
　Hamilton ML3 .... 161 E2
　Paisley PA3 .... 113 E4
St Andrew's Dr W PA3 .... 93 E1
St Andrew's Gdns
　Airdrie ML6 .... 123 D4
　Dalry KA24 .... 191 E4
St Andrew's High Sch G81 .. 94 B4
St Andrew's La G1 .... 241 E1
St Andrew's Pl KA20 .... 206 C1
St Andrew's Prim Sch
　Airdrie ML6 .... 102 C1
　Falkirk FK1 .... 42 B2
St Andrew's RC Cath G1 ... 241 E1
St Andrew's RC High Sch
　G75 .... 180 B3
St Andrew's RC Prim Sch
　G61 .... 75 E3
St Andrew's Rd
　Ardrossan KA22 .... 205 E2
　Glasgow G41 .... 116 C2
　Renfrew PA4 .... 94 B1
St Andrew's Sec Sch G32 .. 119 D4
St Andrew's Sq G1 .... 241 E1
St Andrew's St Ayr KA7 .... 239 D4
　Glasgow G1 .... 241 E1
　Kilmarnock KA1 .... 227 F4
St Andrew's Wlk KA1 .... 227 F4
St Andrews Ave G71 .... 141 D1
St Andrews Cres G41 .... 116 C2
St Andrews Ct
　East Kilbride G75 .... 180 B3
　Motherwell ML1 .... 143 D3
St Andrews Dr
　Bridge Of W PA11 .... 110 B3
　Cumbernauld G68 .... 62 A3
　Gourock PA19 .... 44 A3
St Andrews Gate ML4 .... 141 F3
St Andrews La
　Alexandria G83 .... 27 F2
　Gourock PA19 .... 44 A3
St Andrews Path 🔟 ML9 .. 185 E1
St Andrews Pl Beith KA15 .. 171 D4
　🔟 Falkirk FK1 .... 42 B2
　Kilsyth G65 .... 36 B1
St Andrews St ML1 .... 143 D3
St Andrews Way KA12 ..... 224 C4
St Andrews Wynd G84 ...... 16 C2
St Angela's Prim Sch G53 . 135 E2
St Ann's Dr G46 .... 136 B1
St Anne's Cres FK7 .... 7 F1
St Anne's Prim Sch
　G40 .... 118 A3
St Anne's Prim Sch PA8 ..... 93 E4
St Annes Pl PA8 .... 93 F4
St Annes Wynd PA8 .... 93 E4
St Anthony's Prim Sch
　KA21 .... 205 F1
St Anthony's RC Prim Sch
　Glasgow G51 .... 116 C4
　Johnstone PA5 .... 131 E4
　Rutherglen G73 .... 138 B2
St Athanasius' RC Prim Sch
　ML8 .... 187 F1
St Augustine's Prim RC Sch
　G22 .... 97 E4
St Augustine's RC Prim Sch
　ML5 .... 121 F3
St Barbara's RC
　Prim & Sec Sch G69 ...... 100 B4
St Barchan's Rd PA10 .... 111 D1
St Bartholomew's Prim Sch
　G45 .... 137 F2
St Bartholomew's
　RC Prim Sch G34 .... 101 E1
St Benedict's Prim RC Sch
　G34 .... 100 A1
St Bernadette's
　RC Prim Sch
　Motherwell ML1 .... 163 D4
　Tullibody FK10 .... 4 A1
St Bernard's Prim Sch
　ML5 .... 122 A2
St Bernards Prim Sch
　G53 .... 135 D3
St Blane's Dr G73 .... 137 F3
St Blane's RC Prim Sch
　G72 .... 161 E4
St Blanes Path G23 .... 76 B1
St Bonaventure's RC Prim Sch
　G5 .... 117 E2

St Boswell's Cres PA2 .... 113 D1
St Boswells Dr ML5 .... 122 B2
St Brendan's High Sch
　PA3 .... 112 B3
St Brendan's Prim Sch
　G13 .... 94 C4
St Brendan's RC Prim Sch
　ML1 .... 143 F2
St Bride's Ave G71 .... 141 E4
St Bride's Dr KA23 .... 190 B3
St Bride's Pl KA12 .... 219 E3
St Bride's RC Prim Sch
　G74 .... 160 A1
St Bride's RC Prim Sch
　G71 .... 141 D2
St Bride's Rd Glasgow G43 . 136 B3
　West Kilbride KA23 .... 190 B3
St Bride's Sec Sch G72 ..... 139 D3
St Brides Way G71 .... 141 D2
St Bridget's Prim Sch
　G69 .... 120 A3
St Bridget's RC Prim Sch
　KA25 .... 170 A4
St Brigid's RC Prim Sch
　Glasgow G42 .... 137 E4
　Wishaw ML2 .... 166 A3
St Bryde St G74 .... 159 F1
St Cadoc's Sch G77 .... 156 B3
St Cadoc's Sch G7 .... 139 E2
St Catherine's Prim Sch
　PA3 .... 113 F3
St Catherine's RC Prim Sch
　G21 .... 98 B3
St Catherine's Rd G46 ..... 136 B3
St Catherines Cres ML7 .... 146 C3
St Catherines Rd KA8 .... 236 C1
St Charles Prim Sch PA2 .. 113 F1
St Charles RC Prim Sch
　G72 .... 139 F3
St Charles's Prim Sch G20 . 96 C2
St Clair Ave G46 .... 136 B2
St Clair Terr KA10 .... 229 D1
St Clare's Prim RC Sch
　G15 .... 75 D2
St Clare's RC Prim Sch
　G34 .... 120 B4
St Columba Dr G66 .... 79 F4
St Columba RC Prim Sch
　G66 .... 79 F4
St Columba's High Sch
　Clydebank G81 .... 74 B2
　Greenock PA16 .... 45 D3
St Columba's Prim Sch
　PA13 .... 89 E4
St Columba's RC Prim Sch
　Kilmarnock KA1 .... 228 A4
　Uddingston G71 .... 141 E4
St Columbkille's
　RC Prim Sch G73 .... 138 A4
St Constantine's
　Prim RC Sch G51 .... 115 F4
St Conval's Prim RC Sch
　G43 .... 136 B4
St Crispin's Pl FK1 .... 42 A2
St Cuthbert's Cres KA9 ..... 236 B3
St Cuthbert's Prim RC Sch
　G22 .... 97 D2
St Cuthbert's RC Prim Sch
　ML3 .... 162 A3
St Cuthbert's Rd KA9 .... 236 B3
St Cuthberts High Sch
　PA5 .... 131 E4
St Cyrus Gdns G64 .... 78 B1
St Cyrus Rd G64 .... 78 B1
St David's Ct FK5 .... 23 D1
St David's Pl ML9 .... 185 D2
St David's RC Prim Sch
　PA5 .... 111 E1
St David's RC Sch ML6 .... 104 A1
St Davids Dr ML6 .... 123 E2
St Denis Way ML5 .... 121 F4
St Denis's Prim Sch G31 ... 118 A4
St Dominic's RC Prim Sch
　Airdrie ML6 .... 123 E2
　Glasgow G45 .... 137 F1
St Edmunds Gr G62 .... 55 D2
St Edmunds Prim Sch G53 . 115 E1
St Edward's Prim Sch ML6 . 123 E4
St Elizabeth Seton RC
　Prim Sch G33 .... 119 E4
St Elizabeth's RC Prim Sch
　ML3 .... 183 E4
St Enoch Ave G71 .... 141 E4
St Enoch Pl G1 .... 240 C2
St Enoch Sh Ctr G1 .... 241 D1
St Enoch Sq G1 .... 240 C2
St Enoch Underground Sta
　G1 .... 240 C2
St Eunan's Prim Sch G81 ... 74 B1
St Fergus's RC Prim Sch
　PA3 .... 113 D3
St Fillan's Prim Sch G44 ... 137 D3
St Fillan's RC Prim Sch
　PA6 .... 91 D1
St Fillans Dr PA6 .... 91 D1
St Fillans Rd G33 .... 99 E3
St Flanan Rd G66 .... 59 E1
St Flanan's Prim Sch G66 .. 58 C1
St Francis of Assisi
　Prim Sch
　Cumbernauld G68 .... 82 A4
　Glasgow G69 .... 119 F2
St Francis Prim RC Sch G5 . 117 E2
St Francis Prim Sch PA14 ... 68 C4
St Francis Private Prim Sch
　G43 .... 136 B3
St Francis' RC Prim Sch
　FK2 .... 42 A3

St Francis Xavier Coll ML5 122 B2
St Gabriel's Prim Sch G71 . 141 E4
St Gabriel's RC Prim Sch
　PA16 .... 45 D3
St George's Cross 🔟 G3 ... 97 D1
St George's Cross
　Underground Sta G3 .... 97 D1
St George's Ct FK5 .... 23 D1
St George's Pl 🔟 G20 .... 97 D1
St George's Prim RC Sch
　G52 .... 114 C3
St George's Rd
　ML4 .... 142 A4
St George's Rd Ayr KA8 ... 236 A2
　Glasgow G3 .... 97 D1
St Gerard's Sec Sch G51 .. 116 A4
St Germains G61 .... 75 F2
St Gilbert's RC Prim Sch
　G21 .... 98 B2
St Giles Pk ML3 .... 162 A1
St Giles Sq FK1 .... 41 D3
St Giles Way Falkirk FK1 .... 41 D3
　Hamilton ML3 .... 162 A1
St Gregory's Prim RC Sch
　G20 .... 96 B3
St Helen's Prim Sch
　Bishopbriggs G64 .... 77 E1
　Cumbernauld G67 .... 82 A4
St Helena Cres G61 .... 74 B3
St Hilary's RC Prim Sch
　G74 .... 181 D4
St Ignatius Prim Sch ML2 . 165 D2
St Inan Ave KA12 .... 219 F2
St Inan's Dr KA15 .... 150 B1
St Ives Rd G69 .... 80 C2
St Jame's RC Sch ML5 ..... 121 F2
St James Ave PA3 .... 113 D4
St James Ct ML5 .... 121 F2
St James' Orch FK9 .... 2 B1
St James' Pl KA20 .... 206 C1
St James' Prim Sch G40 ... 117 F3
St James' RC Prim Sch PA3 . 113 E4
St James' RC Prim Sch
　G84 .... 94 B2
St James Rd G4 .... 241 E3
St James' St PA3 .... 113 F3
St James Terr PA13 .... 89 E4
St James Way ML5 .... 121 F2
St Jerome's RC Prim Sch
　G51 .... 115 F4
St Joachim's RC Prim Sch
　G32 .... 119 D3
St Joan of Arc RC Sch G22 . 97 D4
St Joan's Cres KA13 .... 207 F1
St John Bosco Prim Sch
　PA8 .... 72 C2
St John Maxwell Prim Sch
　G43 .... 136 B4
St John Ogilvie Prim Sch
　Irvine KA11 .... 220 A2
　Paisley PA1 .... 114 A2
St John St Ayr KA7 .... 235 F1
　Coatbridge ML5 .... 122 A4
　Prestwick KA9 .... 236 B4
　Stirling FK8 .... 7 D4
St John The Baptist
　Prim Sch G71 .... 141 D3
St John's Ave FK2 .... 42 B3
St John's Ct G41 .... 116 C2
St John's Gate FK6 .... 21 E1
St John's Gdns FK6 .... 21 E1
St John's Gr FK6 .... 21 E1
St John's Pl KA22 .... 205 E1
St John's Pl KA20 .... 206 C1
St John's RC Prim Sch G15 117 D3
St John's Prim Sch KA8 .... 236 A1
St John's Prim Sch
　Barrhead G78 .... 134 B2
　Hamilton ML3 .... 162 B2
St John's Quadrant 🔟 116 C2
St John's RC Prim Sch
　PA14 .... 47 D1
St John's Rd Glasgow G41 . 116 C2
　Gourock PA19 .... 44 C4
St Joseph's Acad KA3 ...... 223 D1
St Joseph's Ct G21 .... 97 F1
St Joseph's Pl G21 .... 97 F1
St Joseph's Prim Sch
　Bonnybridge FK4 .... 40 A2
　Clarkston G76 .... 157 F3
　Clydebank G81 .... 74 B4
　Cumbernauld G67 .... 82 C4
　Glasgow G42 .... 97 D1
　Milngavie G62 .... 54 C1
　Stepps G33 .... 99 F2
St Joseph's RC Prim Sch
　G72 .... 161 E4
St Joseph's RC Prim Sch
　PA16 .... 45 D2
St Joseph's Sch ML5 .... 101 E4
St Joseph's View G21 .... 97 F1
St Josephs Prim Sch G84 ... 16 C1
St Jude's Prim RC Sch
　G33 .... 119 F3
St Julie's Sch G44 .... 137 E2
St Kenneth Dr G51 .... 115 F4
St Kenneth's Prim RC Sch
　G74 .... 159 E2
St Kenneth's RC Prim Sch
　PA15 .... 46 B1
St Kentigerns Rd ML11 .... 215 D3
St Kessogs RC Prim Sch
　G83 .... 27 F4
St Kevin's Prim Sch
　ML1 .... 121 D3
St Kevin's Sch G21 .... 97 F1
St Kilda Bank KA11 .... 220 A1

St Kilda Ct KA11 .... 220 A1
St Kilda Dr G14 .... 95 F2
St Kilda Pl KA11 .... 220 A1
St Kilda Way ML2 .... 165 F3
St Lawrence Pk G75 .... 159 E1
St Lawrence Pl KA21 .... 206 A1
St Lawrence Prim Sch
　PA15 .... 46 A2
St Lawrence St PA15 .... 46 A2
St Leonard St ML11 .... 215 D3
St Leonard's Dr G46 .... 136 B2
St Leonard's RC Prim Sch
　G74 .... 160 B2
St Leonard's Rd Ayr KA7 .. 239 D1
　Lanark ML11 .... 215 D2
St Leonard's Sec RC Sch
　G74 .... 160 B2
St Leonards Sq G74 .... 160 B1
St Leonards Rd G14 .... 160 B1
St Leonards Wlk ML5 ...... 122 B2
St Louise Prim Sch G46 ... 135 E2
St Louise's RC Prim Sch
　G75 .... 180 C3
St Lucy's Prim Sch G67 ..... 62 C2
St Luke's Ave ML8 .... 201 F4
St Luke's Prim Sch KA13 .. 207 D1
St Lukes High Sch G78 .... 155 E4
St Machan's RC Prim Sch
　G65 .... 33 E1
St Machan's Way G65 .... 33 E1
St Machars Rd PA11 .... 110 C4
St Margaret Ave KA24 ..... 191 D4
St Margaret Mary RC
　Sec Sch G45 .... 137 E1
St Margaret Mary's RC
　Prim Sch G45 .... 137 E1
St Margaret's Ave G65 ...... 37 F2
St Margaret's Dr ML2 ...... 164 C1
St Margaret's High Sch
　ML6 .... 123 D4
St Margaret's Pl G1 .... 241 D1
St Margaret's Prim Sch
　PA5 .... 111 F1
St Margaret's RC Prim Sch
　FK7 .... 12 B4
St Margaret's Rd KA22 .... 205 E2
St Mark Gdns G32 .... 118 C3
St Mark St G32 .... 118 C3
St Mark's Prim Sch
　G31 .... 118 C3
St Mark's Prim Sch
　Glasgow G73 .... 138 A3
　Irvine KA12 .... 219 D2
St Mark's RC Prim Sch
　Barrhead G78 .... 134 B1
　Hamilton ML3 .... 183 E4
St Marnock St 🔟 KA1 ...... 227 F4
St Marnock St
　Glasgow G40 .... 118 A3
　Kilmarnock KA1 .... 227 F4
St Marnock's RC Prim Sch
　G53 .... 115 E1
St Martha's RC Prim Sch
　G21 .... 98 A3
St Martin's High Sch PA1 . 113 D2
St Martin's Prim Sch G83 .. 27 F2
St Martin's RC Prim Sch
　G45 .... 137 F1
St Mary's Convent Sch
　G31 .... 117 F4
St Mary's Cres G78 .... 134 B1
St Mary's St ML2 .... 165 D1
St Mary's Hospl ML11 ...... 215 E3
St Mary's La G2 .... 240 C2
St Mary's (Maryhill) Prim
　RC Sch G20 .... 96 B4
St Mary's Pl KA21 .... 205 F1
St Mary's Prim Sch G83 .... 27 F3
St Mary's Prim Sch ML6 .. 104 C3
St Mary's Prim Sch
　Cumbernauld G67 .... 61 F1
　Hamilton ML3 .... 162 B2
　Lanark ML11 .... 215 F1
　Paisley PA1 .... 113 E2
St Mary's RC Prim Sch
　Bannockburn FK7 .... 7 E1
　Cleland ML1 .... 144 A1
　Coatbridge ML5 .... 122 B2
St Mary's RC Prim Sch FK8 . 1 C1
St Mary's RC Prim Sch G83 . 74 A3
St Mary's RC Sec Sch FK6 . 15 F3
St Mary's Rd Bellshill ML4 . 141 F3
　Bishopbriggs G64 .... 77 F1
St Mary's Sec Sch PA16 .... 45 F2
St Mary's Way G82 .... 49 F2
St Mary's Wynd FK8 .... 7 D4
St Marys Gdns G84 .... 134 B1
St Matthew's Prim Sch G84 . 16 B2
St Matthew's Prim Sch
　KA3 .... 223 E1
St Maur's Cres KA3 .... 222 C2
St Maur's Pl KA3 .... 222 C2
St Maurice's Rdbt G68 ...... 61 E1
St Maurices High Sch G68 . 82 A4
St Maurs Gdns KA3 .... 222 C2
St Medan's Pl KA21 .... 206 A1
St Meddans Cres KA10 .... 229 E1
St Meddans St KA10 .... 229 E1
St Meddans St KA10 .... 229 E1
St Michael Dr G84 .... 16 C1
St Michael Rd ML2 .... 164 B1

St Michael's Acad KA13 .... 207 E2
St Michael's Ct G31 .... 118 B3
St Michael's La G31 .... 118 B3
St Michael's Prim Sch
　Dumbarton G82 .... 49 E2
　Moodiesburn G69 .... 81 D1
St Michael's RC Prim Sch
　G31 .... 118 B3
St Michele's Prim Sch
　PA14 .... 68 C4
St Mirin's RC Cath PA1 .... 113 F3
St Mirin's RC Prim Sch
　G44 .... 137 E4
St Mirren Pk
　(St Mirren FC) PA3 .... 113 F3
St Mirren St PA1 .... 113 F2
St Mirren's Rd G65 .... 60 C4
St Modan's High Sch FK7 .... 7 D2
St Modan's RC Prim Sch
　G33 .... 119 D4
St Modan's Way G84 .... 15 D2
St Modans Ct 14 FK1 .... 42 A2
St Monach's Pl KA20 .... 206 E1
St Monance St G21 .... 97 F3
St Monica's RC Prim Sch
　ML5 .... 121 E2
St Monica's RC Prim Sch
　G53 .... 115 D1
St Mungo Ave G4 .... 241 E3
St Mungo Ct PA11 .... 110 C4
St Mungo Pl Glasgow G4 .... 241 E3
　Hamilton ML3 .... 161 E2
St Mungo St G4 .... 241 E3
St Mungo's ML11 .... 215 D2
St Mungo's Acad G40 .... 118 A3
St Mungo's High Sch FK2 .... 42 A3
St Mungo's Prim Sch FK10 ...... 10 B3
St Mungo's Prim Sch PA15 ...... 46 B2
　G4 .... 241 F3
St Mungo's Rd G67 .... 61 F1
St Mungo's Wynd FK10 .... 10 A3
St Nicholas Rd
　Lanark ML11 .... 215 D3
　Prestwick KA9 .... 236 A4
St Ninian St G5 .... 117 E3
St Ninian Terr G65 .... 117 E3
St Ninian's ML11 .... 215 D3
St Ninian's Cres PA2 .... 113 F1
St Ninian's Dr KA22 .... 205 D2
St Ninian's High Sch
　Glasgow G46 .... 136 A1
　Kirkintilloch G66 .... 79 D4
St Ninian's Prim Sch G13 .... 75 E1
St Ninian's RC Prim Sch
　PA19 .... 44 B3
St Ninian's RC Prim Sch
　KA9 .... 236 C4
St Ninian's Rd
　Hamilton ML3 .... 161 F2
　Prestwick KA9 .... 236 A4
St Ninians Pl ML9 .... 198 C1
St Ninians Prim Sch FK7 .... 7 D2
St Ninians Rd
　Cambusbarron FK7 .... 6 C3
　Paisley PA1 .... 113 F1
　Stirling FK8 .... 7 D3
St Ninien's Prim Sch ML3 .... 161 F2
St Oswold's RC Sch G44 .... 137 D3
St Palladius' Prim Sch
　KA24 .... 191 E4
St Palladius Terr KA24 .... 191 E4
St Patrick's ML1 .... 214 C2
St Patrick's High Sch ML5 ...... 122 A4
St Patrick's Prim Sch PA15 ...... 45 F2
St Patrick's RC Prim Sch
　Kilsyth G65 .... 60 B4
　Motherwell ML1 .... 142 C2
　Troon KA10 .... 229 E1
St Patrick's RC Prim Sch
　Denny FK6 .... 21 F2
　Dumbarton G82 .... 50 A2
　Glasgow G3 .... 240 A2
　Shotts ML7 .... 146 C2
St Patrick's Rd ML1 .... 214 C2
St Patrick's Sch ML5 .... 122 A4
St Paul's Prim Sch G14 .... 95 E2
St Paul's RC Prim Sch
　Glasgow G32 .... 119 D2
　Hamilton ML3 .... 162 A3
St Paul's RC Prim Sch
　PA2 .... 112 C1
St Peter's La G2 .... 240 B2
St Peter's Path 13 G4 .... 97 D1
St Peter's Prim Sch
　(Girls & Infs) G11 .... 96 B2
St Peter's RC Prim Sch PA2 .... 133 E4
St Peter's RC Prim Sch
　Dumbarton G82 .... 50 A3
　Hamilton ML3 .... 162 A1
St Peter's St G4 .... 97 D1
St Philip's RC Prim Sch
　G33 .... 99 D1
St Philip's Sch ML3 .... 103 F1
St Phillans Ave KA7 .... 239 D3
St Philomena's RC
　Prim Sch G33 .... 98 A2
St Pius' Prim Sch G15 .... 75 D2
St Quivox Rd KA9 .... 236 A4
St Raymond's RC Sch G45 ...... 137 D1
St Rhonans La G83 .... 27 F2
St Robert's RC Prim Sch
　G53 .... 135 E3
St Roch's High Prim Sch
　G21 .... 98 A1
St Roch's Sec Sch G21 .... 241 F4
St Rollox Brae G21 .... 97 F1

St Ronan's Dr Glasgow G41 .... 136 B4
　Hamilton ML3 .... 183 E4
St Ronan's Prep Sch G41 .... 116 B2
St Ronan's RC Prim Sch
　G83 .... 28 A2
St Ronans Dr G73 .... 138 B2
St Rose of Lima Prim Sch
　G33 .... 99 E1
St Saviour's Sch G51 .... 116 A4
St Serf's Pl FK10 .... 4 A2
St Serf's Prim Sch FK10 .... 4 A2
St Serf's RC Prim Sch
　ML6 .... 103 D1
St Serf's Wlk FK12 .... 4 C3
St Stephen's Cres G73 .... 138 C2
St Stephen's High Sch
　PA14 .... 69 D4
St Stephen's Pl KA20 .... 206 C1
St Stephen's Prim Sch G81 ..... 73 F2
St Stephen's RC Prim Sch
　ML5 .... 122 B3
St Stephen's RC Prim Sch
　G21 .... 97 F1
St Stephens Ave G73 .... 138 B2
St Teiling ML11 .... 215 D3
St Teresa's Prim RC Sch
　G21 .... 97 F1
St Theresa's Prim Sch
　ML1 .... 143 E2
St Thomas Aquinas RC
　Sec Sch G14 .... 95 F2
St Thomas' Prim Sch ML2 .... 165 D1
St Thomas' Prim Sch
　G78 .... 154 B4
St Thomas's Pl FK7 .... 6 C3
St Thomas's Prim Sch
　G33 .... 118 B4
St Thomas's Well FK7 .... 6 B4
St Timothy's RC Prim Sch
　ML5 .... 121 F2
St Valery Dr FK7 .... 7 D2
St Vigeans Ave G77 .... 156 B2
St Vincent Cres Ayr KA7 .... 239 D1
　Glasgow G3 .... 116 C4
St Vincent Crescent La
　G3 .... 116 C4
St Vincent La G2 .... 240 C2
St Vincent Pl
　East Kilbride G75 .... 180 A4
　Glasgow G1 .... 241 D2
　Lanark ML11 .... 215 D2
　Motherwell ML1 .... 163 F4
St Vincent RC Prim Sch
　G46 .... 135 F2
St Vincent St G2 .... 240 B3
St Vincent Terr G3 .... 240 A3
St Vincent's Pl
　G75 .... 180 A3
St Vincent's Sch for the
　Blind & Deaf G32 .... 119 D1
St Winifred's Way ML2 .... 165 D2
St Winning's La KA13 .... 207 E2
St Winning's RC Prim Sch
　KA13 .... 207 E2
St Winning's Rd
　Kilwinning KA13 .... 207 E2
St Winnoc Rd PA12 .... 129 F1
St Winning's Well KA13 .... 207 E2
Salamanca St G13 .... 118 B3
Salasaig Ct G33 .... 119 D4
Salen Loan ML7 .... 147 D2
Salen St G32 .... 115 F3
Saline St ML6 .... 122 B3
Salisbury G74 .... 160 B2
Salisbury Ave KA1 .... 228 C3
Salisbury Cres ML1 .... 163 D4
Salisbury Pl Clydebank G81 .... 73 E3
　Prestwick KA9 .... 236 B4
Salisbury St 2 G5 .... 117 D2
Salkeld St G5 .... 117 D3
Salmon Dr FK1 .... 41 F1
Salmon St PA15 .... 45 F3
Salmona St G22 .... 97 D2
Saltaire Ave G71 .... 141 D3
Saltcoats Rd KA20 .... 217 D4
Saltcoats Sta KA21 .... 216 C4
Salterland Rd G78 .... 134 C2
Saltfield La KA8 .... 235 F1
Saltire Cres ML9 .... 185 E1
Saltmarket G1 .... 241 E1
Saltmarket Pl G1 .... 241 D1
Saltoun La 9 G12 .... 96 B2
Saltoun St G12 .... 96 B2
Saltpans Rd KA8 .... 235 F2
Salvia St G72 .... 138 C3
Samson Ave KA1 .... 228 A2
Sanda Pl Kilmarnock KA3 ..... 223 D3
　Saltcoats KA21 .... 205 F1
Sanda St G20 .... 96 C2
Sandaig Prim Sch G33 .... 119 F3
Sandaig Rd G33 .... 119 F3
Sandale Path G33 .... 161 E3
Sandalwood Ave G74 .... 159 E2
Sandalwood Ct G74 .... 159 E2
Sandbank Ave G20 .... 96 B3
Sandbank Cres
　Alexandria G83 .... 27 F3
　Glasgow G20 .... 96 B3
Sandbank Dr G20 .... 96 B4
Sandbank St G20 .... 96 B3
Sandbank Terr G20 .... 96 B4
Sandbed La 3 KA1 .... 227 F4
Sandbed St KA1 .... 227 F4
Sandend PA8 .... 73 D2

Sandend Rd G53 .... 135 D4
Sanderling Pl PA5 .... 131 E3
Sanderling Rd PA3 .... 113 F4
Sanderson Ave
　Irvine KA12 .... 219 D1
　Uddingston G71 .... 141 E3
Sanderson High Sch G74 ...... 181 E4
Sandfield Ave G62 .... 55 D2
Sandfield Rd KA9 .... 236 B4
Sandfield St G20 .... 96 C3
Sandford Gdns G69 .... 120 A3
Sandgate KA7 .... 238 C4
Sandgate Ave G32 .... 119 E2
Sandhaven Pl G53 .... 135 D4
Sandhaven Rd G53 .... 135 D4
Sandhead Cres ML6 .... 123 F1
Sandhill Gdns KA10 .... 229 F2
Sandholes Rd PA5 .... 111 E3
Sandholes St PA1 .... 113 E2
Sandholm Pl G14 .... 94 C3
Sandholm Terr G14 .... 94 C3
Sandiefield Rd G5 .... 117 E2
Sandielands Ave PA8 .... 93 E4
Sandilands KA10 .... 229 E1
Sandilands Cres ML1 .... 163 D3
Sandilands St G32 .... 119 E3
Sandmill St G21 .... 98 A1
Sandpiper Dr G75 .... 180 A3
Sandpiper Pl G75 .... 180 A3
Sandpiper Rd PA12 .... 129 F1
Sandra Rd G64 .... 78 B1
Sandray Ave PA14 .... 69 D4
Sandringham Ave G77 .... 157 D3
Sandringham Dr G77 .... 157 D3
Sandringham Dr PA5 .... 112 A1
Sandringham La 2 G12 .... 96 B2
Sandringham Terr PA16 ...... 45 F4
Sandwood Cres G52 .... 115 D3
Sandwood Prim Sch G52 ..... 115 D3
Sandwood Rd G52 .... 115 D3
Sandy Ct KA23 .... 190 B2
Sandy Rd Carluke ML8 .... 187 F1
　Glasgow G11 .... 96 A1
　Irvine KA12 .... 219 E1
　Renfrew PA4 .... 94 B1
　Seamill KA23 .... 190 B2
Sandyfaulds Sq 4 G5 .... 117 E2
Sandyfaulds St 6 G5 .... 117 E2
Sandyford Ave ML1 .... 143 E4
Sandyford Pl Glasgow G3 ..... 240 A3
　Motherwell ML1 .... 143 E4
Sandyford Place La G3 .... 240 A3
Sandyford Rd
　Motherwell ML1 .... 143 E4
　Paisley PA3 .... 114 A4
　Prestwick KA9 .... 234 A1
Sandyford St G3 .... 116 B4
Sandyhill Ave ML7 .... 147 D2
Sandyhill Terr KA6 .... 239 F3
Sandyhills Cres G32 .... 119 D2
Sandyhills Dr G32 .... 119 D2
Sandyhills Gr G32 .... 119 D1
Sandyhills Pl G32 .... 119 D2
Sandyhills Prim Sch G32 .... 119 E2
Sandyhills Rd G32 .... 119 E2
Sandyknowes Rd G67 .... 83 D4
Sandylands Cres ML1 .... 163 E3
Sandylands Prom KA21 .... 217 D4
Sandyvale Pl ML7 .... 147 D2
Sannox Dr
　Motherwell ML1 .... 163 D4
　Saltcoats KA21 .... 206 A1
Sannox Gdns G31 .... 118 A4
Sannox Pl Ayr KA8 .... 236 B1
　East Kilbride G75 .... 180 A2
Sannox Rd KA1 .... 222 B1
Sannox View KA8 .... 236 C1
Sannox Way KA8 .... 236 B4
Sanquhar Dr G53 .... 135 D4
Sanquhar Farm Rd KA8 .... 236 B2
Sanquhar Gdns
　Cambuslang G72 .... 140 A1
　Glasgow G53 .... 135 D4
Sanquhar Pl G53 .... 135 D4
Sapphire Rd ML4 .... 142 A2
Saracen Head Rd G1 .... 241 F1
Saracen Prim Sch G22 .... 97 D2
Saracen St G22 .... 97 E2
Sarazen Ct ML1 .... 164 C4
Sardinia La G12 .... 96 B2
Sark Dr KA10 .... 229 F3
Saskatoon Pl G75 .... 159 D1
Saturn Ave PA3 .... 112 C1
Saucel Hill Terr PA2 .... 113 F2
Saucel St PA1 .... 113 F2
Sauchie Ct FK7 .... 7 E2
Sauchie Hospl FK10 .... 10 B4
Sauchie St FK7 .... 7 E2
Sauchiehall La
　Glasgow G2 .... 240 B3
　Glasgow G2 .... 240 C3
Sauchiehall St G2 .... 240 B3
Sauchiesmoor Rd G76 .... 202 A4
Saugh Ave KA3 .... 173 E4
Saughs Ave G33 .... 98 C3
Saughs Dr G33 .... 98 C3
Saughs Gate G33 .... 98 C3
Saughs Pl G33 .... 98 C3
Saughs Rd G33 .... 98 C3
Saughton St G32 .... 118 C4
Saughtree Ave KA21 .... 205 F1
Saunders Ct G78 .... 134 A2
Saunterne Rd KA9 .... 233 E1
Savoy Ct KA7 .... 238 C4
Savoy Pk KA7 .... 238 C4
Savoy St G40 .... 117 F2
Sawers Ave FK6 .... 21 E1
Sawmill Rd G11 .... 95 F1

Sawmillfield St G4 .... 97 D1
Saxon Rd G13 .... 95 E4
Scadlock Rd PA3 .... 113 D3
Scalpay G74 .... 160 B1
Scalpay Pass G22 .... 97 E4
Scalpay Pl Glasgow G22 ..... 97 E4
　Kilmarnock KA3 .... 223 D3
Scalpay St G22 .... 97 E4
Scamadale Rd ML6 .... 84 B2
Scapa St G23 .... 96 C4
Scaraway Dr G22 .... 97 E4
Scaraway Pl G22 .... 97 F4
Scaraway St G22 .... 97 E4
Scaraway Terr G22 .... 97 F4
Scarba Dr G43 .... 136 A3
Scarba Quadrant ML2 .... 164 C1
Scarffe Ave ML3 .... 111 F3
Scargie Rd KA1 .... 227 F2
Scarhill Ave ML6 .... 122 C3
Scarhill St Cleland ML1 .... 144 A1
　Coatbridge ML5 .... 121 F2
Scarletmuir ML11 .... 214 C3
Scarlow St KA14 .... 47 E1
Scarrel Dr G45 .... 138 A2
Scarrel Gdns G45 .... 138 A2
Scarrel Rd G45 .... 138 A2
Scarrel Terr G45 .... 138 A2
Scaur O' Doon Rd KA7 ...... 238 B2
Scaur Rd ML8 .... 201 F3
Scaut of Art (Annexe) G3 .. 240 C4
Schaw Ct Alloa FK10 .... 5 E1
　Bearsden G61 .... 75 F3
Schaw Dr Bearsden G61 ..... 75 F3
　Clydebank G81 .... 74 A3
Schaw Rd PA3 .... 114 A3
Schawpark Ave FK10 .... 5 E1
Schiltron Way FK7 .... 7 E2
Scholar's Gate G75 .... 180 B3
School Ave G72 .... 139 D3
School La Carluke ML8 ...... 187 F1
　Dumbarton G82 .... 49 E2
　Irvine KA12 .... 219 E1
　Lennoxtown G65 .... 57 E4
　Menstrie FK11 .... 4 A4
　Newton Mearns G77 .... 156 B3
　Shotts ML7 .... 167 D4
School Pl KA22 .... 205 D1
School Quadrant ML6 .... 102 C1
School Rd Kilbirnie KA25 .... 149 D1
　Newton Mearns G77 .... 156 B2
　Paisley PA1 .... 114 C3
　Rhu G84 .... 15 E3
　Salsburgh ML7 .... 125 E2
　Stepps G33 .... 99 F3
　Torrance G64 .... 57 E1
　Tullibody FK10 .... 4 A1
　Wishaw ML2 .... 166 A2
School St Chapelhall ML6 .... 123 E1
　Coatbridge ML5 .... 122 A2
　Hamilton ML3 .... 162 B1
　Shotts ML7 .... 146 C2
School Wlk FK5 .... 23 E2
School Wynd
　Kilbirnie KA25 .... 149 D1
　Paisley PA1 .... 113 F3
Schoolhouse La G72 .... 161 E3
Schoolwell St KA20 .... 206 B1
Scioncroft Ave G73 .... 138 B4
Sclandersburn Rd FK6 .... 39 E4
Scone Pl East Kilbride G74 .. 159 E2
　Newton Mearns G77 .... 157 D2
Scone St G21 .... 97 E2
Sconser St G23 .... 76 C1
Scorton Gdns G69 .... 119 F2
Scotas Coll G61 .... 75 E2
Scotia Cres ML9 .... 185 E1
Scotia Gdns ML3 .... 183 E4
Scotia Pl FK2 .... 42 B3
Scotia St ML1 .... 163 E4
Scotland St G5 .... 116 C3
Scotland St W G41 .... 116 C3
Scotsblair Ave G66 .... 79 E4
Scotsburn Rd G21 .... 98 B2
Scotstoun Prim Sch G14 .... 95 D2
Scotstoun Rd FK7 .... 12 C4
Scotstoun St G14 .... 95 D2
Scotstounhill Sta G13 ...... 95 D3
Scott Ave Bowling G60 ..... 72 B4
　Johnstone PA5 .... 131 F4
　Milton Of C G65 .... 58 A4
Scott Cres Alloa FK10 ...... 10 A3
　Cumbernauld G67 .... 82 B4
　Kilmarnock KA1 .... 227 F4
　Troon KA10 .... 229 F2
Scott Ct KA7 .... 238 C4
Scott Dr Bearsden G61 ...... 75 E3
　Cumbernauld G67 .... 82 B4
Scott Gr ML3 .... 162 B1
Scott Hill G77 .... 160 A2
Scott House G67 .... 62 A2
Scott Pl Bellshill ML4 ...... 142 A4
　Johnstone PA5 .... 131 F4
　Saltcoats KA21 .... 205 F1
　Troon KA10 .... 229 E1
Scott Rd Irvine KA12 .... 219 E1
　Kilmarnock KA1 .... 227 F4
　Paisley G52 .... 114 B4
Scott St Alexandria G83 .... 27 F3
　Baillieston G69 .... 120 A2
　Clydebank G81 .... 73 F2
　Glasgow G69 .... 120 A2
　Glasgow, Garnethill G3 ...... 240 B4
　Greenock PA15 .... 46 A3
　Hamilton ML3 .... 162 B1
　Largs KA30 .... 149 D4
　Motherwell ML1 .... 163 F4
　Stirling FK8 .... 2 A1
Scott's Pl ML6 .... 103 D1
Scott's Rd PA1 .... 114 B2

Scottish Exhibition &
　Conference Ctr G3 .... 116 B4
Seabank Rd KA7 .... 235 F1
Seabank St KA21 .... 217 D4
Seabegs Cres FK4 .... 40 A2
Seabegs Pl FK4 .... 39 F2
Seabegs Rd FK4 .... 39 F2
Seafar Rd G67 .... 61 F1
Seafield Ave G61 .... 75 F4
Seafield Cottage La PA16 ... 45 E4
Seafield Cres Ayr KA7 ..... 238 C3
　Cumbernauld G68 .... 60 C1
Seafield Ct
　Ardrossan KA22 .... 205 D2
　Falkirk FK1 .... 41 F1
Seafield Dr
　Ardrossan KA22 .... 205 D2
　Ayr KA7 .... 238 B3
　Rutherglen G73 .... 138 B2
Seafield Rd KA22 .... 238 C3
Seafield Sch KA22 .... 205 D2
Seaforth Ave G61 .... 8 B1
Seaforth Cres Ayr KA8 ..... 236 A2
　Barrhead G78 .... 134 A2
Seaforth La G69 .... 81 D1
Seaforth Pl Bellshill ML4 ... 141 F2
　Stirling FK6 .... 7 D4
Seaforth Rd Ayr KA8 .... 236 A2
　Clydebank G81 .... 74 A1
　Falkirk FK2 .... 24 B1
　Glasgow G52 .... 115 D4
Seaforth Rd N G52 .... 115 D4
Seaforth Rd S G52 .... 115 D4
Seagate Irvine KA12 .... 219 D2
　Prestwick KA9 .... 233 E1
Seagrove St G32 .... 118 B3
Seamill Gdns G74 .... 159 E1
Seamill Path G33 .... 134 C3
Seamill St G53 .... 134 C3
Seamore St 1 G20 .... 97 D1
Seath Ave Airdrie ML6 .... 122 C4
　Langbank PA14 .... 70 B3
Seath Rd G73 .... 118 A1
Seath St G4 .... 117 E1
Seaton Pl FK1 .... 42 B2
Seaview Rd KA21 .... 216 C4
Seaview Terr KA10 .... 230 A2
Seaward La G3 .... 116 C3
Seaward St G41 .... 116 C3
Second Ave Alexandria G83 . 27 F3
　Clydebank G81 .... 74 A2
　Dumbarton G82 .... 50 B1
　Glasgow G44 .... 137 D3
　Irvine KA12 .... 224 B4
　Kirkintilloch G66 .... 79 E1
　Millerston G33 .... 99 D2
　Renfrew PA4 .... 94 B1
　Uddingston G71 .... 120 C1
Second Gdns G41 .... 116 B2
Second Rd G72 .... 161 F3
Second St G71 .... 140 C4
Seddhill Rd PA11 .... 113 F2
Seedhill Rd PA1 .... 114 A2
Seggielea La G13 .... 95 E3
Seggielea Rd G13 .... 95 E3
Segton Ave KA13 .... 207 E2
Selborne Pl G13 .... 95 F3
Selborne Place La G13 ... 95 F3
Selby Gdns G32 .... 119 F3
Selby Pl ML5 .... 101 E1
Selby St ML5 .... 101 E1
Selkirk Ave Glasgow G52 .. 115 E2
　Paisley PA2 .... 133 D4
Selkirk Dr G73 .... 138 B4
Selkirk Pl East Kilbride G74 . 160 B2
　Hamilton ML3 .... 162 C1
Selkirk Rd KA1 .... 228 B4
Selkirk St Blantyre G72 ... 161 E4
　Hamilton ML3 .... 162 C1
Selkirk Way Bellshill ML1 .. 142 A4
　Coatbridge ML5 .... 122 C2
Sella Rd G64 .... 78 B1
Selvieland Rd G52 .... 114 B3
Semphill Gdns G74 .... 160 A1
Sempie St ML3 .... 161 F2
Sempill Ave PA8 .... 72 C1
Semple Ave Bishopton PA7 .. 72 A2
　Lochwinnoch PA12 .... 129 E2
Semple Pl PA3 .... 112 A4
Semple View PA10 .... 236 B3
Senga Cres ML4 .... 142 A4
Sergeant Law Rd
　Paisley PA2, G78 .... 132 C2
　Uplawmoor G78 .... 153 D4
Seright Cres KA3 .... 228 B4
Seright Sq KA3 .... 228 B4
Serpentine Wlk PA15 ..... 46 B2
Service Ct KA10 .... 148 C1
Service St G65 .... 33 E1
Seton Dr FK7 .... 7 E2
Seton La G22 .... 205 E1
Seton Terr 8 G31 ...... 118 A3
Seven Sisters G66 ..... 79 F3
Seventh Ave G71 ...... 140 C4
Seventh Rd G72 .... 161 F3

Severn Rd G75 .... 179 F4
Seward Pl G41 .... 116 C3
Seymour Ave KA13 ...... 207 F1
Seymour Gn G21 .... 180 A4
Seyton Ave G46 .... 136 B1
Seyton La G41 .... 159 F2
Shaftesbury St Alloa FK10 ... 10 A4
  Glasgow G3 .... 240 A3
Shafton Pl G13 .... 95 F4
Shafton Rd G13 .... 95 F4
Shaftsbury Ave G81 ..... 73 F1
Shaftsbury Cres ML1 .... 143 E2
Shakespeare Ave G81 ... 73 F2
Shakespeare St G20 ..... 96 C3
Shalloch Pk KA7 .... 238 B1
Shalloch Pl KA11 .... 220 A1
Shamrock St Glasgow G4 ... 240 B4
  Kirkintilloch G66 ...... 79 E4
Shand La ML8 .... 187 F2
Shand St ML2 .... 165 E1
Shandon Brae G83 ...... 27 F4
Shandon Cres Balloch G83 ... 27 F4
  Bellshill ML4 .... 142 A4
Shandon Pl PA15 .... 46 B1
Shandon Terr ML3 ...... 161 F2
Shandwick St G34 ...... 120 A4
Shangill Ct ML8 .... 186 C2
Shankland La PA15 ..... 46 C1
Shankland Rd PA15 ..... 46 C1
Shanks Ave Barrhead G78 ... 134 B1
  Denny FK6 .... 39 F4
Shanks Cres PA5 .... 111 F1
Shanks Ct KA3 .... 222 C1
Shanks Ind Pk G78 ..... 134 B2
Shanks St Airdrie ML6 ... 103 D1
  Glasgow G20 .... 96 C3
Shanks Way G78 .... 134 B3
Shannon Dr FK1 .... 41 F2
Shannon St G20 .... 96 C3
Shanter Pl KA3 .... 228 B4
Shanter Way KA7 ...... 238 C1
Shanter Wynd KA7 ..... 238 C1
Shantron Rd G83 ...... 27 F3
Shapinsay St G22 ...... 97 E4
Sharon St KA24 .... 191 D4
Sharp Ave ML5 .... 121 E2
Sharp St Gourock PA19 ... 44 C4
  Motherwell ML1 .... 163 D4
Sharphill Ind Est KA21 .. 206 A2
Shavian Terr KA13 ..... 207 F1
Shavin Brae KA7 .... 239 E3
Shaw Ave PA7 .... 72 B2
Shaw Ct PA8 .... 72 C2
Shaw Farm Ind Est KA9 ... 236 C4
Shaw Pl Dalry KA24 .... 191 D4
  Greenock PA15 .... 45 F3
  Linwood PA3 .... 112 A3
  Saltcoats KA21 ...... 206 A1
Shaw Rd Milngavie G62 ... 76 A4
  Newton Mearns G77 ... 156 C2
  Prestwick KA9 .... 233 F1
Shaw St Glasgow G51 ... 116 A4
  Hamilton ML3 .... 199 D4
Shawbank Pl KA1 ...... 228 A4
Shawbridge St G43 .... 136 B4
Shawburn Cres ML3 ... 162 A2
Shawburn St ML3 ..... 162 A2
Shawfarm Ct KA9 ..... 233 E1
Shawfarm Pl KA9 ..... 239 D2
Shawfield Cres ML8 ... 186 C3
Shawfield Dr G5 ...... 117 F1
Shawfield Ind Est G73 .. 117 F1
Shawfield Rd G40 ..... 117 F1
Shawhead Ave ML5 ... 122 A2
Shawhead Cotts ML5 .. 122 A2
Shawhead Prim Sch ML5 ... 122 A2
Shawhill Cres G77 .... 156 C2
Shawhill Rd G41 ...... 136 R4
Shawholm Cres G43 ... 136 A4
Shawlands Acad G41 .. 136 C1
Shawlands Arc G41 ... 136 C4
Shawlands Cross ☒ G41 ... 136 C1
Shawlands Prim Sch G41 ... 136 B4
Shawlands Sta G41 ... 136 B4
Shawmoss Rd G41 .... 116 B1
Shawpark St G20 ..... 96 C3
Shawrigg Rd ML9 .... 185 E1
Shaws Rd ML9 .... 199 E4
Shawstonfoot Rd ML1 .. 145 D1
Shawwood Cres G77 .. 156 C2
Shearer Dr ML3 ...... 183 E4
Shearer Quadrant G83 .. 28 A4
Sheddens Pl G32 ..... 118 C3
Sheddon Ave PA7 .... 72 A1
Sheepburn Rd G71 ... 140 C4
Sheila St G33 .... 98 C2
Sheildhill ☒ G71 .... 140 C4
Sheiling Hill ML3 .... 162 C2
Sheldaig Rd G22 ..... 97 D4
Sheldrake Pl PA5 .... 131 E1
Shellbridge Way KA22 .. 205 E1
Shelley Ct G12 ...... 96 A3
Shelley Rd G12 ...... 96 A3
Shells Rd G66 .... 58 C1
Sherbrooke Ave G41 .. 116 B2
Sherbrooke Dr G41 ... 116 B2
Sherbrooke Gdns G41 .. 116 B2
Sherbrooke Pl G75 ... 159 F1
Sherburn Gdns G69 .. 119 F2
Sherdale Ave ML6 ... 123 E1
Sheriff Park Ave G73 .. 138 A4

Sheriffmuir Rd FK9 ..... 2 B4
Sheriffmuirlands FK9 ... 2 B2
Sherriff La FK5 .... 23 F2
Sherry Dr ML3 .... 162 A1
Sherwood Ave
  Paisley PA1 .... 114 A3
  Uddingston G71 ..... 141 D3
Sherwood Dr G46 .... 136 A2
Sherwood Pl G15 .... 75 D2
Sherwood Rd
  Hurlford KA1 .... 228 C3
  Prestwick KA9 ...... 236 C4
Shetland Ct FK10 ..... 10 A4
Shetland Dr Glasgow G44 ... 137 E2
  Kilmarnock KA3 ..... 223 D3
Shettleston Rd G32 ... 119 D3
Shettleston Sheddings
  G32 .... 118 C3
Shettleston Sta G32 .. 119 D3
Shewalton Dr KA11 ... 225 E3
Shewalton Moss KA11 .. 225 E3
Shewalton Pits
  (Nature Reserve) KA11 .. 224 B4
Shewalton Rd KA11 ... 225 D3
Shiel Ave G74 .... 159 F2
Shiel Ct G78 .... 134 A3
Shiel Dr ML9 .... 184 C3
Shiel Gdns Falkirk FK2 .. 24 B1
  Shotts ML7 .... 147 D2
Shiel Hill KA7 .... 239 D1
Shiel Pl Coatbridge ML5 .. 122 B3
  East Kilbride G74 .... 159 F2
  Irvine KA12 .... 219 E3
Shiel Rd G64 .... 78 A1
Shiel Terr ML2 ...... 165 F3
Shielbridge Gdns G23 .. 76 C1
Shieldaig Dr G73 .... 138 A2
Shieldburn Rd G51 ... 115 E4
Shieldhall Gdns G51 .. 115 E4
Shieldhall Rd G51 ... 115 E4
Shieldhill Prim Sch FK1 .. 66 B3
Shieldhill Rd ML8 ... 201 F4
Shieldmuir St ML2 ... 164 B2
Shieldmuir Sta ML2 .. 164 B2
Shields Ct ML1 ...... 164 A2
Shields Dr ML1 ...... 164 A2
Shields Loan ML1 .... 214 C3
Shields Rd
  East Kilbride G75 ... 180 A2
  Glasgow G41 .... 116 C2
  Motherwell ML1 ..... 164 A2
Shields Road
  Underground Sta G5 .. 116 C3
Shielhope Ct KA11 ... 220 A2
Shieling Pk KA7 ..... 238 C4
Shilford Ave G13 .... 95 D4
Shilford Rd G78 ..... 132 B1
Shillay St G22 ...... 97 F4
Shilliaw Dr KA9 ..... 236 B3
Shilliaw Pl KA9 ..... 236 B3
Shillinghill FK10 .... 10 A3
Shillingworth Pl PA11 .. 110 B3
Shilton Dr G53 ...... 135 E3
Shilton La PA7 ...... 72 C2
Shinwell Ave G81 .... 74 B1
Shipbank La G1 ..... 241 D1
Shiphaugh Pl FK8 .... 2 B1
Shira Terr G74 ...... 160 A1
Shire Way FK10 ..... 9 F3
Shirley Quadrant ML1 .. 163 E2
Shirley's Cl ML11 .... 215 D2
Shirra's Brae Rd FK7 .. 7 F2
Shirrel Ave ML4 ..... 142 A4
Shirrel Rd ML1 ..... 143 D2
Shirva La G65 ...... 59 F2
Shiskine Dr Glasgow G20 .. 96 B4
  Kilmarnock KA3 ..... 222 C2
Shiskine Pl Glasgow G20 .. 96 B4
  Helensburgh G84 .... 16 C1
Shiskine St G20 ..... 96 B4
Sholto Cres ML4 .... 141 E4
Shore Rd Airth FK2 ... 14 B2
  Ayr KA8 .... 235 F1
  Stevenston KA20 .... 217 E4
  Stirling FK8 .... 7 D4
  Troon KA10 .... 229 D1
Shore St Glasgow G40 .. 118 A1
  Gourock PA19 .... 44 C4
  Port Glasgow PA14 .. 47 D1
Shore The FK10 ..... 10 A3
Shortlees Cres KA1 .. 227 F2
Shortlees Prim Sch KA1 .. 227 F2
Shortlees Rd KA1 .... 227 F1
Shortridge St G20 ... 96 C3
Shortroods Ave PA3 .. 113 F4
Shortroods Cres PA3 .. 113 F4
Shortroods Rd PA3 ... 113 E4
Shotts St ML7 ...... 126 C1
Shotts Sta ML7 ..... 119 E4
Shotts Wlk ML7 ..... 146 C2
Shottsburn Rd ML7 .. 126 C1
Shottskirk Rd ML7 .. 146 B3
Shuna Pl Glasgow G20 .. 96 C3
  Newton Mearns G77 .. 156 C4
Shuna St G20 .... 96 C3
Shuttle St Glasgow G1 .. 241 E2
  Kilbarchan PA10 .... 111 D2
  Kilsyth G65 .... 60 B4
  Paisley PA1 .... 113 F2
Sidehead Rd Harthill ML7 .. 127 F3
  Stonehouse ML9 .... 198 C1
Sidland Rd G21 ..... 98 B3
Sidlaw Ave Barrhead G78 .. 134 B1
  Hamilton ML3 .... 161 F1
  Port Glasgow PA14 .. 68 C3
Sidlaw Dr ML2 ...... 164 C2
Sidlaw Foot KA11 ... 220 B1
Sidlaw Pl KA1 ...... 228 A2

Sidlaw Rd G61 ...... 75 D4
Sidlaw Way Chapelhall ML6 .. 123 F1
  Larkhall ML9 .... 184 C3
Sidney St KA21 ..... 216 C4
Sielga Pl G34 ...... 120 A4
Siemens Pl G21 .... 98 A1
Siemens St G21 .... 98 A1
Sievewright St G73 .. 118 B1
Sighthill Loan ☒ ML9 .. 185 D2
Sighthill Prim Sch G21 .. 97 E2
Sighthill Terr ML7 .. 125 D1
Sikeside Pl ML5 .... 122 B3
Sikeside Prim Sch ML5 .. 122 B3
Sikeside St ML5 .... 122 B3
Silk Ho FK1 .... 42 A4
Silk St PA1 .... 113 F3
Silkin Ave G81 ..... 74 B1
Sillars Meadow KA12 .. 219 F1
Silvan Pl G76 ...... 158 A3
Silver Firs ML1 .... 143 E2
Silverbirch Gdns ML3 .. 183 F2
Silverbirch Gr ML3 .. 183 F2
Silverburn Cres ML1 .. 143 E2
Silverburn St G33 .. 118 C4
Silverdale G74 ..... 159 F2
Silverdale Cres ML11 .. 214 C2
Silverdale Ct ML11 .. 214 C2
Silverdale St G31 ... 118 B2
Silverdale Terr ML6 .. 103 F2
Silverfir Ct G5 ..... 117 E2
Silvergrove St G40 .. 117 F3
Silvermuir Ave ML11 .. 215 F4
Silverton Ave G82 .. 50 A2
Silvertonhill Ave ML3 .. 162 C1
Silvertonhill La G82 .. 50 A2
Silvertonhill Pl ML3 .. 183 E4
Silverwells G71 .... 141 D1
Silverwells Cres G71 .. 141 D1
Silverwood Ct G71 .. 141 D1
Silverwood Prim Sch KA3 .. 223 E2
Silverwood Rd KA3 .. 228 B4
Sim St KA3 .... 211 E4
Simons Cres
  Kilmarnock KA1 .... 227 F2
  Renfrew PA4 .... 94 B3
Simonsburn Rd KA1 .. 227 F2
Simpson Ct Clydebank G81 .. 74 A1
  Uddingston G71 .... 140 C3
Simpson Dr
  East Kilbride G75 ... 180 B4
  Saltcoats KA21 ..... 205 F2
Simpson Pl
  East Kilbride G75 ... 180 B4
  Kilwinning KA13 .... 207 F1
Simpson Quadrant G83 .. 28 A4
Simpson St
  Crosshouse KA2 .... 222 A1
  Falkirk FK1 .... 42 A3
  Glasgow G20 .... 96 C2
Simpson Way ML4 ... 142 B4
Simshill Prim Sch G44 .. 137 D2
Simshill Rd G44,G45 .. 137 E2
Simson Ave KA23 ... 190 C2
Sinclair Ave G61 ... 75 F3
Sinclair Cres FK6 .. 21 E1
Sinclair Ct
  Bannockburn FK7 ... 7 F1
  Kilmarnock KA3 .... 222 B2
Sinclair Dr Coatbridge ML5 .. 121 E4
  Fallin FK7 .... 8 B2
  Glasgow G42 .... 136 C4
  Helensburgh G84 ... 16 C2
Sinclair Gdns G64 ... 98 A4
Sinclair Gr ML4 .... 141 F1
Sinclair Pk G75 .... 180 C4
Sinclair Pl
  East Kilbride G75 ... 180 C4
  Falkirk FK2 .... 24 A1
Sinclair St Clydebank G81 .. 94 B4
  Greenock PA15 ...... 46 B2
  Helensburgh G84 .... 16 C1
  Milngavie G62 ...... 55 D1
  Stevenston KA20 .... 206 B1
Singer St G81 ...... 74 B2
Singer Sta G81 ..... 74 A1
Sir Michael Pl
  Greenock PA15 ...... 45 F3
  Paisley PA1 .... 113 E2
Sir Michael St PA15 .. 45 F3
Sir William Wallace Ct
  FK5 .... 23 D2
Sixth Ave PA4 ...... 94 B1
Sixth St G71 .... 120 C1
Skaethorn Rd G20 ... 96 B4
Skaithmuir Ave FK2 .. 24 A2
Skaithmuir Cres FK2 .. 24 A2
Skara Wlk ML2 ..... 165 F4
Skaterigg Dr G13 ... 95 F3
Skaterigg Gdns G13 .. 95 F3
Skaterigg La G13 ... 95 F3
Skelbo Pl G34 ...... 100 B1
Skelbo Pl G34 ...... 100 B1
Skelmorlie Pl
  Kilwinning KA13 .... 207 E2
  Stenhousemuir FK5 .. 23 F2
Skene Rd Glasgow G51 .. 116 A3
  Kilmarnock KA3 ..... 223 E2
Skene St ML7 ...... 40 A3
Skerne Gr G75 ..... 179 F3
Skerrieland Rd KA3 .. 213 D2
Skerray Quadrant G22 .. 97 E4
Skerray St G22 .... 97 E4
Skerryvore Pl G33 .. 119 D4
Skerryvore Rd G33 .. 119 D4
Skibo La G46 ...... 135 F2
Skipness Ave ML8 .. 202 A4

Skipness Dr G51 .... 115 E4
Skirsa Ct G23 ...... 97 D4
Skirsa Pl G23 ...... 96 C4
Skirsa Sq G23 ...... 97 D4
Skirsa St G23 ...... 96 C4
Skirving St G41 .... 136 C4
Skovlunde Way G75 .. 180 C3
Skye G74 .... 160 B1
Skye Ave PA4 ...... 94 B1
Skye Cres Gourock PA19 .. 44 B3
  Old Kilpatrick G60 .. 73 E3
  Paisley PA2 .... 133 E4
Skye Ct Cumbernauld G67 .. 82 B4
  Irvine KA11 .... 225 D4
Skye Dr Cumbernauld G67 .. 82 B4
  Old Kilpatrick G60 .. 73 E3
Skye Gdns G61 ..... 75 D3
Skye Pl Cumbernauld G67 .. 82 B4
  Stevenston KA20 ... 206 C1
Skye Quadrant ML2 .. 165 F3
Skye Rd Cumbernauld G67 .. 82 B4
  Port Glasgow PA14 .. 69 D3
  Prestwick KA9 ...... 233 F1
  Rutherglen G73 ..... 138 B2
Skye St G21 .... 45 E2
Skythorn Way FK1 .. 41 F1
Slaemuir Ave PA14 .. 68 C3
Slaemuir Prim Sch PA14 .. 69 D3
Slakiewood Ave G69 .. 100 C4
Slamannan Prim Sch FK1 .. 86 A4
Slamannan Rd
  Avonbridge FK1 .... 87 F3
  Falkirk FK1 .... 42 A1
  Slamannan FK1 ..... 86 A1
Slatefield G65 ..... 57 E4
Slatefield Ct G31 .. 118 A3
Slatefield St G31 ... 118 A3
Sleaford Ave ML1 .. 163 E2
Slenavon Ave G73 .. 138 B2
Slessor Dr G75 .... 180 C4
Slioch Sq ML1 ..... 143 E2
Sloan Ave KA12 ... 219 E1
Sloan Pl KA8 ...... 236 B1
Sloy St Glasgow G22 .. 97 E2
  Wishaw ML2 .... 165 D1
Small Cres G72 ... 161 E4
Smeaton Ave G64 .. 78 A4
Smeaton St G20 ... 96 C3
Smiddy Ct Kilwinning KA13 .. 207 F2
  Lanark ML11 .... 215 D2
Smiddy Wynd FK12 .. 5 D3
Smillie Pl KA2 ..... 227 E3
Smillie St PA15 .... 46 C1
Smith Art Gallery & Mus FK8 .. 7 D4
Smith Ave
  Crosshouse KA2 .... 170 B3
  Irvine KA12 .... 219 E2
  Wishaw ML2 .... 186 A4
Smith Cres Balloch G83 .. 27 F4
  Clydebank G81 ...... 74 A3
  Kilwinning KA13 .... 207 F2
Smith Dr KA21 ..... 217 D4
Smith Pl FK6 ...... 21 E1
Smith Quadrant ML5 .. 122 B4
Smith St Ayr KA7 .. 239 D4
  Kilmarnock KA3 .... 222 B2
  Falkirk FK2 .... 42 A4
  Glasgow G14 .... 95 F1
  Greenock PA15 ..... 45 F3
  Prestwick KA9 ..... 236 B4
Smithfield Loan FK10 .. 9 F3
Smithhills St PA1 .. 113 F3
Smithston Cotts PA16 .. 45 D2
Smithstone Cres G65 .. 60 C3
Smithstone Ct KA11 .. 219 F3
Smithstone Terr KA13 .. 207 D4
Smithstone Way KA11 .. 219 F3
Smithview ML2 ..... 186 B4
Smithy Brae PA13 .. 89 E4
Smithy Ct G82 ..... 48 A4
Smithycroft ML3 ... 163 D1
Smithycroft Rd G33 .. 98 C1
Smithycroft Sec Sch G33 .. 98 C1
Smithyends G67 .... 62 A3
Smollett Rd G82 ... 50 A2
Smollett St G83 ... 27 E3
Smuggler's Way G84 .. 15 E3
Smugglers Brig Rd ML8 .. 201 D1
Smyllum Pk ML11 .. 215 E2
Smyllum Rd ML11 .. 215 E2
Snaefell Ave G73 .. 138 B2
Snaefell Cres G73 .. 138 B3
Sneddon Ave ML2 .. 165 E1
Sneddon St ML3 ... 161 F3
Sneddon Terr ML3 .. 161 F3
Snowdon Sch Ltd FK8 .. 7 D4
Snowdon Pl
  ☒ Glasgow G5 ..... 117 E2
  Stirling FK8 .... 7 D4
Snowdon Place La FK7 .. 7 D3
Snowdon St ☒ G5 .. 117 E2
Snowdon Terr KA21 .. 190 A3
Snowdrop Sq KA7 .. 239 D2
Snuff Mill Rd G44 .. 137 D3
South Park Dr PA2 .. 113 F1
South Park Gr ML3 .. 162 B2
South Park Prim Sch ML3 .. 183 D2
South Park Rd ML3 .. 162 B2
South Pk ML4 ...... 141 F2
South Pleasance Ave FK1 .. 42 A2
South Portland St ☒ G5 .. 117 E3
South Rd KA24 ..... 202 A4
Port Glasgow PA14 .. 68 C4
  West Kilbride KA23 .. 190 B2
South Robertson Pl ML6 .. 122 C3

Smith Pl FK6 ...... 21 E1
Solway St G40 ..... 117 F1
Somerford Rd G61 .. 75 F1
Somerled Ave PA3 .. 94 A1
Somerset Ave ML3 .. 162 A2
Somerset Pl G3 .... 240 A4
Somerset Place Mews
  G3 .... 240 A4
Somerset Rd KA8 .. 236 A1
Somervell St G72 .. 138 C3
Somerville Ct KA15 .. 150 A1
Somerville Dr
  East Kilbride G75 ... 180 C3
  Glasgow G42 .... 137 D4
Somerville La ☒ G75 .. 180 C3
Somerville Pl KA11 .. 220 A4
Somerville Pl G84 .. 25 C4
Somerville Terr ☒ G75 .. 180 C4
Somerville Way KA11 .. 220 A4
Scommerville Dr KA20 .. 217 F3
Sophia Cres KA12 .. 219 D3
Sorbie Dr ML9 ..... 198 C1
Sorbie Rd Ardrossan KA22 .. 205 E1
  Ardrossan KA22 .... 205 F2
Sorby St G31 ...... 118 B3
Sorley St G11 ..... 95 F1
Sorn St G40 ...... 118 A2
Sorrel Dr KA7 ..... 239 E2
Souillac Dr FK6 ... 21 E1
Soulis St KA3 ..... 223 D1
Sourlie Rd KA11 ... 220 A4
Sourlie Terr KA11 .. 219 F3
Souter Dr KA3 .... 228 B4
Souter Pl KA7 .... 239 D3
Souterhouse Path ML5 .. 121 F3
Souterhouse Rd ML5 .. 121 F3
South Annandale St G42 .. 117 D1
South Approach Rd FK2 .. 24 C4
South Ave Carluke ML8 .. 187 F1
  Clydebank G81 ...... 74 A1
  Hamilton G72 ...... 161 F3
  Paisley PA2 .... 133 F4
  Renfrew PA4 .... 94 B2
South Bank St G81 .. 94 B4
South Bantaskine Dr FK1 .. 42 A2
South Bantaskine Rd FK1 .. 42 A2
South Barrwood Rd G65 .. 60 C4
South Beach KA10 .. 229 E1
South Beach Espl KA10 .. 229 E1
South Beach La KA10 .. 229 E1
South Beach Rd
  Ardrossan KA22 .... 205 E1
  Ayr KA7 .... 235 F1
South Biggar Rd ML6 .. 123 D4
South Brae ML6 .... 57 E4
South Bridge St ML6 .. 123 D4
South Broomage Ave FK5 .. 23 E3
South Burn Rd ML6 .. 122 B4
South Caldeen Rd ML5 .. 122 A3
South Campbell St PA2 .. 113 F2
South Carbrain Rd G67 .. 62 A1
South Chester St G32 .. 119 D3
South Church Pl G83 .. 27 E2
South Circular Rd ML5 .. 122 A3
South Claremont La G62 .. 55 D1
South Commonhead Ave
  ML6 .... 103 D1
South Crescent Rd G82 .. 205 E1
South Crosshill Rd G64 .. 78 A1
South Dean Park Ave
  G71 .... 141 D1
South Dean Rd KA3 .. 223 D3
South Douglas St G81 .. 94 B4
South Dr Kilbirnie KA25 .. 170 A4
  Linwood PA3 .... 112 A3
  Troon KA10 .... 229 F2
South Dumbreck Rd G65 .. 60 A4
South Elgin Pl G81 .. 94 B4
South Elgin St G81 .. 94 B4
South Erskine Pk G61 .. 75 E3
South Exchange Ct G1 .. 241 D2
South Frederick St G1 .. 241 D2
South Gargieston Dr KA1 .. 227 E3
South Harbour St KA7 .. 235 F1
South Hirst Rd ML7 .. 126 C2
South Isle Rd KA22 .. 205 E3
South King St G84 .. 25 C4
South Loan G69 .... 100 B4
South Lodge Ct KA7 .. 238 C3
South Mains Cotts PA6 .. 71 F1
South Mains Rd G62 .. 54 C1
South Medrox St ML5 .. 101 E4
South Melville La FK1 .. 42 A3
South Moraine La G15 .. 75 E1
South Mound PA6 .. 91 E2
South Muirhead Rd G67 .. 62 A1
South Nimmo St ML6 .. 123 D4
South Park Ave G78 .. 134 B1
South Park Dr PA2 .. 113 F1

Society St G31 .... 118 A3
Solar Ct ML9 ...... 199 D4
Sollas Pl G13 ..... 94 C4
Solsgirth Gdns G66 .. 79 F3
Solway Ct ML3 .... 183 D4
Solway Pl
  Chryston G69 ..... 80 B1
  Kilmarnock KA1 ... 228 A2
  Troon KA10 .... 229 F3
Solway Rd G64 .... 78 B1

South Scott St G69 .... 120 A2
South St Cambus FK10 .... 9 D4
  Glasgow G14 .... 95 E2
  Greenock PA16 .... 45 E3
  Houston PA6 .... 91 D1
  Inchinnan PA4 .... 93 C2
  Stirling FK9 .... 2 B1
South Vennel Irvine KA11 ... 220 A2
  Lanark ML11 .... 215 D2
South Vesalius St G32 ...... 119 D3
South View Bellshill ML4 .... 141 F2
  Blantyre G72 .... 140 B1
  Clydebank G81 .... 73 F2
  Stenhousemuir FK5 .... 23 E1
South William St PA5 .... 111 F1
South Woodside Rd
  G4, G20 .... 96 C1
Southampton Dr G12 .... 96 A3
Southampton La G12 .... 96 A3
Southbank Dr G66 .... 79 E4
Southbank Rd G66 .... 79 E4
Southbank St G31 .... 118 B3
Southbar Ave G13 .... 95 D4
Southbar Rd PA8 .... 93 D4
Southbrae Ave PA11 .... 110 A4
Southbrae Dr G13 .... 95 E2
Southbrae La G13 .... 95 F3
Southburn Rd G68 .... 31 E2
Southcroft FK12 .... 4 C3
Southcroft Rd G73 .... 117 F1
Southcroft St G51 .... 116 A4
Southdeen Ave G15 .... 75 D2
Southdeen Rd G15 .... 75 D2
Southend Pl ML4 .... 141 F2
Southend Rd G81 .... 74 A3
Southern Ave G13 .... 95 D4
Southern General Hospl
  G51 .... 115 E4
Southerness Dr G68 .... 62 A3
Southesk Ave G64 .... 77 F1
Southesk Gdns G64 .... 77 F2
Southfield ML5 .... 122 B3
Southfield Ave Paisley PA2 133 F4
  Port Glasgow PA14 .... 68 C4
  Shotts ML7 .... 147 D2
Southfield Cres
  Coatbridge ML5 .... 122 B3
  Glasgow G53 .... 135 E4
  Shotts ML7 .... 147 D2
  Stirling FK8 .... 7 D3
Southfield Dr FK1 .... 86 A3
Southfield Pk KA7 .... 239 D3
Southfield Rd
  Cumbernauld G68 .... 61 E1
  Shotts ML7 .... 147 D2
Southy Newmoor Ind Est
  KA11 .... 224 C4
Southgate
  E East Kilbride G74 .... 159 F1
  Milngavie G62 .... 55 D1
Southhill Ave G73 .... 138 B3
Southhook Rd
  Kilmarnock KA1 .... 222 B1
  Knockentiber KA2 .... 221 F2
Southlea Ave G14 .... 94 C3
Southinch La G14 .... 94 C3
Southlea Ave G46 .... 136 A2
Southloch Gdns [2] G21 ...... 97 F2
Southloch St G21 .... 97 F2
Southmuir Pl G20 .... 96 B3
Southook Row KA11 .... 220 A3
Southpark Ave
  Glasgow G12 .... 96 C1
  Prestwick KA9 .... 236 A4
Southpark La [1] G12 .... 96 C1
Southpark Rd KA7 .... 238 C3
Southpark Terr G12 .... 96 C1
Southview G51 .... 75 E3
Southview Ave G76 .... 157 F3
Southview Cres PA11 .... 90 B1
Southview Ct [2] G64 .... 97 F2
Southview Dr G61 .... 31 D2
Southview Pl G69 .... 100 C3
Southview Rd G63 .... 31 E2
Southview Terr G64 .... 97 F2
Southward Way KA10 ...... 229 F4
Southwold Rd PA1 .... 114 C3
Southwood Dr G44 .... 137 E3
Southwood Rd KA10 .... 233 D3
Soutra Pl G33 .... 119 D3
Spairdrum Rd Airdrie ML6 ... 83 D2
  Cumbernauld G67, ML6 ...... 82 C2
Spalehall Dr ML1 .... 143 F2
Spallander Rd KA10 .... 229 F3
Sparrow Gdns KA1 .... 228 B4
Spateston Rd PA5 .... 131 E4
Spean Ave G74 .... 160 A1
Spean St G44 .... 137 D3
Speedwell Sq KA7 .... 239 D2
Speirs Pl PA3 .... 112 B4
Speirs Rd G61 .... 76 A2
Speirsfield Gdns PA2 .... 113 F2
Speirshall Cl G14 .... 94 C3
Speirshall Terr G14 .... 94 C3
Spence St Bonnybridge FK4 ... 40 A3
  Glasgow G20 .... 96 B4
Spencer Dr PA2 .... 132 C4
Spencer St Clydebank G81 ... 74 A2
  Glasgow G13 .... 95 F4
Spencerfield Gdns ML3 ... 162 C2
Spey Ave Kilmarnock KA1 ... 228 A3
  Paisley PA2 .... 112 C1
Spey Ct Airdrie ML6 .... 123 E3
  Stirling FK7 .... 7 E3
  [2] Wishaw ML2 .... 165 F3
Spey Dr PA4 .... 94 C1
Spey Gdns ML3 .... 183 D4
Spey Gr G75 .... 179 F4

Spey Pl PA5 .... 131 E4
Spey Rd Bearsden G61 .... 75 E1
  Prestwick KA9 .... 233 E1
  Troon KA10 .... 229 F2
Spey St G33 .... 118 C4
Spey Terr G75 .... 179 F4
Spey Wlk ML1 .... 143 D3
Spey Wynd ML9 .... 199 D4
Speyburn Pl KA11 .... 219 F3
Spiers Gr G64 .... 135 F2
Spiers Pl KA15 .... 171 D4
Spiers Rd Houston PA6 ...... 91 D1
  Johnstone PA5 .... 112 A2
  Lochwinnoch PA12 .... 129 D2
Spiers Wharf G4 .... 97 D1
Spiersbridge Ave G46 ...... 135 F2
Spiersbridge La G46 .... 135 F2
Spiersbridge Rd G46 .... 135 F2
Spiersbridge Terr G46 ...... 135 F2
Spiersland Way KA15 ...... 171 E4
Spindlehowe Rd
  Uddingston G71 .... 140 C3
  Uddingston, Tannochside
  G71 .... 141 D4
Spindleside Rd ML1 .... 144 B1
Spinkhill FK2 .... 42 C1
Spinners Gdns PA2 .... 113 D2
Spinners La ML1 .... 144 A4
Spinningdale ML9 .... 198 B1
Spital Rd ML9 .... 198 C1
Spittal Hill FK9 .... 2 B2
Spittal Prim Sch G73 .... 137 F3
Spittal Rd G73 .... 137 F3
Spittal St FK8 .... 7 D4
Spoutmouth G1 .... 241 E1
Sprig Way ML7 .... 127 F3
Spring La ML6 .... 104 C2
Springbank Gdns FK2 .... 42 B3
Springbank Ind Est KA12 .. 224 B4
Springbank Rd Ayr KA8 .... 236 A2
  Paisley PA3 .... 113 E4
  Shotts ML7 .... 146 B3
  Stirling FK7 .... 7 E2
Springbank Terr PA3 .... 113 E4
Springboig Ave G32 .... 119 E3
Springboig Rd G32 .... 119 E3
Springboig St John's Sch
  G33 .... 119 E4
Springburn Mus G21 .... 97 F2
Springburn Pl G74 .... 159 D2
Springburn Rd G21 .... 97 F2
Springburn Sta G21 .... 97 F2
Springburn Way [4] G21 .... 97 F2
Springcroft G69 .... 120 A3
Springcroft Ave G69 .... 120 A3
Springcroft Cres G69 ...... 120 A3
Springcroft Dr G69 .... 120 A3
Springcroft Gdns G69 ..... 120 A3
Springcroft Gr G69 .... 120 A3
Springcroft Rd G69 .... 120 A3
Springcroft Wynd G69 .... 120 A3
Springfield Ave
  Bishopbriggs G64 .... 98 A4
  Paisley PA1 .... 114 A2
  Prestwick KA9 .... 236 B4
  Uddingston G71 .... 140 C3
Springfield Cres
  Bishopbriggs G64 .... 98 A4
  Blantyre G72 .... 140 B4
  Carluke ML8 .... 201 F4
  Uddingston G71 .... 140 C3
Springfield Ct G1 .... 241 D2
Springfield Dr
  Barrhead G78 .... 134 C1
  Falkirk FK1 .... 41 F3
Springfield Gdns ML11 ..... 214 C3
Springfield Park Rd G73 ... 138 B3
Springfield Pk PA5 .... 112 A1
Springfield Prim Sch
  Glasgow G40 .... 118 A1
  Gourock PA19 .... 44 B2
Springfield Quay G5 .... 240 A2
Springfield Rd Airdrie ML6 . 123 F4
  Alloa FK10 .... 10 B4
  Barrhead G78 .... 155 E4
  Bishopbriggs G64 .... 78 A1
  Crosshouse KA2 .... 221 F1
  Cumbernauld G67 .... 62 A2
  Denny FK6 .... 21 F1
  Glasgow G40 .... 118 A2
  Salsburgh ML7 .... 125 D1
  Stirling FK7 .... 7 E2
Springfield Sq G64 .... 98 A4
Springfield Woods PA5 .... 112 A1
Springhead Rd ML7 .... 147 F2
Springhill Ave Airdrie ML6 . 123 D4
  Coatbridge ML5 .... 121 F2
  Crosshouse KA2 .... 226 C4
Springhill Gdns
  Glasgow G41 .... 116 C1
Springhill & Leadloch Rd
  ML7 .... 147 F1
Springhill Pl
  Coatbridge ML5 .... 121 E2
  Glasgow G41 .... 227 F4
Springhill Prim Sch G78 .. 134 A1
Springhill Rd
  Barrhead G78 .... 155 D3
  Clarkston G76 .... 157 F4
  Glasgow G69 .... 120 A3
  Port Glasgow PA14 .... 147 D2
  Shotts ML7 .... 147 D2
Springhill Terr KA11 .... 220 B1
Springhill View ML7 .... 147 D2
Springholm Dr ML6 .... 102 C2
Springkell Ave G41 .... 116 B1

Springkell Dr G41 .... 116 A1
Springkell Gate G41 .... 116 B1
Springkell St PA15 .... 46 A2
Springkerse Ind Est FK7 .... 7 E3
Springkerse Rd FK7 .... 7 E3
Springkerse Rdbt FK7 .... 7 F4
Springside KA23 .... 190 C4
Springside Pl G15 .... 75 D2
Springside Prim Sch
  KA11 .... 220 C1
Springside Terr KA11 ...... 220 C1
Springvale Pk KA7 .... 238 C3
Springvale Pl KA21 .... 216 C4
Springvale Rd KA7 .... 238 C3
Springvale St KA21 .... 216 C4
Springvale Terr [5] G21 ..... 97 F2
Springwell Cres G72 .... 161 F4
Springwell PA11 .... 90 A4
Springwells Ave ML6 ...... 123 E4
Springwells Cres ML6 ..... 123 E4
Springwood Ave FK8 .... 6 C3
Springwood Dr PA13 .... 69 E1
Sprotwell Terr FK10 .... 5 E3
Spruce Ave Blantyre G72 . 161 E4
  Hamilton ML3 .... 162 C1
  Johnstone PA5 .... 112 A1
Spruce Ct Coatbridge ML5 121 F2
  Hamilton ML3 .... 162 C1
Spruce Dr
  Cambuslang G72 .... 139 F2
  Kirkintilloch G66 .... 79 D3
Spruce House KA9 .... 236 A3
Spruce La KA7 .... 239 E3
Spruce Rd
  Cumbernauld G67 .... 62 B2
  Uddingston G71 .... 121 E1
Spruce St G22 .... 97 E3
Spruce Way ML1 .... 143 E2
Sprucebank Ave PA14 ...... 70 B4
Spur Rd KA8 .... 235 F1
Spy's La G84 .... 15 F2
Spynie Pl G64 .... 78 B1
Spynie Way [1] ML2 .... 165 F3
Square The FK7 .... 8 B2
Squire St G51 .... 116 A4
Sraehouse Wynd ML8 ..... 188 A1
Stable Gr PA1 .... 113 D2
Stable Pl G62 .... 54 C2
Stable Rd Milngavie G62 ... 54 C2
  Shotts ML7 .... 147 D3
Stable Wynd KA10 .... 230 A2
Stables The G62 .... 55 D3
Staffa G74 .... 181 E4
Staffa Ave
  Port Glasgow PA14 .... 69 D4
  Renfrew PA4 .... 94 B1
Staffa Ct KA11 .... 225 D4
Staffa Dr Airdrie ML6 ...... 123 F4
  Kirkintilloch G66 .... 80 A4
  Paisley PA2 .... 133 F4
Staffa Pl KA11 .... 42 A1
Staffa Rd G72 .... 138 C2
Staffa St Glasgow G31 .... 118 A4
  Greenock PA19 .... 44 C3
Staffin Gr G23 .... 76 B1
Staffin Rd KA10 .... 229 F3
Staffin St G23 .... 76 C1
Stafflar Dr KA1 .... 227 F2
Stafford Rd PA16 .... 44 C2
Stafford Rd PA16 .... 44 C2
Stafford St Bellshill ML4 .. 141 F2
  Glasgow G4 .... 241 E4
  Helensburgh G84 .... 16 B1
  Kilmarnock KA3 .... 222 C2
Stafford St W G84 .... 16 B2
Staffordway S PA16 .... 44 C2
Stag Ct G71 .... 141 E3
Stag St G51 .... 116 A4
Stag Wynd ML1 .... 164 A2
Staikhill ML11 .... 214 C3
Staineybraes Pl ML6 .... 102 C1
Stairlie Cres KA23 .... 190 B3
Stalker St ML2 .... 164 B2
Stamford St G31, G40 ..... 118 A2
Stamperland Ave G76 ..... 157 F4
Stamperland Cres G76 .... 157 F4
Stamperland Gdns G76 ... 157 F4
Stamperland Hill G76 ...... 157 F4
Stanalane St G46 .... 135 F2
Standalane Kilmaurs KA3 . 222 B4
  Stewarton KA3 .... 211 E4
Standburn Rd G33 .... 98 B3
Stane Prim Sch ML7 .... 147 D2
Stane Rd
  Port Glasgow PA14 .... 68 C4
  Shotts ML7 .... 147 D1
Staneacre Pk ML3 .... 162 C2
Stanecastle Dr KA11 .... 219 F3
Stanecastle Gate KA11 ... 219 F3
Stanecastle Intc KA12 ..... 219 F2
Stanecastle Rd KA11 ...... 219 F3
Stanecastle Sch KA11 ..... 220 A3
Stanecraigs Pl [20] ML2 .. 165 F3
Stanefield Dr ML1 .... 143 D4
Stanely Cres PA2 .... 133 D4
Stanely Ct PA2 .... 133 D4
Stanely Dr PA2 .... 113 E1
Stanely Rd PA2 .... 113 E1
Stanford St G81 .... 74 B1
Stanhope Dr G73 .... 138 B3
Stanhope Pl ML2 .... 186 A4
Stanistone Rd ML8 .... 188 A1
Stanley Ave
  Ardrossan KA22 .... 205 D2
  Paisley PA2 .... 113 D1
Stanley Bvd ML3 .... 161 E2

Stanley Dr Ardrossan KA22 . 205 E2
  Bellshill ML4 .... 142 A3
  Bishopbriggs G64 .... 78 A1
  Bridge Of A FK9 .... 2 A4
  Brookfield PA5 .... 111 E3
Stanley La PA5 .... 111 E3
Stanley Pk Airdrie ML6 ... 123 D4
Stanley Pl Blantyre G72 ... 140 B1
  Saltcoats KA21 .... 216 C4
Stanley Prim Sch KA22 ... 205 E2
Stanley Rd
  Ardrossan KA22 .... 205 E2
  Saltcoats KA22 .... 216 C4
Stanley St Glasgow G41 ... 116 C3
  Hamilton ML3 .... 161 F2
Stanley Street La G41 ..... 116 C3
Stanmore Ave ML11 .... 215 D3
Stanmore Cres ML11 ...... 215 D3
Stanmore Rd
  Glasgow G42 .... 137 D4
  Lanark ML11 .... 215 E3
Stanners La PA15 .... 46 A2
Stanrigg St ML6 .... 104 A1
Stanton Ave FK10 .... 9 E3
Stark Ave Clydebank G81 ... 73 F3
  Falkirk FK1 .... 41 E3
Starling Way ML4 .... 141 F4
Startpoint St G33 .... 119 D4
Station Ave Greenock PA15 . 46 A2
  Howwood PA9 .... 130 C3
Station Brae Irvine KA11 . 220 B1
Station Cres PA4 .... 94 C2
Stanrigg St ML6 .... 104 A1
Station Ct KA14 .... 170 B3
Station Dr Hurlford KA1 .. 228 B3
  Prestwick KA9 .... 233 E1
  Springside KA11 .... 221 D2
Station Pl ML8 .... 187 D3
Station Rd Airdrie ML6 .... 123 F4
  Ayr KA7, KA8 .... 239 D4
  Bannockburn FK7 .... 7 E4
  Bardowie G62 .... 77 D4
  Bearsden G61 .... 75 E2
  Bishopton PA7 .... 72 A1
  Blackridge EH48 .... 107 E1
  Blantyre G72 .... 140 C1
  Bothwell G71 .... 141 D1
  Bridge Of A FK9 .... 1 C4
  Caldercruix ML6 .... 104 C2
  Cambus FK10 .... 4 A1
  Carluke ML8 .... 187 F1
  Clarkston G76 .... 158 A3
  Cleland ML1 .... 144 A1
  Cowie FK7 .... 12 B3
  Dumbarton G82 .... 49 F2
  Dunlop KA3 .... 195 D4
  Glasgow G46 .... 136 B2
  Glasgow, Giffnock G46 ... 136 B2
  Glasgow, Maryhill G20 ..... 96 B4
  Gourock PA19 .... 44 C4
  Hamilton ML3 .... 162 C2
  Helensburgh G84 .... 25 C4
  Howwood PA9 .... 130 C3
  Kilbarchan PA10 .... 111 D1
  Kilsyth G65 .... 36 B1
  Langbank PA14 .... 70 B4
  Larkhall ML9 .... 185 D2
  Law ML8 .... 187 D3
  Lennoxtown G65 .... 57 E4
  Millerston G33 .... 99 D3
  Milngavie G62 .... 55 D1
  Motherwell ML1 .... 143 D2
  Neilston G78 .... 154 B4
  Netherburn ML9 .... 200 B2
  Old Kilpatrick G60 .... 73 D3
  Paisley PA1 .... 113 D2
  Plains ML6 .... 104 A1
  Port Glasgow PA14 .... 47 E1
  Prestwick KA9 .... 233 E1
  Prestwick, Monkton KA9 . 233 E2
  Renfrew PA4 .... 94 C2
  Rhu G84 .... 15 F3
  Shotts ML7 .... 146 C2
  Slamannan ML6 .... 86 A3
  Springside KA11 .... 221 D2
  Stevenston KA20 .... 217 E4
  Stirling FK8 .... 7 D4
  Strathblane G63 .... 31 D2
  Uddingston G71 .... 140 C3
  Wishaw ML2 .... 165 D1
Station Rise PA12 .... 129 C1
Station Row Irvine KA11 .. 225 F3
  Law ML8 .... 187 D3
  Slamannan FK1 .... 86 A3
Station Way G71 .... 140 C3
Station Wynd PA10 .... 111 D1
Stead St Glasgow G1 ...... 241 E4
  Port Glasgow PA14 .... 47 E1
Steading The ML2 .... 165 D3
Steadman Pl KA11 .... 225 D4
Steel St Glasgow G1 .... 241 E1
  Gourock PA19 .... 44 C4
  Wishaw ML2 .... 165 D1
Steele Cres G83 .... 28 A4
Steele Wlk G83 .... 28 A4
Steeple Sq PA10 .... 111 D2
Steeple St PA10 .... 111 D2
Steeples View KA10 .... 229 F4
Stein Sq FK7 .... 7 D2
Stenhouse Ave G69 .... 100 B4
Stenhousemuir Prim Sch
  FK5 .... 23 E2
Stenton Cres ML2 .... 164 B1
Stenton Pl ML2 .... 164 B1
Stenton St G32 .... 118 C4

Stepends Rd Airdrie ML6 . 124 B4
  Plains ML6 .... 104 B1
Stepford Pl G33 .... 119 F4
Stepford Rd G33 .... 120 A4
Stephen Cres G69 .... 119 F3
Stephenson Pl [1] G75 .... 180 B4
Stephenson Sq [2] G75 ... 180 B4
Stephenson St G32 .... 114 C4
Stephenson Terr G75 ...... 180 B4
Stepps Prim Sch G33 .... 99 F3
Stepps Rd Glasgow G33 . 119 E4
  Kirkintilloch G66 .... 79 F1
Stepps Sta G33 .... 99 F3
Steps Rd KA12 .... 219 E2
Steps St FK5 .... 23 E2
Steuart Rd FK9 .... 1 C4
Steven St G83 .... 27 F3
Stevens La ML1 .... 143 D2
Stevens Pl PA19 .... 44 C3
Stevenson Ct FK9 .... 2 A3
Stevenson Pl ML4 .... 142 A4
Stevenson St Carluke ML8 187 F1
  Clydebank G81 .... 73 F2
  Glasgow G40 .... 241 F1
  Kilmarnock KA1 .... 222 B1
  Paisley PA2 .... 113 F2
Stevenston Ct ML1 .... 143 D2
Stevenston Ind Est KA20 . 217 F4
Stevenston Rd
  KA13, KA20 .... 207 D2
Stevenston St ML1 .... 143 D2
Stevenston Sta KA20 ...... 217 E4
Stewart Ave Blantyre G72 161 E4
  Newton Mearns G77 .... 156 C3
  Renfrew PA4 .... 94 A1
Stewart Cres
  Barrhead G78 .... 134 B2
  Wishaw ML2 .... 166 A3
Stewart Ct Barrhead G78 . 134 B2
  Rutherglen G73 .... 138 B4
Stewart Dr Bargeddie G69 121 D3
  Clarkston G76 .... 157 F4
  Clydebank G81 .... 74 A3
  Irvine KA12 .... 219 E2
Stewart Pl Barrhead G78 . 134 B2
  Stewart Pl G78 .... 134 B2
Stewart Quadrant ML1 .... 143 D3
Stewart Rd Ayr KA8 .... 236 B2
  Falkirk FK2 .... 42 B3
  Paisley PA2 .... 133 F4
Stewart St Barrhead G78 . 134 B2
  Bonnybridge FK4 .... 39 F3
  Cambusbarron FK7 .... 6 C3
  Clydebank G81 .... 74 A4
  Coatbridge ML5 .... 122 A2
  Glasgow G4 .... 240 C4
  Hamilton ML3 .... 162 C2
  Milngavie G62 .... 55 D1
Stewartfield Cres G74 ..... 159 E2
Stewartfield Dr G74 .... 159 E2
Stewartfield Rd G74 .... 159 E2
Stewartfield Way G74 ..... 159 E2
Stewartgill Pl ML9 .... 185 F1
Stewarton Acad KA3 ...... 195 F1
Stewarton Cres KA3 .... 223 D3
Stewarton Dr G72 .... 138 C3
Stewarton Rd Dunlop KA3 195 D4
  Fenwick KA3 .... 213 D2
  Glasgow G46 .... 135 F1
  Newton Mearns G77 .... 156 A3
Stewarton St ML2 .... 165 E1
Stewarton Sta KA3 .... 195 F1
Stewarton Terr ML2 .... 165 E1
Stewarts La ML2 .... 165 D1
Stewartville St G11 .... 96 A1
Stinchar Rd KA9 .... 233 E1
Stirling Ave Bearsden G61 . 75 F1
  East Kilbride G74 .... 160 A2
  Irvine KA12 .... 222 B1
Stirling Castle FK8 .... 1 C1
Stirling Dr Bearsden G61 ... 75 E3
  Bishopbriggs G64 .... 77 F2
  Bridge Of A FK9 .... 1 C4
  Johnstone PA5, PA3 .... 111 E1
  Linwood PA3 .... 112 A3
  Rutherglen G73 .... 138 A3
Stirling Enk Pk FK7 .... 7 F4
Stirling F Ed Ctr FK7 .... 7 E3
Stirling Gdns G64 .... 77 F2
Stirling High Sch FK8 .... 7 D3
Stirling Pl Lennoxtown G65 . 57 F4
  Plean FK7 .... 12 B2
Stirling Rd Airdrie ML6 .... 103 D3
  Alexandria G83 .... 27 F1
  Alloa FK10 .... 9 F4
  Alva FK12 .... 4 C4
  Balloch G83 .... 20 A1
  Carluke ML8 .... 187 F2
  Chapelhall ML6 .... 123 F1
  Dumbarton G82 .... 50 B2
  Falkirk FK1 .... 41 F4
  Fallin FK7 .... 8 B2
  Glasgow G4 .... 241 E3
  Kilsyth G65 .... 36 C1
  Larbert FK5 .... 23 D3
  Riggend ML6 .... 83 D2
  Torwood FK5 .... 22 C3
  Tullibody FK10 .... 4 A2
Stirling Royal Infmy FK8 .... 7 D3

Stirling St Airdrie ML6 ...... 123 D4
Alva FK12 ...... 5 D4
Coatbridge ML5 ...... 121 E2
Cumbernauld G67 ...... 62 A2
Denny FK6 ...... 21 E2
Motherwell ML1 ...... 164 A2
Renton G82 ...... 27 E1
Stirling Sta FK8 ...... 7 D4
Stirling Way Glasgow G69 ...... 120 A2
  Renfrew PA4 ...... 94 B1
Stirlingfauld Pl 7 G5 ...... 117 D3
Stirrat St Glasgow G20 ...... 96 B3
  Paisley PA3 ...... 113 E4
Stobbs Cres KA13 ...... 207 F1
Stobbs Terr KA11 ...... 207 F1
Stobcross Bsns Pk 8 G3 ...... 116 C4
Stobcross Rd G3 ...... 116 B4
Stobcross St
  Coatbridge ML5 ...... 122 A3
  Glasgow G3 ...... 240 A2
Stobcross Wynd G3 ...... 116 B4
Stobhill Cotts G21 ...... 98 A4
Stobhill Cres KA7 ...... 239 E3
Stobhill General Hospl
  G21 ...... 98 A3
Stobhill Rd G21 ...... 97 F4
Stobo G74 ...... 160 B2
Stobo Ct G74 ...... 160 B2
Stobo St ML2 ...... 165 E3
Stobs Dr G78 ...... 134 A2
Stobs Pl G34 ...... 100 B1
Stock Ave PA2 ...... 113 F2
Stock St PA2 ...... 113 F1
Stockbridge Cres KA25 ...... 149 D2
Stockholm Cres PA2 ...... 113 F2
Stockiemuir Ave G61 ...... 75 F4
Stockiemuir Ct G61 ...... 75 F4
Stockiemuir Rd
  Bearsden G61 ...... 75 E4
  Milngavie G62 ...... 54 B1
Stocks Rd ML1 ...... 144 C1
Stockwell Pl G1 ...... 241 D1
Stockwell St G1 ...... 241 D1
Stoddard Sq PA5 ...... 112 B2
Stonebyres Ct ML3 ...... 162 A2
Stonecraig Rd ML2 ...... 165 E1
Stonecrop Pl KA7 ...... 239 E2
Stonedyke Cres ML8 ...... 188 A2
Stonedyke Gr G15 ...... 75 D1
Stonedyke Prim Sch G15 ...... 75 D1
Stonedyke Rd ML8 ...... 188 A2
Stonefield Ave
  Glasgow G12 ...... 96 B3
  Paisley PA2 ...... 113 F1
Stonefield Cres
  Blantyre G72 ...... 161 E3
  Clarkston G76 ...... 157 E4
  Paisley PA2 ...... 113 F1
Stonefield Dr PA2 ...... 113 F1
Stonefield Gdns
  Carluke ML8 ...... 187 F2
  Paisley PA2 ...... 113 F1
Stonefield Green PA2 ...... 113 F1
Stonefield Park Gdns
  G72 ...... 161 F4
Stonefield Pk Ayr KA7 ...... 238 B1
  Paisley PA2 ...... 133 F4
Stonefield Pl G72 ...... 161 E3
Stonefield Rd G72 ...... 161 E4
Stonefield St ML6 ...... 103 D1
Stonehall Ave ML3 ...... 162 A1
Stonehaven Rd PA16 ...... 44 C2
Stonehouse Hospl ML9 ...... 198 B1
Stonehouse Prim Sch
  ML9 ...... 198 C1
Stonelaw Dr G73 ...... 138 A3
Stonelaw High Sch G73 ...... 138 B3
Stonelaw High Sch Annexe
  G73 ...... 138 A4
Stonelaw Rd G73 ...... 138 A3
Stonelaw Towers G73 ...... 138 B3
Stoneleigh Pl PA16 ...... 45 E4
Stoneleigh Rd PA16 ...... 45 E4
Stoneside Dr G43 ...... 136 A3
Stoneside Sq G43 ...... 136 A3
Stoney Brae Paisley PA2 ...... 133 F4
  Paisley, Laigh Pk PA3 ...... 113 F3
Stoneyetts Cotts G69 ...... 80 C2
Stoneyetts Rd KA25 ...... 149 D1
Stoneymeadow Rd
  G72, G74 ...... 139 E4
Stoneymollan Rd G82 ...... 26 A3
Stoneywood Pk FK6 ...... 21 D1
Stonyflatt Ave G82 ...... 50 A3
Stonyflatt Rd G82 ...... 50 A3
Stonyhill Ave KA1 ...... 227 F3
Stonyhurst St Glasgow G22 ...... 97 E2
  Glasgow, Firhill G22 ...... 97 D2
Stonylee Rd G67 ...... 62 A1
Stoopshill Cres KA24 ...... 191 F4
Storie St PA1 ...... 113 F2
Stormyland Way G78 ...... 134 B1
Stornoway Cres ML2 ...... 165 F3
Stornoway St G22 ...... 97 E4
Stow Brae PA1 ...... 113 F2
Stow Coll G3 ...... 97 D1
Stow St PA1 ...... 113 F2
Strachan St Bellshill ML4 ...... 142 A2
  Falkirk FK1 ...... 42 A2
Strachur St G22 ...... 97 D4
Strain Cres ML6 ...... 123 D3
Straiton Dr ML3 ...... 161 E1
Straiton St G32 ...... 118 C4
Strand KA15 ...... 171 D4

Strand St KA1 ...... 222 C1
Strandhead KA3 ...... 211 E4
Strang Pl KA9 ...... 236 B3
Strang's Pl FK1 ...... 66 C3
Stranka Ave PA2 ...... 113 E2
Stranraer Dr G15 ...... 75 E1
Stratford G74 ...... 160 B3
Stratford St G20 ...... 96 C3
Strath Carron ML8 ...... 187 D3
Strath Dearn ML8 ...... 187 D3
Strath Elgin ML8 ...... 187 D3
Strath Halladale ML8 ...... 187 D3
Strath Nairn ML8 ...... 187 D3
Strath Naver ML8 ...... 187 D3
Strath Peffer ML8 ...... 186 C3
Strathallan Ct FK9 ...... 2 A2
Strathallan Gdns G66 ...... 79 E4
Hamilton ML3 ...... 183 E3
Stonehouse ML9 ...... 198 C1
Strathavon Cres ML6 ...... 103 D1
Strathayr Pl KA8 ...... 239 D3
Strathblane Cres ML6 ...... 103 D2
Strathblane Prim Sch G63 ...... 31 E2
Strathblane Rd
  Eaglesham G76 ...... 178 C2
  East Kilbride G74 ...... 181 D4
  Hamilton ML3 ...... 183 E3
  Strathblane G63 ...... 198 C1
Strathbran Ct G31 ...... 118 B2
Strathcairn Cres ML6 ...... 123 D2
Strathcarron Dr PA2 ...... 114 A1
Strathcarron Pl 9 G20 ...... 96 B3
Strathcarron Rd PA2 ...... 114 A1
Strathcarron Way PA2 ...... 114 A1
Strathclyde Ave KA22 ...... 205 E2
Strathclyde Bsns Ctr ML1 ...... 142 C2
Strathclyde Bsns Pk ML4 ...... 141 F4
Strathclyde Ct G84 ...... 16 A1
Strathclyde Ctry Pk ML1 ...... 141 F1
Strathclyde Hospl ML1 ...... 163 E3
Strathclyde Path G71 ...... 140 C3
Strathclyde Pl G84 ...... 16 A1
Strathclyde Rd
  Dumbarton G82 ...... 50 A3
  Motherwell ML1 ...... 163 D3
Strathclyde St G40 ...... 118 A1
Strathclyde View G71 ...... 141 D1
Strathclyde Way ML4 ...... 142 B4
Strathcona Dr G13 ...... 96 A4
Strathcona Gdns G13 ...... 96 A4
Strathcona La 11 G75 ...... 180 C4
Strathcona Pl
  East Kilbride G75 ...... 180 C4
  Rutherglen G73 ...... 138 B2
Strathconon Gdns G75 ...... 179 F4
Strathclyde Dr G73 ...... 138 A3
Strathdearn Gr G75 ...... 179 F4
Strathdee Ave G44 ...... 74 A3
Strathdee Rd G44 ...... 136 C5
Strathdon Ave
  Glasgow G44 ...... 136 C1
  Paisley PA2 ...... 113 E1
Strathdon Dr G44 ...... 136 C1
Strathdon Pl G75 ...... 179 F4
Strathdoon Pl KA7 ...... 238 B1
Strathearn Gr G66 ...... 59 D1
Strathearn Rd G76 ...... 157 F3
Strathendrick Dr G44 ...... 136 C2
Strathfillan Rd G74 ...... 159 E1
Strathgryffe Cres PA11 ...... 90 B1
Strathkelvin Ave 12 G64 ...... 97 F4
Strathlachlan Ave ML8 ...... 188 A1
Strathleven Dr G83 ...... 27 F1
Strathmore Pl G82 ...... 49 F2
Strathmallin Cres ML6 ...... 103 D2
Strathmiglo Pl FK5 ...... 23 E2
Strathmore Ave
  Blantyre G72 ...... 140 B1
  Paisley PA1 ...... 114 B2
Strathmore Cres
  Airdrie ML6 ...... 103 D1
  Stirling FK9 ...... 2 A2
Strathmore Dr FK9 ...... 2 A2
Strathmore Gdns G73 ...... 138 B2
Strathmore Pk KA11 ...... 220 A3
Strathmore Pl ML5 ...... 122 B3
Strathmore Rd
  Glasgow G22 ...... 97 D4
  Hamilton ML3 ...... 162 B3
Strathmore Wlk ML5 ...... 122 B3
Strathmungo Cres ML6 ...... 102 C1
Strathnairn Ave G75 ...... 179 F4
Strathnairn Ct G75 ...... 179 F4
Strathnairn Dr G75 ...... 179 F4
Strathnairn Way G75 ...... 179 F4
Strathnaver Gdns G75 ...... 179 F4
Strathord Pl G69 ...... 81 D2
Strathord St G32 ...... 119 D2
Strathpeffer Cres ML6 ...... 103 D1
Strathpeffer Dr G75 ...... 179 F4
Strathspey Cres ML6 ...... 103 D2
Strathtay Ave G44 ...... 136 C1
Strathtummel Cres ML6 ...... 103 D2
Strathview Gr G44 ...... 136 C1
Strathview Pk G44 ...... 136 C1
Strathview Rd ML4 ...... 141 F2
Strathy Pl 13 Glasgow G20 ...... 96 B3
  Kilmarnock KA1 ...... 228 A3
Strathyre Gdns
  Bearsden G61 ...... 76 A3
  Glenmavis ML6 ...... 102 C3
  Moodiesburn G69 ...... 81 D2
Strathyre Rd G72 ...... 161 F3
Strathyre St G41 ...... 136 C4

Stratton Dr G46 ...... 136 A1
Strauss Ave G81 ...... 74 C4
Stravaig Path PA2 ...... 133 D4
Stravaig Wlk PA2 ...... 133 D4
Stravana Terr G45 ...... 137 E1
Stravanan St G45 ...... 137 E1
Stravanan Rd G45 ...... 137 E1
Stravanan St G45 ...... 137 E1
Stravenhouse Rd ML8 ...... 186 C2
Strawberry Field Rd PA6 ...... 91 D1
Strawberrybank Rd KA3 ...... 223 D1
Strawhill Rd G76 ...... 157 F4
Stremabey Ave G73 ...... 138 B2
Striphead FK10 ...... 10 A3
Striven Cres ML2 ...... 165 D1
Striven Dr FK2 ...... 24 B1
Striven Gdns G20 ...... 96 C2
Striven Terr ML1 ...... 162 A1
Stroma Ave PA14 ...... 69 D4
Stroma Ct KA11 ...... 225 E4
Stroma St G21 ...... 98 A1
Stromness St G5 ...... 117 D2
Strone Cres PA15 ...... 46 A2
Strone Gdns G65 ...... 60 A4
Strone Path ML5 ...... 101 E3
Strone Pl ML6 ...... 123 E3
Strone Rd Alexandria G83 ...... 27 F3
  Glasgow G33 ...... 119 D4
Stronend St G22 ...... 97 D3
Stronsay St G21 ...... 98 A1
Stronsay Way KA11 ...... 220 A1
Stronvar Dr G14 ...... 95 D2
Stroud Rd G75 ...... 180 B3
Strowan Cres G32 ...... 119 D2
Strowan St G32 ...... 119 E2
Strowan's Rd G82 ...... 50 B2
Strowan's Well Rd G82 ...... 50 B2
Struan Ave G46 ...... 136 B2
Struan Gdns G44 ...... 137 D3
Struan Rd G44 ...... 137 D3
Strude Howe FK12 ...... 5 D4
Strude Mill FK12 ...... 5 D4
Strude St FK12 ...... 5 D4
Struie St G34 ...... 120 A4
Struma Dr G76 ...... 157 E4
Struther & Swinhill Rd
  ML9 ...... 199 E3
Strutherhill Ind Est ML9 ...... 199 E4
Struthers Ave G64 ...... 228 B4
Struthers Cres G74 ...... 160 A2
Struthers Pl KA10 ...... 229 F3
Struthers Pl KA10 ...... 229 F3
Struthers Prim Sch KA10 ...... 229 F3
Stuart Ave
  Old Kilpatrick G60 ...... 73 D3
  Rutherglen G73 ...... 138 A3
Stuart Dr Bishopbriggs G64 ...... 97 F4
  Lanark ML11 ...... 215 D3
  Larkhall ML9 ...... 185 E1
Stuart Pl KA2 ...... 225 F1
Stuart Quadrant ML2 ...... 164 C1
Stuart Rd Bishopton PA7 ...... 72 A2
  Carmunnock G76 ...... 158 B4
  Dumbarton G82 ...... 50 B2
Stuart St East Kilbride G74 ...... 159 F1
  Old Kilpatrick G60 ...... 73 D3
Stuarton Pk G74 ...... 159 F1
Stuckleckie Rd G84 ...... 17 D1
Sturrock St KA1 ...... 227 F4
Succoth St G13 ...... 95 F4
Sudbury Cres G75 ...... 159 D1
Suffolk Rd PA16 ...... 44 C2
Suffolk St Glasgow G40 ...... 241 E1
  Helensburgh G84 ...... 16 B1
Sugworth Ave G69 ...... 120 A3
Sumburgh St G33 ...... 119 D4
Summer St G40 ...... 117 F3
Summerfield Cotts G14 ...... 95 F1
Summerfield Pl G67 ...... 82 A3
Summerfield St G40 ...... 118 A2
Summerford KA1 ...... 41 E2
Summerford Gdns FK1 ...... 41 E2
Summerlee Cotts ML1 ...... 121 E4
Summerlee Mus ML9 ...... 185 D1
Summerhill Dr G15 ...... 75 D2
Summerhill &
  Garngibbock Rd G67 ...... 82 B2
Summerhill Gdns G15 ...... 75 D2
Summerhill Pl G15 ...... 75 D2
Summerhill Prim Sch G15 ...... 75 D2
Summerhill Rd
  Clarkston G76 ...... 157 F4
  Glasgow G15 ...... 75 D2
Summerhill St ML4 ...... 141 F2
Summerlea Rd
  Glasgow G46 ...... 135 F2
  Seamill KA23 ...... 190 A2
Summerlee Cotts ML1 ...... 121 E4
Summerlee Mus ML5 ...... 121 F4
Summerlee Rd
  Larkhall ML9 ...... 184 C3
  Wishaw ML2 ...... 164 B2
Summerlee St
  Coatbridge ML5 ...... 121 F4
  Glasgow G33 ...... 119 E4
Summerston Sta G20 ...... 96 B4
Summertown Rd G51 ...... 116 A4
Suna Path ML7 ...... 147 D2
Sunart Ave PA4 ...... 94 A2
Sunart Ct ML3 ...... 162 A1
Sunart Gdns G64 ...... 78 B1
Sunart Rd Bishopbriggs G64 ...... 78 B1
  Glasgow G52 ...... 115 F3
Sunart St ML2 ...... 165 D1

Sunbury Ave G76 ...... 157 E4
Sundale Ave G76 ...... 157 E3
Sunderland Ave G82 ...... 49 E2
Sunderland Ct KA25 ...... 170 A4
Sundrum Pl KA13 ...... 207 E1
Sunflower Gdns ML1 ...... 163 F4
Sunningdale Ave Ayr KA7 ...... 239 D2
  Newton Mearns G77 ...... 156 C3
Sunningdale Dr PA11 ...... 110 B3
Sunningdale Rd G23 ...... 96 C4
Sunningdale Sq KA13 ...... 207 E2
Sunningdale Wynd G71 ...... 140 C2
Sunnybank ML7 ...... 146 C3
Sunnybank Dr G76 ...... 157 E3
Sunnybank Gr G76 ...... 157 E3
Sunnybank Rd FK7 ...... 7 D2
Sunnybank St G40 ...... 118 A2
Sunnydale Rd EH48 ...... 107 F2
Sunnydale Rd EH48 ...... 107 F2
Sunnyhill G65 ...... 59 F2
Sunnylaw Dr PA2 ...... 113 D1
Sunnylaw Pl FK1 ...... 41 F2
Sunnylaw St G22 ...... 97 D2
Sunnyside Ave
  Motherwell ML1 ...... 143 D3
  Port Glasgow PA14 ...... 69 D4
  Uddingston G71 ...... 140 C3
Sunnyside Cres ML1 ...... 143 D3
Sunnyside Ct FK10 ...... 10 A3
Sunnyside Dr
  Bargeddie G69 ...... 121 D3
  East Kilbride G74 ...... 157 E4
  Glasgow G15 ...... 75 D1
Sunnyside Oval PA2 ...... 113 F1
Sunnyside Pl
  Barrhead G78 ...... 134 A1
  Glasgow G15 ...... 75 D1
  Motherwell ML1 ...... 143 D3
Sunnyside Prim Sch
  Alloa FK10 ...... 10 A4
  Motherwell ML1 ...... 143 D3
Sunnyside Rd Alloa FK10 ...... 10 A4
  Cleland ML1 ...... 165 D4
  Coatbridge ML5 ...... 122 A4
  Falkirk FK1 ...... 41 F3
  Kilmarnock KA1 ...... 227 F1
  Kirkfieldbank ML11 ...... 214 B3
  Larkhall ML9 ...... 184 B2
  Paisley PA2 ...... 113 E1
Sunnyside Sq E KA1 ...... 227 F1
Sunnyside Sq W KA1 ...... 227 F1
Sunnyside St Falkirk FK1 ...... 41 F3
  Larkhall ML9 ...... 184 B2
Sunnyside Sta ML1 ...... 143 D3
Surcoat Loan FK7 ...... 7 F2
Surrey La 14 G5 ...... 117 D2
Surrey St G5 ...... 117 D2
Susannah St G83 ...... 27 F3
Sussex St G41 ...... 116 C3
Sutcliffe Ct G13 ...... 95 F4
Sutcliffe Rd G13 ...... 95 F4
Sutherland Ave Alloa FK10 ...... 10 B4
  Bearsden G61 ...... 75 F4
  Glasgow G41 ...... 116 B2
  Stirling FK8 ...... 2 B1
Sutherland Dr
  Airdrie ML6 ...... 122 C3
  Denny FK6 ...... 39 E4
  Dumbarton G82 ...... 136 B1
  Glasgow G46 ...... 136 B1
  Kilmarnock KA3 ...... 223 E1
Sutherland La G12 ...... 96 B1
Sutherland Rd ML1 ...... 141 F1
Sutherland St
  Clydebank G81 ...... 74 A1
  Greenock PA16 ...... 45 D2
Sutherland St
  Blantyre G72 ...... 161 E3
  Helensburgh G84 ...... 16 A1
  Paisley PA1 ...... 113 E3
Sutherland Way G74 ...... 160 B2
Sutherness Dr G33 ...... 119 D4
Suttie Way FK9 ...... 1 C4
Sutton Ct KA13 ...... 207 D2
Sutton Pk Cres FK5 ...... 23 F2
Swaledale G74 ...... 159 E2
Swallow Gdns G13 ...... 94 C4
Swallow Rd Clydebank G81 ...... 74 B3
  Wishaw ML2 ...... 165 D2
Swan Pl PA5 ...... 131 E4
Swan St Clydebank G81 ...... 73 F2
  Glasgow G4 ...... 241 D4
Swanson Rd G83 ...... 27 E4
Swanston St G40 ...... 118 A1
Sween Ave G44 ...... 137 D2
Sween Dr ML3 ...... 162 A1
Sween Path ML4 ...... 142 B2
Sweethill Terr ML5 ...... 122 B2
Sweethill Wlk ML4 ...... 142 B4
Sweethope Gdns G71 ...... 141 D1
Sweethope Pl G71 ...... 141 D2
Swift Bank ML3 ...... 161 F1
Swift Cl ML2 ...... 165 D2
Swift Cres G13 ...... 94 C4
Swift Pl East Kilbride G75 ...... 179 F3
  Johnstone PA5 ...... 131 E4
Swindon St G81 ...... 73 F2
Swinhill Rd ML9 ...... 199 E3
Swinstie Rd ML1 ...... 165 E4
Swinstie Vw ML1 ...... 144 B1
Swinton Ave G69 ...... 120 B3

Swinton Cres
  Coatbridge ML5 ...... 121 D2
  Glasgow G69 ...... 120 B3
Swinton Dr G52 ...... 115 D3
Swinton Gdns G69 ...... 120 B3
Swinton Path G69 ...... 120 B3
Swinton Pl Glasgow G52 ...... 115 D3
  Irvine KA11 ...... 220 A4
Swinton Prim Sch G69 ...... 120 B3
Swinton Rd G69 ...... 120 B3
Swinton View G69 ...... 120 B3
Swisscot Ave ML3 ...... 183 D4
Swisscot Wlk ML3 ...... 183 D4
Switchback Rd G61 ...... 75 F1
Sword St Airdrie ML6 ...... 122 C4
  Glasgow G31 ...... 117 F3
Sword's Way FK2 ...... 24 A1
Swordale Pl G34 ...... 120 A4
Sycamore Ave Beith KA15 ...... 150 A1
  Johnstone PA5 ...... 112 A1
  Kirkintilloch G66 ...... 79 E3
  Uddingston G71 ...... 141 E4
Sycamore Cres
  Airdrie ML6 ...... 123 E3
  Ayr KA7 ...... 239 E3
  East Kilbride G75 ...... 180 B3
Sycamore Ct Beith KA15 ...... 150 A1
  Coatbridge ML5 ...... 121 F2
  East Kilbride G75 ...... 180 B3
Sycamore Dr Airdrie ML6 ...... 123 E3
  Clydebank G81 ...... 74 A2
  Hamilton ML3 ...... 162 C1
Sycamore Gr G72 ...... 161 E4
Sycamore Pl
  East Kilbride G75 ...... 180 B3
  Gourock PA19 ...... 44 B3
  Motherwell ML1 ...... 143 E2
  Stirling FK8 ...... 6 C3
Sycamore Way
  Carmunnock G76 ...... 158 B4
  Milton of C G65 ...... 58 B3
Sycamores The FK10 ...... 4 A1
Sydenham La G12 ...... 96 B2
Sydenham Rd G12 ...... 96 B2
Sydes Brae G72 ...... 161 D2
Sydney Dr G75 ...... 180 B4
Sydney Pl 8 G75 ...... 180 B4
Sydney St Clydebank G81 ...... 73 E2
  Glasgow G31 ...... 241 F1
Sykehead Ave ML4 ...... 142 A3
Sykes Terr G78 ...... 154 C2
Sykeside Rd ML6 ...... 122 C2
Sylvania Way G81 ...... 74 A1
Sylvania Way S G81 ...... 74 A1
Symington Pl Falkirk FK2 ...... 24 C4
  Irvine KA11 ...... 224 C4
Symington Prim Sch KA1 ...... 231 E2
Symington Rd N KA1 ...... 231 E2
Symington Rd S KA1 ...... 231 E2
Symington St 11 G75 ...... 180 C4
Syms La KA8 ...... 236 A1
Syriam Pl 10 G21 ...... 97 F2
Syriam St G21 ...... 97 F3

Tabard Pl G13 ...... 95 E4
Tabard Rd G13 ...... 95 E4
Tabernacle La G72 ...... 139 D3
Tabernacle St G72 ...... 139 D3
Taggart Rd G65 ...... 60 C2
Taig Rd G66 ...... 80 A4
Tait Ave G78 ...... 134 B2
Tait Dr FK5 ...... 41 E4
Takmadoon Rd G65 ...... 36 C2
Talbot G74 ...... 160 B2
Talbot Ct G13 ...... 95 D3
Talbot Dr G13 ...... 95 D3
Talbot Pl G13 ...... 95 D3
Talbot Rd G83 ...... 28 A4
Talbot Terr Glasgow G13 ...... 95 D3
  Uddingston G71 ...... 140 C4
Talisman Ave G82 ...... 49 E2
Talisman Cres
  Helensburgh G84 ...... 25 C4
  Motherwell ML1 ...... 142 B1
Talisman Rd Glasgow G13 ...... 95 E3
  Paisley PA2 ...... 132 C4
Talisman Wlk KA21 ...... 206 A1
Talla Rd G52 ...... 115 D3
Tallant Rd G15 ...... 75 D2
Tallant Terr G15 ...... 75 E2
Tam O' Shanter Experience
  KA7 ...... 238 C1
Tam O'Shanter Dr FK7 ...... 12 B4
Tam's Brig KA8 ...... 236 A2
Tamar Dr G75 ...... 179 F3
Tamarack Cres G71 ...... 141 E4
Tambowie Ave G62 ...... 54 C1
Tambowie Cres G62 ...... 54 C1
Tambowie St G13 ...... 95 F4
Tamfourhill Ave FK1 ...... 41 E2
Tamfourhill Ind Est FK1 ...... 41 E2
Tamfourhill Rd FK1 ...... 41 E2
Tammy Dale's Rd KA13 ...... 207 F2
Tamshill St G20 ...... 96 C3
Tanar Ave PA4 ...... 94 C1
Tanar Way PA4 ...... 94 C1
Tandlehill Rd PA10 ...... 111 D1
Tanera Ave G44 ...... 137 E2
Tanera Ct FK1 ...... 42 A1
Tanfield Pl G32 ...... 119 E4
Tanfield St G32 ...... 119 E4
Tankerland Rd G44 ...... 137 D3
Tanna Dr G52 ...... 115 F2
Tannadice Ave G52 ...... 115 E2
Tannahill Cres PA5 ...... 131 E4
Tannahill Dr G74 ...... 160 B2

Tannahill Rd Glasgow G43 .. 136 C3
Paisley PA3 .... 113 D3
Tannahill Terr PA3 .... 113 D3
Tanners Rd FK1 .... 42 A2
Tannery La FK8 .... 2 A1
Tannoch Dr
  Cumbernauld G67 .... 82 C4
  Milngavie G62 .... 55 D2
Tannoch Pl G67 .... 82 C4
Tannoch Rd G78 .... 153 D2
Tannochside Bsns Pk G71 .. 121 D1
Tannochside Pk G71 .... 141 D4
Tannochside Prim Sch
  G71 .... 141 D4
Tannock St Glasgow G22 .... 97 D2
  Kilmarnock KA1 .... 227 F3
Tantallon Ave PA19 .... 43 F3
Tantallon Ct ML8 .... 187 F2
Tantallon Dr
  Coatbridge ML5 .... 101 E1
  Falkirk FK2 .... 24 A2
  Paisley PA2 .... 113 D1
Tantallon Rd PA14 .... 159 E1
Tantallon Rd
  ⑧ Bothwell G71 .... 141 D2
  Glasgow G69 .... 120 A2
  Glasgow, Langside G41 ... 136 C4
Tanzieknowe Ave G72 .... 139 D2
Tanzieknowe Dr G72 .... 139 D2
Tanzieknowe Pl G72 .... 139 D2
Tanzieknowe Rd G72 .... 139 D2
Tappoch Pl FK5 .... 23 D2
Taransay St G51 .... 116 A4
Tarbert Ave Blantyre G72 .. 140 B1
  West Kilbride KA23 ...... 190 C3
  Wishaw ML2 .... 165 D1
Tarbert Ct ML3 .... 162 A1
Tarbet Pl ML8 .... 188 A1
Tarbet St PA19 .... 44 C4
Tarbolton Sq G61 .... 74 B2
Tarbrax Path ML9 .... 147 D2
Tarbrax Way ML3 .... 162 A2
Tarduff Pl FK6 .... 21 D1
Tarff Ave G76 .... 178 C3
Tarfside Ave G52 .... 115 E2
Tarfside Gdns G52 .... 115 E2
Tarfside Oval G52 .... 115 E2
Targe Wynd FK7 .... 7 F2
Target Rd ML1 .... 123 D3
Tarland St G51 .... 115 F3
Tarras Dr PA4 .... 94 C1
Tarras Pl G72 .... 139 E3
Tarryholme Dr KA12 .... 219 E1
Tasker St PA16 .... 45 E3
Tasman Dr G75 .... 180 A4
Tasmania Quadrant ML2 ..... 165 F2
Tassie Dr G74 .... 160 A1
Tassie St G41 .... 136 B4
Tattershall Rd G33 .... 99 E1
Tavistock Dr G43 .... 136 B3
Tay Ave Paisley PA2 .... 112 C1
  Renfrew PA4 .... 94 C2
Tay Cres Bishopbriggs G64 . 78 A1
  Glasgow G33 .... 98 C1
Tay Ct Alloa FK10 .... 10 B3
  East Kilbride G75 .... 179 F4
Tay Gdns ML3 .... 183 D4
Tay Gr G75 .... 179 F4
Tay Loan ML1 .... 143 D3
Tay Pl Dumbarton G82 ...... 50 A4
  Johnstone PA5 .... 131 E4
  Kilmarnock KA1 .... 228 A3
  Larkhall ML9 .... 199 D4
  Shotts ML7 .... 146 C3
Tay Rd Bearsden G61 .... 75 E1
  Bishopbriggs G64 .... 78 A1
  Prestwick KA9 .... 233 E2
  Troon KA10 .... 229 F2
Tay St Coatbridge ML5 ..... 101 E1
  Falkirk FK2 .... 24 B1
  Greenock PA16 .... 45 D3
Tay Terr G75 .... 179 F4
Taybank Dr KA7 .... 239 D2
Tayinloan Dr ML8 .... 202 A4
Taylor Ave
  Alloa FK10 .... 110 C2
  Motherwell ML1 .... 143 E1
Taylor Brown Cl KA3 .... 211 F4
Taylor High Sch ML1 .... 143 D2
Taylor Pl G4 .... 241 E3
Taylor St Alexandria G83 .. 27 E4
  Ayr KA8 .... 235 F1
  Clydebank G81 .... 94 B4
  Glasgow G4 .... 241 E3
Taylor's Rd FK5 .... 23 E1
Taymouth Dr PA19 .... 43 F3
Taymouth St G32 .... 119 D2
Taynish Dr G44 .... 137 D3
Tayside ML1 .... 102 C1
Teak Pl G71 .... 121 E1
Teal Cres G75 .... 179 F3
Teal Ct ML4 .... 141 F4
Teal Dr G13 .... 95 D4
Tealing Ave G52 .... 115 E2
Tealing Cres G52 .... 115 E2
Teasel Ave G53 .... 135 D2
Teawell Rd G77 .... 156 B3

Technology Ave G72 .... 161 E3
Teesdale G74 .... 159 E2
Teign Gr G75 .... 179 F3
Teith Ave PA4 .... 94 C1
Teith Dr G61 .... 75 E2
Teith Pl Cambuslang G72 ... 139 E3
  Kilmarnock KA1 .... 228 A3
Teith St G33 .... 98 C1
Telegraph Rd ML6 .... 105 D4
Telephone La G12 .... 96 B1
Telford Ave ML9 .... 199 E4
Telford Ct Bannockburn FK7 . 7 E1
  Clydebank G81 .... 74 A1
Telford Dr Cumbernauld G67 . 83 D4
  Irvine KA11 .... 219 F1
Telford Rd Cumbernauld G67 . 83 D4
  East Kilbride G75 .... 180 C4
Telford Sq Falkirk FK1 .... 41 F3
Telford St ML4 .... 142 A3
Telford Terr ⑩ G75 .... 180 C4
Teme Pl G75 .... 179 F4
Templand Cres KA24 .... 191 E4
Templand Rd KA24 .... 191 E4
Templar Ave G13 .... 75 E1
Temple Denny Rd FK6 .... 21 E1
Temple Gdns G13 .... 95 F4
Temple Locks Ct ⑥ G13 .... 95 F4
Temple Locks Pl ⑨ G13 .... 95 F4
Temple Prim Sch G13 .... 95 F4
Temple Rd G13 .... 96 A4
Templehill KA10 .... 229 D2
Templeland Rd G53 .... 115 E1
Templerigg Ct KA9 .... 233 E1
Templerigg St KA9 .... 233 E1
Templeton Bsns Ctr G40 ... 117 F3
Templeton Cres KA9 .... 236 B4
Templeton Gdns KA9 .... 236 B4
Templeton St G40 .... 117 F3
Ten Acres FK10 .... 5 D1
Tennant Ave G74 .... 159 D1
Tennant Complex The
  G74 .... 159 D1
Tennant St PA4 .... 94 B2
Tennent St ML5 .... 122 A3
Tennyson Dr G31 .... 118 C2
Tenters Way FK1 .... 113 D2
Tern Pl PA5 .... 131 E4
Terrace Rd PA15 .... 46 A2
Terregles Ave G41 .... 116 B1
Terregles Cres G41 .... 116 B1
Terregles Dr G41 .... 116 B1
Teviot Ave Bishopbriggs G64 . 78 A2
  Paisley PA2 .... 132 C4
Teviot Cres G61 .... 75 E1
Teviot Dr PA7 .... 72 B1
Teviot Pl Cambuslang G72 . 139 F3
  Troon KA10 .... 229 F2
Teviot Sq Port Glasgow PA14 . 68 C3
  Prestwick KA9 .... 233 E2
Teviot St Ayr KA8 .... 236 A2
  Coatbridge ML5 .... 101 E1
  Falkirk FK1 .... 41 F2
  Glasgow G3 .... 116 B4
Teviot Terr PA5 .... 131 E4
Teviot Way G72 .... 139 F3
Teviotdale G77 .... 157 D3
Tewkesbury Rd G74 .... 160 B2
Thane Rd G13 .... 95 E3
Thanes Gate G71 .... 140 C3
Thankerton Ave ML1 .... 142 C1
Thankerton Rd ML9 .... 185 D1
Tharsis St G21 .... 97 F1
Thimble St G82 .... 27 E1
Third Ave Alexandria G83 . 27 F3
  Dumbarton G82 .... 50 B1
  Glasgow G44 .... 137 D4
  Irvine KA12 .... 224 A4
  Kirkintilloch G66 ...... 79 E1
  Renfrew PA4 .... 94 B1
  Stepps G33 .... 99 E3
Third Gdns G41 .... 116 A2
Third Rd G72 .... 161 F3
Third St G71 .... 140 C4
Thirdpart Cres G13 .... 94 C4
Thirdpart Pl KA1 .... 227 E4
Thirlmere G75 .... 179 F3
Thistle Ave FK6 .... 21 E2
Thistle Bank G66 .... 79 E2
Thistle Cres ML9 .... 185 D1
Thistle Gdns ML1 .... 143 D3
Thistle Ind Est FK7 ...... 7 E3
Thistle Pl G74 .... 159 E2
Thistle Quadrant ML6 ..... 103 D1
Thistle Rd ML1 .... 143 D2
Thistle St Airdrie ML6 ... 103 D1
  Alloa FK10 .... 10 B3
  Cleland ML1 .... 144 B1
  Falkirk FK2 .... 42 B3
  Glasgow G5 .... 117 D2
  Kirkintilloch G66 ...... 79 E4
  Paisley PA1 .... 113 E3
Thistle Terr KA20 .... 206 C1
Thistle Wlk KA7 .... 239 E2
Thistledown Gr ML5 .... 122 B3
Thistleneuk G60 .... 73 D4
Thom Hd ML6 .... 45 E2
Thomas Campbell St
  KA21 .... 217 D4
Thomas Muir Ave G64 ...... 98 A4
Thomas Muir High Sch G64 . 98 A4
Thomas Muir La PA15 ...... 46 C1
Thomas Muir St PA15 ...... 46 C1
Thomas St Alexandria G83 . 27 E2
  Paisley PA1 .... 113 D2
Thompson Ave G66 .... 79 F4
Thompson Pl Clydebank G81 . 74 B3
  Slamannan FK1 .... 86 A2

Thompson St
  Glasgow G31 .... 118 A3
  Renfrew PA4 .... 94 B1
Thompson's Cl ML11 .... 215 D2
Thomson Ave
  Johnstone PA5 .... 111 F2
  Wishaw ML2 .... 164 B1
Thomson Cres FK1 .... 41 F2
Thomson Dr Airdrie ML6 ... 122 C3
  Bearsden G61 .... 75 F3
  Bellshill ML4 .... 141 E3
  Motherwell ML1 .... 163 E3
Thomson Gr G72 .... 139 D4
Thomson Pl
  Clydebank G81 .... 74 B3
Thomson St Ayr KA8 .... 236 B1
  Carluke ML8 .... 187 F1
  Johnstone PA5 .... 111 F1
  Kilmarnock KA3 .... 222 C1
Thomson Terr Shotts ML7 .. 146 B3
  Stewarton KA3 .... 211 E4
Thorn Ave G74 .... 158 B2
Thorn Brae PA5 .... 112 A2
Thorn Ct PA5 .... 112 A1
Thorn Dr Bearsden G61 .... 75 E3
  Rutherglen G73 .... 138 B2
Thorn Rd Bearsden G61 .... 75 E3
  Bellshill ML4 .... 142 A3
Thornbridge Ave
  ⑪ Glasgow G12 .... 96 B3
  ④ Glasgow, Garrowhill G69 120 A3
Thornbridge Gdns
  Falkirk FK2 .... 42 C2
  Glasgow G69 .... 120 A3
Thornbridge Rd Falkirk FK2 . 42 C3
  Glasgow G69 .... 120 A3
Thornbridge Sq FK2 .... 42 C3
Thorncliffe Gdns G41 ..... 116 C1
Thorncroft Dr G44 .... 137 E2
Thorndale Gdns FK4 .... 39 D1
Thorndean Ave ML4 .... 142 A2
Thorndean Cres ML4 .... 142 A2
Thornden La G14 .... 95 D2
Thorndene PA5 .... 112 A2
Thorndene Ave ML1 .... 143 E1
Thorndene Ct FK1 .... 41 F1
Thorndyke G74 .... 160 B3
Thorne Rd FK10 .... 4 C1
Thorneyflat Cres KA8 ..... 236 C1
Thorneyflat Pl KA8 .... 236 C1
Thornhill PA5 .... 112 A1
Thornhill La ⑪ G71 .... 141 D2
Thornhill Dr G71 .... 118 B3
Thornhill Path G31 .... 227 F2
Thornhill Rd Falkirk FK2 . 42 B3
  Hamilton ML3 .... 161 F2
Thornhill Way ML5 .... 122 B2
Thornhouse Ave KA12 ...... 219 E1
Thorniecroft Dr G67 ...... 82 B3
Thorniecroft Pl G67 ...... 82 B3
Thornielee G14 .... 160 A1
Thorniewood Gdns G71 ..... 141 D4
Thorniewood Rd G71 .... 140 C4
Thornkip Pl ML5 .... 122 B3
Thornlea Dr G46 .... 136 B2
Thornlea Pl ML11 .... 215 F4
Thornlea St ML8 .... 202 A4
Thornlie Ave G13 .... 95 D3
Thornlie Gill ML2 .... 165 D1
Thornlie Prim Sch ML2 .... 165 D1
Thornliebank Ind Est G46 . 135 F2
Thornliebank Prim Sch
  G46 .... 136 A2
Thornliebank Rd G43 ...... 136 A3
Thornliebank Sta G46 ..... 136 A2
Thornly Park Ave PA2 ..... 133 F4
Thornly Park Dr PA2 ...... 133 F4
Thornly Park Gdns PA2 .... 113 F1
Thornly Park Rd PA2 ...... 133 F4
Thornside Rd PA5 .... 112 A2
Thornton Ave
  Bonnybridge FK4 .... 40 A3
  Crosshouse KA2 .... 221 F1
Thornton La G20 .... 96 C4
Thornton Pl ML3 .... 183 E3
Thornton Rd ML1 .... 158 B1
Thornton St
  Coatbridge ML5 .... 101 E1
Thorntonhall Sta G74 ..... 158 A2
Thorntree Ave Beith KA15 . 150 B1
  Hamilton ML3 .... 183 E4
Thorntree Prim Sch G32 ... 119 D3
Thorntree Way G71 .... 141 E2
Thornwood Ave Ayr KA8 .... 236 C1
  Glasgow G11 .... 96 A1
  Kirkintilloch G66 ...... 79 D3
Thornwood Cres G11 .... 95 F2
Thornwood Dr
  Bridge Of W PA11 .... 110 A4
  Glasgow G11 .... 95 F1
  Irvine KA12 .... 219 E1
  Paisley PA2 .... 113 D1
Thornwood Gdns G11 .... 96 A1
Thornwood Pl G11 .... 96 A2
Thornwood Prim Sch G11 ... 95 F1
Thornwood Quadrant G11 ... 95 F2
Thornwood Rd G11 .... 95 F1
Thornwood Terr G11 .... 95 F1
Thornyburn Terr G69 ...... 120 B2

Thornyburn Pl G69 .... 120 B2
Thornyflat Dr KA8 .... 236 C1
Thornyflat Rd KA8 .... 236 C1
Thornyflat St KA8 .... 236 C1
Thrashbush Ave ML2 .... 165 E2
Thrashbush Cres ML2 ...... 165 E2
Thrashbush Rd ML2 .... 165 E2
Threave Ct ML6 .... 187 F2
Threave Pl G77 .... 156 A3
Three Rivers Wlk G75 ..... 180 A4
Three Sisters Ct KA21 .... 205 F2
Three Stanes Rdbt KA11 ... 224 B3
Threepwood Rd KA15 .... 150 C1
Threestonehill Ave G32 ... 119 E3
Threshold G74 .... 160 A1
Threshold Pk G74 .... 160 A1
Thriplee Rd PA11 .... 110 B4
Thrums G74 .... 160 B3
Thrums Ave G64 .... 78 B1
Thrums Gdns G64 .... 78 B1
Thrush Pl PA5 .... 131 E4
Thrushbush La ML6 .... 103 D1
Thrushbush Quadrant
  ML6 .... 103 D1
Thrushbush Rd ML6 .... 103 D1
Thrushcraig Cres PA2 ..... 113 F1
Thurso Rd G11 .... 96 B1
Thurston Rd G52 .... 115 D3
Thyme Sq ML1 .... 163 F4
Tibbermore Rd ⑫ G11 ...... 96 A2
Tig Rd KA8 .... 236 A2
Tighnasheen Way G72 ...... 140 B1
Till St ML2 .... 165 D3
Tillanburn Rd ML1 .... 143 F2
Tillet Oval PA3 .... 113 E4
Tillie St G20 .... 96 C2
Tillycairn Ave G33 .... 99 E1
Tillycairn Dr G33 .... 99 E1
Tillycairn Pl G33 .... 99 E1
Tillycairn Rd G33 .... 99 E1
Tillycairn St G33 .... 99 F1
Tilt Rd ML2 .... 165 F3
Tilt St G33 .... 98 C1
Timmons Pl FK6 .... 21 E1
Timmons Terr ML6 .... 123 E1
Tinker's La ML1 .... 163 E3
Tintagel Gdns G69 .... 80 C2
Tinto Ave KA1 .... 228 A2
Tinto Cres ML2 .... 165 E1
Tinto Ct G36 .... 78 C2
Tinto Dr Barrhead G78 .... 155 F4
  Cumbernauld G68 .... 61 F1
Tinto Prim Sch G43 .... 136 B3
Tinto Rd Airdrie ML6 ..... 123 D3
  Bearsden G61 .... 75 E3
  Bishopbriggs G64 .... 78 B1
Tinto St ML2 .... 165 E1
Tinto View ML3 .... 183 F4
Tinto Way Cleland ML1 .... 144 A1
  East Kilbride G75 ...... 180 A3
Tintock Dr G66 .... 58 C1
Tintock Rd G66 .... 59 F2
Tinwald Path G52 .... 115 D3
Tiree G74 .... 181 E4
Tiree Ave Paisley PA2 .... 133 E4
  Port Glasgow PA14 ...... 69 D4
  Renfrew PA4 .... 94 B1
Tiree Cres ML2 .... 165 E3
Tiree Ct Cumbernauld G67 . 82 B4
  Irvine KA11 .... 225 D4
Tiree Gdns Bearsden G61 .. 75 D3
  Glenmavis ML6 .... 102 C3
  Old Kilpatrick G60 ..... 73 E3
Tiree Pl Falkirk FK1 ..... 42 A1
  Newton Mearns G77 ...... 156 A3
  Old Kilpatrick G60 ..... 73 E3
Tiree Rd G67 .... 82 B4
Tiree St G21 .... 98 B1
Tirry Ave PA4 .... 94 C1
Tirry Way PA4 .... 94 C1
Titania PA8 .... 93 F4
Titania FK10 .... 10 A4
Titchfield Rd KA10 .... 229 D1
Titchfield St KA1 .... 227 F4
Titchfield Way KA11 ...... 220 A3
Titwood Dr KA3 .... 223 D2
Titwood Rd Glasgow G41 ... 116 B1
  Newton Mearns G77 ...... 156 C1
Tiverton Ave G32 .... 119 E2
Tivoli Ct G75 .... 180 C3
Tobago Pl
  East Kilbride G75 ...... 159 D1
  Glasgow G40 .... 117 F3
Tobago St Glasgow G40 .... 117 F3
  Greenock PA15 .... 45 F3
Tobermory Rd G73 .... 138 B2
Todburn Dr PA2 .... 133 F4
Todd St G31 .... 118 B4
Todhill Ave KA3 .... 222 C2
Todhills G75 .... 180 C4
Todhills N G75 .... 180 C4
Todhills S G75 .... 180 C4
Todholm Cres PA2 .... 114 A1
Todholm Prim Sch PA2 ..... 114 A1
Todholm Rd PA2 .... 114 A1
Todholm Terr PA2 .... 114 A1
Todrig Dr KA1 .... 227 F2
Tofthill Ave G64 .... 77 F1
Tofthill Gdns G64 .... 77 F1
Tofts G77 .... 191 E4
Tofts Cres KA24 .... 191 E4
Tollcross Rd PA5 .... 45 F2
Tolbooth St ⑧ FK1 .... 42 A2
Toll La G51 .... 116 C3
Toll St ML1 .... 163 F3
Toll Wynd ML3 .... 183 E4
Tollbrae Ave ML6 .... 123 D4

Tan – Tow 289

Tollbrae Prim Sch ML6 .... 123 D4
Tollcross Children's Mus
  G32 .... 118 C2
Tollcross Rd G31, G32 .... 118 C2
Tollerton Dr KA12 .... 219 E2
Tollhouse Gdns ML4 .... 142 C3
Tollhouse Way KA11 .... 220 A3
Tollpark Cres ML2 .... 166 A3
Tollpark Pl G68 .... 62 C4
Tollpark Rd G68 .... 62 C4
Tolsta St G23 .... 76 C1
Tom-A-Mhoid G84 .... 15 D2
Tomtain Brae G68 .... 81 F4
Tomtain Ct G68 .... 81 F4
Toner Gdns ML2 .... 186 A4
Tontine Cres G82 .... 49 E4
Tontine La G1 .... 241 E1
Tontine Pk ⑩ 49 E4
Tontine Pl G73 .... 138 C2
Topaz Terr ML4 .... 142 A2
Tophill Entry FK1 .... 41 F3
Toponthank La KA3 .... 223 D3
Toppersfield PA10 .... 111 E1
Torbeg Gdns G75 .... 180 A3
Torbeg House KA9 .... 236 A3
Torbothie Rd ML7 .... 147 D2
Torbreck St G52 .... 116 A3
Torbrex Farm Rd FK7 ...... 7 D2
Torbrex La FK7 .... 7 D3
Torbrex Rd
  Cumbernauld G67 .... 62 A1
  Stirling FK7 .... 7 D2
Torburn Ave Glasgow G46 .. 136 A2
  Plean FK7 .... 12 B1
Tordene Path G68 .... 61 E2
Torgyle St G23 .... 76 B1
Torlea Pl FK5 .... 23 D2
Tormeadow Rd G77 .... 156 B3
Tormore St G51 .... 115 E3
Tormusk Dr G45 .... 138 A2
Tormusk Gdns G45 .... 138 A2
Tormusk Gr G45 .... 138 A2
Tormusk Prim Sch G45 ..... 138 A2
Tormusk Rd G45 .... 138 A2
Torness St G11 .... 96 B1
Torogay Pl G22 .... 97 F4
Torogay St G22 .... 97 E4
Torogay Terr G22 .... 97 E4
Toronto Way G32 .... 139 E4
Torphin Cres G32 .... 119 D4
Torr Ave PA11 .... 89 F1
Torr Cres G84 .... 15 F3
Torr La PA11 .... 89 F1
Torr Rd Bishopbriggs G64 . 78 B1
  Bridge Of W PA11 .... 110 A4
Torr St G22 .... 97 E2
Torran Dr PA8 .... 93 F4
Torran Rd G33 .... 119 F4
Torrance Ave ML6 .... 123 E4
Torrance Cres ML7 .... 57 D1
Torrance Rd
  East Kilbride G74 ...... 159 F1
  Greenock PA15 .... 46 A1
Torrance G64 .... 78 C4
Torrance Rdbt G75 .... 181 D3
Torrance St G21 .... 97 F2
Torranyard Terr ML3 ...... 161 F1
Torriden Pl ML5 .... 121 F3
Torriden St ML5 .... 121 F3
Torridon Ave Falkirk FK2 . 24 B1
  Glasgow G41 .... 116 A2
  Motherwell ML1 .... 143 E2
Torridon Ct FK10 .... 10 B3
Torridon Gdns
  Bearsden G61 .... 75 E4
  Newton Mearns G77 ...... 157 D2
Torrin Loan ML7 .... 147 D2
Torrin Rd G23 .... 76 B1
Torrinch Dr G63 .... 31 D2
Torrington Ave G46 .... 157 D4
Torrington Cres G32 ...... 119 E2
Torrisdale Pl ML5 .... 121 F4
Torrisdale St
  ⑩ Glasgow G42 .... 117 D1
Torry Dr FK12 .... 4 C4
Torryburn Rd G21 .... 98 B2
Torvean Ave ML3 .... 161 F1
Torwood Ave FK5 .... 23 D1
Torwood La G69 .... 81 D2
Torwood Sch FK5 .... 22 C3
Torwoodhill Rd G84 .... 15 F2
Torwoodhill Rd G84 .... 15 F2
Toryglen Prim Sch G42 .... 137 F4
Toryglen Rd G73 .... 137 F3
Toryglen St G5 .... 117 F1
Touch Rd FK7 .... 6 A3
Touchhill Cres FK7 .... 12 B2
Tourhill Rd KA3 .... 222 C2
Tourmaline Terr ML4 ...... 142 A2
Tournai Path G72 .... 161 E4
Toward Ct G72 .... 161 F4
Toward Rd G33 .... 119 E4
Tower Ave G78 .... 134 B2
Tower Cres PA4 .... 94 A1
Tower Dr Gourock PA19 .... 44 B3
  Renfrew PA4 .... 94 A1
Tower Pl Clackmannan FK10 . 10 C3
  Helensburgh G84 .... 16 B1
  Johnstone PA5 .... 112 A1
  Kilmarnock KA1 .... 227 E2
Tower Rd Airdrie G67 ..... 83 D3
  Bearsden G61 .... 56 C2
  Johnstone PA5 .... 111 F1

Tower St Alloa FK10 10 A4
Glasgow G41 116 C3
Tower Terr PA1 113 E2
Tower View FK10 5 F1
Towerhill Ave KA3 222 B3
Towerhill Rd G13 75 E1
Towerlands Farm Rd KA11 220 A2
Towerlands Gate KA11 220 A1
Towerlands Intc KA11 219 F2
Towerlands Prim Sch KA11 220 B1
Towerlands Rd KA11 220 B1
Towers Ct FK2 42 A3
Towers Pl Airdrie ML6 123 F4
Stirling FK9 2 B2
Towers Rd ML6 123 F4
Towerside Cres G53 115 D1
Towerside Rd G53 115 D1
Towie Pl [10] Glasgow G20 96 B3
Uddingston G71 140 C3
Town Burn FK7 6 C2
Town House St FK6 21 F1
Townend KA3 222 B4
Townend La KA24 191 E4
Townend Rd
Dumbarton G82 50 A3
Kilmarnock KA1 227 F2
Townend St KA24 191 E4
Townend Terr KA1 231 E2
Townfoot KA11 220 B1
Townhead Irvine KA12 219 E1
Kilbirnie KA25 149 D1
Kilmaurs KA3 222 B4
Kilwinning KA13 207 E2
Kirkintilloch G66 79 E4
Townhead Ave ML1 142 C4
Townhead Dr ML1 143 F2
Townhead Pl G71 141 D4
Townhead Prim Sch ML5 101 E1
Townhead Rd
Coatbridge ML5 101 E1
Helensburgh G84 17 D1
Newton Mearns G77 156 B2
Saltcoats KA21 217 D4
Townhead St
Beith KA15 171 D4
Hamilton ML3 162 C2
Kilsyth G65 60 B4
Stevenston KA20 206 B1
Stonehouse ML9 198 C1
Townhead Terr PA1 113 E2
Townhill Prim Sch ML3 161 F1
Townhill Rd ML3 161 F2
Townhill Terr ML3 161 F2
Townholm KA3 223 D1
Townmill Rd G31 118 A4
Townsend St G4 97 E1
Tradeston Ind Est G5 117 D2
Tradeston St G5 240 B1
Trafalgar St Clydebank G81 73 F1
Glasgow G40 117 F2
Greenock PA15 45 F2
Trainard Ave G32 118 C2
Tramore Cres KA9 236 B4
Tranent Pl Cleland ML1 144 B1
Glasgow G33 118 C4
Traquair Ave Paisley PA2 132 C4
Wishaw ML2 165 E3
Traquair Dr G52 115 D3
Traquair Wynd G72 161 E4
Treebank Cres KA7 239 E3
Treeburn Ave G46 136 A2
Treemain Rd G46 157 D4
Trees Park Ave G78 134 A2
Treesbank KA13 207 E1
Treesbank Rd KA1 227 F2
Treeswoodhead Rd KA1 228 A1
Trefoil Ave G41 136 B4
Trefoil Pl KA7 239 E2
Trelawney Terr KA20 217 F3
Trent Pl G75 179 F3
Trent St ML5 101 E1
Tresta Rd G23 96 C4
Tribboch St ML9 184 C2
Trident Way PA4 94 B1
Trinidad Gn [3] G75 159 D1
Trinidad Way [7] G74 159 D1
Trinity Ave G52 115 E2
Trinity Cres KA15 150 B1
Trinity Dr Cambuslang G72 139 E2
Dalry KA24 191 D3
Trinity High Sch
Renfrew PA4 94 B2
Rutherglen G73 138 B4
Trinity Way [21] ML9 185 E1
Trinley Rd G13 75 E1
Triton Pl ML4 142 C3
Tron Ct FK10 4 A1
Trondra Path G34 119 F4
Trondra Pl G34 119 F4
Trongate Glasgow G1 241 D1
Stonehouse ML9 198 C1
Troon Ave G75 180 A3
Troon Ct G75 180 A3
Troon Dr PA11 110 B4
Troon Gdns G68 61 F3
Troon Pl G77 157 D2
Troon Prim Sch KA10 229 E2
Troon Rd KA10 230 A2
Troon St G40 118 A2
Troon Sta KA10 229 E1
Trossachs Ave ML1 143 D3
Trossachs Ct G20 97 D2
Trossachs Rd G73 138 B1
Trossachs St G20 97 D2
Troubridge Ave PA10 111 D1
Troubridge Cres PA10 111 D1
Trows Rd ML2 186 A3
Truce Rd G13 95 D4
Truro Ave G69 80 C2
Tryfield Pl KA8 236 A1
Tryst Rd Cumbernauld G67 61 F1
Cumbernauld, Carbrain G67 62 A1
Stenhousemuir FK5 23 E2
Tudhope Cres G83 27 E4
Tudor La S G14 95 F2
Tudor Rd G14 95 F2
Tudor St G69 119 F2
Tulliallan Pl
East Kilbride G74 181 D4
Stenhousemuir FK5 24 A2
Tullibody Rd FK10 4 C1
Tullichewan Cres G83 27 E4
Tullichewan Dr G83 27 E4
Tullichewan Rd G83 27 E4
Tulligarth Pk FK10 10 A4
Tullis St G40 117 F2
Tulloch Gdns ML1 164 A2
Tulloch Rd ML7 147 D2
Tulloch St G44 137 D3
Tulloch-Ard Pl G73 138 B2
Tullymet Rd ML3 183 E4
Tummel Dr ML6 102 C1
Tummel Gn G74 159 F2
Tummel Pl FK5 23 F2
Tummel St G33 98 C1
Tummell Way PA2 112 C1
Tunnel St G3 116 C4
Tuphall Rd ML3 162 B1
Turnberry Ave
[5] Glasgow G11 96 A2
Gourock PA19 44 A3
Turnberry Cres ML5 121 F2
Turnberry Ct KA13 207 D2
Turnberry Dr
Bridge Of W PA11 110 B3
Hamilton ML3 161 E1
Kilmarnock KA1 227 F2
Newton Mearns G77 157 D3
Rutherglen G73 137 F3
Turnberry Gdns
Chapelhall ML6 123 F1
Cumbernauld G68 61 F3
Turnberry Pl
East Kilbride G75 180 A3
Rutherglen G73 137 F2
Turnberry Rd G11 96 A2
Turnberry Wynd
Bothwell G72 140 C1
Irvine KA12 224 B4
Turnbull Ave G83 27 E2
Turnbull Cres G83 27 E2
Turnbull High Sch G64 77 F1
Turnbull St G1 241 E1
Turner Pl KA3 223 D2
Turner Rd Glasgow G21 97 F1
Paisley PA3 113 F4
Turner St ML5 121 F3
Turners Ave PA2 113 D2
Turnhill Ave PA8 93 D4
Turnhill Cres PA8 93 D4
Turnhill Dr PA8 93 D4
Turnhill Gdns PA8 93 D4
Turningshaw Rd PA6 91 F3
Turnlaw G75 180 B3
Turnlaw Rd G72 139 D1
Turnlaw St G5 117 E2
Turnyland Mdws PA8 93 D4
Turnyland Way PA8 93 D4
Turquoise Terr ML4 142 A2
Turret Cres G13 95 E4
Turret Ct FK10 10 B3
Turret Rd G13 95 E4
Turriff St G5 117 D2
Twain Ave FK5 24 A2
Twechar Prim Sch G65 60 A2
Tweed Ave PA2 112 C1
Tweed Cres Glasgow G33 98 C1
Kilmarnock KA1 228 A3
Renfrew PA4 94 C1
Wishaw ML2 165 E3
Tweed Ct ML6 123 E3
Tweed Dr G61 75 E2
Tweed La ML1 143 D3
Tweed Pl PA5 131 E4
Tweed St Ayr KA8 236 A2
Coatbridge ML5 122 A2
East Kilbride G75 179 F4
Greenock PA16 45 D3
Larkhall ML9 185 D1
Tweedmuir Pl ML5 122 B2
Tweedsmuir G64 78 B1
Tweedsmuir Cres G61 75 F4
Tweedsmuir Pk ML3 183 E4
Tweedsmuir Rd G52 115 D3
Tweedvale Ave G14 94 C3
Tweedvale Pl G14 94 C3
Twinlaw St G34 100 B1
Tylney Rd PA1 114 B3
Tyndrum Rd G61 76 A3
Tyndrum St G4 241 D4
Tyne Pl G75 179 F3
Tynecastle Cres G32 119 D4
Tynecastle Path G32 119 D4
Tynecastle Pl G32 119 D4
Tynecastle St G32 119 D4
Tynron Ct ML3 161 F1
Tynwald Ave G73 138 B2
U.P. La G65 60 B4
U.P. Rd G65 60 B4
Uddingston Gram Sch G71 140 C3
Uddingston Rd G71 141 D2
Uddingston Sta G71 140 C3
Udston Hospl ML3 161 F3
Udston Prim Sch ML3 161 F2
Udston Rd ML3 161 F3
Udston Terr ML3 161 F3
Uig Pl G33 119 F3
Uist Ave PA14 69 D4
Uist Cres G33 99 F2
Uist Dr G66 80 A4
Uist Pl ML6 123 E3
Uist St G51 115 F4
Uist Way ML2 165 F3
Ulg Way ML7 147 D2
Ullswater G75 179 F3
Ulundi Rd PA5 111 F1
Ulva St G52 115 F3
Umberly Rd KA1 227 F2
Underwood KA13 207 E3
Underwood Cotts FK7 6 B3
Underwood La PA1 113 E3
Underwood Pl KA1 227 F2
Underwood Rd
Cambusbarron FK7 6 B3
Paisley PA3 113 E3
Prestwick KA9 236 B4
Rutherglen G73 138 B3
Underwood St G41 136 C4
Union Arc KA7 238 C4
Union Ave KA8 236 A2
Union Pl Glasgow G1 240 C2
Larbert FK5 23 D1
Union Rd FK1 41 E3
Union St Alexandria G83 27 F2
Alloa FK10 10 A3
Bridge Of A FK9 2 A4
Carluke ML8 187 F1
Falkirk FK2 42 A4
Glasgow G1 240 C2
Greenock PA16 45 F3
Hamilton ML3 162 B2
Hurlford KA1 228 C3
Kilmarnock KA3 222 C1
Kirkintilloch G66 79 E4
Larkhall ML9 185 D2
Motherwell ML1 143 D2
Paisley PA2 113 F1
Saltcoats KA21 216 C4
Shotts ML7 146 B3
Stenhousemuir FK5 23 F2
Stirling FK8 2 A1
Stonehouse ML9 198 C1
Troon KA10 229 D2
Union Street La G83 27 F2
Unitas Cres ML8 187 F1
Unitas Rd ML4 142 B3
Unity Pk ML7 146 B2
Unity Pl G4 97 D1
Univ of Paisley (Thornly Park Campus) PA2 133 F4
Univ of Stirling (Dept of Nursing & Midwifery, ForthValley Campus) FK1 42 A2
Univ of Strathclyde G1, G4 241 E3
Univ Veterinary Hospl (Univ of Glasgow) G61 96 A4
Universal Rd FK2 42 C4
University Ave G12 96 B1
University Gdns G12 96 B1
University of Glasgow G20 76 A1
University of Paisley PA1 113 E2
University of Stirling FK9 2 B3
University Pl G12 96 B1
University Rd W FK9 2 B3
Unsted Pl PA1 114 A2
Unthank Rd ML4 142 B3
Uphall Pl G33 118 C4
Upland La [2] G14 95 E2
Upland Rd G14 95 E2
Uplawmoor Prim Sch G78 153 D2
Uplawmoor Rd G78 153 F2
Upper Adelaide St G84 16 C1
Upper Arthur St G83 27 E2
Upper Bourtree Ct G73 138 B2
Upper Bourtree Dr G73 138 B2
Upper Bridge St
Alexandria G83 27 E2
Stirling FK8 2 A1
Upper Cartsburn St PA15 46 A2
Upper Castlehill FK8 7 D4
Upper Colquhoun St G84 16 B2
Upper Craigs FK8 7 D4
Upper Crofts KA7 238 C1
Upper Glenburn Rd G61 75 E3
Upper Glenfinlas St G84 16 C1
Upper Hall Rd G84 15 E3
Upper Loaning KA7 238 C1
Upper Mill St ML6 123 D4
Upper Mill Street Ind Est ML6 123 D4
Upper Newmarket St FK1 42 A3
Upper Smollett St G83 27 E2
Upper Stoneymollan Rd G83 27 E4
Upper Sutherland Cres G84 16 A2
Upper Sutherland St G84 16 A2
Upper Torwoodhill Rd G84 15 F2
Ure Cres FK4 40 A3
Urquhart Cres PA4 94 B1
Urquhart Dr
East Kilbride G74 160 A2
Gourock PA19 43 F3
Urquhart Pl G84 16 B2
Urquhart Rd KA3 223 E1
Urrdale Rd G41 116 A3
Usmore Pl G33 119 F3
Vaila Pl G23 97 D4
Vaila St G23 96 C4
Vale Gr FK9 1 C3
Vale of Leven Acad G83 27 E2
Vale of Leven Hospl (General) G83 27 E3
Vale of Leven Ind Est G82 27 F1
Vale Pl FK6 21 F2
Valentine Cres G71 141 D4
Valetta Pl G81 73 E2
Valeview FK5 23 E1
Valeview Terr
Dumbarton G82 50 A3
Glasgow G42 137 D4
Vallantine Cres G71 141 D4
Vallay St G22 97 E4
Valley Ct ML3 162 B1
Valley View G72 139 E3
Valleybank G65 37 E2
Valleyfield
East Kilbride G75 159 E1
Milton Of C G65 58 A3
Valleyfield Dr G68 60 C1
Valleyfield Pl FK7 7 E3
Valleyfield St [2] G21 97 F2
Valleyview Dr FK2 42 A4
Valleyview Pl FK2 42 A4
Vancouver Ct G75 159 D1
Vancouver Dr G75 159 D1
Vancouver La
[17] Glasgow G14 95 E2
[8] Glasgow G14 95 E2
Vancouver Pl G81 73 E2
Vancouver Rd G14 95 E2
Vanguard St G81 74 B1
Vanguard Way PA4 94 B1
Vardar Ave G76 157 E4
Vardon Lea ML1 143 F1
Varna La G14 95 F2
Varna Rd G14 95 F2
Varnsdorf Way ML6 123 F3
Vasart Pl G20 96 C2
Vaults La KA13 207 F2
Veir Terr G82 49 F2
Veitch Pl G65 57 E4
Veitches Ct G81 74 A3
Vennachar St ML7 146 C3
Vennacher Rd PA4 94 A2
Vennal St KA24 191 D4
Vennard Gdns G41 116 C1
Vennel La KA3 211 F4
Vennel St KA3 211 F4
Vennel The FK6 21 F1
Vermont Ave G73 138 A4
Vermont St G41 116 C3
Vernon Bank G74 159 F2
Vernon Dr PA3 112 A3
Vernon Pl KA2 225 F1
Vernon St KA21 216 C4
Verona Ave G14 95 E2
Verona Gdns [4] G14 95 E2
Verona La G14 95 E2
Verona Pl KA22 205 E1
Vesalius St G32 119 D3
Viaduct Circ KA13 207 F3
Viaduct Rd G76 157 F4
Vicar St FK1 42 A3
Vicarfield St G51 116 A4
Vicarland Pl G72 139 D2
Vicarland Rd G72 139 D3
Vicars Rd ML9 198 C1
Vicars Wlk G72 139 D3
Vickers St ML1 163 D4
Victor St ML6 104 A1
Victoria Ave ML8 187 F1
Victoria Cir G12 96 B2
Victoria Cres Airdrie ML6 122 C3
Clarkston G76 157 F4
Irvine KA12 219 E1
Kilsyth G65 60 A4
Wishaw ML2 164 B2
Victoria Crescent La G12 96 B2
Victoria Crescent Pl
[16] G12 96 B2
Victoria Crescent Rd G12 96 B2
Victoria Cross G42 117 D1
Victoria Ct G77 156 B1
Victoria Dr KA10 229 E1
Victoria Dr E PA4 94 B1
Victoria Dr W PA4 94 A2
Victoria Drive Sec Sch G14 95 D2
Victoria Gdns Airdrie ML6 122 C4
Barrhead G78 134 A2
Kilmacolm PA13 69 E1
Paisley PA3 113 E1
Victoria Infmy
Glasgow G42 137 D4
Helensburgh G84 16 C1
Victoria La G77 156 B1
Victoria Meml Cottage Hospl G65 60 A4
Victoria Park Cnr G14 95 E2
Victoria Park Dr N G14 95 F2
Victoria Park Dr S G14 95 F2
Victoria Park Gdns N G11 95 F2
Victoria Park Gdns S G11 95 F2
Victoria Park La N G14 95 E2
Victoria Park La S G14 95 E2
Victoria Park Sch ML8 187 F1
Victoria Park St [27] G14 95 E2
Victoria Pk Ayr KA7 238 C3
Glasgow G14 95 F2
Kilsyth G65 60 A4
Victoria Pl Airdrie ML6 122 C3
Bellshill ML4 141 F2
Kilsyth G65 60 B4
Milngavie G62 55 D1
Rutherglen G73 138 A4
Stirling FK8 7 D4
Victoria Prim Sch
Airdrie ML6 122 C4
Falkirk FK2 42 B3
Glasgow G42 117 D1
Victoria Quadrant ML1 142 C3
Victoria Rd Barrhead G78 134 A2
Brookfield PA5 111 E3
Cumbernauld G68 61 E3
Falkirk FK2 42 B3
Glasgow G42 117 D2
Gourock PA19 44 B4
Harthill ML7 127 F3
Helensburgh G84 16 C1
Kirkintilloch G66 79 E2
Larbert FK5 23 D1
Paisley PA2 113 E1
Rutherglen G73 138 A3
Saltcoats KA21 217 D4
Stepps G33 99 E3
Stirling FK8 7 D4
Victoria Rdbt KA12 219 D1
Victoria Sq
Newton Mearns G77 156 B1
Stirling FK8 7 D4
Victoria St Alexandria G83 27 F2
Alloa FK10 10 A4
Ayr KA8 236 A1
Blantyre G72 161 E4
Dumbarton G82 50 A2
Hamilton ML3 162 A3
Harthill ML7 127 F3
Kirkintilloch G66 79 E4
Larkhall ML9 185 D2
Rutherglen G73 138 A4
Wishaw ML2 166 A2
Victoria Terr
Cumbernauld G68 61 E3
Menstrie FK11 4 A4
Victoria Way KA3 195 F1
Victory Dr PA10 111 D2
Victory Way G69 120 A2
Viewbank G46 136 A2
Viewbank Ave ML6 123 D1
Viewbank St ML5 101 F3
Viewfield ML6 122 C4
Viewfield Ave
Bishopbriggs G64 97 F4
Blantyre G72 140 C1
Glasgow G69 119 F3
Kirkintilloch G66 79 E3
Lochwinnoch PA12 129 D1
Milton Of C G65 58 A3
Viewfield Bsns Ctr KA8 236 A1
Viewfield Dr Alva FK12 4 C3
Bishopbriggs G64 97 F4
Glasgow G69 119 F3
Viewfield La G12 96 C1
Viewfield Rd Ayr KA8 236 A1
Banknock FK4 38 B2
Bellshill ML4 141 F2
Bishopbriggs G64 97 F4
Coatbridge ML5 121 E2
Viewfield St Harthill ML7 127 F3
Stirling FK8 7 D4
Viewglen Ct G45 137 E1
Viewmount Dr G20 96 B4
Viewpark G62 55 D1
Viewpark Ave G31 118 A4
Viewpark Ct G73 138 B3
Viewpark Dr G73 138 A3
Viewpark Gdns PA4 94 A1
Viewpark Pl ML1 163 E3
Viewpark Rd ML1 163 E3
Viewpark Sh Ctr G71 141 E3
Viewpoint Pl G21 97 F3
Viewpoint Rd G21 97 F3
Viking Cres PA6 111 E4
Viking Rd ML6 123 D3
Viking Terr G75 180 C3
Viking Way Glasgow G46 135 F3
Renfrew PA4 94 B1
Villa Bank FK6 21 F1
Villafield Ave G64 78 A2
Villafield Dr G64 78 A2
Villafield Loan G64 78 A2
Village Gdns G72 140 C1
Village Rd G72 139 F2
Vine Park Ave KA3 222 A4
Vine Park Dr KA3 222 A4
Vine St G11 96 A1
Vineburgh Ave KA12 219 E2
Vineburgh Ct KA12 219 D2
Vinicombe La [3] G12 96 B2
Vinicombe St G12 96 B2
Vintner St G4 97 E1
Viola Pl G64 78 B4
Violet Gdns ML8 201 F4
Violet Pl ML1 143 D3
Violet St PA1 114 A2
Virginia Ct G1 241 D2
Virginia Gdns Ayr KA8 236 A1
Milngavie G62 76 B4
Virginia Pl G1 241 D2
Virginia St Glasgow G1 241 D2
Greenock PA15 46 A2
Viscount Ave PA4 94 B1
Viscount Gate G71 140 C3
Vivian Ave G62 54 C1
Voil Dr G44 137 D2
Voil Rd FK9 2 A2
Vorlich Ct G78 134 B1
Vorlich Dr FK1 66 C4

- Vorlich Gdns G61 75 E4
- Vorlich Pl Kilmarnock KA1 228 A2; Stirling FK9 2 A2
- Vorlich Wynd ML1 143 E2
- Vrackie Pl KA1 228 A2
- Vulcan St [5] Glasgow G21 97 F2; Motherwell ML1 163 F4
- Waddell Ave ML6 102 B2
- Waddell Ct Glasgow G5 117 E3; Kilmarnock KA3 222 C2
- Waddell St Airdrie ML6 103 D1; Falkirk FK2 24 B1
- Waggon Rd Ayr KA8 235 F1; Falkirk FK2 42 A4
- Waid Ave G77 156 B3
- Waldemar Rd G13 95 E4
- Walden Rd KA1 228 C3
- Waldo St [3] G13 95 F4
- Walk The FK10 10 A3
- Walker Ave Kilmarnock KA3 228 A4; Troon KA10 229 E3
- Walker Ct G11 96 A1
- Walker Dr Dennyloanhead FK4 39 E3; Elderslie PA5 112 B1
- Walker Path [8] G71 141 D4
- Walker Rd KA8 236 A1
- Walker St Glasgow G11 96 A1; Greenock PA16 45 E3; Kilbirnie KA25 149 D1
- Walkerburn Dr ML2 165 E3
- Walkerburn Rd G52 115 D2
- Walkinshaw Cres PA3 113 D3
- Walkinshaw Rd PA4 93 E2
- Walkinshaw St Glasgow G40 118 A2; Johnstone PA5 112 A2
- Wall Gdns FK1 41 E3
- Wall St FK1 41 E3
- Wallace Ave Bishopton PA7 72 A2; Dundonald KA2 225 F1; Elderslie PA5 112 B1; Stevenston KA20 206 B1; Troon KA10 229 E3
- Wallace Cres Denny FK6 21 E1; Plean FK7 12 B2
- Wallace Ct Kilmarnock KA1 228 C3; Prestwick KA9 236 B4; Stirling FK8 2 A1
- Wallace Dr ML1 185 E1
- Wallace Gdns Stirling FK9 2 A2; Torrance G64 57 D1
- Wallace High Sch FK9 2 A2
- Wallace Monument FK9 2 C2
- Wallace Pl Blantyre G72 140 C1; Cambusbarron FK7 6 B3; Fallin FK7 8 B2; Greenock PA15 45 F3; Hamilton ML3 163 D1
- Wallace Prim Sch PA5 112 B1
- Wallace Rd Irvine KA12 219 E2; Motherwell ML1 143 D1; Renfrew PA4 94 A1
- Wallace St Alloa FK10 10 B4; Bannockburn FK7 7 F1; Clydebank G81 74 A1; Coatbridge ML5 122 A3; Dumbarton G82 50 A2; Falkirk FK2 42 B3; Glasgow G5 117 E3; Greenock PA15 45 E2; Kilmarnock KA1 227 F4; Motherwell ML1 163 E4; Paisley PA3 113 F3; Plains ML6 104 A2; Port Glasgow PA14 47 F1; Rutherglen G73 138 A4; Stirling FK8 2 A1
- Wallace View Kilmarnock KA1 227 F3; Shieldhill FK1 66 B4; Tullibody FK10 4 B2
- Wallace Way ML11 215 E2
- Wallacefield Rd KA10 229 E2
- Wallacehill Rd KA1 227 F2
- Wallacetown Ave KA3 223 D3
- Wallacewell Cres G21 98 A3
- Wallacewell Pl G21 98 A3
- Wallacewell Quadrant G21 98 B3
- Wallacewell Rd G21 98 B3
- Wallbrae Rd G67 83 B4
- Wallneuk Rd PA1 113 F3
- Walls St G1 241 E2
- Wallstale Rd FK7 7 D2
- Walmer Cres G51 116 B3
- Walnut Cres Glasgow G22 97 E3; Johnstone PA5 112 A1
- Walnut Ct G65 58 A3
- Walnut Dr G66 79 D3
- Walnut Pl Glasgow G22 97 E3; Uddingston G71 121 E1
- Walnut Rd Glasgow G22 97 E3; Kilmarnock KA1 227 E4
- Walpole Pl PA5 131 E4
- Walter St Glasgow G31 118 B4; Wishaw ML2 165 D1
- Walton Ave G77 156 B3
- Walton St Barrhead G78 134 B2; Glasgow G41 136 C4
- Wamba Ave G13 95 F4
- Wamphray Pl FK5 179 E4
- Wandilla Ave G81 74 B1
- Wanlock St G51 116 A4
- Ward Ct KA8 236 A2
- Ward Rd KA8 236 A2
- Ward St FK10 10 A3
- Warden Rd G13 95 E4
- Wardend Rd G64 57 D1
- Wardhill Rd G21 98 A3
- Wardhouse Rd PA2 133 E4
- Wardie Pl G33 119 F4
- Wardie Rd G34 120 A4
- Wardlaw Ave G73 138 A4
- Wardlaw Cres East Kilbride G75 181 D4; Troon KA10 230 A2
- Wardlaw Dr G73 138 A4
- Wardlaw Gdns KA11 220 A4
- Wardlaw Pl FK2 24 B1
- Wardlaw Rd Bearsden G61 75 F1; Kilmarnock KA3 223 F3
- Wardneuk KA9 236 B3
- Wardneuk Dr KA3 223 D2
- Wardpark East Ind Est G68 62 C4
- Wardpark North Ind Est G68 62 B4
- Wardpark Pl G67 62 B3
- Wardpark Rd G67 62 B3
- Wardpark South Ind Est G67 62 B3
- Wardrop Pl G74 159 F2
- Wardrop St Beith KA15 171 E4; [2] Glasgow G51 116 A4; Paisley PA1 113 F2
- Wardrop Terr KA15 171 E4
- Wards Cres ML1 121 F3
- Wards Pl KA1 227 F4
- Ware Rd G34 120 A4
- Warilda Ave G81 74 B1
- Warlock Dr PA11 90 B1
- Warlock Rd PA11 90 B2
- Warly Dr KA2 225 F1
- Warly Pl KA2 225 F1
- Warner St KA20 217 E4
- Warnock Cres ML4 142 A2
- Warnock Rd G77 156 B4
- Warnock St G31 241 F3
- Warren Rd ML3 183 E4
- Warren St G42 117 D1
- Warrs Wlk G65 57 F4
- Warriston Cres G33 118 C4
- Warriston Pl G32 119 D4
- Warriston St G33 118 C4
- Warriston Way G33 138 B2
- Warrix Ave G77 156 A2
- Warrix Gdns KA10 232 C4
- Warrix Intc KA11 219 F1
- Warroch St G3 240 A2
- Warwick G74 160 B2
- Warwick Gr ML3 161 F3
- Warwick Hill KA11 220 A3
- Warwick Rd PA16 44 C2
- Warwickhill Rd KA11 222 B1
- Washington Rd G66 79 D4
- Washington St G3 240 B2
- Watchmeal Cres G81 74 B4
- Water La [1] KA1 227 F4
- Water Rd G78 134 B2
- Water Row G51 116 A4
- Water St KA11 47 E1
- Waterbank Rd G76 158 B3
- Watercut Rd KA13 219 D4
- Waterfoot Ave G53 135 E4
- Waterfoot Rd G76, G77 157 D2
- Waterfoot Row G76 157 E2
- Waterfoot Terr G53 135 E4
- Waterford Ct G46 136 A1
- Waterlands Gdns ML8 188 A2
- Waterlands Pl ML8 187 D2
- Waterlands Rd ML8 187 D2
- Waterloo Dr ML11 215 D3
- Waterloo Gdns G66 58 B1
- Waterloo La G2 240 C2
- Waterloo Rd Lanark ML11 215 D3; Prestwick KA9 236 A3
- Waterloo St G2 240 C2
- Watermill Ave G66 79 F4
- Watermill Gr PA2 112 C1
- Watersaugh Dr ML1 144 A1
- Watersedge Ct G68 44 C2
- Waterside Ave KA11 219 D2
- Waterside Ct KA1 227 F4
- Waterside Dr G77 156 B2
- Waterside Gdns Carmunnock G76 158 B4; Hamilton ML3 162 C1
- Waterside Rd Carmunnock G76 158 B3; Kilwinning KA13 207 F2; Kirkintilloch G66 79 F4
- Waterside St Glasgow G5 117 E2; Kilmarnock KA1 227 F4
- Waterslap KA3 213 D1
- Waterston Way PA12 129 E2
- Waterworks Cotts G77 177 D2
- Wateryetts Dr PA13 69 E3
- Watling Ave FK1 41 E3
- Watling Dr FK1 41 E3
- Watling Gdns FK1 41 E3
- Watling Pl G75 159 D1
- Watling St Falkirk FK1 41 E3; Motherwell ML1 142 B1; Uddingston G71 140 C4
- Watson Ave Linwood PA3 112 A3; Rutherglen G73 138 A4; Stonehouse ML9 199 D2
- Watson Cres G65 60 C4
- Watson Pl Blantyre G72 161 D4
- Watson Rd FK5 39 E2
- Watson St Blantyre G72 161 E4; Falkirk FK2 42 A3; Glasgow ML1 241 E1; Kilmarnock KA3 228 A4; Larkhall ML9 199 D4; Motherwell ML1 163 F3; Uddingston G71 140 C3
- Watson Terr KA12 219 E1
- Watsonville Pk ML1 163 F3
- Watstone Rd ML9 199 D1
- Watt Cres ML4 142 A4
- Watt Ct KA24 191 E4
- Watt Gdns FK1 41 F3
- Watt La PA11 110 C4
- Watt Low Ave G73 137 F3
- Watt Pl Greenock PA15 46 A3; Milngavie G62 54 C2
- Watt Rd Bridge Of W PA11 110 B4; Glasgow G52 115 D4
- Watt St Airdrie ML6 103 E1; Glasgow G5 116 C3; Greenock PA16 45 F3
- Wattfield Rd KA7 238 C3
- Waukglen Ave G53 135 D1
- Waukglen Cres G53 135 C2
- Waukglen Dr G53 135 D2
- Waukglen Gdns G53 135 D2
- Waukglen Path G53 135 D2
- Waukglen Pl G53 135 D2
- Waukglen Rd G53 135 D2
- Waulking Mill Rd G81 74 B4
- Waulkmill Ave G78 134 B2
- Waulkmill Pl KA1 228 A4
- Waulkmill St G46 135 F2
- Waulkmill Way G78 134 B2
- Waverley G75 160 B2
- Waverley Ave Helensburgh G84 25 D4; Kilmarnock KA1 222 B1
- Waverley Cres Cumbernauld G67 82 B4; Hamilton ML3 161 F2; High Bonnybridge FK4 40 A2; Kirkintilloch G66 79 E4; Lanark ML11 215 E2; Stirling FK8 2 B3
- Waverley Ct Bothwell G71 141 D1; Helensburgh G84 16 B1
- Waverley Dr Airdrie ML6 103 D1; Rutherglen G73 138 B4; Wishaw ML2 165 D2
- Waverley Gdns Elderslie PA5 112 B1; Glasgow G41 116 C1
- Waverley Pl KA21 205 F1
- Waverley Rd Paisley PA2 132 C4; Stenhousemuir FK5 23 E1
- Waverley St Coatbridge ML5 102 A1; Falkirk FK2 42 A4; Glasgow G41 116 C1; Greenock PA16 45 E2; Hamilton ML3 161 F2; Larkhall ML9 199 D4
- Waverley Terr Blantyre G72 161 E3; Dumbarton G82 49 D2; Stenhousemuir FK5 23 E1
- Waverley Way ML9 198 C1
- Weardale La G33 119 E4
- Weardale St G33 119 E4
- Weaver Ave G77 156 B4
- Weaver Cres ML6 123 D3
- Weaver La PA10 111 D3
- Weaver Pl G75 179 F4
- Weaver Row 7 D2
- Weaver St G4 241 E3
- Weaver Terr PA2 114 A2
- Weavers Ave PA2 113 D2
- Weavers Cotts PA10 111 D2
- Weavers Gate PA1 113 D2
- Weavers Rd PA2 113 D2
- Weavers Way ML9 198 C1
- Weavers Wlk ML1 215 D2
- Webster Groves ML2 165 E3
- Webster St Clydebank G81 94 C4; Glasgow G40 118 A2
- Wedderlea Dr G52 115 D3
- Wee Cl KA15 171 D4
- Wee Sunnyside Rd ML3 184 A1
- Weensmoor Rd G53 134 C2
- Weeple Dr PA3 112 A3
- Weighhouse Cl PA1 113 F2
- Weighhouse Rd ML8 187 F2
- Weir Ave Barrhead G78 134 B1
- Weir Pl Greenock PA15 46 B2; Kilbirnie KA25 149 D1; Law ML8 186 C2
- Weir Rd Ardrossan KA22 205 E2; Ayr KA8 235 F2
- Weir St Coatbridge ML5 122 A4; Falkirk FK1 42 B3; Greenock PA15 46 A3; Paisley PA3 113 F3
- Weirston Rd KA13 208 A2
- Weirwood Ave G69 120 A3
- Weirwood Gdns G69 119 F2
- Welbeck Cres KA10 229 D1
- Welbeck Mews KA10 229 D1
- Welbeck Rd G53 135 D2
- Welbeck St Greenock PA16 45 E4; Kilmarnock KA1 228 A4
- Weldon Pl G65 60 C2
- Welfare Ave G72 139 E2
- Well Gn G43 136 B4
- Well La G65 57 E4
- Well Rd Bridge Of A FK9 2 A4; Kilbarchan PA10 111 D2; Lanark ML11 215 D2
- Well St Paisley PA1 113 E3; Wishaw ML2 165 D1
- Welland Pl G75 179 F4
- Wellbank Gdns KA23 190 B3
- Wellbank Pl G71 140 C3
- Wellbrae Larkhall ML9 185 D1; Stonehouse ML9 198 C1
- Wellbrae Rd ML3 162 A1
- Wellbrae Terr G69 80 C1
- Wellcroft Pl G5 117 D2
- Wellcroft Rd ML3 161 F2
- Wellcroft Terr ML3 161 F2
- Wellesley Cres G75 179 F4
- Wellesley Dr G75 179 F4
- Wellfield Ave G46 136 A2
- Wellfield St G21 97 F2
- Wellgate ML11 215 D2
- Wellgate Ct ML11 215 D2
- Wellgate Dr FK9 2 B4
- Wellgate St ML9 185 D2
- Wellgatehead ML11 215 D2
- Wellgreen Pl FK8 7 D3
- Wellhall Ct ML3 162 A2
- Wellhall Rd ML3 162 A2
- Wellhead Ct ML11 215 D2
- Wellhouse Cres G33 119 F4
- Wellhouse Prim Sch G33 119 F4
- Wellhouse Rd G33 119 F4
- Wellington Ave KA3 228 B4
- Wellington La Ayr KA7 238 C4; Glasgow G2 240 C2
- Wellington Pl Clydebank G81 73 E2; Coatbridge ML5 121 E3; Kilmarnock KA3 222 C1; Wishaw ML2 186 B4
- Wellington Rd G65 78 A2
- Wellington Sch KA7 238 C4
- Wellington Sq KA7 238 C4
- Wellington St Airdrie ML6 103 D1; Glasgow G2 240 C2; Greenock PA15 45 F2; Kilmarnock KA3 222 C1; Paisley PA3 113 E3; Prestwick KA9 236 A3; Wishaw ML2 164 B3
- Wellington Terr ML11 214 C3
- Wellington Way Greenock PA15 45 F2; [POI] Renfrew PA4 94 B1
- Wellknowe Ave G74 158 B1
- Wellknowe Pl G74 158 B2
- Wellknowe Rd G74 158 B2
- Wellmeadow Cl G77 156 B3
- Wellmeadow Gn G77 156 B3
- Wellmeadow Rd G43 136 A3
- Wellmeadow St PA1 113 E2
- Wellmeadow Way G77 156 B3
- Wellpark KA7 238 C1
- Wellpark Ave KA3 228 B4
- Wellpark Cres FK7 6 C2
- Wellpark Ct KA3 228 B4
- Wellpark La KA3 216 C4
- Wellpark Pl KA3 228 B4
- Wellpark Rd Banknock FK4 38 B1; Motherwell ML1 163 F3; Saltcoats KA21 216 C4
- Wellpark St G31 241 F2
- Wellpark Terr Bonnybridge FK4 40 A3; Neilston G78 154 B3
- Wells St G81 73 F2
- Wellshot Dr G72 138 C3
- Wellshot Prim Sch G32 118 C2
- Wellshot Rd G32 118 C2
- Wellside Ave ML6 103 D1
- Wellside Dr G72 139 E2
- Wellside Pl FK1 42 A3
- Wellside Quadrant ML6 103 D1
- Wellsquarry Rd G74 159 E3
- Wellstead St G21 97 E2
- Wellwood Ave ML11 215 D3
- Wellwynd ML6 122 C4
- Wellyard La PA16 44 B2
- Wellyard Way PA16 44 B2
- Welsh Dr Blantyre G72 161 E3; Hamilton ML3 183 E4
- Welsh Gdns FK9 2 A4
- Welsh Pl KA21 205 E1
- Wemyss Ave G77 156 B4
- Wemyss Bay St PA15 45 F2
- Wemyss Dr G68 60 C1
- Wendur Way PA3 113 E4
- Wenlock Rd PA2 113 E1
- Wensleydale G74 159 E2
- Wentworth Dr G23 76 C1
- Wentworth Sq KA13 207 E2
- Wesley St ML6 122 C4
- West Abercromby St G84 16 B2
- West Academy St ML2 164 C2
- West Ave Carluke ML8 187 F1; Hamilton ML3 161 F3; Motherwell ML1 143 D1; Plains ML6 104 A2; Renfrew PA4 94 B2; Stepps G33 99 E3; Uddingston G71 141 E3
- West Barmoss Ave PA14 68 C4
- West Benhar Rd ML7 127 D2
- West Blackhall St PA15 45 F3
- West Boreland Rd FK6 21 E1
- West Bowhouse Way KA11 220 A3
- West Bowhouse Workshops KA11 220 A3
- West Brae PA1 113 E2
- West Bridge St FK1 42 A3
- West Bridgend G82 49 F2
- West Buchanan Pl PA2 113 E2
- West Burn La PA15 195 F1
- West Burn Rd PA15 45 F3
- West Burnside G65 60 B4
- West Byrehill Ind Est KA13 207 D1
- West Campbell St Glasgow G2 240 C3; Paisley PA1 113 D2
- West Canal St ML5 121 F4
- West Carmuirs Loan FK5 40 C3
- West Chapelton Ave G61 75 F2
- West Chapelton Cres G61 75 F2
- West Chapelton Dr G61 75 F2
- West Chapelton La G61 75 F2
- West Clyde St Helensburgh G84 16 B1; Larkhall ML9 185 D1
- West Coats Prim Sch G72 138 C3
- West Coats Rd G72 138 C3
- West Cres KA10 229 F2
- West Ct G81 73 F2
- West Dhuhill Dr G84 16 B2
- West Doura Ave KA21 205 F1
- West Doura Way KA13 207 E2
- West Dr Airdrie ML6 123 F3; Larbert FK5 23 D1
- West End KA24 191 D4
- West End Dr ML4 141 F2
- West End Gdns FK10 10 A3
- West End Pl ML4 141 F2
- West Fairholm St ML3 184 C3
- West Faulds Rd ML11 215 F3
- West Fullarton St KA1 222 C1
- West Gate ML2 165 E2
- West George La G2 240 C3
- West George St Coatbridge ML5 122 A4; Glasgow G2 240 C3; Kilmarnock KA1 222 C1
- West Glebe Terr ML3 162 B1
- West Glen Gdns PA13 69 F1
- West Glen Rd Kilmacolm PA13 69 F1; Kilmacolm PA13 70 A1
- West Gr KA10 229 F2
- West Graham St G4 240 C4
- West Greenhill Pl G3 116 C4
- West Hamilton St ML1 163 F3
- West High St G66 58 B1
- West James St FK12 5 D3
- West Johnstone St FK12 5 D3
- West Kilbride Prim Sch KA23 190 B3
- West Kilbride Rd KA24 191 D4
- West Kilbride Sta KA23 190 B3
- West King St G84 16 A1
- West Kirk St ML6 122 C4
- West Kirklands Pl KA24 191 D4
- West La PA1 113 D2
- West Langlands St KA1 222 C1
- West Lennox Dr G84 16 A2
- West Link Rd FK9 2 B3
- West Lodge Gdns FK10 9 F4
- West Lodge Rd PA4 94 A2
- West Main St ML7 127 F3
- West Mains Ind Est FK3 42 C4
- West Mains Rd East Kilbride G74 159 E1; Falkirk FK3 42 B4
- West Montrose St G84 16 B1
- West Murrayfield FK7 7 E1
- West Nemphlar Rd ML11 214 B3
- West Netherton St KA1 227 F4
- West Nile St G1 241 D3
- West Park Cres KA3 222 A4
- West Park Dr KA3 222 A4
- West Park Sch KA2 221 F1
- West Port KA11 214 C2
- West Portland St KA10 229 D1
- West Porton Pl PA7 71 F2
- West Princes St Glasgow G4 96 C1; Helensburgh G84 16 B1
- West Quay PA15 45 F3
- West Rd Irvine KA12 219 D2; Kilbarchan PA10 111 D2; Port Glasgow PA14 47 D1; Torrance G64 57 D1
- West Regent La G2 240 C3
- West Regent St G2 240 C3
- West Rossdhu Dr G84 16 B2
- West Row G84 16 B2
- West Sanquhar Rd KA8 236 A2

West Scott Terr ML3 .... 162 B1
West Shaw St
 Greenock PA15 .... 45 F3
 Kilmarnock KA1 .... 227 F3
West St Clydebank G81 ...... 94 C4
 Glasgow G5 .... 117 D3
 Paisley PA1 .... 113 E2
West Sta ML3 .... 162 B2
West Stewart St
 Greenock PA15 .... 45 F3
 Hamilton ML3 .... 162 B2
West Stirling St FK12 .... 4 C4
West Street
 Underground Sta G5 ...... 117 D3
West Thomson St G81 .... 74 A2
West Thornlie St ML2 .... 165 D1
West Vennel FK10 .... 10 A3
West View Dunlop KA3 .... 195 D4
 Waterside KA3 .... 213 F2
West Wellbrae Cres ML3 .. 183 D4
West Whitby St G31 .... 118 B2
West Woodside Ave PA14 ... 68 C3
West Woodstock St KA1 .... 227 F4
Westacres Rd G77 .... 156 A2
Westbank Ct 7 G12 .... 96 C1
Westbank La G12 .... 96 C1
Westbank Quadrant G12 .... 96 C1
Westborne Gdns G84 .... 16 B1
Westbourn Bldgs PA15 .... 45 F3
Westbourne Ave KA9 .... 236 B4
Westbourne Cres 75 E3
Westbourne Rd G61 .... 75 E3
Westbourne Gardens La 25
 G12 .... 96 B2
Westbourne Gdns KA9 ...... 236 B4
Westbourne Gdns N 27
 G12 .... 96 B2
Westbourne Gdns S G12 ..... 96 B2
Westbourne Gdns W 28
 G12 .... 96 B2
Westbourne Rd G12 .... 96 A2
Westbourne Terrace La N 26
 G12 .... 96 B2
Westbourne Terrace La S 3
 G12 .... 96 A2
Westbrae Dr G14, G13, ... 95 F2
Westbrae Rd G77 .... 156 C3
Westburn Ave
 Cambuslang G72 .... 139 E3
 Falkirk FK1 .... 42 A2
 Paisley PA3 .... 113 D3
Westburn Cres
 Clydebank G81 .... 74 A4
 Rutherglen G73 .... 137 F4
Westburn Farm Rd G72 ... 139 D3
Westburn Rd
 Cambuslang G72 .... 140 A3
 Cambuslang, Westburn G72 . 139 E3
Westcliff G82 .... 49 D2
Westclyffe St 3 G41 .... 116 C1
Westcott Pl ML11 .... 215 E3
Westcraigs Pk EH48 .... 107 E2
Westcraigs Rd
 Blackridge EH48 .... 107 E2
 Harthill ML7 .... 127 F3
Westend G61 .... 76 A1
Westend Ct ML8 .... 186 C2
Westend Park St G3 .... 240 A4
Wester Park Pl G31 .... 96 A1
Wester Carriaghhill PA2 ... 113 F1
Wester Cleddans Prim Sch
 G64 .... 78 A1
Wester Cleddens Rd G64 .. 78 B1
Wester Common Dr G22 .... 97 D2
Wester Common Prim Sch
 G22 .... 97 D2
Wester Common Rd G22 ... 97 D2
Wester Mavisbank Ave
 ML6 .... 122 C4
Wester Moffat Ave ML6 .. 123 F4
Wester Moffat Cres ML6 .. 123 F4
Wester Moffat Hospl ML6 . 123 F4
Wester Myvot Rd G67 .... 82 A2
Wester Rd G32 .... 119 E2
Westerburn St G32 .... 118 C3
Westercraigs G31 .... 117 F4
Westerdale G74 .... 159 E2
Westerfield Rd G76 .... 158 B2
Westerglen Rd FK1 .... 42 A1
Westergreens Ave G66 ...... 79 E3
Westerhill Rd G64 .... 78 B2
Westerhouse Ct ML8 .... 187 E1
Westerhouse Rd G34 .... 120 A4
Westerkirk Dr G23 .... 76 C1
Westerlands 34
 Newton Mearns G77 .... 156 A2
 Stirling FK8 .... 2 A3
Westerlands Gdns G77 .... 156 A2
Westerlands Gr G77 .... 156 A2
Westerlands Pl G77 .... 156 A3
Westerlea Ct KA9 .... 2 A3
Westerlea Dr KA9 .... 2 A3
Westermains Ave G66 ...... 79 D4
Western Ave Falkirk FK2 ... 42 A3
 Rutherglen G73 .... 137 F4
Western Cres KA23 .... 170 A4
Western Infmy G11 .... 96 B1
Western Isles Rd G60 .... 73 E3
Western Rd
 Cambuslang G72 .... 139 D2
 Kilmarnock KA3 .... 223 D2
Westerton Cowie FK7 .... 12 B4
 Lennoxtown G65 .... 57 F4

Westerton Ave
 Bearsden G61 .... 95 F4
 Clarkston G76 .... 158 A3
 Larkhall ML9 .... 185 D1
Westerton Dr FK9 .... 2 A4
Westerton La G46 .... 158 A3
Westerton Sta G61 .... 75 F1
Westerton Terr FK2 .... 24 B2
Westfield Dumbarton G82 .. 49 E2
 Kilbirnie KA25 .... 170 A4
Westfield Ave G73 .... 137 F4
Westfield Cres G61 .... 75 F1
Westfield Dr Bearsden G61 . 75 F1
 Cumbernauld G68 .... 81 F4
 Glasgow G52 .... 115 D3
 Greenock PA16 .... 45 E4
 Kilmalcolm PA13 .... 89 D4
Westfield Ind Area G68 .... 81 F3
Westfield Pl
 Cumbernauld G68 .... 81 E3
 Denny FK6 .... 21 F1
Westfield Prim Sch G68 .... 81 F4
Westfield Rd Ayr KA7 .... 238 C2
 Cumbernauld G68 .... 81 F4
 Glasgow G46 .... 136 A2
 Kilsyth G65 .... 36 A1
 Motherwell ML1 .... 143 E4
 Port Glasgow PA14 .... 68 C4
Westfield Rdbt FK7 .... 42 C3
Westfield St FK2 .... 42 C3
Westfields G64 .... 77 F2
Westgarth Pl G74 .... 159 D2
Westgate Way ML4 .... 141 F2
Westhouse Ave G73 .... 137 F4
Westhouse Gdns G73 ...... 137 F4
Westland Dr G14 .... 95 E2
Westland Drive La 20 G14 . 95 E2
Westlands Gdns PA2 .... 113 E1
Westlea ML6 .... 123 D3
Westminster Pl FK5 .... 23 F2
Westminster Terr 3 G3 .. 116 C4
Westmoor Cres ML1 .... 227 E4
Westmoreland St G42 .... 117 D1
Westmorland Rd PA16 ...... 44 C2
Westmuir Pl G73 .... 137 F4
Westmuir St G31 .... 118 B3
Weston Pl KA9 .... 236 B3
Weston Terr KA23 .... 190 B3
Westpark Ct KA20 .... 217 F4
Westpark Dr PA3 .... 113 D3
Westport G75 .... 159 D1
Westport St G65 .... 60 B4
Westray Ave
 Newton Mearns G77 .... 156 B4
 Port Glasgow PA14 .... 69 D3
Westray Cr G22 .... 97 E3
Westray Ct G67 .... 82 C4
Westray Pl
 Bishopbriggs G64 .... 78 B1
 Glasgow G22 .... 97 E4
Westray Rd G67 .... 82 C4
Westray Sq G22 .... 97 E4
Westray Terr FK1 .... 42 B1
Westray Wynd 2 ML2 .... 165 F3
Westside Gdns G11 .... 96 B1
Westview Cres FK10 .... 4 B1
Westward Way KA10 .... 229 F4
Westwood Ave Ayr KA8 ... 236 C1
 Glasgow G46 .... 136 A2
Westwood Cres Ayr KA8 .. 236 C1
 Hamilton ML3 .... 162 B1
Westwood Dr ML1 .... 144 C1
Westwood Gdns PA3 .... 113 D3
Westwood Hill G75 .... 180 A4
Westwood Quadrant G81 . 74 B1
Westwood Rd
 East Kilbride G75 .... 180 A4
 Glasgow G43 .... 136 A3
 Wishaw ML2 .... 166 A3
Westwood Sq G75 .... 180 A4
Weymouth Cres PA19 .... 44 C3
Weymouth Dr G12 .... 96 A3
Whamflet Ave G34 .... 120 B4
Whangie The G63 .... 29 D3
Wharry Rd FK12 .... 4 C4
Whatriggs Rd KA1 .... 228 A2
Wheatfield Rd Ayr KA7 ... 238 C4
 Bearsden G61 .... 75 E1
Wheatholm Cres ML6 ...... 103 D1
Wheatholm St ML6 .... 103 D1
Wheatland Ave G72 .... 161 E4
Wheatland Dr ML11 .... 214 C3
Wheatlandhead Ct G72 .. 161 E4
Wheatlands Ave FK4 .... 40 A3
Wheatlands Dr PA10 .... 111 D2
Wheatlands Farm Rd
 PA10 .... 111 D2
Wheatlandside ML11 ...... 214 C3
Wheatley Cres G65 .... 60 B4
Wheatley Loan G64 .... 98 B4
Wheatley Rd
 Saltcoats KA21 .... 206 A1
 Stevenston KA20 .... 206 C1
Wheatpark Rd ML11 .... 214 C2
Whifflet Ct ML5 .... 122 A3
Whifflet Sq ML5 .... 122 A3
Whifflet Sta ML5 .... 122 A3
Whin Ave G78 .... 134 A2
Whin Hill G74 .... 160 A2
Whin Hill Rd KA7 .... 239 D1
Whin Loan G65 .... 59 E4
Whin Pl G74 .... 160 A3
Whin St G81 .... 74 A2
Whinfell Dr G75 .... 180 A3
Whinfell Gdns G75 .... 180 A3
Whinfield Ave KA9 .... 236 B3

Whinfield Gdns KA9 .... 236 A3
Whinfield Rd Glasgow G53 . 135 D2
Whinfield Sch G53 .... 135 D2
Whinhall Ave ML6 .... 102 C1
Whinhall Rd ML6 .... 102 C1
Whinhill Cres PA15 .... 46 A1
Whinhill Rd Glasgow G53 . 115 D2
 Greenock PA15 .... 46 A2
 Paisley PA2 .... 114 A1
Whinhill Sta PA15 .... 46 A2
Whinknowe ML9 .... 199 F4
Whinney Gr ML2 .... 165 F2
Whinnie Knowe ML9 .... 184 C1
Whinpark Ave ML4 .... 141 F2
Whinriggs ML9 .... 198 B1
Whins of Milton Sch FK7 ... 7 D1
Whins Rd Alloa FK10 .... 10 B4
 Glasgow G41 .... 116 B1
 Stirling FK7 .... 7 D3
 Troon KA10 .... 229 F4
Whinwell Rd FK8 .... 2 A1
Whirlie Dr PA6 .... 111 D4
Whirlie Rd PA6 .... 91 D1
Whirlies Rdbt The G74 .... 160 A2
Whirlow Gdns G69 .... 120 A3
Whirlow Rd G69 .... 120 A3
Whistleberry Cres ML3 ... 162 A4
Whistleberry Dr ML3 ...... 162 A4
Whistleberry Ind Est ML3 162 A4
Whistleberry Pk ML3 ...... 162 A4
Whistleberry Rd ML3 ...... 162 A4
Whistlefield Ct G61 .... 75 F2
Whitacres Path G53 .... 135 D2
Whitacres Rd G53 .... 135 D2
Whitburn St G32 .... 118 C4
White Ave G82 .... 50 A2
White Cart Rd PA3 .... 113 F4
White Craig Rd KA22 ...... 205 E2
White St Ayr KA8 .... 236 A2
 Clydebank G81 .... 94 B4
 Glasgow G11 .... 96 B1
Whiteadder Pl G75 .... 179 E4
Whitecraigs Pl G23 .... 96 C4
Whitecraigs Sta G46 ...... 157 D4
Whitecrook Prim Sch G81 74 B1
Whitecrook St G81 .... 74 B1
Whitefield Ave G72 .... 139 D2
Whitefield Rd G51 .... 116 B3
Whitefield Terr G65 .... 33 E1
Whitefield Ct G82 .... 50 B3
Whiteford Cres G82 .... 50 B3
Whiteford Ct ML3 .... 183 E3
Whiteford Pl G82 .... 50 B3
Whiteford Rd PA2 .... 114 A1
Whiteford View KA7 .... 239 E4
Whitegates PI FK1 .... 41 E2
Whitehall Ave KA9 .... 236 B4
Whitehall St G40 .... 240 A2
Whitehaugh Ave PA1 ...... 114 A3
Whitehaugh Cres G53 .... 135 D2
Whitehaugh Dr PA1 .... 114 A3
Whitehaugh Rd G53 .... 135 D2
Whitehill Ave Airdrie ML6 . 103 D1
 Cumbernauld G68 .... 61 E1
 Kirkintilloch G66 .... 58 C1
 Stepps G33 .... 99 E3
Whitehill Cres
 Carluke ML8 .... 187 F2
 Clydebank G81 .... 74 C4
 Kirkintilloch G66 .... 58 C1
Whitehill Farm Rd G33 ..... 99 E3
Whitehill Gdns G31 .... 118 A4
Whitehill Gr G77 .... 156 C1
Whitehill Pl FK8 .... 7 D3
Whitehill Rd Bearsden G61 . 75 E3
 Hamilton ML3 .... 162 A3
Whitehill Sec Sch G31 .... 118 A4
Whitehill St G31 .... 118 A4
Whitehill Street La G31 ... 118 A4
Whitehill Terr ML11 .... 214 C2
Whitehills PA8 .... 73 F3
Whitehills Dr G75 .... 180 C4
Whitehills Pl G75 .... 180 C4
Whitehills Terr G75 .... 180 C4
Whitehirst Park Rd KA13 . 207 D2
Whitehope Green KA11 ... 220 A2
Whitehorse Wlk G75 .... 180 A4
Whitehouse Rd FK7 .... 7 E4
Whitehurst G61 .... 75 E3
Whitehurst Park Prim Sch
 G61 .... 75 E3

Whitehurst Park 75 E2
Whiteinch Prim Sch G14 ... 95 E2
Whitekirk Pl G15 .... 75 D1
Whitelaw Ave ML5 .... 101 F3
Whitelaw Cres ML4 .... 142 B2
Whitelaw St
 Blackridge EH48 .... 107 E1
 Glasgow G20 .... 96 B4
Whitelaw Terr G65 .... 59 F2
Whitelea Ave PA13 .... 89 E4
Whitelea Cres PA13 .... 89 E4
Whitelee G75 .... 180 B3
Whitelee Cres G77 .... 156 A3
Whitelee Gate G77 .... 156 A3
Whitelees Prim Sch G67 ... 62 C3
Whiteless Rd
 Cumbernauld G67 .... 62 C3
 Greenock PA15 .... 46 C1
 Lanark ML11 .... 203 F1
 Lanark ML11 .... 215 E2
Whitelees Rdbt G67 .... 62 C3
Whiteloans G71 .... 141 D2
Whitemoss Ave
 East Kilbride G74 .... 159 F1
 Glasgow G44 .... 136 C2
Whitemoss Gr G74 .... 160 A1

Whitemoss Rdbt G74 ...... 160 A1
Whitepond Ave ML4 .... 141 F2
Whites Bridge Ave
 Paisley PA2 .... 112 C2
 Paisley PA3 .... 113 D3
Whites Bridge Cl PA3 ..... 113 D3
Whites' Loan ML11 .... 215 E3
Whiteshaw Ave ML8 .... 187 E1
Whiteshaw Dr ML8 .... 187 E1
Whiteshaw Rd ML8 .... 187 D2
Whiteside Rd KA9 .... 236 B4
Whiteside Terr KA9 .... 236 B4
Whitestone Ave G68 .... 61 D1
Whitevale St G31 .... 118 A4
Whitewisp Ct KA11 .... 220 A2
Whitfield Dr KA8 .... 236 B2
Whithope Rd G53 .... 134 C2
Whithope Terr G53 .... 134 C2
Whithorn Cres G69 .... 80 C2
Whitlawburn Ave G72 .... 138 C2
Whitlawburn Rd G72 ...... 138 C2
Whitlawburn Terr G72 .... 138 C2
Whitlees Cres KA22 .... 205 E2
Whitlees Ct KA22 .... 205 F2
Whitletts Ct KA8 .... 236 C1
Whitletts Prim Sch KA8 .. 236 C2
Whitletts Rd KA8 .... 236 B1
Whitriggs Rd G53 .... 134 C2
Whitslade St G34 .... 99 F1
Whitslade St G34 .... 100 A1
Whitsun Dale G74 .... 159 E2
Whittagreen Ave ML1 ..... 143 E2
Whittagreen Cres ML1 .... 143 E1
Whittagreen Ct ML1 .... 143 E2
Whittinghame Dr G12 ...... 96 A3
Whittinghame La G12 .... 95 F3
Whittington St ML5 .... 122 A3
Whittle Pl KA11 .... 219 F1
Whittle Rd ML8 .... 236 B2
Whittliemuir Ave G44 .... 136 C2
Whitton Dr G46 .... 136 C2
Whitton St G20 .... 96 B4
Whitworth Dr G81 .... 74 A1
Whitworth St G20 .... 97 D3
Whyte Ave
 Cambuslang G72 .... 138 C3
 Irvine KA12 .... 219 E1
Whyte Cnr G82 .... 50 C1
Whyte St ML7 .... 127 F3
Wick Ave ML6 .... 122 C2
Wickets The PA1 .... 114 A2
Wickham Ave G77 .... 156 B3
Wide Cl ML11 .... 215 D2
Wigton Ave G77 .... 156 B4
Wigtoun Pl G67 .... 62 A2
Wildcat Rd KA23 .... 190 B3
Wilderness The FK2 .... 14 B2
Wildman Rd ML4 .... 187 D4
Wilfred Ave G13 .... 95 E4
Wilkie Cres ML9 .... 185 D1
Wilkie Loan ML4 .... 142 A4
Wilkie Rd G71 .... 141 D3
William Booth Pl FK7 .... 7 D2
William Dr ML3 .... 183 E4
William Mann Dr G77 ..... 156 B2
William St Clydebank G81 . 74 A3
 Coatbridge ML5 .... 122 A3
 Glasgow G3 .... 240 A3
 Greenock PA15 .... 46 A3
 Hamilton ML3 .... 162 A3
 Helensburgh G84 .... 17 D1
 Johnstone PA5 .... 111 F2
 Kilmarnock KA3 .... 222 C1
 Kilsyth G65 .... 60 B4
 Paisley PA1 .... 113 E2
 Port Glasgow PA14 .... 47 D2
Williamfield Ave KA7 ...... 239 D2
Williamfield Gr KA12 ...... 219 D2
Williamfield Pk KA12 ...... 219 D2
Williamsburgh Prim Sch
 PA1 .... 114 A3
Williamsburgh Terr PA1 .. 114 A3
Williamson Ave
 Dumbarton G82 .... 50 A2
 Falkirk FK1 .... 24 A1
Williamson Dr G84 .... 16 C1
Williamson PI Falkirk FK2 . 42 B4
 Johnstone PA5 .... 112 A1
Williamson St
 Clydebank G81 .... 74 A2
 Falkirk FK1 .... 42 A2
 Glasgow G31 .... 118 B2
Williamwood Dr G44 ...... 136 C1
Williamwood High Sch
 G76 .... 157 E4
Williamwood Pk G44 ...... 136 C1
Williamwood Pk W G44 .. 136 C1
Williamwood Sta G44 ..... 136 B1
Willie Mar's Brae KA3 .... 223 D1
Willie Ross Pl KA3 .... 223 E2
Willison's La PA14 .... 47 E1
Willock Pl G20 .... 96 C4
Willock St KA1 .... 227 F3
Willockston Rd KA10 ...... 229 F1
Willoughby Dr G13 .... 95 F3
Willoughby La G13 .... 95 F3
Willow Ave
 Bishopbriggs G64 .... 98 A4
 Elderslie PA5 .... 112 B1
 Kirkintilloch G66 .... 79 E3
Willow Cres ML5 .... 122 A2
Willow Ct G75 .... 180 A3
Willow Dr Airdrie ML6 .... 123 E4
 Banknock FK4 .... 38 C1
 Blantyre G72 .... 161 E4
 Johnstone PA5 .... 112 A1
 Milton Of C G65 .... 58 B3
Willow Gdns KA11 .... 219 F3

Willow Gr ML1 .... 143 D3
Willow La Glasgow G32 .. 119 D1
Willow Pk G64 .... 98 A4
Willow Pl G69 .... 239 E2
Willow Pl Johnstone PA5 . 112 A1
 Uddingston G71 .... 141 E4
Willow Rd KA1 .... 227 E4
Willow St G13 .... 95 F4
Willow Way ML2 .... 162 C1
Willowbank ML9 .... 185 D3
Willowbank Cres 6 G3 .... 96 C1
Willowbank Gdns G66 ...... 79 E4
Willowbank Prim Sch G3 .. 96 C1
Willowbank Sch ML5 ...... 121 F3
Willowbank St G3 .... 240 A4
Willowburn Rd KA15 ...... 170 C4
Willowdale Cres G69 ...... 120 A2
Willowdale Gdns G69 ..... 120 A2
Willows The G53 .... 135 D2
Willows The
 Carmunnock G76 .... 158 C4
 Tullibody FK10 .... 4 A1
Willowyard Ind Est KA15 170 C4
Willowyard Rd KA15 .... 170 C4
Wills Rd KA8 .... 236 B1
Willwood Rd ML2 .... 165 E4
Wilmot Rd G13 .... 95 E3
Wilsgait St ML1 .... 144 B1
Wilson Ave Denny FK6 ...... 21 F1
 Falkirk FK1 .... 41 E3
 Irvine KA12 .... 219 E2
 Kilmarnock KA3 .... 228 A4
 Linwood PA3 .... 112 A3
 Troon KA10 .... 230 A1
Wilson Ct KA15 .... 150 A1
Wilson Dr
 Bannockburn FK7 .... 7 E1
 Falkirk FK1 .... 41 E3
Wilson Gdns FK1 .... 41 E3
Wilson Pl Dundonald KA2 . 225 F1
 East Kilbride G74 .... 160 A2
 High Bonnybridge FK4 ...... 40 B2
 Newton Mearns G77 .... 156 B2
Wilson Rd Falkirk FK1 ...... 41 E3
 Shotts ML7 .... 146 C1
Wilson St Airdrie ML6 ..... 122 C4
 Alexandria G83 .... 27 F3
 Ayr KA8 .... 236 A1
 Beith KA15 .... 150 B1
 Coatbridge ML5 .... 122 A3
 Glasgow G1 .... 241 D2
 Hamilton ML3 .... 162 A3
 Larkhall ML9 .... 185 D1
 Motherwell ML1 .... 163 F4
 Paisley PA1 .... 113 F2
 Port Glasgow PA14 .... 47 F1
 Renfrew PA4 .... 94 B2
Wilson's Rd ML1 .... 144 C4
Wilton Crescent La G20 ... 96 C2
Wilton Dr G20 .... 96 C2
Wilton Rd ML8 .... 202 A4
Wilton St Coatbridge ML5 . 101 E1
 Glasgow G20 .... 96 C2
Wiltonburn Path G53 ..... 135 D2
Wiltonburn Rd G53 .... 135 D2
Wilverton Rd G13 .... 95 F4
Winburne Cres ML3 .... 162 A2
Winchester Ave FK4 .... 21 F2
Winchester Avenue Ind Est
 FK6 .... 21 F2
Winchester Dr G12 .... 96 A3
Windelstraw Ct KA11 ..... 220 A2
Windermere St ML4 .... 141 F2
Windermere G75 .... 179 F3
Windhill Cres G43 .... 136 A3
Windhill Pl G43 .... 136 B3
Windhill Rd G43 .... 136 A3
Windlaw Ct G45 .... 137 E1
Windlaw Gdns G44 .... 136 C1
Windlaw Park Gdns G44 . 136 C1
Windlaw Prim Sch G45 .. 137 F1
Windlaw Rd
 Carmunnock G76 .... 158 B4
 Glasgow G45 .... 137 E1
Windmill Ct ML1 .... 163 F3
Windmill Rd ML3 .... 162 B2
Windmillhill St ML1 .... 163 F3
Windmillhill St ML1 .... 163 F3
Windrow Terr ML2 .... 165 E4
Windsor Ave Falkirk FK1 ... 41 F2
 Newton Mearns G77 .... 156 C3
Windsor Cres
 Clydebank G81 .... 74 A2
 Elderslie PA5 .... 112 A1
 Falkirk FK1 .... 41 F2
 Paisley PA1 .... 114 A3
Windsor Ct ML8 .... 187 F1
Windsor Dr Denny FK6 ...... 21 E2
 Falkirk FK1 .... 41 F2
 Glenmavis ML6 .... 102 C2
Windsor Path 8 ML9 ...... 185 E1
Windsor Pl Shotts ML7 ... 146 C3
 Stirling FK8 .... 7 D4
Windsor Quadrant ML8 .. 187 F1
Windsor Rd Falkirk FK1 ..... 41 F2
 Motherwell ML1 .... 143 D3
 Renfrew PA4 .... 94 B1
Windsor St
 Coatbridge ML5 .... 121 F2
 Glasgow G20 .... 240 A4
 4 Glasgow, Woodside G20 97 D1
 Menstrie FK11 .... 4 A2
 Shotts ML7 .... 146 C3
Windsor Terr G20 .... 97 D1
Windsor Wlk G71 .... 141 D4

Windward Pk KA7 .... 239 D1
Windward Rd G75 .... 159 D1
Windy Yetts G65 .... 59 F2
Windyedge Cres G13 .... 95 E3
Windyedge Pl G13 .... 95 E3
Windyedge Rd ML1 .... 144 B2
Windyhill Pk G77 .... 157 F1
Windyridge ML3 .... 162 C1
Windyridge Pl G72 .... 161 E4
Winehouse Yett KA2 .... 225 F1
Winfield Ave G72 .... 138 C4
Wingate Ave KA24 .... 191 D4
Wingate Cres G74 .... 160 B2
Wingate Dr G74 .... 160 B2
Wingate Pk G74 .... 160 B2
Wingate St ML2 .... 164 C2
Wingfaulds Ave KA24 .... 191 D4
Wingfield Gdns G71 .... 141 D1
Winifred St G33 .... 98 B2
Winning Ct G72 .... 140 C1
Winning Quadrant ML2 .... 164 B2
Winning Row G31 .... 118 B3
Winnipeg Dr G75 .... 180 A4
Winstanley Wynd KA13 .... 207 E3
Winston Ave KA9 .... 236 B4
Winston Cres G65 .... 57 E4
Winston Rd G84 .... 17 D1
Wintergreen Ct G72 .... 159 E2
Wintergreen Dr G74 .... 159 E2
Winton Ave
Eaglesham G76 .... 178 C2
Glasgow G46 .... 136 B1
Kilwinning KA13 .... 207 E2
Winton Cir KA21 .... 216 C4
Winton Cres G72 .... 161 E4
Winton Ct KA22 .... 205 E1
Winton Dr G12 .... 96 B3
Winton Gdns G71 .... 140 C4
Winton La
Ardrossan KA22 .... 205 E1
Glasgow G12 .... 96 B3
Winton Pk G75 .... 159 D1
Winton Pl KA22 .... 205 E1
Winton St
Ardrossan KA22 .... 205 E1
Saltcoats KA21 .... 216 C4
Wirran Pl G13 .... 94 C4
Wishart Ave G81 .... 74 B4
Wishart Dr FK7 .... 7 E2
Wishart St G4, G31 .... 241 F3
Wishaw Acad (Prim) ML2 .... 165 D1
Wishaw High Rd ML1 .... 165 E4
Wishaw Low Rd ML1 .... 165 D4
Wishaw Rd ML2 .... 186 C4
Wishaw Sta ML1 .... 165 D1
Wishawhill St ML2 .... 164 C2
Wisner Ct G64 .... 135 F2
Wisteria La ML8 .... 201 F4
Wiston St G72 .... 139 F3
Witch Rd KA3 .... 222 C1
Witches Linn KA22 .... 205 D2
Witchill Pl KA3 .... 222 C1
Witchill Sch KA3 .... 222 C1
Witchknowe Ave KA1 .... 227 F3
Witchknowe Ct KA1 .... 227 F2
Witchknowe Rd KA1 .... 227 F3
Witchwood Ct ML5 .... 101 E1
Witcutt Way ML2 .... 164 C1
Woddrop St G40 .... 118 A1
Wolcott Dr G72 .... 161 E4
Wolfe Ave G77 .... 156 B4
Wolfe Rd ML1 .... 42 B2
Wolseley St G5 .... 117 E2
Wood Aven Dr G74 .... 159 E2
Wood Avens FK10 .... 4 B1
Wood Cres
Kilwinning KA13 .... 207 F2
Motherwell ML1 .... 142 C1
Wood Farm Rd G46 .... 136 A1
Wood Gr KA11 .... 220 B1
Wood La G64 .... 98 B4
Wood Pk KA7 .... 239 D2
Wood Pl G63 .... 31 D2
Wood Quadrant G81 .... 94 C4
Wood Rd KA10 .... 229 D1
Wood St Airdrie ML6 .... 103 E1
Coatbridge ML5 .... 121 F4
Glasgow G31 .... 118 A4
Greenock PA16 .... 45 E4
Kilwinning KA13 .... 207 F2
Motherwell ML1 .... 163 F4
Paisley PA2 .... 114 A2
Wood View
Motherwell ML1 .... 143 D3
Shotts ML7 .... 166 C4
Woodbank Cres
Clarkston G76 .... 157 F3
Johnstone PA5 .... 111 F1
Woodbank Ct G83 .... 27 E4
Woodbank Gdns G83 .... 27 E4
Woodbank Rd KA2 .... 221 F1

Woodburn Ave
Airdrie ML6 .... 122 C3
Balloch G83 .... 28 A4
Blantyre G72 .... 161 F4
Clarkston G76 .... 157 F3
Kilwinning KA13 .... 207 F2
Woodburn Cres FK4 .... 39 F2
Woodburn Dr FK10 .... 4 C1
Woodburn Gdns FK2 .... 42 C3
Woodburn Pl PA6 .... 111 F4
Woodburn Rd Beith KA15 .... 171 E4
Falkirk FK2 .... 42 B3
Glasgow G43 .... 136 B3
Motherwell ML1 .... 143 E4
Woodburn St Falkirk FK2 .... 42 C3
Motherwell ML1 .... 163 F4
Woodburn Terr ML9 .... 165 E1
Woodburn Way Alva FK12 .... 5 D3
Cumbernauld G68 .... 61 E1
Milngavie G62 .... 55 D1
Woodcroft Ave G11 .... 95 F2
Woodfale ML1 .... 163 E2
Woodend G C32 .... 119 F1
Woodend Dr
Glasgow G13 .... 95 F3
Paisley PA1 .... 114 B2
Woodend Gdns G32 .... 119 E1
Woodend La G13 .... 95 F3
Woodend Oval KA6 .... 239 F1
Woodend Pl PA5 .... 112 A1
Woodend Rd Ayr KA7 .... 239 D1
Carluke ML8 .... 188 A1
Glasgow G32 .... 119 F1
Rutherglen G73 .... 138 A2
Woodend St G84 .... 16 A1
Woodfarm High Sch G46 .... 136 A2
Woodfield G71 .... 141 E3
Woodfield Ave Ayr KA8 .... 236 A3
Bishopbriggs G64 .... 98 A4
Woodfield Cres KA8 .... 236 A2
Woodfield Dr ML6 .... 103 E1
Woodfield Rd KA8 .... 236 A2
Woodfoot Pl G53 .... 135 D2
Woodfoot Quadrant G53 .... 135 D2
Woodfoot Rd
Glasgow G53 .... 135 D2
Woodford Pl PA3 .... 112 A3
Woodford St G41 .... 136 C4
Woodgreen Ave G44 .... 137 E3
Woodgreen Wynd KA13 .... 207 E3
Woodhall ML1 .... 143 D4
Woodhall Ave
Calderbank ML6 .... 123 D1
Coatbridge ML5 .... 121 F2
Hamilton ML3 .... 162 A2
Motherwell ML1 .... 142 C3
Woodhall Cottage Rd
ML6 .... 123 E1
Woodhall Mill Rd ML6 .... 123 D1
Woodhall Pl ML5 .... 121 F2
Woodhall Rd
Braidwood ML8 .... 201 E1
Calderbank ML6 .... 123 D1
Wishaw ML2 .... 165 F2
Woodhall St
Chapelhall ML6 .... 123 E1
Glasgow G40 .... 118 A1
Woodhall Sta PA14 .... 48 A1
Woodhall Terr PA14 .... 69 D4
Woodhead Ave
Bothwell G71 .... 141 D1
Cumbernauld G68 .... 81 F4
Kirkintilloch G66 .... 79 E4
Woodhead Cres
Hamilton ML3 .... 183 D4
Uddingston G71 .... 140 C4
Woodhead Ct G68 .... 81 F4
Woodhead Gr G68 .... 81 F4
Woodhead Pl G68 .... 81 F4
Woodhead Prim Sch ML3 .... 183 D4
Woodhead Rd
Chryston G69 .... 100 A3
Cumbernauld G68 .... 81 F4
Glasgow G53 .... 135 D3
Woodhead Terr G69 .... 100 A4
Woodhead View ML8 .... 81 F4
Woodhill Cres KA11 .... 220 A3
Woodhill Gr KA3 .... 222 A3
Woodhill Prim Sch G64 .... 78 B1
Woodhill Rd
Blackridge EH48 .... 107 D2
Bishopbriggs G64 .... 98 A1
Kilmarnock KA3 .... 222 C2
Woodholm Ave G44 .... 137 E3
Woodhouse Ct G16 .... 158 A3
Woodhouse St G13 .... 95 F4
Woodilee Cotts G66 .... 79 F3
Woodilee Hospl G66 .... 79 F3
Woodilee Ind Est G66 .... 79 F3

Woodilee Rd
Kirkintilloch G66 .... 79 F3
Motherwell ML1 .... 143 F2
Woodland Ave Airdrie ML6 .... 123 E2
Kirkintilloch G66 .... 79 D4
Paisley PA2 .... 133 F4
Woodland Cres
Cambuslang G72 .... 139 E2
Eaglesham G76 .... 178 B3
Woodland Gdns
Carmunnock G76 .... 158 B4
Hamilton ML3 .... 162 C1
Woodland Pl ML2 .... 205 E2
Woodland Terr ML9 .... 185 E1
Woodland Way
Cumbernauld G67 .... 62 A2
Denny FK6 .... 39 E4
Woodlands Alloa FK10 .... 5 F1
Glasgow G46 .... 135 F2
Woodlands Ave
Bothwell G71 .... 141 D2
Gartcosh G69 .... 100 C3
Irvine KA12 .... 219 E2
Law ML8 .... 187 D3
Woodlands Cres Ayr KA7 .... 239 D2
Bothwell G71 .... 141 D2
Falkirk FK1 .... 42 A2
Glasgow G46 .... 135 F2
Johnstone PA5 .... 131 F4
Woodlands Ct
Alexandria G83 .... 27 E4
Glasgow G46 .... 135 F1
Woodlands Dr
Coatbridge ML5 .... 121 E4
Glasgow G4 .... 96 C1
Motherwell ML1 .... 142 C3
Woodlands Gate
Glasgow G3 .... 240 A4
Glasgow, Thornliebank G46 .... 135 F2
Woodlands Gdns G71 .... 141 D2
Woodlands Gr
Kilmarnock KA3 .... 223 D2
Milngavie G62 .... 55 D2
Woodlands High Sch FK1 .... 42 A2
Woodlands Pk G46 .... 135 F2
Woodlands Pl
Coatbridge ML5 .... 121 E4
Kilmarnock KA3 .... 223 D2
Woodlands Prim Sch
Irvine KA12 .... 219 E2
Linwood PA3 .... 112 A3
Woodlands Rd
Glasgow G3 .... 240 A4
Glasgow, Thornliebank G46 .... 135 F1
Motherwell ML1 .... 163 F2
Woodlands St
Milngavie G62 .... 55 D1
Motherwell ML1 .... 163 F2
Prestwick KA9 .... 236 A4
Woodlands Terr
Bothwell G71 .... 141 D2
Glasgow G3 .... 240 A4
Woodlands The ML4 .... 142 B2
Woodlea Ave ML6 .... 123 E2
Woodlea Cres KA2 .... 221 F1
Woodlea Ct KA2 .... 221 F1
Woodlea Dr Glasgow G46 .... 136 B2
Hamilton ML3 .... 183 E4
Woodlea Gdns FK10 .... 5 D1
Woodlea La PA19 .... 45 D4
Woodlea Pk G66 .... 10 A4
Woodlea Pl ML6 .... 103 E1
Woodlinn Ave G44 .... 137 D3
Woodmill KA13 .... 207 F1
Woodmill Dr G64 .... 57 E1
Woodmill Gdns G64 .... 81 F3
Woodneuk La G69 .... 100 C3
Woodneuk Rd
Gartcosh G69 .... 100 C3
Glasgow G53 .... 135 D3
Woodneuk St ML6 .... 123 E1
Woodneuk Terr G69 .... 100 C3
Woodrow ML1 .... 143 D4
Woodrow Ave
Kilmacolm PA13 .... 69 E1
Motherwell ML1 .... 143 D1
Woodrow Cir G41 .... 116 B2
Woodrow Pl G41 .... 116 B2
Woodrow Rd G41 .... 116 B2
Woodside Houston PA6 .... 91 E1
Motherwell ML1 .... 142 C4
West Kilbride KA23 .... 190 B2
Woodside Ave
Bridge Of W PA11 .... 90 B1
Glasgow G46 .... 136 A2
Hamilton ML3 .... 162 C1
Kilmarnock KA3 .... 227 E3
Kilsyth G65 .... 60 C4
Kirkintilloch G66 .... 79 E3
Rutherglen G73 .... 138 B4

Woodside Cres
Alexandria G83 .... 27 F3
Barrhead G78 .... 134 B1
Glasgow G3 .... 240 A4
Paisley PA1 .... 113 E2
Motherwell ML2 .... 166 A3
Woodside Ct
Cambusbarron FK7 .... 6 B3
Falkirk FK1 .... 42 A2
Woodside Dr
Calderbank ML6 .... 123 D1
Eaglesham G76 .... 157 E1
Woodside Gdns
Carmunnock G76 .... 158 B4
Clarkston G76 .... 157 E4
Coatbridge ML5 .... 121 E2
Woodside Gr FK5 .... 41 E4
Woodside La PA5 .... 111 E3
Woodside Pl Dunlop KA3 .... 195 E4
Fallin FK7 .... 8 B2
Glasgow G3 .... 240 A4
Uddingston G71 .... 141 E4
Woodside Place La G3 .... 240 A4
Woodside Prim Sch ML3 .... 162 B1
Woodside Rd Alloa FK10 .... 4 C1
Brookfield PA5 .... 111 E3
Carmunnock G76 .... 158 B4
Forrestfield ML6 .... 106 A2
Stirling FK8 .... 2 A2
Tullibody FK10 .... 4 A1
Woodside Sec Sch G3 .... 116 C4
Woodside St
Chapelhall ML6 .... 123 E1
Coatbridge ML5 .... 121 E2
Motherwell ML1 .... 164 A2
New, Stevenston
ML1 .... 143 D2
Woodside Terr
Clackmannan FK10 .... 10 C2
Falkirk FK1 .... 42 A2
Glasgow G3 .... 240 A4
Woodside Terrace La G3 .... 240 A4
Woodside Wlk ML3 .... 162 C1
Woodstock Ave
Glasgow G41 .... 116 B1
Kirkintilloch G66 .... 79 E4
Lanark ML11 .... 215 E2
Paisley PA2 .... 132 C4
Woodstock Dr
Lanark ML11 .... 215 D2
Wishaw ML2 .... 165 E2
Woodstock Pl KA1 .... 222 C1
Woodstock Rd
Greenock PA16 .... 45 E2
Lanark ML11 .... 215 D2
Woodstock Sch KA1 .... 227 F4
Woodstock St KA1 .... 227 F4
Woodstock Way PA2 .... 132 C4
Woodstone Ct G84 .... 15 F2
Woodvale Ave Airdrie ML6 .... 123 E2
Bearsden G61 .... 76 A1
Rutherglen G46 .... 157 D4
Woodvale Dr PA3 .... 113 D3
Woodview G71 .... 141 E4
Woodview Dr Airdrie ML6 .... 123 D3
Bellshill ML4 .... 142 B4
Woodview La ML6 .... 123 D3
Woodview Rd ML9 .... 199 D4
Woodview Terr ML3 .... 162 A2
Woodville Pl G51 .... 116 A3
Woodville St G51 .... 116 A3
Woodwynd KA13 .... 207 F2
Woodyard Rd G82 .... 49 D2
Woodyett Pk G76 .... 157 F3
Woodyett Rd G76 .... 157 F3
Wooer St ■ FK1 .... 42 A2
Wordie Rd FK7 .... 7 E1
Wordsworth Way G71 .... 141 D2
Works Ave G72 .... 139 F3
Workshops ML1 .... 122 A3
Worsley Cres G77 .... 156 B4
Wotherspoon Dr KA15 .... 150 A1
Wrangfie Ave PA4 .... 94 B2
Wraes Ave G78 .... 134 B1
Wraes View G78 .... 133 F1
Wraisland Cres PA7 .... 71 F2
Wrangholm Cres ML1 .... 143 D2
Wrangholm Dr ML1 .... 143 D2
Wren Ct ML4 .... 141 E4
Wren Pl Johnstone PA5 .... 131 E4
Wishaw ML2 .... 165 D2
Wren Rd PA16 .... 45 D2
Wright Ave G78 .... 134 A1
Wright St Falkirk FK2 .... 42 A3
Renfrew PA4 .... 94 B1
Wright Way ML1 .... 143 D2
Wrightfield Pl KA7 .... 238 C1
Wrightlands Cres PA8 .... 93 F4
Wyburn Pl KA8 .... 236 A2
Wye Cres ML5 .... 101 E1
Wykeham Pl G13 .... 95 E3

Wykeham Rd G13 .... 95 E3
Wylie G74 .... 160 B3
Wylie Ave Alexandria G83 .... 27 E2
Newton Mearns G77 .... 156 B4
Wylie Pl G82 .... 27 F1
Wylie St ML3 .... 162 B1
Wylie Rd KA21 .... 217 D4
Wynd The Alva FK12 .... 5 D4
Cumbernauld G67 .... 62 A3
Wyndford Dr G20 .... 96 B3
Wyndford Pl ■ G20 .... 96 B3
Wyndford Prim Sch G20 .... 96 B3
Wyndford Rd
Cumbernauld G68 .... 62 B4
Glasgow G20 .... 96 B3
Wyndford Terr G71 .... 141 D2
Wyndham Ct G12 .... 96 B2
Wyndham St G12 .... 96 B2
Wynnyard Gdns G75 .... 180 A4
Wyper Pl G31 .... 118 A3
Wyvil Ave G13 .... 75 F1
Wyvis Ave Bearsden G61 .... 75 E4
Glasgow G13 .... 94 C3
Wyvis Gdns KA1 .... 228 A2
Wyvis Pl Glasgow G13 .... 94 C4
Irvine KA11 .... 220 A2
Shotts ML7 .... 147 D2
Wyvis Quadrant G13 .... 94 C4
Wyvis Rd KA1 .... 228 A2

Yair Dr G52 .... 115 D3
Yardley Pl FK2 .... 24 A1
Yarside Rd KA3 .... 222 A4
Yarrow Cres Bishopton PA7 .... 72 B1
Wishaw ML2 .... 165 D2
Yarrow Ct G72 .... 139 F3
Yarrow Gardens La ■ G20 .... 96 C2
Yarrow Gdns G20 .... 96 C2
Yarrow Pk G74 .... 160 A1
Yarrow Rd G64 .... 78 A2
Yarrow Way G72 .... 161 E4
Yate St G31 .... 118 A3
Yerton Brae KA23 .... 190 B2
Yetholm St G14 .... 94 C3
Yetholm Terr ML3 .... 161 F2
Yett Rd ML1 .... 143 E2
Yetts Ave PA13 .... 69 E1
Yetts Cres G66 .... 79 F4
Yetts Hole Rd ML6 .... 102 A3
Yetts The FK7 .... 6 B3
Yew Dr G21 .... 98 A2
Yew Pl PA5 .... 111 F1
Yews Cres ML3 .... 162 A3
Yieldshields Rd ML8 .... 189 E2
Yoker Ferry Rd G14 .... 94 C3
Yoker Mill Gdns G13 .... 94 C4
Yoker Mill Rd G13 .... 94 C4
Yoker Prim Sch G13 .... 94 C3
Yoker Sta G81 .... 94 B4
Yokerburn Terr G81 .... 94 B4
Yonderton Pl KA23 .... 190 B2
York Dr Falkirk FK2 .... 42 B3
Rutherglen G73 .... 138 B3
York Rd PA16 .... 44 C3
York St Ayr KA8 .... 235 F1
Clydebank G81 .... 74 A2
Falkirk FK2 .... 42 B3
Glasgow G2 .... 240 B2
Wishaw ML2 .... 165 D1
York Street Lane KA8 .... 235 F1
York Way PA4 .... 94 B1
Yorke Pl KA1 .... 222 C1
Yorke Rd KA10 .... 229 E1
Yorkhill Par G3 .... 96 B1
Yorkhill St G3 .... 116 B4
Young Ave KA10 .... 229 E3
Young Pl East Kilbride G75 .... 181 D3
■ Uddingston G71 .... 141 D4
Young Rd ML11 .... 215 F3
Young St Ardrossan KA22 .... 205 E1
Ayr KA8 .... 235 F1
Clydebank G81 .... 74 A2
Wishaw ML2 .... 165 D1
Young Terr G21 .... 98 A2
Young Wynd ML4 .... 142 A4
Younger Dr KA9 .... 233 E1
Younger Quadrant G64 .... 78 A1
Yukon Terr G75 .... 180 A4
Yvetot Ave ML11 .... 215 D2
Yvetot Ct ML8 .... 187 F2

Zambesi Dr G72 .... 140 B1
Zena Cres G33 .... 98 B2
Zena Pl G33 .... 98 B2
Zena St G33 .... 98 B2
Zetland Pl FK2 .... 24 C2
Zetland Rd G52 .... 114 C4

STREET ATLASES ORDER FORM

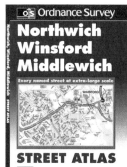

PHILIP'S

The Street Atlases are available from all good bookshops or by mail order direct from the publisher. Orders can be made in the following ways. **By phone** Ring our special Credit Card Hotline on **01933 443863** during office hours (9am to 5pm) or leave a message on the answering machine, quoting your full credit card number plus expiry date and your full name and address. **By post or fax** Fill out the order form below (you may photocop it) and post it to: **Philip's Direct, 27 Sanders Road, Wellingborough, Northants NN8 4NL** or fax it to: **01933 443849**. Before placing an order by post, by fax or on the answering machine, please telephone to check availability and prices.

COLOUR LOCAL ATLASES	PAPERBACK	
	Quantity @ £3.50 each	£ Total
CANNOCK, LICHFIELD, RUGELEY	☐ 0 540 07625 2	➢
DERBY AND BELPER	☐ 0 540 07608 2	➢
NORTHWICH, WINSFORD, MIDDLEWICH	☐ 0 540 07589 2	➢
PEAK DISTRICT TOWNS	☐ 0 540 07609 0	➢
STAFFORD, STONE, UTTOXETER	☐ 0 540 07626 0	➢
WARRINGTON, WIDNES, RUNCORN	☐ 0 540 07588 4	➢

COLOUR REGIONAL ATLASES	HARDBACK	SPIRAL	POCKET	
	Quantity @ £10.99 each	Quantity @ £8.99 each	Quantity @ £5.99 each	£ Total
BERKSHIRE	☐ 0 540 06170 0	☐ 0 540 06172 7	☐ 0 540 06173 5	➢
	Quantity @ £10.99 each	Quantity @ £8.99 each	Quantity @ £4.99 each	£ Total
MERSEYSIDE	☐ 0 540 06480 7	☐ 0 540 06481 5	☐ 0 540 06482 3	➢
	Quantity @ £12.99 each	Quantity @ £9.99 each	Quantity @ £4.99 each	£ Total
DURHAM	☐ 0 540 06365 7	☐ 0 540 06366 5	☐ 0 540 06367 3	➢
EAST KENT	☐ 0 540 07483 7	☐ 0 540 07276 1	☐ 0 540 07287 7	➢
WEST KENT	☐ 0 540 07366 0	☐ 0 540 07367 9	☐ 0 540 07369 5	➢
EAST SUSSEX	☐ 0 540 07306 7	☐ 0 540 07307 5	☐ 0 540 07312 1	➢
WEST SUSSEX	☐ 0 540 07319 9	☐ 0 540 07323 7	☐ 0 540 07327 X	➢
	Quantity @ £12.99 each	Quantity @ £9.99 each	Quantity @ £5.50 each	£ Total
GREATER MANCHESTER	☐ 0 540 06485 8	☐ 0 540 06486 6	☐ 0 540 06487 4	➢
TYNE AND WEAR	☐ 0 540 06370 3	☐ 0 540 06371 1	☐ 0 540 06372 X	➢
	Quantity @ £12.99 each	Quantity @ £9.99 each	Quantity @ £5.99 each	£ Total
BIRMINGHAM & WEST MIDLANDS	☐ 0 540 07603 1	☐ 0 540 07604 X	☐ 0 540 07605 8	➢
BUCKINGHAMSHIRE	☐ 0 540 07466 7	☐ 0 540 07467 5	☐ 0 540 07468 3	➢
CHESHIRE	☐ 0 540 07507 8	☐ 0 540 07508 6	☐ 0 540 07509 4	➢
DERBYSHIRE	☐ 0 540 07531 0	☐ 0 540 07532 9	☐ 0 540 07533 7	➢
EDINBURGH & East Central Scotland	☐ 0 540 07653 8	☐ 0 540 07654 6	☐ 0 540 07656 2	➢

STREET ATLASES ORDER FORM

UR REGIONAL ATLASES

	HARDBACK	SPIRAL	POCKET	£ Total
	Quantity @ £12.99 each	Quantity @ £9.99 each	Quantity @ £5.99 each	
GOW & West al Scotland	☐ 0 540 07648 1	☐ 0 540 07649 X	☐ 0 540 07651 1	➤ ☐
TH PSHIRE	☐ 0 540 07471 3	☐ 0 540 07472 1	☐ 0 540 07473 X	➤ ☐
H PSHIRE	☐ 0 540 07476 4	☐ 0 540 07477 2	☐ 0 540 07478 0	➤ ☐
FORDSHIRE	☐ 0 540 06174 3	☐ 0 540 06175 1	☐ 0 540 06176 X	➤ ☐
RDSHIRE	☐ 0 540 07512 4	☐ 0 540 07513 2	☐ 0 540 07514 0	➤ ☐
REY	☐ 0 540 06435 1	☐ 0 540 06436 X	☐ 0 540 06438 6	➤ ☐
WICKSHIRE	☐ 0 540 07560 4	☐ 0 540 07561 2	☐ 0 540 07562 0	➤ ☐
TH KSHIRE	☐ 0 540 06330 4	☐ 0 540 06331 2	☐ 0 540 06332 0	➤ ☐
KSHIRE	☐ 0 540 06329 0	☐ 0 540 06327 4	☐ 0 540 06328 2	➤ ☐
	Quantity @ £14.99 each	Quantity @ £9.99 each	Quantity @ £5.99 each	£ Total
CASHIRE	☐ 0 540 06440 8	☐ 0 540 06441 6	☐ 0 540 06443 2	➤ ☐
NGHAMSHIRE	☐ 0 540 07541 8	☐ 0 540 075426 6	☐ 0 540 07543 4	➤ ☐
FORDSHIRE	☐ 0 540 07549 3	☐ 0 540 07550 7	☐ 0 540 07551 5	➤ ☐

CK AND WHITE REGIONAL ATLASES

	HARDBACK	SOFTBACK	POCKET	£ Total
	Quantity @ £11.99 each	Quantity @ £8.99 each	Quantity @ £3.99 each	
TOL AND N	☐ 0 540 06140 9	☐ 0 540 06141 7	☐ 0 540 06142 5	➤ ☐
	Quantity @ £12.99 each	Quantity @ £9.99 each	Quantity @ £4.99 each	£ Total
DIFF, SWANSEA AMORGAN	☐ 0 540 06186 7	☐ 0 540 06187 5	☐ 0 540 06207 3	➤ ☐
T ESSEX	☐ 0 540 05848 3	☐ 0 540 05866 1	☐ 0 540 05850 5	➤ ☐
T ESSEX	☐ 0 540 05849 1	☐ 0 540 05867 X	☐ 0 540 05851 3	➤ ☐

to: Philip's Direct,
anders Road, Wellingborough,
hants NN8 4NL

ree postage and packing

ll available titles will normally
ispatched within 5 working days
eceipt of order but please allow
o 28 days for delivery

Please tick this box if you do
wish your name to be used
ther carefully selected
anisations that may wish to send
information about other
ucts and services

stered Office: Michelin House,
ulham Road, London SW3 6RB

stered in England
ber: 3597451

I enclose a cheque / postal order, for a **total** of ☐

made payable to *Octopus Publishing Group Ltd,* or please debit my

☐ Access ☐ American Express ☐ Visa ☐ Diners

account by ☐

Account no

☐☐☐☐ ☐☐☐☐ ☐☐☐☐ ☐☐☐☐

Expiry date ☐☐ ☐☐

Signature..

Name..

Address...

....

....POSTCODE

PHILIP'S

Ordnance Survey

MOTORING ATLAS Britain

The best-selling *OS Motoring Atlas Britain* uses unrivalled and up-to-date mapping from the Ordnance Survey digital database. The exceptionally clear mapping is at a large scale of 3 miles to 1 inch (Orkney/Shetland Islands at 5 miles to 1 inch).

A special feature of the atlas is its wealth of tourist and leisure information. It contains comprehensive directories, including descriptions and location details, of the properties of the National Trust in England and Wales, the National Trust for Scotland, English Heritage and Historic Scotland. There is also a useful diary of British Tourist Authority Events listing more than 300 days out around Britain during the year.

Available from all good bookshops or direct from the publisher:
Tel: 01933 443863

The atlas includes:

◆ 112 pages of fully updated mapping
◆ 45 city and town plans
◆ 8 extra-detailed city approach maps
◆ route-planning maps
◆ restricted motorway junctions
◆ local radio information
◆ distances chart
◆ county boundaries map
◆ multi-language legend